The Palgrave Handbook of Embodiment and Learning

"In the Anthropocene, a time when the fate of the planet is determined largely by humans, it has become difficult to differentiate between nature and culture. There is hardly any nature remaining that has not been impacted by humans. In view of this, the body - the place where nature and culture meet - is becoming increasingly important for human identity, our understanding of humanity and the processes by which we live and learn. In our bodies, nature and culture are inextricably interwoven. The body is a clear manifestation of what all human beings have in common, what is different because of culture and what is individual and unique. This is why processes of embodiment and learning are so important both for society and the individual. In the cultural and social sciences, and also in the natural, technological and life sciences, this insight is now widely accepted. This handbook contains contributions by scholars from a variety of academic backgrounds who use different scientific paradigms to examine diverse processes of embodiment and learning. Main references are theoretical and empirical approaches of philosophy, historical anthropology and cultural or social anthropology. In the processes of embodiment and learning, the senses, the emotions and practical knowledge come into their own. Education is seen as the development of the whole person. The handbook makes an important contribution especially to the advancement of educational practice."

Anja Kraus • Christoph Wulf
Editors

The Palgrave Handbook of Embodiment and Learning

palgrave
macmillan

Editors
Anja Kraus
Department of Teaching and Learning
(Ämnesdidaktik)
Stockholms universitet
Stockholm, Sweden

Christoph Wulf
Anthropology and Education
Freie Universität Berlin
Berlin, Germany

ISBN 978-3-030-93000-4   ISBN 978-3-030-93001-1   (eBook)
https://doi.org/10.1007/978-3-030-93001-1

© The Editor(s) (if applicable) and The Author(s), under exclusive licence to Springer Nature Switzerland AG 2022
This work is subject to copyright. All rights are solely and exclusively licensed by the Publisher, whether the whole or part of the material is concerned, specifically the rights of translation, reprinting, reuse of illustrations, recitation, broadcasting, reproduction on microfilms or in any other physical way, and transmission or information storage and retrieval, electronic adaptation, computer software, or by similar or dissimilar methodology now known or hereafter developed.
The use of general descriptive names, registered names, trademarks, service marks, etc. in this publication does not imply, even in the absence of a specific statement, that such names are exempt from the relevant protective laws and regulations and therefore free for general use.
The publisher, the authors, and the editors are safe to assume that the advice and information in this book are believed to be true and accurate at the date of publication. Neither the publisher nor the authors or the editors give a warranty, expressed or implied, with respect to the material contained herein or for any errors or omissions that may have been made. The publisher remains neutral with regard to jurisdictional claims in published maps and institutional affiliations.

Cover illustration: Thomas Aichinger / VWPics / Alamy Stock Photo

This Palgrave Macmillan imprint is published by the registered company Springer Nature Switzerland AG.
The registered company address is: Gewerbestrasse 11, 6330 Cham, Switzerland

Contents

Introduction: Embodiment—A Challenge for Learning and Education   1
Anja Kraus and Christoph Wulf

Part I   Philosophical and Historical Underpinnings   19

Promoting Embodiment Through Education in the Anthropocene   23
Renaud Hétier and Nathanaël Wallenhorst

Embodiment Through Mimetic Learning   39
Christoph Wulf

Awareness as a Challenge: Learning Through Our Bodies on a Planet in Crisis   61
Mariagrazia Portera

Building Blocks of a Historical Overview of 'Tacit Knowledge'   75
Kristina Brümmer, Thomas Alkemeyer, and Robert Mitchell

The Antinomies of Pedagogy and Aporias of Embodiment: A Historical and Phenomenological Investigation   91
Norm Friesen

vi   Contents

Embodied Cognition: A Methodological and Pedagogical Interpretation   107
Christian Rittelmeyer

Part II   The Pedagogical Relationship and Professionalism   129

Knowledge of Pathos   133
Shoko Suzuki

Pedagogical Tact: Reconstruction of a Bodily Moment of the Pedagogical Relationship   145
Anja Kraus and Thomas Senkbeil

Gestures in the Classroom   163
Regula Fankhauser and Angela Kaspar

Vulnerability: A Basic Concept of Pedagogical Anthropology   179
Daniel Burghardt and Jörg Zirfas

Pedagogical Relationships as Relationships of Power   193
Kathrin Audehm

Part III   Body, Sociality and Learning   209

The Performativity of Learning   213
Birgit Althans

The Embodied Other: Mimetic-Empathic Encorporations   229
Léonard Loew

The Embodiment of Gender in Childhood   245
Anja Tervooren

The Adult-Child Co-existence: Asymmetry, Emotions, Upbringing   259
Tatiana Shchyttsova

Contents   vii

Alterity and Emotions: Heterogeneous Learning Conditions and Embodiment   277
Anja Kraus

Part IV   Body, Space and Learning   291

Movement and Touch: Why Bodies Matter   295
Gabriele Klein

Like Water Between One's Hands: Embodiment of Time and the Ephemeral of Dance   311
Gabriele Brandstetter

Materiality and Spatiality of Bodily Learning   325
Arnd-Michael Nohl and Morvarid Götz-Dehnavi

Body-Related Learning Processes in Museums   341
Bernd Wagner

Part V   Body, Virtual Reality and Mindfulness   355

Technical Mediation of Children's Onlife Worlds   357
Michalis Kontopodis and Kristiina Kumpulainen

Creative and Artistic Learning in Post-digital Youth Culture: Results of a Qualitative Study on Transformations of Aesthetic Practices   367
Benjamin Jörissen, Martha Karoline Schröder, and Anna Carnap

Mind the Body: Mindfulness Meditation as a Spiritual Practice Between Neuroscience, Therapy and Self-awareness   383
Andreas Nehring

Part VI   Classroom Practices   403

The Role of Bodily Experience for Learning Designs   407
Staffan Selander

viii   Contents

Mathematics Learning: Structured Ways of Moving *With*   419
Nathalie Sinclair and Eva Jablonka

Social Choreographies in Primary School Education   437
Cornelie Dietrich and Valerie Riepe

On the (In)Visibility of Postcolonial Subjectivation: Educational Videography Research in Glocalised Classrooms   457
Juliane Engel and Cristina Diz Muñoz

Music as an Embodied Learning Experience   479
Tiago de Oliveira Pinto

Part VII   Bodies in Times of Glocalizations   501

Embodiment of the Values System in Indigenous African Society   505
Michael Omolewa and Adetola Adejo

Embodiment in Education in the Islamic World   519
Reza Arjmand

The Body in Education: Conceptions and Dimensions in Brazil and Latin America   541
Karina Limonta Vieira

Cultivating a Gentle Body: A Chinese Perspective   561
Hongyan Chen

The Body and the Possibility of an Ethical Experience of Education: A Perspective from South Asia   577
Srajana Kaikini

Notes on Contributors

Adetola Adejo is an assistant lecturer and a PhD student in the Department of History and International Studies at Babcock University, Nigeria. Her research interests focus on food politics, food security and climate change with reference to their impact on states' relations.

Thomas Alkemeyer is Professor of Sociology and Sociology of Sport at the Carl von Ossietzky University of Oldenburg, Germany. His main research interests are sociological theories of practice, sociology of the body and of sport, subjectivation research and cultural analysis of the present.

Birgit Althans received her doctorate in 1998 with "Der Klatsch, die Frauen und das Sprechen bei der Arbeit" (Campus 2000). From 2000 to 2008 she was a research assistant to Prof. Christoph Wulf at the Free University of Berlin in the Department of Anthropology and Education/General Pedagogy and in the Sonderforschungsbereich (SFB) "Cultures of the Performative". In 2005 she received Habilitation with "Masked Desire. Female Social Reformers between Social Work and Management" (Campus 2007) from the Freie Universität (FU) Berlin. Since 2018 she is Professor of Pedagogy at the Kunstakademie Düsseldorf. Her research interests include pedagogical and historical anthropology, gender and cultural studies, early management history and organisational theory and qualitative methods.

Reza Arjmand is Associate Professor of Education at Linnæus University, Sweden. He has written extensively on Islamic education and everyday life of Muslims. His recent publications include "Sexuality and Concealment among Iranian Young Women" (*Sexualities*, 2019); "Ephemeral Space Sanctification and Trespassing Gender Boundaries in a Muslim City" (*Storia Urbana*, 2019);

Handbook of Islamic Education (2018) and *Public Urban Space, Gender and Segregation: Women-Only Urban Parks in Iran* (2017).

Kathrin Audehm is Professor of Pedagogy with a focus on education and heterogeneity at the University of Cologne, Germany. Her main areas of work are ethnographical and theoretical research on performative practices, on authority and power relations in the field of education, the interferences between socialization and habitualization and gender constructions in popular culture.

Gabriele Brandstetter is Professor of Theatre and Dance Studies at Freie Universität Berlin, Germany, Director of the Center of Movement Studies (ZfB) and Co-director of the International Research Center "Interweaving Performance Cultures". Her research focus is on history and aesthetics of dance from the eighteenth century until today; theatre and dance of the avant-garde; contemporary theatre and dance, performance, theatricality and gender differences; and concepts of body, movement and image.

Kristina Brümmer is a research assistant in the working group "Sociology and the Sociology of Sports" of the Institute of Sport Science at the Carl von Ossietzky University of Oldenburg, Germany. Her research focuses on processes of subjectivation, coordination and learning in high-performance team sport. She works with sociological theories of practice, knowledge, technology and the body as well as methods from qualitative social research (especially ethnography, videography and interviews).

Daniel Burghardt is a Professor of Educational Science with a focus on inequality and social education at the University Innsbruck, Austria. His main areas of work are pedagogical anthropology, pedagogical theory of space and critical pedagogy.

Anna Carnap is an education researcher and a lecturer at the Friedrich-Alexander University of Erlangen-Nuremberg and the Humboldt University of Berlin, Germany. Her research interest is dedicated to the intertwining relation of situated practice, the visible and the sayable, society and its change. Her researches had yet taken place in the fields of school, social media and gender.

Hongyan Chen is an associate professor at the Institute of International and Comparative Education, East China Normal University, China, and Director of the Intercultural Education and Communication Research Center. She obtained her PhD from the Free University of Berlin, Germany. She is the principal investigator of the National Project "Educational Ritual and the

Urbanization of China". She has written papers in international conferences (USA, Germany, Korea, New Zealand and China) and journals including books and chapters. Her research fields include ritual and mimetic learning in education, intercultural education, urbanisation and school reforms in modern China and picture-interpretation as qualitative method.

Morvarid Götz-Dehnavi is working as the Chair for Education Science at the Helmut Schmidt University, Hamburg, Germany, since 2006, with her main focus on history of education, political socialisation, child and youth research and qualitative methodology.

Tiago de Oliveira Pinto is UNESCO Chair Holder on Transcultural Music Studies and Head of the Department of Musicology at the University of Music Franz Liszt, Weimar, and Friedrich Schiller University, Jena, Germany. De Oliveira Pinto is Former Professor of Social Anthropology at the University of São Paulo, Brazil, and Director of the Brazilian Cultural Institute in Germany. He was a visiting scholar at universities in the US, South Africa and several other European and Brazilian universities. He is the author of books and numerous chapters and papers on music in Latin America and in Africa, on music as living cultural heritage, international cultural policy and methodological issues in musicology and anthropology.

Cornelie Dietrich is Professor of Educational Sciences at the Humboldt University of Berlin, Germany, with a focus on primary school education and co-director of the Interdisciplinary Center of Research in Education (IZBF). Her main research interests are cultural anthropology in school and childhood studies, theory of arts education and language education and theory of care.

Juliane Engel holds a professorship at the Institute for Pedagogy, Goethe University Frankfurt, Germany. Her work focuses on theories and empirical studies of relational subjectivation and videography research in cultural studies. In her most recent research project on "Glocalized Lifeworlds", she investigated ethical judgements of students in the context of heterogeneous interpretations and (post)digital learning cultures. She has developed responsive methodologies in the context of qualitative educational and social research in schools and other fields of socio-cultural education.

Regula Fankhauser studied philosophy and German literature in Berne, Berlin and Zurich, where she received her doctorate in 1998. She actually holds a position as a senior researcher at the Berne University of Teacher Education, Switzerland. Her research focuses on teacher educational training, classroom teaching and aesthetic literacy. She currently leads a project on personalised learning.

Norm Friesen is a professor in the Department of Educational Technology at the College of Education, Boise State University, USA. He has recently translated and edited Klaus Mollenhauer's *Forgotten Connections: On Culture and Upbringing* (2014) as well as a book on *Existentialism and Education in the Thought of Otto Friedrich Bollnow* (Palgrave Macmillan, 2017). He is also the author of *The Textbook and the Lecture: Education in the Age of New Media* (2017).

Renaud Hétier is Professor of Pedagogy at the Catholic University of the West (UCO), France. Some of his books include *Cultivate Attention and Care in Education. At the Source of Wonderful Tales* (Rennes, PURH, 2020), *Humanity Against the Anthropocene* (Paris, PUF, 2021) and *Presence and Digital in Education* (ed. Bord de l'eau, 2021, in French).

Eva Jablonka is Professor of Mathematics Education at Freie Universität Berlin, Germany; she has held positions at King's College, London, Great Britain, and Luleå University of Technology, Sweden. Her main research interests include mathematics classrooms in different cultures, effects of curricula and transitions between sectors of education on access to different forms of mathematical practice and mathematization as a social process.

Benjamin Jörissen is Full Professor of Education with a focus on Culture and Aesthetics and Chairholder of the UNESCO Chair in Arts and Culture in Education at the Friedrich-Alexander-Universität Erlangen-Nürnberg (Germany). The Chair's research aims to contribute to an understanding of the role of aesthetic, arts, and cultural education in a transforming and diverse world, including digitization, postdigital culture, as well as UNESCO-related and postcolonial perspectives. Jörissen is a member of the European Academy of Sciences and Arts, member of the UNESCO UNITWIN Network Arts Education Research for Cultural Diversity and Sustainable Development, as well as a member of the German Council for Arts and Cultural Education (Rat für Kulturelle Bildung).

Srajana Kaikini is Assistant Professor of Philosophy in the Division of Humanities and Social Sciences and Division of Literature at the School of Interwoven Arts and Sciences, Krea University, India. Her works span across philosophy, writing, teaching and curatorial/artistic practice, reflected in her formal education in architecture, aesthetics, curation and philosophy, alongside a continuing engagement with music, dance and design.

Angela Kaspar has a teacher's degree and studied applied ethics and social theory in Berne and Zurich, Switzerland, and Jena, Germany. Since 2015 she has been working as a research assistant at Berne University of Teacher Education and as a lecturer at Lucerne University of Teacher Education. Her main research focus is intersectional research and career choice in the context of personalised learning.

Gabriele Klein is Professor of Sociology with focus on human movement science, dance and performance studies at University of Hamburg, Germany. Her English publications include books like *Dance (and) Theory* (2013, with G. Brandstetter), *Emerging Bodies* (2011, with S. Noeth) and issues like *On Labour and Performance* (Performance Research 2012, with B. Kunst) as well as numerous articles like "Urban Choreographies in: The Oxford Handbook of Dance and Politics" (2017). Her last monograph is entitled *Pina Bausch's Dance Theater: Company, Artistic Practices and Reception* (2020).

Michalis Kontopodis is a professor and Chair of Global Childhood and Youth Studies at the School of Education, University of Leeds, Great Britain. In collaboration with a wide network of academics, practitioners, NGOs, community organizations and policy makers, Kontopodis conducts research on inclusive and equitable quality education and children's well-being in a global perspective. His books, edited volumes and journal articles have been published in six languages.

Anja Kraus is Professor of Arts and Culture Education at the Stockholm University, Sweden. Her research interests are corporeality in educational contexts; phenomenological, ethnographical and theoretical research on practices; transcultural learning; teacher education; and different questions within arts education and pedagogical anthropology.

Kristiina Kumpulainen is Professor of Education at the University of Helsinki, Finland, and an associate professor at Simon Fraser University, Canada. She has written widely on communication, learning and education in the digital age including publications on multiliteracies, children's agency as well as visual and participatory research methodologies. She serves as the co-editor of Elsevier's journal *Learning, Culture and Social Interaction*.

Léonard Loew is a lecturer in the Social Sciences Department at the Hochschule für Technik und Wirtschaft des Saarlandes, Saarbrücken, Germany. He has studied history, philosophy and educational sciences, and made his PhD with a thesis on the history of the empathy-idea. His main focuses in research are the history of ideas in pedagogy, historical semantics and social theory of the psyche, ethics and epistemology of the educational relationship.

Robert Mitchell is a research assistant at the Institute of Sociology, Johannes Gutenberg University of Mainz, Germany; scientific coordinator of the research center 'Human Differentiation' at the JGU Mainz. Capitalizing on his experience as a professional ballet dancer, his autoethnographic research focuses on movement systems, his most recent work comparing ballet and taijiquan. His research interests are sociological theory, sociology of the body, practice theories and (auto-)ethnography.

Cristina Diz Muñoz is a research assistant at the Institute of Secondary School Pedagogy, Goethe University Frankfurt, Germany. Her work focuses on notions of difference and knowledge as well as on representation practices within the school context—especially from a postcolonial perspective. Her PhD project analyses digital-aesthetic forms of reflection as paradigms of inquiry on the emergence of subject positionings in the classroom.

Andreas Nehring is Professor of Religious Studies and Intercultural Theology at the University of Erlangen, Germany. His main areas of work are theories in religious and cultural studies, postcolonial theologies, transcultural processes of exchange and communication between Europe and India, Buddhist modernism and its western expressions.

Arnd-Michael Nohl studied educational science, psychology and Islamic studies in Heidelberg, Germany; Ankara, Turkey; and at the Freie Universität (FU) Berlin, where he received his doctorate in 2001. After positions as research assistant (1997–2001 FU Berlin, 2001–2004 University of Magdeburg), he was Assistant Professor of Intercultural Education at the FU Berlin from 2004 to 2006 and since then he has been Full Professor of the Foundations of Education at the University of the Federal Armed Forces/ Helmut Schmidt University, Hamburg.

Michael Omolewa, Ph.D. is Emeritus Professor of the History of Education at the University of Ibadan, Nigeria, member of the Council of the International African Institute in the UK and of the Centre for Black Culture and International Understanding. He served as the president of the 32nd session of the General Conference of UNESCO and on editorial boards of many learned journals including the *Paedagogica Historica: International Journal of the History of Education*, *Journal of African American History* and the *International Review of Education*.

Mariagrazia Portera is Junior Research Fellow in Aesthetics at University of Florence, Italy, after being a post-doctoral fellow at the Universities of Rijeka, Berlin, Zagreb and Edinburgh. She holds a PhD in Philosophy from the

University of Florence. She has worked on themes concerning the history of aesthetics between the eighteenth century and nineteenth century in Germany; her current areas of interest are contemporary aesthetics, the role of habits in philosophy and in aesthetics and the relationship between aesthetics, biology and neurosciences.

Valerie Riepe is a scientific associate in the Art and Design Department at the University of Europe for Applied Sciences, Campus Hamburg, Germany. Her main research interests are the theorisation of (in)equality, cultural and social theory of body and embodiment as well as ethnographic methods and methodology.

Christian Rittelmeyer was Professor of Pedagogy at the University of Göttingen, Germany. His main areas of work are theory and history of education, pedagogical anthropology, psychology of child development, empirical and phenomenological research methods and aesthetic education.

Martha Karoline Schröder is a consultant for media education and e-learning at the Saxony-Anhalt State Institute for School Quality and Teacher Education, Leipzig, Germany. Her research focuses on transformation processes of cultural practices in the post-digital age.

Staffan Selander is Professor Emeritus of Education in the Department of Computer and Systems Sciences at Stockholm University, Sweden. He is the founder of the e-journal *Designs for Learning* (and the bi-annual conferences) and has during the last ten years focused on designs for learning, multimodal knowledge representations and cultures of recognition.

Thomas Senkbeil PhD, is associate in profession and professionalization research at the University of Education FHNW. His main areas of work are pedagogical anthropology, social pedagogy, educational philosophy and critical culture sciences.

Tatiana Shchyttsova is a professor in Philosophy at the Department of Social Sciences and Director of the Center for Research of Intersubjectivity and Interpersonal Relations at the European Humanities University, Vilnius, Lithuania. Her main areas of work are philosophical anthropology, phenomenology of intersubjectivity, social philosophy and theories of emotions.

Nathalie Sinclair is a professor at Simon Fraser University, Burnaby, Canada, and Canada Research Chair in Tangible Mathematics Learning. Her main research interests are in the use of technology in mathematics thinking and learning, in the aesthetics of mathematical activity and in posthuman theories

xvi Notes on Contributors

that seek to understand the co-construction of material and cultural processes as they pertain to mathematics knowing.

Shoko Suzuki is Professor of Educational Philosophy at the Kyoto University, Japan; principal investigator of the Center for Advanced Integrated Intelligence, National Research Institute Riken, Japan; and a visiting researcher at Research Institute for Information and Communications Policy, Ministry of Internal Affairs and Communications, Japan. In 2009–2010 he was a visiting professor at Free University of Berlin. Her recent publication is "Redefining Humanity in the Era of AI—Technical Civilization" ("Paragrana—Zeitschrift für Historische Anthropologie", 2020).

Anja Tervooren is Professor of Education and Childhood Studies at the University of Duisburg-Essen, Germany. Her research is situated in the fields of ethnography and inclusion, and doing difference in childhood and youth. She completed her PhD from the Free University of Berlin, worked at Goethe University Frankfurt and held a professorship at the University of Hamburg prior to joining her current institution.

Karina Limonta Vieira holds a Doctorate Degree in Education from Universidade Estadual Paulista, São Paulo, Brazil, with doctoral internship at Interdisciplinary Center for Historical Anthropology, Freie Universität Berlin. She is member of Gesellschaft für Historische Anthropologie and International Network of Historical-cultural Anthropology. Her research interests include foundations of education, anthropology of education, mimesis, cultural learning and body.

Bernd Wagner is Professor of Social Science Education at the University of Leipzig, Germany. His main areas of work are intercultural and political education in primary school lessons of social science, primary school children in museums, early education and objects of museum collections, anthropological research in childhood education and education for sustainability.

Nathanaël Wallenhorst is an associate professor at the Catholic University of the West (UCO), France. Some of his books are *The Anthropocene Decoded for Humans* (Le Pommier, 2019, in French), *Educate in Anthropocene* (ed. with Pierron, Le Bord de l'eau 2019, in French) and *Resistance, Resonance: Learn to Change the World with Hartmut Rosa* (ed. Le Pommier, 2020, in French).

Christoph Wulf is Professor of Anthropology and Education and a founding member of the Interdisciplinary Centre for Historical Anthropology at Freie Universität Berlin, Germany. He has been a visiting professor or been involved in research projects at many universities across the world. Major research areas include historical and cultural anthropology, educational anthropology, rituals, gestures, emotions, imagination, intercultural communication, mimesis, aesthetics, epistemology and Anthropocene. His books have been translated into 20 languages. He is the vice-president of the German Commission for UNESCO.

Jörg Zirfas is Professor of Pedagogy with a focus on pedagogical anthropology at the University of Cologne, Germany. His main areas of work are pedagogical and historical anthropology, philosophy of education, pedagogical ethnography and psychoanalysis, cultural education and aesthetic education.

List of Figures

The Antinomies of Pedagogy and Aporias of Embodiment: A Historical and Phenomenological Investigation

Fig. 1   One, two, … three, four, five, six   100
Fig. 2   Let's try Alizé or Marie, then. What was the new number we
          just learned?   101
Fig. 3   Wake up, will you? *Seven!*   101
Fig. 4   Lopez briefly looks away and sighs   103

Materiality and Spatiality of Bodily Learning

Fig. 1   Photogram at 00:01 (copyright: the authors)   336

Creative and Artistic Learning in Post-digital Youth Culture: Results of a Qualitative Study on Transformations of Aesthetic Practices

Fig. 1   Hybrid creative practices using the example of the case vignette
          'Lara and Lara'   377

Mathematics Learning: Structured Ways of Moving *With*

Fig. 1   Exhibits in the Friedrich-Froebel-Museum in the Thuringian town
          Bad Blankenburg, in the house that the practitioner and theorist of
          early pedagogy used for his first kindergarten. The images refer to the
          Spiel und Beschäftigungskasten No. 3 (play and activity box No 3). (a)
          Some of the forms of knowledge and gestures used to interact with
          the cubes; (b) some of the forms of beauty. (Source: the author's own
          photos)   421
Fig. 2   Picture of a master and disciples using counting rods from the
          Seijutsu Sangaku Zue 1795; according to Volkov (2018, p. 152) a

xx   List of Figures

	collection of pictures related to computation methods by Miyake Katataka (1663–1746). (Source: Public domain, Wikimedia Commons (https://upload.wikimedia.org/wikipedia/commons/4/47/Counting_board.jpg))	423
Fig. 3	(a) A 2-regular orientations of C_6^2 in their stylised form; (b) the drawing on the backboard. (Source: diagram by graduate student Finn, Menz (2015), Figs. 6–18 (left) p. 199; Fred's diagram, Menz (2015), Figs. 6–16 (right), p. 196)	430
Fig. 4	A permutation of four letters achieved by swapping the last two. (Source: the author's own diagram)	430
Fig. 5	A diagram showing all six permutations of the letters a, e and r in a transposition graph. (Source: the author's own diagram)	431

Social Choreographies in Primary School Education

Fig. 1	Source: Authors' own picture	442
Fig. 2	Source: Authors' own picture	444
Fig. 3	Source: Authors' own picture	447
Fig. 4	Source: Authors' own picture	450
Fig. 5	Source: Authors' own picture	450
Fig. 6	Source: Authors' own picture	451
Fig. 7	Source: Authors' own diagram	452

On the (In)Visibility of Postcolonial Subjectivation: Educational Videography Research in Glocalised Classrooms

Fig. 1	Physical learning and education processes in the classroom's world trade game are here portrayed from a high-angle camera shot: wide shot of the classroom from above. (Source: Authors' own picture)	463
Fig. 2	Touch: A student is holding her breath while trying to stop a hand reaching for a piece of paper. (Source: Authors' own picture)	464
Fig. 3	Body and technology: An isolated, lonely student interacts with the audio recorder and then addresses the camera directly. (Source: Authors' own picture)	464
Fig. 4	Wanting to participate in class activities, a student reaches for a pair of scissors. Another student wants to push the first one out of her territory; her hand gestures express distancing attempts. (Source: Authors' own picture)	465
Fig. 5	A student holds another in a headlock while looking at a girl. Neither of the girls at the table looks at what the other students are doing; they smile and keep on working. (Source: Authors' own picture)	465

Music as an Embodied Learning Experience

Fig. 1   Short extract of a transcription of a drumming piece sequence
from a silent film, based on a 'frame-to-frame' analysis
(Kubik, 1984, p. 216)   484

Fig. 2   Photo: Rubab master Ustad Ghulam Hussein with pupil, from
Kabul: the master and his student on stage in Weimar (University
of Music Franz Liszt, 2015)   493

Introduction: Embodiment—A Challenge for Learning and Education

Anja Kraus and Christoph Wulf

The aim of this handbook is to show that embodiment is far more important in learning and education than is often assumed. Modern cognitive science has also reached this conclusion, having recognized that consciousness and cognitive processes need a physical body with which to interact, without which they would not exist. This has long been known in the fields of Anthropology, Cultural Studies and the Humanities. In recent decades, however, it has become considerably more important. In many societies and in many sciences, there is an increased interest in the body and the concept of embodiment. Today, there is hardly any scientific discipline which is not expressly interested in processes of embodiment. The chapters in this handbook, therefore, bring together a wide range of interdisciplinary scholarly research on embodiment from different countries in many areas of society, focusing especially on children and young adults. In situating the body at the centre of educational practices and research, the authors follow historical, conceptual, empirical and practical educational approaches and traditions. The core argument is as follows: on a superficial level, education appears to be designed by normative requirements and largely without regard to bodily

---

A. Kraus (✉)
Department of Teaching and Learning (Ämnesdidaktik), Stockholms universitet, Stockholm, Sweden
e-mail: anja.kraus@su.se

C. Wulf
Anthropology and Education, Freie Universität Berlin, Berlin, Germany
e-mail: christoph.wulf@fu-berlin.de

© The Author(s), under exclusive license to Springer Nature Switzerland AG 2022
A. Kraus, C. Wulf (eds.), *The Palgrave Handbook of Embodiment and Learning*,
https://doi.org/10.1007/978-3-030-93001-1_1

needs and corporeal interactions. However, thorough analysis reveals that education is composed of a broad spectrum of bodily expressions, forms of 'corporeal regulation', personal abilities, motivations, subjective perceptions, individual peculiarities and the like. These aspects play a major role in learners' success. Here, we can see a historical development in terms of focusing on bodies as vehicles of learning. In former times young adults' bodies were viewed either as obstacles to learning due to factors such as weakness and deviance, or as objects, as in the context of physical education or training lessons.

The handbook forms part of a development in the Humanities in which there has been a re-evaluation of the body. The book provides an overview of corporeality and embodiment from both theoretical and empirical perspectives. It focuses on seven areas in which the processes of embodiment and learning in the field of education are particularly important. Before turning to these, however, it is important to define the frame of reference of our research.

There was an explicit interest in the body in the progressive education of Europe and America at the end of the nineteenth and the first half of the twentieth centuries, and this interest was then developed further in Educational Anthropology over the last 50 years under the influence of Anthropology and General Pedagogics when it became an important area of education and Educational Science research (Wulf, 2013, 2022b). This development was supported by a number of research projects in the Humanities and Social Sciences which highlighted the important social role of the body. There were important insights into the role played by the 'performative' and the 'material turn' in our understanding of the body—this will be explored further below (Wulf and Zirfas, 2007; Nohl, 2011). It became clear that incorporating the world is dependent on our imagination and that this generates emotions of many kinds. Studies show that many embodiment processes generate practical knowledge (Kraus, 2008–2012). A considerable part of this knowledge is implicit or tacit. This is where we see the limits of theoretical language-based research. Tacit or wordless knowledge is practical knowledge that is important for social and pedagogical action (Kraus et al., 2021). This knowledge is indispensable for the social changes that must be made as a consequence of the many negative effects of the Anthropocene (Wallenhorst and Wulf, 2023).

1   Historical Perspectives

The body has become an increasingly important subject in the Humanities, Social Sciences and Cultural Studies for almost 50 years now. In the early 1980s there was a growth in studies on the body (Feher et al., 1983). It is therefore completely acceptable to speak of a "return of the body" (Kamper and Wulf, 1982). From the very beginning of this early research it was clear that there is no single scientific discipline that can claim the body as its own topic, and also that new fields of knowledge were emerging with different thematic approaches and research methods. New forms of knowledge were appearing (that were sometimes contradictory), not only because of their interdisciplinary nature but also because they were intercultural (Wulf and Kamper, 2002).

From a historical point of view there were several reasons for the body becoming a central subject of research in the Humanities, with new conceptions of the world and humanity. One reason lies in the fact that the traditional 'western' division between body and spirit was unsatisfactory. It had led to an increase in processes of abstraction, which has distanced, disciplined and instrumentalized the body. With the increase in digitalization there has been a further intensification of these processes of rationalizing the body, seeing it in terms of economic factors, taking away its materiality, all of which can be seen as a result of this division (Kontopodis et al., 2017). We have become increasingly aware of the appropriation of the body for purposes that have nothing to do with human bodiliness (that has been suffered in silence) and also of the destructive effects of this development on many societies and the life on our planet. Human bodies with their diverse senses, passions and desires have become forced into a control mechanism of prohibitions and rules and subjected to many forms of repression. Critical Theory, for example, has seen this as a consequence of the increasing abstraction, the media transformation of our world and the transformation into images, in many instances, there has been an increase in psychogenic and sociogenic illnesses. Many of these are related to the undesirable side-effects of a social dynamic that is oriented towards growth and progress, with side-effects which have expedited climate change, the depletion of non-renewable resources and fast-growing rubbish mountains. In leisure, art and culture we see a marked increase in the desire for bodily experiences to compensate for this abstraction. This can be interpreted as a desire to find new ways to live and new meanings in our lives and a less destructive relationship with nature and our own bodies.

2 Continental Educational Science and Educational Anthropology

In the Humanities and Social Sciences, the reception and development of the paradigm of the body has been different across the countries of Europe, and this is still the case. The same is also true of the field of education where there have always been different assumptions in different countries on what pedagogy is about. In this book you will find a collection of chapters that picks up on a variety of traditions and premises that have coloured the way the body and embodiment have become an important subject in society and education. In Germany, for example, there were two important developments which we will briefly mention.

One development relates to the concept of 'Bildung' which has become a central concept in education since the early nineteenth century. Johann H. Pestalozzi prepared the ground for this in some ways but the concept was influenced and made popular by Immanuel Kant, Wilhelm von Humboldt, Friedrich Schleiermacher and many others (Wulf, 2022b). In the 20th century, it came to our attention through Progressive Education, and it was then picked up by the Frankfurt School that emphasized the political dimension that had received too little attention until then. In the present day there are controversial discussions about using the concept to characterize quantitative metric empirical studies as well. The concept of 'Bildung' differs from the English tradition of 'education' which is understood predominantly as a task performed in the context of school. 'Bildung' goes further, and the emphasis is placed on the activity and the responsibility of subjects for their own 'Bildung'. 'Bildung' is not limited to teaching and learning in school and to an education that is going to be useful or vocational. The goal is a fully rounded person, morally, politically and aesthetically, who has the capability of judging and forming critical opinions.

The second development that led to seeing the body and embodiment as issues in the field of education was based on discussions in Anthropology and Educational Anthropology which played an increasingly important role in German Educational Science from the 1960s onwards. The understanding of Anthropology and Educational Anthropology that formed the basis of this again differed from the customary understanding of the concepts in the English-speaking world. Anthropology was understood first and foremost as four paradigms. Two of these were based on what is common to all humanity (Wulf, 2013). They were hominization (Roberts, 2011) and Philosophical Anthropology that had its inception in Germany in the first half of the twentieth century (Scheler, 2009; Plessner, 1981; Gehlen, 1988). The other two paradigms were Historical Anthropology that grew up at the same time in France around the Ecole des Annales (Burke, 1991; Bloch, 1964) and Cultural or Social Anthropology or Ethnology that became popular in several European countries (Kuper, 1973). Subsequently, views which were based rather more on general characteristics of the human body and on incorporation were combined with views which emphasized that what was special about the body and what was imprinted differently depending on cultural and historical factors. Educational Anthropology was also swayed by this, changing its focus from being predominantly philosophical, developing instead into a historical, cultural, educational anthropology. Educational anthropology today considers theoretical philosophical, historical and ethnographic research important (Wulf and Zirfas, 2014). The anthropological approach has helped with the understanding and research of embodiment and learning as being on the one hand something common to us all and on the other as a process that is culturally and historically different. In the globalized world of the Anthropocene in which human beings largely determine the fate of the planet and where it is essential to put right what has gone badly wrong in a completely different way, an anthropological view of things together with the educational practices based on this are of key importance. Perhaps this will also mean that the sustainability goals will be achieved (UN, 2015). If education approaches the human body, embodiment and learning in a conscious and respectful way, then educational anthropology and education will be able to play an important part in fulfilling this task (Wallenhorst and Wulf, 2023).

3   Learners as Human Beings

A further reason for 'rediscovering the body' in education is because corporeality plays an especially important role for children and young people. Our relationship to our body changes depending on our age and what we experience as pleasurable or repulsive, what draws our attention or what doesn't interest us at all, and also depending on how we evaluate something (Kraus, 2000). This plays a particularly important role in school and classroom education (Kraus, 2008–2012).

Seen in a more general way, as young people's personalities develop it becomes clear that listening, being spoken to by another person and perceiving the world through hearing are of central importance for the incorporation of the world into their imaginary. The fact that we hear ourselves when we speak plays a key role in the forming of the subject and intersubjectivity. The senses are also extremely important in the way we experience the world. It is through smell, taste and touch that we perceive and (more or less implicitly) understand the world, its objects, other people and also ourselves. It is through the senses that we experience the alterity of the world and are able to become individuals and subjects (Michaels and Wulf, 2014; Wulf, 2016). Physical movements are also important. They lead to incorporations which transform the outside world into the world inside us and transform the inner world of our imaginary into the outside world. Lakoff and Johnson (1999) have detected several directions of perception: source–path–goal; up–down; into–out of; towards–away from; straight–curves, which are bound to the positions and movements of the body and which are essential for our balance and physical orientation in space.

4   Corporeality and Senses

"'Corporeality' is a term that can be used to signify the body as social actant" (Gilleard and Higgs, 2013, p. 17). Our corporeality conveys and performs individuality, such as specific dispositions, age, gender, a certain social upbringing and cultural imprint. Corporeality is the *conditio sine qua non* for all individual life. As one cannot position oneself outside of one's perceptions, corporeality largely evades transparency and reflection. It can neither be fully grasped nor expressed. Maurice Merleau-Ponty expressed this from a phenomenological point of view: "In so far as it sees or touches the world, my body can therefore be neither seen nor touched. What prevents its ever being an object, ever being *completely constituted* [M.-P's emphasis] is that it is the instance by which there are objects" (Merleau-Ponty, 1962, p. 92). According to phenomenology, all reality appears in the first hand as sensual impressions, non-articulable perceptions, subliminal thoughts and as the origin of speaking in silence. As our body is our 'natural I and as such the subject of perception', we are our body, without any distance. Thus, we cannot have a complete consciousness about our living body. The bodily orientation in an individual or situational field of seeing, acting or speaking is a 'point zero'. At the point zero—where we always already are—we become (tacitly) aware of *how* one deals with something and *how* practices relate to their contexts. This is where Meyer-Drawe (2008) locates the experience of learning. Learning, thus, lacks evidence regarding its starting point and process—it is an occurrence. In learning, former knowledge is rejected and new features enter familiar contexts: an inner estrangement enables us to respond to things we do not yet know. Thus, we do not gain knowledge, insight and understanding only in an active way. Rather we experience and learn by dealing with multiple disruptions, chiasms and fissures. After we have learnt something, then all of a sudden things make sense in a kind of archaic and persistent way, as if this sense had been there forever.

It is our senses that primarily enable us to connect with others and the world outside our own body and also to perceive ourselves (Michaels and Wulf, 2014). There are three aspects that clarify the process of embodiment and perceptions. The first is based on the physical attributes of *homo sapiens* and, as the prerequisite for our sensory experiences, is the same for all humans. The second aspect denotes the historical and cultural differences in human perception. There are differences depending on whether people live in the Middle Ages or in the present day, in Europe or in China. The third aspect is determined by the uniqueness of each individual person which distinguishes them and their lifeworlds from all other people. All our sensory perceptions are constituted through the working together of these three aspects, which are merged into an inextricable nexus in which the individual aspects can no longer be differentiated from each other. The senses cannot be seen in isolation. The way we understand the senses determines how we understand our bodies and vice versa. Michael Polanyi described this situation thus: "Our body is the only assembly of things known as most exclusively by relying on our awareness of them for attending to something else… we make sense of the world, we rely on our tacit knowledge of impact made by the world on our body and the complex of our body these impacts" (Polanyi, 1974, pp. 147, 148). Bourdieu drew our attention to the fact that our social habitus is the consequence of a multidimensional embodiment (Bourdieu, 1984, 1990) in the course of which embodied identities and embodied practices are formed, through which we are socially engaged and historically situated within social and personal time: Embodiment encompasses all those actions performed by the body or on the body which are inextricably oriented towards the social. As living beings and living bodies we react to our social environment: we learn and act.

5   Performativity

The growing interest in the body and embodiment is also connected to the discovery of the cultural importance of performativity, performance arts and the performativity of theatrical staging and productions. Performativity highlights a central aspect of social action and behaviour. Here the meanings of actions are not predominantly interpreted in words. What is central are the staging and performance and the skills that a situation demands. It is the social staging and performance of actions and ways of behaving that are important. The quality of people's social relations depends very much on 'how' people use their bodies, that is, the physical distance they keep, their stance and posture and gestures. All of these convey to other people more than the conscious intentions of their actions. The bodily qualities of actions also suggest intersubjective and social relations, interpretations and meaning, views of the future and so on. In order to give a full picture of processes of embodiment in education we investigate here how social and educational action comes about and the extent to which it is intermeshed with language, deeds and imagination (see also Kress et al., 2021), how its uniqueness is a result of social and cultural frameworks (Resina and Wulf, 2019).

Based on the premise that pedagogy is a science of actions, that is, a practical science to be practised (Wulf, 2003), performativity in the act of education acquires a special importance in the processes of embodiment and learning. Since performative practices place an emphasis on valid norms, rules and certainties, they can have a conserving and stabilizing effect as well as one that transforms or subverts a situation at hand. The execution of performative acts contains the possibility of disempowering and changing the norms and rules in their very execution, treating them in an ironical way and questioning their unquestionability.

Performative acts also have a dimension that refers back to itself, identifies and exemplifies itself. They do not definitively refer to something outside of themselves but to something within themselves; they do what they mean; their meaning is to be found in their execution. By being executed they portray a reality; they create 'their' reality as 'the' reality in question (Wulf and Zirfas, 2007, 2014).

Social knowledge can be grasped as performative knowledge that has been acquired through the execution of social practices (Wulf et al., 2010). Here we see that the corporeality of the people performing the actions, from the performativity perspective, seen as elements of staging and performance, is of central importance. Social actions are symbolic arrangements of the human body. When we consider performativity, it is a question of how the links between language, power and action that make up social action determine our world and thus also education (Wulf et al., 2001; Wulf and Zirfas, 2007).

From the performativity point of view, we realize that not only norms but also objects, spaces theories about, bodies and artefacts play a part in everything we do, and this means that what happens in an educational context need to be rethought. The performativity concept locates the body as the site and medium of all that we do. In empirical research, the performative turn involves a micro-analytic examination of various practices. The performative

Introduction: Embodiment—A Challenge for Learning and Education

turn entails a revision of the existing theoretical approaches to educational practices and learning by drawing our attention to tacit, that is, unwritten, unofficial and unintended but effective features and practices and, in this context, to corporeality (Kraus et al., 2021). From a methodological point of view, a social setting is then not seen as merely 'given', but as 'constituted' by historical and cultural conventions, conceptual approaches, methodological and methodical presuppositions and the like.

6   Mimetic Processes

In recent years there have been three approaches to researching and demonstrating the important role of mimetic processes in the incorporation of knowledge. The first of these shows how mimetic processes were conceptualized historically in European philosophy from Plato to Derrida. It also shows how these processes were developed as important ways of handing down culture from one generation to the next. According to the mimesis approach, embodiment takes place by means of copying, 'wanting to become like', 'becoming similar to' or assimilation. Acting mimetically also means expressing, 'bringing something into being' or even anticipating something that does not yet exist (Gebauer and Wulf, 1995, 1998).

A second approach that has demonstrated the importance of mimetic processes for the incorporation of social relations was developed as part of Evolutionary Anthropology. Here investigations have shown that although elementary forms of mimetic learning do take place also in non-human primates, human beings (and small children in particular) have the special capacity to learn mimetically (Tomasello, 1999). In young children's striving to become similar to adults or older siblings we find the motivation to understand causal connections between the objects of the world and the communicative intentions of other people in gestures, symbols and constructions. Accordingly, event schemas and object categories are formed through dependence on others (Tomasello, 2008).

Thirdly, research on mirror neurons has shown that we reproduce what we have perceived in our brains in the very process of perceiving it. For example, an act of violence elicits similar processes in the person perceiving it to those in the person committing it. This incorporation happens because of the mirror neuron system (Rizzolatti & Sinigaglia, 2008; Jacoboni, 2008).

Mimetic abilities are interwoven with such bodily processes and often counteract social abstraction processes. They form a bridge to what is outside of us, to the world and to other people. Thus, the focus on mimetic learning softens the strict split between subject and object and the sharp difference between 'is' and 'ought'. What we have instead is an understanding of something 'in between', which is experienced in a person's assimilation of an outside world or another person. Mimetic processes contain rational elements; however, they go beyond this. As mimetic processes allow us to get really close to objects, they are indispensable for our understanding. Whereas modern rational thinking relates to the isolated subject of cognition, the mimetic processes take place in a network of relationships between subjects. The mimetic creation of a symbolic world makes reference to other world views and draws other people into our own world. It recognizes the exchange between world and subject and the aspect of power that this contains.

The history of mimetic processes in education and human development is also the history of the struggle for the power to create symbolic worlds, for the power to portray oneself and others and the power to interpret the world in one's own way or else to fit in or perhaps be forced into doing so. In this way, especially in the field of education and socialization, mimesis is also part of the history of power structures.

7 Imagination

Imagination plays an essential role in the embodiment that takes place through mimetic processes. Imagination helps to transform the outside world into the inner world and the inner world into the outside world (Wulf, 2022a). Imagination is the force that creates images, that expresses itself in images and that can be understood in images. In a general sense, inner and outer 'images' include feelings, atmospheres and other 'imaginations', that is sounds, traces of touch, smell and taste. In the imagination on the one hand what is absent is present; but on the other, the imagination is also materially absent. The representative character of the imagination lies in this paradoxical structure. The representative power of imagination makes it possible to transform and incorporate the outside world into the inside world and the inside world into the outside world. The spectrum of possible changes in this process ranges from minimal deviations to major innovations and inventions. While a psychoanalytic perspective, for example, tends to point to the limited possibilities of emotions changing (Kraus, 2000), an aesthetic perspective emphasizes the creative possibilities of the individual. Perceptions of both the external world and internal images can generate emotions. An example of this are perceptions of erotic situations in the outside world or the perception of erotic images in the imagination. The erotic images of the imagination can precede and evoke emotions; they can become their medium and accompany them; as well as they can be a consequence of emotions.

Arnold Gehlen (1988) sees imagination as rooted in the life of the human body and its origin in the vegetative system and understands it in connection with the excess drive of humans. For André Leroi-Gourhan, the development of the imagination has its starting point in the muscular activities in connection with movement, food and sex (Leroi-Gourhan, 1993). Marcel Jousse (1974) sees the emergence of the imagination in the mimetic actions of people directed towards the processes of nature. Despite their different points of view, these authors agree that imagination is closely related to people's physical activities, emotions and actions and is therefore essential for embodiment: the imagination creates representations of emotions in the world of ideas and is, thereby, an important prerequisite for the ability to communicate emotions. Imagination also brings emotions to light in dreams, visions and hallucinations and enables them to be created in works of culture, in art and literature, theatre, music and architecture, as well as in politics, business and technology (Wulf, 2022b). While imagination and emotion are universal human life conditions, historically and culturally they manifest themselves differently (Huppauf and Wulf, 2009). They unfold differently under different historical and cultural conditions.

8   Emotions

Processes of embodiment produce feelings. This is true both of perceptions of the world that are based on the senses and also of processes of the imagination which bring to our consciousness imaginary worlds that are not really present, such as those created in literary texts for example. In teaching and learning feelings and the formation of feelings are of central importance. They are important in how people lead their lives. There are no embodiment processes that do not affect the emotions which are important in the constitution of the person and of individuality (Michaels and Wulf, 2012).

The truth of this was seen in Johann Gottfried Herder's response to Descartes' *cogito ergo sum*: "I feel! I am" (Herder, 1960, p. 282). Feeling is understood here as a guarantee of being, of human existence. For Herder, people experience themselves in their feelings, in the immediate presence of feeling, of touching. The feeling derived from the sense of touch is the sense that determines the emotions. On the one hand, emotions are similar, while, on the other hand, they are different from person to person. Emotions are socially and culturally shaped, that is, they are incorporated and communicated linguistically, medially and normatively. Many emotions are generated and conveyed in interactions; they are the result of relationships with other people and with the world. Emotions are understood neither as essence nor as-mere social and cultural constructions. Emotions have a bio-social character. From such an understanding of emotion a number of challenges arise that require further exploration. These include the relationship between emotion and body, in particular between emotion and movement, emotion and action, emotion and ritual, emotion and memory, emotion and language, emotion and imagination.

In contrast to the extensive experimental research into emotions, which often tends to regard emotions as being independent of their historical and cultural contexts and draws universal conclusions in a way that is not always acceptable, the focus of anthropological and historical research as well as historical-anthropological research is on the particularity resulting from a situation and a context. There seems to be a limited number of basic emotions, but there are numerous shades, blends and overlays between these so that many emotions are ambiguous (Kraus et al., 2021). Every time emotions are new, but also known at the same time; we know them, but not well enough; much has been said about them, but no language can capture them fully; they surprise, cannot be tied down, they change and evade control. Even in memory they appear differently. Emotions are fluid; that makes it difficult to make them objects of cognition; there is a difference that is hard to resolve between their dynamic movement and the claim to distanced objective knowledge.

The commercialization of emotions permeates all areas of human relationships in capitalist societies (Martin et al., 2003; Gobé, 2001). Not only commercialization, but also the politicization of emotions plays an important role in all societies and cultures. In particular where politics becomes populist, emotions are used, or rather misused, for example, by playing with people's fears and hopes in order to achieve political goals (Furedi, 2005).

9 Tacit Knowledge

As we have seen, in research on embodiment and learning we keep coming up against the limitations of a knowledge that can be expressed in language. We experience the difference between what can be put into words and the perception and learning processes of the senses and the body. The research on iconic and performative knowledge has shown that the insights gained here are quite different from those that can be expressed and portrayed in language. Much of the learning that is done by the body takes place on an unconscious level or via the senses and movements of the body (Kraus et al., 2021).

With his distinction between 'knowing how' and 'knowing that', Gilbert Ryle had already in the 1940s drawn attention to the fact that there are different forms of knowledge, the practical implementations of which, described as 'knowing how', are difficult to research (Ryle, 1990; Collins, 2010). With these methods, the focus is not on the acquisition of factual knowledge that can be expressed linguistically. On the contrary, 'knowing how' describes a skill that enables the person to act. 'Knowing how' is learned in mimetic processes by relating to the practices of other people. An example of this is rituals. Rituals are not statements, reasons or explanations themselves, but they transport such. They must be staged and performed in order to come into force. The knowledge required for rituals is a performative, practical knowledge, which differs from the knowledge needed for the description, interpretation and analysis of rituals. One can see here that 'knowing how' is practical knowledge—an embodied skill that is visible in a person's performance (Wulf, 2006).

A practice such as driving a car is only learned if the explanation of how to learn was understood. But constantly remembering the explanation is not necessary to execute the action. An action cannot be 'skilfully' performed as long as this remembering is necessary. Learning happens through embodiment, through which the person gets the skill to do something, that is, to drive a car. Practical skill is thus a form of knowledge that requires attention and social recognition; in the words of Gilbert Ryle (1990, p. 33): "Successful practice precedes its actual theory". Types of practical knowledge are constitutive for many sciences such as Medicine, Law and Education. In this regard, embodiment and learning are decisive for all everyday and professional knowledge.

10 The Structure of the Handbook

This handbook develops the awareness that, as the agent, medium and addressee of education and socialization, the body plays a central role in learning and education in several specific ways. In line with its goals the handbook is divided into seven parts, each one of which has its own short introduction.

1. Part I consists of various "Philosophical and Historical Underpinnings" which help to put the subject into context. It includes chapters on how the subject can be anthropologically and socially classified as part of the Anthropocene, on the embodiment of cognition, on attentiveness, on tacit

knowledge and on the importance of mindfulness and the intergenerational and antinomic foundations of pedagogy.

2. Part II moves on to examine "The Pedagogical Relationship and Professionalism". In view of the vulnerability of the body, here the focus is on the significance of power, how power is expressed in educational gestures, and on the need for a tactful approach in enculturation and socialization.

3. Part III, "Body, Sociality and Learning", continues to develop and analyse questions around enculturation and socialisation. Mimetic and performative processes underpinning education and the embodiment of learning are examined. These chapters show that learning based on embodiment is focused on other people and that experiences of alterity and gender play a key role in the engendering of emotions.

4. Part IV, "Body, Space and Learning", examines the importance of movement and touch, of temporality, space and materiality in processes of embodiment. Embodiment is to be seen as a multisensory, multimodal process. This is illustrated with examples from the worlds of dance, museums and school.

5. In Part V, "Body, Virtual Reality and Mindfulness", our attention turns to the forms of embodiment that result from the processes of digital transformation and also the role of mindfulness in the development of individuality and subjectivity.

6. In Part VI, "Classroom Practices", the focus turns to school learning processes, how they are designed and choreographed and the 'structured ways of acting together with others', with an example from a mathematics lesson. A conscious approach to embodiment can play a role in postcolonial subjectivation. Through the sharing of music a conscious approach to embodiment can help lead to important aesthetic experiences.

7. Part VII and final section, "Body in Times of Glocalization", considers the importance of research into the processes of embodiment for the reciprocal interchange between global and local, general and particular points of view. Studies relating to China, India, Nigeria, Brazil and the Islamic world show that in the world of the Anthropocene what is needed is for local, regional and global perspectives to be interconnected if we are to meet the challenges that lie before us on various levels. And here it is corporeality, embodiment and learning that create an awareness of difference just as they also promote mutual understanding.

We would like to express our gratitude to Elizabeth Hamilton for reviewing the language in many sections of the handbook and to Silas de Saram and Zinnia Lautner for their help in preparing the manuscript for printing.

References

Bloch, M. (1964). *The Feudal Society*. University of Chicago Press.

Bourdieu, P. (1984). *Distinction: A Social Critique of the Judgement of Taste* (R. Nice, Trans.). Harvard University Press.

Bourdieu, P. (1990). *The Logic of Practice* (R. Nice, Trans.). Stanford University Press.

Burke, P. (1991). *The French Historical Revolution: The Annales School, 1929–89*. Stanford University Press.

Collins, H. (2010). *Tacit and Explicit Knowledge*. University of Chicago Press.

Feher, M., Naddaf, R., & Tazi, N. (Eds.). (1983). *Fragments for a History of the Human Body*. Zone. Cambridge. Ass. Distributed by MIT.

Furedi, F. (2005). *Politics of Fear. Beyond Left and Right*. Continuum Press.

Gebauer, G., & Wulf, C. (1995). *Mimesis. Culture, Art, Society*. California University Press.

Gebauer, G., & Wulf, C. (1998). *Spiel, Ritual, Geste. Mimetisches Handeln in der sozialen Welt*. Rowohlt.

Gehlen, A. (1988). *Man: His Nature and Place in the World*. Columbia University Press.

Gilleard, C., & Higgs, P. (2013). *Ageing, Corporeality and Embodiment* (pp. 17–33). Anthem Press.

Gobé, M. (2001). *Emotional Branding. The New Paradigm of Connecting Brands to People*. Allwo.

Herder, G. J. (1960). Aus Herders Nachlass. In H. D. Irmscher (Ed.), *Euphorion* (Vol. 54, pp. 281–204). IV. Folge.

Huppauf, B., & Wulf, C. (Eds.). (2009). *Dynamics and Performativity of Imagination. The Image between the Visible and the Invisible*. Routledge.

Jacoboni, M. (2008). *Mirroring People*. Farrar, Straus and Giroux.

Jousse, M. (1974). *L'anthropologie du geste*. Gallimard.

Kamper, D., & Wulf, C. (Eds.). (1982). *Die Wiederkehr des Körpers*. Suhrkamp.

Kontopodis, M., Varvantakis, C., & Wulf, C. (Eds.). (2017). *Global Youth in Digital Trajectories*. Routledge, Taylor, and Francis Group.

Kraus A. (2000). *Nihilismus, Sprache und Wahrnehmung. Zur Anthropologie Lacans und Merleau-Pontys*. Dissertation. Berlin: Freie Universität. https://doi.org/10.17169/refubium-10915

Kraus, A. (Ed.). (2008–2012). *Körperlichkeit in der Schule—Aktuelle Körperdiskurse und ihre Empirie* (Vol. I–V). Athena.

Kraus, A., Budde, J., Hietzge, M., & Wulf, C. (Eds.). (2021). *Handbuch Schweigendes Wissen. Erziehung, Bildung, Sozialisation und Lernen* (2nd ed.). Beltz Juventa.

Kress, G., Selander, S., Säljö, R., & Wulf, C. (Eds.). (2021). *Learning as Social Practice. Beyond Education as an Individual Enterprise*. Routledge.

Kuper, A. (1973). *Anthropologists and Anthropology: The British School, 1922–1972*. Pica Press.

Lakoff, G., & Johnson, M. (1999). *Philosophy in the Flesh. The Embodied Mind and Its Challenge to Western Thought*. Basic books.

Leroi-Gourhan, A. (1993). *Gesture and Speech*. MIT Press.

Martin, B., Anleu, S. R., & Zadoroznyj, M. (2003). Editor's Introduction to the Special Issue 'Commercializing Emotions'. *Journal of Sociology, 39*(4), 331–333.

Merleau-Ponty, M. (1962). *Phenomenology of Perception* (C. Smith, Trans.). Motilal Banarsidass Publishers.

Meyer-Drawe, K. (2008). *Diskurse des Lernens*. Fink.

Michaels, A., & Wulf, C. (Eds.). (2012). *Emotions in Rituals and Performances*. Routledge.

Michaels, A., & Wulf, C. (Eds.). (2014). *Exploring the Sense*. Routledge.

Nohl, A.-M. (2011). *Pädagogik der Dinge*. Klinkhardt.

Plessner, H. (1981). Die Stufen des Organischen und der Mensch. In H. Plessner (Ed.), *Gesammelte Schriften* (Vol. 4). Suhrkamp.

Polanyi, M. (1974). *Personal Knowledge. Towards a Post-Critical Philosophy. A Chemist and Philosopher Attempt to Bridge the Gap Between Fact and Value, Science and Humanity*. The University of Chicago Press.

Resina, J. R., & Wulf, C. (Eds.). (2019). *Repetition, Recurrence, Returns. How Cultural Renewal Work*. Lexington Books/Roman & Littlefield.

Rizzolatti, G., & Sinigaglia, C. (2008). *Mirrors in the Brain. How Our Minds Share Actions and Emotions*. Oxford University Press.

Roberts, A. (2011). *Evolution. The Human Story*. Dorling Kindersley.

Ryle, G. (1990). *Collected Papers*. Thoemmes.

Scheler, M. (2009). *The Human Place in the Cosmos*. Northwestern University Press.

Tomasello, M. (1999). *The Cultural Origins of Human Cognition*. Harvard University Press.

Tomasello, M. (2008). *Origins of Human Communication*. MIT Press.

UN. (2015). *Goals for Sustainable Development*. UN.

Wallenhorst, N., & Wulf, C. (Eds.). (2023). *Handbook of the Anthropocene*. Springer Nature.

Wulf, C. (2003). *Educational Science: Hermeneutics, Empirical Research, Critical Theory*. Waxmann.

Wulf, C. (2006). Praxis. In J. Kreinath, J. Snoek, & M. Stausberg (Eds.), *Theorizing Rituals: Issues, Topics, Approaches, Concepts* (pp. 395–411). Brill.

Wulf, C. (2013). *Anthropology. A Continental Perspective*. University of Chicago Press.

Wulf, C. (Ed.). (2016). *Exploring Alterity in a Globalized World*. Routledge.

Wulf, C. (2022a). *Human Beings and their Images. Imagination, Mimesis, Performativity*. London et al.: Bloomsbury.

Wulf, C. (2022b). *Education as Human Knowledge in the Anthropocene*. An Anthropological Perspective. Routledge.

Wulf, C., Althans, B., Audehm, K., Bausch, C., Göhlich, M., Sting, S., Tervooren, A., Wagner-Willi, M., & Zirfas, J. (2010). *Ritual and Identity: The Staging and Performing of Rituals in the Lives of Young People*. Tufnell Press.

Wulf, C., Göhlich, M., & Zirfas, J. (Eds.). (2001). *Grundlagen des Performativen. Eine Einführung in die Zusammenhänge von Sprache, Macht und Handeln.* Juventa.

Wulf, C., & Kamper, D. (Eds.). (2002). *Logik und Leidenschaft, Erträge historischer Anthropologie.* Reinhard.

Wulf, C., & Zirfas, J. (2007). Performative Pädagogik und performative Bildungstheorien. Ein neuer Fokus erziehungswissenschaftlicher Forschung. In C. Wulf & J. Zirfas (Eds.), *Pädagogik des Performativen. Theorien, Methoden, Perspektiven* (pp. 7–40). Beltz.

Wulf, C., & Zirfas, J. (2014). Performativität. In C. Wulf & J. Zirfas (Eds.), *Handbuch Pädagogische Anthropologie* (pp. 515–524). VS Springer.

Part I
Philosophical and Historical Underpinnings

In the light of the fact that we are now living in the globalised world of the Anthropocene, that is in a situation in which human beings have become a power that determines the fate of the planet, there is an urgent need to rethink the relationship between nature and culture. Nature hardly exists today in a form that is unaffected, unmoulded even, by humans and their cultures. There is a close interconnection between nature and culture and it is no longer easy to tell them apart. The reciprocal interaction between nature and culture affects the way we understand the human body. We come to realise the degree to which this understanding is culturally determined. If we want to understand humans today we have to take into account the effect we have on nature and the effect nature has on us, which gives us an understanding of how nature and culture are closely interwoven in our cultural and social activities. In view of these insights it is clear that in the context of embodiment and learning we have to consider the entanglements and interdependence of nature and culture.

In their introductory chapter (Chap. 2), *Renaud Hétier* and *Nathanaël Wallenhorst* focus on the challenges for education, development and socialization of the younger generation in the Anthropocene. They use the example of COVID-19, showing how this pandemic not only endangers many people's lives but also leads to a crisis in the economic and political as well as the cultural and social structures of societies. In time of crisis transformations take place in all areas of human life. Bodily experiences that were previously quite natural are no longer a matter of course. We are becoming more and more disembodied, with images and abstractions attaining ever more importance. At the same time, we can realise how valuable living bodily experiences are.

20   Philosophical and Historical Underpinnings

In the field of education, the detriment to the body and corporeality shows the great importance of embodiment in learning as well as in social and cultural life.

In mimetic processes, a creative re-creation takes place in which learners learn and incorporate new knowledge, through using their senses, body movements and imagination (*Christoph Wulf* [Chap. 3]). Mimetic processes are a fundamental part of education and human development. For a long time, it was even thought that education takes place entirely through mimetic processes, so that no distinction was made between mimesis and education. Mimetic processes make clear the extent to which humans are social beings who need other humans as role models for their own development.—Children try to become like adults. They need their attention, appreciation and care. Mimetic processes are not only related to other people and their cultural and social actions but also important in the incorporation of social and cultural spaces and situations. They are essential if we are to understand the world around us, and develop practical knowledge. The central significance of mimetic processes for the phylogenetic and ontogenetic development of humanity has been the subject of research not only in historical anthropology but also in evolutionary anthropology and neuroscience.

Chapter 4 by *Mariagrazia Portera* ties in with this. She shows that the changes that the Anthropocene demands of us should not be purely theoretical but must lead to changes in the way we act and behave. Such transformations are only possible if our insights become part of our bodily experience and lead to practical knowledge. For this to happen new attitudes and habits must be developed. In the face of the many negative developments in the Anthropocene, comprehensive changes to correct people's behaviour are needed. In the field of education there is a need for body-based strategies and practices that target sustainability. At present, however, we are still unsure of the extent to which habits that have developed over long periods of time can change as a result of insight and knowledge and can be replaced by new habits.

Chapter 5 by *Kristina Brümmer, Thomas Alkemeyer* and *Robert Mitchell* illustrates the fact that numerous processes are necessary for social changes to take place, processes that cannot be rationally planned, structured and brought to fruition. Also forms of knowledge are required that cannot be put into words. The distinction between 'knowing that' and 'knowing how' and research studies on the importance of implicit, tacit and silent knowledge have highlighted how important certain forms of non-scientific knowledge are if social change is to take place. This is particularly true of important areas of practice such as Medicine, Law and Education in which the performativity of what is practised dominates over academic knowledge. Up until now in the Anthropocene hardly any research has been done on connections between the negative effects of human actions and behaviour, the recognition or the growing uncertainty and complexity of human knowledge and the new understandings of the human body.

Norm Friesen's chapter (Chap. 6) about antinomies of pedagogy serves as an example of the search for such a new understanding, which he traces back to Socrates' exposition of ignorance as fundamental to insight and knowledge, then explaining heteronomy as being constitutive for freedom in education. Pedagogical antinomies are seen as a 'fluctuating between different perceptions and value judgements' in an 'also … but'. From a phenomenological perspective, the body is the central factor in 'integrating and manifesting opposed phenomena simultaneously'. Merleau-Ponty's concept of the flesh describes awareness and expression as emerging in the simultaneity of mind and body, sensed and sensing, subject and object. Friesen's analysis of a film sequence of a teacher and pupil shows that semantic and material effects and communicational shifts are brought about when the teacher touches the child. In this way, it highlights and explores the striking isomorphism of the embodied and the pedagogical—both as fields and as processes.

Learning processes have a distinct corporeal aspect without which it would not be possible to fully understand them. This is clear in *Christian Rittelmeyer*'s chapter (Chap. 7) which examines embodied cognition. The premise here is that the entire body shapes the features of cognition. Accordingly, mental constructs and the performance of various cognitive tasks are dependent on the motoric and perceptual system and on bodily interactions with the environment, such as physiognomic imitation and corporeal habituation of cultural patterns. Rittelmeyer replaces the concept according to which assumptions about the world are built into the structure of the organism through information-processing by the brain like a computer by a 'biological-organic epistemology without a neurocentric narrowing of perspective'. In the scientific field, he describes the use of visualising or imaging techniques in order to render visible body processes that are normally invisible, thus proving philosophical theories. Rittelmeyer describes so-called mindreading that is the reading of facial expressions by neural mirroring, as an example of basing scientific results on corporeal processes and the conditions under which they take place. He sees the consequences of the embodiment approach for pedagogy in the recognition of the importance of the sensomotoric system of the body for cognitive activity. The aim of this research lies in 'anthropologically substantiating more comprehensive and corporeal didactics'.

Promoting Embodiment Through Education in the Anthropocene

Renaud Hétier and Nathanaël Wallenhorst

1 Introduction

The COVID-19 pandemic is partly linked to the Anthropocene; unquestionably, it is a characteristic marker thereof. The concept of the Anthropocene originated in geology in the early 2000s; it refers to the new geological period which Earth's system has entered due to the impact of human activities. The advent of the Anthropocene means we have had a permanent impact on Earth's habitability, both for humans and for all living things. This scientific concept, which is increasingly heavily imbued with militant and political meanings, marks the point at which human survival is under threat.

We can even go so far as to say that COVID-19 is an Anthropocene disease—a tangible manifestation of the ecological and political threats that come with the dawn of the Anthropocene. This poses a particular problem in view of what we have experienced in recent times. The pandemic is (or has been) a crisis. However, it is something that can be overcome, and consigned to a particular slice of time, with a clearly demarcated beginning and end. The Anthropocene Epoch, on the other hand, has no foreseeable end. There is no way in which we can get through the Anthropocene, and then return to an earlier way of life—it marks a point of no return. We now have no choice but to try and organize human society against a geological backdrop that has been

---

R. Hétier (✉) • N. Wallenhorst
Catholic University of the West, Angers, France
e-mail: Renaud.hetier@uco.fr; nwallenh@uco.fr

© The Author(s), under exclusive license to Springer Nature Switzerland AG 2022
A. Kraus, C. Wulf (eds.), *The Palgrave Handbook of Embodiment and Learning*,
https://doi.org/10.1007/978-3-030-93001-1_2

irreversibly changed. The Anthropocene is characterized by countless crises (COVID-19 being just one example). One of the characteristics of this pandemic is that it has altered and reshaped our relationship with bodies: the human body in relation to the animal body and with the body politic, and the way in which we experience the living world.

During the pandemic, we in our physical bodies have been kept apart—imprisoned, even—as the result of political decisions. This is a clear indicator that the Anthropocene has begun. Now, in the field of education, we need to reflect on new ways of thinking. How can we plant the seeds of a relationship with the body which is characterized, firstly, by its inclusion in the creative and resilient living world? That world itself will, undoubtedly, be able to weather the coming storm, though humanity's endurance is less certain. Is it possible to fully grasp the concept of embodiment, in the Anthropocene Epoch, against the backdrop of Enlivenment?[1]

2   When Politics Separates and Confines Bodies

In France, during the lockdowns in the years 2020 and 2021, public spaces were off limits until further notice. Everyone had to stay home, so as not to overload hospital resuscitation departments, which simply were not set up to cope with so widespread health crisis. The aim was to prevent people dying at home or on the streets for lack of treatment—though COVID-19 patients often died *in spite* of the professional care they received. The slogans exhorted everyone to stay home 'to save lives'—starting with their own. Suddenly, everyone was acutely aware of the timeframe over which the crisis was unfolding. Nothing, apparently, is more effective than an emergency in shutting down our ability to think clearly. During the first few weeks of lockdown, powerful emotions (especially distress and anguish) came flooding to the fore, with rationality fading into the background. It can be said that our ability to think and to deliberate were simultaneously affected. That is, a state of emergency makes people think in terms of immediacy (their actions are guided by instinct and emotion rather than rationality)—a knee-jerk reaction, where actions take the path of least resistance. Politics, however, requires us to think in the long term and to deliberate rationally. We found ourselves faced with a formidable problem: political

---

[1] This chapter was written by two Frenchmen, in the wake of months of lockdown to combat the COVID-19 pandemic. The perspective expressed in this chapter—particularly in the first part—is that of a Frenchman, and relates specifically to the political context in France. [*Nevertheless, the general points about the human experience apply quite readily in other sociocultural contexts*].

and intellectual function in an emergency represent a veritable contradiction in terms. The healthcare measures, including but not limited to the lockdown, meant the populace was restricted in unprecedented ways. The strategy may have effectively suppressed the spread of the virus, but only because sufficient information was promulgated to enable everyone to fully grasp the reality of the danger, and appreciate that the measures were genuinely necessary. Hence, the general point must be conceded: we ceased to use public spaces in full knowledge and with our full consent.[2] As individuals, though, each person attached different levels of priority to (a) their physical safety and (b) their freedom (freedom of body, movement and contact).

This crisis is symptomatic of globalization and of the Anthropocene. Many factors have contributed to the dawn of the Anthropocene, but prominent among these are the unlimited exploitation and global exchange of resources. Such unrestricted exchanges bring organisms into contact which have, hitherto, been independent of one another, and allow them to circulate far and fast. In that respect, COVID-19 is a disease of global capitalism, which also is related, in part, to the Anthropocene. Today, it is clear that unlimited human exploitation of ecosystems disrupts the balance between animals, plants and pathogens. The pandemic must be understood in the context of the Anthropocene (and papers and newspaper articles show that epidemics are breaking out ever more rapidly—Grandcola and Valo 2020; Mouterde 2020; Thiaw 2020). In addition, COVID-19 first appeared in China—the 'reactor core' of modern economic globalization—and, in the space of only a few weeks, spread all over the world. As far as the Anthropocene is linked with global capitalism (this new geological period could even be said to be 'Capitalocene' and 'Globalocene'), the pandemic is, at its very origin, 'anthropocenic'.

The COVID-19 crisis saw a certain type of authoritarianism, which we believe is symptomatic of political desolation.[3] This remark needs to be put into context. Today, the world over, there is an extremely pervasive, and subjective, sense of insecurity. Though the world is safer today than it has ever been, everyone appears to be afraid of everything. For example, parents seem

---

[2] Note that in the digital age in which we live, there is less and less need to actually move in order to connect with others, or to engage in some form of struggle.

[3] Since the 1980s, with the disastrous policies of Ronald Reagan, Margaret Thatcher and later, François Mitterrand, neoliberalism has become the policy of those in power. We have witnessed the scuttling of the political system: as the State has been reduced in importance, politics has taken a back seat. However, this has meant that politicians have to actively support the economic sector (it cannot survive without this support): with the high-risk game of finance, with all the losses and crashes that come with it, costs are incurred that businesses cannot cover (damage to the environment, pollution cleanup, dismantling of factories etc.).

to be constantly worried about the safety of their children, who spend far less time outside than did previous generations—today's children are much too busy with digital technologies. In the face of COVID-19, most governments implemented restrictive health measures, because of some kind of emotional communion or contagion (which can surely be analyzed from the perspective of mimicry). This suggests politics is no longer playing the role it should—to *convert* emotions (tragedy, in the words of the Ancient Greeks) into *logos*, elaboration and debate (the agora, the City). In addition, given the astonishing progress in science, each human being is increasingly in a position to control events (thus, we are no longer powerless, as we were in the Middle Ages, when we did not know how to protect ourselves from the Black Death). The approach adopted stems from the principle of precaution, with anxiety being exploited to achieve safety. Finally, as a result, we have also entered a period of extreme litigiousness. For this reason, all authority figures have become extremely defensive (think of the nightmare faced by mayors who had been ordered to reopen schools, while trying to ensure the safety of the children in those classrooms). Above all else (be it political or health-related), they rush to protect themselves from potential complaints (in fact, formal complaints were lodged against government ministers themselves).

The management of the COVID-19 pandemic is indicative not of the return, so sorely needed, to normality in politics, but rather of a political void. In France, the government has been given unlimited power in dealing with the crisis; the National Assembly has been bypassed entirely, with its debates becoming irrelevant—in the name of 'managing the crisis effectively'. This means, however, that many authoritarian decisions have been made that are no longer 'political', if that term is understood as what emerges from regulated debate in our institutions. A campaign was launched, calling on people to 'stay home to save lives', and the message was relayed by vast numbers of YouTubers, influencers, private citizens, associations or other professional organizations without critical distance. What does 'saving lives' really mean? What is a 'life' when stripped of all social, cultural and political roots? What are these 'lives' that need protecting? Do we as citizens really want to be 'protected' by the State? By 'protecting' us, the State strips us of our duty to participate in world affairs. But should the State not, instead, be facilitating our involvement and democratic exposure?

Since the days of ancient Athens, politics has offered the opportunity for public presence and '*corps-à-corps*'[4] (in-person) discussion. Today, though, we

---

[4] '*Corps-à-corps*' refers to a relationship of proximity between at least two bodies, which may be erotic, tender or agonistic.

are caught in a paradox, between a political vacuum (the State has stepped back, allowing commercial interests to become prevalent; and people's physical bodies have been confined) and an excessive focus on authoritarianism, security and health (saturating the public consciousness with anguish and blame). Indeed, while it is the right response from a health perspective, the solution deployed is profoundly unsatisfactory from a political standpoint: in the long term, it is dangerous—all the more so if it lasts for a long time or is repeated. The limitation of physical liberties has accelerated in recent times. The rise of virtual technologies has already limited physical motion in our daily lives. This foreshadows the human condition in the Anthropocene, with the combination of two components. Firstly, there is growing inhospitality that will lead to defensive behavior, with people shutting themselves off. Secondly, there is an increasing sense of insecurity (resulting from increasing demographic shifts, and burgeoning inequality). As a result, people take refuge in safe havens (the richest among us are currently investing in New Zealand, among other places) and barricade themselves in 'strongholds'.[5] Thus, the Anthropocene could be marked by the overflow of humanity across the planet, causing the human body to 'retreat' into enclosed, private spaces. That is to say, it is not only the COVID-19 pandemic that has weakened political action, but rather the Anthropocene, which is sure to last a few thousand years, at least. Anthropogenic effects, which cause irreversible harm to our planet, seem to be due to a form of unrestrained pleasure-seeking (especially consumption). This is physical enjoyment, and as such, fits in perfectly with a material approach (consumption of the world). An 'effective' political decision would be to try to constrain physical bodies and limit such enjoyment—by force if necessary, if individuals refuse to comply—in the context of an authoritarian State. Such an approach would limit access to resources (energy, food, items, travel etc.) and also sanction any excesses (obesity, unnecessary travel, consumption of toxic products, excessive reproduction etc.) in a fashion reminiscent of *The Handmaid's Tale*. Ultimately, we must ask, beyond a trend toward authoritarianism or totalitarianism, what becomes of democratic public function without physical presence—without '*corps-à-corps*' debate. This is a problem in itself, in our hyperspecialized and hyper-technical societies: today, it is no longer enough—as it was in Socrates' time—to know oneself and examine one's thoughts in order to be a true citizen. Decisions often need to be based on knowledge that is not necessarily widely accessible

---

[5] Such is the case, for example, in Brazil—see https://www.courrierinternational.com/article/1999/10/07/quand-les-riches-bresiliens-vivent-en-etat-de-siege

('expert knowledge'). There is always the risk that technology will dilute the essence of democracy.

The Anthropocene will undoubtedly have an increasing impact on our bodies, both physically and politically. COVID-19 affords us the opportunity to prepare for that impact by forging bonds (as some have done with gestures of solidarity: taking care of caregivers, singing on balconies, screening movies on the sides of buildings, manufacturing facemasks instead of lingerie etc.). We can also forge similar connections with the living world as a whole, by taking back possession of arenas for expression, exchange and conviviality that are too often neglected, in order to cultivate our sense of belonging to a 'common people'.

3   A Regression of the Experience of Bodily Interaction

COVID-19 is not the first disease to tear us apart from one another. Even when the Black Death was ravishing Europe, our ancestors learned social distancing. Advances in hygiene and medicine have meant we have been able to drop our guard. However, in the 1980s, the HIV epidemic made contact with others dangerous once more. Admittedly, HIV affected only intimate relations, and solutions could be found; but something changed: the bodies of others became potential sources of danger, and we had to learn to protect ourselves. Even by putting on a condom, we are putting a certain distance between ourselves and others, introducing a foreign body object into the naked '*corps-à-corps*' experience. With COVID-19, which is far less deadly than was HIV before triple therapy was developed, the harsh measures taken may mean greater social distancing for a long time to come. The experience of lockdown is one of complete removal—or imprisonment—of the body. Yet even after lockdown ends, some of its effects remain. To be unable to touch with our hands, and to see the other person's face, detracts directly from the very thing that makes us human. Remember that the *homo* genus came about by straightening the body and gait, thus freeing the hands to manipulate objects, and allowing the face, open to the horizon, to finally communicate. It is likely that our haptic habits will soon resume in our private relationships, but professional or public relations will remain marked by physical distance, which will mark a cultural transition. France—a Latin country with a rather tactile culture—will likely come into line with the more reserved, aloof cultures of the English-speaking world and Scandinavia.

Epidemics could be interpreted as time-localized 'accidents', whose impact continues to be felt over time to varying degrees. In the Western world, we have all but forgotten the Plague. However, there is a gradual cultural evolution toward greater bodily distancing. There are several contributing factors. The first is urbanization: concentrating a large population in a limited space, inevitably leads to a certain degree of anonymity. While we still greet each other on a path (whether we are running or walking), we typically do not exchange greetings on a city sidewalk. The next factor is the capitalist system, in which humans are viewed as exploitable resources. Capitalism has no hesitation in displacing people (human commodities: the best example is to be found in the centuries of slavery), or bringing them together *en masse* (e.g., in factories and workshops in the industrial era). This system uproots individuals, and causes them to experience a certain degree of isolation, even amid a crowd of others. As Tocqueville noted, the establishment of democracy marks another turning point. Prefiguring H. Rosa's treatise on social acceleration (2010), Tocqueville stated:

> [D]emocratic peoples are grave, because their social and political condition constantly leads them to engage in serious occupations; and they act inconsiderately, because they give but little time and attention to each of these occupations [...]. (1990, p. 188)

Hand in hand with democracy comes individualism (which is linked to equality), and a sense of self-importance, self-recognition and confidence in one's own activity. Individuals, who are increasingly overwhelmed, are paying less and less attention to others, which widens the chiasm between them. This trend is constantly being amplified by the phenomenon of social acceleration, which Rosa highlights.

In the West, at least, we see another anthropological viewpoint emerge in the eighteenth century, both in culture and in education. Norbert Elias notes that vision—the sense which requires least closeness—is given certain priority in our society. Claudine Haroche (2008, p. 170) points out:

> Since vision is less threatening to the social order than touching, it becomes necessary to avoid physical contact, and make eye contact only. Establishing contact—letting glimpses of kindness, or especially warmth, show through; being touched or moved by another, a peer, by his condition—will tend, for a variety of reasons, to decline. They will be supplanted by distance, coldness, hardness, insensitivity; an attitude of observation, evaluation, calculation, resulting in interchangeability and indifference to one's peers.

This emotional distancing from one another is linked to bodily distancing, and a retreat from the phenomena resulting from physical presence: the sense of closeness but also movement. Elias notes that

> the pleasures of the eyes and ears become ever more intense, richer, more subtle and more widespread, while the pleasures of the flesh are increasingly limited by commandments and prohibitions. (Elias, 1991, p. 163)

These remarks are of value for our analysis: we see how a certain inhibition of the body, and particularly of '*corps-à-corps*' interaction, with the attending physical contact, is partly linked with lending too much importance to 'what is left'—that is, remote perception. We shall examine this point in depth in the next paragraph.

Postman (1996) noted in 1983 that modern media (television, especially) tend to expose children to what he called 'adult secrets', including violence and sexuality, from which they had been sheltered since the late Middle Ages, by the division of adults and children imposed by the schooling system. Of course, this trend has practically skyrocketed with the advent of the internet and free access to pornography. The aim here is to analyze this evolution from the perspective of the role the body now has. Plainly, today's children are not in the same situation as those in the Middle Ages, who were frequently exploited and often abused. Through their screens, though, children are indeed exposed to a great deal of violent imagery. This violence of images (Houssier, 2008) creates fascination, and the experience is all-consuming. This phenomenon can be analyzed in the context of excitation of the scopic drive. For children and adolescents, screens are so pervasive that, without a doubt, we can point to 'overstimulation'. Screens represent a pleasure which is difficult to get away from (so they create a certain dependency). This addiction also inhibits the potential of other senses and impulses, and reduces overall mobility. When we speak of a 'fixed gaze', we are referring to the immobility of that gaze. We can also say, though, that such a gaze hypnotizes and immobilizes the viewer themselves. It seems that digital technology, and the digital industry, has found a way to literally alienate digital 'consumers' by seizing their attention in an unrelenting grip (Stiegler, 2008). The immobilizing effect on their bodies is even more powerful. This explains how children— who, it must be recognized, have a pressing *need* to move around—find themselves immobilized: screens—especially video game screens—provide them with constant movement, stimulating the scopic drive. This stimulation is redoubled, since users can make the images move by interacting with the game.

Such immobilization also helps keep people apart from one another, leading to a sort of voluntary confinement. In addition, we can wonder about the more general process of virtualization (Lévy, 1995). Here, the term refers to a general process by which humans mediate their interactions with others. This began, at the dawn of humanity, with the use of primitive tools and the development of language, and it continues today through the burgeoning presence of technology. Not only does technological development mean ever-more 'machines' are being interposed between humans, and between people and the outside world; the world itself has become one of hyper-communication. In other words, we increasingly connect with others and with the world through languages, objects and images. The crisis of resonance which Rosa describes (2018, 2020) can also be interpreted as over-mediation. Texts and images have become more striking than real-world events; virtual universes mean that the living of real life is now only optional; and the world has been reduced to what our devices can comprehend. When, today, do we present ourselves to the world, to nature, to life around us, without some form of mediation? Only in the context of a sexual experience can we have an 'unarmored' and 'naked' relationship with someone else, without the intercession of any external objects—just with our bodies (provided the experience is not tainted by the compulsion to conform to pornographic ideals). The advance of virtualization and digital technology ultimately marginalizes the *agōn* and *eros* of the '*corps-à-corps*' experience (Hétier, 2014). This trend culminates with the creation of avatars (Tisseron, 2012). The body itself becomes virtualized. Our sense of our own bodies practically evaporates, being traded for constant virtual movement (in a form of 'transcendental life'), and we develop a false sense of immortality (given that, in the digital world, one can always simply respawn).

4 Restoring a Bodily Experience of the Living World: Promoting Embodiment Through Education in the Anthropocene, Against the Backdrop of Enlivenment

What can be done, in education, to lay the foundations to enable people to have a different type of relationship with their own bodies? How can we, as educators, encourage a relationship with the body that interacts with the living world, through the flesh? How do we approach active participation in the living world? The contemporary German biologist and philosopher Andreas

Weber, whose work follows on from Critical Theory, developed by the Frankfurt School (closely connected to Rosa's research), proposes a particularly interesting shift of thought in order to comprehend embodiment in the Anthropocene. We should think of our awareness of the world, not only from the standpoint of Enlightenment similar to that which gave rise to the Industrial Revolution, but also from the standpoint of a form of Enlivenment for the Anthropocene. This concept is particularly present in two of Weber's works: the first, co-written with his fellow philosopher Hildegard Kurt, *Lebendigkeit sei! Für eine Politik des Lebens. Ein Manifest für das Anthropozän* (2015) (Towards Cultures of Aliveness: Politics and Poetics in a Postdualistic Age—an Anthropocene Manifesto) and the second, *Enlivenment. Eine Kultur des Lebens. Versuch einer Poetik für das Anthropozän* (2016) (no official English translation found).

What we need to do, in Weber's view, is supplement Enlightenment by steering contemporary societies toward reintegration with the living world. What Weber proposes is that intellectuals shift focus away from Enlightenment and onto vitalization. In each of Weber's works written in German, he uses the term 'Enlivenment', a word he invented, undoubtedly to highlight the parallel with the term *Enlightenment*, and emphasize the importance of adopting this paradigm in the way in which we think, and in the way in which human society is organized. The word refers to a form of dynamics intrinsic to living creatures, which must be allowed to be expressed and to spread, bringing the human experience along with it.

Enlivenment is based on what we have in common—what we share with other creatures: living and feeling. This concept discards the idea of separation between humans and the natural world. The premise is that humans' notion of total dominion over the living matter that constitutes us is nothing more than an illusion. In our modern way of living, everything has been seized upon as 'culture', and we have developed the belief that we are superior to nature. Weber decries an approach to the world based on mechanisms designed with efficiency in mind. Rather, his approach to the world, which Kurt echoes in their coauthored manifesto, is 'A process of creative relations and interpenetration allowing us to experience and express' (Weber, & Kurt, 2015, p. 11). This view is rooted in the current revolution of biological thinking, 'similar to the revolutions in physics [...] through relativity theory and quantum physics' (p. 11). In fact, '[h]umans and nature are one, because creative imagination and feeling expression are natural forces' (Weber & Kurt, 2015, p. 11).

Above all, Enlivenment celebrates vitality. Life holds irrepressible and subversive power and creativity, which simply cannot be contained or influenced.

Furthermore, it is the vitality of others (both human and non-human) and of our environment that makes our own existence possible. The crux of this notion is that, far from being exceptional in comparison to other lifeforms, we humans are an integral part of a vast web of life. Fundamentally, life is beyond our control, as it *should* be, according to Weber's idea of Enlivenment. It is precisely by recognizing and embracing our place in this infinitely interconnected fabric of life that we will be able to survive the Anthropocene. The power of vitality and solidarity between all living things can offer hope, so it is crucial we do not view ourselves as being, in any way, removed from the rest of that web. Enlivenment refers to the conception of life as a creative practice, as opposed to a technical exercise. The idea of Enlivenment, upon which the manifesto places particular emphasis, hinges on the need to fundamentally alter the way in which we think about human beings: we must think about the ways in which we are connected to the rest of the living world—in terms of the biological fundaments of life.

Weber cites the American poet and eco-philosopher Gary Snyder, and his view of the wild as a process beyond human control. It is not by controlling the Earth that life will be made better; it is by participating in the natural intercourse of existence. That represents a major shift from our current practices. The 'human adventure' (understood as this inclusion of humanity within the living world, characterized by the uncertainty and malleability of its anthropological fate) has a role to play. We have the possibility to participate more fully in this web of solidarity between all living beings. Such participation is possible, but it is poetic, and is diametrically opposite to human control of our environment.

Enlivenment can be viewed as a form of second Enlightenment ('Aufklärung 2.0') (Weber, 2016, p. 25). Andreas Weber criticizes Enlightenment and its ideology of death, where everything around us is viewed as inert matter. (It should, however, be remembered that Enlightenment was a highly multifaceted concept—a fact which Weber seems to overlook somewhat when constructing his argument). Weber's work follows on from Max Horkheimer and Theodor W. Adorno's critique in their *Dialectic of Enlightenment* (1972). Horkheimer and Adorno highlight how the ideology of Enlightenment did not only bring freedom, but also contributed to catastrophic totalitarianism. However, it should be recognized that in this criticism of Enlightenment, Horkheimer and Adorno did not put forward any alternative approach. This is what Weber set out to do by proposing the concept of Enlivenment. Thus, Weber's work is directly connected to Hartmut Rosa's approach, which also follows on from the Frankfurt school's Critical Theory. In addition, alongside the concept of resonance, Rosa develops an alternative concept: a kind of political proposition. Enlivenment is a 'corrective' type of concept. The concepts of Enlivenment and resonance are closely intertwined. For instance, Weber frequently uses the term *Verbindung*, which can be translated as a relationship, link or connection. The concept of Enlivenment lends an additional biological foundation to the concept of resonance (in addition, e.g., to the mirror neurons which Rosa describes).

The poetics of Enlivenment criticize, firstly, neo-Darwinism, with the idea of biological optimization, and secondly, neo-liberalism, with its quest for economic efficiency (Weber, 2016, p. 45). These two paradigms may, at times, seem sufficient to encapsulate our current knowledge of how the world works. However, they fail to recognize any commonality among humans, and between humanity and the rest of the living world. (Both theories also ignore cooperative dynamics). In Enlivenment, Andreas Weber shows that the anthropological concepts based on individual competition, at the heart of our biological (Darwinism) and economic (liberalism) function, are linked to the way in which we have historically viewed reality. Weber suggests shifting our perspective. The world is not a never-ending war of every person for him or herself. We need to supplant the bio-liberal principles that guide our scientific, political and educational decisions with the dynamics and principles of Enlivenment. Being aware of one's own vitality is the foundation upon which to build a connection with nature and other living organisms. While education in the Anthropocene entails education in resonance, it also involves educating in favor of Enlivenment (both experiential, allowing us to feel our immersion in the living world, and cognitive, learning to overcome the dominant Cartesian rationale). The term Enlivenment is deliberately chosen so as to closely relate to and link in with the ideas of Enlightenment. It is not a question of replacing rational thought and empirical observation with poetics, but of being able to interlink different rationalities. It is a question of allowing science, politics and society to regain interest in sensitivity to the lives both of human beings and of other creatures.

Enlivenment is the cornerstone of a policy of civilization that can come about through establishing a culture of vitality, whose purpose is to allow us to survive the Anthropocene Epoch. Thus, Enlivenment counters the ideas about nature which tend to shape political positions. Firstly, nature is not efficient. Quite the contrary—it is continually wasteful: fish, amphibians and insects have to lay millions of eggs in order for just a few to reach maturity. Another example of this inefficiency is the fact that warm-blooded animals use 90% of their energy simply to keep their metabolism running. Secondly, the biosphere is not growing. The biomass of the biosphere is in balance (with only very slight variations). Thus, nature is characterized by a steady state.

Thirdly, no new species has ever appeared as a result of competition for resources. Rather, it is new cooperation and symbioses (or simply chance) that allow new forms of life to emerge. Fourthly, nature affords resources enough for everyone; the prime example of this is solar energy, which is abundant enough for all living things. Thus, we can conclude that, with symbioses and cooperation, all species should be able to coexist. Fifthly, the concept of ownership has no place in the biosphere. The body itself is not the property of the creature which inhabits it, given that it must interact with its environment and is characterized by exchanges of matter (Weber, 2016, pp. 55–57). In view of the above observations, Andreas Weber developed biopoetics as a model of living relationships.

What is particularly interesting in Weber's philosophical and political thinking is that the dawn of the Anthropocene should not crush all hope. On the contrary, the vitality of life means we can embrace revitalization and renewed solidarity in our lives, with our existences becoming political capital. The Earth, and the living macro-ecosystem upon it, shows us what we must do if we are to survive the Anthropocene. We are not masters of the Earth; rather, the Earth—and the web of life which inhabits it—is master of us. From this perspective, Enlivenment breaks with all forms of anthropocentrism.

5   Conclusion

The global crisis that is COVID-19 reveals uncomfortable truths about human society today. It has forced us to face up to accelerated, intensified manifestations of trends that are already at work in our societies: notably, political weakness, and heavy investment in security to compensate, sometimes with the unmistakable tang of authoritarianism. This has a major impact on our freedoms and, in particular, the ability to actually be with one another physically, be it for social interaction or for debate. This is part of a longstanding historical tendency to create distance between us. The role of digital devices in this trend cannot be underestimated, as they facilitate communication, but bypass the need for physical presence and '*corps-à-corps*' interaction. Andreas Weber reminds us how nature possesses vital power, and how the living world is inextricably linked to a complex environment. Humankind's Promethean error is, without a doubt, losing sight of our corporeal nature, by which we are firmly grounded in the natural world and on our planet. From an educational perspective, we need to completely re-examine individuation, and with it, the idea of autonomy. Even before we begin to look at the catastrophic consequences of individualism, the shaping of an individual identity must go hand in hand with an awareness of, and regular reflection on, interdependence (Second Convivialist Manifesto): interdependence which is experienced through daily life in the flesh—interdependence with others, with the living world and with the world itself. It is a concrete, dynamic and collaborative task, whose aim must be to 'give life' (Hétier, 2019, 2021) to all that we can.

References

Adorno T. W., & Horkheimer, M. (1972 [1944]). *Dialectic of Enlightenment*. Herder and Herder.

Elias, N. (1991). *La société des individus*. Fayard.

Grandcola, P., & Valo, M. (interview). (2020). Coronavirus: L'origine de l'épidémie de Covid-19 est liée aux bouleversement que nous imposons à la biodiversité. *Le Monde*, https://www.lemonde.fr/sciences/article/2020/04/04/pandemies-nous-offrons-a-des-agents-infectieux-de-nouvelles-chaines-de-transmission_6035590_1650684.html

Haroche, C. (2008). *L'avenir du sensible. Les sens et les sentiments en question*. PUF.

Hétier, R. (2014). Aspiration numérique et mise à distance du corps. *Recherches en éducation, 18*, 122–131. http://www.recherches-en-education.net/IMG/pdf/REE-no18.pdf

Hétier, R. (2019). Apprendre à faire vivre. In N. Wallenhorst & J. P. Pierron (Eds.), *Éduquer en Anthropocène*. Le bord de l'eau.

Hétier, R. (2021). Faire vivre. In N. Wallenhorst & C. Wulf (Eds.), *Dictionnaire d'anthropologie prospective*. Vrin.

Houssier, F. (Ed.). (2008). *La violence de l'image*. In Press.

Internationale convivialiste. (2020). *Second manifeste convivialiste*. Actes Sud.

Lévy, P. (1995). *Qu'est-ce que le virtuel?* La Découverte.

Mouterde, P. (2020). Coronavirus: la dégradation de la biodiversité en question. *Le Monde*, https://www.lemonde.fr/sciences/article/2020/04/04/coronavirus-la-degradation-de-la-biodiversite-en-question_6035591_1650684.html

Postman, N. (1996 [1982]). *Il n'y a plus d'enfance*. Insep Consulting.

Rosa, H. (2010 [2005]). *Accélération*. La Découverte.

Rosa, H. (2018 [2016]). *Résonance. Une sociologie de la relation au monde*. La Découverte.

Rosa, H. (2020). *Rendre le monde indisponible*. La Découverte.

Stiegler, B. (2008). *Prendre soin de la jeunesse et des générations*. Flammarion.

Thiaw, I. (2020). Coronavirus: Les animaux qui nous ont infectés ne sont pas venus à nous; nous sommes allés les chercher. *Le Monde.* https://www.lemonde.fr/idees/article/2020/03/29/coronavirus-la-pandemie-demande-que-nous-re-definissions-un-contrat-naturel-et-social-entre-l-homme-et-la-nature_6034804_3232.html

Tisseron, S. (2012). *Rêver, fantasmer, virtualiser. Du virtuel psychique au virtuel numérique.* Dunod.

Tocqueville, A. (1990). *De la démocratie en Amérique.* Vrin.

Weber, A. (2016). *Enlivenment. Eine Kultur des Lebens. Versuch einer Poetik für das Anthropozän.* Matthes und Seitz.

Weber, A., & Kurt, H. (2015). *Lebendigkeit sei! Für eine Politik des Lebens. Ein Manifest für das Anthropozän.* Think Oya.

Embodiment Through Mimetic Learning

Christoph Wulf

In many mimetic processes the body plays a central role which is often not obvious. This is true especially for mimetic processes in which body-based learning takes place. In mimetic processes a creative re-creation takes place in which learners learn and incorporate new knowledge, through using their senses, body movements and imagination (Brandstetter & Wulf, 2007). In these processes learning and education take place. They make clear the extent to which humans are social beings who need other humans and their approach to culture and society as role models for their own development. People behaving in a mimetic way are both active and passive at the same time. Mimetic processes are directed toward other people and the way they behave and are driven by an active urge to become like them. Since people acting mimetically use other people as role models, they have a receptive attitude toward them and absorb or incorporate them into themselves. Mimetic behavior is an interweaving of active and receptive elements. The result is not a simple copying of other people and the way they act. What happens is far more that the people acting mimetically become similar to their role models in a way that is specific to them. The result is a new way of behaving which is both similar and different at the same time.

For Josephine and Karlotta.

C. Wulf (✉)
Anthropology and Education, Freie Universität Berlin, Berlin, Germany
e-mail: christoph.wulf@fu-berlin.de

© The Author(s), under exclusive license to Springer Nature Switzerland AG 2022
A. Kraus, C. Wulf (eds.), *The Palgrave Handbook of Embodiment and Learning*,
https://doi.org/10.1007/978-3-030-93001-1_3

Infants and small children relate to the people with whom they live: parents, elder siblings, other relatives and acquaintances. They try to be like them, by, for example, answering a smile with a smile. However, they also initiate responses in adults by using skills they have already acquired (Dornes, 1993; Stern, 2003). These early exchanges also enable small children to learn new forms of behavior, language and feelings. They learn to evoke their own feelings toward other people and to elicit them in others. Initially, the mimetic actions of infants and children do not allow for a separation of subject and object; this occurs only at a later stage of development. At first, the world is perceived as magical, that is, not only humans but also objects are experienced as being alive. As rationality becomes more developed the capacity to experience the world in this way gradually becomes less central. However, it is this capacity upon which children draw to transform the external world into images in mimetic processes and to incorporate them into their internal image worlds (Gebauer & Wulf, 1995).

In his autobiography, *Berlin Childhood around 1900*, Walter Benjamin (2006) illustrated how children incorporate their cultural environments in processes of assimilation. During these processes, children assimilate aspects of the parental home, such as the rooms, particular corners, objects and atmospheres. They are incorporated as 'imprints' of the images and stored in the child's imaginary world, where they are subsequently transformed into new images and memories that help the child gain access to other cultural worlds. Culture is handed on by means of these processes of incorporating and making sense of cultural products. The mimetic ability to transform the external material world into images, transferring them into our internal worlds of images and making them accessible to others enables individuals to actively shape cultural realities (Wulf, 2022a; Gebauer & Wulf, 1998, 2003).

These processes encompass not only our modes of dealing with the material products of culture, but also social relationships and forms of activity and the way social life is staged and performed. This involves forms of practical knowledge that are learned mimetically in body-oriented, sensory processes and enable people to act competently in institutions and organizations (Wulf, 2006b). This knowledge is learnt in rituals and gestures (Wulf, 2005); and this is how institutions become rooted in the human body. Images, schemas and movements are learnt in mimetic processes, and these render the individual capable of action. Since mimetic processes involve products of history and culture, scenes, arrangements and performances, these processes are among the most important ways of handing down culture from one generation to the next. Without our mimetic abilities, cultural learning and 'double inheritance', that is, the handing down of cultural products along with biological inheritance, which enables culture to change and develop, would not be possible (Wulf, 2022a, b).

Cultural learning is mimetic learning, which is at the center of many processes of education and self-education. It is directed toward other people, social communities and cultural heritages and ensures that they are kept alive. Mimetic learning is a sensory, body-based form of learning in which images, schemas and movements needed to perform actions are learnt. This occurs largely unconsciously, and it is this that is responsible for the lasting effects that play an important role in all areas of cultural development (Kraus et al., 2021). 'Becoming similar' to the world in mimetic actions becomes an opportunity to leave egocentrism, logocentrism and ethnocentrism behind and to open oneself to experiences of otherness (Wulf, 2006a, 2016). However, mimetic processes are also linked to aspirations to forms and experiences of higher levels of life, in which vital experiences can be sought and found. As the experience of love, mimetic movements invoke "the power to see similarity in the dissimilar" (Adorno, 1978, p. 191). No knowledge is possible without the production of similarities, without mimesis. It is certainly taken as true for scientific knowledge that mimesis is indispensable in the process of knowing.

> Cognition itself cannot be conceived without the supplement of mimesis, however that may be sublimated. Without mimesis the break between subject and object would be absolute and cognition impossible. (Adorno, 1982, p. 143)

If a mimetic element is indispensable in scientific knowledge, it is at the heart of cultural experience (Michaels & Wulf, 2020). These processes are of central importance for our understanding of the human situation in the globalized world of the Anthropocene (Wallenhorst & Wulf, 2022, 2023).

1   Social Learning and Culture

Recent studies in the field of primate research have shown that although elementary forms of mimetic learning can be found in other primates as well, human beings are especially capable of mimetic learning. In the light of the research into the social behavior of primates and in comparison with them, studies in the field of developmental psychology and cognitive psychology over recent years have managed to pin down some characteristics of mimetic learning in humans at a young age and to ascertain the special nature of mimetic learning in babies and small children. Michael Tomasello sums up these abilities of toddlers as follows:

[…] they identify with other persons; perceive other persons as intentional agents like the self; engage with other persons in joint attentional activities; understand many of the causal relations that hold among physical objects and events in the world; understand the communicative intentions that other persons express in gestures, linguistic symbols, and linguistic constructions; learn through role-reversal imitation to produce for others those same gestures, symbols, and constructions; and construct linguistically based object categories and event schemas. (Tomasello, 1999, p. 161).

It is through these abilities that young children become able to participate in cultural processes. They can take part in enactments of the practices and skills of the social group in which they live and acquire the cultural knowledge of that group in this way (Wulf & Baitello, 2018). The abilities described are indicative of the central importance of role models for mimetic learning processes in young children. These processes can be understood as mimetic processes. The ability to identify with other persons, to see them as individuals who act intentionally and to direct their attention toward something together with them is due to the mimetic desire of the child to emulate adults, to become like them. It is this desire to become similar to older people that motivates children to understand causal relationships between the objects of the world, to comprehend the intentions of other people as they communicate them in gestures, symbols and constructions and to develop categories of objects and event schemata. Infants as young as nine months are already in possession of these abilities that are inherent in the human mimetic capacities and not available to other primates at any point in their lives.

2 Mirror Neurons

These insights were confirmed by research in the neurosciences that began to prove humans differ from other primates by the fact that they are equipped in a special way to discover the world in mimetic processes (Rizzolatti & Signigaglia, 2008; Jacoboni, 2008). The reason for this is the mirror neuron system. The analysis of the way mirror neurons function shows how recognition of other people, their actions and intentions is dependent on our capacity for movement. The mirror neuron system appears to enable the human brain to relate observed movements to our own capacity for movement and to recognize the importance of this. Without this mechanism we would perceive the movements and actions of other people but we would not know what their actions mean and what they are really doing. The mirror neurons are a physiological condition for us to be able to act not only as individuals but also as social beings. They are important in mimetic behavior and learning, gestural and verbal communication and understanding the emotional reactions of other people. The perception of someone's pain or disgust activates the same areas of the brain that would be activated if we were feeling these things directly ourselves. Although there are also non-human primates that have mirror neurons, the system is more complex in human beings. Unlike non-human primates, humans have the capacity to differentiate between transitive and intransitive movements and to select types of action and the sequence of actions that constitute these types. They can also become active in actions that are not carried out in reality but are merely imitated. The mirror neuron system enables us to grasp the actions of other people, and not just isolated actions but also sequences of actions. In addition, numerous experiments have shown something that primate research also proved to be true for children during the first year of life, that is, that the mirror neuron system does not only process observed actions but also the intentions lying behind these actions. If we see somebody completing an action then their movements have a direct meaning for us. The same is true of our actions and the way they are understood by other people. Moreover, experiments have also shown that the quality of the movement system and the mirror neuron system represents necessary, although insufficient, conditions for mimetic behavior. Further neuronal processes would be needed for processes to arise that are more than simply repetition, but rather processes in which people become mimetically similar to the world and other people.

Mimetic processes are initially directed toward other people. It is in mimetic processes that infants and toddlers refer to the people with whom they live, that is, their parents, older brothers and sisters and other relatives and acquaintances. They try to make themselves similar to these people, for instance by responding to a smile with a smile. However, they also elicit the corresponding responses from the adults by employing the abilities they have already learned. In these early interactive processes toddlers also learn about feelings, for example. They learn to produce them in themselves in relation to other people and to evoke them in other people. Their brains evolve in interactions with their environments; this means that certain of their potential capacities develop, while others decline. The cultural conditions of this early phase of life are inscribed in the children's brains and bodies. Anyone who has not learned to see, hear, feel or speak at an early age cannot learn these abilities adequately at a later stage. To begin with there is no separation between subject and object in the mimetic referencing of infants and toddlers. At this point their perception of the world is magical, that is, not only the people but also the things are experienced as animate. This ability to experience the world becomes lost as we develop reason, but it contains important opportunities for us to change the outside world into images and absorb it into our inner image world.

3   Anthropological Approaches

We can describe social and cultural actions as mimetic if, firstly, as movements they refer back to other movements, secondly, they can be understood as physical performances or stagings and, thirdly, they are stand-alone actions that can be understood in their own terms and that refer to other actions or worlds. This means that actions such as mental calculations, decisions, reflex or routine behavior and also one-off actions and actions that break the rules are not mimetic (Gebauer & Wulf, 1998). In order to better understand the cultural significance of mimetic processes there are seven aspects that I would identify.

1. The linguistic origin of the term 'mimesis' and the historical context of the way it was originally used point to the role that mimetic processes play in the staging of cultural practices and the culture of performativity (Gebauer & Wulf, 1995).
2. Mimesis must not be seen as simple copying as in making photocopies. What it is, is far more a creative human capacity which assists in the creation of new things (Gebauer & Wulf, 1998; Wulf, 2013a, b, 2022a, b).
3. The performativity of social and cultural actions and behavior is an important prerequisite for mimetic learning processes (Wulf et al., 2001; Wulf & Zirfas, 2007, 2014).
4. In the arts and aesthetics mimetic processes have an important role to play. However it is important to recognize that mimesis is not restricted to aesthetics. It is, in fact, an anthropological concept which has a distinct aesthetic element (Wulf, 2022a).
5. It is through mimetic processes that the collective and individual imaginary of a historical time and a culture comes into being. In the imaginary an interweaving of past, present and future takes place. It is a center upon which social and cultural actions are based (Hüppauf & Wulf, 2009; Wulf, 2022a).
6. Through mimetic processes we gain practical knowledge, which is silent, body-based knowledge and is important for how we live with our fellow human beings (Wulf, 2006b; Kraus, et al., 2021).

7. Mimetic processes do not only have positive effects. Through their blurring of boundaries and contagious nature they can also lead to violence. This happens, for example, when rivalry is whipped up through mimetic processes, or when scapegoats are created or responsibility is delegated to groups and crowds (Girard, 1977, 1986).

4 Mimesis as a Concept of Historical Anthropology

If we look at the history of the concept of mimesis, we see clearly that it is an anthropological concept. As far as we know today it was in Sicily, the home of mime artists, that the concept of mimesis first came to the Greek culture. A linguistic analysis of the history of the term reveals that the word mimesis has something to do with 'mimos', performed by a mime artist. The chief task of the mimos is not to imitate or to create something similar but to put on a comic farce, to behave as a mime artist. This activity refers to the everyday culture of simple folk who would perform vulgar scenes from their way of life in order to entertain rich people at their celebrations. The stagings and performances developed were often ribald and disrespectful. It has been confirmed by many sources as being the origin of the term mimesis in performative, cultural practices, and it had a pronounced sensory aspect, relating to movements of the body. In the fifth century B.C.E. the term 'mimesis' was widely used in Ionia and Attica. In the Platonic era the term mimesis was already commonly used to refer to processes of imitation, emulation and striving to be like something (Else, 1958).

In Greece, it was considered that poets played an important role in educating the next generation, and in his third volume of *The Republic* Plato examines the way in which literary works unfold their educative effect. He believes that the characters and actions in works of literature inscribe themselves into the imaginary of young people through mimetic processes. These images are so powerful that young people cannot resist their effects. Therefore, it is important to be very careful in selecting the stories and images that are intended to take possession of the young people's image worlds. Other content, however, should be kept away from the young. Plato therefore sees mimetic processes as being useful for educating and socializing. This is where cultural knowledge is created and passed on. Aristotle, like Plato, is also convinced that people have an innate ability to behave mimetically. "The instinct of imitation is implanted in man from childhood, one difference between him and other animals being that he is the most imitative of living creatures, and through imitation learns his earliest lessons; and no less universal is the pleasure felt in things imitated" (Aristotle, 2013, Part IV).

5   Mimesis as Creative Imitation

Mimesis means making oneself similar to something or a person, emulating them, but also 'portraying', 'representing' or 'expressing' something. Mimetic behavior or action means relating to another person or another 'world' with the intention of becoming similar to them. It can refer to the relationship with a given, represented 'reality', in which case it describes a representational relationship. But mimetic behavior can also refer to the 'imitation' of something that has never even existed, such as the representation of a myth, that has only ever existed in this representation and which is based on no known model outside of this representation. Behaving and acting mimetically have a productive function. Mimetic behavior does not necessarily refer back to a 'reality'; it can also relate to a sign for a word, image or action (Gebauer & Wulf, 1995, 2003).

The capacity to identify with other person, to see them as intentional agents and to focus our attention on something alongside them is linked with the desire to understand the Other through using our imagination to become like them. This desire to become like the Other is also the prerequisite for understanding the intentions of other people as they communicate them in gestures, symbols and constructions and for developing categories of objects and event schemata and grasping the causal connections between the objects of the world.

Unlike processes of mimicry, where the person simply adjusts to the given conditions, mimetic processes simultaneously produce both similarities to and differences from other situations or people to which or whom they refer to (Deleuze, 1994). By "making ourselves similar" to situations we have previously experienced and to culturally shaped worlds, we acquire the ability to orient ourselves in a social field. Through participating in the life practices of other people we expand our own lifeworlds and create new ways of acting and experiencing for ourselves. In this process, receptivity and activity overlap and the given world becomes interwoven with our individuality as we relate to it mimetically. We recreate situations we have experienced previously or the world outside us and make them our own by duplicating them. Not until we have confronted the earlier situation or the outside world do we attain our individuality. Not until this process takes place does the excess drive of which we had been unaware become shaped into personal wishes and needs. The confrontation with the outside world and the development of the self take place in the same system. The outer and inner worlds gradually become increasingly similar and can only be experienced in this reciprocal relationship. Thus, similarities develop between inside and outside and they begin to correspond to each other. We make ourselves similar to the outside world and change in the process. In this transformation our perceptions of the external world and of ourselves are altered.

6   Mimesis and Performativity

As performance and action, mimesis denotes, firstly, the human capacity to stage and perform internal images, imaginings, happenings, stories, series of actions and so on. It also denotes the ability to make oneself similar to the performativity of social and aesthetic actions as one observes them, by means of which one makes them one's own. The differing requirements of the processes of mimetically becoming similar to role models give rise to different results. It is the differences in these processes of becoming similar and appropriation that have resulted in diversity (Wulf, 2022b; Wulf & Zirfas, 2007; Wulf et al. 2001b).

The capacity for performative social action is acquired in mimetic processes. For example, in mimetic processes people develop levels of skill in games, exchanging gifts or ritual actions that differ from one culture to another (Bilstein et al., 2005). If one is to be able to learn to act 'correctly' in each situations, then it is necessary to have practical knowledge that is acquired by means of sensory, body-based learning processes in the corresponding fields (Benthien & Wulf, 2001). The cultural characteristics of particular social actions can also only be grasped through mimetic rapprochement. Practical knowledge and social actions have a historical and cultural basis.

7   Aesthetic Experience in Mimetic Processes

Mimetic processes lead to aesthetic experiences (Adorno, 1984). A piece of music only has aesthetic value if it is performed, when the notes become sounds and when these sounds are recreated in a mimetic process and made to resonate both in the performer of the music and also the listener. This is also the case when we read a literary work and the language and images have to be brought to life by means of mimetic processes (Csikszentmihalyi, 1990).

And finally, this process also takes place when we look at works of art which are recreated by mimetic seeing, by means of which they become images in a person's imaginary (Belting, 2011; Wulf, 2013b; Paragrana, 2014).

When we appropriate an image mimetically it is possible to distinguish two phases that run into each other. In the first phase the picture is there before the eyes of the person viewing it, and in the second it has already been absorbed into the 'internal' image world. In the first phase it is a question of overcoming a mechanical way of seeing, which takes in images like any other objects and deals with them by 'knowing what they are'. A way of seeing that already knows the meaning that the image is supposed to have provides protection against being overwhelmed by images. This way of seeing reduces the possibilities of seeing. In acts of seeing that are consciously mimetic the aim is to recreate and make the work of art one's own. This mimetic process requires spending time in front of the work of art, shedding what is familiar and discovering the unfamiliar. The mimetic appropriation of a work of art requires stopping a while and being prepared to be gripped by it.

In the second phase, as a consequence of mimetic seeing, the image is already part of the internal image world, the imaginary. A mimetic 'becoming similar' to the image has now taken place. This process of becoming similar is always incomplete and can continue to reach new levels of intensity. Holding an image that has been internalized in this way in one's imagination is good practice for one's concentration and imaginative powers. Since the image is reproduced by the imagination it constantly has to be recreated and held fast against the stream of intrusive images that appear inside us. It has to resist the inherent compulsion to disappear. This activity of the imagination is mimetic and represents an element of every creative production of an image.

Aesthetic experience is an experience of the Other, captured so beautifully by Rimbaud in his *Je est un autre*. René Char's observation about poems is also valid for works of art: they know something about us that we don't know. They contain an element of surprise that cannot be anticipated and which is often not quite rational; we feel it before we understand the meaning of the works. Mimetic processes work toward recreating them through us seeing them and absorbing them into our 'internal' image world with the aid of our imagination. The re-creation of images is a process of mimetic appropriation which accepts the images with all their pictorial qualities, into the world of our imagination and memory. Our mimetic appropriation of the images is directed toward us absorbing into our bodies their pictorial quality, which is a given before, during, after and beyond all interpretation.

When images have been absorbed into the 'internal' image world then they form points of reference for interpretations that can also change over the course of one's life. Whatever the interpretations may be, the repeated handling of images is an act of appropriation, of discovery even. It involves concentration and devotion to the re-creation of imaginary images and repeatedly demands that the images be 'refreshed' by seeing the real images or their reproductions. The mimetic encounter with images means that we dispense with preconceptions. Retracing their shapes and colors with our eyes requires us to suppress the images and thoughts that rise up 'inside' us as we look at them. It demands that we hold the image fast with our eyes, that we open ourselves up to its pictorial qualities and surrender ourselves to it. The mimetic process involves the observer making himself 'similar' to the picture as he recreates it through seeing, incorporates it and through this image expands his 'internal' image world.

Mimetic seeing is both active and passive; it is directed toward the world and at the same time receives the world. In the history of seeing there have been different interpretations of the extent to which it is active and the extent to which it is passive. Since Maurice Merleau-Ponty, if not before, we assume that the world, together with the images created by human beings, is also looking at us. The look is chiastic (Merleau-Ponty, 1968, 2002); world and human being meet and cross over. Mimetic seeing plays an important role in the way we deal with images. It is a way of us opening ourselves up to the world. By becoming similar to the images, we expand our world of experience. We take an imprint of the world and incorporate it into the image world of our minds. By retracing the shapes and colors as we look at them, the material and its structures, these become transformed into the internal world and become part of the imaginary. In such a process we incorporate the uniqueness of the world with all its historical and cultural distinctiveness. Here it is important to protect the world and image from quick interpretations which may, for example, grasp and interpret the image linguistically but do not do full justice to the pictorial character of the 'image'. Instead, it is a question of bearing with the uncertainty, ambiguity and complexity of images without wanting to establish clear-cut answers. By retracing them mimetically we expose ourselves to the ambivalence of the world and images. In this process it is a question of learning this section of the world, or the image, 'by heart'. In the case of images that means we must close our eyes and by using a mimetic process create the image we have seen in our 'mind's eye' and focus our attention on the image, fend off other images that float up from the stream of images in our mind and 'hold on to it' as an image through our concentration and the power of our thoughts. The re-creation of an image through contemplation is the first step; holding on to it, working on it, bringing it to life by repeatedly referring back in one's imagination to the original are further steps in a mimetic confrontation with images. The reproduction of an image through contemplation and staying with it and paying full attention to it are no lesser achievements than trying to interpret it. Educational processes require the interweaving of these two aspects involved in understanding images.

8 How Mimetic Processes Create the Imaginary

Mimetic processes help to create the imaginary of individuals, communities and cultures. The imaginary can be understood as an ensemble of images, sounds, touch, smell and taste. The imagination remembers, creates, combines and projects images. It creates reality. At the same time, reality helps the imagination to create images. The images of the imagination have a dynamic character, structuring perception, memory and projections of the future. The images interconnect with each other following the rhythmical movements of the imagination. Not only everyday life, but also literature, art and the performing arts provide an inexhaustible number of images. Some appear to be stable and unchanging. In contrast, others are subject to historical and cultural change. The imagination continuously creates new meanings and images. Interpretations of the world are developed using these images created by the imagination (Wulf, 2022a; Hüppauf & Wulf, 2009).

The imagination has a strong performative power, by means of which it produces and performs social and cultural actions. The imagination helps create the world of the imaginary, which includes images stored in the memory, images of the past and the future. As part of our inner world the images that are incorporated in the imaginary are references to the outer world. There are many factors that determine which images, structures and models become part of our imaginary. In these images the fact that the outer world is both present (in our mind's eye) and absent at the same time is inextricably interwoven. Images emerging from the imaginary are transferred by the imagination to new contexts. Image networks develop, with which we transform the world, and which determine our view of the world.

It is the fact that the imagination is essentially performative that results in the images of the social field constituting a central part of the imaginary (Wulf & Zirfas, 2007). We find there the power structures of social relationships and social structures. Many of these processes have their roots in our childhood and take place to a large extent unconsciously. It is in childhood that we learn to perceive social constellations and arrangements. These early visual experiences and the images resulting from them play an important and essential role in our visual understanding of the world. We understand the social actions that we see because historical and cultural structures and mental images that arise as part of our lives play a part in everything we perceive. We see social actions and relate to them as we perceive them. As a result, these actions become more important for us. If the actions of other people are directed toward us, they inspire us to forge a relationship with them; a response on our part is expected. In each case the images of our imagination are important in forming the relationship. Embedded in an action, we perceive the actions of the other and act mimetically.

9   Mimetically Acquired Practical Knowledge

The ability to act socio-culturally is acquired from early childhood on in mimetic learning processes. People develop the skills of playing, exchanging gifts and ritual actions in mimetic processes, which vary from culture to culture. To be able to act, practical knowledge is required, which is acquired through sensual, body-related mimetic learning processes in the corresponding fields of action. The respective cultural characteristics of social action are captured in mimetic approaches. Practical knowledge and social actions are strongly historically and culturally shaped (Wulf, 2006a, 2013a; Wulf et al., 2001a, 2004, 2007, 2010, 2011). Wherever we act with reference to an already existing social practice thereby creating a social practice ourselves, a mimetic relationship between the two arises. This is the case when we perform a cultural practice, when we act according to a social model, when we physically express a social idea. In mimetically executed cultural practices there is always the creation of something particular and new. How this is judged does not result from the mimetic process itself but is the result of normative considerations.

In mimetic learning processes, previous cultural actions are repeated (Resina & Wulf, 2019). They are staged, performed and thus performative (Wulf et al., 2001b; Wulf & Zirfas, 2007). In this process, the reference is not made by theoretical thinking, but aisthetically, that is, with the help of the senses; compared to the first social action, the second action distances itself from it in that it does not directly deal with it, does not change it, but performs it again; in this process, the mimetic action both shows and performs something; its performance in turn generates its own sensuous qualities. Mimetic processes relate to cultural worlds already made by humans, which can be either real or imaginary.

The dynamic nature of social acts is related to the fact that the knowledge required for their staging is practical social knowledge. As such, it is less subject to rational control than is analytical knowledge. Practical knowledge is not reflexive, self-aware knowledge. It only becomes so in the context of conflicts and crises, where the actions arising from it need justification. If social practice is not questioned, practical knowledge remains semi-conscious. Like habitus knowledge, it comprises images, schemata and forms of action that are used in the scenic performance of social actions without any conscious thought being required for whether they are appropriate or not. They are 'simply known' and used for the staging of social practice (Wulf, 2006b, 2016).

Practical knowledge also includes body movements, which are used to arrange scenes of social behavior. By means of controlling body movements, a controlled practical knowledge emerges, which—stored in the body memory—enables the staging of corresponding forms of social behavior. This knowledge is related to the social forms of behavior and performance developed in a community and is therefore a particular knowledge, limited in its general value, in mimetic processes an imitative change and shaping of preceding worlds takes place. This is what makes mimetic acts innovative. Social practices are mimetic if they relate to other actions and can themselves be understood as social arrangements that represent independent social practices as well as having a connection to other actions. Social actions become possible through the emergence of practical knowledge in the course of mimetic processes. The practical knowledge relevant to social actions has a physical, playful, historical and cultural side; it is formed in face-to-face situations and is semantically ambiguous; it has imaginary components, cannot be reduced to intentionality, contains an excess of meaning and is manifested in the social stagings and performances of religion, politics and everyday life (Kress et al., 2021; Kraus et al., 2021).

10   How Mimesis Can Lead to Violence

Mimetic processes do not always lead to social or cultural actions or behavior that we would regard in a positive light. When rituals or prohibitions in social situations lose their power to set limits, mimetic processes can generate violence. An example of this is violence that arises in groups or crowds, where individuals pass the responsibility for their violent actions onto the group or crowd. This happens to a varying degree in bullying in the media, on the internet, in the world of work and in school. In one of my research projects

'Balance—Rhythm—Resonance' we examined a social situation which almost led to the creation of a scapegoat (Paragrana, 2018, pp. 81–136). An interdisciplinary study by psychoanalysts, dance specialists, conversation researchers, educationalists and ethnologists analyzed a teaching conflict in a primary school class which could have led to someone becoming a scapegoat. It looked not only at the way the pupils behaved but also the attempts of the teacher (which not everyone evaluated in the same way) to prevent this from happening. There were many surprising insights but one thing that emerged was how infectious mimetic processes can be and how they have the potential to generate violence.

Awareness of the 'infectious nature' of mimetic processes is the basis of an influential theory of the origins of social violence (Girard, 1977). The mimetic acquisition of attitudes and behavioral patterns creates competition and rivalry between the imitators and those imitated, which can trigger violence. A contradictory situation arises—the fact that the imitators strive to acquire characteristics from those they are imitating is in conflict with the fact that both parties aspire to be different and to assert their uniqueness. This paradoxical situation leads to an increase in the potential for social violence.

Actions containing great emotional intensity seem to trigger the mimetic processes to a high degree; the infectious nature of laughter, love and violence is proverbial. In many early cultures, acts of violence were answered with acts of violence. This resulted in a vicious circle of violence that increased the extent and intensity of these acts. Not infrequently, the cohesion of societies was threatened by this; their response was to use prohibitions and rituals to attempt to control the mimetically intensified violence (Girard, 1987).

In mimetic crises where violence breaks out and cannot be suppressed by the use of prohibitions and rituals, a scapegoat might be ritually sacrificed in order to help to end the crisis. A potential victim would be selected by common agreement, designated as the scapegoat and sacrificed. The community was bound together by 'mimetic antagonism', that is, by an alliance against the victim, who had been declared the enemy. A defenseless person was usually chosen unanimously, whose death would not unleash any further violence. Although the sacrifice was itself an act of violence, it was expected to bring an end to the mimetic circle of violent acts. The community came together in solidarity in the act of violence against the victim. This action gave them, to all appearances, the opportunity to free themselves from their own inherent violence (Girard, 1986).

The crisis was ended by the following mechanism of reversal. On the one hand, the victim was made responsible for the violence inherent in society. This ascribed to the victim a power that he or she did not have; yet it still enabled the society to relieve itself of the burden of its own potential for violence. On the other hand, the victim was given the power of reconciliation, which occurred in the society after his or her death. Both cases involve processes of attribution and transference that are intended to ensure that the sacrifice will have the expected results. The return of peace was interpreted as proof that the victim was responsible for the mimetic crisis. This assumption was, of course, an illusion. It was not society that was suffering from the aggression of the victim, but the victim who was suffering from the violence of society. In order for this mechanism of reversal to function, it was important that people should not be aware of these two processes of transference onto the victim. If people realized the truth of what was happening, the victim would lose his or her reconciliatory, liberating power (Dieckmann et al., 1997; Wimmer et al., 1996).

11   Summary and Outlook

1. The concept of mimesis differs from imitation or simulation in that it relates to something outside of us that we connect with and make ourselves similar to. We cannot, however, 'dissolve' or lose ourselves in it, and therefore we will always be different from it. This 'something outside of us', toward which children and young people gravitate, can be another person, part of the environment or an artificially constructed imaginary world. Whichever it is, what takes place is a connecting with the world outside us. As our senses and imagination transform this outside world into internal images, sounds and the worlds of touch, smell and taste, living experiences arise which are inextricably bound to our physical bodies (Michaels & Wulf, 2014).
2. Mimetic processes are an intrinsic part of our human corporeality and thus they begin at a very early age. They take place before 'I and thou' become split and before the separation of subject and object, and they have an important role to play in psychological and socio-development and the development of the persona. They are closely bound up with early complexes and imaginings and extend into the preconscious. Because they are cemented into the earliest processes of 'becoming a body' through birth, weaning and desire, their effects are very comprehensive.
3. Even before the development of thought and language, the child experiences the world, the other person and themselves mimetically. Their mimetic processes are tied to the various senses. As they learn motor skills the gift for mimesis plays an especially important role. However even the

acquisition of language is unthinkable without mimetic processes. In early childhood, mimetic behavior is *the* way of life.

4. Mimetic processes are also involved in the awakening and evolving of sexual desire. A gender identity is developed and there is a realization of gender difference. Desire relates mimetically to other desires; it is contagious—it infects and is infected; it develops a dynamic which often comes into conflict with the intentions of the subject. Conceptions that have already evolved are modified and new ones tried out. References to other drafts and experiments continue to be developed. Many of these processes take place unconsciously.

5. Mimetic processes support the polycentricity of the individual. They extend into layers of corporeality, sensuality and desire which are constituted by forces other than those of the conscious mind. These include aggression, violence and destruction, all of which are aroused and developed in mimetic processes. In group and crowd situations they can be particularly effective, since in these situations an individual's personal control center and sense of responsibility are replaced by the authority of the masses, which enables destructive actions to take place by means of an intoxicating infection, actions which the individual would not have been capable of on their own.

6. In the family, school and workplace the values, attitudes and norms embodied by these institutions are internalized by children, young people and adults through mimetic processes. As the discussion of the hidden curriculum has shown, the values that are really effective in the institution can go completely against its conscious, intended self-image. Analysis of the institution, a critique of its ideology, bringing in consultants and making institutional changes can bring these contradictions to the fore, thus providing a basis for remedial action.

7. The same is true of the developmental, educative and socializing effects of individual people. These too take place far more in mimetic processes than is generally assumed. Here too there is a discrepancy between the teacher's or educator's perception of themselves and the effects of their actual actions. In many cases the unconscious and unintentional effects of a teacher's personality have a long-lasting influence on children and young people. The way individual teachers feel, think and make judgments is conveyed largely mimetically. In each particular case assimilation or rejection play a different role, the effects of which are hard to measure. Another factor that makes it difficult to evaluate the effect of the way the teacher behaves is that the same behavior is evaluated differently depending on a person's stage of life.

8. It becomes clear in memory images that mimetically making places, spaces and objects one's own is of major importance for child development. Children relate to their environments through mimesis from early childhood onward, and they experience them as "peopled with animate beings". They expand themselves into this world by making themselves similar, absorb it into their internal imaginary worlds and broaden their skills and knowledge in this way. Since these worlds are always historically and culturally determined and the objects in them have meaning, that is, they are symbolically encoded, the children and young people become encultured in these mimetic processes.

9. Objects and institutions, imaginary figures and practical actions are embedded in societal power relations which are also conveyed, along with other information, through the processes of becoming similar. They are learned and experienced in mimetic processes, but they are not usually grasped to begin with. If mimetic experiences are to be fully fathomed they need to be analyzed and reflected upon. It is frequently the case that they can only be appropriately assessed and judged once this work of analysis and reflection has been done. Mimetic processes are important prerequisites for the development of lively experiences. Analysis and reflection are required for these experiences to develop.

10. Mimetic processes are ambivalent. The impulse to become similar is inherent in them and can be carried through independently of the value of the world that has gone before. Thus, in mimetic processes people can make themselves similar to things that are stiff and lifeless which block their development or lead it in the wrong direction. Mimesis can degenerate into simulation and mimicry. However, it can also result in a child or young person expanding into the world around them; it can bridge the gap to the outside world. Characteristically making ourselves similar to the outside world through mimesis is a non-violent process. The aim is first and foremost not to shape or alter the world, but rather to develop and grow in our encounter with it.

11. Mimetic processes can teach us to relate to other people in a non-instrumental way. Mimetic movements leave the other person as they are and do not attempt to change them. They are open to what is foreign in that they allow it to remain as it is and approach it, but do not try to dissolve the difference. The mimetic impulse to make ourselves similar to what is other accepts this difference; it forgoes clarity or non-ambiguity for the sake of the otherness of the other, who could only be rendered unambiguous by being reduced to the same, to something that is familiar.

By forgoing clarity, we ensure that our experience will be rich and the alien different.

12. In mimetic movements we interpret a world that went before that has already been interpreted from a world that we have created symbolically. This means that we re-interpret a world that is already interpreted. This is true even when we repeat or simply reproduce. Thus, a gesture that is made over and over again creates meaning structures that are different from those it produced when it was made for the first time. It takes an object or an event out of its usual context and produces a perspective that differs from that in which the pre-existing world was perceived. Taking out of context and the switching of perspectives are characteristics of aesthetic processes that are connected with the close affinity between mimesis and aesthetics, seen since Plato. Mimetic re-interpretation is a novel perception, *a seeing as* (Wittgenstein). In mimetic actions there is an intention to recreate a symbolically constructed world in such a fashion that it is seen as a specific one.

References

Adorno, T. W. (1978). *Minima Moralia: Reflections on a Damaged Life* (E. F. N. Jepcott, Trans.). Verso.

Adorno, T. W. (1982). *Against Epistemology. A Metacritique. Studies in Husserl and the Phenomenological Antinomies* (W. Domingo, Trans.). Basil Blackwell.

Adorno, T. W. (1984). *Aesthetic Theory* (C. Lenhardt, Trans.). Routledge and Kegan Paul.

Aristotle. (2013). Poetics (A. Kenny, Trans.). Oxford World's Classics.

Belting, H. (2011). *An Anthropology of Images*. Princeton University Press.

Benjamin, W. (2006). *Berlin Childhood Around 1900*. Belknap Press of Harvard University Press.

Benthien, C., & Wulf, C. (Eds.). (2001). *Körperteile. Eine kulturelle Anatomie*. Rowohlt.

Bilstein, J., Winzen, M., & Wulf, C. (Eds.). (2005). *Anthropologie und Pädagogik des Spiels*. Beltz.

Brandstetter, G., & Wulf, C. (Eds.). (2007). *Tanz als Anthropologie*. Wilhelm Fink.

Csikszentmihalyi, M. (1990). *Flow. The Psychology of Optimal Experience*. Harper and Row.

Deleuze, G. (1994). *Difference and Repetition* (P. Patton, Trans.). Athlone Press.

Dieckmann, B., Wulf, C., & Wimmer, M. (Eds.). (1997). *Violence. Nationalism, Racism, Xenophobia*. Waxmann.

Dornes, M. (1993). *Der kompetente Säugling*. Fischer.

Else, G. F. (1958). Imitation in the 5th Century. *Classical Philology, 53*, 73–90.

Gebauer, G., & Wulf, C. (1995). *Mimesis: Culture, Art, Society*. University of California Press.

Gebauer, G., & Wulf, C. (1998). *Spiel, Ritual, Geste. Mimetisches Handeln in der sozialen Welt*. Rowohlt.

Gebauer, G., & Wulf, C. (2003). *Mimetische Weltzugänge*. Kohlhammer.

Girard, R. (1977). *Violence and the Sacred*. Johns Hopkins University.

Girard, R. (1986). *The Scapegoat*. The Johns Hopkins University Press.

Girard, R. (1987). *Things Hidden since the Foundation of the World*. Stanford University Press.

Hüppauf, B., & Wulf, C. (Eds.). (2009). *Dynamics and Performativity of Imagination. The Image between the Visible and the Invisible*. Routledge.

Jacoboni, M. (2008). *Mirroring People*. Farrar, Straus and Giroux.

Kraus, A., Budde, J., Hietzge, M., & Wulf, C. (Eds.). (2021 [2017]). *Handbuch Schweigendes Wissen. Erziehung, Bildung, Sozialisation und Lernen*. Beltz Juventa.

Kress, G., Selander, S., Säljö, R., & Wulf, C. (Eds.). (2021). *Learning as Social Practice. Beyond Education as an Individual Enterprise*. Routledge.

Merleau-Ponty, M. (1968). *The Visible and the Invisible* (C. Lefort, Ed. and A. Lingis, Trans.). Northwestern University Press.

Merleau-Ponty, M. (2002). *Phenomenology of Perception. An Introduction* (C. Smith, Trans.). Routledge.

Michaels, A., & Wulf, C. (Eds.). (2014). *Exploring the Senses*. Routledge.

Michaels, A., & Wulf, C. (Eds.). (2020). *Science and Scientification in South Asia and Europe*. Routledge.

Paragrana. Internationale Zeitschrift für Historische Anthropologie. (2014). Art and Gesture. 23(1) (M. Gall, E. Friedlander, C. Wulf, & M. Zuckermann, Eds.).

Paragrana. Internationale Zeitschrift für Historische Anthropologie. (2018). Balance—Rhythmus—Resonanz. 27(1) (G. Brandstetter, M. B. Buchholz, A. Hamburger, & C. Wulf, Eds.).

Resina, J. R., & Wulf, C. (Eds.). (2019). *Repetition, Recurrence, Returns. How Cultural Renewal Works*. Lexington Books.

Rizzolatti, G., & Signigaglia, C. (2008). *Mirrors in the Brain. How Our Minds Share Actions and Emotions*. Oxford University Press.

Stern, D. (2003). *Die Lebenserfahrung des Säuglings*. Klett-Cotta.

Tomasello, M. (1999). *The Cultural Origins of Human Cognition*. Harvard University Press.

Wallenhorst, N., & Wulf, C. (Eds.). (2022). Humains - *Dictionnaire d'anthropologie prospective*. Vrin.

Wallenhorst, N., & Wulf, C. (Eds.). (2023). *Handbook of the Anthropocene*. Springer Nature.

Wimmer, M., Wulf, C., & Dieckmann, B. (Eds.). (1996). *Das zivilisierte Tier. Zur Historischen Anthropologie der Gewalt*. Fischer.

Wulf, C. (2005). *Zur Genese des Sozialen: Mimesis, Performativität, Ritual*. Transcript.

Wulf, C. (2006a). *Anthropologie kultureller Vielfalt. Interkulturelle Bildung in Zeiten der Globalisierung.* Transcript.

Wulf, C. (2006b). Praxis In. In J. Kreinath, J. Snoek, & M. Stausberg (Eds.), *Theorizing Rituals: Issues, Topics, Approaches, Concepts* (pp. 395–411). Brill.

Wulf, C. (2013a). *Anthropology. A Continental Perspective.* The University of Chicago Press.

Wulf, C. (2013b). *Das Rätsel des Humanen. Eine Einführung in die Historische Anthropologie.* Brill.

Wulf, C. (2016). *Exploring Alterity in the Globalized World.* Routledge.

Wulf, C. (2022a). *Human Beings and their Images. Imagination, Mimesis, Performativity.* Bloomsbury.

Wulf, C. (2022b). *Education as Human Knowledge in the Anthropocene. An Anthropological Approach.* Routledge.

Wulf, C., Althans, B., Audehm, K., Bausch, C., Göhlich, M., Sting, S., Tervooren, A., Wagner-Willi, M., & Zirfas, J. (2001a). *Das Soziale als Ritual: Zur performativen Bildung von Gemeinschaft.* Leske and Budrich.

Wulf, C., Althans, B., Audehm, K., Bausch, C., Göhlich, M., Sting, S., Tervooren, A., Wagner-Willi, M., & Zirfas, J. (2010). *Ritual and Identity: The Staging and Performing of Rituals in the Lives of Young People.* The Tufnell Press.

Wulf, C., Althans, B., Audehm, K., Bausch, C., Jörissen, B., Göhlich, M., Mattig, R., Tervooren, A., Wagner-Willi, M., & Zirfas, J. (2004). *Bildung im Ritual: Schule, Familie, Jugend, Medien.* Springer VS.

Wulf, C., Althans, B., Audehm, K., Blaschke, G., Ferrin, N., Göhlich, M., Jörissen, B., Mattig, R., Nentwig-Gesemann, I., Schinkel, S., Tervooren, A., Wagner-Willi, M., & Zirfas, J. (2007). *Lernkulturen im Umbruch: Rituelle Praktiken in Schule, Medien, Familie und Jugend.* Springer VS.

Wulf, C., Althans, B., Audehm, K., Blaschke, G., Ferrin, N., Kellermann, I., Mattig, R., & Schinkel, S. (2011). *Die Geste in Erziehung, Bildung und Sozialisation Ethnografische Fallstudien.* Springer VS.

Wulf, C., & Baitello, N. (2018). *Sapientia Uma arqueologia de saberes esquecidos.* Edições Sesc SP.

Wulf, C., Göhlich, M., & Zirfas, J. (Eds.). (2001b). *Grundlagen des Performativen. Eine Einführung in die Zusammenhänge von Sprache, Macht und Handeln.* Juventa.

Wulf, C., & Zirfas, J. (Eds.). (2007). *Pädagogik des Performativen. Theorien, Methoden, Perspektiven.* Beltz.

Wulf, C., & Zirfas, J. (Eds.). (2014). *Handbuch Pädagogische Anthropologie.* Springer VS.

Awareness as a Challenge: Learning Through Our Bodies on a Planet in Crisis

Mariagrazia Portera

As Carlisle (2018) points out, 'habit'—a word coming etymologically from the Latin *habitus* (*habeo*, to have), which is in turn a calque of the Greek *hèxis* (from *echein*, to have, to hold a form through time)—designates a genuinely interdisciplinary concept, extensively used in botany, mineralogy, zoology and of course anthropology and the human and social sciences. As she puts it, "mineralogists refer to the habits of crystals; botanists to the habits of plants; of course, animals, including humans, have habits—and in each case, 'habit' means a shape or pattern of growth. [...] Habits are the 'way' in which [...] an all-encompassing unity expresses or manifests itself in diverse forms of life" (Carlisle, 2018, p. 105). The last few years have witnessed an impressive resurgence of interest in the notion of 'habit' across a wide range of contemporary fields of inquiry: philosophers turn to the concept to investigate its significance to the historical development of Western thought (Carlisle, 2010, 2018; Sparrow & Hutchinson, 2013); neuroscientists look into the role that habits play in the functioning of the human mind and identify the neural and psychological underpinnings of habitual behaviour (Graybiel, 2008); anthropologists, political scientists and sociologists tap into habits as a key notion to explain social dynamics and collective behaviour (Latour, 2013; Pedwell, 2017). It is a matter of fact that habits pervade our social and mental life to a great extent (see Bargh, 1997): "during much of our waking lives, we act

---

M. Portera (✉)
University of Florence, Florence, Italy
e-mail: mariagrazia.portera@unifi.it

© The Author(s), under exclusive license to Springer Nature Switzerland AG 2022
A. Kraus, C. Wulf (eds.), *The Palgrave Handbook of Embodiment and Learning*,
https://doi.org/10.1007/978-3-030-93001-1_4

according to our habits, from the time we rise and go through our morning routines until we fall asleep," writes neuroscientist Ann Graybiel (2008, p. 360). This centrality of habits to the human individual and social life is notoriously a key point in William James' theory of human behaviour: according to the father of modern psychology, "when we look at living creatures from an outward point of view, one of the first things that strikes us is that they are bundles of habits" (James, 1890, p. 104).

In the wake of this recent rise of the concept, the main aim of this article is to try to figure out what role habits and habitual behaviour may play in tackling complex and multifaceted issues such as the current environmental crisis, with particular reference to the challenge posed by the fact that, as has been argued, the vast majority of our habits seem to unfold beneath the level of consciousness.

Understanding human behaviour is indeed crucial if we are to effectively address issues such as the current environmental crisis. As scholars working in the newly established, multidisciplinary matrix called 'Environmental Humanities' (Neimanis et al., 2015, p. 69) have recently pointed out, "at the heart of global change in the 21st century" there are

> human choices and actions—questions of human behaviour, habits, motivation that are embedded in individual practices and actions, in institutional and cultural pathways, and in political strategies. (Holm et al., 2015; see also Wallenhorst, 2019; Wallenhorst & Wulf, 2022)

But in what sense are human habits relevant to the current environmental crisis? Is it reasonable to expect individuals to change their habits to mitigate the effects of the environmental crisis? And since habits are usually understood as unfolding beneath the level of consciousness, what strategies can be appealed to in order to face the new challenges?

The recent resurgence of interest in the notion of habit should not obscure the fact that the concept has a very long and rich history and it is far from being a term of recent coinage. Philosophical analysis of habit dates back as far as the work of Aristotle (particularly his *Nicomachean Ethics*) and the notion cuts across all schools and traditions until the present day, from Descartes and Kant to Felix Ravaisson and the American pragmatists, from Pierre Bourdieu to today's cognitive scientists. As Barandiaran and Di Paolo (2014) have shown, any philosopher over the last 2000 years has commented on or written at least a couple of lines about the concept of habit, recognized as a key term in any attempt to make sense of the human mind and behaviour.

In the second half of the twentieth century, however, habits—particularly in the field of the study of the human mind—gradually lost ground to more recent (at that time) notions such as 'representation,' 'module,' 'information-processing device.' The advent of cognitivism, representationalism and computationalism in the 1950s and 1960s brought about a decline in the academic and scientific interest in habits, which lasted at least until the beginning of the 1990s. Over the last decade, the emergence of the new paradigm of 4E cognition (*e*mbodied, *e*mbedded, *e*xtended and *e*nactive) has led to a re-assessment of the notion as one of the foundations of a new conception of the human mind.

As Alva Noë points out in his 2009 book *Out of Our Heads: Why You Are Not Your Brain, and Other Lessons from the Biology of Consciousness*, "traditional approaches to the mind in cognitive science," such as the computationalist and (hard-) representationalist ones,

> have failed to appreciate the importance of habit, for they start from the assumption that the really interesting thing about us human beings is that we are very smart. We are deliberators, we are propositional, we use reason. (ibid., p. 98)

The intellectualist, computationalist and representationalist stance, the roots of which according to Noë date back to Plato, sees human beings at their best as habit-free. Humans' distinctive nature, in his view, is supposed to reveal "itself precisely in the fact that [human beings]" decide, plan and act relying on pure reason and that they "rise above mere habit and act from principles" (ibid.). Is this approach to human nature able to grasp the specificity of our way of thinking and behaving? According to the proponents of the 4E cognition paradigm, the reverse is true. As Noë argues, we can make deliberations, act and carry out plans not because we are endowed with pure reason, but because we have bodies, that is, because our bodies can learn, which means they can contract habits. In a word, we are *Homo sapiens* because we have (and are) habitual bodies. Even skills so sophisticated such as mathematical expertise and the ability to speak two or more languages would not be possible if we had no habits:

> If I am working on a mathematical problem, I may be pushing my understanding to its limits, but this is only possible because of my confident mastery of the more basic skills (such as counting) on which I depend. (ibid., p. 99)

In other words, solving a mathematical problem is only possible because more basic skills such as counting have become a 'habit,' on which I can confidently rely without paying too much conscious attention to the mechanisms of its execution. There is a difference, in Noë's account, between an expert and a novice: an expert, e.g. a pianist has habits, which enables her to perform her task in the smoothest and therefore most effective way; a novice—let us think, for instance, of a boy who has just started to play the piano for the first time—must pay attention to every single gesture and movement of his actions, which sound then fairly 'mechanical.' It has been demonstrated (ibid., p. 100) that the level of brain activation decreases in experts (compared to novices) when they engage in the performance of tasks which they master efficiently; in this sense, it may be said that "expertise requires precisely the absence of care and deliberation"—that is, requires habits—"that the intellectualist wrongly takes to be the hallmark of our mental lives" (ibid., p. 101).

The conclusion to which Noë comes sounds very much like William James in its spirit: "Human beings are creatures of habit. Habits are central to human nature […]. Only a being with habits could have a mind like ours" (ibid., pp. 97–98). If we want to understand how the human mind works, why we behave in the way we do and how it is possible to promote more sustainable and pro-environmental behaviour, we need to turn the spotlight on our embodied, embedded, partially unconscious (but not utterly impermeable to cognition) habits. Indeed, our habits have very much to do with our learning bodies.

Perhaps no one as effectively and clearly as Maurice Merleau-Ponty has brought to the fore in the twentieth century the relationship between habits and the human body. In his *Phenomenology of Perception* (1945), he understands 'habit' as a 'rearrangement and renewal of the corporeal schema,' an ability to feel 'at home' in the environment by incorporating new motoric significances, that is, by acquiring bodily familiarity with instruments and tools (Merleau-Ponty, 1945, p. 164). If I take up the habit of driving my car or if a blind man takes up the habit of relying on his stick to walk, the car and the stick cease to be seen as "objects with a size and volume which is established by comparison with other objects" (ibid., p. 165) and become an extension of the living body, the more so the deeper the habit of using them. Merleau-Ponty chooses the example of a woman who types so regularly (for work) that she contracts a habit of type-writing: her habit is neither cognitive knowledge (based on representations) nor a Pavlovian involuntary action; rather, it is a non-representational, embodied and embedded 'knowledge in the hands,' a feeling of being familiar with the type-writer as if it were a sensitive extension of her own body. As Merleau-Ponty puts it,

> it is possible to know how to type without being able to say where the letters which make the words are to be found on the banks of keys. To know how to

type is not, then, to know the place of each letter among the keys, nor even to have acquired a conditioned reflex for each one, which is set in motion by the letter as it comes before our eye. (ibid., p. 166)

To know how to type is instead a habit, that is, a rearrangement of my own body in connection with environmental factors or elements. It is because our bodies can learn, which means because they can be moulded and shaped by experience, that we are able to take up habits. This point is very clearly brought out by William James in the fourth chapter of his *Principles of Psychology* (1890), in which he discusses habits and their role and relevance to human experience. "The phenomena of habit in living beings are due to the plasticity of the organic materials of which their bodies are composed" (James, 1890, p. 68); plasticity, as a defining feature of organic materials, is understood by James as "the possession of a structure weak enough to yield to an influence, but strong enough not to yield all at once" (ibid.).

Now, what have our easily moulded bodies and habits to do with the current environmental crisis? A growing body of recent literature has addressed the question as to how climate change and the current environmental crisis can be mitigated through personal actions and the acquisition of better environmental habits (Howell, 2018; Steg & Vlek, 2009; Farrow, et al., 2017; Knussen & Yule, 2008); there is today

an urgent need for a robust theory of consumption that addresses how habits form, how they change and how policy can contribute to the formation of new habits that are less environmentally intrusive. (Wilhite, 2015, p. 100)

Examples of simple environmental (bad) habits are: leaving the light on when nobody's in the room; leaving the tap running while brushing the teeth; buying more food than needed (thus increasing the amount of waste); regularly leaving household electrical appliances on standby mode instead of switching them off and other similar patterns of behaviour. Project Drawdown®, a non-profit organization which has emerged in the last few years as one of the leading resources in providing climate solutions, offers lists of actions, to be performed both on the collective-global and on the individual level, that are useful to tackle effectively the environmental and climate issues (https://drawdown.org/solutions/table-of-solutions). It is important to notice that each of these (apparently) minor behavioural patterns (leaving the lights on, leaving household equipment on standby mode etc.), which we perform in most cases automatically, without being completely aware of what we are doing while we are doing it and which are potentially environmentally harmful, reveals a more general propensity (acquired, not innate) to think of natural resources as if they were infinite and of us, human beings, as if we were the ultimate and only masters of the planet. Each of them, to put it differently, taps into a more general, 'neo-liberal' habit of thinking that is specific to the Anthropocene 'milieu.'

Let us dwell for a moment on the fact that human beings are never completely aware of their habitual actions as they perform them. According to William James, one of the laws of habit is that it "diminishes the conscious attention with which our acts are performed" (James, 1890, p. 74). As James explains,

> if an act requires for its execution a chain, *A, B, C, D, E, F, G,* etc., of successive nervous events, then in the first performances of the action the conscious will must choose each of these events from a number of wrong alternatives that tend to present themselves; but habit soon brings it about that each event calls up its own appropriate successor without any alternative offering itself, and without any reference to the conscious will, until at last the whole chain, *A, B, C, D, E, F, G,* rattles itself off as soon as A occurs, just as if A and the rest of the chain were fused into a continuous stream. (James, 1890, pp. 74–75; for an insightful discussion of the relationship between habit and attention, alternative to the Jamesian approach, see Magrì, 2019)

This means that, if we start to perform habitually an environmentally harmful behavioural pattern, with one repetition after another the whole action will result in becoming easier and easier, the attention with which it is performed lower and lower, up to the point of it being executed unconsciously. But then, if the current environmental crisis is worsened by our non-environmentally friendly habits, how should we grasp and change them since they unfold beneath the level of consciousness?

On 19 August 2020, *The Guardian* published an article by Damian Carrington featuring climate activists Greta Thunberg, Luisa Neubauer, Anuna de Wever and Adélaïde Charlie:

> "Looking back [over two years], a lot has happened. Many millions have taken to the streets, and on 28 November 2019, the European parliament declared a climate and environmental emergency," Thunberg said. "But over these last two years, the world has also emitted over 80 bn tonnes of CO_2. We have seen continuous natural disasters taking place across the globe. Many lives and livelihoods have been lost, and this is only the very beginning." The young activists pointed out that "when it comes to action, we are still in a state of denial. The gap between what we need to do and what's actually done is widening by the

minute." It seems, Thunberg and her fellow activists recognized, that the climate emergency is a "fact which most people refuse to accept. Just the thought of being in a crisis that we cannot buy, build or invest our way out of seems to create some kind of mental short-circuit. This mix of ignorance, denial and unawareness is the very heart of the problem."

These last words by the climate activists are relevant: here we are confronted again, as it emerged while discussing the notion of habit in general, with *unawareness* as being at the very heart of the environmental issue. Why does it seem that our minds and habitual bodies are, as it were, 'designed' to refuse or at least to struggle to accept the reality of the environmental crisis?

In a book published a few years ago, *Reason in a Dark Time. Why the Struggle Against Climate Change Failed and What it Meant for Our Future* (2014), Dale Jamieson offers a few answers to this question. First, it seems that a sort of evolutionary bias is at work with the environmental crisis: we, as evolved animals which have passed through the sieve of natural selection, struggle to recognize problems like climate change.

> We have a strong bias toward dramatic movements of middle-size objects that can be visually perceived, and climate change does not typically present in this way. The onset of climate change is gradual and uncertain rather than immediate and obvious. Increments of climate change are usually barely noticeable, and even less so because we re-norm our expectations to recent experiences. (Jamieson, 2014, p. 102)

That is, even less so because we have a strong tendency to habituate ourselves and to get accustomed even to the most extra-ordinary experiences, provided that they are repeated often enough. This is all the more evident today, in a world whose spatial and temporal boundaries have inevitably narrowed and in which, at least in the Western countries, the socio-economic system forces us to be as flexible and fast as possible. Devising good solutions to mitigate the environmental crisis, however, implies a number of time-consuming efforts, the results of which might require many years before becoming tangible.

As Jamieson (2014) points out, other psychological mechanisms inhibit action: "The scale of a problem like climate change can be crippling. When we do not feel efficacious with respect to a problem, we often deny that it exists" (ibid., p. 103). In his view, the problem with climate change and the environmental issues is that they must be thought rather than sensed [...]. Even if we succeed in thinking that something is a threat, we are less reactive than if we sense that it is a threat. Consider the difference between touching a hot stove and being told that the stove is hot. Scientists are telling us that the world is warming, but we do not sense it and so we do not act. (ibid.)

Here again, the issue at stake is that of 'bodily' unawareness: how is it possible to make our bodies—our habitual bodies—feel and sense the climate change? Indeed, if we do not feel the environmental crisis, and if we do not feel and sense (i.e., if we are not aware of) the harmful impact on the environment exerted by some of our habits, how might we contribute to the mitigation of the current environmental crisis?

In this final section of my paper I would like to present two models of answers to the question with which I concluded the preceding one. On the one hand, recently there have been proposals aiming at 'by-passing' the question of the awareness of our (bad) environmental habits, ultimately considering our lack of awareness not to be crucial or decisive in enabling us to grasp and eventually change our habits. On the other hand, a line of research has lately emerged focusing on the development of new, non-intellectualist and non-cognitivist tools that are useful for making people aware of their environmental habits, under the premise that, without awareness, no modification or transformation of our habits would ever be possible. Let us start with the first proposal.

Theories of sustainable environmental habits have been put forward in the last few years. These approaches revolve around the notions of 'affordance' and 'nudge' (see, for instance Lehner et al., 2016; Kaaronen, 2017). It is stressed that in order to steer people towards more sustainable behaviour it is not necessary to make them aware of their, largely automatic, environmentally unsustainable habits, rather it is enough and indeed much more effective to implement minor changes ('affordances,' 'nudges') to the everyday infrastructures and architectures so that people can be pushed into environmentally friendly behaviour. In other words, independently of us being aware or not of our habitual behaviour, a suitably equipped and designed environment will gently 'force' us to make the best choices and to act in the most nature-friendly way. 'Affordance,' as is well known, is a concept coined and brought to the fore by the American psychologist James Gibson in the 1960s and fully developed in his masterpiece *The Ecological Approach to Visual Perception* (1979). Gibson defines 'affordances' as follows:

The affordances of the environment are what it offers the animal, what it provides or furnishes, either for good or ill. The verb to afford is found in the dictionary, but the noun affordance is not. I have made it up. I mean by it something that refers to both the environment and the animal in a way that no existing term does. It implies the complementarity of the animal and the environment. (Gibson, 1979, p. 127)

Affordances are 'possibilities for action': for example, the curved handle of my breakfast mug invites me to grip it in a certain way; it is, in this sense, an 'affordance.' Less well known is perhaps the concept of the 'nudge,' put forward by University of Chicago economist Richard H. Thaler and Harvard Law School Cass R. Sunstein in a book published in 2008 under the title *Nudge: Improving Decisions About Health, Wealth, and Happiness.* According to the authors,

A nudge [...] is any aspect of the choice architecture that alters people's behaviour in a predictable way without forbidding any options or significantly changing their economic incentives. To count as a mere nudge, the intervention must be easy and cheap to avoid. Nudges are not mandates. Putting the fruit at eye level counts as a nudge. Banning junk food does not. (ibid., p. 9)

Nudges are not just affordances: they are affordances designed by someone specifically with the aim of letting people carry out a certain action or take a certain decision. The main premise underlying the theory of the nudge is, of course, that people usually do not make choices and take decisions in their best interests; pushed by ignorance, emotions, feelings and other non-rational factors, humans end up in most cases with reasoning very badly. An example of the application of nudging to promote environmental causes in food consumption (through the modification of the physical environment) are changes in the positioning, accessibility and visibility of products on the supermarket shelves, for instance, to reduce meat consumption (and therefore the huge impact of meat consumption on the environment).

There have been critical voices concerning the idea of applying nudging to promote behavioural change, both on a theoretical and on an empirical basis. As Pedwell (2017) has argued, for instance, the nudge theory focuses on pernicious habits with the idea of getting rid of them without the 'active' and fully aware cooperation of individuals and without addressing the more complex question of how 'intelligent,' malleable and more sustainable habits can be formed; moreover, it targets isolated individuals alone—seen more as consumers than as citizens—instead of communities, groups and their shared values. In a word, it seems that the 'libertarian-paternalist' approach based on nudging is just another facet of the manipulative, neo-liberal habit of hyper- and quick-consuming that has dominated so far in the Anthropocene. On an empirical basis, a recent study by Hagmann et al. (2019)—among other pieces of research following the same lines—has demonstrated that a nudge-based approach with the aim of promoting the reduction of carbon emissions (instead of a carbon tax, which imposes direct costs on consumers) would be in the long term more detrimental than beneficial to the environmental cause. As the researchers propose, "nudges aimed at reducing carbon emissions could have a pernicious indirect effect if they offer the promise of a 'quick fix' and thereby undermine support for policies of greater impact" (ibid., p. 484). Moreover, nudges risk providing the "false hope that problems can be tackled without imposing considerable costs" (ibid.). Tiefenbeck et al. (2013) have shown, in a similar vein, that people who were nudged to reduce their water consumption ended up with increasing their use of electricity, which is an example of behavioural spill-over that risks undermining the effectiveness of the nudge approach as a whole.

Being fully aware of our behavioural patterns, including our environmental habits and the energy- and time-consuming efforts required to modify them, seems then to be crucial if we are to promote *truly effective* pro-environmental change. This is why in recent years—with the current resurgence of interest in the concept of habit—a stimulating body of research has emerged addressing alternative ways to make people aware of their habits. I stress the term 'alternative,' since a purely cognitive, in a broad sense intellectualist or rational approach to our embodied habits is assumed not to be enough to grasp them and eventually change them. As Carlisle (2010, pp. 141–142) has argued,

> Awareness of habit has to be cultivated at the level of sensations, feelings, and involuntary thoughts [...]. Developing the faculty of awareness of passive phenomena [...] can gradually enable a person to discriminate between habits in order to choose which to maintain and which to resist.

In this sense, an interesting path that environmental scientists have started to explore has to do with the possible interconnections between policy-making, the behavioural sciences and mindfulness, understood as a practice through which individuals are invited to develop 'sensitive awareness'—awareness on the level of the body, see Shusterman (2008)—of the present moment through meditation techniques (see Lilley et al., 2014; Armstrong, 2015; Amel et al., 2009). In the contemporary consumer culture, in which "we are constantly separated, even at the most basic sensory level, from the very systems we rely on, such that many of us do not even know we are in the middle of environmental crises" (Amel et al., 2009, p. 14), that is, we do not even feel or sense the crisis and how our habitual behaviour impacts on it, cultivating awareness and gaining 'sensitive attention' through mindfulness training might be useful if we are to increase sustainable behaviour.

This proposal has, however, its lights and shadows. In this final part of the section, I would like to draw attention to the target of the two proposals—the nudge-based and the mindfulness-based: in fact, both target isolated individuals.

While the nudge theory sees individuals as consumers unable to choose what is in their best interest and who must, therefore, be gently forced or nudged towards certain options or actions, mindfulness-based approaches try to make individuals fully aware of the impact, effects and consequences of their own (habitual) behaviour, with particular reference, in this case, to environmental and sustainability issues. But are we sure that, on the one hand, maintaining individuals in their condition of unawareness, through nudging, or, on the other hand, burdening them with the full awareness of the whole chain of environmental consequences of their acts are the only two options available to tackle the environmental crisis effectively? Let us consider, for instance, the various plans and projects aimed at promoting pro-environmental behaviour which have been carried out in the UK over the last few years by the Department for Environment, Food and Rural Affairs (DEFRA) (see Shove, 2010). The vast majority of these projects were inspired by the so-called ABC approach, where A stays for 'attitude,' B for 'behaviour' and C for 'change.' As Shove (2010, p. 1274) argues, "the popularity of the ABC framework is an indication of the extent to which responsibility for responding to climate change is thought to lie with individuals whose behavioural choices will make the difference."

The point with approaches like this is that they place "responsibility squarely on the individual CO2 addict and in the same move [deflect] attention away from the many institutions involved in structuring possible courses of action and in making some very much more likely than others" (ibid., p. 1280). This is, in my opinion, a criticism worth considering which can be applied not only to a nudge-based approach to climate change but also, at least to some extent, to certain mindfulness-based approaches. Indeed, these new, embodied, sensitive, *habit*-based strategies (such as nudges and mindfulness) can be much more beneficial for the environmental cause if we bring to the fore their potential to contribute to a *sense of community* and *political belonging* (broadly understood), rather than just individualist thinking. Let us consider, for instance, experiences such as the international Councils on the Uncertain

Human Future (https://councilontheuncertainhumanfuture.org), launched in 2014 at Clark University, USA, and now internationally widespread, which are initiatives of collective reflection relying on mindfulness techniques, meditation, storytelling and the sharing of scientific data, with the aim of building collaborative insight on climate change and the ecological crisis. Experiences like these might help people truly share in the *joint* effort towards a more sustainable way of living.

References

Amel, E. L., Manning, C. M., & Scott, B. A. (2009). Mindfulness and Sustainable Behavior: Pondering Attention and Awareness as Means for Increasing Green Behavior. *Ecopsychology, 1*(1), 14–25.

Armstrong, A. (2015). Mindfulness and Sustainability: Happy Bedfellows. In R. Robison (Ed.), *Sustainability: New Questions, New Answers* (pp. 68–72). Global Sustainability Institute. ARU.

Barandiaran, X. E., & Di Paolo, E. A. (2014). A Genealogical Map of the Concept of Habit. *Frontiers in Human Neuroscience, 8*, 522. https://doi.org/10.3389/fnhum.2014.00522

Bargh, J. A. (1997). The Automaticity of Everyday Life. In R. S. Wyer (Ed.), *Advances in social cognition* (Vol. X, pp. 1–61). Erlbaum.

Carlisle, C. (2010). "Between Freedom and Necessity: Félix Ravaisson on Habit and the Moral Life". *Inquiry, 53*(2), 123–145.

Carlisle, C. (2018). Habit, Practice, Grace: Towards a Philosophy of Religious Life. In F. Ellis (Ed.), *New Models of Religious Understanding* (pp. 97–115). Oxford University Press.

Farrow, K., Grolleau, G., & Ibanez, L. (2017). Social Norms and Pro-environmental Behavior: A Review of the Evidence. *Ecological Economics, Elsevier, 140*(C), 1–13.

Gibson, J. (1979). *The Ecological Approach to Visual Perception*. Houghton Mifflin.

Graybiel, A. M. (2008). Habits, Rituals, and the Evaluative Brain. *Annual Review of Neuroscience, 31*, 359–387.

Hagmann, D., Ho, E. H., & Loewenstein, G. (2019). Nudging Out Support for a Carbon Tax. *Nature Climate Change, 9*, 484–489.

Holm, P., et al. (2015). Humanities for the Environment. A Manifesto for Research and Action. *Humanities, 4*(4), 977–992.

Howell, R. (2018). Carbon Management at the Household Level: A Definition of Carbon Literacy and Three Mechanisms that Increase It. *Carbon Management, 9*(1), 25–35.

James, W. (1980 [1890]). *The Principles of Psychology*. Henry Holt and Company.

Jamieson, D. (2014). *Reason in a Dark Time. Why the Struggle Against Climate Change Failed and What It Meant for Our Future*. Oxford University Press.

Kaaronen, R. O. (2017). Affording Sustainability: Adopting a Theory of Affordances as a Guiding Heuristic for Environmental Policy. *Frontiers in Psychology, 8*, 1974. https://doi.org/10.3389/fpsyg.2017.0197

Knussen, C., & Yule, F. (2008). 'I'm Not in the Habit of Recycling': The Role of Habitual Behavior in the Disposal of Household Waste. *Environment and Behavior, 40*, 683–702.

Latour, B. (2013). *An Inquiry Into the Modes of Existence: An Anthropology of the Moderns.* Harvard University Press.

Lehner, M., Mont, O., & Heiskanen, E. (2016). Nudging: A Promising Tool for Sustainable Consumption Behaviour? *Journal of Cleaner Production, 134*(A), 166–177.

Lilley, R., Whitehead, M., Howell, R., & Jones, R. (2014). *Mindfulness, Behaviour Change and Engagement in Public Policy. An Evaluation.* Retrieved October 7, 2020, from https://changingbehaviours.wordpress.com/2014/10/10/mindfulness-and-behaviour-change-an-evaluation/

Magrì, E. (2019). Situating Attention and Habit in the Landscape of Affordances. *Rivista Internazionale di Filosofia e Psicologia, 10*(2), 120–136.

Merleau-Ponty, M. (2002 [1945]). *Phenomenology of Perception.* Routledge.

Neimanis, A., Åsberg, C., & Hedrén, J. (2015). Four Problems, Four Directions for Environmental Humanities. *Ethics and Environment, 20*(1), 67–97.

Noë, A. (2009). *Out of Our Heads: Why You Are Not Your Brain, and Other Lessons from the Biology of Consciousness.* Hill and Wang.

Pedwell, C. (2017). Habit and the Politics of Social Change: A Comparison of Nudge Theory and Pragmatist Philosophy. *Body and Society, 23*(4), 59–94.

Shove, E. (2010). Beyond the ABC: Climate Change Policy and Theories of Social Change. *Environment and Planning A: Economy and Space, 42*(6), 1273–1285.

Shusterman, R. (2008). *Body Consciousness: A Philosophy of Mindfulness and Somaesthetics.* Cambridge University Press.

Sparrow, T., & Hutchinson, A. (Eds.). (2013). *A History of Habit: From Aristotle to Bourdieu.* Lexington Books.

Steg, L., & Vlek, C. (2009). Encouraging Pro-environmental Behaviour: An Integrative Review and Research Agenda. *Journal of Environmental Psychology, 29*(3), 309–317.

Thaler, R. H., & Sunstein, C. R. (2008). *Nudge: Improving Decisions about Health, Wealth, and Happiness.* Yale University Press.

Tiefenbeck, V., Staake, T., Roth, K., & Sachs, O. (2013). For Better or for Worse? Empirical Evidence of Moral Licensing in a Behavioral Energy Conservation Campaign. *Energy Policy, 57*(C), 160–171.

Wallenhorst, N. (2019). *L'Anthropocène expliqué aux humains.* Le Pommier.

Wallenhorst, N. & Wulf, C. (2022). *Humains – un dictionnaire d'anthropologie prospective.* Vrin.

Wilhite, H. L. (2015). The Problem of Habits for a Sustainable Transformation. In K. L. Syse & M. L. Mueller (Eds.), *Sustainable Consumption and the Good Life* (pp. 100–110). Routledge.

Building Blocks of a Historical Overview of 'Tacit Knowledge'

Kristina Brümmer, Thomas Alkemeyer, and Robert Mitchell

1 Introduction: (Re-)Turning to Tacit Knowledge

Since the 1990s, there have been a number of shifts in cultural studies that have caused an upheaval, each (re-)emphasising elements of the social that have either been forgotten or never quite recognised in a pivotal manner. For instance, alongside focusing on language, signs and semiotic structures in the so-called linguistic turn, since the 1990s there has been a move towards a transdisciplinary methodological re-orientation around the terms 'practice' and 'practices' within the so-called practice turn. A central impetus of this 'turn around' is the rejection of an (over-)theorised perspective that only perceives the 'nitty-gritty,' 'real' material and embodied being-in-the-world when it happens to present an obstacle to cognitive and intellectual processes. Instead, in a multiplication of different turns and resurgences, other aspects of

---

K. Brümmer (✉)
University of Hamburg, Hamburg, Germany
e-mail: Kristina.bruemmer@uni-hamburg.de

T. Alkemeyer
University of Oldenburg, Oldenburg, Germany
e-mail: thomas.alkemeyer@uni-oldenburg.de

R. Mitchell
University of Mainz, Mainz, Germany

© The Author(s), under exclusive license to Springer Nature Switzerland AG 2022
A. Kraus, C. Wulf (eds.), *The Palgrave Handbook of Embodiment and Learning*,
https://doi.org/10.1007/978-3-030-93001-1_5

the social are given the limelight: the *body turn* focuses on the role of the body as a mediator, while a *renaissance of pragmatism* also considers embodied knowledge to be pivotal; the *performative turn* addresses the performative nature of the social, that is, that it does not simply reside in structures, but must be enacted; the *spatial turn* predictably puts the role of spaces in the foreground, and the *material turn* looks to material settings and artefacts. From a practice-theoretical perspective, the issue is then how all these aspects (co-)constitute social order(s) and their human—and non-human—co-actors participating in them. Thus, it is both a premise and a corollary of these theoretical (re-)orientations that humans are no longer viewed as rational reflexive, primarily cognising entities, standing in opposition to the disorder of everyday life, but rather "carnally" as entities of "flesh and blood" (Wacquant, 2015) who are anchored in multiple ways to their being-in-the-world, just as—to loosely quote Marx—they equally make their own circumstances and, thus, form themselves or, rather, their selves. From this perspective, all perception and knowledge—or in praxeological parlance, perceiving and knowing—is co-constituted by practical doing. Indeed, even thinking is conceived as a component of 'real' practice.

In the sociology of knowledge, this re-orientation corresponds to the replacement of the question "*who* knows something?" with the more fundamental question, "*how* can something be known in the first place?" (Hirschauer, 2008, p. 87). Whereas a Platonic-Cartesian approach only bestows the term 'knowledge' on what can be expressed in language and terminology, thus exalting the *theoria* and its hard-earned glimpse of eternal and immovable ideas as the highest of mankind's achievements, practice theories (re-)discover concepts of knowledge that were displaced or stigmatised as irrational by the epistemocentric mainstream of Western philosophy (Hetzel, 2008, p. 29). A central aspect here is a re-turn towards skilful embodied navigation in the world around and with things, people, spaces and situations which is founded upon an intimate sense of being-in-the-world. Such implicit or "empractical" (Stekeler-Weithofer, 2005) 'know how,' which is intrinsically tied to practices being performed, has been postulated, among others, by such philosophers as Heidegger, Wittgenstein, Fleck, Polanyi and Merleau-Ponty.

Thus, the approaches detailed here share the more or less strong programmatic ambition to critique systematically the otherwise dominant assumption that 'theory' takes epistemological precedence over 'practice.' Instead, the aim is to rehabilitate "other knowledge" (Böhle et al., 2001), an aim which itself could stem from current times and circumstances, living in a 'second modernity,' characterised by a resurgence of ambiguity and uncertainty arising in making conscious thought, intentional planning and reflexive regulation seem less important vis-à-vis situationally adequate action via (socialised) intuition and a 'feeling for the situation' (Beck & Bonß, 2001).

Such clarity of impetus notwithstanding, in the relevant (inter-)disciplinary discourse it is not uncontroversial what the characteristic features of such 'other,' generally 'silent' knowledge are. Indeed, the question can even be raised whether one is dealing with knowledge in a sensible usage of the term at all, or whether the term 'knowledge' should be reserved for verifiable content that can be articulated (e.g., Schneider, 2012, p. 87).

Terminological disagreements aside, in our view, in the current re-evaluation of what is known as tacit knowledge there are five fundamental assumptions. First, it does not exist of its own accord in an independent, purely theoretical state, but rather is entwined with practice. Subsequently, second, human bodies are not mere executive organs of mental intentions and intellectual planning, but rather themselves (co-)agents developing their own 'intelligence' through practice (comprehensive discussion by Keller & Meuser, 2011). Third, this embodied knowledge of skill (in the sense of a strict concept of knowledge) cannot be represented or verbalised or only with difficulty (Loenhoff, 2012, p. 62). As 'silent knowledge' in this sense, it can, fourth, only be acquired via practical experience. Lastly, fifth, in contrast to knowledge in line with the Platonic-Cartesian model, its value is not measured according to the criterion of universally and abstractly determined truth, but rather exclusively according to its effects, that is, with regard to whether it enables action which is adequate for the situation.

In sum, compiling a comprehensive conceptual history of tacit knowledge poses an impossible task because it entails summarising a history of an epistemological issue that is present even when the term itself does not (yet) make an explicit appearance. Thus, our contribution here must of necessity be highly selective. Consequently, our aim is to provide an overview of the most important aspects, especially of those approaches that have played and/or still play a pivotal part in the current discussion. In so doing, this overview details diverse approaches along three broad disciplinary boundaries depicting the respective phenomena being focused upon and the solution which is being sought by referring to this 'other' knowledge. Subsequently in the third and final section, we consider critically the interconnected (new) concepts of practice and knowledge that are steadily gaining influence in the wake of these cultural turns.

2 Tacit Knowledge in Diverse Disciplines

2.1 Philosophy

In philosophy, with materialism, anthropology, phenomenology and pragmatism, there is no dearth of approaches providing a counterbalance to the Cartesian conception of the subject.

Although Karl Marx was not primarily endeavouring to develop the concept of implicit knowledge in his critical discussion of Feuerbach's anthropological materialism, in his Theses on Feuerbach (1845), Marx nevertheless postulates a primacy of practice, that is, sensuous human activity vis-à-vis theoretical contemplation revealing a common denominator between his practice philosophy and other anti-Cartesian philosophies similarly engaged in locating the development of subjectivity, mind and meaning first and foremost in practice. Consequently, all knowledge is entwined in concrete enactments of everyday life and is in this sense implicit in practice.

In his ontological hermeneutic, Martin Heidegger (2001, §§ 31–33) conceives of one's relation to and in the world not in a contemplative but a practical sense. As Loenhoff (2012, p. 50) emphasises, the main drive here is the manual handling of everyday tools and instruments that bestows an understanding of the world upon actors before theoretical insight has even begun. This primary mode of understanding proceeds as a practical orientation towards a familiar world filled with objects which are ready to be handled manually, that is, are 'ready-to-hand' in Heidegger's terminology. Therefore, primary understanding is a practical skill. The depth of this understanding reveals itself in interpretative acts vis-à-vis the objects that are ready-to-hand, not primarily formulated in lingual form but already expressed non-lingually, for example, in the creative handling of objects in the world. Thus, Heidegger subverts the widely held position of equating explication with verbality or even linguality for that matter (ibid., p. 60). By reconstructing the origins of theoretical discovery on the foundation of practical handling with what is ready-to-hand, he succeeds in not completely untethering even the most abstract forms of contemplation from their material prerequisites (ibid., p. 56). Cognition and reflexion are driven by real-world occurrences when what is ready-to-hand becomes conspicuous, obtrusive or recalcitrant, for example, by causing a disruption, thus stepping out of their otherwise inconspicuous standby-mode into the mode of being 'present-at-hand'. Hence, the foundation of all knowledge lies in such circumspect skilfulness in the world. Moreover, the everyday handling of objects and language "already is with

Others" (ibid., p. 162) is, in this sense, irreducibly social. Meaning that this knowledge is dependent on intersubjective recognition so that it would be fallacious to conceive of it as exclusively the corporeal skill of a single individual or their body.

With the aim of understanding how humans orientate themselves in the world, in his philosophy of perception the French phenomenologist Maurice Merleau-Ponty (1998) postulates the primordial interwovenness of the living body[1] and the world. He describes how, before any kind of analysis can take place, we perceive objects via the medium of the lived body, in turn, creating these objects in the first place (ibid., p. 92). All—even scientific—cognition, thought and action are mediated via the anchor of the living body in contexts of meaning. Perception is neither reduced in a sensory manner to a purely passive reception of impressions nor idealistically to an accomplishment exclusive to cognition, but is instead conceived of as a process filling the world with meaning and, thus, constituting 'world'. Vis-à-vis the body as an object among objects, the lived body (*corps vivant, corps propre*) differentiates itself analytically in that it is never fully in view, never fully in perception's grasp, featuring an "intentionality" (Merleau-Ponty, 1998, p. 137) of its own, an "opening upon the world" (ibid., p. 117), a "being in and towards the world" (ibid., p. 106): by 'inhabiting' the world, it co-develops the objects it perceives as meaningful; they are immediately "present as the immanent term of [one's] practical intentions" (Wacquant, 1992, p. 21). Thus again, it is not theoretical-abstract knowledge that is the primary access point to the world but rather practical intentionality and practical knowledge housed in the living body.

A further important point of reference in current discussions around the interconnectedness of practice, bodies and knowledge is to be found in Ludwig Wittgenstein's later work. Here (meaningful) order in thought and in the world is conceived of as starting from the close relationship between an active subject and the world (Wittgenstein, 1970, 1971). Following Wittgenstein, subjects and their actions are structured according to the suggestions and demands the subject receives from and in the world. The subject does not primarily perceive objects in the world in an abstract manner, but instead mainly from the concrete angle of how they can be used. In this sense, action and understanding are viewed as practical responses to demands from objects: practical understanding of their material-symbolic handling qualities (Gebauer, 2009, p. 64). Pivotal here is the concept of the 'language game'

---

[1] Attempts to translate phenomenological terms for the lived experience of the body (e.g., *Leib* in German) vis-à-vis the body as an object or instrument (e.g., *Körper*) are always somewhat fraught. Using 'living' rather than the more common 'lived body' follows Sara Heinämaa's (1999, p. 128, fn. 6) suggestion for translating Merleau-Ponty's *corps vivant*.

with which Wittgenstein underscores that lingual descriptions and words accrue their meaning through their practical handling in the world, that is, within a social usage context, and that such accrued meaning does not precede their usage. Thus, the acquisition of a language game and, concurrently, of adequate rule-abiding behaviour goes hand in hand with the corresponding constitution of the body. Ultimately, Wittgenstein (1970) traces back all certainties in our thinking and acting to language games, the material structure of the body and its ability to (re-)act in and to the world.

For the American pragmatists William James, Charles Sanders Peirce and John Dewey the important issue—this time more figuratively than literally—is the 'nature' of knowledge. Their focus is not on abstract-theoretical knowledge which precedes and guides action, but rather on knowledge with regard to its practical effects in everyday life. Indeed, instead of locating mind, knowledge, thought and subjectivity outside of practice, pragmatism focuses on their practical social constitution (Hetzel, 2008). Critical in this regard is the term *experience*, which is especially pronounced in Dewey's (1929) work which differentiates between primary experience as the "unanalyzed totality" (ibid., p. 8) of unprocessed impressions in everyday life vis-à-vis secondary experiences as "derived and refined products" (ibid., p. 4) that are "discriminated by reflection out of primary experience" (ibid., p. 8). By observing these different types of experience, Dewey criticises the intellectualistic tendency to place the products of reflection and the explicit articulation of knowledge above primary experience.

Following in the tradition of both Wittgenstein and pragmatism, the British philosopher Gilbert Ryle devotes a whole book titled *The Concept of Mind* (2002) to the cause of elevating skill ('knowing how') vis-à-vis theoretical knowledge ('knowing that'). Ryle charges (post-)Cartesian philosophy with following the (categorically) mistaken and dogmatic 'official doctrine' that action can only be classed as intelligent if an actor considers plans and rules ex ante, forms intentions and recalls theoretical knowledge (ibid., pp. 15–16). Ryle demonstrates how this dogmatic position leads to an infinite regress by assuming that the practical performance of an intelligent action is always preceded by some sort of "spectral" (ibid., p. 20), rule-like mechanisms according to the "double-life theory" (ibid., p. 18) of mind versus body. Ryle uses the fact that something can be done skilfully without the capability of articulating explicit rules to re-evaluate the term 'intelligence,' assigning it not to incorporeal acts of the 'mind,' but rather locating it in practice as the manner in which acts are physically carried out. Consequently, here again, it is practical performance which precedes theorisation. Moreover as, in this view, skill is not the result of propositional knowledge, Ryle finds that skill is the result of "a disposition, but not a single-track disposition like a reflex or a habit" (ibid., p. 46). It is a multi-track or complex disposition acquired by practice which not only lays the foundation for routines, but also allows for the variable adjustment in execution vis-à-vis demands in situ (ibid., 45ff.).

Within the philosophy of science, 'other' knowledge is primarily an epistemological issue with regard to studying the (pre-)conditions of (scientific) cognition, knowledge and discovery. Here Michael Polanyi, one of the most notable authors of the current re-discovery of 'other' knowledge, offers a sound critique of what he described as an "erroneous scientific world view" (Polanyi, 1970, p. 971) narrowing knowledge down to only that which is scientifically substantiated. Polanyi begins from "the fact that 'we can know more than we can tell'" (Polanyi, 2009, p. 4, original emphasis) and builds the argument that even explicit, seemingly objective and completely objectifiable knowledge, for example, a mathematical theory, is built upon an epistemological foundation which it can never fully encapsulate. Polanyi calls this foundation the 'tacit dimension.'[2]

2.2 Psychology/Social Learning Theory

For psychology and social learning theory, tacit knowledge provides a path on their primary mission of explaining *how* humans are enabled to act competently in the world. With the intention of sounding out the boundaries of artificial intelligence vis-à-vis the faculties of their human counterparts, Stuart and Hubert Dreyfus put forward a model of skill acquisition following the development from novice to expert, which was met with a positive response in the psychological and educational study of expertise. According to Dreyfus and Dreyfus (1986), the type of formal-analytical approach deemed to be the highest form of intelligent action in intellectualistic theories absolutely does *not* represent how human expertise works, but rather depicts the approach of beginners. The latter, namely, plan their course of action and analyse situations thoroughly before doing anything; experts, however, act based on a wealth of experience quickly and intuitively—instead of being analytical and distanced their approach is holistic. When it comes to experts, alongside case- and situation-specific tacit knowledge, there is a

---

[2] A similarly positioned, albeit less often noted critique of the hypostatising of scientific thought (Schützeichel, 2012, p. 118) is to be found in the work of Karl Mannheim (1982), specifically his distinction between conjunctive and communicative cognition. Whereas Polanyi views tacit knowledge in conjunction with an individual body, Mannheim conceives of conjunctive cognition as a fundamentally collective act, operating in communities and resting upon shared experience (ibid., p. 194ff.; also Schützeichel, 2012).

higher level of reflection at work: their actions are accompanied by "deliberative rationality" (ibid., p. 36). Such contemporaneous thinking-in-action is also described by Donald Schön in his book, *The Reflexive Practitioner* (2009, p. 21), as 'reflection-in-action.' It enables adepts and masters to react instantaneously to contingencies in situ, adapting their actions accordingly, and departing from established routine.

Whereas Dreyfus and Dreyfus focus on individual practitioners, Jean Lave and Etienne Wenger (1997) adopt a collectivistic perspective in their communities-of-practice approach. They begin by wondering how newcomers learn to participate in practices and—eventually—become recognised members of a community of practitioners. The authors analyse practical knowledge as being shared between participants. A central concept of this practice-theoretical learning theory is "legitimate peripheral participation" (ibid., p. 27), according to which practical competence is acquired by being increasingly engaged in respective practice(s). In this view, learning is not a top-down process of authoritative instruction, but rather occurs in interaction in which all participants learn 'communally' together in practice. Here then, practical knowledge is framed primarily as a carrier of traditions. The strength of the communities-of-practice approach is describing how novices gradually gain in competence, reproduce proficiency and become carriers of established practices themselves. However, the concomitant weakness of this approach with its emphasis on tradition is that it is less well equipped to explain change vis-à-vis "persistence and perpetuation" (Nicolini, 2012, p. 85).

Similarly, the assumption that learning and practice are inseparably conjoined characterises activity theory. The starting point here is the observation that the relationship of humans and their environment is mediated materially, that is, via artefacts and symbols. In this view, not only practical faculties, but also 'high' mental functions are constituted in and by the handling of objects (ibid., p. 103). This is exemplified by Alexei Nikolajewitsch Leontjew's (1973, p. 239) description of how a child's hand movements learning to use a spoon gradually succumb to the objective logic of handling this object: while learning the child converts what are at first involuntary movements into object-adequate skilful movements. By this, the child unlocks the objective-social material meaning (Holzkamp, 1995, p. 282), which is literally 'objectified' in and by the spoon, conforming to it and, thus, gradually gaining competence in the practice of eating and, in turn, displaying recognisable social form.

2.3   Sociology

In sociology, 'other' knowledge is primarily discussed under the aspect of its historical and societal contingency and its importance for the construction, reproduction and transformation of social order(s). With regard to conceptualisation and nomenclature of this knowledge, there are several different proposals (see, e.g., Hirschauer, 2008 for an overview):

Marcel Mauss influentially speaks of "techniques of the body" to denote people's everyday actions by which social order is produced. Specifically, this term refers to historically and culturally variable "ways in which from society to society men (sic!) know how to use their bodies" (Mauss, 1973, p. 70). Techniques of the body are socially regimented, becoming 'second nature' through drill and training, in turn securing the continuity of given order(s).

Ethnomethodology builds on the concept of tacit knowledge in that it takes social order(ing) to be primarily created not by the "formal analytic" (Garfinkel, 2002, p. 94) efforts of sociologists, but by the methodical workings of people in everyday life. In this sense, founding figure Harold Garfinkel sees sociality and social order(ing) as an interactive, local "practical accomplishment" (Garfinkel, 2011, p. 9) of members via specific ethno-methods and skills (ibid., p. vii). Here, action, interaction and order are not attributed to pre-existing structures or occult, explicit rules or knowledge. Instead, ethnomethodology pivotally focuses on how in the doing of members' methods they make themselves unavoidably, due to their social nature, "reportable and observable" (Sharrock & Anderson, 1986, p. 56), that is, in ethnomethodological parlance, "accountable" (Garfinkel, 2011, p. 33).

In a similar vein, albeit with marked differences, in his diverse studies of the "interaction order" (Goffman, 1983), Erving Goffman gets to grips with the "relations in public" (Goffman, 1971) of meaning and action. He considers the processes by which humans navigate around each other and their social surroundings, taking people at 'face value,' viewing their bodies as displays of knowledge delivering information about emotional states, intentions and so on to others, but also back to the body's occupants (Hirschauer, 2008). Exemplary here is Goffman's depiction of people's literal navigation of the social world, namely, in pedestrian traffic. Here, order is constituted by an interplay of mainly automatic bodily displays on the one hand— 'externalizations,' 'body glosses' or 'intention displays'—which constitutes the gestural pre-emption of practical intentionality, and 'scanning' on the other as the practically embedded sensory-corporeal perception going beyond mere visual observation (Goffman, 1971, p. 11).

For the current re-orientating turns, Pierre Bourdieu's praxeology is without doubt highly influential. His concepts of habitus and 'sens pratique,' the "logic of practice" (Bourdieu, 1990) sociologically re-utilise Merleau-Ponty's postulate of the primordial interwovenness of the lived body and the world, albeit admittedly in a manner mostly incompatible with phenomenology (Wacquant, 1992, p. 20, fn. 35). Similar to Merleau-Ponty, Bourdieu does not view the comprehending, 'competent' body simply as 'a given,' but emphasises instead how it is first and foremost constituted out of relations in practice. In practices of differently structured social fields, the human organism principally "open to the world" (Bourdieu, 2000, p. 134) forms a net of dispositions encompassing schemata of perception, cognition and judgement which, in turn, for example, as milieu- or gender-specific habitus proceeds to work as a motor of production of practices beyond conscious societal or self-control. When the condition of a fit between incorporated structures of the habitus and the objectified structures of a social field holds, the habitus functions as a quasi-intuitive practical logic, enabling the creation of ways of acting which are "[o]bjectively 'regulated' and 'regular' without being in any way the product of obedience to rules" (Bourdieu, 1990, p. 53).[3] The logic of practice manifests itself at a basal level as corporeal intuition vis-à-vis expectations of a given social field, a feeling for the 'correct' gestures, stature and movements fitting with one's social status and the situation at hand, that is, a socialised sensibility for a sensorially experienced world (also Wacquant, 1992, 20, fn. 36). Although Bourdieu's primary goal was to understand the reproduction mechanisms of social inequality, he nevertheless strives to describe habitus as a source of creative and transformative power (e.g., Bourdieu, 2000, pp. 128–163), carrying the potential for "practical reflection" in moments of discord and disruption (ibid., pp. 162–163).

In the broad field of science and technology studies, sociologist Harry Collins (2010) concerns himself explicitly with 'tacit and explicit knowledge' within his work on scientific expertise and describing scientific practice, especially with regard to artificial intelligence. A unique feature of his approach is the critical attempt to take the term of tacit knowledge to its conceptual limits, destroying his own "belief in tacitness" (Collins, 2001, p. 108). This involves two steps: first is a demystification of the tacit, clarifying that what is meant by 'tacit' "only makes sense when it is in tension with explicit knowledge" (Collins, 2010, p. 78), and is, thus, "parasitic on the notion of the explicit" (ibid., p. 85). Ultimately, this turns the relation of these two forms of knowledge on its head, not focusing on the otherwise often prevalent

---

[3] Anthony Giddens' (1984) term "practical consciousness" is similarly conceived.

fascination with silent knowledge but finding instead "nothing strange about things being done but not being told [...]. What is strange is that anything *can* be told" (ibid., p. 7, original emphasis). Second, by considering tacit knowledge with regard to what actually limits explication, Collins (ibid., pp. 85–138) attempts to get a better grasp of the concept. Thus, he distinguishes three kinds which are increasingly resistant to explication: relational, somatic and collective tacit knowledge. In brief, *relational* tacit knowledge remains tacit due to 'contingencies' of social organisation. *Somatic* tacit knowledge is represented by the skills of bike riding, rock climbing, tap dancing and so on. Considering the focus of other approaches on the body mentioned here, Collins sees no real obstacle to explicating what humans do with their bodies as evidenced by the transfer of these skills to machines and robots. Instead of the knowledge slumbering in human bodies, for Collins it is *collective* tacit knowledge "which is the irreducible heartland of the concept" (ibid., p. 119). This is knowledge which only humans acquire by virtue of their being embedded in society, illustrated, for example, by the difference between the somatic knowledge of learning a sequence of dance steps in contrast to knowing how to improvise these steps in a fitting manner (ibid., p. 123).

3   In Conclusion: Speaking for Silent Knowledge in Current Sociological Practice Theories

The re-evaluation of 'other' knowledge and the recognition of the body as a carrier *of* and an agent *in* practices are at the core of current turns in the cultural and social sciences, bringing practice(s) back in, which in many current practice-sociological approaches are considered to be highly significant, if not the basic building blocks of the social (e.g., Reckwitz, 2002; Schatzki, 2002; Shove et al., 2012). These sociological approaches—at least partially—have a tendency, as Andreas Reckwitz (2002, p. 255) succinctly puts it, to view practices as "routines: routines of moving the body, of understanding and wanting, of using things, interconnected in a practice" so that, in this account, "[f]or practice theory, the nature of social structure consists in routinization."

However, this equation of practical knowledge with routines harbours the risk of functional reductionism in that it seems to lean heavily on the depiction of the frictionless flow of practice(s) and, thus, primarily predict the iteration of what has gone before. Focusing on the main flow of practice(s) rather than, say, on distributaries or anabranches, entails viewing implicit knowledge only in contexts in which it 'functions appropriately' according to whatever situative, systemic or theoretical goals one takes as a framework.

This is a somewhat surprising conceptual blind spot when one considers the theoretical roots predating and often feeding into practice theories such as Bourdieu's (1977) Algeria studies, focusing on how practices break down.[4] Such an understanding of tacit knowledge is the result of a specific external perspective on practices from which they are hypostatised, frozen in time as unitary entities that are performed *on* bodies or, more pointedly, "recruit" (Shove et al., 2012, 63 pp.) bodies for their aims and goals in order to imprint on them the requisite knowledge for their reproduction. This perspective leaves other features and capabilities of tacit knowledge such as its moments of reflection or its creative-transformative potential in the dark which are indeed emphasised by, for example, Ryle or Dreyfus and Dreyfus, or Bourdieu who attempts, alongside the consideration of pre-figuring social structures, to also capture the participants' perspective. Only by getting down into 'the trenches,' and taking the (imaginary) position of 'peeking over diverse participants' shoulders' does it become clear that practices do not present themselves as identical entities, but rather are refracted in different ways depending upon the standpoint whence they are viewed, and, moreover, their performance continually produces the potential for conflict, confusion, problems and disorder (Brümmer & Mitchell, 2014), which, on the one hand, participants are required to deal with and, on the other, offer the opportunity to seize the "potential of the situation" (Jullien, 2004, p. 15) and to pursue one's own position-dependent interests. In this light, tacit knowledge appears as a factor in local coping strategies and problem-solving, that is, as orientation-in-action in which moments of reflexive corporeal feelings and of reflection are always present.

Moreover, there is a concomitant risk of the frictionless depiction of practices, namely, an ableistic bias with regard to the bodies involved in them. This is because there is then an in-built tendency to gravitate towards harmonious performances of (hyper-)able bodies such as is the case when soldiers march, acrobatic or dance troupes perform daring or visually aesthetic feats, or highly skilled martial arts practitioners teach their techniques. There can be good theoretical and methodological reasons for considering such perspicuous cases of practices' performance. Nevertheless, a course correction focusing more on disharmonious, amateurish embodiments of practices and the concomitant

---

[4] See also Judith Butler's (1990) detailing of omnipresent "trouble" in everyday practices reproducing gender, or, more broadly, Critical Theory emphasising that theories should not presuppose the workings of the societies they observe.

struggles, mismatches and failures involved seems prudent (Alkemeyer et al., 2017, pp. 73, 76; Brümmer, 2015, pp. 66–70) as does moving away from (hyper-)ability in bodies, towards moments when bodies are unable or unavailable with regard to the practical accomplishment of a given practice (Alkemeyer, 2019), thus, considering "bodily inabilities," aiming to focus on how "(some) bodies cannot do (some) things" (Boll & Lambrix, 2019, p. 261) rather than their moments of glory in meticulously put together and rehearsed choreographies.

Conceptual issues aside, as far as the future of tacit knowledge goes, due to its close ties with practice theories, the tacit dimension likely shares its fate with them. Therefore, Collins' previously detailed effort to dispense with the tacit or fundamental debates regarding perceived flaws in practice theories with regard to the transmission of knowledge (Turner, 1994) or neuroscientific discoveries such as mirror neurons can all have serious repercussions for how tacit knowledge is conceived, as can the development of artificial intelligence and any other non- or post-human subjects for that matter.[5] At the same time, these issues provide the opportunity for further empirically grounded contributions to the discussion of tacit knowledge with regard to its explicability (re-)conceptualising it in the light of the ever-changing flow of practice.

References

Alkemeyer, T. (2019). Bedingte Un/Verfügbarkeit. Zur Kritik des praxeologischen Körpers. *Österreichische Zeitschrift für Soziologie, 44*, 289–312.

Alkemeyer, T., Buschmann, N., & Michaeler, M. (2017). Critique in Praxis: Arguments for a Subjectivation Theoretical Expansion on Practice Theory. In M. Jonas & B. Littig (Eds.), *Praxeological Political Analysis. Routledge Advances in Sociology* (Vol. 196, pp. 67–83). Routledge.

Beck, U., & Bonß, W. (Eds.). (2001). *Die Modernisierung der Moderne*. Suhrkamp.

Böhle, F., Bolte, A., Drexel, I., & Weißhaupt, S. (2001). Grenzen wissenschaftlich-technischer Rationalität und, anderes Wissen'. In U. Beck & W. Bonß (Eds.), *Die Modernisierung der Moderne* (pp. 96–105). Suhrkamp.

Boll, T., & Lambrix, P. (2019). Editorial. *Österreichische Zeitschrift für Soziologie, 44*, 261–267.

Bourdieu, P. (1977). *Algeria 1960*. Cambridge University Press.

Bourdieu, P. (1990). *The Logic of Practice*. (R. Nice, Trans.). Stanford University Press.

---

[5] For the practice theoretical debate on mirror neurons, see Omar Lizardo's (2007) argument for their explanatory power and Turner's (2007) reply dampening expectations of their supposed utility.

Bourdieu, P. (2000 [1997]). *Pascalian Meditations* (R. Nice, Trans.). Polity Press.

Brümmer, K. (2015). *Mitspielfähigkeit. Sportliches Training als formative Praxis.* transcript.

Brümmer, K., & Mitchell, R. (2014). Becoming engaged. Eine praxistheoretisch-empirische Analyse von Trainingsepisoden in der Sportakrobatik und dem Taijiquan. *Sport und Gesellschaft, 11*, 157–186.

Butler, J. (1990): Gender Trouble. *Feminism and the Subversion of Identity.* New York: Routledge

Collins, H. (2001). What Is Tacit Knowledge? In T. Schatzki, K. Knorr Cetina, & E. von Savigny (Eds.), *The Practice Turn in Contemporary Theory* (pp. 107–119). Routledge.

Collins, H. (2010). *Tacit and Explicit Knowledge.* The University of Chicago Press.

Dewey, J. (1929). *Experience and Nature.* George Allen, and Unwin.

Dreyfus, H., & Dreyfus, S. (1986). *Mind over Machine. The Power of Human Intuition and Expertise in the Era of the Computer.* Basil Blackwell.

Garfinkel, H. (2002). *Ethnomethodology's Program. Working Out Durkheim's Aphorism* (A. W. Rawls, Ed. and Introduced). Rowman & Littlefield Publishers.

Garfinkel, H. (2011 [1967]). *Studies in Ethnomethodology.* Polity Press.

Gebauer, G. (2009). *Wittgensteins anthropologisches Denken.* Beck.

Giddens, A. (1984). *The Constitution of Society: Outline of the Theory of Structuration.* Polity Press.

Goffman, E. (1971). *Relations in Public. Microstudies of the Public Order.* Basic Books.

Goffman, E. (1983). The Interaction Order: American Sociological Association, 1982 Presidential Address. *American Sociological Review, 48*, 1–17.

Heidegger, M. (2001 [1962]). *Being and Time* (J. Macquarrie & E. Robinson). Blackwell.

Heinämaa, S. (1999). Simone de Beauvoir's Phenomenology of Sexual Difference. *Hypatia. A Journal of Feminist Philosophy, 14*, 114–132.

Hetzel, A. (2008). Zum Vorrang der Praxis. Berührungspunkte zwischen Pragmatismus und kritischer Theorie. In A. Hetzel, J. Kertscher, & M. Rölli (Eds.), *Pragmatismus—Philosophie der Zukunft?* (pp. 17–57). Velbrück.

Hirschauer, S. (2008). Körper macht Wissen: für eine Somatisierung des Wissensbegriffs. In K.-S. Rehberg (Ed.), *Die Natur der Gesellschaft. Verhandlungen des 33. Kongresses der Deutschen Gesellschaft für Soziologie in Kassel* (pp. 974–984). Campus. 2.

Holzkamp, K. (1995). *Lernen. Subjektwissenschaftliche Grundlegung.* Campus.

Jullien, F. (2004 [1996]). *A Treatise on Efficacy. Between Western and Chinese Thinking* (J. Lloyd, Trans.). University of Hawai'i Press.

Keller, R., & Meuser, M. (Eds.). (2011). *Körperwissen.* VS.

Lave, J., & Wenger, E. (1997). *Situated Learning: Legitimate Peripheral Learning.* Cambridge University Press.

Leontjew, A. N. (1973 [1931]). *Probleme der Entwicklung des Psychischen.* Fischer-Athenäum.

Lizardo, O. (2007). 'Mirror Neurons,' Collective Objects and the Problem of Transmission: Reconsidering Stephen Turner's Critique of Practice Theory. *Journal for the Theory of Social Behavior, 37,* 319–350.

Loenhoff, J. (2012). Zur Reichweite von Heideggers Verständnis impliziten Wissens. In J. Loenhoff (Ed.), *Implizites Wissen. Epistemologische und handlungstheoretische Perspektiven* (pp. 49–66). Velbrück.

Mannheim, K. (1982). *Structures of thinking* (D. Kettler, et al., Text and Trans.). Routledge, and Kegan Paul.

Marx, K. (1845). *Thesen über Feuerbach.* http://www.mlwerke.de/me/me03/me03_005.htm.

Mauss, M. (1973 [1935]). Techniques of the Body. *Economy and Society, 2,* pp. 70–88.

Merleau-Ponty, M. (1998 [1962]). *Phenomenology of Perception* (C. Smith, Trans.). Routledge.

Nicolini, D. (2012). *Practice Theory, Work and Organization. An Introduction.* Oxford University Press.

Polanyi M. (1970). Science and Man. *Proceedings of the Royal Society of Medicine, 63,* pp. 969–976. https://www.ncbi.nlm.nih.gov/pmc/articles/PMC1812163/pdf/procrsmed00292-0145.pdf.

Polanyi, M. (2009 [1966]). *The Tacit Dimension.* University of Chicago Press.

Reckwitz, A. (2002). Toward a Theory of Social Practices. A Development in Culturalist Theorizing. *European Journal of Social Theory, 5,* 243–263.

Ryle, G. (2002 [1949]). *The Concept of Mind.* The University of Chicago Press.

Schatzki, T. (2002). *The Site of the Social: A Philosophical Account of the Constitution of Social Life and Change.* Pennsylvania State University Press.

Schneider, H. J. (2012). Können, Wissen, Zuschreibung. Begriffliche Vorschläge im Ausgang von Wittgenstein. In J. Loenhoff (Ed.), *Implizites Wissen. Epistemologische und handlungstheoretische Perspektiven* (pp. 67–90). Velbrück.

Schön, D. (2009). *The Reflective Practitioner. How Professionals Think in Action.* Ashgate.

Schützeichel, R. (2012). Implizites Wissen' in der Soziologie. In J. Loenhoff (Ed.), *Implizites Wissen. Epistemologische und handlungstheoretische Perspektiven* (pp. 108–128). Velbrück.

Sharrock, W., & Anderson, B. (1986). *The Ethnomethodologists.* Ellis Horwood Limited.

Shove, E., Pantzar, M., & Watson, M. (2012). *The Dynamics of Social Practice. Everyday Life and how it Changes.* Sage.

Stekeler-Weithofer, P. (2005). *Philosophie des Selbstbewußtseins. Hegels System als Formanalyse von Wissen und Autonomie.* Suhrkamp.

Turner, S. (1994). *The Social Theory of Practices. Tradition, Tacit Knowledge, and Presuppositions.* The University of Chicago Press.

Turner, S. (2007). Mirror Neurons and Practices: A Response to Lizardo. *Journal for the Theory of Social Behavior, 37,* 351–371.

Wacquant, L. (1992). Toward a Social Praxeology: The Structure and Logic of Bourdieu's Sociology. In P. Bourdieu & L. Wacquant (Eds.), *An Invitation to Reflexive Sociology* (pp. 1–59). Polity Press.

Wacquant, L. (2015). For a Sociology of Flesh and Blood. *Qualitative Sociology, 38*, 1–11.

Wittgenstein, L. (1970). *Über Gewissheit*. Suhrkamp.

Wittgenstein, L. (1971). *Philosophische Untersuchungen*. Suhrkamp.

The Antinomies of Pedagogy and Aporias of Embodiment: A Historical and Phenomenological Investigation

Norm Friesen

1 Introduction: The Antinomies of Pedagogy

It may sound strange to think of possibilities for both educational theorizing and practice as bound by antimonies, paradoxes, tensions and double binds. To see education in this way is no longer to regard it as entirely germane either to the gradual amelioration promised by progressive education or to claims of functional optimization offered by (educational) psychology. Instead, it is to see education as it has been depicted in both canonical and contemporary sources in German and Northern European Educational sciences—in other words—by continental pedagogy.[1]

Whether new or old, the idea that the practical pedagogical field is marked by antipodes, paradoxes, tensions and aporia has long been important in the history of educational ideas. It can be traced as far back as Socrates' dialectic, his method of arriving at knowledge or the 'truth' through question and answer, dialogue and dispute. Referencing Socrates' early exchanges in particular, Meyer (2018) explains:

---

[1] For more about continental pedagogy, please see: Friesen, N. & Kenklies, K. (2023). Continental pedagogy & curriculum. In Tierney, F. Rizvi, K. Ercikan (Eds.) *International Encyclopedia of Education 4th ed.* Elsevier. https://doi.org/10.1016/B978-0-12-818630-5.03028-1.

N. Friesen (✉)
Boise State University, Boise, ID, USA
e-mail: normfriesen@boisestate.edu

© The Author(s), under exclusive license to Springer Nature Switzerland AG 2022
A. Kraus, C. Wulf (eds.), *The Palgrave Handbook of Embodiment and Learning*,
https://doi.org/10.1007/978-3-030-93001-1_6

> In these aporetic dialogues, the double dimension of Socrates' questioning is most clearly revealed: on the one hand, questioning is used in order to reach the truth about the question debated, on the other hand, when Socrates questions, he puts the interlocutor himself in question by attacking his alleged knowledge. (p. 115)

Such dialogues are aporetic, expressive of contradiction and paradox, in multiple senses: They not only show that truth and knowledge is reached through its opposite—doubt, scepticism and ignorance—but they also expose the ignorance and impotence underlying individuals' presumed knowledge and mastery. Often, the only certainty and knowledge that Socrates arrives at in these dialogues is that he (or his interlocutor) *doesn't* know and *isn't* certain. Wisdom, paradoxically, arises through the realization of one's own ignorance.

A number of lesser-known links connecting Socrates with contemporary understandings of education are of German origin; they include Kant and the theologian and hermeneutician Friedrich Schleiermacher. Kant casts education as intrinsically oppositional or paradoxical in a question for education: "How do I cultivate [the child's] freedom under [conditions of] constraint?" This question and Kant's ambivalent response—"I shall accustom my pupil to tolerate a constraint of his freedom, and I shall at the same time lead him to make good use of his freedom" (2007, p. 447)—reappear frequently in educational discourses of Northern Europe. As Helsper (2001) has remarked of the German context, Kant's "paradox" has come to represent a "foundational" opposition, one which has "repeatedly been seen as an object for reflection and reformulation" (p. 85). Young toddlers must be barred from stairways and other dangers to freely exercise their newly found ability to walk, just as teenagers must first study (e.g., for the driver's exam and other tests) before they can go on to enjoy the privileges of driving or many other freedoms of adulthood (e.g., to choose to go on to university).

Kant's opposition has often been seen as constituting a paradox—rather than an opposition or antinomy—with "paradox" implying a kind of mutual exclusivity in which one side can be affirmed only at the expense of the other (e.g., see Schlömerkemper, 2018, p. 29). According to this conception, the removal of access to stairways and other dangers for the young toddler can only be realized at the expense of their freedom to roam as they please. However, to understand Kant's question in this way can be seen as interpreting freedom in a manner that is limiting—specifically as "freedom *from*," as what political theorist Isaiah Berlin refers to as "negative liberty" (1969, p. 120). Freedom in this sense then can only be the *absence* of any constraint and interference, with any degree of heteronomy or intrusion from outside deemed to be a limitation. On the other hand, 'freedom *to*' or what Berlin has called "positive liberty"; Berlin, 1969, p. 121 sees such heteronomy as being *integral* to freedom: One is free in this sense not simply to do something according to one's wishes; instead, one is free, for example, to have access to higher education, to be protected by the law or to vote in elections. To enjoy such freedoms not only presupposes a degree of heteronomy, external interference or even constraint; it is also to see such heteronomy or constraint as positively *constitutive* of such freedom: To be protected by the law is to submit to it, just as to cast one's vote is to constrain oneself to a highly structured political system. Similarly, a toddler's freedom to walk (safely) is constituted precisely *through* certain safety measures or limitations—just as a teenager's freedom to drive or participate in higher education is meaningful only in ways that involve rules and restraints.

Understanding education in terms of paradoxes and antinomies receives its fullest and most sustained treatment only a few decades after Kant in F.D.E. Schleiermacher's *Lectures on Education*.[2] The entirety of these lectures can be seen as structured through a dialectic that works to define, heighten and resolve the differences between the widest range of opposed terms. These include the opposition or antimony of individuality versus collectivity (e.g., doing justice to both the unique student and the class as a whole) as well as of the present and the future in the life of the child (e.g., as captured by Dewey's insistence that "education" be "a process of living and not a preparation for future living" 1897, p. 79). Of particular importance in this chapter is Schleiermacher's opposition of 'support' and 'counteraction.' Schleiermacher understands this opposition in ethical terms, specifically in terms of what is 'good' and to be 'supported' and what is *not* and to be 'counteracted':

> From one perspective we act according to the maxim that education should and must be nothing but the awakening and the support of the Good in preparation for the [child's] entry to larger circles of life. ... From the other perspective we [should] act according to the maxim that education should and must be nothing but counteract[ion] [...] comprehensively counteracting that which is objectionable. (Schleiermacher, 2000, p. 59; 2022, n.p.)

Both as parents and teachers, we go out of our way to encourage and assist with words and rewards behaviour in children that we see as good; and we counteract—discourage, correct, redirect—those things we view less

---

[2] The fact that Schleiermacher also contributed substantially to theories of education—in addition to theories of hermeneutics and to theology—is little known in English. Passages from Schleiermacher's Lecture provided here are from a translation that will soon be in press.

favourably. Do we necessarily know in advance precisely how and why such support or counteraction might occur? Theory, Schleiermacher admits, cannot dictate precisely what should happen in practice. He concludes his initial discussion of support and counteraction by saying that "we … have to leave it to life itself to decide what should be done from moment to moment" (2000, p. 62, 2022, n.p.). It is the realm of practice, in other words, in which the opposition between support and counteraction is resolved.

A very similar approach to the practical antinomies and tensions of education—one that includes Kant's question and a number of Schleiermacher's oppositions—has been taken up in a range of contemporary sources on educational practice and professionalization, with a particular focus on teacher education. Contributions by Werner Helsper (e.g., 1996, 2001, 2002) and others (e.g., Hainschink & Zahra-Ecker, 2018; Schlömerkemper, 2018) posit that such oppositions are constitutive of the structure of the field of pedagogical practice itself: "According to this understanding," as Helsper (2001) explains, "antinomies are constitutive for pedagogical teacher action. To try to suspend them would be to eliminate the pedagogical nature of the action itself" (p. 87). Or as Hainschink and Zahra-Ecker (2018) say,

pedagogical action is comprised of constitutive contradictions and/or antinomies which cannot be suspended, but only engaged with reflectively […]. Learning how to balance their opposed polarities is a constitutive element of [teacher] professionalization. (pp. 179, 182; for an English-language discussion, see: Didolet et al., 2019)

Prominent in these contemporary discussions is an antinomy that is in some ways already implied in the tensions between freedom and constraint, support and counteraction as well as individuality and collectivity. This is the opposition of proximity and distance. Again, with an unmistakable emphasis on practice, Werner Helsper (2002) explains:

A problem of professional pedagogical action is also evident in the repeated accusations that teachers neglect their educational duty through the distanced "transmission" of curriculum content. But if they were to orient themselves completely to the individual [student], then allegations would soon arise that they are improperly inserting themselves in the private realm of the child and their family. (p. 25)

To also invoke Schleiermacher's oppositions of support and counteraction *and* individuality and collectivity, one could say that the teacher must closely *support* and guide students, and attend to them carefully—both as a group and as individuals. At the same time, though, the teacher must treat any one student like any other and retain sufficient distance to effectively remain a teacher rather than a friend—and be prepared to appropriately counteract, redirect and correct the student.

In his 2017 book, *Antinomic Interpretations of Pedagogical Processes*,[3] Jörg Schlömerkemper outlines how pedagogical antimonies in general are to be understood. In particular, he argues against a purely "binary understanding" of pedagogical oppositions, as if dealing with opposites was just "a question of alternative positioning and decision-making in the sense of 'either/or' 'good/bad' or 'true/false.'" Instead, Schlömerkemper continues,

> From a more sophisticated perspective, it becomes a matter of situations and structures in which two aspects, requirements or demands which are (almost) of the same weight … but that are nonetheless dialectically intermixed. Briefly put, one can at this point say: It should not be a matter of a polarizing 'either/or' but of a consistent 'also … but.' (p. 28)

To understand freedom and constraint, support and counteraction or proximity and distance not as an 'either/or' but as an 'also … but' is to understand them as oppositions that can be addressed through a certain *ambivalence* in pedagogical practice. Ambivalent awareness and practice is one which, for example, presents to the child any offer of choice or freedom within a given set of constraints. It is one that sees a moment of correction or redirection ('counteraction') as something also containing an element of affirmation and support. Schlömerkemper (2018) describes this type of 'ambivalent' practice as a

> fluctuation between different perceptions and value judgments in which one assesses matters first one way and then another, without desiring or having to decide between them. Both can be seen as simultaneously valuable ('-valent'). Ambivalences can be seen as a more moderate form of antinomy, because the two poles actually are not mutually exclusive. (p. 29)

For example, in the case of the freedom and constraint of the young child learning to walk, a parent might well prefer greater restraint immediately after the child suffers an injury while walking, but alternatively, might choose greater freedom when the child is among family. Similarly, a teacher might choose the 'pole' represented by the individual versus the collective (and also support over counteraction) in order to give a challenged but hard-working

---

[3] *Pädagogische Prozesse in antinomischer Deutung.*

student a grade that is more generous than one that would be prescribed by class evaluation curve or rubric. In any case, though, their affirmation of one side will never be final or absolutely definitive, but instead ambivalent, one that is well aware of the value of an opposite course of action (e.g., of evaluation that does not take individual differences into account). It is this oscillation between the dominance and latency of one pole or another—or the embrace of two opposed possibilities simultaneously—which then constitutes what can be called the dynamics or 'dialectics' of pedagogical thought and action.

2 The Aporias of Embodiment

If the dialectical structures and dynamics of pedagogical thought and action can be seen as embedded in pedagogical situations, or as constitutive of pedagogical professionalism or the pedagogical 'field' itself, then the dialectic of the lived body is manifest rather differently. As the study of lived experience, phenomenology shows the body to appear as a kind of dynamic meeting point or 'nexus,' more a verb or a process than an object or thing. In its dynamism, the body appears to integrate and manifest opposed phenomena simultaneously.

Phenomenology has conventionally understood the body in terms of the foundational notion of intentionality; the idea that our awareness is always an awareness of *something*, and that in everyday life, we regard this 'something' in a particular way; we see this something-*as-something*: A tree is shade on a hot summer day just as a doorway might be a place for refuge on a windy or rainy one. The body is typically seen as having a mediating, enabling and sometimes constitutive role in the subject's engagement in 'intentional' action, not only taking us to the cooling shade of a tree or protection from the cold and rain, but also being literally the source of experiences of heat, shade, cold and protection to begin with. The lived body is, as Edmund Husserl says, a 'point of interchange' between the physical and psychical worlds (e.g., see Cantista & Martins, 2002, p. 537); it is part of our everyday projects and (in this sense) of our "project-ions" in the world (e.g., Heidegger, 1962). Writing in 1945 in the *Phenomenology of Perception*, Maurice Merleau-Ponty develops this further in saying that "consciousness is being toward the thing through the intermediary of the body"—with the body, in turn, presenting "our general means of having a world" (1945/2012, pp. 140, 147). The body is expressive both of nature and culture, and of biological necessity and human freedom:

The Antinomies of Pedagogy and Aporias of Embodiment... **97**

[E]verything [bodily] is constructed and everything is natural, in the sense that there is no single word or behaviour that does not owe something to mere biological being—and, at the same time, there is no word or behaviour that does not break free from animal life that does not deflect vital behaviours [...] through a sort of *escape* and a genius for ambiguity [*équivoqu*] that might well serve to define man. Behaviours create significations that are transcendent in relation to the anatomical structure and yet immanent to the behaviour as such. (Merleau-Ponty, 2012, p. 195)

We are simultaneously biological and cultural, with our every word and move expressing our anatomical and our physiological limitations and possibilities—while also expressing something about our individuality, our kinaesthetic 'style,' our mood and about the culture into which we are socialized. In initial congruence with the 'dialectics' of pedagogical practice, Merleau-Ponty describes these opposites as being negotiated with an 'ambiguity' (*équivoque*; a close etymological cousin of ambivalence) that, he emphasizes, may be nothing less than *definitive* of what it is to be *human*.

Later, however, Merleau-Ponty rejects the mentalist bias implicit in the primacy of 'consciousness' in our relation to the world and in seeing the body (merely) as the 'intermediary' or 'space' for our more-or-less conscious plans and devices. The body, as Merleau-Ponty later comes to see, can no longer be viewed just as a meeting point for opposites like object and subject, mind and world. In *The Visible and the Visible*, he instead casts the body as *simultaneously* mind and world, object and subject, sensible and sentient. Body is flesh (*chair*[4]), simultaneously constitutive of body, mind *and* world, marked above all by its 'visibility.' To properly designate it, Merleau-Ponty (1968) explains, "we should need the term 'element,' in the sense it was used to speak of water, air, earth, and fire, that is, in the sense of a *general thing*" (p. 139). The body, moreover, is emergent as the 'intertwining' (*entrelacs*[5]) of self and world, characterized as "two phases" in a single process or as the "obverse and reverse" (p. 138) sides of a leaf or of two leaves:

We say therefore that our body is a being of two leaves, from one side a thing among things and otherwise what sees them and touches them; we say, because it is evident, that it unites these two properties within itself, and its double belongingness to the order of the 'object' and to the order of the 'subject' reveals to us quite unexpected relations between the two. (p. 137)

---

[4] *La chair*, like the word 'flesh' has both material and also antiquated (mostly Biblical) connotations regarding the body.

[5] *Entrelacs* also refers to fine tracery, also suggesting things like a latticework, maze or tangle.

The body is both subject and object, sensed and sensing, and it unites these oppositions doubly—arguably in both material and experiential terms. And the quite unexpected relations between the two orders can be seen to include the oppositions of the "phenomenal body and objective body" (p. 136), "passivity" and "activity," 'the visible' and 'the seer,' 'material' and 'spiritual' (p. 139), as well as the "In Itself" and the "For Itself" (p. 137). On its own, the body can realize these opposed possibilities in multiple ways and senses; it shifts from one sense modality to another; it touches, hears and sees itself and it combines activity and passivity in myriad habits, dispositions and ways of "being." However, shortly after describing these aspects as the "two leaves" of the body, Merleau-Ponty (1968) puts this initial characterization into question:

> One should not even say, as we did a moment ago, that the body is made up of two leaves … it would be better to say that the body sensed and the body sentient are […] two segments of one sole circular course which […] is but one sole movement in its two phases. And everything said about the sensed body pertains to the whole of the sensible of which it is a part, and to the world. (pp. 137, 138)

Here, Merleau-Ponty's emphasis is not exclusively on the lived body itself, but on this body's relation to the world. World and body are the same visible substance, mirroring each other not only in sensory and material qualities, but also in these sense of the body as what Merleau-Ponty calls an "exemplar sensible"—as the basis or the measure for what we see and experience in the world. This can be seen to extend from the 'foot' of a mountain through the 'torso' of a work to the 'head' of a bed. The body, as Merleau-Ponty (2012) says, is "caught up in the tissue of the things," "draw[ing]" this tissue "entirely to itself, incorporat[ing] it, and, with the same movement, communicat[ing] to the things upon which it closes over that identity without superimposition" (p. 138).

The oppositions of sensed and sentient, object and subject, touched and touching, visible and seeing—together with the myriad complexities and permutations to which they give rise—can be seen to form consistent antipodes in Merleau-Ponty's account. Insofar as the body is both nature and culture, both enabling and constraining of movements and habits, one might add to Merleau-Ponty's oppositions a version of the Kantian paradox of freedom and constraint as well: Our embodiment is the precondition for both our liberty as well as our own ultimate limitation. However, unlike Schlömerkemper's account of antinomic ambivalences, Merleau-Ponty here is suggesting that we do *not* fluctuate or switch emphasis from any one set of bodily aporia—whether between subject and object, nature and culture, sensing and sensed—at will. Both in the *Phenomenology of Perception* or *The Visible and the Invisible*, the body's or the flesh's ambiguity, its two sides or phases tend to appear less as a "fluctuation ... in which one assesses matters first one way and then another" (as Schlömerkemper described the antipodes of pedagogical practice; p. 29) and more as always-already interwoven and interlaced. The "genius for ambiguity" that Merleau-Ponty (2012) earlier says might well be definitive for the human appears decisively aporetic—much more as a 'both ... and' rather than an 'either/or.' In *The Visible and the Invisible*, this ambiguity is arguably expanded to become not simply a characteristic of the body, but as a comprehensive but fractured ontological paradox of fleshly existence as a whole. Here, Merleau-Ponty describes the flesh as

> a being in latency, and a presentation of a certain absence [...] prototype of Being, of which our body, the sensible sentient, is a very remarkable variant, but whose constitutive paradox already lies in every visible [...] our body commands the visible for us, but it does not explain it, does not clarify it, it only concentrates the mystery of its scattered visibility; and it is indeed a paradox of Being, not a paradox of man, that we are dealing with here. To be sure, one can reply that, between the two 'sides' of our body [...] there is an abyss that separates the In Itself from the For Itself. (p. 136)

Merleau-Ponty's ontology of the flesh, then, is one emphatically marked by paradox, and the abyss or gap that characterizes it arises arguably in that any opposition that it might integrate or manifest is never fully complete or symmetrical: As an 'element,' flesh is 'decentered' (p. 138) and the dynamism and multiplicity of this decentring it is never fully self-identical. The interweaving, interleaving and intertwining that is Merleau-Ponty's *entrelacs* may be both an intricate pattern as much as it also is a dynamic *process* or *event*. As I now go on to show, this pattern, process or event unfolds in a way that suggests a remarkable isomorphism with the antinomic polarities of pedagogical theory and practice.

3 Pedagogy and the Body: A Video Example

Merleau-Ponty's emphasis on the dynamism of the *lived* body-as-flesh and Schlömerkemper's (and others') focus on the antinomies of concrete pedagogical *practice* suggest that both accounts are ripe for illustration and elaboration through careful situational observation and interpretation. Theory alone can arguably only go so far in addressing dynamic, lived and concretely practical phenomena. Consequently, I briefly consider a 95-second video clip from the 2002 French documentary of a one-room country schoolhouse, *Etre et Avoir*—a film often noted for its intimate portrayal of teacher Georges Lopez's patient work with his young students (clip available at: https://vimeo.com/223987444). This particular sequence shows Lopez at the right side of kindergartner Letitia, sitting together with her peers. They have just learned to write the number seven. The teacher's arm rests on the back of Letitia's chair, and his left hand is close to Letitia's left shoulder; his right hand is generally pointing at the worksheet in front of them both (Figs. 1, 2 and 3).[6]

Letitia counts slowly: One, two, … three, four, five, six …	Six.
Teacher: What comes after six? … What comes next? …. What did you draw just now? … What was that red one? … What did we learn today?	Letitia begins counting again: One, two, three, four, five, six …
	—And then comes? …
	Marie: Seven.
	What comes after six?
Student (off camera): She can't remember?	Marie just said it.
Teacher: Let's try Alizé or Marie, then. What was the new number we just learned?	Teacher, forcefully (forming his hand into a fist and gently nudging Letitia's left shoulder while looking at her directly): Wake up, will you? *Seven!*
Marie (off camera): Seven.	
Teacher: Who does seven come after?	
After?	
Six? It comes …	Letitia looks at the teacher briefly.
It comes after nine.	Count again now.
All right ….	Letitia: Six.
We haven't learned nine yet.	What did Marie say after six?
Teacher: After six!	She said?
	Letitia, very quietly: Seven.

Fig. 1 One, two, … three, four, five, six

---

[6] *Due to copyright restrictions, traced and sketched renderings of the original images are used.*

Fig. 2 Let's try Alizé or Marie, then. What was the new number we just learned?

Fig. 3 Wake up, will you? *Seven!*

Lopez, to summarize, spends the 95 seconds of the sequence, nudging and coaxing, trying to elicit the word 'seven' from little Letitia. He is met only with meagre success when Letitia almost inaudibly articulates the word in the final moment of their exchange (Fig. 3).

The delicate entwinement of subject and object, nature and culture, feeling and felt, touching and touched, seeing and seen are instantiated in myriad ways in this segment. This is perhaps best evoked by thinking of Merleau-Ponty's account of self and world as "two segments of one sole circular course … one sole movement in its two phases" (1968, p. 138). With his arm already around the back of Letitia's chair, and his finger pointing on the worksheet, the teacher is in *near* tactile contact with Letitia for most of the clip. This becomes *direct*—but carefully modulated—contact in the final third or quarter of the video when the teacher's left hand forms a fist which gently nudges Letitia's shoulder. This has the effect of transferring their communication to a visual modality, resulting in a moment of direct eye-contact.

Vision and visibility, subject and object undergo a similar mutual entwinement as the teacher and Letitia look out to and communicate with the other children who are also at the table (but generally off-screen; Fig. 2). Again, thinking of Merleau-Ponty's description of the dynamics of the flesh, we might—with some imagination—see this circular movement as being instantiated between Lopez, Letitia, the sheet in front of them, as well as among the other children in this scene on multiple occasions and in multiple ways. A kind of fleshly circuit, both semantic and material, consisting of both gesture and word, question and response, activity and passivity can be seen to traverse this scene numerous times in the course of the 95 seconds captured here. Particularly in the exchanges and contact between Lopez and Letitia, this traversal becomes so rapid as to be effectively simultaneous. The equivocality or paradox manifest in the body and the world, in other words, rapidly incorporates not only Lopez and Letitia, but also the others around them.

Beginning with Kant's pedagogical paradox of freedom and constraint, one could say that the tension between these two opposites is more-or-less palpable at every moment in this clip: Letitia is of course significantly constrained by the exercise itself (only one correct digit follows the number six) as well as physically by Lopez with his arm around her chair. At the same time, however, Lopez's aim is to have Letita say the number 'seven' in sequence, something which would be meaningless if it were directly forced, or if someone else's answer were accepted in its place. The body (primarily Lopez's) takes up, with apparent and perhaps even conscious purpose, the valence of necessity, of limitation and of constraint. But it does so in order that, in however muted a way, its opposite—a voluntary moment of expression and freedom—might be realized. In other words: *Embodiment, like other communicative events, can take up one valence in a pedagogical opposition while still not entirely eliminating the other.*

The opposition of *distance* and *proximity* both underscores and qualifies this conclusion. Lopez's physical proximity to Letitia, despite the insistence it communicates, can only be justified—both institutionally and interpersonally—if it is *not* total, if it allows a particular *degree* of freedom and *distance*. Lopez subtly modulates this distance in a number of ways: Approaching the middle of the clip, Lopez can be said to figuratively expand the distance between himself and Letitia as he adjusts his position and looks to the other students for their answers. While his glance and his attention leave Letitia for a few seconds, his left hand simultaneously comes closer to her shoulder and it seems likely that she can sense this. *The body can thus be said to enact* both *distance and proximity in aporetic simultaneity.*

Lopez's gentle nudge of Letitia on the shoulder and the clear moment of eye-contact that follows, however, rapidly collapse any distance between the two, and it is at this significant moment that Merleau-Ponty's dynamic of the flesh is most literally realized: Subject and object, touching and touched, the visible and the seer literally become "one sole movement in its two phases" (p. 138). Through mutual eye-contact in particular, a particular kind of "mutual enfolding" can be achieved, as Merleau-Ponty (1960/1964, p. 17) explains:

> I look at him. He sees that I look at him. I see that he sees it. He sees that I see that he sees it … even though in principle reflections upon reflections go on to infinity, vision is such that the obscure results of two glances adjust to each other, and there are no longer two consciousnesses with their own teleology but two mutually enfolding glances.

At the same time, of course, such moments of mutually enfolded proximity can also give way to responses of distantiation and withdrawal, as seems to be suggested (on Letitia's part) in Fig. 4. The body, in short, can move almost imperceptibly between pedagogical antinomies and is capable not only of moments of proximity and entwinement but also of distance and disentanglement.

Needless to say, the univocal contact of touch and mutual eye 'contact' is sustained for only a moment as the body's aporetic character and the tensions of embodied and pedagogical oppositions (or is it biological or psychological necessity?) lead Lopez to sigh slightly and look away (Fig. 4). Considering these and other moments from the clip specifically in the light of Schleiermacher's opposition of *support* and *counteraction* further underscore the manifest ambivalence of Lopez's actions—especially when they are viewed both in terms of his pedagogical responsibilities and of Letitia's own possible experience: Is his arm around Letitia a gesture of *support* or is it a way of confining and *counteracting* her inattention? Is his nudging of her shoulder a moment in which she is encouraged and supported or when she is interrupted

Fig. 4 Lopez briefly looks away and sighs

and reprimanded? Is his look into her eyes in the moment that follows one of confirmation or correction? One might also ask something similar regarding Lopez's tone of voice, which is slightly more insistent with Letitia than with the others. Does it provide a supportive emphasis, or does it have the effect of a type of counteraction? Although Letitia's shrinking or avoidant position in Fig. 4 may suggest a certain refusal or withdrawal, we have access neither to Lopez's precise purposes nor to Letitia's experience.

Regardless, the body in these senses is potentially expressive of a kind of *escape* from determination, and of a particularly human 'genius for ambiguity': It not only combines nature and culture as well as subject and object, sensing and sensed, touching and touched, but in pedagogical situations, its embrace of these aporia appears to waver equivocally between a definitive manifestation either of support or counteraction, of proximity or distance and of freedom or constraint. The body, in other words, is ambivalent and aporetic in its expressions in a way that takes it beyond definitive meaning or decidability.

To reference Schlömerkemper (2018), the ambivalence of the body takes on a form that is inextricably 'both … and' rather than 'either … or,' a pedagogical ambivalence which, through embodied engagement, "both poles can [potentially] be done justice" (p. 28). At the same time, though, this embodied ambivalence does not unambiguously indicate the kind of conscious decision-making foregrounded in Schlömerkemper's and others' accounts of pedagogical antinomies: It is neither a conscious "fluctuation between different perceptions and value judgments" nor a matter of the explicit "recognition [of] and … reflection [on] which weight the poles retain or should be granted," as Schlömerkemper (ibid.) puts it (p. 32). In phenomenological terms, it is not so much a question of the early Merleau-Ponty's (2012) "consciousness … toward the thing through the intermediary of the body" (p. 147) but rather, of the body "unit[ing] … two properties within itself" (1968, p. 137), exhibiting a kind of "double belongingness" to both support and counteraction, freedom and constraint (p. 137). Although it readily gives expression to ambivalence that can do justice to antonymic both poles, the body often does not appear as the instrument of discrete conscious purposes.

4   Conclusion: A Fissured Intertwining

The character of the body as simultaneously sensing and sensed, receptive and expressive, passive and active, material and spirit can thus be said to give it a unique power to communicate ambiguity and ambivalence. It alone is arguably able to grant space and freedom while remaining immediately (if not also insistently) present; only it can be supportive while at the same time redirecting and counteracting. Only it can even form a fist but use it only most gently to nudge the fledgling student. The body, moreover, accomplishes this in a way that still leaves little doubt that it is indeed communicating. While we can debate the precise meaning of their communications, we certainly cannot question that the gestures and glances of Lopez and Letitia mean *something*. At the same time, this 'something' is obscured not only by the body's ambivalent and aporetic nature, but also by what Merleau-Ponty has referred to as an "abyss" or gap (1968, p. 146). Just as such a "fissure" (p. 235) separates what can be seen as objectively given from what is subjectively taken up, so too does the most palpable non-coincidence and non-identity separate Lopez's overall purpose from Letitia's apparent detachment.

The body, to speak more generally, displays a striking isomorphism, and an inextricable intertwining with pedagogical practice: Both are characterized by types of aporia and dialectical patterns in which tensions between expression and receptivity, word and action, support and counteraction and freedom and restraint (and much more) all intersect and vie for significance. And the body is doing this always already, exceeding both conscious intention and instructional planning. Finally, both the body and pedagogical practice are arguably marked by a sort of non-coincidence—one that keeps an intercorporeal dynamic in play, and the adult's pedagogical responsibility continuously alive.

References

Berlin, I. (1969). Two Concepts of Liberty. In I. Berlin (Ed.), *Four Essays on Liberty* (pp. 118–172). Oxford University Press.

Cantista, M. J., & Martins, M. M. (2002). Phenomenology: Corporeity and Intersubjectivity in Husserl; the Most Significant Influences of Husserl. In A. K. Tymieniecka (Ed.), *Phenomenology World-Wide: Foundations, Expanding Dynamics, Life-Engagements* (pp. 532–543). Springer.

Dewey, J. (1897). My Pedagogic Creed. *School Journal, 54*(January), 77–80.

Didolet, S., Lundin, S., & Krüger, J. O. (2019). Constructing Professionalism in Teacher Education. Analytical Tools from a Comparative Study. *Education Inquiry, 10*(3), 208–225. https://doi.org/10.1080/20004508.2018.1529527

Hainschink, V., & Zahra-Ecker, R. A. (2018). Leben in Antinomien–Bewältigungsdispositionen aus arbeitsbezogenen Verhaltens- und Erlebensmustern. *Pädagogische Horizonte, 2*(2), 179–194.

Heidegger, M. (1962). *Being and Time*. Harper.

Helsper, W. (1996). *Pädagogische Professionalität: Untersuchungen zum Typus pädagogischen Handelns*. Suhrkamp.

Helsper, W. (2001). Antinomien des Lehrerhandelns—Anfragen an die Bildungsgangdidaktik. In U. Hericks, J. Keuffer, H. C. Kräft, & I. Kunze (Eds.), *Bildungsgangdidaktik—Perspektiven für Fachunterricht und Lehrerbildung*. Springer.

Helsper, W. (2002). Pädagogisches Handeln in den Antinomien der Moderne. In H.-H. Krüger & W. Helsper (Eds.), *Einführung in Grundbegriffe und Grundfragen der Erziehungswissenschaft*. Springer.

Kant, I. (2007 [1803]). Lectures on Pedagogy. In G. Zöller & R. B. Louden (Eds.), *Anthropology, History and Education*. Cambridge University Press.

Merleau-Ponty, M. (1960/1964). *Signs*. Northwestern University Press.

Merleau-Ponty, M. (1968). *The Visible and the Invisible*. Northwestern University Press.

Merleau-Ponty, M. (2012). *Phenomenology of Perception*. Routledge.

Meyer, M. (2018). Dialectic and Questioning: Socrates and Plato. *Revue internationale de Philosophie, 2*(284), 113–129.

Schleiermacher, F. D. E. (1826/2022). *F.D.E. Schleiermacher's Outline of the Art of Education: A Translation and Discussion*. Peter Lang.

Schleiermacher, F. D, E. (2000). *Texte zur Pädagogik: Kommentierte Studienausgabe, 2* (M. Winkler & J. Brachmann, Eds.). Suhrkamp.

Schlömerkemper, J. (2018). *Pädagogische Prozesse in antinomischer Deutung: Begriffliche Klärung und Entwürfe für Lernen und Lehren*. Beltz Juventa.

Embodied Cognition: A Methodological and Pedagogical Interpretation

Christian Rittelmeyer

1 Regarding a New Research Field and Its Significance for Education

For some decades, a new research-supported view of cognitive and learning processes with titles such as *Embodiment, Grounded Cognition, Corporeal Turn* or *Embodied Cognition* has been gaining importance and appears to be informative for education and pedagogical practice. The underlying assumption is that the constitutive conditions of all our perceptive and cognitive activities, even highly abstract thoughts, have their basis in elementary corporeal processes outside of the brain (Nathan, 2014; Pecher & Zwaan, 2005; Shapiro, 2019; Sheets-Johnstone, 2009). Research in this area has made it clear that our thoughts and imagination are to a considerable extent determined by our gestures, gesticulations and body postures, by the way we move spatially, our changing body temperature and heart function, our fine-motor skills and many other corporeal activities (Goldin-Meadow & Beilock, 2010; Rittelmeyer, 2010; Ruggieri, 2003; Simms, 2008). The basic concept of embodiment of cognitive activities (including the emotions that are tied up with these) consists of a *body feedback hypothesis*: Actual perception of or empathetic feeling for our fellow human beings occurs, for example, not only when we register gestures and gesticulations of the other person within the

---

C. Rittelmeyer (✉)
University of Goettingen, Göttingen, Germany
e-mail: rittelmeyer@keerl.net

© The Author(s), under exclusive license to Springer Nature Switzerland AG 2022
A. Kraus, C. Wulf (eds.), *The Palgrave Handbook of Embodiment and Learning*,
https://doi.org/10.1007/978-3-030-93001-1_7

brain but also through very subtly *imitating or simulating* these in a *corporeal* manner that usually goes unnoticed. From an embodiment perspective, the elegant hand movements of a lecturer as she explains her concepts are not only an *expression* of a psychological disposition but always also an *impression* experienced by the speaker from the periphery of her body that will not least determine her thoughts over the course of the lecture.

Thus, *embodied cognition* is not about physical processes that accompany perceptive and cognitive activities, but about certain mental and perceptive capabilities that are made possible in the first place by such intentionally controlled corporeal processes and postures. From the perspective of a *psychology of the senses*, embodiment processes are an interaction between exteroceptive and interoceptive senses. The former 'externally directed' senses allow us to perceive the exterior world (e.g. seeing, hearing, smelling); the latter 'internally directed' senses relate to the perception of one's own body (e.g. sense of balance, sense of own motion, sense of tension and relaxation, sense of pain or physical well-being). A person looking at the face of another sees the face but also feels an *empathetic gesture within his own body* through physiognomic imitation, which is also unconsciously transmitted to the motor area of his brain via his sense of motion; he does not only see it but *experiences* it. Thus, every external perception is always (usually unconsciously) accompanied by a perception of one's own body.

Contrary to traditional terminology according to which the brain or the 'centre' is differentiated from the rest of the body or the 'periphery', embodied cognition states that messages of one's own peripheral body constitute elements of thinking and perception; for example, the hand gestures of the lecturer will determine her unconscious *self-perception* and, thus, the cognitive orientation of the lecture. However, embodied cognition is not only to be understood as a whole-body phenomenon but also as a cultural phenomenon since the talk is directed at a specific audience and the lecturer is acting intentionally in a certain individual and social situation as well as within a specific cultural milieu. This 'environmental approach' is not emphasised by all researchers in the field but increasingly gaining significance within the embodiment discourse. The body becomes the "extended mind" (Aizawa, 2014), its theoretical description an "enactive approach" (Paolo & Thompson, 2014; Varela et al., 1991). Points of contact exist with respect to cultural science and philosophic descriptions of cultural patterns (e.g. as gender-related role ascriptions) that are corporeally habituated and then also determine thoughts and cognition (e.g. Maurice Merleau-Ponty, Jean-Paul Sartre or Michel Foucault).

Some researchers regard this empirically substantiated anthropological approach as a critical and new psychological paradigm, also for pedagogics. According to the research team of Daniel Casasanto and Katinka Dijkstra, a more humane and holistic view of the human being is taking the place of the long-dominant computer-cognition analogy within neuro and cognitive sciences (Casasanto & Dijkstra, 2010). Embodiment researchers Jaak Panksepp and Colwyn Trevarthen similarly perceive a change from an "over-intellectualised, computer-based view" to human cognitive activity and communication for gaining insight into the original basis of all cognition within our entire corporeality (Panksepp & Trevarthen, 2009, p. 110). In her empirical study on the impact of certain basic forms of movement (soft, angular, flowing, growing, shrinking etc.) with respect to cognitive activities, psychologist Sabine C. Koch also postulated a mental change within psychology that turns away from the computer analogy (the brain as the central information-processing control organ) to a biological-organic epistemology without a neurocentric narrowing of perspective (Koch, 2011, p. 39). With respect to pedagogics, the Italian researcher Umberto Margiotta even refers to embodiment theories as a 'New Deal for Education in the XXI Century' and a 'Copernican Revolution for the Education Sciences' (Margiotta, 2017). Time and again, criticism of the brain-computer comparison that is common at the moment is striking in connection with such statements: "The paradigmatic disembodied, unembedded device is the digital computer, which has served as a metaphor for a cognitive agent since the 1950s" (Michaels & Palatinus, 2014).

Meanwhile embodiment research is also discussed in education, albeit still rudimentarily (Gomez-Paloma, 2017; Katz, 2013; Trumpp, 2012). The necessity to overcome over-intellectualised learning methods in favour of methods of learning which involve the body is often the topic within this context. Although the 'corporeality' of educational processes has been addressed more often in German specialist pedagogic literature and although insights gained from embodied cognition research are increasingly being discussed from an educational perspective, to my knowledge there has been only little attempt to provide a systematic analysis of these insights, in lesson planning for example (Bilstein & Brumlik, 2013; Hildebrandt-Stratmann et al., 2013; Kraus, 2009; Laging, 2017; Wulf et al., 2011). Three problem areas, which become apparent upon closer analysis of research activities, are most likely the reason for this.

One problem is that numerous research findings are available in statistical form and usually only apply to the specific social groups—this raises questions of the validity of theses findings for educational practice. Thus, some studies show, for example, that teaching methods that use gestures seem to improve performance in arithmetic and language among subgroups of pupils. Further in-depth studies would be needed in order to understand these correlations and decide whether such research results are helpful for educational work in primary schools. Indeed, there is currently much broad neurological, cultural-historical and developmental-psychological discussion about these effects offering explanations as to why learning-relevant impacts are only observable in subgroups (Ifrah, 2000; Menninger, 1969; Roux et al., 2003; Rowe & Goldin-Meadow, 2009). The connection between arithmetic or linguistic abilities and motoric skills becomes apparent when children count with their fingers and, for example, hold up three fingers to show their age (Alibali et al., 2014; Armstrong, 1995; Bremmer & Roodenburg, 1991; Corballis, 2003; Feyereisen & DeLannoy, 1991; Goldin-Meadow & Beilock, 2010; Kaschak et al., 2014; Macedonia, 2019). Rather, as will be shown later, this empirical result concerns the challenge of developing a fundamental *educational body posture/style* aligned with the students' individualities that are expressed in the teacher's gestures and gesticulations in a way that is appropriate and makes sense for the learning situation; it is about *cultivating embodied cognition* (see also Soliman & Glenberg, 2014).

A *second* problem for the educational evaluation of embodiment studies is that research almost always seeks to answer very specific questions (Rittelmeyer, 2014, Chapter 5; Rittelmeyer, 2016, Chapter 4). How does body posture influence thinking and how does thinking while walking compared to while standing or sitting affect creative problem-solving? In the schoolyard: how does the distance adolescents keep between each other while talking unconsciously define their relationship to each other? How do short walks through urban or natural areas affect metabolic processes in the brain or heart function and what emotions of relaxation or stress and what kinds of *lived experiences* of these environments are generated in the process? When hearing words such as 'kick' or 'catch', why are precisely those motoric areas in the brain activated that control actual kicking or catching motions? What does it mean for embodied cognition that when we read those parts of texts where scenes of movement are described, centres in the brain are active that go back to highly subtle movements of the mouth and facial expressions, that is physical articulation of what we are reading of which we are not consciously aware and which is invisible to external observers? How can we explain that people assume systematic and individualistic body postures and assert that they cannot think properly when prompted to change their position? How can it be that events associated with certain body postures are remembered better later on when the same postures are assumed again?

These few examples serve to show that it is not merely a multitude of *questions* that make the research field increasingly confusing. Various *research methods* are also used, each one of which has something special to offer. In addition to classic survey and observation methods, we are thinking chiefly of imaging and medical techniques such as functional magnetic resonance imaging (fMRI) for examining the brain, electromyographic methods for visualising highly subtle muscle activities, measurements of the heart rate and breathing rhythm, transcranial magnetic stimulation for determining motoric activities in the mouth area—such as the tongue—while reading texts with strong emotional messages, examinations of blood flow in the thoracic region or metabolic activity in the brain, for example by means of laser infrared spectroscopy. According to the embodiment thesis, what is most important is what happens to our perceptions and cognitive processes when various physical activities take place and how these effects can be explained. It is these newer scientific examination methods and apparatuses with which we visualise body processes that are normally invisible such as metabolic activities in the brain or micro-motions of facial muscles. Although the embodied cognition theorem has a long history, which has been referenced time and again in various publications (such as the phenomenological studies of Maurice Merleau-Ponty, Edmund Husserl, Martin Heidegger or the German *Lebenskraft* [life-force] debate), it is only through these measurement devices and procedures that have proved to us what previously was purely theoretical knowledge—that is mere assertions, self-observations or assumptions. For this reason, we can understand why people are talking of a new paradigm for pedagogics (Macedonia, 2019; McCarthy et al., 2016; Shapiro & Stolz, 2018).

However, philosopher Shaun Gallagher has pointed out with good reason that knowledge of this philosophical-phenomenological tradition can guard against behaviouristic errors and narrow theoretical perspectives that sometimes occur within the context of embodiment research (Gallagher, 2014). Thus, imitating another person's happy or sad facial expression through fine-motoric mimicry has often been examined by asking the question whether this approach provides a better understanding of the other person's emotions and moods than without such corporeal resonances. However, other studies have shown that one's own—imitative or contrary—body posture, breathing, heart rate, gestures and gesticulations are important for understanding and empathising with another person (Nummenmaa et al., 2013; Oosterwijk & Barrett, 2014). Thus, a summary of research results in regard to certain individual questions would have to allow for an *imagination* of these various corporeal activities from many individual studies in order to arrive at a psychological understanding.

A *third* problem when attempting to draw pedagogical inferences from embodiment studies relates to some terminological and methodological ambiguities in the research. Such problems are raised time and time again by proponents of the classic cognition theory in particular (Shapiro, 2019). Thus, the implicit assumption of embodiment proponents that the term *body* refers to *the whole physical body minus the brain* is astounding. With respect to numerous research projects, one must also ask whether this research actually proves that a function of human bodies *constitutively* determines cognition. If people who tend towards sociability tend on average to perceive objects as being closer to them than unsociable people do, then the question arises whether this actually supports the embodiment thesis or rather points to the well-known fact that different people observe their environment differently according to their individual personality, the way they live, their interests and so on (Casasanto, 2014). This was extensively examined in the 1960s under the title *Social Perception Research* and is also not contested by proponents of classic cognition theories. From a cognition-theoretical perspective, the question of who guesses distances with greater accuracy is also important; yet a new form of cognition is not associated with this.

The philosopher and cognitive scientist Alvin I. Goldman offers an enlightening and informative exposition of these controversies in his illustration of a fundamental problem of many embodiment studies: "Opening or closing the eyes affects one's perception" (Goldman, 2017). In other words, many assertions from the embodiment faction simply make the trivial statement that our perception depends on our body organs (such as our senses). However, any classic cognition theorist would also claim the same but then also emphasise that the messages received through the body are processed in the *brain* as cognitions and perceptions. Goldman therefore proposes to examine embodiment research according to a logical procedure suggested by him as to whether the results can be better explained by classic cognition theories or embodiment theories. An example that is transferable to other areas of embodiment research should at least visualise the outlines of this procedure and at the same time elucidate that the reflections of Goldman clearly discern which perspectives interpreted embodied cognition research uncovers for pedagogical practice and for education.

2 What Special Learning Experiences Does Embodied Cognition Make Possible?

So-called *mindreading* is specifically addressed in the third chapter of his book: "the capacity to identify the mental states of others (e.g., their beliefs, desires, intentions, goals, experiences, sensations, and also emotion states)" (Goldman, 2017, p. 63). The perception of emotion in another person's face is highlighted as a special form of mindreading (Face-based Emotion Recognition, FaBER), for example the ability to accurately detect expressions of disgust or fear in the facial expression of another person. However, these deliberations can also be related to other communication forms via which 'mindreading' is activated—gestures, gesticulations, linguistic intonation or interaction partners (e.g. Stefani & Marco, 2019). Many classic cognition theories assume that such facial expressions of other people are identified based on previous knowledge as in regard to feelings of disgust, for example, that is based on a certain theory about such feelings. Goldman (2017) refers to this cognition theory as *theory-theory* (TT) since it is a theory about the theoretical interpretation of such emotions in daily life. He refers to the competing theory as the *simulation theory* (ST) since the theory assumes that one can only understand another person's emotions via visual mindreading if one comprehends it *physically* within oneself, simulates or reproduces it sensomotorically—for example in the form of so-called facial mimicry, the mimicking imitation of another person's physiognomic expression. In other words, one must *reactivate* one's own emotional experiences *sensomotorically* in order to understand another person's emotional facial expression. Which of the two theories better explains an expression of disgust or fear in the face of another person?

Studies have also been performed on patients with *brain damage* in the areas that are critical for the development of feelings of fear and disgust. These people do not or hardly show any feelings of fear or disgust in situations that would normally evoke such feelings. However, surprisingly, they were also partially or wholly incapable of perceiving these emotional manifestations in the facial expressions of other people. In further studies, brain scans have shown that certain brain areas are active during face-based recognition of disgust that also control these feelings—the authors conclude that "appreciation of visual stimuli depicting other's disgust is closely linked to the perception (i.e., experience) of unpleasant tastes and smells" (Goldman, 2017, p. 67). It must be pointed out that *experience* is referenced here as in many other studies of this kind as a sensomotoric *lived experience*, which, as emphasised by

114   C. Rittelmeyer

Goldman, can hardly be explained with the TT assumption but quite well with the simulation theory.

The research findings of Bruno Wicker et al. (2003), which Goldman also incorporates in his conscientious step-by-step argumentation, are also interesting in this regard. Wicker et al. (2003) report:

> We performed an fMRI study in which participants inhaled odorants producing a strong feeling of disgust. The same participants passively viewed movies of individuals smelling the contents of a glass (disgusting, pleasant, or neutral) and expressing the facial expressions of the respective emotions. (Ibid., p. 655)

According to the TT theory, one would expect that the *real odour* activates the respective brain areas, for example for olfactory perception, but the *observation* of the respective facial reactions stimulates the visual and prefrontal cortex. However, this was not primarily the case: The perception of facial reactions, as of disgust for example, experienced by another person and the feeling of disgust experienced in one's own self activate the *same brain region responsible for smelling*. "This suggests that the understanding of the facial expressions of disgust as displayed by others involves the activation of neural substrates normally activated during the experience of the same emotion" (ibid., p. 657).

Thus, the group of researchers follows the simulation theory (ST) in this regard (to which Goldman also subscribes) and sees its results as proof for "the idea that we perceive emotions in others by activating the same emotion in ourselves" (ibid., p. 660)—whereas the 'activation' is an actual sensomotor (and not solely a mental) process. Studies cited by the authors in which electrical stimulation of the brain regions responsible for feelings of disgust produced "unpleasant sensations in the mouth and throat" (ibid., p. 660) show that peripheral body reactions are possibly also involved (see also Susskind et al., 2008). As a side note it must be mentioned that the *hearing* of words expressed with distinct tongue movements is accompanied by fine-motor tongue movements—this as well can be better explained with the simulation theory (ST) than with the theory-theory (TT) (Fadiga et al., 2002).

However, Wicker et al. emphasise that the processes described by them refer to elementary corporeal activities in which the autonomous nervous system plays a special role. If one specifically imagines the perception of foul-smelling substances and the observance of facial reactions, one will certainly discover that manifold thoughts and reflections experienced in daily life become important that can more readily be ascribed to TT. Goldman also emphasises this as he analyses these studies on face-based mindreading. He talks about 'hybrid explanatory models' within this context. The differentiation of 'cognitive and emotional empathy' also calls attention to these connections of sensomotoric and theoretical-discursive perceptions of other people. The former type of cognition deals with deliberations such as 'What is making this person so unhappy?'; the latter is about self-perceiving actual *empathy* for the emotional state of another human being (Drimalla et al., 2019; Drimalla, 2019).

As frequently referenced in the study by Wicker et al. as well as in Goldman's analysis, it is striking that an *understanding* of these emotions is only made possible in the first place based on corporeal recapitulation of such emotions observed in others. Goldman here even quotes the *German* word *Verstehen* [understanding] as he references the work of Wilhelm Dilthey (1833–1911) and his differentiation between 'Verstehen' [understanding] and 'Erklären' [explaining] (Goldman, 2017, pp. 176–181; see also Faulstich, 2014). He grasps 'the Verstehen heuristic as an alternative to TT'. Here *Verstehen* of another person (also in regard to his emotional facial expressions) is to be understood within the meaning of a deeper empathetic perception. This active engaging with the other is to be differentiated from mere observation or reflecting about another person. In this context it should be mentioned that in the embodiment theory the Cartesian 'I think, therefore I am' is replaced by 'I act, therefore I am' as attributed to Husserl and Merleau-Ponty (e.g. Gallagher, 2014; Vignemont, 2014). Reflections and research interpretations of the described type therefore seem to substantiate the assumption that embodied cognition does not necessarily lead to realisations that are inaccessible to perception in accordance with the mode of classic cognition theories. In its hybrid forms as well, it rather seems to make a much more compassionate, deeper understanding possible. In light of the volitional character of embodied cognition, one may quote the often-translated saying of the Chinese philosopher Confucius, which already contains an indication of the *pedagogical* aspects of embodiment theory: 'Tell me and I will forget, show me and I may remember; involve me and I will understand.'

However, in further activities of embodied cognition, this *understanding* is articulated differently than in social interaction. For example, when I am intensely reflecting while sitting on a chair and I observe myself, I notice that my perception of the environment is blurred—accommodation and convergence movements of the eyes have apparently ceased. As soon as I see clearly again as I observe myself, I notice that the environment has a distracting function. Thus, the body 'says' on a highly elementary level of experience that it partially retreats with its sensory organs from the environment and wholly focuses on the thinking self. It is not a reflective but a *pre-reflective*

116   C. Rittelmeyer

understanding in the moment of concentration. The same is true for self-observation while walking through altering changing natural landscape during which I notice that my thoughts change from one idea to the next rather than remaining focussed on a single topic (Oppezzo & Schwartz, 2014). These deliberations also apply to other areas of embodiment, for example with respect to physiological processes while experiencing colours in school buildings (Rittelmeyer, 2013), with respect to the role of gestures, body postures and gesticulations during school lessons (Wulf et al., 2011) or with respect to the change of heart and breathing function in certain positively or negatively experienced natural environments (Frohmann et al., 2010). The previously mentioned *phenomenological self-observation* with respect to certain phenomena of one's own body and its cognitions combined with research—critically examined according to Goldman—seems very helpful to me. Finally, I would like to give an example of this process which also demonstrates the educational possibilities (for teaching in schools for example) that are suggested. Once again, I take the well-studied phenomenon of 'facial/visual mimicry' as an example.

When looking at a sad or happy facial expression, one notices something peculiar in regard to one's own self. It is nearly impossible to produce a contrary emotional expression, for example a happy and exuberant mood when seeing the (real or depicted) sad face of another person (Ekman, 2004). One's *own facial expression* seems to be constitutive for the perception of another person's emotional expression as well as for the development of one's own similar empathic mood. What happens in us if we observe the laughing face of another person? (Rittelmeyer, 2014, Chapter 5). How can it be that we perceive an emotional expression in this face? According to a common neurological explanation, the *same* brain cells are active that also control the *real* facial expression of the observed face when, for example, looking at a laughing or angry face. These cells are therefore referred to as mirror neurons, because the perceiving person mirrors or simulates the observed facial expression in the motor brain area (Bauer, 2006; Decety & Ickes, 2009). This neuronal mirroring is what allows us to empathise with another person, thereby substantiating our empathic capability (Harmon-Jones & Winkielman, 2007).

However, as previously mentioned, various studies have also shown that we often activate exactly the same facial muscles that are needed to manifest the observed expression when observing unambiguous facial expressions (or their respective depictions). However, this *real* facial mirroring in the form of extremely subtle muscle activities is invisible to external observers and only verifiable by means of certain electromyographic measures (facial EMG responses: Ruggieri et al., 1986; Dimberg et al., 2000; Dimberg & Petterson, 2000; Oberman et al., 2007). Thus, by mimicking the physiognomy of the perceived person micro-motorically, we corporeally experience the expressed mood and do not merely register it apathetically; its physical incorporation becomes an emphatic sensation. Numerous studies have meanwhile been performed on 'visual mimicry' in regard to viewing emotional physiognomic gestures of other people; a prominent assumption among these is that peripheral motor activities are the *trigger* for central representations of emotional experiences (Drimalla, 2019; Singer, 2006; Strack et al., 1988). The facial expression of the perceiver is therefore not merely an expression of cerebrally 'processing' what was observed, but at the same time also a *director* of thoughts and emotions in a reciprocal process between the 'centre' (the brain) and the 'periphery' (the facial expression). Various electromyographic studies have shown that such activities of visual mimicry can also be fundamental for *imagining* facial expressions, for instance while *reading* a novel or *hearing* certain descriptions (Ito et al., 2009; Johnstone et al., 2006). It seems that so-called deep reading, that is a pronounced and empathetic engagement while reading is also promoted by such corporeal-mimetic resonances.

However, we must learn to activate these corporeal resonances in a manner that is appropriate to the situation—strong imitative mimetic actions (e.g. during intense grief reactions) limit the consciousness and thinking capacity while weak imitative mimetic actions make us cold and apathetic to the world. Both extremes are part of life—but lead to social malfunctions if allowed to dominate the actions of the individual. A compulsive imitation of another person's facial expression is a symptom of *echolalia*. The opposite reaction, that is remaining completely unaffected by the facial expressions of another person, is generally referred to as social coldness but is perhaps also a specific expression of behaviour referred to in specialist literature as *aggressive conduct disorder (ACD)*. There are indications that an unaffected, apathetic observation of pain inflicted on another person is partially due to missing mirroring processes in the brain—and therefore presumably to a lack of corporeal resonance and a lack of mimetic articulation of the expression of pain (Decety et al., 2009; Likowski et al., 2012; Osborn & Derbyshire, 2010; Rymarczyk et al., 2018).

According to the resonance model of embodied cognition, the multimodal interaction of senses for the described *empathy with a facial expression* (e.g. while seeing images of humans) can be characterised as follows: The face of another person is received visually through the *sense of sight*; a mimicking imitation follows, which is not consciously perceived by the perceiving or the observed person but nonetheless registered by the *kinetic sense* and transmitted to the brain whereby *empathy and thus a deeper realisation* of the happy or friendly mood of the other person is possible—not merely an apathetic registration. One may presume that such empathy with the emotions of another person is only made possible on account of these *real micro-imitations* by means of a *physical* experience with the other person. Facial expressions are only one element of mimicry, as it is also performed, as numerous studies have shown, via other bodily organs such as arm movements, body postures, foot placements and so on. The expression 'kinaesthetic empathy', which is also used in research literature, thereby becomes understandable (Zaboura, 2009).

If facial micro-motions are so important for the perception of other people and their emotional states, moods and so on, the following research question arises: What happens with respect to social sensitivity when muscles that are important for mimicking activities are dulled? We would expect that the empathic abilities are lower when lacking this corporeal resonance (although only statistical tendencies can be discerned due to the complexity of such processes). Of course, experiments such as these have already been performed, for example, by covering up certain facial areas with bandages (Oberman et al., 2007; Ponari et al., 2012). For other studies, the cosmetic agent Botox was injected into various facial areas. Among other uses, the medication Botox reduces so-called crow's feet by numbing or paralysing certain facial muscles. These experiments actually showed a decrease in the empathic abilities of many research participants. Thus, the injection of Botox into the facial muscles that are also responsible for empathic mimetic reactions resulted in the reduced ability among many research participants to properly discern emotional messages in texts compared to untreated persons—which suggests that there are micro-motor activities of facial expressions even for *imagined* moods and feelings in other people. Similar effects have been demonstrated for the identification of emotional messages in images (Davis et al., 2010; Havas et al., 2010).

As already mentioned, some studies have shown that reading emotionally engaging texts is accompanied by very subtle, specific muscle activities of the face that, for some readers at least, seem to be important for understanding what they are reading (Niedenthal et al., 2009). However, a person's own facial expressions can also change their emotional mood. Test subjects were asked to hold a pen between either their lips or their teeth with their mouth open. As they did so, they were supposed to evaluate how funny they thought a caricature was. Statistics showed that the second group found the image funnier than the first group. The researchers explained this effect by saying that if you hold a pen between your teeth it is specifically the muscles that are used for laughing that are activated (Koch, 2011, p. 55).

As already stated, it is difficult for us to be sad when focussing on a happy facial expression (and vice versa). As researcher David Havas stated in connection with the Botox study, when observing an unhappy face, the brain normally sends an impulse to the periphery to generate a micro-motor 'frown'; this fine-motor, facial mirroring, which outsiders cannot necessarily see, is then transmitted as a characteristic impression of motion to the brain or *mirrored back*, whereby the emotional message becomes *experienceable*. However, this corporeal gesture is inhibited by the medication given, and the ability to understand the emotional message is impeded. These effects were very strong in some persons but weak or even non-existent in others. For we must remember that our understanding of a facial expression or a described emotion, as numerous research projects have shown, can also be moderated by other corporeal activities such as how someone sits to read. Personal idiosyncrasies seem to be important for visual/facial mimicry. For example, some studies have shown that mimetic behaviour occurs more often with persons who, according to tests, are especially empathetic as they react with strong imitative fine-motor activity to the facial expression of fear or disgust in others (Rymarczyk et al., 2016).

After this short excursion into studies on micro-mimetic resonance, the initial example can now be analysed in greater detail and we will examine what the implications are for *education*. For example, it is difficult for us to produce a sad, angry or happy mood when we observe a contrary facial expression. The same is true for physiognomic expressions that we observe in other people or images (whereas such micro-mimetic reactions are probably not activated when we perceive them only fleetingly). However, the example of the apathetic observation of pain in other people (Aggressive Conduct Disorder) elucidates that not all individuals are capable of such mimicry. In everyday social life it is also true to a certain extent that such imitation processes can be moderated—for example, when a grieving friend speaks to us with an unhappy facial expression, we unconsciously do not imitate this facial expression but speak with a serious, yet encouraging facial expression in order to comfort our friend—however, this presupposes that we are able to precisely assume the socially appropriate *mood*. It is possible that this friend now gets the impression of a comforting encounter when he reacts with at least slight imitations to the facial expression (Drimalla et al., 2019; Hess & Fischer, 2016; Seibt et al., 2015). It is a question of reciprocal resonances although corporeal social interaction also indicates a much more basic function of such facial activities and, in a further sense, embodiment processes. If we look more deeply at this tactful interaction we see that it is an expression of *a process of (self-) education* that has already taken place. The socially appropriate form of interaction that is also articulated in the face is preceded by a life of relatively complex experience and learning in the course of which the correlation between such social and incorporated abilities has been developed. On an abstract level it is possible to initially maintain that the forms of expression in this bodily repertoire of behaviour and action, this bodily instrument of successful communication must be developed. However, what needs to be developed cannot be separated from what can only happen within the context of general (self-)education because it is always a more specific expression of one's own educational experiences. From this we see that a careful phenomenological observation of an important individual example of Embodied Cognition, the mimicking resonance of the facial expressions (and moreover certainly also bodily postures, gestures, movement) of another person clarifies the *mind-body-environment-approach*. The following example illustrates what *incorporation* of culture or specifically also morals means. People living about 150 years ago were not disturbed by physical violence towards children in families or schools nor by the sight of public executions. However, seeing things like this evokes *corporeal* reactions of horror and empathy among most people today. Moral convictions and cultural attitudes have 'incarnated' themselves (in the words of Merleau-Ponty) so that most people feel strong empathetic resonances that also *motivate* them to intervene in such situations (De Mause, 1974; Gersch, 2015; Soliman & Glenberg, 2014; Strejcek & Zhong, 2014).

Based on research results, it seems to me that, whatever form it takes, *Embodied Cognition* as cultural education that produces resonances expresses the total education of head, heart and hand, of thinking, feeling and volition, and of intellectual and aesthetic worlds of experience. This becomes even more apparent when we look beyond facial expressions to body postures, forms of movement, gestures, physiological processes and so on that form a kind of 'concert' of these varied corporeal activities (Stefani & Marco, 2019).

In an article, neuroscientist Manuela Macedonia describes how insights gained from embodiment research can inspire teaching and learning practices in schools, highlighting the learning of foreign languages, mathematics and also basic spatial thinking, which is fundamental for technical professions.

> Most educational programs follow theories that are mentalistic, i.e. they separate the mind from the body. At school, learners sit, watch, listen, and write. The aim of this paper is to present embodied learning as an alternative to mentalistic education. (Macedonia, 2019, online)

She views this type of more rationalistic teaching which ignores the body as being part of the tradition of Descartes mind-body dichotomy (1596–1650), which has also had a significant impact on the cognitive sciences of the current time. We 'still' learn with the mind; the body contains our vital organs and allows us to move around. However, embodiment research has made it clear that our cognitive activities are interwoven into the sensomotor system of the body. For example, numerous brain areas are activated when grasping an apple with the hand and observing it. These brain areas are related to the form, colour, odour, motor function while peeling, taste and so on of the object. The renewed perception of the object is thus a reactivation of the multisensory or multimodal perception of the fruit. The perception as well as the imagining of the object or of another person will be far richer and livelier if comprehensive and numerous sensuous experiences that are essential for the observed objects have played a role in what has been experienced before.

In a botany class, one can observe a rose on the computer screen or through virtual reality goggles (Smart, 2014). One can observe it in nature from the side, the top and as a shape in space by activating the sense of balance and kinetic sense and thereby come close to the concept of the rose in accordance with its 'essence' while also training one's multimodal resonance capabilities at the same time. One can also observe its metamorphosis from stem leaf to flower more precisely and perceive the underlying movement pattern of expansion and contraction; ultimately, one can also feel the prickly thorns and capture the typical forms of the plant in a drawing: All this is meant by a multimodal approach to reality (Blackwood, 2012; Bockemühl, 1997). Observing resonances of the body and their cognitive function results in concrete demands for teaching that stimulates the senses but at the same time has a phenomenological orientation, which again leads us to the question of whether we have to fear deprivation of the senses and experience if the body is left out of teaching and onscreen media, virtual reality goggles and so on *come to dominate* (Rittelmeyer, 2018). Manuela Macedonia (2019, online) summarises the mind-body dichotomy in these words: "All this is to say that mind and body are intertwined with each other and that Cartesian theories of the mind cannot be the reference for educationalists any longer".

However, anyone who looks carefully at the international development of preschool and school educational theory will notice that this change has been coming for a long time. There are still educational theories which disregard the body, which the author has described as 'mentalistic'. At the same time, there are many teaching methods being developed and tested in educational institutions, without the protagonists being consciously aware of it, that are oriented towards the insights of embodiment research and often have an artistic-craft emphasis. Such teaching methods often align with the saying of the Chinese philosopher Confucius that I quoted earlier: 'Tell me and I will forget, show me and I may remember; involve me and I will understand.'

Thus, German *cultural schools*, for example, attempt to create lessons for science and mathematics as well that *in an inspired way* appeal to the whole body through aesthetic elements (such as theatre, dance, music, landscape painting, see Fuchs & Braun, 2018). Similar intentions are associated with the so-called STEAM concept, whereby Sciences, Technology, Engineering and Mathematics (the classic STEM concept) are complemented by 'Arts' (e.g. Skorton & Bear, 2018). And some schools in the U.S. are envisaging how to design rooms as so-called *Da Vinci Studios* within the context of new building planning in which the 'hard separation of science and art' is to be suspended and it will be possible to experience "various paths of thinking" (Nair, 2014, p. 94). Thus, awareness of the most important role of the embodiment paradigm for education and teaching already exists to a large extent in public or pedagogical institutions. However, both now and in the future educationally oriented embodiment research will have to perform the important task of *anthropologically substantiating* more comprehensive and corporeal didactics.

References

Aizawa, K. (2014). Extended Cognition. In L. Shapiro (Ed.), *The Routledge Handbook of Embodied Cognition* (pp. 31–38). Routledge.

Alibali, M., Bonoddo, R., & Hostetter, A. (2014). Gesture in Reasoning. In L. Shapiro (Ed.), *The Routledge Handbook of Embodied Cognition* (pp. 150–159). Routledge.

Armstrong, D. F. (1995). *Gesture and the Nature of Language*. Cambridge University Press.

Bauer, J. (2006). *Warum ich fühle, was du fühlst. Intuitive Kommunikation und das Geheimnis der Spiegelneurone*. Heyne.

Bilstein, J., & Brumlik, M. (Eds.). (2013). *Die Bildung des Körpers*. Beltz.

Blackwood, J. (2012). *Geometry in Nature*. United Kingdom: Floris Books.

Bockemühl, J. (1997). Aspekte der Selbsterfahrung im phänomenologischen Zugang zur Natur der Pflanzen, Gesteine, Tiere und der Landschaft. In G. Böhme & G. Schiemann (Eds.), *Phänomenologie der Natur* (pp. 149–189). Suhrkamp.

Bremmer, J., & Roodenburg, H. (Eds.). (1991). *A Cultural History of Gesture*. Polity Press.

Casasanto, D. (2014). Body Relativity. In L. Shapiro (Ed.), *The Routledge Handbook of Embodied Cognition* (pp. 108–117). Routledge.

Casasanto, D., & Dijkstra, K. (2010). Motor Action and Emotional Memory. *Cognition, 115*, 179–185.

Corballis, M. C. (2003). *From Hand to Mouth: The Origins of Language*. Princeton University Press.

Davis, J. I., Senghas, A., Brandt, F., & Ochsner, K. N. (2010). The Effects of BOTOX Injections on Emotional Experience. *Emotion, 10*, 433–440.

De Mause, L. (Ed.). (1974). *The History of Childhood*. The Psychohistory Press.

Decety, J., & Ickes, W. (Eds.). (2009). *The Social Neuroscience of Empathy*. MIT Press.

Decety, J., Michalska, K. J., Akitsuki, Y., & Lahey, B. B. (2009). Atypical Empathic Responses in Adolescents with Aggressive Conduct Disorder: A Functional MRI Investigation. *Biological Psychology, 80*, 203–211.

Dimberg, U., & Petterson, M. (2000). Facial Reactions to Happy and Angry Facial Expressions: Evidence for Right Hemisphere Dominance. *Psychophysiology, 37*, 693–696.

Dimberg, U., Thunberg, M., & Elmehed, K. (2000). Unconscious Facial Reactions to Emotional Facial Expression. *Psychological Science, 1*, 86–89.

Drimalla, H. (2019). *On Facial Mimicry and Empathy*. Dissertation Humboldt-Universität Berlin, Germany.

Drimalla, H., Landwehr, N., Hess, U., & Dziobek, I. (2019). From Face to Face: The Contribution of Facial Mimicry to Cognitive and Emotional Empathy. *Cognition and Emotion, 33*, 1672–1686.

Ekman, P. (2004). *Gefühle lesen*. Elsevier.

Fadiga, L., Craighero, L., Buccino, G., & Rizzalotti, G. (2002). Speech Listening Specifically Modulates the Excitability of Tongue Muscles: A TMS Study. *European Journal of Neuroscience, 15*, 399–402.

Faulstich, P. (2014). Lernen: Erfahrung – Wahrnehmen und Handeln. In P. Faulstich (Ed.), *Lerndebatten* (pp. 35–60). Transcript.

Feyereisen, C. F., & DeLannoy, J. B. (1991). *Gestures and Speech*. Cambridge University Press.

Frohmann, E., Grote, V., Avian, A., & Moser, M. (2010). Psychophysiologische Effekte atmosphärischer Qualitäten der Landschaft. *Schweizerische Zeitschrift für Forstwesen, 161*, 97–103.

Fuchs, M., & Braun, T. (Eds.). (2018). *Kulturelle Unterrichtsentwicklung*. Beltz.

Gallagher, S. (2014). Phenomenology and Embodied Cognition. In L. Shapiro (Ed.), *The Routledge Handbook of Embodied Cognition* (pp. 9–18). Routledge.

Gersch, L. (2015). *Das inkarnierte Ethos (Embodied Ethics)*. Dissertation Freie Universität Berlin, Germany.

Goldin-Meadow, S., & Beilock, S. L. (2010). Action's Influence on Thought: The Case of Gesture. *Perspectives on Psychological Science, 5*, 664–674.

Goldman, A. I. (2017). *Joint Ventures. Mindreading, Mirroring, and Embodied Cognition*. Oxford University Press.

Gomez-Paloma, F. (Ed.). (2017). *Embodied Cognition. Theories and Applications in Education Science*. Nova Publishers.

Harmon-Jones, E., & Winkielman, P. (Eds.). (2007). *Social Neuroscience: Integrating Biological and Psychological Explanations of Social Behavior.* Guilford Press.

Havas, D. A., Glenberg, A. M., Gutowski, K. A., Lucarelli, M. J., & Davidson, R. J. (2010). Cosmetic Use of Botulinum Toxin – A Processing of Emotional Language. *Psychological Science, 21*, 895–900.

Hess, U., & Fischer, A. (Eds.). (2016). *Emotional Mimicry in Social Context.* Cambridge University Press.

Hildebrandt-Stratmann, R., Laging, R., & Moegling, K. (Eds.). (2013). *Körper, Bewegung und Schule.* Prolog.

Ifrah, G. (2000). *The Universal History of Numbers.* Wiley.

Ito, T., Tiede, M., & Ostry, D. J. (2009). Somatosensory Function in Speech Perception. *PNAS, 106*, 1245–1248.

Johnstone, T., van Reekum, C., Oakes, T., & Davidson, R. (2006). The Voice of Emotion: An FMRI Study of Neural Responses to Angry and Happy Expressions. *Social Cognitive Affective Neuroscience, 1*, 242–249.

Kaschak, M., Jones, J., Carranza, J., & Fox, M. (2014). Embodiment and Language Comprehension. In L. Shapiro (Ed.), *The Routledge Handbook of Embodied Cognition* (pp. 118–126). Routledge.

Katz, M.-L. (Ed.). (2013). *Moving Ideas. Multimodality and Embodied Learning in Communities and Schools.* Lang.

Koch, S. (2011). *Embodiment. Der Einfluss von Eigenbewegung auf Affekt, Einstellung und Kognition.* logos.

Kraus, A. (Ed.). (2009). *Körperlichkeit in der Schule* (p. 2). Athena.

Laging, R. (2017). *Bewegung in Schule und Unterricht.* Kohlhammer.

Likowski, K., Mühlberger, A., Gerdes, A., Wieser, M., Pauli, P., & Weyers, P. (2012). Facial Mimicry and the Mirror Neuron System: Simultaneous Acquisition of Facial Electromyography and Functional Magnetic Resonance Imaging. *Frontiers in Human Neuroscience, 6*, 214. https://doi.org/10.3389/fnhum.2012.00214

Macedonia, M. (2019). Embodied Learning: Why at Schools the Mind Needs the Body. *Frontiers in Psychology, 10*, 2098. https://doi.org/10.3389/fpsyg.2019.02098

Margiotta, U. (2017). Embodied Cognition and the Cognitive Modifiability. A New Deal for Education in the XXI Century. In F. G. Paloma (Ed.), *Embodied Cognition. Theories and Applications in the Education Science* (pp. 49–73). Nova Publishers.

McCarthy, J., Hilger, S., Sullivan, H., & Saul, N. (2016). *The Early History of Embodied Cognition 1740–1920. The Lebenskraft-Debate and Radical Reality in German Science, Music, and Literature.* Brill Rodopi.

Menninger, K. (1969). *Number Words and Number Symbols: A Cultural History of Numbers.* MIT Press.

Michaels, C., & Palatinus, Z. (2014). Ten Commandments for Ecological Psychology. In L. Shapiro (Ed.), *The Routledge Handbook of Embodied Cognition* (pp. 19–28). Routledge.

Nair, P. (2014). *Blueprint for Tomorrow. Redesigning Schools for Student-Centered Learning.* Harvard Education Publ.

Nathan, M. (2014). Grounded Mathematical Reasoning. In L. Shapiro (Ed.), *The Routledge Handbook of Embodied Cognition* (pp. 171–183). Routledge.

Niedenthal, P. M., Winkielman, P., Mondillon, L., & Vermeulen, N. (2009). Embodiment of Emotion Concepts. *Journal of Personality and Social Psychology, 96*, 167–178.

Nummenmaa, L., Glerean, E., Hari, R., & Hietanen, J. K. (2013). Bodily Maps of Emotion. *PNAS (Proceedings of the National Academy of Sciences), 111*, 646–651.

Oberman, L., Winkielman, P., & Ramachandran, V. (2007). Face to Face: Blocking Facial Mimicry Can Selectively Impair Recognition of Emotional Expressions. *Social Neuroscience, 2*, 167–178.

Oosterwijk, S., & Barrett, L. (2014). Embodiment in the Construction of Emotion Experience and Emotion Understanding. In L. Shapiro (Ed.), *The Routledge Handbook of Embodied Cognition* (pp. 250–260). Routledge.

Oppezzo, M., & Schwartz, D. (2014). Give Your Ideas Some Legs.: The Positive Effect of Walking on Creative Thinking. *Journal of Experimental Psychology, Learning, Memory, and Cognition, 40*, 1142–1152.

Osborn, H., & Derbyshire, S. W. G. (2010). Pain Sensation Evoked by Observing Injury in Others. *Pain, 148*, 268–274.

Panksepp, J., & Trevarthen, C. (2009). The Neuroscience of Emotion in Music. In S. Malloch & C. Trevarthen (Eds.), *Communicative Musicality. Exploring the Basis of Human Companionship*. Oxford University Press.

Paolo, E., & Thompson, E. (2014). The Enactive Approach. In L. Shapiro (Ed.), *The Routledge Handbook of Embodied Cognition* (pp. 68–78). Routledge.

Pecher, D., & Zwaan, R. (Eds.). (2005). *Grounding Cognition. The Role of Perception and Action in Memory, Language, and Thinking*. Cambridge University Press.

Ponari, M., Conson, M., D'Amico, N., Grossi, D., & Trojano, L. (2012). Mapping Correspondence Between Facial Mimicry and Emotion Recognition in Healthy Subjects. *Emotion, 12*, 1398–1403.

Rittelmeyer, C. (2010). The Human Body as a Resonance Organ: A Sketch of an Anthropology of the Senses. *Research Bulletin, 15*, 9–12.

Rittelmeyer, C. (2013). *Einführung in die Gestaltung von Schulbauten*. Farbe und Gesundheit.

Rittelmeyer, C. (2014). *Aisthesis. Zur Bedeutung von Körperresonanzen für die ästhetische Bildung*. Kopaed.

Rittelmeyer, C. (2016). *Bildende Wirkungen ästhetischer Erfahrungen*. Beltz Juventa.

Rittelmeyer, C. (2018). *Digitale Bildung. Ein Widerspruch*. Athena.

Roux, F. E., Boetto, S., Sacko, O., Chollett, F., & Tremoulet, M. (2003). Writing, Calculating, and Finger Recognition in the Region of the Angular Gyrus: A Cortical Stimulation Study of Gerstmann Syndrome. *Journal of Neurosurgery, 99*, 716–727.

Rowe, M. L., & Goldin-Meadow, S. (2009). Differences in Early Gesture Explain SES Disparities in Child Vocabulary Size at School Entry. *Science, 323*, 951–953.

Ruggieri, V. (2003). *Semeiotica di Processi psicofisiologici e psicosomatici*. Il Pensiero Scientifico Editore.

Ruggieri, V., Fiorenza, M., & Sabatini, N. (1986). Visual Decodification through microimitation. *Perceptual and Motor Skills, 62*, 475–481.

Rymarczyk, K., Zurawski, L., Jankowiak-Siuda, K., & Szatkowska, I. (2016). Emotional Empathy and Facial Mimicry for Static and Dynamic Facial Expressions of Fear and Disgust. *Frontiers in Psychology, 7*, 1853. https://doi.org/10.3389/fpsyg.2016.01853

Rymarczyk, K., Zurawski, L., Jankowiak-Siuda, K., & Szatkowska, I. (2018). Neural Correlates of Facial Mimicry. *Frontiers in Psychology, 9*, 52. https://doi.org/10.3389/fpsyg.2018.00052

Seibt, B., Mühlberger, A., Likowski, K., & Weyers, P. (2015). Facial Mimicry in Its Social Setting. *Frontiers in Psychology, 6*, 1122. https://doi.org/10.3389/fpsyg.2015.01122

Shapiro, L. (2019). *Embodied Cognition* (2nd ed.). Routledge.

Shapiro, L., & Stolz, S. (2018). Embodied Cognition and Its Significance for Education. *Theory and Research in Education, 17*, 19–39.

Sheets-Johnstone, M. (2009). *The Corporeal Turn. An Interdisciplinary Reader*. Imprint Academic.

Simms, E. (2008). *The Child in the World. Embodiment, Time, and Language in Early Childhood*. Wayne State University Press.

Singer, T. (2006). The Neuronal Basis and Ontogeny of Empathy and Mind Reading: Review of Literature and Implications for Future Research. *Neuroscience Biobehavior Review, 30*, 855–863.

Skorton, D., & Bear, A. (Eds.). (2018). *The Integration of the Humanities and Arts with Sciences, Engineering and Medicine in Higher Education*. The National Academic Press. https://doi.org/10.17226/2498

Smart, P. R. (2014). Embodiment, Cognition, and the World Wide Web. In L. Shapiro (Ed.), *The Routledge Handbook of Embodied Cognition* (pp. 326–334). Routledge.

Soliman, T., & Glenberg, A. (2014). The Embodiment of Culture. In L. Shapiro (Ed.), *The Routledge Handbook of Embodied Cognition* (pp. 207–219). Routledge.

Stefani, E., & Marco, D. (2019). Language, Gesture, and Emotional Communication: An Embodied View of Social Interaction. *Frontiers in Psychology, 10*, 2063. https://doi.org/10.3389/fpsyg.2019.02063

Strack, F., Martin, L., & Stepper, S. (1988). Inhibiting and Facilitating Conditions of the Human Smile: A Nonobtrusive Test of the Facial Feedback Hypothesis. *Journal of Personality and Social Psychology, 54*, 768–777.

Strejcek, B., & Zhong, C.-B. (2014). Morality in the Body. In L. Shapiro (Ed.), *The Routledge Handbook of Embodied Cognition* (pp. 220–230). Routledge.

Susskind, J., Lee, D., Cusi, A., Feimann, R., Grabski, W., & Anderson, A. (2008). Expressing Fear Enhances Sensory Acquisition. *Nature Neuroscience, 11*, 843–850.

Trumpp, N. (2012). Embodiment Theory and Education: The Foundations of Cognition in Perception and Action. *Trends in Neuroscience and Education, 1*, 15–20.

Varela, F. J., Thompson, E., & Rosch, E. (1991). *The Embodied Mind*. MIT Press.

Vignemont, F. (2014). Acting for Bodily Awareness. In L. Shapiro (Ed.), *The Routledge Handbook of Embodied Cognition* (pp. 287–305). Routledge.

Wicker, B., Keysers, C., Plailly, J., Royet, J.-P., Gallese, V., & Rizzalotti, G. (2003). Both of Us Disgusted in *My* Insula: The Common Neural Basis of Seeing and Feeling Disgust. *Neuron, 40*, 655–664.

Wulf, C., Althans, B., Audehm, K., Blaschke, G., Ferrin, N., Kellermann, I., Mattig, S., & Schinkel, S. (2011). *Die Geste in Erziehung, Bildung und Sozialisation. Ethnographische Feldstudien*. Springer VS.

Zaboura, N. (2009). *Das empathische Gehirn. Spiegelneurone als Grundlage menschlicher Kommunikation*. Springer VS.

Part II

The Pedagogical Relationship and Professionalism

Tactful behaviour is based on acknowledging the other person to be of equal value, even if the other person is not (yet) able to behave as an equal in terms of social responsibility, etc., as in the case of a child. Tact is a requirement for the success of pedagogical actions. There is a close connection between tact and behaving mimetically. Tact can lead to an exchange between people based on mutual respect, in the course of which each person reveals herself in a way that corresponds to her own conceptions and self-image, as long as this does not infringe the rights of other people. Tact is associated with the aesthetic side of pedagogical actions without which they are simply disciplinary measures. As in aesthetic action, also in tactful action there is a mimetic exchange between the body of the person acting and the addressee of her actions. Such exchange necessitates openness and a readiness to perceive the other person. Tact as a body-based aesthetic sensitivity is a prerequisite of the social effect of gestures, rituals and other social practices. The conscious use of gestures as an aid in education and child-rearing involves bodily practices that become a medium for teaching and learning. Vulnerability as a bodily condition of life and as a form of knowledge delimits action.

Sensitivity and discretion must be exercised by adults towards children, and this can be described as pedagogical tactfulness (*Shoko Suzuki* [Chap. 8]). When being pedagogically tactful, a person responds in a caring way to the circumstances at hand. Pedagogical tact arouses emotion. Tact functions as a 'mode of knowledge'. In contrast to reason and cognition (*logos*), tact relates to the body and its feelings. The author shows how the knowledge of pathos of pedagogical tactfulness is related to other educational 'techniques', which Suzuki explains as an expression of *phronesis*, which is a type of wisdom relevant to practical action, implying both good judgement and good character and habits. Suzuki also elucidates Kitaro Nishida's 'logic of place' as being determined by 'the richness of the nothingness'. The logic of place constitutes an ever-changing cosmos, 'in which all things resonate'. In pedagogical tact, bodies resonate with each other by encompassing all living things. This experience has an association with the tranquil state of Zen enlightenment.

In Chap. 9 pedagogical tact is identified as body-based mindfulness (*Anja Kraus* and *Thomas Senkbeil*). Pedagogical tact involves assumptions that are proved by practice. Instant judgements or decisions are made. The practitioners steadily improve their tact in a non-quantifiable way, through tacit knowledge. The authors present a small-scale empirical study. Finally, pedagogical tact is defined as corporeal social awareness for social equality, by which offensive, defensive behavior or power games can be avoided. However, as pedagogical tact is associated with proximity and touch it can, in principle, also be associated with violation or harm. At the same time, tact has the didactic function of changing the way students engage with the content of a lesson so that superficial knowledge and confusion gradually turns into analysis and reflection. From the didactic perspective, the question is also raised how the evaluation of performance and pedagogical tact can operate together.

Gestures are important means for enabling classroom communication to function well (*Regula Fankhauser* and *Angela Kaspar* [Chap. 10]). On the one hand, gestures are strongly related to language, thinking and imagination. They 'are not learnt through language and thought, but in performances and mimetic processes'. Gestures do not merely follow and support verbal expressions; they even have the potential to replace, resist and undermine language. The authors' videography on how teachers perceive and interpret certain physical movements in the classroom shows the ambiguity of gestures. As the meaning of gestures in social interaction is often unclear, a gesture can also convey manipulative, debasing, harmful ways of dealing with the children. This is the case, for example, when a teacher reacts to her own irritation by a pupil's disruptive signals by drawing on social and cultural stereotypes. The authors conclude that gestures only then signify the school rules and the sovereignty of the teacher, when the 'hegemony of the linguistic is restored' and when the gestures in the classroom follow an integrative institutional logic.

The incorporation of social power structures in educational processes is a consequence of the potential vulnerability of the human body (*Daniel Burghardt* and *Jörg Zirfas* [Chap. 11]). Vulnerability is an aspect of the human body that is often overlooked. It is an anthropological fact. Vulnerabilty is (in life and online) omnipresent in the face of harm, suffering and disaster. Humans are, in a pathic way, exposed to their vulnerability. Vulnerability is corporeally, socially and culturally contextualised through an expansion of experience, and involves the awareness of what might happen next in a concrete situation. In its situatedness, contingency, relativity and relationality and in all its corporeal, social and cultural dimensions, vulnerability can be seen as knowledge regarding 'potentially harmful actions or cause-effect relationships' that is required in order to prevent violence and harm. In pedagogical situations this is of special relevance, because 'actual physical harm cannot be attributed to a single cause'. An individual's resilience and self-preservation instincts are largely based on the ability to anticipate possible dangers. This, in turn, assumes a deep sense of vulnerability as being the 'dark side' of 'enlightened' times.

When tactful behaviour and gestures and rituals are used in an educational way in institutions like schools, they take place in social fields that are permeated by power structures (*Kathrin Audehm*). The author of Chap. 12 presents well-known concepts about bodies as bearers of politico-cultural forces and dynamics, not least in pedagogical contexts, namely the ideas of Max Weber, Michel Foucault and Pierre Bourdieu. Audehm elaborates their analytic contribution to pedagogy. The exercise of power is defined as the ability to exercise one's will over others (Weber), as power of action, instrumental power and authoritative power. Bourdieu and Foucault refer to the discursive means of power and the mechanisms and formulae behind the 'belief in the legitimacy of domination'. We can learn from them how power structures are practised and how they become absorbed into human bodies. Audehm is interested not only in these interpretations of the networks of power and their role(s) in the field of education but also in what is tacitly assumed and what is ignored in each of the reference-concepts. At the same time, she stresses that pedagogy must prove itself every day in terms of mutuality, recognition and trust. Herein lies the opportunity for pedagogical authority and practice to prevent violence.

Knowledge of Pathos

Shoko Suzuki

The daily life of a school is a collection of inexpressible knowledge. For example, it begins in the morning when we welcome students to school. They come to school with the rhythms of life that they have developed in their own homes. The student who leaves home to come to school having been in an argument with his parents over something trivial. The student whose conversation with a friend last night about something that's bothering her has stuck in her mind. Or the student who has spent some quality time with her family and is excitedly anticipating the upcoming holidays. The mental rhythms created by these various shades of emotions swirl around the classroom in the morning. On the other hand, teachers, too, stand in front of their students, tinged with the rhythms generated by time spent at home. The morning 'homeroom' time is a place to regulate and tune in to the complex rhythms of the mind.

The teacher must keep track of what each student is doing through daily interactions. Lately, a certain student has been having trouble concentrating in class and is often defiant when I, as her teacher, pay attention to her. There is something of a hidden anger that comes through. Why is it that she is unable to listen to others honestly/openly? Is it because she is distrustful of the people around her? Or she may have lost confidence in herself. Is she trying to cope with sadness? The teacher must be sensitive to each student's

---

S. Suzuki (✉)
Kyoto University, Kyoto, Japan
e-mail: shoko.suzuki.ue@riken.jp

© The Author(s), under exclusive license to Springer Nature Switzerland AG 2022
A. Kraus, C. Wulf (eds.), *The Palgrave Handbook of Embodiment and Learning*,
https://doi.org/10.1007/978-3-030-93001-1_8

temperament and current situation when focusing attention on them in the classroom. Also, when reprimanding a student in front of other students, the teacher must be aware of the message of the reprimand in the eyes of other students who are watching, who may perceive it as a message without hurting the pride of the reprimanded student.

J.F. Herbart (1776–1841), a German philosopher who was a pioneer in the field of philosophical psychology and established pedagogy as a discipline for teachers, explored the practicalities of teachers' judgements and decisions that underpin daily school life and described it as 'pedagogical tact' (*pädagogischer Takt*) (Herbart, 1802). Pedagogical tact, as a mediating term (*Mittelglied*) between the theory and practice of education, enables teachers to make quick judgements and decisions. This tact, he said, must be honed until it becomes a skilful technique that works by synthesizing the teacher's various techniques for educational practice. Pedagogical tact, therefore, can be said to be a skill of judgement, or 'phronesis-techne.' To become a master of tact, it is necessary to start by noticing the function of tact in various aspects of practice, that is to say, it is necessary to clarify the function of tact, to extract the various elements that compose it, and to clarify the network of relationships between the elements in terms of how it functions. The first task is to discover the function of educational tact in the daily actions of the school (Blochmann, 1950; Heyd, 1995; Muth, 1962).

Pedagogical tact is a technical term used by Herbart to describe the professional skill of the teacher. In the same way, the tact of a great doctor can be seen as a single glance to assess a patient's condition in an instant. Tact, as an everyday word, comes from the Latin word *tactus*, which means the sense of touch. It also means an inner feeling produced by contact. In musical terminology, tact means a conductor's baton, the time signature, and rhythm. From the eighteenth century onwards, the term 'tact' has been commonly used to describe the delicate emotions necessary for social interaction, as well as the ability to avoid harming others. As the urban concentration of modernization progressed, new manners of socializing came to be demanded, and tact came to attract people's attention as a knack for human interaction. Being tactful, or to be full of tact, was considered important in this context (Gödde & Zirfas, 2012; Suzuki, 2014; Burckhardt, Krinninger, & Seichter, 2015).

The term 'tactful teacher' is also used to describe a teacher who can relate to his or her students in the most appropriate way. It also works in relationships between people. Tact is a measure of the distance between people, or in other words, a measure of the heart. The distance between people is not visible, but it is possible to measure this interpersonal distance through comprehensive sensibility that mobilizes all the five senses. Tact is the ability to read the invisible distance and the quality of the distance that lies between the self and others, the atmosphere and mood of a place. We can perceive the subtle folds of our mind such as mood, state of mind, and comfort of others through their facial expressions, tone of voice, and the atmosphere of a place. Tact is a practical knowledge that enables us to take appropriate actions in our daily practice, and it is a physical knowledge that enables us to respond appropriately to situations in a physical manner (De Certeau, 1980; Detienne & Vernant, 1974; Raphals, 1992).

Knowing and understanding a particular student is not enough to know and understand her objective data, for example, date of birth, height, weight, how many seconds she ran the 100 metres during the last sporting event, what her marks were last semester, or any of the many other data accumulated in student records. The teacher must have a comprehensive understanding of the messages that this student sends out with her whole body—her words, expressions, and attitudes, as well as her own experience of what makes her happy and what makes her sad, what she looks at, and what she longs for. Moreover, the teacher must know it not as a scientist observes and measures a subject, but as a teacher, seeing a being of flesh and blood, who opens up and shows her true face to the teacher. On the one hand, the teacher is trying to get to know his or her students, and on the other hand, the students are also diagnosing how well the teacher has the ability and capacity to understand them. The basis of this relationship is a mutual act of knowing.

In various scenes encountered in daily life at school, teachers and students are (1) reading the backgrounds of the actions (performances) of the people who compose those scenes, that is, the ambiguity of the actions; (2) seeing how those scenes weave together into the present, tomorrow, and future of the people in those scenes and positioning them in a time-space framework (*cosmos*); and (3) understanding the meaning of the various elements that make up the scene as symbols. The field of education is a vital, living thing. It is a product of improvization. It is created by all the people in the room. A place is created in such a way that it is impossible to know who intended to create it that way. The power of the place is the situational power that makes the relationship between teacher and student emerge. In this sense, tact can be seen as giving power to the place while making use of the power of the place.

1 Touch the World/Touch Life

Let us look more deeply at the function of tact from the phenomenological point of view. First, the sense of touch is a fundamental sense for human beings. I would like you to close your eyes, put your hands together, and enjoy the sensation of the right hand touching the left hand for a while. After that, try to feel the sensation of your left hand touching your right hand. With your hands together, it is not clear whether your right hand is touching your left hand, or your left hand is touching your right hand. Touching and being touched happen simultaneously, which is a characteristic of the sense of touch. The way you set your consciousness determines which hand you touch, and which hand you feel is being touched. From a Descartes point of view, I am on the side that senses and perceives the object. But my hand is not only on the side of the perceiving subject, but also on the side of the perceived, or perceived object, at the same time. Touching and being touched—isn't this a fundamental human trait? Maurice Merleau-Ponty (1908–1961) focused on the ambiguity and ambivalence of the 'I' as both the owner of the hand that touches and the owner of the hand that is touched and tried to restore the 'I' as an entity (Merleau-Ponty, 1964). In the 1920s in Japan the Kyoto School, which attempted to build up this school of thought, described the 'I' that emerges in such ambiguous situations as 'the unparticipating' of the subject and the object. They also called the experience that arises 'the boundary of consciousness and unconsciousness,' where subject and object are undifferentiated, 'pure experience' (Nishida, 1911; Suzuki, 2012).

Tactile sensation can be positioned as a common-sense or somatic sense that cooperates with various other senses such as vision, hearing, and balance, and coordinates these various senses with the body. Also, tact, as a sense of touch, has a meaning similar to rhythm. Our internal rhythm is linked to the external rhythms of the world through the movements of our bodies, including dance. It is not a coincidence that various rituals and events have long been conducted according to the rhythm of the changing seasons. We internalize the rhythms of the universe and nature through rituals and ceremonies. As proof of this, events and rituals invite human beings to sense this rhythm through dances and music, and the internal rhythm and the rhythms of the universe and the natural world intersect and resonate with each other, creating a world of resonance.

Moreover, tact does not work only in direct contact. It also has the function of reproducing and recalling in an image the feeling induced by the sense of touch as if we feel we were touching it without touching it. This is the reason why tact starts from the meaning of touch, but also includes the meaning of emotional change that occurs within oneself through contact with others.

New-born babies are held in their mothers' arms, and while holding milk in their mouths, feel the heartbeat of their mothers' breasts. This contact with their mothers, exchanged through skin-to-skin contact, is the beginning of children's contact with the outside world. As children begin to move around, they experience the weight and texture of objects by grasping and holding them. When they stand on two feet, they know where they are in the space of the room, which is referred to as the spatial sense of knowing one's place, the balanced sense of being able to move around without falling, and the sense of physical position. And at last, we come to understand the relationship and distance between ourselves and the outside world. The function of vision not only allows us to measure the distance between ourselves and an object without touching it directly, but it is also related to our sense of touch and physical balance. Tactile perception and physical balance are also related to spatial perception. This leads to the sense of knowing one's place in a society or group, or even the sense of knowing the size of one's existence, or the sense of being able to move harmoniously and assert oneself in a place. It can be said to be an organ in contact with the outside world, yet it is not only in direct contact with things but also connects the outside world and the inner world through its mediating action as a rhythm.

The German philosopher Immanuel Kant (1724–1804) referred to "the tact of an acrobat walking a tightrope" because he believed that tact is a spontaneous power of judgement that acts anticipatively during an action (Kant, 1781). The acrobat walks on a single rope. He walks across the rope, keeping his eyes on the path ahead and constantly making decisions as he goes. This is the sense of always moving forward, rather than standing still and looking straight down. Leading on from this, Kant thought of tact as the wisdom of a tightrope walker's synthesis of that instantaneous judgement and physical sensation. In the classroom, the teacher makes countless instantaneous judgements and decisions in order to create a flow. The wisdom used is probably what Kant calls the acrobat's tact. The movement itself is unstable, but there is something stable in that instability, something vague, but we can say that instability is the sense of securing a certain point. It is a function of maintaining movement in equilibrium, in each moment of that movement. It is a kind of dynamic equilibrium, a kind of false focus. In education, the teacher feels the quality of time and space of time and their own position in the flow of time and the field of education. They think about where they are in the field, where their hearts are, and how to measure pauses.

The work of tact in harnessing the power of place is anthropological in the sense that it is characterized by three elements: performativity, symbolism, and cosmology (Wulf, 2013). To put it another way, tact transforms the ordinary and commonplace into a place of resonance. The power of rhythmic resonance echoes among all the people and things present, but also generates special rhythms, repeatedly diffusing and converging in various directions. What we experience in the here and now is not only one immediately apparent meaning but may become a trigger for some kind of awakening in the form of something gained or clarified today, tomorrow, the next day, one year later, or ten years later in the lives of those who are present. Through its rhythmic resonance, the tact submerges deep within the human body and forms a cosmology that involves not only living things but also non-living things.

2 Those Who Have Suffered, Have Learned: *Ta Pathemata Mathemata*

The tact of judgements and decisions must be honed as a skill to increase the probability that they will be successfully optimized. Herbart also shared this thought.

Waza in Japanese (*techne, ars, Kunst*, skill) is honed through use in real situations. Tact is refined through actual use. No matter how much you learn the theory of pedagogy, if you cannot apply it effectively in your daily practice, you cannot say that you have learned it. It is important to analyse the experiences encountered in daily educational practice and reflect on them not only at the cognitive level but also at the emotional level. It is necessary to reflect on the meaning of the experience for oneself and prepare for the next experience by activating the image and adjusting one's psychological state for the next practice. It is a practice that feeds on experience. The practice of *waza* also requires another *waza*, '*waza* of *wazas*,' 'skill of skills,' which entails looking over the practice itself and assessing the process of its practice, called meta-*waza* or meta-skill. In other words, e.g. a craftsman refines his craftsmanship through the process of creating his work and tact can be seen as having a similar dual structure to *waza* (Suzuki, 2010).

To make experience a true source of sustenance, it is necessary to set within oneself a fundamental principle, a rule or law of education, to analyse experience in the light of it, to anticipate the situation to come, and to make an effort to open up one's work prospects with it. It is not, however, something that can be learned by following what one is told in a book. The fundamental principle must be imbued in each teacher until he or she becomes an eye for education, an eye for students, an eye for himself or herself, in other words, a framework for seeing things, a framework for thinking (*Gedankenkreis*), until the pedagogical horizon becomes a 'home-grown' one (Herbart, 1806). It is just like extracting elements that are meaningful to you from the things you encounter through your daily experiences and linking them to how you should act in the future and how you should do your work and your work prospects. It is a map in our minds, so to speak. Pedagogy and its theories must be presented in such a way as to draw a single map on which we can list the relationships between its core elements. With the map in hand, the beginner walks around the unknown world, and in the process draws his or her map according to personal interests and perspectives. The fundamental principle of education is acquired through each experience so that the beginner learns how to recognize and respond to situations in various educational situations, how to interact with students, and how to apply mental techniques, that is to say, to develop a map in his or her mind, an eye for discernment (Suzuki, 2007; Blaß, 1972).

What is noteworthy about the refinement of Herbart's tact is that it encourages us to look back at each thing we have experienced in the past, paying attention to the buzzing of the emotional side of the mind, as well as the images that prepare us for what we will experience in the future. The key to action in any given situation, which unfolds through contact with the world and the rhythms of resonance that arise within and outside the self through contact with life, and the tact of utilizing the power of that situation, is the key to the attraction of the imaginary world that takes place in the teacher before the situation arises. Herbart knew that the emotional impact of the experience was the key opportunity to imprint experience deep into the body. This is exactly what the ancient Greek proverb says: 'He who suffers will learn.'

Moreover, the imagery sessions of future-oriented experience require an intense imagination, as if one were actually experiencing the scene. Herbart's creation of instructional plans for lesson development is adopted by teachers in today's Japanese schools and used in their classes. However, the lesson plans are never a timetable. The lesson plans, which are used to imagine a particular scene, serve as a compass in the preparation process and must be forgotten once in the actual classroom. This plan, submerged in the body through forgetting, is said to contribute to the optimization of action through the action of remembering, to adapt it to the various modes of occurrence of the actual situation, which are different from what was expected.

Images of future experience are inscribed in the body. When we summarize what we experienced in words or tell a story to others, it is edited and remembered as a story in a way that is appropriate to the place and the person to whom it is told. On the other hand, what is felt through the experience is submerged deep in the body without being verbalized. It can be said that the experiential knowledge that escapes segmentation through language is stored deep within the body. Even though we may not have done such things for decades, we can suddenly find ourselves doing things we learned to do as children, such as riding a bicycle or swimming. One day we can simply do them— a physical memory. The lullaby your mother sang to you a long time ago comes out of your mouth without you even knowing it. The body, more than we think, underlies our experiences and the way we change and develop through these experiences.

A technique is expressed through its use, or in other words through the actions and behaviour of the user of the technique. It is impossible to separate a technique from its user's body and see it in isolation. Moreover, to master a technique it is not enough to master the theory and principles behind it. If we cannot make a technique work in the most appropriate way in the situation at the very moment when it is needed, and if we cannot make it work as wisdom through the body, it is necessary to learn to understand it through the body, as the expressions 'to acquire' and 'to know' imply. If you don't cultivate it, you can't say that you have acquired the skill in the true sense of the word. A skill will blossom at the right time (Suzuki, 2019; Yuasa, 1993).

3 Knowledge of *Pathos*: Knowledge of the Emotional and Physical Body

The knowledge that became dominant under the modern scientific worldview was characterized by universalism, which presupposes a homogeneous time and space, logicism, which emphasizes significance through linguistic segmentation, and objectivism, which eliminates and demonstrates subjective arbitrariness. In terms of clarification of the material world, the modern scientific method has achieved great things. However, it must be admitted that it has neglected to grasp in detail the situation of each person living here and now, the specificity of each individual, the characteristics of the senses and the body that mix subjectivity and objectivity, the realm of expression that is beyond the reach of linguistic segmentation, and the ambiguity of situations.

Kitaro Nishida, the founder of the Kyoto School, who in the 1920s explored the possibility of dialogue between Western and Eastern philosophy, regarded the conscious field as a "field" and presented it as a "logic of place" (Nishida, 2011; Suzuki, 2012). Nishida, who studied Western philosophy and practised Zen, presented the "logic of place" and the "actional intuition" that operates therein. Nishida's 'logic of place' was developed through his discussion of the functioning of consciousness (awareness) in terms of a form of judgement. Nishida was sceptical about the fact that epistemology had been developed from the opposition between subjectivity and objectivity. According to him, the root of cognition is to reflect the self in the self, and to be conscious is to reflect the self itself in the field of one's consciousness. This act of reflection is the place of 'at work' where action-oriented intuition works. According to Nishida, it is the logical form of judgement that expresses consciousness most clearly.

In the formal logic, judgement refers to the inclusion of the subject, which is the individual, in the predicate, which is the general, commonly referred to as the universal, or in other words 'the particular is in the general.' It is inclusion, but another way of looking at it is that the general particularizes itself, or, in other words, it is self-limiting. For a judgement to be valid, this self-limiting general, the concrete general, is necessary. This concrete general person is exactly what Nishida calls 'place,' a place focus that reflects the self. Self-awareness is the function of reflecting the self in the self. The human knowledge system is composed of infinite layers of such ordinary people, and in the direction of the subject, we can see an infinitely deep intuition, and at the same time, in the direction of the predicate, we can recognize an infinite number of generalities that surround it. Thus, Nishida attempted to turn from the position of subject-logicism, which had been a common assumption in Western philosophy, to that of predicate logicism. He grounded all existence in a predicative substratum, namely nothingness. For him, the place of nothingness was not the absence of something but was presented as a bottomless and abundant world (Nishida, 1987; Nishitani, 1991; Pinovesana, 1997).

However, because his logic of place was conceived in the context of Zen enlightenment in religious practice, Nishida's logic of place itself cannot help but be associated with the tranquil state of enlightenment. Nishida focused on the comprehensive relationship in the formal logic to establish an intuition of action as something that works at work, but it cannot be said that he was able to sufficiently reveal the diversity and complexity of the richness of nothingness as a dynamic system of places. The richness of the nothingness of a place must be a cosmos that generates an infinite number of beings and meanings, is always changing, and in which all things resonate.

The cosmos as an organic, qualitative space is ubiquitous. In the microcosm of the individual body there is a concentration of the macrocosm, in which dense meaning and specificity reside. Moreover, situations and things are multifaceted, and various meanings are woven into a multi-layered tapestry behind them, in which it is possible to read various meanings according to the angle from which we view them. Moreover, the composition of experience through physical interaction is filled with the performative bodily expressions of the people who participate in it.

If cosmology, symbolism, and performance-based knowledge are theatrical or anthropological knowledge, and modern scientific knowledge is knowledge of logos, centred on language and cognition, then we can say that this knowledge is the knowledge of pathos that resides in feelings and bodies. This kind of knowledge of pathos is often thought to be cultivated through practice. Religious practices are attempts to lead to metamorphosis and to achieve access to, or realization of, the divine through the application of certain programmed transformations to consciousness and the body. It is an attempt to achieve metamorphosis with the awakening and expansion of the body and mind through various attempts at fasting, meditation, *zazen*, waterfall, *gyoza*, and so on. It seeks to escape from the control of the fundamental force that regulates the daily rhythm and speed of the body, namely gravity, which is the fundamental mechanism that controls the body. It can be said that it is an attempt to free oneself from this gravity that regulates life's inconvenience and to obtain the purity and freedom of the spirituality and divinity of the inner cosmos. Freeing oneself from the everyday speed of life through the reconfiguration of space-time is nothing less than shifting one's body and mind into a completely different kind of pace and rhythm from the everyday speed of enlightenment and mystical experiences by changing the mechanism and field of intellect and sensitivity through the practice of intervention through the body. Mystical and enlightenment experiences are made possible by removing the boundaries of intellect and sensibility that are regulated by the speed of daily life.

The world in which the rhythms of the universe (cosmos) called the body resonate with each other will encompass all living things, and even non-living things and objects. Today, when artificial intelligence is embedded in various information networks, including computers, and constitutes a kind of information sphere, humans will be positioned as actors in the environmental intelligence that makes the information sphere function (Floridi, 2014; Berberich et al., 2020). We humans, who are letting go of our attachment to our bodies, are now eager to confirm our humanity through mindfulness, connecting our bodies and minds. What another path is there for us to take?

References

Berberich, N., Nishida, T., & Suzuki, S. (2020). Harmonizing Artificial Intelligence for Social Good. *Philosophy & Technology, 33*, 613–638.

Blaß, J. L. (1972). *Pädagogische Theoriebildung bei Johann Friedrich Herbart.* Anton Hain.

Blochmann, E. (1950). Der pädagogische Takt. *Die Sammlung. Zeitung für Kultur und Erziehung, 5*, 712–722.

Burckhardt, D., Krinninger, D., & Seichter, S. (2015). *Pädagogischer Takt.* Brill Schöningh.

De Certeau, M. (1980). *L'Invention du Quotidien. Vol. 1, Arts de Faire.* Paris: Union générale d'éditions, pp. 10–18. [*The Practice of Everyday Life.* Translated by Steven Rendall, University of California Press, 1984].

Detienne, M. J.-P., & Vernant, J.-P. (1974). *Les ruses d'intelligence: la Metis des grecs.* Paris: Flammarion et Cie. [*Cunning Intelligence in Greek Culture and Society.* Translated by Lloyd, J. Branch Line 1977].

Floridi, L. (2014). *The Fourth Revolution. How the Infosphere is Reshaping Human Reality.* Oxford University Press.

Gödde, G., & Zirfas, J. (Eds.). (2012). *Takt und Taktlosigkeit über Ordnungen und Unordnungen in Kunst, Kultur und Therapie.* transcript.

Herbart, J. F. (1802). *Zwei Vorlesung über Pädagogik.* In Kehrbach, K., Flügel, O., and Fritsch, Th. (eds.). *Johann Friedrich Herbarts Sämtliche Werke*(=SW). Langensalza 1887–1912, Neudruck Aalen 1964, SW I, pp. 279–290.

Herbart, J. F. (1806). Allgemeine Pädagogik aus dem Zweck der Erziehung abgeleitet. *SW, II*, 1–139.

Heyd, D. (1995). Tact: Sense, Sensitivity, and Virtue. *Inquiry, 38*(3), 217–231.

Kant, I. (1781). Kritik der reinen Vernunft. In *Critique of Pure Reason.* (Guyer, P., & Wood, W., Trans. and ed.). Cambridge University Press, 1988.

Merleau-Ponty, M. (1964). *Le Visible et l'invisible, suivi de notes de travail*, texte établi par Claude Lefort (1968). *The Visible and the Invisible* (Lingis, E., Trans.). Northwestern University Press.

Muth, J. (1962). *Pädagogischer Takt.* Quelle & Meyer.

Nishida, K. (1911/1990). *An Inquiry into the Good* (Abe, M., & Ives, C., Trans.). Yale University Press.

Nishida, K. (1987). *Intuition and Reflection in Self-consciousness* (Viglielmo, V. H., and Takeuchi, Y., & O'Leary, J. S., Trans.). State University of New York Press.

Nishida, K. (2011). *Place and Dialectic: Two Essays by Nishida Kitaro* (Krummel, J. W. M., & Nagatomo, S., Trans.). Oxford University Press.

Nishitani, K. (1991). *Nishida Kitaro* (Yamamoto, S., & Heisig, J. W., Trans.). University of California Press.

Pinovesana, G. (1997). *Recent Japanese philosophical Thought 1862–1996.* Japan Library.

Raphals, L. (1992). *Knowing Words. Wisdom and Cunning in the Classical Traditions of China and Greece*. Cornell University Press.

Suzuki, S. (2007). Takt als Medium. *Paragrana – Internationale Zeitschrift für Historische Anthropologie, 17*(1), 145–167.

Suzuki, S. (2010). *Takt in Modern Education*. Waxmann.

Suzuki, S. (2012). The Kyoto School and. In J. F. Herbart, P. In Standish, & N. Saito (Eds.), *Education and the Kyoto School of Philosophy. Pedagogy for Human Transformation* (pp. 41–53). Springer.

Suzuki, S. (2014). Takt. In C. Wulf & J. Zirfas (Eds.), *Handbuch pädagogische Anthropologie* (pp. 295–301). VS Springer.

Suzuki, S. (2019). Etoku (会得) and Rhythms of Nature. In J. R. Resina & C. Wulf (Eds.), *Repetition, Recurrence, Returns. How Cultural Renewal Works* (pp. 131–146). Lexington Books.

Wulf, C. (2013). *Anthropology. A Continental Perspective*. University of Chicago Press.

Yuasa, Y. (1993). *The Body, Self-Cultivation, and Ki-Energy*. State University of New York Press.

Pedagogical Tact: Reconstruction of a Bodily Moment of the Pedagogical Relationship

Anja Kraus and Thomas Senkbeil

1 Topic

Pedagogy is broadly understood as a technique for teaching or a particular kind of description of practices connecting actions with a pedagogical ethos. This ethos contains the feeling for acting considerately and sensitively toward the state of mind of each individual. Therefore, the pedagogical ethos is an integral part of pedagogical practice. This contribution deals with the question of how pedagogical ethos takes place in practice. The hypothesis is that by means of pedagogical tact such conjunctive experiences are created in the classroom that are supposed to awaken own purposes and tasks toward the school subjects among the younger; pedagogical tact withdraws from standardization. In a first step, in order to elaborate the empirical indicators' respective criteria on which one can draw this tactful behavior, the hypothesis will be approached by a case study on filmed teacher practice, analyzed by using the Documentary Method. In a second step, some of these criteria will be epistemologically tagged.

A. Kraus (✉)
Department of Teaching and Learning (Ämnesdidaktik),
Stockholms universitet, Stockholm, Sweden
e-mail: anja.kraus@su.se

T. Senkbeil
University of Applied Sciences and Arts Northwestern Switzerland,
Solothurn, Switzerland
e-mail: thomas.senkbeil@puk.zh.ch

© The Author(s), under exclusive license to Springer Nature Switzerland AG 2022
A. Kraus, C. Wulf (eds.), *The Palgrave Handbook of Embodiment and Learning*,
https://doi.org/10.1007/978-3-030-93001-1_9

2 The Pedagogical Relationship

The relationship between pedagogue and child follows a specific social ethos. Even if this ethos is to a great deal imposed by a national government, in the context of pedagogical practice the guiding beliefs and ideals are perceived mostly as personal. Thus, "[...] ethos, first of all, refers to the character demonstrated by the speaker—the person who is working through his or her words (logos) to affect the thoughts and feelings (pathos) of the audience" (Friesen & Osguthorpe, 2018, p. 257). In the case of the pedagogical ethos, the "logos" of the teacher usually reveals concepts of right and wrong conduct, as well as it systematizes ethical principles and imparts forms of defending them.

In Europe, one already looks back on a long tradition of the pedagogical relationship being a central topic in interpretive studies of education; "[...] themes of *student-teacher relations* and *pedagogies of relation* are common in both empirical and theoretical literature" (Friesen, 2017, p. 743). The most famous approaches to the ethos of the student-teacher relationship are Plato's didactics of maieutics as a form of a cooperative argumentative dialogue between individuals, hereby exercising critical thinking and drawing out the unproven opinions of an individual. Supposedly, up to today, the teaching method to develop the content by asking the students questions, mostly frontal instruction, is the most common form of teacher-directed classroom practice worldwide.

However, teaching does not only consist of stepwise knowledge building and instruction. It also requires a sense for the individual. The difference in age, maturity, and responsibility makes it necessary to act caringly and appropriately to the very capability and quality of experience of the under-aged. The pedagogical ethos, thus, contains the feeling for acting considerately and sensitively for the state of mind of each individual. As mentioned previously, depending foremost on feelings and intuition—not in the least also giving the reason for continuous reflection:

> Situational predicaments that can be *solved* by techniques and procedures are not ethical predicaments. And so pedagogy is both the tactful ethical practice of our actions as well as the doubting, questioning, and reflecting on our actions and practices. (van Manen, 2015, p. 33)

In this contribution, we focus on sensitivity and active thoughtfulness in a pedagogical relationship and in the immediacy of the moment as grasped by the concept of pedagogical tact. The term pedagogical tact was coined by

Johann Friedrich Herbart (1776–1841). Herman Nohl (1879–1960) was the first to give the term pedagogical relation explicit description and definition in this sense, while the phenomenologist Max van Manen established the term in the English-speaking realm by interpreting the pedagogical ethos as pedagogical tact. Van Manen is also one of the first educationalists who dedicated his empirical scientific research on pedagogical tact as a relational phenomenon. Friesen and Osguthorpe (2018) extended the phenomenological concept of tact to research specifically on teacher-student relationships in the so-called pedagogical triangle. We will thus foremost adhere to van Manen's concept on tact and Friesen and Osguthorpe's adaptation of this concept to didactics. According to van Manen, pedagogical tact is tentative acting, prompt reflection, contemplation, as well as referring to the educator's preunderstandings and orientations. van Manen (2015) highlights: "Tact is the active embodiment, the body-work of thoughtfulness" (ibid., p. 105).

Our contribution is about highlighting pedagogical tact as permanently reflecting ethical and moral standards in bodily terms, and as self-reflection. Instead of regarding mind and body as separate spheres, the mind as moving, hearing, seeing, and the body as getting moved, heard, and seen, phenomenologically, the body is seen as both, as a *sensorium* and *responsorium*, at once; bodily response ranges from sensations to spontaneous judgment (Waldenfels, 2002, 2011).

3 Tact as a Pedagogical Term

Etymologically speaking, tact derives from the Latin *tactus*, meaning touch, from *tangere* to touch. In the context of pedagogy, this turns into a figurative sense. Here, touch means to handle in order to interfere with, alter, or otherwise affect another person; it means to come into, or be in mutual contact with somebody. The purpose of pedagogy is to set goals within the school subjects and tasks among the younger that they can regard as their own. Therefore, the adult will always in a specific way orient his or her actions to the child's or adolescent's; "[…] to be tactful is to be thoughtful, sensitive, perceptive, discreet, prudent, judicious, sagacious, perspicacious, gracious, considerate, cautious, careful" (van Manen, 2015, p. 103). Tact corresponds with a mindful quality of reflection and perceptiveness, which van Manen declares as the body-work of thoughtfulness in the uniqueness of the situation of being and acting *with* a child. –

Related terms are *intact*, meaning untouched, uninjured, and *tactile* refers to touch, which means to handle or feel something with the intent to appreciate or understand it in more than merely an intellectual manner. We should notice that touch can also imply violation or harm. (van Manen, 2015, p. 103)

We will come back to this. In the frame of classroom education, not only the teacher-pupil relationship but also content learning plays a central role: The students are expected to instantly connect to the content of a lesson through their former experiences and knowledge, then via study and learning, while the teacher is supposed to have an advanced and didactic knowledge approach to the content. In the pedagogical situation, the teacher thus intends to change the relations of the students to a lesson's content from superficial knowledge and confusion to stepwise analysis and reflection. The aim is to develop the student's subject knowledge and to replace unnecessary uncertainty by (self-) confidence. The students, teacher(s), and the content form the so-called didactical triangle, which is

[...] an elementary, heuristic structure that can be used to highlight and analyze the specific interrelationships and interactions between teacher, student and content (e.g., student lessons, exercises, and projects) in a given pedagogical situation. (Friesen & Osguthorpe, 2018, p. 256)

Tact by then is present

[...] as means by which teacher candidates might navigate between the means-ends thinking embodied in standardized teaching and testing on the one hand, and the dangers of unsustainable demoralization on the other. (ibid., p. 256)

According to Meinert Meyer (2003), good—more modest, the most purposeful—lessons have a well-recognizable structure, for example, there is a common thread and the lesson steps, objectives, content, roles, and tasks are clear. The teacher acts consistently. Rules, rituals, and open spaces are discussed with the students. The proportion of real learning time is high; the atmosphere encourages learning. Meaningful communication, which gets ensured, for example, through the participation of the pupils in planning, as well as through a culture of conversation, allows the students' feedback. Other purposeful features are method variety, individual support, intelligent practice, and a prepared environment. Performance expectations are clear, the tasks are adapted to the performance of the students. The students receive a swift, subsidizing feedback on their learning progress. Some of the aspects of a purposeful lesson are actively directed by the teacher. Others are part of school socialization. Others are mediated situationally, non-theoretically and implicitly, being experience-based and physically mediated, action-guiding orientations (Bohnsack, 2010), which are shared collectively. Such collective orientations are generated on the content, as well as on the relationship level.

The ultimate aim of classroom education insists to let pupils experience and learn things in order to make them their own. However, the educational will cannot simply be transferred to the students' minds. As far as pedagogical aims and intentions foremost concern personality development, they do not only presuppose the technological rules of a how-to-do. Every educational situation is moreover about to create a conjunctive experiential space.

Conjunctive experiences are fundamental, existentially meaningful relationships that determine the socialization of individuals and are shared with others. These can be, for example, milieu, generation, gender or organization specific experiences. (Asbrand, 2011, no page)

School education can generally be understood as

[…] group-specific conjunctive experiential space and individual lesson sequences as situation-specific or object-related experiential spaces in which processes of knowledge genesis occur. (Martens et al., 2015, p. 51)

Both, the initiation of orientation by the teacher and their handling of the orientation figures of the children, proceed more or less tactfully in a pedagogical sense; thus, a special kind of knowing-in-action is involved. Donald Schön (1987) coined the concept of educational practical knowledge and reflection as follows:

Reflection-in-action has a critical function, the structure of knowing-in-action […] we may, in the process, restructure strategies of action, understandings of phenomena, or ways of framing problems […]. Reflection gives rise to on-the-spot experiments. We [teachers] think out and try out new actions intended to explore the newly observed phenomena, test our tentative understandings of them, or affirm the moves we have invented to change things for the better. (ibid., p. 28f.)

According to the term pedagogical tact, such reflection-in-action cannot be, in all regards, formulated in propositional terms but requires the normative quality of sensitivity and active thoughtfulness in the immediacy of the moment. To be tactful, it is indispensable that someone is present, attentive, and able to get the learner's attention, cautiously triggering her/his affects and concern, as well as responding to a situational need for creating some emotional coolness and distance.

> Often tact involves a holding back, a passing over something, which is nevertheless experienced as influenced by the student to whom the tactful action is directed. (van Manen, 2015, p. 102)

By steadily holding a sensitive balance between tackling child and content, and withdrawing from influence, attentive presence in terms of pedagogical tactfulness (ideally) encourages learning.

However, under classroom conditions, pedagogical tact toward each individual is done under time pressure and as successful sensitive handling with certain unavailability, as well as with paradoxes and pedagogical aporia. Jörg Zirfas and Günter Gödde (2012) translate the common predicates of Johann F. Herbart's lectures of pedagogy 1802 with a call for the principle of mediation characterized by "1. quick, 2. rational ('evaluation and decision'), 3. flexible ('not uniform') and 4. taking individuality into account" (1997, p. 1269). Herbart (ibid.) describes that in pedagogical situations a decision or action is required in case of lack of time. The temporal dimension of tact concerns pedagogical methods, attitudes, and goals. However,

> [...] to quickly sense or know the right thing to do in a particular situation means to rely on knowledge or sense that is implicit, and even emotional, rather than explicit and logical. (Friesen & Osguthorpe, 2018, p. 258)

As snap judgments or decisions may not always be right, practitioners steadily improve their tact as quickly recallable tacit knowledge. Tact happens based on their skills in anticipating the possible consequences of their actions. The practical knowledge needed here gets embodied and imparted via mimetic forms of adaptation to the environment, for example, in ritual settings and dynamics in terms of cultural staging and actions.

> Cultural staging and actions are understood less as performances of a psychological, social or religious text, but rather as an arrangement of social institutions with a performative surplus, e.g., in the dramaturgy and organization of ritual interactions and their effects, the scenic-mimetic expressivity, the performance and staging character and the practical knowledge of social action. (Wulf & Zirfas, 2005, p. 12)

In incorporating knowledge through mimetic processes, emotions play the central role (Gebauer & Wulf, 1996). Jakob Muth (1962) outlines the importance of mutual thoughtfulness in order to arouse (generate) tuned social polyphony and a coherent choreography in pedagogy. However, as this tuning also concerns the question of what it means to be human and to grow up toward adulthood, it is always also up to discussion.

> Pedagogical tactful action, for its part, can be described as the ability to [quickly] see and make use of what is available in a given situation for ends that are specifically pedagogical—that are for the good of the student and for his or her learning. (Friesen & Osguthorpe, 2018, p. 257)

To sum up, purposeful teaching means to authorize pupils to learn by themselves through a clear structuring of teaching, a high proportion of real learning time, learning-promoting climate, clarity of content, meaningful communication, individual support, and transparent expectations of performance. However, the pedagogical authorization of the learners depends on pedagogical tact as not to be reduced to standardized requirement in properly performing a pedagogue's work, but the central quality in relation to what we understand of being a good pedagogue and teacher (Suzuki, 2010).

4 Pedagogical Tact as an Epistemological Term

To make pedagogical tact an instrument for a precise definition, Immanuel Kant's student Herbart in 1802 describes the translation of abstract theory into concrete pedagogical practice as pedagogical tact. This departs from the argument that all the pedagogical concepts contain theoretically based assumptions that wished education might occur. If an assumption gets approved by practice, the concept in question gets justified by practical evidence. At times it may also turn out that a concept needs to be changed, refined, or supplemented. Tact is an important advisor in this.

> Ever since Kant had discussed objections to his [Kant's] moral doctrine from the perspective of theory and praxis, and then spurned on again through the controversies of the young Hegelians, it had become common to deal with the link between theory and praxis as a relation, or even as a relation that mirrored itself. (Luhmann & Schorr, 2000, p. 204)

Thus, in practical pedagogy the meaning of a concept is the result of clarifying the more or less experimental elements of pedagogical reality by the capability of the pedagogue to recognize the own emotions and those of the children, discern between the different feelings, and label them appropriately, as well as to use emotional information to guide thinking and behavior. Accordingly, one can regard pedagogical terms as heuristic hypotheses, characterized by their own mode of evidence, as well as linked with alternative concepts in an interpretative manner. This also counts for the specialist term pedagogical tact. How do such heuristics proceed and how does their evidence shape up?

In Herbart's first *Lecture on Pedagogy* in 1802 (see Herbart, [1802] 1997), he describes tact as

> [...] a mode of action that is less the result of one's thinking, but instead gives vent to one's inner movement, expressing how one has been affected from without, and exhibiting one's emotional state. (Herbart quoted by van Manen, 2015, p. 209)

van Manen (2015) with a phenomenological perspective writes, for example, about student teachers:

> By observing and imitating how the teacher animates the students, walks around the room, uses the board, and so forth, the student teacher learns with his or her body, as it were, how to feel confident in this room, with these students. This confidence is an affective quality that makes teaching easier; rather, this confidence is the active knowledge itself, the tact of knowing what to do or not to do, what to say or not to say. (ibid., p. 183)

Confidence is active knowledge and becomes a habit and even skill. Then it is a practical corporeal knowledge forming the basis of the capability to communicate with others and, thus, allowing for original and spontaneous access to the world; at the same time, it includes moral and ethical aspects (see above). With a phenomenological perspective, the question will be asked how confidence is obtained.

The most important reference point of the phenomenological perspective is the learning-with-the-body approach oriented to the lifeworld as experienced in an immediate way.

> Phenomenology can be adopted to explore the unique meanings of any pedagogical experience or phenomenon, such as the experience of care, recognition, patience, encouragement, hope, respect, humbleness, and so forth. (van Manen, 2015, p. 40)

Moral and ethical dimensions of human existence in general can be approached by the phenomenological concept of the alien—*alien* is not to be misunderstood as deadly and aggressive extraterrestrial, as one might instantaneously think, but moreover as the other person as far as we cannot conquer or grasp her as such. Waldenfels (2011) coined the *phenomenology of the alien* by departing from the point that

> [...] each order [also that of perceiving another person as somebody who is not me] has its blind spot in the form of something unordered that does not merely constitute a deficit [...] In other words: the fact of reason is itself not reasonable. (ibid., p. 13)

His idea is that we experience the other by realizing such a blind spot, that is, the disruptions, fissures, and distances you feel within yourself. Here the other appears to you as what s/he, in fact, is: not you. As the pedagogical relation is grounded in the respect of the other as alien, also the concept of pedagogical tact plays around just this blind spot of all human orientation and thinking. This process of alienation of one's own firm structures of performative forms of presentation and expression enables an extension of the inner world "[...] through the aesthetic-mimetic recording of exterior and enables vivid experiences" (Wulf, 2010, p. 292).

However, blind spots may at first glance imply the lack of the usual social or ethical standards, that is, anomy (Durkheim, 1951), which overall lacks scholarly sharpness. To not fall into this trap demands awareness of where pedagogy ends, that is, its ethical limits and the pedagogical irresponsibility.

5 The Ethics of Pedagogical Tact

The limits of pedagogical tact are tactlessness as an intuitive deviation (Adorno, 1984); van Manen (2015) writes:

> [...] someone who is tactless is considered to be hasty, rash, indiscreet, imprudent, unwise, inept, insensitive, mindless, ineffective, and awkward. In general, to be tactless means to be disrespectful, ill-considered, blundering, clumsy, thoughtless, inconsiderate, and stupid. (ibid., p. 103)

Someone is especially tactless and out of tact (even out of tactlessness) if his/her action implies violence, deriving, for example, from ethnocentrism or racism, sexual harassment, or harm. Violence is usually connected to the visible body. However, with the sign of human civilization,

> [...] the rebellion against dominance, which due to its subtle institutionalization and shifting from physical torture to civilized discipline has become increasingly invisible and thus less transparent and eventual radical, continues to be topic of critical thinking. (Meyer-Drawe, 1990, p. 41)

According to Foucault (1995), social control and authority are not just imposed by social requirements or norms. Social violence inscribes itself on human corporeality. Socially mediated emotions and judgment become embodied, as part of our dispositions they form morality and routines. Such bodily inscriptions are the main power factors and, in the first place, the most effective instruments of authoritarian violence. Experiences of violence are inscribed on the body and precipitate an individual self-dynamic. With this perspective, e.g. child abuse can be theoretically grasped (Kraus, 2012).

Is it possible to react preventively in a situation of violence? Waldenfels does not give a definite answer; he stresses that violence, quasi-anonymously, creates an impersonal social situation, which makes it difficult to react to it: "Violence cannot be traced back to the initiative or property of individuals or groups, nor to a mediating authority, nor to encoded rules" (Waldenfels, 2002, p. 174). Violence is, in a way, anarchist. It is a social happening. Violence acts in a manner of its own and degrades all passively affected, and even the active participants to silent figures. Even if the offenders are the initiators and bear the social guilt for it, there is no possibility of winning over violence in its own terms. In order to be able to enter a dialogue again, one must respond to this stripping of authority and limited sphere of influence over violence. Non-violent acting is not just a question of exercising the will to suppress somebody's urge to perform inner aggressions; it is rather an active battle with a cultivated form of compulsion, which takes physical and also collective shape (Butler, 2015). Accordingly, there are no other means than tact for entering a dialogue again. Tact in the case of violence deals with forms of alienation and social expectations by making tuned social polyphony, coherent choreography, and dialogue possible again. However, tact is not measurable. One can also pretend tact, not least in order to hide one's violent behavior.

To come back to the pedagogical practices in the classroom: Our hypothesis is that in the classroom pedagogical tact is indispensable in creating conjunctive experiences with the aim to awaken own purposes and tasks toward school subjects among the younger. The questions to be answered by analyzing the empirical material are: What are the empirical indicators respective criteria on which we can draw tactful behavior? Is there any chance to tag some of these criteria from the external perspective, for example, by observing behavior or practices? How may violence and tact relate to each other?

6   Case Study

The lesson in the subject cluster natural sciences, biology, in this case, took place in March 2015 in the seventh grade (8 girls, 7 boys) of an integrated comprehensive school in Cologne/Germany. There were in total 40 lessons documented on film. All involved persons and teachers gave their permission to be recorded; those persons whose permissions were not procured were not filmed. For the case study, the sequence from minute 16:10 to minute 18:38 is chosen. The chosen sequence appears as characteristic of the entire lesson, firstly, in terms of the characteristics of pedagogical tact as presented above. The competence goal of lesson in grade 7 is: "Students can use microscopic examinations to explain that plants and other living things consist of cells" (MSW, 2013, p. 62); in the classroom, the technical term osmosis is mentioned.

The analysis of the material is based on the Documentary Method (Bohnsack, 2010) that departs from the assumption that the interlocutors share common orientation figures and, thus, conjunctive experiential spaces in their verbal contributions and gestures. Such orientation figures are generated by means of focusing metaphors as well as by negative counter-horizons. The film sequence we have chosen consists of all these features. The analysis of the lesson sequence is conducted in three steps: The transcription is interpreted in a formulating and then in an analytical-reflective way, together with a type formation. The analysis follows the hypothesis, that in the classroom pedagogical tact is indispensable in creating conjunctive experiences with the aim to awaken purposes toward the school subjects and tasks among the pupils that are their own. Hence, targeted teaching means authorizing the students to learn for themselves through a clear structuring of the lessons, a high proportion of real learning time, an atmosphere conducive to learning, clarity of content, meaningful communication, individual support, and transparent performance expectations.

Transcription of the film sequence:

T.   Who dares to do this? (…) Maria, Daniel? () Pardon? Yes.

T.   Very good. <u>Maria</u> is doing exactly right: one hand on the back: I_ Do you remember what the part is called? () Christian?

Ch.   _I Tripo::d.

T.   () Exactly, the tripod and?

Ch.   _I Foo::t.

T.   _I Precisely.

T.	Then we put- ah right Daniel, you still wanted (.) I_ ?
D.	_I Should I now also say how we do that with the- ().
T.	I_Maybe we'll bring someone else to the front. Maria maybe you go to your table again-. Who does it, the: Christoph, Could you do that?
C.	_I What?
T.	Over here, how to work with a microscope. You'll get it explained, you just have to (show it).

The addressed student Christoph gets up, comes to the teacher's desk, and stands with expectant expression and turned to class behind the electron microscope. The teacher gives him some space.

T.	What does Christoph do with the slide when the object is lying on it?
D.	So first put the plug in properly.

The teacher steps aside and the student carefully unwinds the cable from the electron microscope, not knowing where to look for a power outlet.

T.	We put it in the pocket; (soft laugh in the classroom).
D.	Then we rotate at the () I_lens
T.	_I Exactly we rotate it around first so we have a little space to move, therefore (.)
T.	**First** we do the project? Exactly Daniel.
D.	Yes, then we turn on the projectile on the side below.
T.	_I Exactly, that's the big pipe (). We look from the side; First take a small magnification of the lenses of the lens revolvers, take a small size, look that you get as close as possible. And then?
D.	When it's at the bottom, we turn on the light and see what happens.
T.	Very good. **Then it's time**, that we make a little drawing and then comes our big change, namely the osmotic effect that we want to prove. What are we going to do **next**?
C.	Ma:y I go to my place?
T.	Gladly.
T.	What are we going to do next? What are we going to do then, Maria?

6.1 Formulating Interpretation

At the beginning of the selected sequence, the teacher (T.) notes the name of a student on a merit-board that is clearly visible on the edge of the blackboard. The merit-board is used in all lessons as a pedagogical means of recognition, or disapproval of student contributions. Accordingly, it is divided into two columns. In the left-hand column many names are listed already for this lesson; it is reserved for good performance. The right column for disapproval is empty. T. asks if there is someone in the class who dares to demonstrate *something* to the class. As a matter of course, he names two female names and casually writes a name on the merit-board. The student Maria reports and gets invoked. She hesitantly asks if she is allowed to demonstrate *it*, and when prompted (*yes please*), she goes to the side table, picks up the electronic microscope, and carefully places it on the teacher's desk. For this she gets praised by the teacher. He reflects her movements by saying: *Very good. M. is doing exactly right*. Then he picks up the microscope, puts it on the floor, and keeps it in sight for the class. The student Maria says something hardly audible. However, T. directs the view to the class and asks for the correct designation. Christian gets addressed and he gives the correct answer, slowly and with audible difficulties in verbal expression. T. notes his name on the merit-board. T. requests student Daniel to act; Daniel asks in an equally fragmented manner back what he is required to do. T. leaves the question unanswered and addresses the class. Maria is asked to seat herself and she is visibly satisfied with this task. T. asks student Christoph to continue, whereupon Christoph reacts with an astonished *What?* T. asks him with a firm and nice voice to show how to work with the microscope and offers him his assistance. T. stands upright and calmly directed to the class. Christoph comes to the teacher's desk and looks expectantly into the classroom. The teacher steps aside and Christoph takes the position of the teacher, he looks satisfied, then following the instructions of the pupil Daniel. The teacher asks the class how Christoph (correctly) uses the slide. Daniel suggests first connecting the electronic microscope to a power source. Apparently, there is no outlet, as Christoph searches for it in vain. T. puts the power plug into his pocket, commenting this with a smile. The students in the class start to laugh. The next instruction refers to the lens, which is to be placed in a work-safe position. T. instructs the action itself; although he praises Daniel, student Christoph takes the microscope and puts it in front of him. Daniel and T. instruct Christoph to place the apparatus in the correct position. T. praises Daniel's remarks again, gives a thumbs-up, and introduces the next lesson sequence by noting that it is time for everyone to

6.2 Reflective Interpretation and Type Formation

sketch the osmotic effect. At the same time, he announces something new and asks the question what that could be to the class and then to Maria. Christoph politely asks whether he can sit back on his seat and the teacher says *gladly*, politely expressing agreement.

6.2 Reflective Interpretation and Type Formation

In this sequence of a lesson, we recognize the following conjunctive experiential spaces, more accurate, the existential contexts of experience and practical knowledge, out of which habitual correspondences and action-guiding, that is, atheoretical sets of knowledge derive:

1. Good performance: This focusing metaphor manifests itself in the use of the merit-board only appreciating the pupils' performance. At the same time, this creates a counter-horizon to the otherwise usual practice of using the merit-board in class more likely to disapprove their lesson contributions.
2. Confidence and gradual transfer of responsibility to the students: First, the teacher gives the pupils an advance of trust, which he continues to increase up to the point of co-operation and, in a way, even to hand over the responsibility for the lessons to them. At the beginning of the lesson, he tries to take the pupils out of reserve by asking for a brave one. After a brief passage of instruction, he addresses a girl as a co-operation partner with an own will (*ah right D., you still wanted (.) I_?*). However, T. does not (yet) pursue it. Someone else is supposed to do the work. A boy gets addressed who reacts ignorantly. The teacher offers him his assistance. The fact that the boy then surrenders expectantly to the class can be read as a vote of confidence based on previous experience. By stepping aside, the teacher gives the stage to the student, and then even the role of an expert, when he starts to act together with the female pupil who gives him instructions. Thereby, the teacher solves small problems and gives some hints. However, by asking whether he himself is correct and what is it that comes afterward, the teacher plays the ball back to the students in the sense of *you know better*. For the class, the performance of the specialist pupils thus must appear as excellent. After completing the demonstration, the entire class gets asked to make a drawing of what no one has seen yet: osmosis. The teacher does not say exactly what to do but asks the students. They will maybe answer that the microscope will make osmosis visible. This gives them certain authorship about the further course of the lesson.

3. Harmonic teamwork: During the setup of the microscope, the two acting students and the teacher make the impression of a perfectly coordinated scientific team. Thereby, specialist knowledge gets focused in a mostly corporeal way.
4. Counterbalance to school assessment systems: Due to the exclusively positive performance rating, the merit-board as a means of assessment is used only for appreciation. Neither learning progress gets measured, nor are support-oriented feedbacks on possible improvement given.
5. There is no violence to be perceived.

7 Summary and Outlook

Pedagogical tact cannot be rationally anticipated and measured. However, it is a component of teacher professionality and of the theory-praxis relation that is remaining an outstanding issue of research on education.

> Concepts of learning and education that take their negativity into account has already been the focus of extensive theoretical research […]. The empirical application and further development of such approaches is still, however, missing. Pedagogically valuable areas of conflict, as well as the tacit dimensions of pedagogy, must still be thoroughly investigated. (Kraus, 2016, p. 146)

In the analysis, the pedagogical tact of the teacher turned out as letting the pupils experience and learn things in order to make them their own by holding back and successively passing over responsibility to them. The teacher does this with words, movements, and gestures. It is obvious in the data that the orientation frames of the pupils are mostly missing self-confidence, being afraid of not to know, or of being held back. The orientation frames are taken into account by the teacher by performing humbleness and understatement, and by explicitly replacing their unnecessary uncertainty by (self-)confidence. An important reference in this process is specialist knowledge that gets ascribed to the acting students, and not the teacher, as it is usually. The learning demands are adapted to the pupils' possibilities. However, there is no transparency in terms of the performance expectations, and the pupils seem to have done fine, however simple their contribution to the lesson was. There are no proposals for performance improvement. The merit-board is used rather to subvert the assessing function of school, and not to support it. This can be read as a form of protest against the performance evaluation at school, which would be violence degrading the active participants to silent figures and undermining pedagogical tact. Indeed, pedagogical tact and violence form a kind of gray zone in terms of reflection, as their corporeal dimension is not easily graspable. Violence can be implicitly performed right within actions that are explicitly declared as pedagogically tactful. At the same time, in a pedagogical situation, one needs pedagogical tact to prevent violence. From this point of view, the question for further (empirical) examination is how performance evaluation and pedagogical tact can operate together.

References

Adorno, T. (1984). *Minima Moralia*. Suhrkamp.
Asbrand, B. (2011). *Dokumentarische Methode*. Retrieved November 11, 2020, from http://www.fallarchiv.uni-kassel.de/lernumgebung/methodenlernpfade/dokumentarische-methode/
Bohnsack, R. (2010). *Rekonstruktive Sozialforschung. Einführung in qualitative Methoden*. Barbara Budrich.
Butler, J. (2015). *Notes Toward a Performative Theory of Assembly*. Harvard University Press.
Durkheim, È. (1951). *Suicide*. Free Press.
Foucault, M. (1995). *Discipline and Punish: The Birth of the Prison*. Second Vintage Books Edition.
Friesen, N. (2017). The Pedagogical Relation Past and Present: Experience, Subjectivity and Failure. In: *Curriculum Studies, May*, pp. 743–756. Retrieved November 8, 2020, from https://www.tandfonline.com/doi/abs/10.108 0/00220272.2017.1320427
Friesen, N., & Osguthorpe, R. (2018). Tact and the Pedagogical Triangle. The Authenticity of Teachers in Relation. *Teaching and Teacher Education, 70*, 255–264.
Gebauer, G., & Wulf, C. (1996). *Mimesis Culture Art Society*. California University Press.
Herbart, J. F. (1997 [1802]). Erste Vorlesung über Pädagogik. In D. Benner (Ed.), *Johann Friedrich Herbart: Systematische Pädagogik, Bd. 1, Ausgewählte Texte* (pp. 43–46). Dt. Studien – Verlag.
Kraus, A. (2012). Diskurse, Sexualität und Macht in pädagogischen Kontexten. In A. Kraus (Ed.), *Körperlichkeit in der Schule. Aktuelle Körperdiskurse und ihre Empirie. Sexualität und Macht* (pp. 109–132). Oberhausen.
Kraus, A. (2016). *Perspectives on Performativity. Pedagogical Knowledge in Teacher Education*. Waxmann.
Luhmann, N., & Schorr, K.-E. (2000). *Problems of Reflection in the System of Education*. Waxmann.

Martens, M., Asbrand, B., & Spieß, C. (2015). Lernen mit Dingen. Prozesse zirkulierender Referenz im Unterricht. *ZISU, 1*, 48–65. https://doi.org/10.3224/zisu.v4i1.21314

Meyer, H. (2003). Zehn Merkmale guten Unterrichts. Empirische Befunde und didaktische Ratschläge. *Pädagogik, 55*(10), 36–43.

Meyer-Drawe, K. (1990). *Illusionen von Autonomie. Diesseits von Ohnmacht und Allmacht des Ich*. Kirchheim.

MSW: Ministry for School and Further Education North Rhine-Westphalia. (2013). *Kernlehrplan für die Gesamtschule. Sekundarstufe I in Nordrhein-Westfalen Naturwissenschaften Biologie, Chemie, Physik*. Retrieved November 8, 2020, from https://www.schulentwicklung.nrw.de/lehrplaene/lehrplan/130/KLP_GE_NW.pdf

Muth, J. (1962). *Pädagogischer Takt*. Quelle & Meyer.

Schön, D. A. (1987). *Educating the Reflective Practitioner: Towards a New Design for Teaching and Learning in the Professions*. Jossey-Bass.

Suzuki, S. (2010). *Takt in Modern Education*. Waxmann.

van Manen, M. (2015). *Pedagogical Tact: Knowing What to Do When You Don't Know What to Do*. Left Coast Press Inc.

Waldenfels, B. (2002). *Bruchlinien der Erfahrung*. Suhrkamp.

Waldenfels, B. (2011). *Phenomenology of the Alien: Basic Concepts*. Northwestern University Press.

Wulf, C. (2010). *Mimesis, Performativity, Ritual*. Transcript.

Wulf, C., & Zirfas, J. (2005). *Ikonologie des Performativen*. Fink.

Zirfas, J., & Gödde, G. (2012). *Takt und Taktlosigkeit. Über Ordnungen und Unordnungen in Kunst, Kultur und Therapie*. Transcript.

Gestures in the Classroom

Regula Fankhauser and Angela Kaspar

1 Introduction

Gestures play an important role in everyday school and teaching, even if they are rarely explicitly addressed. Gestures such as the pupils' hands going up or the raised index finger of the teacher are emblematic of teaching and learning. Often, their meaning seems to be immediately clear. They are institution-specific in nature; their use stands for the role-forming behaviour that students and teachers perform every day. The student's raised hand shows his or her willingness to respond and desire to learn. With their raised index finger, the teachers make it clear that they can demand the attention of the pupils and rebuke inappropriate behaviour. The two emblematic gestures can easily be translated into language by replacing them with a corresponding verbal statement.

In contrast, other gestural actions that accompany, support or disrupt lessons are semantically more difficult to grasp. Is a glance at the clock or out of the window an educational gesture? Is there something gestural about leaning back on a chair or resting one's head on the desk? And if so, what do these gestures convey?

R. Fankhauser (✉)
University of Teacher Education Berne, Bern, Switzerland
e-mail: regula.fankhauser@phbern.ch

A. Kaspar
University of Teacher Education Lucerne, Lucerne, Switzerland

© The Author(s), under exclusive license to Springer Nature Switzerland AG 2022
A. Kraus, C. Wulf (eds.), *The Palgrave Handbook of Embodiment and Learning*,
https://doi.org/10.1007/978-3-030-93001-1_10

In gestures, language and body interlock in a way that might be sometimes entirely clear but not always. Therefore, we wish to examine the conceptual question of what constitutes a gesture and what meaning it acquires in interactive processes of teaching. For this, it seems useful to establish a provisional heuristic definition. In this article we understand gestures as a physical manifestation that occurs as part of a continuum of movement. A gesture is characterised by the fact that it stands out or is accentuated, that is, it is an interruption of the movement pattern that may be noticeable to a greater or lesser degree (Luehrs-Kaiser, 2000). This physical accentuation is significant, even if the meaning is not always clear and often remains unconscious. Gestures are physical, non-verbal expressions and yet are inextricably linked to language, thinking and imagination (McNeill, 1992; Wulf, 2011). Their relationship to language, to a greater or lesser extent, structures the wide range of gestures we are familiar with. At one end of the spectrum, we find gestures which are clear and obvious in their meaning, and at the other end gestures which remain opaque and diffuse and are difficult to translate into language.

School is a field characterised by the "hegemony of the linguistic" (Falkenberg, 2013, p. 5). In other words, a world where language dominates. The initiation into this world goes hand in hand with disciplining and immobilising the child's body (Langer, 2008). Nevertheless, silent practices such as gestures are omnipresent in schools and lessons. They can support, replace or undermine verbal expressions. As different as the relationship of gestures to linguistic expressions is, just as different is their relationship to institutional order. Gestural actions—both by teachers and by pupils—can follow institution-specific objectives. Gestural expressions—especially from pupils— can also compete with and disregard these objectives. Such gestural expressions mark a boundary of institutional logic and force their representatives to react.

In the following we focus on student gestures which are interpreted as annoying or disruptive. We are focusing our attention on the perspective that the teachers take. What gestural actions in the classroom do they find disruptive or annoying? Why and in what respect do they feel disrupted or annoyed? And what meaning do they ascribe to fleeting physical expressions?

To answer these questions, we will proceed in three stages. To begin with, we will focus on ritualised gestures and the work done on them in educational gesture research. The subject of our study came out of this research—student gestures of resistance. Secondly, we will further differentiate this subject with reference to theoretical concepts by Goffman. The third stage is to apply the areas and questions that arise to empirical material and to refine them. Finally, we will use our findings to expand the knowledge base of educational gesture research.

2   Ritualised Gestures

In the German-speaking field of discourse, anthropologically oriented gesture research, which emerged from the Berlin Study on Rituals, has a different conception of gestures to linguistic approaches (Kellermann & Wulf, 2011; Wulf, 2010, 2011). Linguistic, semiotic communications and media-theoretical approaches typically consider the phenomenon of gestures as one of many modalities involved in a fundamentally multi-modal process; the body is conceived as part and parcel of language and communication (Müller et al., 2014). Gestures are considered to illustrate, complement or counteract speech. In contrast, Wulf (ibid.) and his research group emphasise the autonomy of a physical-gestural expression. Gestures cannot be replaced by language. They are understood as fleeting but significant movements of the body in which—often unconsciously—emotions and moods are expressed. Gestures cannot be reduced to speech. But despite this autonomy, gestures are thought as inextricably interwoven with language.

The Berlin Study on Rituals focuses on institutionally preformed gestures. Many gestural performances that can be observed in school and education have a ritual character. This can be illustrated by the example of a school enrolment ceremony at which the new pupils are presented with a sunflower (Wulf, 2011, p. 18): With the handing over of the sunflower the pupils are accepted at school; the admission to the school is supposed to be the prelude to a happy time at school. The different moments of the celebration are condensed and intensified in the gesture. The meaning of the gesture—a welcome and congratulations—is immediately understandable to all those taking part in the celebration, without having to translate it into language. This is an emblematic gesture in Posner's sense (Posner, 1986): the handing over of the sunflower is a gesture that is consciously and intentionally used to convey a certain message.

Ritualised gestures are omnipresent in schools and lessons. Kellerman and Wulf (2011) distinguish different forms: *space-constituting gestures* define, for example, where the stage and the auditorium are located. When the teacher points to the blackboard with an arm movement, she turns the blackboard space into a stage on which knowledge is brought out publicly, that is, in front of the pupils watching. *Gestures of institutional typification* physically and symbolically indicate that someone is a student or a teacher. Pupils putting up their hands can serve as an example here. *Theatrical gestures* in turn accompany and intensify lecture and presentation sequences. And finally, *gestures of hierarchisation* stage claims to authority.

The main function of school rituals is community building and initiation into the institution. The repeated performance of ritualised practices generates continuity and coherence; it has an inclusive character. In the performance of institution-specific, ritualised gestures, the legitimacy of the institution and its order is confirmed. Gestures are not learnt through language and thought but in performance and mimesis. Through physical-symbolic reconstruction, the validity of the institution is constantly updated anew. Students who imitate and practise institution-specific gestures become part of the institution through mimesis. Imitation has the function of initiation: practising and participating in a collective social practice in which social positions are allocated and stabilised. The power-related character of many ritualised gestures can thus be obvious. The exercise of affirmative, institution-specific gestures is associated with a subjection to the institution and its normative logic (Gebauer & Wulf, 1998; Müller & Posner, 2004). When students refuse, parody or counteract ritualised gestures, this may easily be interpreted as resistance by the teacher. Then, they call into question the legitimacy of the institution.

3   Disruptive Gestures

These ritualised, institution-specific gestures are opposed by many bodily actions, whose semantic status is more difficult to determine. Many of them are not obvious and therefore do not attract attention. They get lost in the flow of permanent movements. Some, however, emerge from this flow. These are mainly movements of pupils which are perceived as accentuated by teachers who have to observe pupils as part of their job. For example, a pupil shifting once on their chair is likely to go unnoticed, while a sustained rocking is obvious and considered to be articulating something, which can be significant for the teacher. Thus, under certain circumstances, rocking can lead to the disruption of lessons.

Such expressions arise from a particular situation and cannot be read in isolation. Many of them serve the purpose of community building among peers: roving glances, a brief nod of the head, a fleeting turning towards or away from the body. If these articulations are understood as 'disruptive' or 'resistant', they appear to interrupt the institutional logic of order. More unspecific gestural practices are not always bound to language and often not at all. They are silent articulations that react responsively to the language-dominated teaching situation.

Thus, e.g. playing with objects during a lesson in the classroom can be a gesture of resistance that marks the "boundary of the discourse in class" (Falkenberg, 2013, p. 5). Even a brief high-five or a small kick—all these "mini-performances" (Alkemeyer, 2000, p. 394) as they are common among peers—can be a sign that the children are escaping the institutional requirements and trying to establish their own fleeting territory within the institutional framework by means of peer practices. However, whether these are conscious and intentional disruptions are not yet clear.

We are confronted here with a difficulty that affects gestures in general, but which is particularly true in the case of rather diffuse, difficult-to-read gestures among peers: their "situational contingency" (Kellermann & Wulf, 2011, p. 27). In order to address this difficulty, we draw on theoretical considerations by Irving Goffman.

In his microsociological studies Goffman observes gestural behaviour in specific interactions (Goffman, 1974). Gestures here are practices that arise in and from the situation. According to Goffman, gestures are expressive elements of an interaction and they have higher contingency as linguistic utterances. However, Goffman distinguishes between gestures with less contingency and those with more. The former are described as situated, the latter as situational (Goffman, 1981). Situated gestures can be dissociated from the situation in which they occur. One might say they have an emblematic character. The raised hand of the pupil can again be taken as an example: although it is paradigmatic for the situation of the pupil in the classroom, it can be taken out of the classroom situation and be fully understood in another. By contrast, situative gestures originate in the situation; their meaning remains tied to it and cannot be understood without it.

Perception and interpretation play a key role in the understanding of gestures, especially situational gestures. Gestural actions in general appear as a moment of physical presence, which can be read by the other person as a kind of art display. The intention or even the calculation that lies behind a gesture must be interpreted and anticipated by the interacting partner (Goffman, 1970). What is shown in the gestural representation gains its meaning firstly in the way it is read and through the reaction of those that perceive and interpret what is shown and to what it refers. What is crucial in the meaning of the gesture is not only the intention of the originator but also the perception, interpretation and reaction of the viewer. For the latter, the 'frame' is ineluctable: Goffman introduces the institutional concept of gestural meaning-construction with the concept of the 'frame'. Frames are schemes that organise experience. They define the situation in which an event occurs. Otherwise meaningless aspects may become meaningful by a 'frame'. A frame enables "its user to locate, perceive, identify and label a seemingly infinite number of concrete occurrences defined in its terms" (Goffman, 1974, p. 21). It helps the individual "in deciding what it is that is going on" (ibid., p. 26). It is the frame which—like a stage setting—situates, accentuates and dramatises the events that happen within it. The frame predefines what type of situation the events present and how it should be understood. Frames are models learnt through socialisation which help 'read' situations as significant and meaningful. The process of framing is indispensable, especially for situational gestures. The framework determines whether the accentuated movement of a body or body part appears significant.

Let us return to the mini-performances that take place in the classroom among peers—all the short glances, the little pushes, the teasing articulated in gestures—and ask ourselves to what extent these can be understood as classroom disruption.

Educational teaching research, which deals with teaching disorders, speaks of a 'semantic instability' of the subject and highlights the role of perspectival perception (Makarova et al., 2014, p. 137). Actions that are perceived as disruptive could, for example, differ considerably depending on whether there is a high or low level of disruption in the classroom. The evaluation of the disruption and the feeling of being disrupted are also dependent on underlying norms (Walter & Walter, 2014). If we limit instances of disruption to motoric phenomena and gestures, the lack of clarity is increased: the question as to whether a certain movement is perceived as exposed and meaningful, and also whether it can be ascribed the significance of a (deliberate) disruption, is highly dependent on the perspective of the viewer and the underlying system of values of the person who interprets the gestures. In other words, the meaning of situational gestures is of high semantic instability. To decide what happens in the classroom during a small gestural intermezzo requires an appropriate framing. It is the framework which helps to identify and name the incident and thus to remedy its 'semantic instability'.

Despite the lack of clarity in defining the subject, class disruptions are a fact and teachers are given training to learn and practice gestures and body postures as a preventative means of avoiding class disruptions (Pille, 2009). Having preventative and intervention options in relation to class disruptions is a key part of classroom management and the subject of wide research. However, less attention has been paid to the process of perception and interpretation which leads the teacher to define an incident in the classroom as class disruption. Why does a teacher perceive a certain physical movement in the classroom as obvious and meaningful? And as disruptive? And how does the process of verbalisation, in which a silent incident in the background moves into the language-dominated foreground, take shape?

Or with reference to Goffman: which frame is applied by the teacher to localise and identify a gesture of resistance? And what is the relationship between this frame and the institutional system of logic?

4   Case Study

To investigate these questions, we will be considering empirical material from a research project financed by Berne University of Teacher Education. The study deals with the role of bodies in teaching. It focuses on the teachers' perspective and examines how they perceive and interpret body-bound teaching practices. We worked with the method of video elicitation (Henry & Fetters, 2012). Here, the videographic material serves to support processes of perception and interpretation that are bound to the filmed situation. An image is used as a stimulus to recall scenes that occurred and to verbalise the tacit knowledge that is activated. It is particularly the silent, body-focused practices which come to the fore through the image, and whose meaning can be reconstructed.

In our case, the informants, teachers, had their lessons filmed and then they discussed scenes in a guided interview. The direction was left up to them in a number of ways: firstly, they determined which teaching sessions were recorded with which camera angle. Secondly, they selected sequences for the interview from the extensive video material. It was therefore up to the teachers which (body) practices were chosen. The interview guide was developed based on the concept of 'Professional Vision' (Sherin, 2007). The test subjects were each asked to freely formulate their thoughts on a sequence. This question of associations with a 'scene' was followed by questions in which the video sequences were described, interpreted, explained or evaluated. The transcriptions of the interviews were openly coded according to the principle of increasing abstraction in a first step, axially in a second, and selectively in a third. In a contrasting approach, a typology was finally developed which generalises the concepts of perception and interpretation of body-related teaching practices across all analytic sequences (Glaser, 1965).

As we are focusing in this article on the subject of disruptive gestures, and we are investigating just one aspect of the project, that is, how do social agents (in this case the teacher) construct meaning with regard to the perception of gestures of resistance. We are interested in what physical movements are perceived by teachers as obvious gestures, what meanings they ascribe to them and, in doing so, what interpretive frames they use.

In the following case we begin by describing the generative normative context. Including an extract from an interview, we look at the teacher's/informant's understanding of learning and what role she assigns to the body and body-focused teaching practices. We then focus on interview passages in which the teacher talks about gestures that she describes as disruptive and analyse what she says in reply to the questions of the pupils.

The teacher, whom we will call Anna, has several years of professional experience and teaches at a primary school in an urban area in Switzerland. Her class is an integration class, so the size of the class is smaller than a regular class.

Anna's beliefs are based on progressive educational ideas and this motivates the way she thinks and acts in a school-based situation. The pupils' well-being is the focus of Anna's activities. She considers school often to be rigidly controlled and regimented; she considers the discipline that is implemented through, among other things, controlling the children's bodies, to be detrimental to their development. Anna therefore considers it her task, to create a space, in which children can feel free. She develops an idealised concept of the body as the site where children experience the freedom to be themselves.

She considers those lessons that involve free sequences of movements or dance improvisation in particular to be ideal learning opportunities, because they give the children the space to discover and express themselves.

The following quotation demonstrates Anna's fundamental ideas:

Anna: [...] School is something very structured, where in a lot of things the children have to always do what the teacher says. For me, I always try, in PE and elsewhere, to create opportunities where they can do something themselves. So that it's not about always just following and doing what they've been told. Within this frame I create and with the clearly set boundaries, I allow as much freedom as possible. But just [...], always within it, everyone can be free, without disrupting someone else in their freedom. That's what it's about for me. [...].

The quote illustrates that—from Anna's point of view—school is generally closely associated with order and discipline that limit the freedom of the individual. She distances herself from this institutional demand to conform that is imposed on the children by repeatedly arranging less-structured teaching sequences in opposition to the movements that are imposed on them. Her aim is to create more creative scope for children. She wants students not only to practise institutionalised gestures but also to explore the expressive possibilities of physical movement.

Particularly in PE, she wants to create the opportunity for less coordinated, rule-free, gestural-physical expressions to allow them to support children's development. The freedom of pupils should be as comprehensive as possible. It is only limited if the freedom of others is restricted. In a protected environment created by the teachers, and primarily through free movement, everyone should be able to 'express or find themselves' equally.

Anna demonstrates to us during the research period with some of the video sequences she selects for the meetings, how she implements her idea of ideal teaching. For example, she focuses on a sequence from gymnastics in which she gives the children the task of moving to a piece of music in the room and using a scarf creatively. Anna sees this scene as an opportunity for the pupils to experience themselves as being in charge of themselves through determining their movement themselves and 'to find themselves' through it.

In addition to these positive examples, Anna's video elicitation repeatedly focuses on gestures that she describes as disturbing. In the following we will concentrate on interview excerpts in which she discusses such a scene. The scene occurs at a moment of transition from one part of the lesson to the next.

The pupils are asked to sit down in a circle. The pupil Arsim uses gestures to claim a specific space in the circle. He puffs out his chest and approaches Jari, bumps him with his chest and slaps him lightly on the back of the neck.

While looking through the video material, Anna immediately got stuck on this scene. She played it back several times and was horrified by what she saw. The scene disturbed her so much that she turned away from it and watched more footage before returning to the sequence and discussing it. In answer to the question about the meaning of the sequence it becomes clear that Anna understands this gestural behaviour as a crude demonstration of power and locates its origin outside school.

> Anna: For me that's a typical breaktime/playground situation and I know that these children and their fathers often act like that in conflicts. It is a display of power, it's about showing who's top dog, marking their territory. I know that these children grow up with posturing like that, that it's part of their daily life. Of course, as a teacher with my objective and my view of humanity: I don't want posturing like that in my classroom. They already have the awareness, but it's so firmly rooted, if the cousin behaves like that and achieves something, and the

dad does it and achieves something, so of course it is very plausible that it's a behaviour that brings success and that you'll do it too. Because a behaviour that's beneficial, you'll keep it, no matter what the teacher says, and one that's not beneficial, you'll give it up.

For Anna, the gestural behaviour of the pupils comes from spaces outside the classroom, in particular from the family space, which she perceives as being patriarchally structured. Anna interprets the gestures of Arsim as a demonstration of power which he's learnt from his father. In her interpretation she uses metaphors from the animal world, so she reads his gestures as showing who's 'top dog' and marking their 'territory'. The gestures are seen as animal and uncivilised behaviours reflecting a child's tough life. In Anna's view, they are gestures that are distant from school and inadequate, that express illegitimate male claims to power and space. Such 'posturing' is learnt in socialisation processes in the family.

Anna removes the gestures from the specific situation and shifts in her interpretation to a more general level. Arsim's gestures become the gestures of fathers and cousins. Anna focuses on the aspect of power that is demonstrated in the gestures and states that she won't tolerate behaviour like that in the classroom, that is, in her territory. She justifies this by reference to her 'remit' as teacher—although it's not clear what she includes in this—and also by a conception of humanity that seems incompatible to her with the pupil's dominant behaviour. Her teaching appears here as a corrective to the (gestural) behaviours acquired in the children's social milieu. Anna considers it her duty to prevent gestures entering the classroom from outside school that represent (alternative) claims to power. So, the bodies of the two pupils are seen as conditioned by family and gender-specific influences from which they must be 'liberated'.

To Anna it's clear that the pupils are in a field of tension: the behaviour that is associated with success in the family sphere of influence does not belong in the code of values at school. Moreover, at this point, for the first time it seems that the pupils' behaviour is not only a threat to the other pupils, but that the gestures also question the authority of the teachers, whose voice is not heard.

In her description and interpretation of the gestures, which are understood to be power-based, Anna has so far referred to the influence of social background and family environment and the gender norms that accompany them. In the following passage Anna talks specifically about this aspect and mentions the family's migration background:

Anna: Simply the posture, when he pulls back his shoulders, and speaks with a stronger accent than he actually has: "What are you doing here?" [Speaks with an aggressive, sharp tone with a foreign accent]. And his posture makes him seem bigger than he is, with his body and his shoulders back, his head up and an aggressive look. And then this gesture, a hit on the back of the head, is for me a very strong demonstration of power. [...] And his cousin once visited the school [...] And he is in the 4th class. And came into the classroom like this. And then I said, "You are welcome to visit", but then I also said how I'd like his posture to be different, I'd like it different from that because I'm in charge here. [GRINS] and it's no one but me who can act like that here.

Alongside the boys' gestures, which are discussed extensively here, Anna refers to another characteristic, namely the foreign accent of Arsim. She not only mentions but also imitates it. Through this re-enactment Anna emphasises the student's ethno-cultural background. The gestures of Arsim (and another student) are therefore turned into gestures shaped by socio-cultural origin and gender.

The last part of text in the sequence reveals another key aspect in the analysis: in her story about the cousin visiting the school it is clear that the power-associated behaviour of Arsim is not only problematic because it affects one or more pupils. What is revealed here is that Anna sees it as a threat to the teacher-pupil hierarchy. By making it clear that she only acts 'like that' because she's the 'boss' here, she shows her own claim to power in the classroom. The pupils' behaviour is seen by her not only as an attack on the freedom of other pupils, but also as an attack on her as a teacher.

In summary, it can be asserted that Anna considers free physical self-expression to be the ideal. According to her conception, it is through this that the real 'self' finds expression. The aim of their reform-driven pedagogically oriented teaching is to enable such free movement sequences again and again and thus create an alternative to physical standardisation through school discipline.

Anna engages with gestural behaviour in the video conversations, which irritates or disturbs her. The analysis of such a sequence illustrates that Anna understands the gestures of a student as an illegitimate demonstration of power. Other interpretations, for example, that the slap on the back of the head could be understood as a playful gesture among peers, are ignored. The gestures are power-based in Anna's perception because they reflect the space-consuming behaviour of male family members. For Anna, these physical performances by the student are shaped by his ethno-socio-cultural background.

In this interpretation the bodies of the students become over shaped and thus unfree bodies dominated by an archaic outside world.

The gestures are disturbing for Anna for various reasons: not only do they oppress the classmate, but in Anna's reading they also represent male dominant behaviour which also attacks her as a teacher and thus the institutional logic. Above all, however, the student's behaviour undermines Anna's belief in the free, authentic self. She considers it her task to put a stop to these gestures that she sees as power-infused and to release the bodies from their conditioning.

In her interpretation, she does not reflect on her own involvement in the school hierarchy. She is consistently critical of her students' power-based demeanour. Her claim to power as a teacher, however, seems to be unproblematic for her. She reinstates her own defining power by devaluing the pupils' gestures and their family background.

The micro-scene, which led to extensive explanations in the video elicitation, provides the starting point for the discussion with the teacher. A brief, silent incident between two pupils sets off an extensive discussion where the teacher justifies her views. Her perception of the scene is connected with various associations in the teacher's mind. The silent scene between the two pupils must, we conclude, represent a type of threat; the wilfulness evident in the gesture provokes the teacher to define the incident by drawing on models from her past experience.

As a teacher Anna functions within a specific pedagogical frame. She is guided by progressive educational views and wants to create free spaces in her lessons in which the children can develop with the help of free and improvised movement sequences. In this way she wants to make it possible for an 'authentic' self to express itself and grow. The short gestural interactive sequence between the two pupils is seen by the teacher as an attack on this educational model: the small scene questions its ideal of the innocent, free and authentic child.

The teacher reacts to this irritation with the attempt to decode the body-related, fleeting incident using concepts of social differentiation: she explains the pupils' behaviour in terms of their social and cultural conditioning. With reference to Goffman, it can be asserted that she constructs a situated gesture from a situative one. She disengages the gesture which the pupil performed in the short interval, from the classroom situation and generalises it as a gesture of a male from a migration background. Instead of understanding the small mini-performance that takes place on the fringes of the classroom as part of a peer situation into which she as a teacher may have limited insight, she turns it into an emblematic gesture which she considers to be culturally determined.

In such a gesture, teachers are confronted with norms, values and behaviour that are diametrically opposed to those of the school as an institution. The teacher frames the gesture as an actualisation of an off-school code and therefore as a disturbance.

The teacher tries to explain the disruptive gesture she has observed as being ethno-culturally motivated and she attempts to impose her norm-based school rules of interaction. There are two mutually exclusive conceptions at play here: on the one hand the concept of the free and authentic child that is part of the liberal educational theory she espouses, and the other is the world outside education that impacts negatively on the children in a gender-specific and socio-cultural specific way. The former is normalised, while the latter is excluded as intolerable. Her evaluation can only be understood against the background of certain values and norm systems, the questioning of which the teacher experiences as an attack on her professional self-image, her authority and the institutional order.

5   Conclusion

Our analysis focuses on how gestures are perceived and interpreted in the context of school and education. By focusing on disruptive gestures, we were interested in investigating what behaviour is perceived by the teacher as dissenting and why. Both, in drawing attention to the gesture and, in the way, she describes and interprets it, the teacher draws on institutional framing to re-establish the disturbed order.

The interlocking of feeling threatened and institutional framing in the perception and interpretation of gestures of resistance seems to us to be an important outcome of our research. The feeling of insecurity generated arises not only from the disruption to the content of the lesson and the teaching concept, but perhaps more from the physical performance of such gestures. In our view, the fact that the micro-scene performed in gestures generates such a heated discussion explaining and justifying the reaction is more to do with the quality of the gestural action per se, that is, its physicality, than with the content of the gestural incident. This small gestural incident perhaps has such an impact precisely because it is both silent and blatant at the same time. Accentuated in its appearance, but diffuse in its meaning, it seems to threaten not only the teacher's self-conception, but also to challenge the institutional logic.

Educational gesture research has hitherto dealt mainly with ritualised gestures. Ritualised gestures confirm the institutional order; they stage and execute its norms and rules in an intensified way that can be experienced on an aesthetic level as well. In this way they do not touch the 'hegemony of the linguistic' or disrupt the world where language dominates, which characterises the institution of school. In contrast, resistant gestures elude this logic. They call the institutional order into question and destabilise it. What happens silently backstage shows the limitations of the language-dominated front of stage. In the interpretation of the event by the teacher, the events are brought from the back to the front of the stage and the institutional 'hegemony of the linguistic' is restored. The aim of that is to stabilise the position of the teacher and the order which he or she represents.

References

Alkemeyer, T. (2000). *Zeichen, Körper und Bewegung. Aufführungen von Gesellschaft im Sport*. Freie Universität.

Falkenberg, M. (2013). *Die Schweigsamkeit des Schulischen*. Lucius & Lucius.

Gebauer, G., & Wulf, C. (1998). *Spiel, Ritual, Geste: Mimetisches Handeln in der sozialen Welt*. Rowohlt.

Glaser, B. G. (1965). The Constant Comparative Method of Qualitative Analysis. *Social Problems, 12*, 436–445.

Goffman, E. (1970). *Strategic Interaction*. University of Pennsylvania Press.

Goffman, E. (1974). *Frame Analysis. An Essay on the Organization of Experience*. Harper & Row.

Goffman, E. (1981). *Strategische Interaktion*. Hanser.

Henry, S. G., & Fetters, M. D. (2012). Video Elicitation Interviews: A Qualitative Research Method for Investigating Physician-Patient Interactions. *Annals of Family Medicine, 10*(2), 118–125.

Kellermann, I., & Wulf, C. (2011). Gesten in der Schule. Zur Dynamik körperlicher Ausdrucksformen. In C. Wulf, B. Althans, K. Audehm, F. N. Blaschke, I. Kellermann, R. Mattig, & S. Schinkel (Eds.), *Die Geste in Erziehung, Bildung und Sozialisation. Ethnographische Feldstudien* (pp. 27–82). Springer Verlag für Sozialwissenschaften.

Langer, A. (2008). *Disziplinieren und entspannen: Körper in der Schule—eine diskursanalytische Ethnographie*. transcript.

Luehrs-Kaiser, K. (2000). Exponiertheit als Kriterium von Gesten. In M. Egidi, O. Schneider, M. Schöning, I. Schütze, & C. Torra-Mattenklott (Eds.), *Gestik: Figuren des Körpers in Text und Bild* (pp. 43–52). Gunter Narr.

Makarova, E., Herzog, W., & Schönbächler, M.-T. (2014). Wahrnehmung und Interpretation von Unterrichtsstörungen aus Schülerperspektive sowie aus Sicht der Lehrpersonen. *Psychologie in Erziehung und Unterricht, 61*, 127–140.

McNeill, D. (1992). *Hand and Mind: What Gestures Reveal about Thought.* The University of Chicago Press.

Müller, C., Cienki, A., Fricke, E., Ladewig, S. H., McNeill, D., & Tessendorf, S. (Eds.). (2014). *Body—Language—Communication. An International Handbook on Multimodality in Human Interaction.* De Gruyter.

Müller, C., & Posner, R. (Eds.). (2004). *The Semantics and Pragmatics of Everyday Gestures: Proceedings of the Berlin Conference April 1998.* Weidler.

Pille, T. (2009). Organisierte Körper. Eine Ethnographie des Referendariats. In T. Alkemeyer, K. Brümmer, R. Kodalle, & T. Pille (Eds.), *Ordnung in Bewegung. Choreographien des Sozialen. Körper in Sport, Tanz, Arbeit und Bildung* (pp. 161–178). transcript.

Posner, R. (1986). Zur Systematik der Beschreibung verbaler und nonverbaler Kommunikation. Semiotik als Propädeutik der Medienanalyse. In H. G. Bosshardt (Ed.), *Perspektiven auf Sprache. Interdisziplinäre Beiträge zum Gedenken an Hans Hörmann* (pp. 267–313). De Gruyter.

Sherin, M. G. (2007). The Development of Teachers' Professional Vision in Video Clubs. In R. Goldman, R. Pea, B. Barron, & S. J. Derry (Eds.), *Video Research in the Learning Sciences* (pp. 383–395). Routledge.

Walter, P., & Walter, C. (2014). *Müssen Lehrer streng sein? Unterrichtsstörungen und Klassenmanagement in der Schülerwahrnehmung.* Lit.

Wulf, C. (2010). Der mimetische und performative Charakter von Gesten. Perspektiven für eine kultur- und sozialwissenschaftliche Gestenforschung. *Paragran. Internationale Zeitschrift für Historische Anthropologie, 19*(1), 232–245.

Wulf, C. (2011). Auf dem Weg zu einer erziehungswissenschaftlichen Gestenforschung. Eine Einleitung. In C. Wulf, B. Althans, K. Audehm, G. Blaschke, N. Ferrin, I. Kellermann, R. Mattig, & S. Schinkel (Eds.), *Die Geste in Erziehung, Bildung und Sozialisation. Ethnographische Feldstudien* (pp. 7–26). Springer VS.

Vulnerability: A Basic Concept of Pedagogical Anthropology

Daniel Burghardt and Jörg Zirfas

1   Introduction

In recent decades, the term 'vulnerability' has come to occupy a central position in many areas of science. For approximately 30 years, the term has been the subject of intense discussion around the world in areas of medical science such as psychology, sciences such as economics, ecology and geography and also in the technical sciences of computer science and engineering, in social and cultural sciences such as sociology and political science, and lastly in areas of the humanities such as literature, philosophy and theology. Finally, interest in this term has been increasingly in evidence over the last few years in studies of education in the German-speaking world (Burghardt et al., 2017).

It is possible to link the heightened interdisciplinary use of the term 'vulnerability' to a series of quite diverse developments in recent times that would appear to make it necessary to devote increased consideration to the vulnerability of objects, systems, groups or individuals. Without going into detail at this point, we can cite the following keywords in regard to these developments: environmental catastrophe, poverty, financial crisis, international

---

D. Burghardt (✉)
University of Innsbruck, Innsbruck, Austria
e-mail: daniel.burghardt@uni-koeln.de

J. Zirfas
University of Cologne, Cologne, Germany

© The Author(s), under exclusive license to Springer Nature Switzerland AG 2022
A. Kraus, C. Wulf (eds.), *The Palgrave Handbook of Embodiment and Learning*,
https://doi.org/10.1007/978-3-030-93001-1_11

terrorism, pandemic diseases, hacker attacks and the war and refugee situation. All these developments increase awareness of vulnerability because they literally open our eyes to the fact that despite all our security systems, despite advances in many areas of science and despite discernible economic, political or educational improvements in many countries, vulnerability remains an ineluctable fact of human existence.

In this respect, vulnerability can be identified as a trend in various scientific disciplines beginning in the decade of the 1990s. This development is significant, since it forms a counterpoint to the theories and concepts that have dominated social and cultural studies for several decades. The ideal subject projected in these theories can be roughly characterised by autonomy, competence, empowerment, personal responsibility and health. Pedagogy has been no exception to this. Here too, the prevailing image is one of an autonomous, strong, newly resilient and infinitely optimistic subject. We begin to suspect that these qualifiers are less a description of the subject than a prescription for the subject, inasmuch as humans appear in anthropological terms as vulnerable beings: humans are subject to injury and violation; in many situations their lives prove to be fragile and brittle; in their living conditions, they are capable of both inflicting and suffering harm and, at the end of their lives, they are inevitably confronted with their finite nature and mortality. It can be stated as an anthropological premise that humans are vulnerable beings because they are physical, social, cultural and reflective creatures. Humans are susceptible to harm because they are both physically and emotionally vulnerable, because they can suffer physical wounds or be deprived of recognition and participation (Popitz, 1992, p. 43ff.). Included under the term 'vulnerability' is the exposure or susceptibility of a person, social group, object or system faced with existing dangers, risks, crises, stresses, shocks or recent occurrence of harmful events (Bürkner, 2010, p. 24).

To date, therefore, systematic conceptualisation of pedagogical issues has only partially conformed to debates within the discipline. Of course, many pedagogical ideas broached by educational studies in recent years—such as recognition, solidarity, inclusion or pedagogical rhythms—are often implicitly related to different forms of exposure. In this way, the vulnerabilities of the addressees (such as pupils) as well as those engaged in pedagogical acts (such as teachers) are negotiated; educational and instructional practices are brought into focus; and institutional, organisational and societal conditions that increase vulnerabilities of all kinds are analysed. Up to this point, however, scarcely any systematic attempts at a vulnerable pedagogy exist. Changing this one-sided focus is the concern of the *Cologne Vulnerability Research Group*, which for several years has devoted itself to the task of filling this research need (Burghardt et al., 2016, 2017; Stöhr et al., 2019; Zirfas, 2017). The following discussion is intended to make this effort plausible through a historical and anthropological approach.

2 Historical Dimensions

2.1 A Modern Debate

Vulnerability is an interdisciplinary term. Bürkner summarises the common denominator of the various approaches as follows: 'Vulnerability' is understood to mean

> the exposure or susceptibility of a person, social group, object or system faced with existing dangers, risks, crises, stresses, shocks or recent occurrence of harmful events. The violation or injury generally refers to a situation where essential functions are restricted or cease to exist. A key condition of vulnerability is the insufficient coping capacity of individuals, groups or systems. (Bürkner, 2010, p. 24)

Moreover, the term is used metaphorically, displaying a broad spectrum of meaning ranging from damage, loss, illness to fault, setback, shock or defeat.

Against this backdrop, it can be established historically that since the beginning of the modern era, themes such as susceptibility, suffering, fragility, frailty and finiteness have increasingly become topics for debate. These were defined as expressions of a defect or unacceptable imperfection and as weaknesses to be corrected. To this end, an entire arsenal of "anthropo-techniques" (Sloterdijk, 2009) was developed with the function—which they still possess—of immunising humans against their vulnerability, compensating for defects, overcoming faults and breaking down social dependencies. In effect, a systematic attempt was made to take preventive steps against all phenomena that could be subsumed under the term 'vulnerability' by engaging individual empowerment and legal measures to attenuate the force of their effects and to overcome vulnerability through technological advancement.

This modern combat against vulnerability reveals a certain similarity to the problem of theodicy. If God was responsible for vulnerability and suffering in the medieval Christian world, modern humanism placed this responsibility on human beings. If 'God is dead', as Nietzsche maintained, the consequence of this fact was not merely that man was seeking to replace him but also that man himself would now be responsible for the evil in the world. There was a growing awareness that disease, suffering, poverty and violence no longer need to be tolerated as immutable fate but are to some extent conditioned by individuals and society and can be overcome. As a result, the assertion that human suffering must simply be accepted or even understood as the purpose or meaning of life finds little acceptance today. More common is the assumption that human beings are creatures who generally do not want to suffer—and many would add, do not need to suffer. And even more: at least under modern conditions, the experience of harm, suffering, pain and so on is always coupled with the demand to eliminate or overcome it. This observation is related to one of the first main findings of our research: many descriptions and interpretations of vulnerability have a normative dimension in the sense that they characterise vulnerability as a scourge to be overcome. Vulnerability appears as a double-sided concept directly linking facticity with normativity, description with prescription. Those who detect vulnerability—of whatever kind—are almost unanimous in their call for it to be 'eliminated'. It is not a coincidence that Nietzsche's Zarathustra states it thus: "Woe saith: Hence! Go!" Experience indicates, however, that, for its part, the strategy of 'elimination' not uncommonly produces new suffering and new vulnerability. In this respect, vulnerability is a dialectical issue.

This becomes clear from current debates, which have to do less with reflections on theodicy than with a conception of pathodicy. These would refer to René Girard's conception of sacrifice and the sacrificial lamb in his historical studies of violence, Emmanuel Lévinas's ethical formulation of responsibility in view of the susceptibility of the face, Jacques Derrida's deconstructive margins at the limits of life, Judith Butler's political theory of a performative vulnerability and, finally, the debates and developments taking place since 1947 in the area of human rights that imply the goal of a world 'without fear and misery'. In this respect, the modern era also writes a history of vulnerability, but one that so far exists in ideas at best. This history describes a different image of human beings and a distinct understanding of a subject not centred on sovereignty and agency or on integrity, autonomy and authenticity, but commencing instead with sensibility, passivity, fragility and decentrality. Such a history would be required above all to emphasise physical susceptibility and fundamental social vulnerabilities. It would also need to show, however, that vulnerability is closely intertwined with other keywords, especially those of the modern era such as contingency, plurality, complexity, openness, unpredictability and flexibility, and that its link to these terms imbues it with important but mostly implicit and hidden significance.

The increasing awareness of vulnerability, which is connected to the ambivalence of uncertainty and risk, pain and suffering on the one hand and of

Vulnerability: A Basic Concept of Pedagogical Anthropology 183

prevention and elimination of suffering on the other, is a product of the modern world. While many areas of life and certitude are brittle, fragile and suspect, there is now also an increased awareness of their contingency and vulnerability. What can be thoroughly significant for this development are the important efforts undertaken by modern medicine to achieve as much freedom from pain as possible for sick (and even healthy) people. This nonetheless indicates that especially where potential or actual harm can be traced to human actions or living conditions that society has created, the project to overcome this harm is a political one (as is shown quite clearly by what is happening today and the current debate over 'care'). The social movements of the late nineteenth and twentieth centuries also illustrate how social inequity creates social vulnerability. Providing a perspective on this are the various 'movements': the women's movement, the 'lesbian/gay movement', the 'disability rights movement' or the anti-racist movements, which also offer indications of violated forms of self-esteem and the social *exposure* of certain societal groups to political conditions.

The increasing awareness of vulnerability outlined here is also revealed in the respective debates carried on in recent years in the social sciences. Especially worthy of mention is Ulrich Beck's "risk society" (Beck, 1992). In a modern age that has become reflective, Beck identifies, two significant changes which he seeks to define as signatures of the age—namely, that post-modern or post-industrial society, along with its self-induced catastrophes, has itself led to a change in the modern world. Yet these developments have a bearing not only on society but also on its subjects. Beck brings this to a double risk: here the risk society, there the risk biography (cf. Dederich & Burghardt, 2019). Following the ideas of Beck, the discussion now includes the concepts of a "fatigue society" (cf. Han, 2010) with its uncertainties and helplessness, an "assisted society" (Brumlik, 2002), a "fear society" (Bude, 2014) and an "imperilled life" (Butler, 2004), each concept with various means of social fears, vulnerabilities and susceptibilities. Appearing now alongside the ideal concept of the subject as the "entrepreneurial self" (Bröckling, 2007) is its exhausted and overwhelmed antithesis with disorders such as depression, attention deficit syndrome, borderline status or burnout (Ehrenberg, 2010; Fuchs et al., 2018).

As a result, it is probably not a coincidence that writings in *critical sociology* such as those by Stephan Lessenich or Hartmut Rosa regularly evoke vulnerable subject types. Lessenich writes of an activated self that nonetheless has a tendency to make excessive demands, while Rosa, against the background of his "acceleration society", postulates a stand-off in which subjects appear above all to have lost their vibrancy (Lessenich, 2008; Rosa, 2016).

These and other studies indicate that vulnerability has been seen by various disciplines as a relevant topic for several decades and, accordingly, that it has been the subject of research activities. The advent of explicit discourse on vulnerability in these disciplines therefore constitutes a response to the dark side of wide-ranging modernisation and civilisation processes and their effects in diverse areas of life, especially in the twentieth century.

3 The Century of Catastrophe

The twentieth century is also termed the *Century of Catastrophe*. In the past century, wars and episodes of terror and violence became the focus of history to such an extent that the perspectives of victims and the afflicted, questions of insecurity and risk, issues of fragility and passivity—in short dimensions of vulnerability—were both explicitly and implicitly included as elements of disparate theories and models of this period.

Chronologically, the century is also termed the 'short' twentieth century—extending from the outbreak of World War I (1914) to the break-up of the Soviet Union from 1989 to 1991; at the same time, we find expressions such as the Age of Extremes (Hobsbawm) or even the Century of Genocide. When we speak about this century, we are speaking about a hundred years of world wars, world economic crises, atomic bombs and worst-case scenarios, of Auschwitz, fascism, environmental catastrophes, hunger crises; of the Cold War, the Third World and the Middle East Conflict. Following the dissolution of the USSR, however, the melodramatic announcement of the End of History (Fukuyama) did not prove true. History took an uncertain step further, and the end of the twentieth century was ultimately rocked by drifts towards re-nationalisation and new forms of warfare. Once again, the triumphal procession of Western democracies was and is called into question, following in the wake of globalised capitalism.

We cannot, however, characterise the twentieth century as a coherent string of disasters. Historians have now generally agreed that the decades between the 'seminal catastrophe of World War I' (Kennan) and the end of World War II indeed constituted a catastrophic era: a time in which very few contemporaries would probably have regarded the humanisation of the world as a good bet. Yet the historic alliance against German fascism between liberal capitalism and socialism began a brief epoch—there are those who even speak of a Golden Age—of economic growth and relative prosperity in the Western world. It not only started a never-before-seen commodities and arms race on a worldwide scale but also transformed space into a field of technological conquest strategies, rang at the end of colonialism and cleared the way for manifold local independence and emancipation movements.

Moreover, a technical revolution in communication technologies took place in the final third of the twentieth century, and reference to the Digital Age became increasingly part of the lexicon. The world had at last become a 'Global Village' (McLuhan) with its corresponding dependencies and interdependencies. Finally, with the oil crisis and the reflection on the ecological 'limits to growth' (Club of Rome), an era of mastery of long-standing difficulties and transnational strategic solutions was opened that still affects us today.

The twentieth century has taught us how people are capable of eradicating their cultural achievements and themselves. It showed us that a large portion of humanity continues to live under brutal and inhuman conditions in the face of a wide range of advancements in political, economic, technical, medical and other areas. In the short twentieth century, not only did the world's population triple but more people perished and were systematically and industrially murdered than ever before (Hobsbawm, 1994).

4   The Defenceless Subject

It is no coincidence, therefore, that even the problems of the 'subject' were for the first time radically expounded in this century. In the studies of the mind that were only established in universities in their present form towards the end of the nineteenth century, this development (originally taken up by Sigmund Freud) of the wounding of the subject, who is no longer the 'master' of its own consciousness, proceeds through Critical Theory's analysis of an authoritarian characterology to the declaration of the death of the subject by several variants of post-structuralism. One could speak of a 'subject of extremes', fitted out in the twentieth century with narcissistic and technological fantasies of omnipotence, stepping forward in self-justification and observing in the process that it could never sufficiently safeguard the tenets of the self—whether these tenets were now taken to include the unconscious, capital, power, language or the body.

In twentieth-century subject philosophies, the self-determined and idealised subject of the Enlightenment is no longer the focus, replaced by the death wish subject (Freud), the barbaric subject (Adorno), the stigmatised self (Goffman), the face of the Other (Lévinas), the fragile subject (Butler) or the foreign (Waldenfels). In the twentieth century, therefore, a new understanding of the subject is discernible, a different anthropology in which human beings take centre stage as a vulnerable subject in the drama of their own story, a story no longer told solely from the optimistic perspective of progress.

5   A Different Anthropology

Against such historical backgrounds, anthropology too has altered its approach. More recent research in the context of pedagogical anthropology (Wulf & Zirfas, 2014) assumes that it is in many respects arguable to speak of a human essence or core. A better approach is to widen our perspective and ask, from a pedagogical-anthropological perspective, what constitutes human beings and, in turn, to what extent these are tied to processes of upbringing, education and socialisation. Up to this point, the following dimensions have been singled out (with no claim to completeness) as essential anthropological issues: spatiality, temporality, individuality, sociality, physicality, culturality and liminality (Zirfas, 2004).

All these dimensions have their respective vulnerabilities. In spatiality, these involve proximity and distance or constriction and dilation. Included under temporality are time limits, finitude or, conversely, accelerations. With respect to individuality, we can take as examples identities that foster either affiliation or stigmatisation, while the vulnerability of the social being is characterised in the modern age by the loss of traditions and the eroding of relationships. Physical vulnerabilities are tied to pain and suffering; those in culturality to symbolic and linguistic actions; and lastly, a liminality approach presents various forms of boundary violations.

6   Dimensions of Physical Susceptibility

What follows is a focus on the physical dimension from an anthropological perspective. Since the 1970s, the body has occupied a central place in social and cultural studies. Pedagogical anthropology has likewise focussed its interest on social issues. Accordingly, seeing the importance of the body in its social context leads us to highlight questions concerning its vulnerability. In this endeavour, following Plessner's distinction between having a body and being a body, Bittner's triad of the human being's sensual body, implement body and appearance body, and Funke-Wieneke's extension of this notion to include the categories of symbolic body and social body, it therefore becomes possible to consider physical vulnerability on additional levels.

At the outset, the Plessner conception can be employed to distinguish between an external-to-the-body and internal-to-the body vulnerability. There is a difference between speaking about the body using the medical categories of possible damage and injury and discussing the bodily experience of this vulnerability, as well as between observing the capacity for pain from the perspective of a third party and broaching the subject from the ego perspective (Dederich, 2013, pp. 79ff.).

If we combine these two aspects under the term 'physical vulnerability', this means firstly that people are susceptible as bodily physical beings, that they can contract disease and suffer pain; in (disability) pedagogy, accordingly, physical vulnerability is generally found under the heading of children's health or violence against children. And in pedagogy, the history of violence against children is a long and sobering one: over the centuries, all manner of child killings, mistreatment, selectiveness, exploitation, abuse and punishment have been the constant companions of 'pedagogical' interactions with (disabled) children. Since the eighteenth century, against the background of various pedagogical reform movements (social developments related to children and youth, didactics, learning theory etc.), there has been increasing acceptance of the belief that children have a right to violence-free education.

Another form of vulnerability is sensual, extending in the broadest sense to possible impairment of the sensory organs. In issues of vulnerability, the sense of pain is arguably of greatest interest due to the specific information it can provide regarding a person. Here it is possible to distinguish the experience of ego-related feeling of pain from personalised suffering in relation to pain (Diaconu, 2013, p. 79). People can feel vulnerable to pain but do not need to suffer. Chronic experiences of vulnerability related to pain and suffering are difficult to envisage. Above all, they refer to the fact that pain represents not only a physical and physiological condition but also the negative physical sensations linked to the attempt to alleviate and overcome this condition. The ego's passivity and feelings of impotence and helplessness are expressed in pain. "The ego feels susceptible and abandoned to an alien power—an anonymous, impersonal agent" (ibid., p. 81). This connexion refers to the fact that the very experiences of pain and suffering can also enhance sensibility to the pathic and to vulnerability.

Perhaps the vulnerability of the body that we see is the most immediately and commonly accessible anthropological form. This vulnerability is primarily virulent in the 'disabled body' (Krüger-Fürhoff, 2001). The disabled body can be identified from the following characteristics: injury, mutilation, fragmentation, violence, opening, death as well as transience, disintegration, wounding, abuse, disgust and compassion. And it is not coincidental that Goffman (1963) orients his studies towards the stigmatisation of features of this body, which appears in a 'conspicuous' way. Persons with 'disabled bodies' frequently confront scrutiny of a pejorative nature on the part of those who seek to demonstrate the inferiority and harmfulness of the one being stigmatised. And this close examination will cause them problems in forming a positive self-image.

Another distinction by Goffman takes place between the discredited (persons with known stigmata) and the discreditable (those disabled by a potential stigma not yet known in the environment). Anyone who has faced such images of negative identity as 'discredited' or 'discreditable' but was unable to ward them off through skilful identity and stigma management will have scant opportunity to demonstrate the capacity to be more than that or other than that—or to do more than that or other than that—which is defined within this vocabulary range of institutional stigmatisation. Moreover, Goffman makes it clear that divergence from normality and the stigmatisation and labelling associated with such divergence basically affects everyone, although of course in different ways and to varying degrees.

From an anthropological perspective, symbolic susceptibility, more recently also frequently paraphrased as 'emotional susceptibility' and 'degradation', is conditioned by our capacity to understand symbols. Communicative beings who can comprehend signs and symbols are able to comprehend not only (linguistic) actions by sympathetic others but also the actions of those who wish them harm. This vulnerability therefore requires the ability to understand other individuals as intentional persons who pursue specific goals through their actions and to understand themselves as someone who can be 'impaired' by these actions. Individuals can be regarded as symbolically susceptible to the extent that they have a sense of self-esteem and can respond resentfully to symbolic susceptibilities (Giesinger, 2007, p. 41).

When words not only function as weapons but are themselves weapons that inflict harm based on "language as a thing" (Gehring, 2007, p. 213) and experienced as a "blow", the question then arises as to what kind of vulnerability they encounter and what kind is generated by the language itself. Assuming that people are symbolic beings that exist both in and through 'language' (in its broader sense as a system of signs)—a thesis that remains to be spelled out in terms of language philosophy, phenomenology, development theory and cultural theory—then relations to oneself, to others and to the world are linguistic in nature: more specifically, they are an outgrowth of the speech of others. This development can take a 'positive' or 'negative' direction—that is, language would have the power to engender vulnerability because, on the one hand, it would have a 'homoeopathic' effect: it produces a specific (negative) understanding and a specific (negative) self-assessment in us in the context of language. And on the other hand, it would also have an 'allopathic' effect because that which is physical, emotional and motivational (also unconscious?) is also permeable with respect to language, is affected by it, and can therefore be experienced as physical harm. In this respect, language would have not only a linguistic but a somatic effect. Here, symbolic harm would be relevant—not intrinsically but only for a particular individual in situations where, under certain conditions, inclusion of a cultural parlance, a special way of speaking, is also understood as an 'insult' (Herrmann et al., 2007).

Finally, vulnerability as a social body applies to those linked to others through relationships and for whom the permeability of their own body is linked to others. Discrimination, stigmatisation and other forms of rejection, especially in relationships that are meaningful for children and youth, generally have a significant impact on emotional, cognitive, volitional and behaviour-related wellbeing—that is, on physical structures as well as on physical and psychological wellness. These particularly affect the self-confidence and self-worth of the one experiencing discrimination and create conditions for rejection, devaluation and a perceived lack of belonging. They therefore act counter to a basic human desire for social acceptance and integration into a community.

The results of relationship research, psychoanalysis and infant research make clear that social relations are especially significant with regard to issues of vulnerability. In turn, this is probably linked to social experiences in the early stages of life. Infant research, which has continued to grow in importance in recent decades in the area of the human and social sciences, has shown, based on the earliest childhood self-genesis, that from the very start, relationships to other people and objects are constitutive in every respect, not merely for the nascent relationship to self but also for the educational process. The genesis of the earliest self-relationship in the form of a 'proprioceptive self' is directly linked to the experience of sociality even if this is addressed here at a very proximal and otherwise quite undifferentiated level. Above all, the issue of vulnerability must be broached against the backdrop of a physical-social relationship; from an anthropological perspective, vulnerability arising from physical relationships must be appraised as tremendously significant for human life.

7 Conclusion

With a view to the lack of terminological precision revealed in many contributions on the subject, we wish to stress yet again that the term 'vulnerability' refers to a *potentiality*—that is, to requirements, possibilities and prospects. In concrete terms, this means the following: vulnerability is synonymous not with being harmed or violated (an equation between the potentiality for vulnerability and the reality of harm having appeared quite frequently in relevant literature) but only with the possible or probable capacity to be harmed or violated.

This understanding of the term is also important for pedagogy because it opens up the possibility on the one hand of inquiring about causes and requirements both for specific susceptibilities or vulnerabilities and for potentially harmful actions or cause-effect relationships. On the other hand, an essential preventative feature is associated with it. Knowledge regarding potentially harmful actions or cause-effect relationships is required if these are to be alleviated and actual harm is to be prevented. Moreover, the understanding of vulnerability as a potentiality stresses its relativity and relationality. There is no vulnerability *per se*; it does not simply exist but is rather perceived and comprehended only in specific contexts that are linked to corporeality, sociality and culturality.

The previously explained understanding of the term has a further implication: that vulnerability must be recognised as contingent upon such contexts. This means several things: first, that change from the possibility of harm into the reality of harm is not inevitable but only potential. Even where all conditions are present for the actualisation of vulnerability, the harm can fail to materialise because of the affected individual's pronounced resilience, for example, or fortunate circumstances, or well-functioning protection factors. But the opposite side is also conditional: since, in many cases, actual physical harm cannot be attributed to a single cause, conditions of the potentiality of harm based on processes of cognizance, assessment and decision-making or even on recognition policies that make vulnerability visible. Because vulnerability itself is conditional, this makes it a problematic locus: questions about who counts as vulnerable, how, to what extent and in what way, are consigned to a system of discursive and non-discursive elements, of interests and power configurations.

Among other conclusions, this leads to the insight that not all people are vulnerable in the same way. In this respect, it is possible to make distinctions between different types of vulnerability: children and the infirm, elderly or disabled as well as persons labelled as having an 'immigrant background' and currently refugees as well appear at first glance to be more vulnerable than adult, young, healthy and able-bodied individuals. But what does this initial impression tell us from an anthropological point of view? Adults can also become ill, the youth can suffer from lovesickness, the healthy can be involved in an accident and non-disabled individuals can become unemployed. In this sense, vulnerability occurs as an experience to which people are 'exposed' even under seemingly optimum conditions of resilience and empowerment. Vulnerability appears as the latent 'dark' and pathic side that is recalled whenever any kind of harm or danger occurs. Vulnerability lies in wait like a shadow in the brightly lit and fully enlightened modern age.

References

Beck, U. (1992). *Risk Society: Towards a New Modernity*. Sage.

Bröckling, U. (2007). *Das unternehmerische Selbst. Soziologie einer Subjektivierungsform*. Suhrkamp.

Brumlik, M. (2002). Die betreute Gesellschaft—Grenzen oder Entgrenzung der Pädagogik. In O. Hans-Uwe (Ed.), *Erziehungswissenschaft: Politik und Gesellschaft* (pp. 99–110). Leske + Budrich.

Bude, H. (2014). *Gesellschaft der Angst*. Hamburger Edition HIS Verlag.

Burghardt, D., Dederich, M., Dziabel, N., Höhne, T., Lohwasser, D., Stöhr, R., & Zirfas, J. (2016). Vulnerabilität in verschiedenen Wissenschaften: Ein Überblick. In *Behinderte Menschen. Zeitschrift für gemeinsames Leben, Lernen und Arbeiten 2/2016* (pp. 19–31). Steirische Vereinigung für Menschen mit Behinderung.

Burghardt, D., Dederich, M., Dziabel, N., Höhne, T., Lohwasser, D., Stöhr, R., & Zirfas, J. (2017). *Vulnerabilität. Pädagogische Herausforderungen*. Kohlhammer.

Bürkner, H. (2010). *Vulnerabilität Forschungsstand und sozialwissenschaftliche Untersuchungsperspektiven*. Working Paper No. 43, Erkner, Leibnitz-Institut für Regionalentwicklung. Retrieved November 5, 2019, from https://leibniz-irs.de/fileadmin/user_upload/IRS_Working_Paper/wp_vr.pdf

Butler, J. (2004). *Precarious life: the powers of mourning and violence*. Verso.

Dederich, M. (2013). *Philosophie in der Heil- und Sonderpädagogik*. Kohlhammer.

Dederich, M., & Burghardt, D. (2019). Riskante Modernisierung. Ulrich Becks Theorie der sozialen und individuellen Verwundbarkeit. In R. Stöhr, D. Lohwasser, N. Napoles, D. Burghardt, & M. Dederich (Eds.), *chlüsselwerke der Vulnerabilitätsforschung* (pp. 169–183). Springer VS.

Diaconu, M. (2013). *Phänomenologie der Sinne*. Reclam.

Ehrenberg, A. (2010). *The Weariness of the Self: Diagnosing the History of Depression in the Contemporary Age*. McGill-Queen's University Press.

Fuchs, T., Iwer, L., & Micali, S. (Eds.). (2018). *Das überforderte Subjekt—Zeitdiagnosen einer beschleunigten Gesellschaft*. Suhrkamp.

Gehring, P. (2007). Über die Körperkraft von Sprache. In S. Herrmann, S. Krämer, & H. Kuch (Eds.), *Verletzende Worte. Die Grammatik sprachlicher Missachtung* (pp. 211–228). transcript.

Giesinger, J. (2007). *Autonomie und Verletzlichkeit. Der moralische Status von Kindern und die Rechtfertigung von Erziehung*. transcript.

Goffman, E. (1963). *Stigma: Notes on the Management of Spoiled Identity*. Prentice-Hall.

Han, B. (2010). *Müdigkeitsgesellschaft*. Matthes & Seitz.

Herrmann, S., Krämer, S., & Kuch, H. (Eds.). (2007). *Verletzende Worte. Die Grammatik sprachlicher Missachtung*. transcript.

Hobsbawm, E. (1994). *The Age of Extremes: The Short Twentieth Century 1914–1991*. Penguin Group.

Krüger-Fürhoff, I. (2001). *Der versehrte Körper. Revisionen des klassizistischen Schönheitsideals*. Vandenhoek & Ruprecht.

Lessenich, S. (2008). *Die Neuerfindung des Sozialen. Der Sozialstaat im flexiblen Kapitalismus*. transcript.

Popitz, H. (1992). *Phänomene der Macht* (p. 2). Mohr Siebeck.

Rosa, H. (2016). *Resonanz: Eine Soziologie der Weltbeziehung*. Suhrkamp.

Sloterdijk, P. (2009). *Du musst Dein Leben ändern. Über Anthropotechniken*. Suhrkamp.

Stöhr, R., Lohwasser, D., Napoles, N., Burghardt, D., Dederich, M., Krebs, M., & Zirfas, J. (2019). *Schlüsselwerke der Vulnerabilitätsforschung*. Springer VS.

Wulf, C., & Zirfas, J. (Eds.). (2014). *Handbuch Pädagogische Anthropologie*. Springer VS.

Zirfas, J. (2004). *Pädagogik und Anthropologie. Eine Einführung*. Kohlhammer.

Zirfas, J. (2017). Das vulnerable Subjekt. In G. Taube, M. Fuchs, & T. Braun (Eds.), *Handbuch Das starke Subjekt: Schlüsselbegriffe in Theorie und Praxis* (pp. 149–157). kopaed.

Pedagogical Relationships as Relationships of Power

Kathrin Audehm

1 Perspectives on Power: From Property to Network

Pedagogical relationships are power relationships. Not only do individuals educate other individuals, but education can be understood, according to Friedrich Schleiermacher and Émile Durkheim, as a social practice in which the older generation bears the responsibility for conveying and passing on cultural achievements to the younger generation and for educating them to behave morally. Therefore, pedagogical relationships are based on the pedagogical generational difference, and at least asymmetrical to hierarchical relationship—classically expressed—between educators and pupils, which is reinforced by pedagogical practice. If power is in education like 'a stake in the flesh' (Mayer-Drawe, 2001, p. 12), this not only refers to the social entanglement of the educational sector in power relations but also to the inherent power form of educational practices and processes.

Following on Max Weber, the term 'power' is sociologically amorphous and means in general every chance to enforce one's own will against others (Weber, 1972, pp. 28 f.) and achieve obedience, whether or not it is grounded in voluntary submission or reached by means of compulsion or violence. Therefore, the term includes a wide range of asymmetrical social constellations and

K. Audehm (✉)
University of Cologne, Cologne, Germany
e-mail: kathrin.audehm@uni-koeln.de

© The Author(s), under exclusive license to Springer Nature Switzerland AG 2022
A. Kraus, C. Wulf (eds.), *The Palgrave Handbook of Embodiment and Learning*,
https://doi.org/10.1007/978-3-030-93001-1_12

phenomena (Paris, 2015, p. 7) like concrete and directly interpersonal relationships, relationships in organisations or institutions, state power, and social relations in general.

In educational science, too, the concept of power is becoming increasingly blurred, in the German-speaking discourse initially accompanied by a radical critique of power in schools as an ideological state and coercive apparatus in the 1970s (Wellendorf, 1973). In addition, canonical texts are subjected to a critical re-reading (Rutschky, 1977) and since the 1980s and 1990s supplemented by (uncountable) educational-historical and empirical studies, which refer mainly to the power-critical works of Michel Foucault and Pierre Bourdieu. In the 2000s, the power-critical perspectives were belatedly but finally complemented by in-depth investigations and reappraisals of sexual violence, especially in boarding schools (Baldus & Utz, 2011; Thole et al., 2012).

The ability to exercise power over others is based on fundamental human characteristics. These include the fundamental dependence on material living environments and living conditions, the vulnerability of the human body and the need for recognition of one's own social existence by others, the urgency to be able to act in social situations, to orient oneself in the social living environment, and to interpret it, thereby not only to exist but to lead one's own life and to help shape one's own, individual, collective, and social future in the course of life. Based on this, basic types of power can be identified: Action power, instrumental, and authoritative power, as well as the power of data setting (Popitz, 2009, p. 22ff.). Nevertheless, power is not an anthropological constant; rather, historically and culturally different variants of power exist that play out in the field-, organisation-, and milieu-specific entanglements (Rieger-Ladich, 2014, p. 287).

Exercising power could initially mean gaining power over others. If asymmetries are condensed into power hierarchies, one can speak of a domination-like organisation of social relationships. Rulership refers to an institutionalised relationship of superiority and subordination, whereby power initially appears as a relationship of ownership and possession. From this point of view, rulership is exercised by those who succeed in using their economic, political, and cultural resources profitably, accumulating them as capital, and thereby gaining control over its purposes. In this perspective, the thoughts of the ruling class are therefore also 'the ruling thoughts in every epoch' (Marx & Engels, 1962, p. 46). Domination depends on mutual recognition. Thus, someone is only king or queen because their subjects behave like subjects and they in turn do so because they believe they are subjects (Marx, 1962, footnote 21, p. 72).

Max Weber distinguishes between three ideal types of legitimate rulership or authority (Weber, 1972, p. 124), whose characteristic features, occurrence, and development he explains socio-historically and socio-theoretically in *Economy and Society*. The type of charismatic rulership occurs primarily in times of upheaval and is based on an extraordinary devotion with which vassals, comrades, and conspiratorial communities recognise charisma as a superhuman gift of special persons such as religious and military leaders. In contrast to this, traditional authority is based on everyday belief or an inner attitude, guiding, for example, children, students, or journey(wo)men to recognise the honour and prestige of parents, priests, or master teachers but also customs and traditions. And finally, rational authority is based on an ingrained discipline and refers to the set of rules of an organisation and its goals, such as the Prussian bureaucracy with its files and official channels or scientific management in a Fordist-organised company with its assembly lines and stopwatches. Here, those who act in it serve not so much persons as a cause.

The type of rational authority in particular underlines, that the legitimation of power is based not only on conscious recognition but also on social experience or 'discipline' (Weber, 1972, p. 681). Furthermore, this type shows, exercising power is not limited to interpersonal relationships.

Weber's ideal type of rational authority has similarities with Foucault's type of disciplinary power. However, while Max Weber searches for legitimate reasons for domination, Michel Foucault and Pierre Bourdieu show that the legitimisation of domination cannot be detached from practical as well as discursive means of power, because these secretly co-produce the reasons for legitimisation. This makes the rationality of the recognition of power generally suspect, but especially the efforts of education and training become suspect.

The belief in the legitimacy of domination does not dissolve into a 'false', ideological consciousness, but is maintained, renewed, and stabilised by incorporated knowledge of action, interpretation, and experience, which has been laboriously and painfully practised—certainly on both sides of the power relation. Thus, in all types of aristocracies (including educated aristocracies), elites entrust their most valuable legacy and cultural heritage to the body and bodily discipline (Bourdieu, 1990, p. 89). In this perspective, power works with bodies and embeds itself in them. In this perspective, there is hardly any room for resistance or any forms of autonomy; instead, power and the body are welded together in mutual complicity. Nevertheless, the power form of pedagogical relations is productive, and their disciplining effects enable both educational processes and educational discourses.

While Bourdieu hardly distinguishes (symbolic) power from violence, according to Foucault, violence occurs in relation to persons when power is not only directed at their subjugation, but at their destruction and destroys them themselves as already subjugated subjects. Violence is not the antithesis of power and relations of power do not suddenly change into relations of violence. Rather, they are gradual, fluid transitions.

2 Incorporation as Disciplining and Educating Effect of Power Techniques

Since the 1970s, Michel Foucault has developed a whole 'toolbox' (Lorey, 2015, p. 31) for analysing different technologies of power. In particular, in *Discipline and Punish*, a theory of power unfolds which has challenged educational science (Rieger-Ladich, 2002, p. 360). In contrast to sovereign power, which focuses on revenge and is directed at death, discipline or disciplinary power is directed at the seizure, capture, and cultivation of human life (Demirović, 2015, p. 73 f.). It unfolds in a multifaceted, diffused web of power relations and possesses its own logic or political economy, which does not so much punish as educate. The political economy of disciplinary power is composed of a political and scientific register that are intertwined. What is new about the techniques of discipline are their steadiness, detail, and inescapability.

The political register includes (1) the distribution of bodies in space by enclosing, parcelling, and assigning functional positions within the framework of a hierarchy, with which the bodies are localised in a network of relations (Foucault, 1994, p. 188) and living tableaus are created; (2) the temporal control of activities (ibid., p. 193ff.) through the narrowing of time grids, the decomposition of activities into sequences of individual acts and their elements, whereby bodies and gestures are put together as in writing (ibid, p. 195ff.) and bodies and tools are interconnected in manoeuvres. Added to this are (3) the organisation of developments, achieved through exercises and secured through examinations, which at the same time differentiate the abilities of the individuals (ibid., p. 205) and finally (4) the combination of forces in the form of the training of tactics.

The military and school techniques and exercises are linked to techniques of control and normalising sanction, and the performance of individuals is measured against norms along which their behaviour is aligned. If the disciplining efforts are successful, the individuals confined in hospitals, factories, schools, and prisons are homogenised along the norms and in the process they become efficient.

The scientific register includes (1) hierarchical surveillance in the form of potentially permanent observation and a network of mutually controlling gazes, as well as (2) normative sanction, which, through prohibitions and subtle punishments, establishes a micro-justice of time, performed activities, and sexuality, and in which punishment is always only one element in a system of reward, dressage, and correction (ibid., p. 231), such as the donkey bonnet or class of disgrace at school. Both techniques are combined (3) in the examination as the great technique of disciplinary power. In examination the practices of observational control and normalising sanction become intertwined. And while disciplinary power makes itself invisible in its techniques, it imposes visibility on the bodies that are measured, tested, useful, and taught (ibid., p. 241).

The political and the scientific register are interwoven and produce an organic knowledge of the body (Foucault, 1976, p. 109), which becomes the object of observation and control. The scientific register thus produces a dark and secret archive of pedagogical knowledge. The 'elegance of discipline' (Foucault, 1994, p. 31) simultaneously subjects bodies and aligns and enhances their performance. The disciplined, educated, efficient, and useful bodies are machines that, by means of their activities, produce the effects themselves to which they are subject. The individual bodies thus exhibit certain characteristics and subjectivise themselves in their subjugation. Thus, the domination of persons has given away to the 'power of the norm' (ibid., 1994, p. 237).

The immediate entanglement of objectified reification and subjectivising submission is carried out in Bentham's panopticon, an apparatus of power characterised by greatest transparency, infinite control, and surveillance of those who learn, work, recover, or are imprisoned within it. The panopticon thus appears as a *perpetuum mobile* of the concealed power of discipline (ibid., p. 279) that knows no evasion.

Power no longer emanates from state apparatuses and strategic positions or switching points of domination, but appears as a network of power techniques and practices, effective as strategic dispositions of subject positioning and self-regulation. Power is therefore not so much something that someone possesses, but something that unfolds (ibid., p. 38). Power produces subjects with particular characteristics as well as objectivated, scientific knowledge. Power therefore does not mainly have a repressive effect but acquires a productive character (ibid.).

With disciplinary power, power acquires a material character and can no longer be limited as an interpersonal relationship. Rather, it appears as an incorporated relationship of norming and normalising factors of practical exercise and discursive knowledge. These factors of subjection, which include usefulness and performance, are based on constant, subjectivising practice and assert themselves like an organically regulating functional compulsion. Disciplinary power thus undermines the notion of an autonomously acting subject just as much as it makes clear that subjects are not given as entities a priori, but rather their capacities and action power develop within the framework of processes of subjectivation, which are at the same time entangled in and bound up with power relations.

Power becomes a productive force because it produces subjects capable of action as well as discourses that functions as power-knowledge complexes. This makes it difficult to distinguish between social exercises and discursive practices as well as between techniques of power and practices of power. Furthermore, the question of the extent of the impact of discourses on subjects arises, how pervasive the power effects of techniques and discourses are, and how they dock onto or generate experiential knowledge. Foucault, however, has no conception of the process of incorporation; the entanglement of power techniques and subjective bodies remains an effect resulting from a functional logic that no longer knows a justifying centre and yet asserts itself as a general and total compulsion. Moreover, Foucault's concept of disciplinary power ignores the problematics of recognising power and bodies appear as crucial media of unrecognised processes of subjectivation—in other words, individuals become subjects 'without a cause'.

Subsequently, Foucault elaborates an overall technology of power. Disciplinary power is a subtype and, along with population policy, belongs to bio-power, which is aimed at preserving and promoting life. Bio-power complements sovereignty power and governmentality, and all three types of power do not follow one another as hegemonic power blocks, but form an irreducible triangle. Finally, pastoral power is added to this triangle as a unique, Christian occidental art of guiding souls and constantly intervening in the conduct of life. This type of power in particular guides people to orientate themselves to what is permitted without prohibitions and to follow it voluntarily. In the unfolding of the power types, it becomes clear that power relations are fragile, unstable, and reversible. And while the type of disciplinary power knows no simultaneous disciplining and rebelling, Foucault will then state: 'Where there is power, there is resistance' (Foucault, 1983, p. 92).

Foucault's theory of power welds the body with power techniques. Although the process of incorporation is described, a theoretical concept to explain this process is missing. Such a concept, which also includes the problem of subjective (individual as well as collective) recognition of power relations, is provided by the habitus concept.

3 Education as a Social-Magical Process of Habitus Transformation

The concept of habitus has many fathers. John Locke already introduced the terms 'habit' and 'disposition' in his essay *Some Thoughts Concerning Education* (1693). Education purposefully builds habits of thought and behaviour based on repetition. Dispositions are internal habits that trigger actions and often elude observation (Oelkers, 2004, p. 335). John Dewey also understands dispositions as basic mental attitudes that in turn guide and structure further action. According to Karl Mannheim, all human knowledge is based on bodily activities with their touches, sensual experiences, and emotional stimuli, which enable an existential absorption of a counterpart into consciousness qua contagion and transmission (Mannheim, 1980, pp. 206 f.). This experience of contagion lies before the separating distinction between subject and object, takes place in bodily co-presence, and is the background or a basic mood in which all further knowledge resides (ibid., p. 215). The bodily existence and the bodily being-boundness of thinking create so-called conjunctive knowledge as a component of a total mental habitus, whereby the separation of body and mind is abolished.

Bourdieu's concept mainly refers to Aristotle's *hexis*, Panofsky's *habitus*, and Weber's *ethos*, whereby, unlike John Locke, newborns are not considered blank slates. Mannheim's concept is ignored in Bourdieu's writings; the main difference between the two concepts lies in their treatment of power issues. While in Mannheim's concept the habitus binds itself to things through bodily practice and thereby forms a capacity for their practical mastery—for example, in riding a bicycle or playing a musical instrument, in Bourdieu's concept the power relations are incorporated through bodily cognition and transferred into the dispositions of the habitus, which are burned into them like 'indelible tattoos' (Bourdieu, 2001, p. 181). In Bourdieu's notion the body itself becomes an instrument of knowledge and the recognition of power at the same time (Audehm, 2017, pp. 173ff.).

According to Bourdieu, social and symbolic power are closely interwoven, articulated through the habitus, which is both structured by the social structures of social fields of play and struggle and effective as a *modus operatum*, and in turn, as a *modus operandi*, structures practices and principles of classification, symbolic sifting, and ordering. Education contributes decisively to the generation and transformation of habitualised dispositions and can be understood as a practice by which social power relations are transferred into the power of symbols, whereby symbolic power helps to disguise the social power relations on which it is based. This applies to all social formations and their forms of education, whereby the organisation of education in the form of schools, which includes universities, does not differ significantly from other forms.

In their *Foundations of a theory of symbolic violence*, Pierre Bourdieu and Jean-Claude Passeron (1973) refer to the works of Karl Marx, Max Weber, and Émile Durkheim. Similar to Marx, social and symbolic power are interdependent, but in contrast to classical Marxist perspectives on ideology, they stand in dynamic relations to each other and, symbolic power has a force of its own that it adds to social power relations and is therefore not merely a superstructure phenomenon. In contrast to Max Weber (excepted his version of rational authority), symbolic power, which enforces meanings as generally recognised and legitimised, is not reduced to interpersonal relations and thus, for example, cultural artefacts are attributed authority—without conceding a dynamic character to it. And similarly, to Émile Durkheim, it is assumed that social facts become social constraints, but unlike Durkheim's version, these are not equally valid and compelling for all members of a society.

In Durkheim's version, the moral authority of a society achieves resounding effects, on the one hand through rituals, on the other through education. Using the example of Australian totem cults, Durkheim underlines that collective bodily performances—especially ritual dances—generate a special 'electricity' (Durkheim, 1998, p. 297) and that ritual gatherings of individuals arouse in them 'a common passion' (ibid.). During the ecstatic invocation of collective symbols, individuals go completely out of themselves and thus become a collective body, and transforming themselves into a community, whereby they would experience its moral authority with feelings of 'awe' (Durkheim, 1998, p. 285). However, the ecstasy does not last, so the ritual gatherings would have to be repeated. Another form is education, where the children to be educated appear strangely passive and educational practices are compared to hypnosis (Durkheim, 1972, pp. 44 f.).

With Durkheim, education is directed towards the formation of a social being, in that individual aptitudes are developed, and the socialised human beings form enlightened moral behaviour. In this process, teacher's authority becomes the preferred means of pedagogical action. This authority is based on a preconception of knowledge, experience (ibid., p. 45), and morality (ibid.,

p. 47), supplemented with—in this respect it is similar to priestly authority—personal conviction in the task to which the teacher is called and commissioned by virtue of his or her office (ibid., p. 48). Authority here is essentially institutional authority, which is fulfilled through exemplary, neither vain nor petty or reserved, pedagogical action (ibid.).

For Bourdieu and Passeron, too, those who act in the pedagogical field as educators are charged with educating. Educational instances can be parents as well as teachers. Educational processes are composed of pedagogical action, work, and authority, whereby pedagogical work has a transformative character (Bourdieu & Passeron, 1973, p. 51) in that it is directed towards the transformation of a habitus that is considered perfect, enduring, and transferable to other fields, which in turn generates practices of a legitimate culture after education has ceased. Education in general—as well in families or social groups and communities as at schools—thus becomes the decisive basis for the effectiveness of symbolic power, whose recognition is guaranteed in the dispositions of the habitus. Insofar the individuals become subjects 'with a cause', grounded in their social experience and practical knowledge—although Bourdieu himself uses the term social agents and strictly avoids the term subject.

The connection between education and the recognition of symbolic power is elaborated by Bourdieu in discussion with Austin's speech act theory, whereby he generalises the social function of entrance examinations to French elite universities in a social-functionalist perspective and calls them rituals of institution. He thus directs the perspective away from the symbolic confirmation of a social transition towards the aspect of the legitimising, sanctifying, and traditionalising effect of rituals, whose main social function is to institutionalise social differences (Bourdieu, 1990, pp. 84 f.).

Examination rituals separate those who just pass from those who have already failed, that means they separate those, who are very likely to become elites, and those who are at least handicapped in the capital-circuit and race for social positions (Audehm, 2001, p. 150). Thus, like circumcision rituals drawing an arbitrary boundary in a broad spectrum of behaviours: Circumcision rituals separate practices of still childlike and female from already male behaviour.

Moreover, in a theatrical and communicative act, the instituted are assigned an identity that is imposed on them 'in front of all eyes' (Bourdieu, 1990, p. 88) and defines a social existence like a categorical imperative. This definition encompasses the totality of social attributes and attributions produced by the act of institution, which thus becomes a performative utterance intended to produce what it signifies (ibid., p. 87).

As exceptional and outstanding cases of social meaning-making, investiture rites have a 'performative logic' (Bourdieu, 2001, p. 150) that is not easily broken, its effectiveness depends on the magnitude of the authority with which the utterance is performed (Bourdieu, 1990, p. 79). The recognition of ritual as well as extra-ritual authorities is guaranteed in the dispositions of habitus that secure the collective belief of the ritually acting in the social differences institutionalised in the ritual (ibid., p. 79) and that result from pedagogical work as work on incorporation.

However, ritually drawn boundaries and identity assignments are not self-evident. Rather, every setting of difference includes the danger of its transgression. By entrusting their cultural legacy to bodily disciplining, social groups counter the danger of transgressing boundaries (ibid., p. 88ff.). This results in a strange cycle of social magic (Audehm, 2008, p. 130): On the one hand, rituals as symbolic action complexes attain their social efficacy due to incorporation work that has already been done; on the other hand, it is not sufficiently secured by this, which is why further, disciplinary incorporation work takes place that is not left to coincidence.

The social-magical process of collective recognition of symbolic demarcations is dependent on bodily performances and their repetition. This opens up performative gaps between the coincidence of symbolic sense-making and the social understanding of meaning of the ritually acting, who are already educated and yet continue to be educated.

While the analysis of the functioning of entrance examinations explains the effectiveness of symbolic power and seems to give it a resounding impact, the question arises, especially from a pedagogical perspective, of subjective stubbornness, which can be based not only on a reflexive distancing but also on a practical-strategic distancing. Docking on the levers of habitualised dispositions to recognise authority can encounter un-adapted and incoherent habitual dispositions (Bourdieu, 2001, p. 206ff.). Moreover, rituals become less tangible as social-magical boundary barriers within a hierarchically ordered context of instruction and interpretation but play out as dynamic practices of institution within a complex and heterogeneous, social-cultural discursive web.

In discursive webs, 'struggles for the *definition* of "reality"' (Bourdieu, 1990, p. 99, emphasis in original) take place. Rituals as performative utterances encounter '[…] the practical (i.e., unspoken, unsystematic and more or less contradictory) schemata' (ibid., p. 103) of the habitus, which in turn generate classification practices and principles with which the powerful symbolic practices are individually and collectively evaluated.

Even if Bourdieu himself remains sceptical about the capacity for resistance, the dispositions of the habitus, which—as misrecognition or belief—lead to the delegation of power, through which the authorised discourse first acquires its authority (ibid., p. 79), do not force social actors into a performative logic that would be all-powerful, it is just not easy to break through. With recourse to Bourdieu's concept of habitus, both recognition and disregard, obedience as well as opposition, approval as well as criticism can be explained—also for the pedagogical field and its discourses and debates on educational systems, concepts, and reforms and not least with regard to the inherent power relations of pedagogical practice. Pedagogical authority, which, like all recognised power, is based on the recognisers transferring their power of recognition to the commissioned and appointed, does not represent property, but can rather be understood as an element of symbolic practice whose performative logic cannot rely on fixed and institutionally secured hierarchies and responsibilities.

4 Conclusion: Notes and Outlook on Character, Materiality, and Performativity of Pedagogical Authority

Pedagogical authority depends on recognition and trust and must prove itself in everyday pedagogical life. Recognition refers to a hierarchical difference between educators and those to be educated, whereby the pupils recognise the responsibility and competences, especially the knowledge and experience advantage, of the educators and follow them and their instructions more or less willingly. Those who educate with authority can therefore, in principle, do without coercion and violence.

The recognition of pedagogical power does not work unilaterally; rather, educators must trust in the basic willingness of their counterpart to obey, without being able to constantly demand or negotiate this or explicitly justify its necessity and meaningfulness. Moreover, recognition knows different degrees, ranging from absolute respect and obedience to just reserved willingness and critical scrutiny, and it can be withdrawn at any time. Pedagogical authority thus has a fragile, gradual, dynamic, and reciprocal character (Helsper, 2009, p. 69ff.; Paris, 2009, p. 38ff.).

The pedagogical authority of schoolteachers, representing systems of school rules and cultural values, consists of analytically distinguishable dimensions that are, however, inseparably interwoven in pedagogical practice. These include the institutional dimension, which is manifested in the sanctioning power of the teacher and consists mainly in his or her power to grade pupils' performance, determined and secured by the teaching office. The pedagogical expertise as the second dimension consists not only of subject knowledge but is shown in the mastery of the didactic art of conveying educational content as well as in classroom management, which includes both the organisation of lessons and the ability to guide classes. Added to this is personal authority, which manifests itself in the teacher's exemplary and appreciative as well as disciplinary behaviour and convincing appearance. These dimensions create the teacher's balance of authority and depend both on norms and values of the concrete school culture and on norms and values outside the school.

Currently, a continuing crisis of pedagogical authority is observed, with the discourse of crisis referring to various factors, disturbing the balance of the teacher's authority. Following the discourse, the crisis emanates mainly from a crisis of the institutional dimension. The (claimed) historically declining radiance of the school (Paris, 2009, p. 51) and the increasing insecurity of school investments are cited, as are such contradictory factors as the advanced democratisation of pedagogical generational relations and school-cultural transformations with their declining ritualisations (Fend, 1998, p. 179), or the constant, neo-conservative pressure on schools to constantly reform and perform (Paris, 2009, p. 52 f.). In addition, youth cultural influences and decreasing educational efforts in general would put pressure on the dimension of subject matter competence (ibid., p. 54 f.), which is further intensified by digitalisation and globalisation processes.

In addition to abstract-generalised assessments, assuming the integration of the educational sector into socially effective power relations, qualitative and ethnographic empirical studies assume both, the powerful social embedding of educational sector (Helsper, 2009, p. 67) as well that teachers individually as in the college, and schools themselves as institutions can react to changes in social power relations and are not helpless in the face of these (ibid., p. 80).

Empirically, structural variants of dealing with pedagogical authority can be identified, which play in different fields of force of pedagogical authority. Teacher's authority is straddled between the poles of 'charismatic' or comprehensive and 'function-oriented' or limited authority (ibid., p. 74), which themselves are distinguished in the field of a lower and higher level. At the lower level of an authority that is granted rather than demanded by pedagogical concepts and practices, the field of limited authority is exemplified in the pedagogical figure of a virtuoso piano teacher, the field of charismatic authority by a spiritual master (ibid.). At the higher level of a demanded authority, the force field of limited authority is shown, for example, in the figure of a competent mathematics teacher at the grammar school and in the force field of comprehensive authority in the figure of the Waldorf teacher (ibid.).

Furthermore, considerations of educational theory recur by means of deconstructivist references to the principally opaque, context-related, and derived character of authority, whose origin cannot be determined, and which thus cannot be justified (Wimmer, 2009). In this respect, pedagogical authority is in a constant crisis and the current crisis scenarios can be read as a 'crisis of crisis' (Reichenbach, 2011, p. 34).

The empirical studies in the German-speaking educational science discourse of pedagogical authority refer in particular to Max Weber's considerations but limit themselves to the interpersonal character of pedagogical authority. Although the power of spatial arrangements, material props and bodily practices is reflected in educational discourse, the interplay, overlaps, and ruptures of the performative power of the spatial, material, and bodily elements of pedagogical practice have only recently been focussed on in ethnographic studies.

The materiality and performativity of pedagogical authority co-determined by bodily exercise, observation, and examination in power-knowledge complexes as well as by practical recognition, which is generated and structured by the habitus, require further reflection and investigation in educational science. Through lenses, inspired by practice theory, educational investigations note the historical character of power relations and fields and the power of practical knowledge—in critical following and reflecting Bourdieu's and Foucault's legacy. This can be executed in an undogmatic and doubly critical manner, both inspired by a critique of domination and at the same time remains sceptical of the resounding impacts of pedagogical power techniques and practices, paying attention to both the dynamic relations between sociomaterial and performative factors of pedagogical practice and the dynamic relations between the pedagogical sector and other fields of power.

References

Audehm, K. (2001). Die Macht der Sprache. Performative Magie bei Pierre Bourdieu. In C. Wulf, M. Göhlich, & J. Zirfas (Eds.), *Grundlagen des Performativen. Eine Einführung in die Zusammenhänge von Sprache, Macht und Handeln* (pp. 101–128). Juventa.

Audehm, K. (2008). Die Kaffeekanne und die Autorität des Vaters: Familienmahlzeiten als symbolische Praxen. In R. Schmidt & V. Woltersdorff (Eds.), *Symbolische Gewalt. Herrschaftsanalyse nach Pierre Bourdieu* (pp. 125–144). UVK.

Audehm, K. (2017). Habitus. In A. Kraus, J. Budde, M. Hietzge, & C. Wulf (Eds.), *Handbuch Schweigendes Wissen. Erziehung, Bildung, Sozialisation und Lernen* (pp. 167–178). Beltz Juventa.

Baldus, M., & Utz, R. (Eds.). (2011). *Sexueller Missbrauch in pädagogischen Kontexten. Faktoren. Interventionen. Perspektiven.* VS Verlag für Sozialwissenschaften.

Bourdieu, P. (1990). *Was heisst Sprechen? Die Ökonomie des sprachlichen Tausches.* Braumüller.

Bourdieu, P. (2001). *Meditationen. Zur Kritik der scholastischen Vernunft.* Suhrkamp.

Bourdieu, P., & Passeron, J.-C. (1973). *Grundlagen einer Theorie der symbolischen Gewalt.* Suhrkamp.

Demirović, A. (2015). Sex Machine oder: Die Führung der Individuen durch Sexualität. In B. Bargetz, G. Ludwig, & B. Sauer (Eds.), *Gouvernementalität und Geschlecht. Politische Theorie im Anschluss an Michel Foucault* (pp. 62–89). Campus.

Durkheim, É. (1972). *Erziehung und Soziologie.* Pädagogischer Verlag Schwann.

Durkheim, É. (1998 [1912]). *Die elementaren Formen des religiösen Lebens.* Suhrkamp.

Fend, H. (1998). *Qualität im Bildungswesen. Schulforschung zu Systembedingungen, Schulprofilen und Lehrerleistung.* Juventa.

Foucault, M. (1976). *Die Mikrophysik der Macht.* Merve.

Foucault, M. (1983). *Der Wille zum Wissen.* Sexualität und Wahrheit, 1. Suhrkamp.

Foucault, M. (1994 [1975]). *Überwachen und Strafen. Die Geburt des Gefängnisses.* Suhrkamp.

Helsper, W. (2009). Autorität und Schule—zur Ambivalenz der Lehrerautorität. In A. Schäfer & C. Thompson (Eds.), *Autorität* (pp. 65–83). Ferdinand Schöningh.

Lorey, I. (2015). Das Gefüge der Macht. In B. Bargetz, G. Ludwig, & B. Sauer (Eds.), *Gouvernementalität und Geschlecht. Politische Theorie im Anschluss an Michel Foucault* (pp. 31–61). Campus.

Mannheim, K. (1980 [1924]). *Strukturen des Denkens.* Suhrkamp.

Marx, K. (1962 [1864]). Das Kapital (Vol. 1). In Marx-Engels-Werke, MEW, 23. Dietz.

Marx, K., & Engels, F. (1962 [1845–1846]). Die deutsche Ideologie. Kritik der neuesten deutschen Philosophie in ihren Repräsentanten Feuerbach, B. Bauer und Stirner, und des deutschen Sozialismus in seinen verschiedenen Propheten. In *Marx-Engels-Werke*, MEW, 3, pp. 9–530. Dietz.

Mayer-Drawe, K. (2001). Erziehung und Macht. *In Vierteljahreszeitschrift für wissenschaftliche Pädagogik, 77*, 446–457.

Oelkers, J. (2004). Erziehung. In D. Benner & J. Oelkers (Eds.), *Historisches Wörterbuch der Pädagogik* (pp. 303–340).

Paris, R. (2009). Die Autoritätsbalance des Lehrers. In A. Schäfer & C. Thompson (Eds.), *Autorität* (pp. 37–63). Ferdinand Schöningh.

Paris, R. (2015). *Der Wille des Einen ist das Tun des Anderen. Aufsätze zur Machttheorie.* Velbrück Wissenschaft.

Popitz, H. (2009). *Phänomene der Macht.* Mohr.

Reichenbach, R. (2011). *Pädagogische Autorität. Macht und Vertrauen in der Erziehung.* Kohlhammer.

Rieger-Ladich, M. (2002). *Mündigkeit als Pathosformel. Beobachtungen zur pädagogischen Semantik.* UVK.

Rieger-Ladich, M. (2014). Macht und Gewalt. In C. Wulf & J. Zirfas (Eds.), *Handbuch Pädagogische Anthropologie.* Springer VS.

Rutschky, K. (1977). *Schwarze Pädagogik.* Ullstein.

Thole, W., Baader, M., Helsper, W., Kappeler, M., Leunzinger-Bohleber, M., Reh, S., Sielert, U., & Thompson, C. (2012). *Sexualisierte Gewalt, Macht und Pädagogik.* Barbara Budrich.

Weber, M. (1972 [1922]): *Wirtschaft und Gesellschaft. Grundriß der verstehenden Soziologie.* Tübingen: Mohr.

Wellendorf, F. (1973). *Schulische Sozialisation und Identität. Zur Sozialpsychologie der Schule als Institution.* Beltz.

Wimmer, M. (2009). Zwischen Zwang und Freiheit. Der leere Platz der Autorität. In A. Schäfer & C. Thompson (Eds.), *Autorität* (pp. 85–120). Ferdinand Schöningh.

Part III

Body, Sociality and Learning

The human body is a social body: it learns through relating to other human beings and testimonies of their culture. As soon as a child is born, from the experience of birth onwards the child's complete and lasting dependence on other people is clear. From an early age our survival depends on other people and, furthermore, on the community. Something that is often overlooked is the fact that learning is more than an individual and fully governed process. This is especially true of mimetic processes in which children begin to discover the world. In these early processes, the body plays a central part.

Performativity, that is how cultural and social actions are staged and performed, plays an important role in the success of mimetic processes. These involve a productive imitation of the outside world in the form of other people and cultural and social phenomena (*Birgit Althans* [Chap. 13]). In the performativity of actions, corporeality, the event character of actions and the cultural nature of dealing with the materiality of things are expressed. In the performativity of actions, we find more than the mere realization of the intentions that lie behind them. The quality and effect of actions depend on *how* people use their bodies, what physical distance they keep, what stances they adopt and what gestures they use. In conclusion, it can be said that performativity denotes the execution of a speech act (Austin), the ostentatious activity of an individual (Goffman), the power of discourse in the constitution of gender (Butler), the creation of the social world in rituals and gestures (Berlin Study on Rituals and Gestures), and the aesthetic effect of artistic performances. Through language alone the performativity of social action does not lead to the experience of alterity. Althans analyses the role of the performativity of actions in the context of gender formation and focuses aspects of the new materialism. 'Learning by doing' is examined as a performative practice of embodiment.

Since pedagogy is a practical science, the practical knowledge and the performativity acquired in mimetic processes play an important part in the education of the next generation of children (*Léonard Loew* [Chap. 14]). The interaction of body, consciousness and society results in the formation of an individual's identity. This forms the matrix for the way the individual sees the world and humanity. Mimetic and performative processes make us familiar with what is foreign to us, that is with the alterity of the world. Processes of incorporation are initiated by physical desire, instincts and feelings. What emerges is a somatic understanding of otherness that can only be partially explained by language and that shows the importance of implicit knowledge for social action. Thus, we appropriate the world not by the use of words but by through techniques of our bodies. The repetition of social actions in certain social situations leads to the development of a habitus, which creates coherence and similarity in mimetic social actions. In this appropriation process, what is foreign to us becomes transferred into our inner world in a manner that is determined by the habitus. The result is the gradual formation of structures of both individual and collective identity.

On the basis of similar insights, Chap. 15 focuses on gender as embodiment. In the practices of daily life gender-specific behaviour is learnt, expressed, repeated and incorporated. *Anja Tervooren* shows how the embodiment of gender starts in early childhood. Not only the characteristics of gender are specific to each phase of life but also the social gender relations transform during the life span. Especially to highlight is the physical dependency of children. Enactments of gender and the analysis of gender hierarchies in society are done in dichotomous or in ambiguous terms. Tervooren presents deconstructive approaches of gender research to analyse forms of the embodiment of gender as empirical phenomena. She demonstrates the complexity and the interweaving of differences and argues for gender research in the framework of educational anthropology, in which gender as embodiment is conceived as concern with the development of children.

Tatiana Shchyttsova in Chap. 16 illustrates the complexity of physical experiences by looking at relationships between adults and children. She rejects two common interpretations of this asymmetry: the presupposition of the child's immaturity combined with subordination, and the ideal of the 'spontaneous natural creativity of the child, free from conventional social normativity'. She rejects both ideas and the corresponding pedagogical concepts as being subject-centred thinking. Instead, she highlights the 'being-with-one another' of the adult and child and explains their 'intriguing relatedness' in terms of emotions, using anxiety as an example. The child's anxiety relates to being faced with options that are as yet unknown. 'Pedagogy as a science arises out of the adult's primary, pre-scientific concern about how to bring up children.' Pre-reflexive trust on the side of the child corresponds with patience on the adult's side. Shchyttsova draws the consequence: 'It is the child's being-in-touch with the poetic that allows the child not to lose existential balance and productive openness in his or her anxiously-curious state of mind'.

Anja Kraus in Chap. 17 investigates the idea that all humans are equal in fundamental worth or moral status. This is expressed in the principle of 'egalitarian difference', according to which culture is conveyed less by cultural authorities than by persons. Individuals are seen as recipients, as well as agents of culture. An individual carries out culture with his/her unique blend of experiences, perspectives and backgrounds, and culture links the innate dispositions of a person to his/her outer personality, and to generic potentialities and specific performances. Corporeality, the body and embodiment as well as historically created systems of meaning play a central role here. Involved are not least challenges by alterity, violence and 'the differend' (Lyotard) as integral aspects of culture. As pedagogy is about enabling the young to eventually take ownership of their learning and their lives, it is also about enabling them to deal with the menacing experiences of alterity, violence and 'the differend'. In this contribution, the principle of egalitarian difference, as well as historically created systems of meaning, are presented as possible approaches to deal with cultural difference in some of its facets.

We see through these chapters how body-based processes facilitate appropriation and esteem of the foreign, as well as a detachment from it. It is through these processes that the conceptual world and the practical knowledge of individuals are formed. For these processes to succeed, their body-based performative aspects are essential. Instincts, desire, emotions and body techniques all play an important role. Uniqueness and alterity are interwoven in the learning individual and their corporeality.

The Performativity of Learning

Birgit Althans

The complex process of learning, described in terms of neurophysiology and cognitive science, is seen as the interconnection of certain muscular and motor actions of the limbs of the learning body with the brain areas, neurons and synapses responsible for them.—Theories on learning hardly fall within the remit of educational science after the end of the twentieth century, but rather within that of psychology or the neurosciences. After the corona pandemic in 2020–2021 revealed the need to catch up in the digital organization of knowledge transfer, the subdisciplines of educational science, school pedagogy, teaching science and didactics are currently dealing with the intensified organization of the provision of learning environments and multi-media 'learning settings' in order to organize the daily routines of knowledge transfer as free of disruptions as possible. The fact that this is not yet entirely successful from a media-didactic point of view becomes apparent by the increasing number of children and young people who use YouTube tutorials privately to help them with their schoolwork. So, what has a performative effect on learning in the twenty-first century? The techniques of teaching? Digital technologies or the mediating bodily practices in learning situations? Or is it rather the interplay, the intertwining of digital technology and learning bodies, the use of knowledge scanning and mediating technology or the bodies that absorb and process the knowledge? "The home, workplace, market, public arena, the body itself—all

---

B. Althans (✉)
Kunstakademie Düsseldorf, Düsseldorf, Germany
e-mail: Birgit.Althans@kunstakademie-duesseldorf.de

© The Author(s), under exclusive license to Springer Nature Switzerland AG 2022
A. Kraus, C. Wulf (eds.), *The Palgrave Handbook of Embodiment and Learning*,
https://doi.org/10.1007/978-3-030-93001-1_13

can be dispersed and interfaced in nearly infinite, polymorphous ways" (Haraway, 2016a, p. 33). But even the bodies, according to Haraway, are now generated with their needs by the technologies themselves: "Communications technologies and biotechnologies are the crucial tools recrafting our bodies" (Haraway, 2016a, p. 33). For postmodern biology, according to Haraway, bodies are no more than organic-technological artefacts, biomedically repairable, neuroscientifically conditionally programmable:

> Late twentieth-century machines have made thoroughly ambiguous the difference between natural and artificial, mind and body, self-developing and externally designed, and many other distinctions that used to apply to organisms and machines. Our machines are disturbingly lively and we ourselves frighteningly inert. (Haraway, 2016a, p. 37)

Nevertheless, not only technologies but also human bodies act actively, performatively in these environments dominated by (learning) technologies, generating themselves, their materiality and difference from others again and again in the processes of their processual 'becoming'.

In its presentation of the performativity of learning, this article refers on the one hand to classical concepts of the performative, but perspectively—with a view to learning in increasingly digitally shaped lifeworlds—it incorporates approaches from Donna Haraway's and Karen Barad's feminist philosophy of science and New Materialism (Barad, 2003), which assumes a reciprocal performativity of human and non-human bodies.

> If performativity is linked not only to the formation of the subject but also to the production of the matter of bodies, as Butler's account of 'materialization' and Haraway's notion of 'materialized refiguration' suggest, then it is all the more important that we understand the nature of this production. [...] All bodies, not merely 'human' bodies, come to matter through the world's iterative intra-activity—its performativity. (Barad, 2003, pp. 808, 823)

By all means reference is made to the breadth of theories of the performative:

> Indeed, performativity has become a ubiquitous term in literary studies, theater studies, and the nascent interdisciplinary area of performance studies, prompting the question as to whether all performances are performative. [...] I propose a specifically posthumanist notion of performativity—one that incorporates important material and discursive, social and scientific, human and nonhuman, and natural and cultural factors. (Barad, 2003, p. 808)

On the other hand, this assumption of a reciprocal performativity of human and non-human bodies is supposed to be illustrated using classical educational theories as well. Here, also, the article follows approaches of New Materialism and its reception practice of a 'diffractive methodology' (Barad, 2013, p. 60), which advocates a respectful 'thinking through each other' of different disciplinary approaches and knowledge practices that are not normally thought together. This is done especially in relation to the formula—usually attributed to John Dewey—that almost imposes itself in regard to the performative: 'learning by doing'.

Surprisingly, Donna Haraway's trenchant, ironic, late twentieth-century analyses of a society on the verge of closely intertwining artificial and natural intelligence, artificial and natural body parts, set out in her *Cyborg Manifesto* (Haraway, 2016a), can be linked surprisingly well with the no less ironically formulated positions of the philosopher of education John Dewey at the beginning of the twentieth century, which he set out in *Democracy and Education* (2004). He, too, addressed the handling of learning, knowledge-consuming and knowledge-producing bodies in the educational and teaching apparatuses of the schools he examined at the beginning of the twentieth century. After the presentation of the performativity inherent in 'learning by doing' (1), the performativity of learning will be differentiated by means of two further examples of physical learning: Learning in the entanglement with other species (2) and learning as a bodily experience of immersion into other elements, in swimming and in imaginary and digital worlds (3)

1 Learning by Doing—Performativity of Learning

The formula 'learning by doing', mostly attributed to the American educational philosopher John Dewey, can almost be used as a definition of the concept of the performative: That one learns by doing, performing, practically trying something out. Dewey used the formula extremely sparingly and relatively late, a total of 11 times in the text *Schools of Tomorrow* (Dewey & Dewey, 1915), written together with his daughter Evelyn Dewey, and in a brief reference in *Democracy and Education* (2004). In his very detailed overview, *From Aristotle to Dewey. Vom Ursprung der Maxime 'Learning by doing'* (2011), Michael Knoll reconstructs the long genealogy of the formula, which can be traced as an adaptation and translation practice from Aristotle via Comenius and Friedrich Fröbel to the discourse production of the New Education,

Kindergarten and Progressive Education movements in North America in the nineteenth and first half of twentieth centuries. Aristotle laid the foundation of the formula in the Nicomachean Ethics, in which he stated his conviction that virtuous, ethical behaviour and professional skill were rather learned through practical (re-)doing, than through simple (theoretical) instruction:

> For that which we must do after we have done it, we learn by doing it. Thus, by building one becomes a builder, and by playing the zither one becomes a zither player. (Aristotle., 1985, p. 27f., [author's translation])

This describes for physical-practical actions in situations of learning or instruction what the English philosopher of language John L. Austin stated for use of language in 1961 in *How to Do Things with Words*: Even through speech, when properly contextually framed, actions, acts are performed, meanings are established. Austin called this process performing, performative. The term, Austin said, "comes, of course, from 'to perform': one 'performs' actions. It is meant to imply that one who makes such an utterance is thereby performing an action" (Austin, 1979, p. 27f.). At the centre of Austin's concept, then, is the focus on practical performance, in which concrete meaning becomes visible: "by saying something, we *do* something" (Austin, 1979, p. 33). For example, Donald Trump's infamous "*You are fired*", often uttered both in the TV series *The Apprentice* and during his time as US president, is, when uttered by a person endowed with institutional power to a person who can be fired, a speech act that performs an action: The person thus addressed is then in effect dismissed. The speech act is therefore about saying something in a coherent context in front of an audience, in front of spectators or in front of listeners, about performing an action in front of their eyewitnesses. Therefore, in teaching-learning situations, in classical face-to-face teaching, there are always performances in front of an audience. A school class constitutes itself performatively new by saying its greetings: "Good morning, Mr/Mrs …" and "Good morning, class …", acts of demonstrating knowledge or not-knowing by pupils become assessed performances through teachers' comments in front of class. Thus, if a situation of pedagogical instruction, or a teaching-learning situation as outlined by Aristotle on the basis of building or playing the zither, is regarded as a speech act, then it is split into a linguistic and bodily consummation that is perceived as intertwined in the action itself. Austin would emphasize the differently framed speech acts in learning situations, Aristotle the importance of bodily accomplishment, the 'embodiment' of knowledge acquisition. In this, the aforementioned focus on something that was only explicitly articulated in the arts in Europe and the USA in *performance art* since the 1960s and 1970s. The theatre scholar Mayte Zimmermann describes the focus on 'performance', the physical action, from the perspective of theatre pedagogy:

> a radical shift towards the performance of actual (physical) actions in a public setting. What moves into the focus of the scenic event with these works is not the meaning-bearing, but rather the meaning-generating or simply sensual dimension of a scenic event as such, which is no longer measured by its functioning ('right/wrong'). (Zimmermann, 2020, [author's translation])

Aristotle, and subsequently Comenius, Fröbel and, albeit in a limited way, Dewey, did something similar with regard to pedagogical situations, emphasizing the importance of bodily action for learning, which will be shown later. The philosopher Sybille Krämer points out that Plato, too, in his Socratic dialogues, emphasized the importance of the physical accomplishment of knowledge. The dialogues themselves represent a physical performance of the staging of a pedagogically framed question-answer game, an obviously physically performed knowledge, presented in the form of a theatrical dialogue. For Plato, as George Steiner pointed out in *Lessons of the Master*, had begun his career as a dramatist (Steiner, 2004, p. 33). Plato also emphasizes the importance of physical comprehension in relation to mathematical knowledge, as the philosopher Sibylle Krämer shows in her analysis of a famous example from the dialogue *Menon*:

> That mathematical knowledge can be acquired through one's own activity is demonstrated by the Menon scene. Socrates draws a square in the sand and a slave boy is given the task of doubling it. In the first attempt, the boy doubles one side and then sees from the resulting square that this is wrong because it is too big. The next step of extending the side by half a distance also proves to be wrong because—as can easily be seen from the drawing—a square much too large is still created. The boy gets into an aporia, he confesses to not knowing his way around. Finally, after several attempts, he finds the solution, which is to build the square on the diagonal of the initial square, which then actually has twice the area. [...] In the course of his graphic experiments, the boy not only develops a positive knowledge, but can also—in the first step—learn about his ignorance, his error. What he finally acquires is a 'knowledge of how', a know-how of how to perform the square mediation geometrically. Moreover, it is revealing that Socrates actually compares this 'knowledge how' with a spatial knowledge of movement, namely with knowing 'the way to Larissa'. (Plato, 1990, cited in Krämer, 2018, p. 26, [author's translation])

Krämer concludes from this that Plato thus not only introduces the 'conception of knowledge as wayfinding' into philosophy but also emphasizes the importance of the 'embodiment of knowledge', that it is precisely

> the sensualisation of the senseless, the concretion of the abstract, the embodiment of ideal objects, which constitute the artifice and analytical potential of scientific—and precisely also philosophical—knowledge. (Krämer, 2018, p. 28, [author's translation])

But, once again back to Aristotle's example, who relates his description of learning to more manual arts, such as building and playing the zither, who, however, in his description of learning to build, underestimates the part that 'non-human actors' have in the learning process: The materials involved in building, such as sand, stone or wood, or the zither involved in playing the zither, also have an influence on learning in their materiality and also have a performative effect: "All bodies, not merely 'human' bodies, come to matter through the world's iterative intra-activity—its performativity" (Barad, 2003, p. 823).

Aristotle's focus on the physical process of learning was taken up again by Johann Amos Comenius in his *Didactica Magna* (1657) in the section 'Method for the Arts':

> Activity should be learned through activity. Craftsmen do not stop their apprentices by contemplation, but lead them immediately to work, so that they learn forging by forging, sculpting by sculpting, painting by painting, dancing by dancing. Therefore, in the schools, writing should be learned by writing, speaking by speaking, singing by singing, arithmetic by arithmetic. (Comenius, 1982, p. 142, [author's translation])

In the US, this was first expressed as 'learning by doing' by Henry Barnard in the *Journal of Education* in the nineteenth century:

> Each study should be learned by practice; writing by writing, singing by singing, etc. The master must perform the thing before the scholar, without tiresome explanation. [...] Rules should not be given without examples. Artisans understand this well. None of them would give their apprentice a lecture upon this trade, but would show him how he, the master, went about it, and then would put the tools into his hands, and show him how to do the like and to imitate himself. Doing can be only learned by doing, writing by writing, painting by painting. (Comenius, 1858, pp. 266; 290)

The Performativity of Learning   219

In further translations of Comenius, the formula is repeated and condensed: "Let things that have to be done be learned by doing them" (Laurie, 1881, p. 116). The often over-complex formulations of the German kindergarten inventor Friedrich Froebel and his theory of learning through the materiality of play—according to Knoll, the third strand of the genealogy of the 'learning by doing' formula—also became 'education by doing' and 'children learn by doing' in the extremely successful American adaptation of Froebel's kindergarten movement, which was pushed by the women's movement as early as the 1880s (cf. Knoll, 2011, p. 5). In the American translation, Froebel's complex theory of 'human education' (1982) is so abridged that it made kindergarten education downright 'mainstream' in cultural discourse. Froebel's 'learning by doing' in kindergarten became so popular that the inventor of the 'skyscraper', the American architect Louis Sullivan, who was also Frank Lloyd Wright's teacher, titled his teaching instructions to young architects, written in the form of fictional Socratic dialogues, *Kindergarten Chats* (Sullivan, 1979). In his memoirs, Frank Lloyd Wright also emphasizes the influence that the physical exercise and playing with Fröbel's 'materials' had on his later artistic development:

> My mother learned from Froebel that children must not draw according to the random manifestations of nature until they have mastered the basic forms lying behind those manifestations. First, cosmic and geometric elements had to be made visible to the child's mind. [...] For several years I sat at the small kindergarten table, over which longitudinal and transverse lines were drawn at intervals of ten centimetres, so that squares of ten centimetres were formed, there I played, among other things, on these 'unit lines' with the square (cube), the circle (sphere) and the triangle (tetrahedron or tripod)—they were smooth maple blocks. Scarlet cardboard triangles (60°–30°), five centimetres long on the short side, with white undersides, were smooth triangular sectors with which I could lay patterns—make designs—according to my own imagination. Eventually I had to make designs with other means. But the smooth cardboard triangles and maple blocks were most important. Even today I can feel them in my fingers. (Wright, 1966, p. 15f, [author's translation])

Here Wright retrospectively describes something that John Dewey was to work out in his use of the formula 'learning by doing': The importance of cognitive reflection on the practical experience of physically carrying out the learning process! Like Haraway, Dewey frames his observations of the school system of his time quite ironically. In particular, he problematizes the constant suppression of students' bodily needs in the classroom situation.

The very word pupil has almost come to mean one who is engaged not in having fruitful experiences but in absorbing knowledge directly. Something which is called mind or consciousness is severed from the physical organs of activity. The former it then thought to be purely intellectual and cognitive; the latter to be an irrelevant and intruding physical factor. (Dewey, 2004, p. 152)

At the same time, Dewey refers to the physical basis of all learning processes:

For the pupil has a body, and brings it to school along with his mind. And the body is, of necessity, a wellspring of energy; it has to do something. (Dewey, 2004, p. 153)

Knowledge is absorbed with the body, but at the same time this body repeatedly causes interruptions and irritations in the teaching situation, its suppressed energies make students and teachers alike nervous. In the school context, the body and its organs are regarded merely as 'tools' for the acquisition of knowledge:

Even, however, with respect to the lessons which have to be learned by the application of 'mind', some bodily activities have to be used. The senses—especially the eye and the ear—have to be employed to take in what the book, the map, the blackboard, and the teacher say. The lips and vocal organs, and the hands, have to be used to reproduce in speech and writing what has been stowed away. The senses are then regarded as a kind of mysterious conduit through which information is conducted from the external world into the mind; they are spoken of as gateways and avenues of knowledge. (Dewey, 2004, p. 154)

Here it becomes apparent that Dewey, unlike his classical predecessors Plato and Aristotle cited above, also sees the significance of 'things'—in Haraway's and Barad's understanding of the 'non-human actors'—in situations of learning. In learning situations, he sees interplay with the sensory organs of the body, also conceived as tools, in reciprocal performativity. Although Dewey refers to the formula 'learning by doing' when he formulates: "Experience is primarily an active-passive affair; it is not primarily cognitive" (Dewey, 2004, p. 152), something else is central to his theory of education. In order to come to cognition, to the experience of thinking, which he defines as "the discernment of the relation between what we try to do and what happens in consequence" (Dewey, 2004, p. 157), it takes more than the practical performance of an action. For him, the processual, unfinished thinking, the accomplishment of 'thinking research', seems to constitute the essence of the learning process: "thinking is a process of inquiry, of looking into things, of investigating" (Dewey, 2004, p. 160f.). He relates this to the conceptual history of learning:

> The Greeks acutely raised the question: How can we learn? For either we know already what we are after, or else we do not know. In neither case is learning possible; on the first alternative because we know already; on the second, because we do not know what to look for, nor if, by chance we find it can we tell that it is what we were after. [...] Nevertheless, the twilight zone of inquiry, of thinking, exists. The possibility of hypothetical conclusion, of tentative results, is the fact which the Greek dilemma overlooked. The perplexities of the situation suggest certain ways out. We try these ways, and either push our way out, in which case we know we have found what we were looking for, or the situation gets darker and more confused—in which case we know we are still ignorant. Tentative means trying out, feeling one's way along provisionally. (Dewey, 2004, p. 161)

For Dewey, the 'thinking experience' or the 'experience of thinking' that is central to learning arises at the moment when everyday routines and certainties—as in the *Menon* example cited above—are shaken and real reflection becomes necessary. This in turn initiates a different process of (bodily-sensory-motorical) action and thought, both of which Dewey sees as constitutive of learning in their interconnectedness. Asked in, 1949, on his 90th birthday, about the formula 'learning by doing', Dewey replied:

> I don't believe people learn merely by doing. The main points are the ideas that a man puts into his doing. Unintelligently doing will result in his learning the wrong thing. (Fine, 1949, p. 31)

Following this, two further perspectives on the performativity of learning will be described.

2 Entanglements: The Performativity of Learning With and From Others

Philosophical anthropology likes to cite the premature birth of humans and the associated dependence on others as the reason for the ability to learn; or the imageability of humans and the impetus for human sociality. In his extremely popular evolutionary history *A Brief History of Humankind* (Harari, 2011), the Israeli historian Yuval Noah Harari describes the special neediness of human mammals compared to other species:

[C]ompared to other animals, humans are born prematurely, when many of their vital systems are still underdeveloped. A colt can trot shortly after birth; a kitten leaves its mother to forage on its own when it is just a few weeks old. Human babies are helpless, dependent for many years on their elders for sustenance, protection and education. [...] Raising children required constant help from other family members and neighbors. It takes a tribe to raise a human. Evolution thus favored those capable of forming strong social ties. In addition, since humans are born underdeveloped, they can be educated and socialized to a far greater extent than any other animal. (Harari, 2011, p. 11)

The resulting malleability or imageability of the human being in dependence on recognition by others is described by Hegel in his *Phenomenology of Spirit* as the master-servant paradox (Hegel, 1998). Judith Butler reads Hegel's famous scene about the emergence of human self-consciousness, the 'struggle for recognition', as an educational novel, even as an educational journey, an optimistic narrative of adventure and edification, a pilgrimage of the spirit (Butler, 2012), which she also finds receivable as a theatrical production.

Hegel's provisional scenes, the stage of self-certainty, the struggle for recognition, the dialectic of lord and bondsman, are instructive fictions, ways of organizing the world which prove to be too limited to satisfy the subject's desire to discover itself as substance. (Butler, 2012, p. 21)

She goes even further: Hegel's descriptions of the subjects 'tragic blindness' in becoming a subject remind her in their predictability of comic scenes:

Like such miraculously resilient characters of the Saturday morning cartoons, Hegel's protagonists always reassemble themselves, prepare a new scene, enter the stage armed with a new set of ontological insights—and fail again. (Butler, 2012, p. 21)

An undoubtedly performative reading of the Hegelian master-servant paradox! Butler made the concept of the performative extremely popular through her analysis of the emergence of gender identities in *Gender Trouble* (Butler, 1990): She described the emergence of gender identity as an entanglement of speech act—'That's a girl'—and physical performance of social gender identity of the subjects themselves. It is precisely this treatment of the performative by Butler, as well as her theory of materiality, that is criticized by Karen Barad and Donna Haraway's New Materialism as being too limited "on the materialization of 'human' bodies" (Barad, 2003, p. 825). For Barad's conception of the performative has to be applied: "All bodies, not merely human bodies, come to matter through the world's iterative intra-activity—its performativity" (Barad, 2003, pp. 808; 823).

Moreover, according to Donna Haraway, taking her perspective on evolutionary theory and pedagogies, we acquire knowledge not only from other humans but also from other species. She links her earlier analyses of technology-based entanglements of human and non-human actors to learning experiences with other 'companion species', in her case with dogs. Haraway starts her view of learning from others by looking at her early cyborg text, from the perspective of technocultures.

> In the 'Cyborg Manifesto', I tried to write a surrogacy agreement, a trope, a figure for living within and honoring the skills and practices of contemporary technoculture without losing touch with the permanent war apparatus of a nonoptional, postnuclear world and its transcendent, very material lies. Cyborgs can be figures for living with contradictions, attentive to the nature-cultures of mundane practices. [...] However, cyborg reconfigurations hardly exhaust the tropic work required for ontological choreography in technoscience. I have come to see cyborgs as junior siblings in the much bigger, queer family of companion species. (Haraway, 2016b, p. 102f.)

For Haraway, Companion Species means more than *Companion Animals*:

> Companion animals can be dogs, horses, cats or other beings willing to make the leap to the biosociality of service-dogs, family members or team members in cross-country sports. Generally speaking one does not eat one's companion animals (or get eaten by them); and one has a hard time shaking colonist, ethnocentric, ahistorical attitudes towards those who do (eat or get eaten). (Haraway, 2016b, p. 106)

With the concept of 'companion species', she is more concerned with casting a common—human and non-human—perspective on living conditions in technocultures and thereby also benefiting from the vitality, the different sensory abilities and sensitivities of other species:

> I take *interpellation* from the French poststructuralist and Marxist philosopher Louis Althusser's theory for how subjects are constituted from concrete individuals by being 'hailed' through ideology into their subject positions in the modern state. Today, through our ideologically loaded narratives of their lives, animals 'hail' us into account for the regimes in which they and we must live. We 'hail' them into our constructs of nature and culture, with major consequences of life and death, health and illness, longevity and extinction. We also live with each other in the flesh in ways not exhausted by our ideologies. (Haraway, 2016b, p. 108f.)

Haraway provides a very vivid example from her personal environment: The joint 'training' of her godson Marco and her dog puppy Cayenne, which at the same time points to the great importance of the performative framing of teaching-learning situations. Both dog and child are 'educated' at the same time. They learn together, as does the observer:

> Like many of her breed, Cayenne was a smart and willing youngster, a natural to obedience games. Like many of his generation raised on high-speed visual special effects and automated cyborg toys, Marco was a bright and motivated trainer, a natural to control games. […] Entranced, Marci at first treated her like a microchip-implanted truck for which he held the remote controls. He punched an imaginary button; his puppy magically fulfilled the intentions of his omnipotent, remote will. […] I, an obsessive adult who came of the age in the communes of the late, 1960s, was committed to the ideals of intersubjectivity and mutuality in all things, certainly including dog and boy training. […] Marco was at the same time taking karate lessons, and he was profoundly in love with his karate master: this fine man understood the children's love of drama, ritual, and costume, as well as the mental-spiritual-bodily discipline of his martial art. *Respect* was the word and the act that Marco ecstatically told me about from his lessons. He swooned at the chance to collect his small, robed self into the prescribed posture and bow formally to his mater or his partner before performing a form. Calming his turbulent first-grade self and meeting the eyes of his teacher or his partner in preparation for demanding, stylized action thrilled him. Hey, was I going to let an opportunity like that go unused in my pursuit for companion species flourishing? 'Marco', I said. 'Cayenne is not a cyborg truck; she is your partner in a martial art called obedience. You have learned how to perform respect with your body and your eyes. Your job is to teach the form to Cayenne. Until you can find a way to collect her galloping puppy self calmly and to sit still, you cannot let her perform the 'sit' command. (Haraway, 2016b, p. 132f.)

What Haraway shows here is not only a productive interplay of different species and generations, the interlocking effectiveness of different cultural values and performative framings of a teaching-learning situation. She also presents her conviction of the great importance of learning from and with other species:

> It is also my belief that as he learned to show her the corporeal posture of cross-species respect, she and he became significant others for each other. (Haraway, 2016b, p. 134)

Me, the author, experienced a similarly productive interplay of learning when riding, together with the 'companion species' horse with which humanity shares a long stretch of its evolutionary history (Raulff, 2014). I was lucky enough to be taken into the lessons of a well-known cross-country-rider as a teenager. Here, together with the horses I trained and moved there, I was always seen as part of an inseparable 'structure' by glances from outside. The horses and I were, each separately, in the process of 'becoming'. We were 'nothing yet', we were in training, in which we could only 'become something' in the eyes of the riding instructor if both sides made the necessary effort. Horse-and-me were only perceived together, in the ritual staging and performance of our joint learning in the riding lesson. When moving together in the riding situation, 'horse-and-me' formed a 'through-one-another-through' (Barad, 2013, p. 60) swinging unity in the joint forward movement:

> Through their reaching into each other, through their 'prehensions' or graspings, beings constitute each other and themselves. Beings do not preexist their relatings. (Haraway, 2016b, p. 98)

In the movement itself, 'horse-and-me' had different parts in the common movement, which, however, changed both of us in every common hour, formed our corporeality, and constantly (formed) in our respective individuality as human and non-human actors.

However, according to the last thesis, we cannot only learn from other species, but also from other elements.

3 Learning as a Physical Experience of the Other: Immersion into the Other Element

Something that is mentioned repeatedly in the context of 'learning by doing' is swimming. It is used again and again as a strong metaphor for learning a skill or practice that has to be learnt immediately, performed immediately. Already Dewey's predecessors used it:

> We learn to do a thing, by doing it, [...] I learned how to fall into the pond, the other day, by falling in; but I learned at the same time how to swim. That is the way, he [the director of the school] says, to learn everything; by being pushed in, as the little birds are pushed out of their nests to learn to fly. You can't learn to swim without going into the water. (Brooks, 1882, p. 243)

Dewey points out in *Democracy and Education* that one cannot learn to swim on dry land. John Maddox, one of his students and a curriculum expert, explains this again:

> As Professor Dewey insists, we learn to swim by swimming in water, not on a bench in practice; to talk by talking to people about things that interest us and them; we think by solving our own problems, not by exercises in logic; we acquire skill as we work, not by preliminary formal exercise. (Maddox, 1924, p. 149)

The special thing about learning to swim is the associated immersion in another element. The American digital media professor Janet H. Murray used this metaphor to describe the experience of entering virtual reality simulations, digital gaming practices, at the end of the twentieth century.

> The experience of being transported to an elaborately simulated place is pleasurable in itself, regardless of the fantasy content. Immersion is a metaphorical term derived from the physical experience of being submerged in water. We seek the same feeling from a psychologically immersive experience that we do from a plunge in the ocean or swimming pool: the sensation of being surrounded by a completely other reality, as different as water is from air, that takes over all of our attention, our whole perceptual apparatus. (Murray, 1997, p. 98f.)

That is why the passionate swimmer, author and playwright John von Düffel focuses precisely on this very physical moment of immersion, the experience of the 'performative materiality' (Barad, 2003) of another element:

> Whoever goes into the water must master a transition that should not be underestimated, a transformation from the solid to the liquid, from the reliable to the unpredictable, from one form of existence to another. (Von Düffel, 2016, p. 16, [author's translation])

Although he was a competitive swimmer in his youth and has been in the water almost every day of his life since then, the foreign, the materially quite different element still frightens him. Von Düffel understands his physical respect for exposing himself to this element while swimming as a transformational experience in which his body entrusts itself to the materiality of the other element. Together, water and body create a new movement:

> Every swimmer knows that. He knows that from the moment he dives in, he is alone with the water, and he can only hope that it will carry him. He knows that he has to summon up all his willpower in order to survive in this element, and

he also knows that this is not enough. Ultimately, it is thanks to the favour of the water that this will is transformed into movement and he glides through the pool with swift, supple strokes, as if there were no resistance between the water and his movement, as if swimming and being swum were one. (Von Düffel, 2002, [author's translation])

Von Düffel compares this transformational option with the process of writing. This, too, resembles immersion in another element and must be carried out physically.

In the beginning there is always immersion, the change from one familiar element to another, foreign one. I were lying if I said it didn't cost me any effort at all. On the contrary. Entering the world of water or a story always means saying goodbye to the life one is living at the moment. And this farewell is not always easy. Often you have to tear yourself away from the people and comforts that surround you. There are many things one would rather do, because the element of swimming and writing knows no more considerations from the moment of immersion. One is at its mercy, completely and utterly. (Von Düffel, 2002, p. 11, [author's translation])

Similar to what Haraway described for the interaction with the 'companion species', obviously the bodily experience of surrendering the floating body(ies) to the very other element can enable an experience of thinking that Dewey already described: "It is seeking, a quest, for something that is not at hand" (Dewey, 2004, p. 161) and: "the discernment of the relation between what we try to do and what happens in consequence" (Dewey, 2004, p. 157). Even when swimming in water, 'learning by doing' becomes performative. It remains important to note: Learning results from the shared, reciprocal performativity of non-human (water) and human (body) materiality. "Through their reaching into each other, through their 'prehensions' or graspings, beings constitute each other and themselves" (Haraway, 2016b, p. 98).

References

Aristotle. (1985). *Nikomachische Ethik*. Meiner.
Austin, J. L. (1979). *Zur Theorie der Sprechakte*. Reclam.
Barad, K. (2003). Posthuman Performativity. Toward an Understanding of How Matter Comes to Matter. *Gender and Sciences. New Issues, 23*(3), 801–831.
Barad, K. (2013). *Diffraktionen: Differenzen, Kontingenzen und Verschränkungen von Gewicht*. LIT Verlag.

Brooks, B. A. (1882). *Those Children and Their Teacher*. Putnam.

Butler, J. (2012 [1987]). *Subjects of desire: Hegelian reflections in twentieth-century France*. Columbia University Press.

Butler, J. (1990). *Gender Trouble*. Routledge.

Comenius, J. A. (1858). *The School of Infancy: An Essay on the Education of Youth, During Their First Six Years: to which is Prefixed a Sketch of the Life of the Author*. W. Mallalieu.

Comenius, J. A. (1982). *Didactica Magna. Die vollständige Kunst, alle Menschen alles zu lehren*. Klett-Cotta.

Dewey, J., & Dewey, E. (1915). *Schools of Tomorrow*.

Dewey, J. (2004 [1916]). *Democracy and Education. An Introduction to the Philosophy of Education*. Aakar Books.

Fine, B. (1949). John Dewey at 90. *New York Times*, 19.10.1949. pp. 31-39.

Fröbel, F. (1982). *Die Spielgaben*. Edited by Hoffmann, E. Stuttgart.

Harari, Y. N. (2011). *Sapiens. A Brief History of Humankind*. Random House.

Haraway, D. (2016a [1985]). Cyborg Manifesto. Science, Technology and Socialist Feminism in the Late Twentieth Century. In Haraway, D., (ed.) *Manifestly Haraway*, pp. 3-90. University of Minnesota Press.

Haraway, D. (2016b). The Companion Species Manifesto. Dogs, People, and Significant Otherness. In D. Haraway (Ed.), *Manifestly Haraway* (pp. 91–198). University of Minnesota Press.

Hegel, G. W. F. (1998 [1807]). *Phenomenology of spirit*. Motilal Banarsidass Publ.

Krämer, S. (2018). 'Kartographischer Impuls' und 'operative Bildlichkeit'. Eine Reflexion über Karten und die Bedeutung räumlicher Orientierung beim Erkennen. In *ZFK*, H.1, pp. 19-31.

Laurie, S. S. (1881). *John Amos Comenius, Bishop of the Moravians, His Life and Educational Works*. K. Paul, Trench and Company.

Maddox, W. A. (1924). Development of Method. In I. L. Kandel (Ed.), *Twenty-Five Years of American Education. Collected Essays* (p. 149). Macmillan.

Murray, J. H. (1997). *Hamlet on the Holodeck: The Future of Narrative in Cyberspace*. Free Press.

Plato. (1990). *Menon*. Reclam.

Raulff, U. (2014). *Das letzte Jahrhundert der Pferde. Geschichte einer Trennung*. Beck.

Steiner, G. (2004). *Der Meister und seine Schüler*. Hanser.

Sullivan, L. H. (1979). *Kindergarten Chats and Other Writings*.

Von Düffel, J. (2002). Schwimmen und Schreiben. Über den Autor als Amphibium. In J. Von Düffel (Ed.), *Wasser und andere Welten* (pp. 9–14). Dumont.

Von Düffel, J. (2016). *Gebrauchsanweisung fürs Schwimmen*. Piper.

Wright, F. L. (1966). *Ein Testament. Zur neuen Architektur*. Rowohlt.

Zimmermann, M. (2020). Performativität und Performance. In M. Zimmermann, K. Westphal, & Arend, & H. Lohfeld (Eds.), *Theater als Raum bildender Prozesse* (pp. 39–47). Athena.

The Embodied Other: Mimetic-Empathic Encorporations

Léonard Loew

1 Introduction

In the following article, the processes of socialization and education are to be shown as genuinely physical in a mimetic-empathic sense. The socialization of the individual is ensured through the embodiment of the concrete others (in representation of the general others), namely: through the mimetic incorporation of observed and imitated or appropriated body expressions. This includes both, the pure body behavior and the somatic emotional correlates/semantics. For this purpose, various theoretical elements should be used, including the theory of body techniques by Mauss, Bourdieu's conception of habitus, psychoanalytic considerations on 'introjection' and the mimesis concept. All these theories show in addition to the meaningful aspects of mimetic-empathic embodiments also their power-shaped character. Anthropological considerations on the vitality and emotionality of the body as well as on the embodiment of empathy serve to reveal the connection between (intermediate) corporeality, imagination/simulation and social rituality/gestures.

The concept of the soma (German: *Leib*) is used here for the subjectively perceptible body sensations, in contrast to the body (German: *Körper*). A body is visible (e.g. in the mirror), e.g. in relation to the bodies of others

---

L. Loew (✉)
Hochschule für Technik und Wirtschaft des Saarlandes, Saarbrücken, Germany
e-mail: leonard.loew@htwsaar.de

© The Author(s), under exclusive license to Springer Nature Switzerland AG 2022
A. Kraus, C. Wulf (eds.), *The Palgrave Handbook of Embodiment and Learning*,
https://doi.org/10.1007/978-3-030-93001-1_14

(which one perceives as material-spatially founded objects). Robert Gugutzer (2006, p. 4538) illustrates this difference as follows:

> For example, the body of a blind person who walks down the street with his cane ends at the hand with which he leads his cane. The soma of the blind person extends beyond this bodily limit, namely to the end of the stick with which he feels resistance on the ground.[1]

2 The Other

The other is always part of one's own identity as far as the ego is originally decentered, toward the social, in the form of the other. Peter Berger and Thomas Luckmann (1967) therefore locate personal identity at the intersection of body, consciousness and society. Maurice Merleau-Ponty goes on the search for traces of the other, who is neither only in things, nor in his body. Therefore, according to Merleau-Ponty (1984), there is nowhere to accommodate the other; in fact, we are not settling him anywhere; he is nowhere and at the same time always there, as a silent partner and guest inside, from behind he slides into my perception. In this sense, Emmanuel Lévinas (1969) describes the other as transcendence, which bursts open the ego by ruling over me. Via his living in the 'other', a (social) processual decenteration and pluralization of the ego takes place throughout life, which at the same time gains its identity. Because the other also has an original access to the world, he doubles the problem of contingency (which can be described as the anthropological cornerstone), because he could experience everything differently than I and I can, therefore, become radically insecure (Luhmann, 1979). In this sense, the other functions as the social antithesis of the individual, from whom the latter draws its existence in an act of dialectical entanglement. The other is a moldering underground, often unconsciously, in the form of a calming community, but also as a disquieting difference, "as a subject at my back who (co-) constitute my world" (Angehrn, 1999, p. 50).

In this sense, it is to speak of an identity-for-others, whereby the others, according to Ronald D. Laing (1973) and his colleagues, are representing a kind of identity construction kit of the ego. Each individual resembles a polyphonic jumble of voices that, in its deepest depths, drowns out, confuses and

---

[1] For a more detailed reflection of this difference, see Lindemann (1996) and Gugutzer (2002); on the phenomenology of corporeality, see Waldenfels (2000); on a theory of corporeal intersubjectivity interested in education, see Meyer-Drawe (2001).

simultaneously produces all subjective expressions like he "obstinate murmur of a language that speaks as if by itself" (Foucault, 1965). In this sense, "the unconscious [...] is the other who speaks in us" (Ruhs, 2010, p. 43) or also: the unconscious is the other's discourse. Lacan (1988) speaks of the ego as an object built like an onion from nothing but successive identifications. The other therefore appears individually and at the same time in plural: as the others who form the stumbling block for a 'game' of identity-difference, in which the individual finds himself as an altered individual and at the same time as the sum of identified, incorporated others. The ego is thus constituted in a socially existential and anthropologically profound way through a multitude of alterations (Laing et al., 1966). The other as the others finds lifelong and everyday entrance into the ego, whereby he is "not only outside, but also within the individual" (Wulf, 2002, p. 83). In doing so, according to Christoph Wulf (2002, p. 88), in the act of mimetic adaptions and identifications, the other will be physically "transferred into the own world of symbols; the relationship with him is embodied".

3 The Desire of Body: Instincts and Feelings

According to Niklas Luhmann (1982) the consciousness is everywhere and nowhere in the world; it finds its reference point in one's own body and derives its identity from it. The unconscious too, in the form of multifaceted, overlapping and ambivalent, often paradoxical feelings, is reflected in the "social formatting of body states" (Fuchs, 2016, p. 228). Consciousness and especially the unconscious are not structured egologically, but relationally. Therefore, the affectivity of the human being, his instinct-determined experience is always defined as a relationship event: "Instinct is [...]: body need 'in-relation-to'" (Lorenzer, 1972, p. 17). The body, as an object of desire as well as one's own body as a subject of desire and at the same time as an object of being desired, forms the matrix of affective sociality. For although the modern psyche is shaped by processes verbalization, "[t]he physical needs [...] remain melted into the context of meaning formed by language" (Lorenzer, 1972, p. 67). Nevertheless, it is precisely this fact that forms the ground for the (political and social) instrumentalization of such embodied desire.

This form of "institutionalized body formation" (Busch, 1987, p. 107) can be found in the "symbolic layers of communicative action", that have been growing since modern times, and "which [...] put on to the intimate, sensual figures of experience", whereby "the pleasure of naming intimacy" appears as the "burden of discursivation" (Busch, 1987, p. 112). The discursivation of the body, with its affects, its instincts and desires and its irreducible sensations, objectifies the emotional-somatic subject to a body-object. In this way, those 'asocial' vitality and affectivity of the individual that could put it in a resistant relationship to society will be pushed out (see Foucault, 1976b). In the history of mankind, the body has been tried again and again to control precisely, because it is predisposed to resist the social order and rationality pattern or, better said, to slip under them, as the other of social order, as the downside of culture, as nature.

4   The Expression of Body: The Somatic Understanding of the Other

In this sense, the understanding of the alien psychic, no less a form of exercise of power, is conceived even in this way, by observation and decryption of bodies. Because socialization consists in the fact that the individual "externalizes his own being into society" and at the same time internalizes society in turn incorporated its objective reality (Berger & Luckmann, 1967), the body of the other exercises social-epistemic control. This may cause the intention to deprive the other of the disturbing, because of strange moment. The body as the vehicle of being-to-the-world and pivot of the world (Merleau-Ponty, 1968) is accordingly discursively discussed and practiced as a medium of empathy. Herder (1963, p. 16) already spoke of a "force in the soul" that "works on other souls as well as on bodies" and thus views the psyche "not […] through such boards from the soul [as alien psyche, LL] divorced", how this, according to him, "separates the brackets of our metaphysics". Gustav Fechner (1907, p. 9) exemplarily illustrated (and confirmed) this epistemological-ethical problem of the inside-outside split (which corresponds to a subject-object dichotomy) when he wrote: "I show the soul with one inward, the body with one finger turned outward".

For this reason, the 'inside' of the other must be derived from its outside, from the externally sensually objectified soma *as* body. For example, Husserl (1987, p. 20) writes: "me, other people […] are only experiences through the sensual experience of their physical bodies". Since only one's own body appears as a feeling body, as a soma, according to Husserl (1987, p. 100), immediate empathy with the other is impossible, "every meaningful reference to a possible us or we remains [eliminated]". The personal ownership and authorship of everything bodily donates individuality. On the other hand, the somatic isolation is the reason why one has no direct access to the inner life of the

The Embodied Other: Mimetic-Empathic Encorporations   233

other. To realize external psychic knowledge, "the thematic ray of activity is initially straight to the body" (Husserl, 1964, p. 56). There is no other psychic without a body. Empathy necessarily consists in the fact that "[t]he whole inwardness of fellow human beings [...] is 'projected' into them by the observer, felt into them" (Volkelt, 1922, p. 41). It is only through this detour of interpretation that "[t]he alien soul life [...] becomes accessible through empathy with the bodily exterior" (Volkelt, 1922, p. 41). The semantics of the inside-outside duality causes and literally forces that empathy is played across bonds. Understanding the psyches of others has hermeneutical status, as a lifelong challenge of a process-related, constantly renewed and repeated (re) construction of foreign meaning formation in the medium of one's own meaning formation.

The analytical evaluation of the corresponding empathy discourses (see Loew, 2020a, 2020b, 2021) shows that the arguments are always based on an astonishingly uniform pattern. Introspection is an evident means of knowledge. Therefore, a classic three-rule method is used to resolve the unknown variable of the alien psychic by means of this known variable and the corresponding middle link, the body-soul mechanics of the human being, which is assumed to be known. In this respect, there is always a conclusion from the individual to the general and back again to the individual (by analogy). The decisive 'link' is the body, namely in its unity as (1) individual body and (2) 'collective body', which, coupled to semantics of human being, contains general functional laws apart from all idiosyncrasies. The assumption of a fundamental equality of human inner-outer mechanics is therefore very decisive for the condition of the possibility of empathy: because all people show approximately the same body reactions to similar sensations, the individual can deduce from his own sensations about the experience of the other (Merleau-Ponty, 1986).[2]

Thus, the body of the other is also (imaginatively) "grasped as a soma and not as a physical body among other bodies in the world", in order to be able to "comprehend foreign sensory fields" (Fidalgo, 1985, p. 81f.) (in fictional sense) to come to a plausible interpretation of what is going on inside someone else. Johannes Volkelt (1920, p. 124f.) speaks in this context of trans-subjectivity, which is supposed to guarantee this simulative access to the inner side of the other. This super-subjectivity is, according to the idea, achieved by starting from a general physicality, which is linked to human being, in addition to the individual body. As a result, when one melts the affect of the other

---

[2] On the inner-outer duality, "The soul is planted in the body like a stake in the ground [...] or better: the soul is the body's cavity, the body is the swelling of the soul".

into the perceived strange gesture, the individual behavior of the other is associated with an 'objective' meaning of the gesture, whereby the melting of the strange self into gesture will be realized and in this way the affect loses its ego-affiliation. The body behavior of the other is therefore no longer understood as completely individual, so to speak hyper-subjective and therefore socially epistemically inaccessible, but as part of a bodily somatic intersubjectivity, which is an act of incorporation mediated sensitively to the other (Schmitz, 1997). Merleau-Ponty (2012) describes this process in an astonishingly similar form. According to him communication, the understanding of gestures, is based on the reciprocal correspondence of my intentions and the gestures of the other, my gestures and the intentions of the other, which are expressed in his behavior. Then it is as if his intentions reside in my body and mine in his body. In this context, empathy also takes place in an act of unconscious communication, which, precisely because of its somatic conveyed character, always manifests itself before all rational transformations and subsequent narratives and undermines them. Merleau-Ponty points out, that generations upon generations have 'understood' and performed sexual gestures before a philosopher was able to define their intellectual meaning. Through the body we understand the other (Merleau-Ponty, 2012).

5 The Incorporation of the Other

5.1 Body Techniques

Marcel Mauss (1936) describes how the act of understanding and incorporation of foreign gestures is concretely designed with his concept of body techniques that explain why and how people in society traditionally use their body. For example, different marches or gaits are learned and practiced in different societies. As a further example, Mauss cites the specific posture of clergymen, especially nuns, which can be recognized by the "closed fists" (ibid.). In this context, Jean-Claude Schmitt (2000) also showed in his cultural-historical study how one becomes a monk by unlearning everyday gestures and learning sacred gestures.[3] That the body techniques described by Mauss can in extreme cases reach to the learning of killing-techniques is shown in an impressive and entertaining way in the classic film *Léon—The Professional* (1994).

---

[3] For an anthropological and pedagogical analysis of these findings, see Gebauer and Wulf (1998).

The Embodied Other: Mimetic-Empathic Encorporations 235

According to Mauss (1936), body techniques take place as an original and existential act of imitative education, in which the not yet established successor generations, especially the children who are power-shaped marginalized, imitate the behavior of the established adults that is promising and that is at the same time so easily embodied. In this way, every day, self-evident and unquestioned body techniques such as washing become social imperatives that must be internalized. It is important to imitate physically, since these techniques indicate what everyone knows and learns, and what he must do under all circumstances. In this sense, body techniques function not only as neutral structural forms of a society, but at the same time as micropolitical practice of power-shaped systems of rule, which as systems of meaning and behavior over the "security of ready-to-use movements" install a "domination of the conscious over emotion and unconsciousness in the individual" (ibid.). Nonetheless, as a complement to this aspect of power, a collectively coordinated and ritualized body behavior such as "[r]hythmic [...] shouting, drumming, clapping" can also be a phenomenon of "solidary incorporation" that is eminently important for social stability (Schmitz, 1997, p. 145).

5.2 Habitus

Bourdieu's habitus concept is also suitable for describing the incorporation of the other as a fundamental axiom of sociality. It is not just about the habitus as the result of the social entering into the body (Bourdieu & Wacquant, 1992), but also can be said: the body is in the social world (Bourdieu, 1982). Bourdieu (1977) defines the genuinely bodily part of the habitus, the 'hexis', as an "incorporated myth, the permanent way of giving oneself, speaking, walking, and in it: to feel and think". The premise is as plausible as it is complex: it is the unconscious, bodily somatic sensations and formations that determine the social place and the identity of the individual, even before rational narratives and controls begin. Because, according to Bourdieu (1977), education uses the body as a memory aid, it trains the 'wild body', 'the a-social eros', in order to impress a social structure into it, by means of which the structured body forms the behavior and experience possibilities of the individual socially compatible. The effectiveness of this social training is that one's own body, as a sensitive and feeling soma, is simply too close to one's own experience, to one's own self, to defend itself against this imprint. Therefore, the habitus inevitably remains unconscious, so that social ideologies and concepts of order will be incorporated in the guise of an implicit pedagogy and its "meaningless commands as 'hold yourself straight' or 'don't hold the knife in your left hand'" (ibid,). Once internalized, one can then no longer so easily free oneself from this unreflected, self-evident facts of bodily somatic being (in the social world), which means being an ego. Social imprint has become (a part of) individual identity. The incorporation of the habitus encloses a reproduction of existing power and domination relationships and the resulting constitution of unconsciously consensual spaces of possibility and normality.

The incorporation of the habitus implies collectivization in a repressive sense and at the same time the condition for the possibility of social integration and stability. The commonly shared forms of subjectivity create a habitual-social familiarity which, on the basis of shared behavioral expectations and modes of experience, generates an inclusive community consciousness and reciprocal understanding. When the habitus enters into a relationship with a social world of which it is the product, then it moves 'like a fish in water' and the world seems natural to him (Bourdieu & Wacquant, 1992). Then, the other is perceived as a similar counterpart, as an alter ego.

5.3   Introjection

The psychoanalytic theory of introjection describes a process in which "objects [i.e. people, LL] [...] get from 'outside' to 'inside'", but "it does not necessarily imply a reference to the body boundary" (Laplanche & Pontalis, 1992, p. 235), so can stay also imaginative/psychic. If one regards introjection in the bodily sense as the assimilation of something previously foreign (Hirsch, 2000) and thus as a transformation of the 'alien foreign' into the 'own foreign' (Kämpfer, 1999), the result is the perspective of a psycho-somatic socialization and learning theory. The power effects that arise can be set analogously to the theory of aggressor identification (cf. Ferenczi, 1933; Freud, 1936). They imply the internalization and embodiment of those gestures and habitus that were (forcibly) adopted by the powerfully experienced caregivers. The child who is in psychological-emotional, political, economic and physical dependency not only orientates itself on the bodily behavior of the significant others, who embody the order of the generalized others (cf. Mead, 1967), but also necessarily adopts this due to the lack of alternative possibilities. Because the limited social field of the individual, especially the tight family space, offers only a few possibilities of escape, so it is assumed that the incorporated gestures and the associated identifications still exist when the pressure from others has subsided. This type of embodied superego becomes increasingly abstract over time from the specific reference persons and the (pressure) situations associated with them. It remains as an 'impersonal' component of one's own ego: as the other, which is now one's own (Freud, 1969, p. 503).

5.4 Mimesis

The processes already described by the terms body technique, habitus or introjection can also be combined with the concept of mimesis. The mimetic-empathic incorporation of the other as appropriation of the symbolically mediated, socialized body behavior can already be found in ancient theater (cf. Plato, 2012; Aristotle, 1967) and takes place in modern times via analog, but above all via virtualized others (Silverstone, 2008, p. 233) in literature (cf. Jannidis, 2004, pp. 166ff.), television/cinema (cf. Eder, 2005; Wulff, 2005), in computer games (cf. Herzig et al., 2018; Tillmann & Weßel, 2018) or on the internet (cf. Döring, 2013; Flasche, 2018). The fact that "individuals do not dispose of their bodies autonomously", but rather have a habitually stamped "social body" (Hirschauer, 1994, p. 673), is above all evident in the virulent representations of the mass media, which guarantee "a permanent scenic visualization of social reality" by "connecting bodies, people and knowledge" (ibid., p. 675). In this way, given order patterns are represented in socially pre-structured power relations and will be mimetically "learned and experienced, but mostly not recognized" (Wulf, 2014, p. 100).

The mimetic-empathic incorporation of the perceived behavior has a performative side in addition to the repressive side. The body behavior that has been learned is not simply reproduced or copied, but rather 'presented' within the framework of individual strategies of appropriation (Wulf, 1997b, p. 1015).[4] Although with it a "complex relationship [of, L.L.] imagination, language and body" (ibid., p. 1016) condenses, "mimetic processes [...] mostly refer to existing settings" (ibid., p. 1021). Therefore, the mimetic-empathic incorporation of the other always functions at the same time as an "insertion into the [...] [existing, LL] structure and power relations" (Wulf, 1994, p. 33). These microsocial processes of socialization could be, in a socialization-theoretical reading of Foucault (1976a), viewed as 'microphysics of power'. The body as a medium of social inequalities and asymmetrical power relations (cf. Mörgen, 2014) as well as a medium of self-discipline/self-optimization was already instrumentalized in earlier times. Totalitarian political systems in particular have made use of the body to establish and stabilize their ideologies. According to the motto: 'burn' it into the mind through the

---

[4] On the character of mimesis as (re)presentation, see also Scheffel (2006, p. 85f.) and Hamburger (1968, p. 260).

body (cf. Schöpfs-Potthoff, 1984; Alkemeyer & Richartz, 1993; Hermann, 1993; Peiffer, 1993).

It is and has always been the gestures in which 'man [embodies]' (Wulf, 1997a, p. 516), which at the same time only are established on the basis of a "historical-cultural power-structured context" (ibid., p. 520). In this way one becomes an 'other', a profound and fundamental transformation takes place: an 'alteration' (Wulf, 2008, p. 345) of the ego and the body, through which the individual is always the other. One is me and at the same time always the other, the society. On the one hand, this represents a hard, violent act of socialization and pedagogy, at the same time it forms the educational basis for learning processes in the sense of mimetic-empathic incorporations. They decenter and simultaneously enrich the ego through a plurality of different perspectives. Showing and bodily demonstration and the previous and subsequent imitation are constitutive for the acquisition of new skills and the learning expansion of the ego (see Polanyi, 1966; Hirschauer, 2008; Keller & Meuser, 2011; Schindler, 2011; Alkemeyer & Brümmer, 2016).

6   Conclusion

The body-sensitive mechanics of mimetic-empathic incorporation, with empathy as its psychic-phenomenal correlate, are the "inner side of imitation" (Lipps, 1923, p. 120f.). Physical imitation builds the foundation of an embodied society/sociality. Embodied socialization happens through 'othering', that is, through pluralistic, decentering and gestural-based 'alterations' of the ego. That means that identification achievements are constitutive for the educational-culture socialization of the individual. Embodied learning and embodied sociality could be checked for plausibility with different theoretical models. In any case, one can draw the conclusion from our considerations that empathic-mimetic incorporations do not work exclusively through the (directly) imitation of the other, but also through performative appropriation and imaginatively simulated participation. Empathy turns out as the paradigmatic base of a pedagogical link between the bodily somatic, emotional and cognitive matrix of the human being. In this respect, embodied empathy forms a highly effective social-anthropological foundation of learning, which is exemplarily expressed in the following observation of a tightrope walker:

> I perform the movements […] in the acrobat himself. According to my direct consciousness, I am in him; so I'm up there. I am transferred there. Not next to the acrobats, but exactly where he is. Now this is the full meaning of 'empathy'. (ibid., p. 122)

References

Alkemeyer, T., & Brümmer, K. (2016). Körper und informelles Lernen. In T. Burger, M. Harring, & M. D. Witte (Eds.), *Handbuch informelles Lernen. Interdisziplinäre und internationale Perspektiven* (pp. 493–509). Beltz Juventa.

Alkemeyer, T., & Richartz, A. (1993). Inszenierte Körperträume. Reartikulationen von Herrschaft und Selbstbeherrschung in Körperbildern des Faschismus. In U. Herrmann, and U. Nassen (eds.), Formative Ästhetik im Nationalsozialismus. Intentionen, Medien und Praxisformen totalitärer ästhetischer Herrschaft und Beherrschung. *Zeitschrift für Pädagogik, 31*, 77–90.

Angehrn, E. (1999). Selbstverständigung und Identität. Zur Hermeneutik des Selbst. In B. Liebsch (Ed.), *Hermeneutik des Selbst—Im Zeichen des Anderen. Zur Philosophie Paul Ricoeurs* (pp. 46–69). Alber.

Aristotle. (1967). *Poetics* (translated with an Introduction by G. F. Else). The University of Michigan.

Berger, P., & Luckmann, T. (1967). *The Social Construction of Reality. A Treatise in the Sociology of Knowledge*. Anchor Books/Random House.

Bourdieu, P. (1977). *Outline of a Theory of Practice*. Cambridge University Press.

Bourdieu, P. (1982). *La leçon sur la leçon*. Minuit.

Bourdieu, P., & Wacquant, L. J. D. (1992). *An Invitation to Reflexive Sociology*. The University of Chicago Press.

Busch, H.-J. (1987). Subjektgeschichte als Sozialisationsgeschichte. In J. Belgrad, B. Görlich, H.-D. König, & G. S. Noerr (Eds.), *Zur Idee einer psychoanalytischen Sozialforschung. Dimensionen szenischen Verstehens* (pp. 103–117). Fischer.

Döring, N. (2013). Wie Medienpersonen Emotionen und Selbstkonzept der Mediennutzer beeinflussen. Empathie, sozialer Vergleich, parasoziale Beziehung und Identifikation. In W. Schweiger & A. Fahr (Eds.), *Handbuch Medienwirkungsforschung* (pp. 295–310). Springer VS.

Eder, J. (2005). Die Wege der Gefühle. Ein integratives Modell der Anteilnahme an Filmfiguren. In M. Brütsch, V. llcdigcr, U. von Keitz, A. Schneider, & M. Tröhlel (Eds.), *Kinogefühle. Emotionalität und Film* (pp. 225–242). Schüren.

Fechner, G. T. (1907). *Über die Seelenfrage. Ein Gang durch die sichtbare Welt, um die unsichtbare zu finden*. Voß.

Ferenczi, S. (1933). Sprachverwirrung zwischen den Erwachsenen und dem Kind. *Internationale Zeitschrift für Psychoanalyse, 19*, 5–15.

Fidalgo, A. C. (1985). *Der Übergang zur objektiven Welt. Eine kritische Erörterung zum Problem der Einfühlung bei Edith Stein*. Universität Würzburg.

Flasche, V. (2018). Jugendliche Bricolagen—Eine Spurensuche zwischen digitalen und analogen Räumen. In M. Pietraß, J. Fromme, P. Grell, & T. Hug (Eds.), *Jahrbuch Medienpädagogik 14. Der digitale Raum—Medienpädagogische Untersuchungen und Perspektiven* (pp. 35–54). Springer VS.

Foucault, M. (1965). *Madness and Civilization: A History of Insanity in the Age of Reason.* Tavistock.

Foucault, M. (1976a). *Mikrophysik der Macht. Über Strafjustiz, Psychiatrie und Medizin.* Merve.

Foucault, M. (1976b). *The History of Sexuality. The Will to Knowledge.* Allen Lane.

Freud, A. (1936). *Das Ich und die Abwehrmechanismen.* Internationaler psychoanalytischer Verlag.

Freud, S. (1969). Neue Folge der Vorlesungen zur Einführung in die Psychoanalyse. In S. Freud (Ed.), *Studienausgabe, Band 1: Vorlesungen zur Einführung in die Psychoanalyse und Neue Folge* (pp. 447–610). Fischer. (New Introductory Lectures on Psycho-Analysis 1933).

Fuchs, P. (2016). *Der Fuß des Leuchtturms liegt im Dunkeln. Eine ernsthafte Studie zu Sinn und Sinnlosigkeit.* Velbrück.

Gebauer, G., & Wulf, C. (1998). *Spiel, Ritual, Gesten. Mimetisches Handeln in der sozialen Welt.* Rowohlt.

Gugutzer, R. (2002). *Leib, Körper und Identität. Eine phänomenologisch-soziologische Untersuchung zur personalen Identität.* Springer VS.

Gugutzer, R. (2006). Leibliches Verstehen. Zur sozialen Relevanz des Spürens. In K.-S. Rehberg (Ed.), *Soziale Ungleichheit, kulturelle Unterschiede. Verhandlungen des 32. Kongresses der Deutschen Gesellschaft für Soziologie in München* (pp. 4536–4546). Campus.

Hamburger, K. (1968). *Die Logik der Dichtung.* Klett.

Herder, J. G. (1963). Vom Erkennen und Empfinden der menschlichen Seele, Bemerkungen und Träume. In Nationale Forschungs- und Gedenkstätten der klassischen deutschen Literatur in Weimar (Ed.), *Herders Werke in fünf Bänden* (Vol. 3, pp. 5–69). Aufbau Verlag.

Hermann, U. (1993). Formationserziehung. Zur Theorie und Praxis edukativformativer Manipulation von jungen Menschen in der Zeit des Nationalsozialismus. In U. Herrmann & U. Nassen (Eds.), Formative Ästhetik im Nationalsozialismus. Intentionen, Medien und Praxisformen totalitärer ästhetischer Herrschaft und Beherrschung. *Zeitschrift für Pädagogik*, Beiheft; 31, pp. 101–112. Beltz Juventa.

Herzig, B., Schelhowe, H., Robben, B., Klar, T.-M., & Aßmann, S. (2018). Design von Interaktionsräumen für reflexive Erfahrung—Wie werden im Digitalen Medium implementierte Modelle erfahr- und verstehbar. In M. Pietraß, J. Fromme, P. Grell, & T. Hug (Eds.), *Jahrbuch Medienpädagogik 14. Der digitale Raum—Medienpädagogische Untersuchungen und Perspektiven* (pp. 135–156). Springer VS.

Hirsch, M. (2000). Das Fremde als unassimiliertes Introjekt. In U. Streeck (Ed.), *Das Fremde in der Psychoanalyse. Erkundungen über das 'Andere' in Seele, Körper und Kultur* (pp. 213–224). Psychosozial.

Hirschauer, S. (1994). Die soziale Fortpflanzung der Zweigeschlechtlichkeit. *Kölner Zeitschrift für Soziologie und Sozialpsychologie, 46*, 668–692.

Hirschauer, S. (2008). Körper macht Wissen. Für eine Somatisierung des Wissensbegriffs. In K.-S. Rehberg (Ed.), *Die Natur der Gesellschaft. Verhandlungen des 33. Kongresses der Deutschen Gesellschaft für Soziologie in Kassel 2006* (pp. 974–984). Campus.

Husserl, E. (1964). *Erfahrung und Urteil. Untersuchungen zur Genealogie der Logik.* Claassen & Goverts.

Husserl, E. (1987). *Cartesianische Meditationen. Eine Einleitung in die Phänomenologie.* Meiner.

Jannidis, F. (2004). *Figur und Person. Beitrag zu einer historischen Narratologie.* De Gruyter.

Kämpfer, H. (1999). Das eigene Fremde und das fremde Fremde. Aus der Behandlung eines magersüchtigen Jugendlichen. *Analytische Kinder- und Jugendlichen-Psychotherapie. Zeitschrift für Theorie und Praxis der Kinder- und Jugendlichen-Psychoanalyse, 100,* 43–60.

Keller, R., & Meuser, M. (Eds.). (2011). *Körperwissen.* Springer VS.

Lacan, J. (1988). *The Seminar, Book I. Freud's Papers on Technique, 1953–1954* (J.-A. Miller, Ed., J. Forrester, Trans.). W.W. Norton and Co. (*Das Seminar. Buch I: Freuds technische Schriften.* Walter.)

Laing, R. D. (1973). *Das Selbst und die Anderen.* Kiepenheuer & Witsch.

Laing, R. D., Philipson, H., & Lee, A. R. (1966). *Interpersonal Perception: A Theory and a Method of Research.* Tavistock Publications.

Laplanche, J., & Pontalis, J.-B. (1992). *Das Vokabular der Psychoanalyse.* Suhrkamp.

Lévinas, E. (1969). *Totality and Infinity.* Duquesne University Press.

Lindemann, G. (1996). Zeichentheoretische Überlegungen zum Verhältnis von Körper und Leib. In A. Barkhaus, M. Mayer, N. Roughley, & D. Thürnau (Eds.), *Identität, Leiblichkeit, Normativität. Neue Horizonte anthropologischen Denkens* (pp. 146–175). Suhrkamp.

Lipps, T. (1923). *Ästhetik. Psychologie des Schönen und der Kunst. Erster Teil: Grundlegung der Ästhetik.* Voß.

Loew, L. (2020a). Im Schatten des Körpers—Pädagogische Beratung zwischen körperlicher Präsenz und Virtualität. In N. Kutscher, T. Ley, U. Seelmeyer, F. Siller, A. Tillmann, & I. Zorn (Eds.), *Handbuch Soziale Arbeit und Digitalisierung* (pp. 215–228). Beltz Juventa.

Loew, L. (2020b). Einfühlung als allgemeines Bildungsgut der Aufklärung. Die Renaissance einer religiösen Idee. In A. Conrad, A. Maier, & C. Nebgen (Eds.), *Bildung als Aufklärung. Historisch-anthropologische Perspektiven* (pp. 369–384). Böhlau.

Loew, L. (2021). *Inside Out: Empathie-Spiele. Eine Ideengeschichte der Einfühlung von der Antike bis zur Gegenwart.* Logos.

Lorenzer, A. (1972). *Zur Begründung einer materialistischen Sozialisationstheorie.* Suhrkamp.

Luhmann, N. (1979). *Trust and Power.* Wiley.

Luhmann, N. (1982). *The Differentiation of Society.* Columbia University Press.

Mauss, M. (1936 [1934]). Les techniques du corps. *Journal de Psychologie, 32*, 3–4. Reprinted in Mauss, Sociologie et anthropologie, 1936, PUF.

Mead, G. H. (1967 [1934]). *Mind, Self, and Society*. University of Chicago Press.

Merleau-Ponty, M. (1968). *The Visible and the Invisible, Followed by Working Notes* (A. Lingis, Trans.). Northwestern University Press.

Merleau-Ponty, M. (1984). Die Wahrnehmung des Anderen und der Dialog. In M. Merleau-Ponty, *Die Prosa der Welt, Übergänge. Texte und Studien zu Handlung, Sprache und Lebenswelt*, ed. R. Gathoff & B. Waldenfels (Vol. 3, pp. 147–161). Fink.

Merleau-Ponty, M. (2012). *Phenomenology of Perception*; new trans. D. A. Landes. Routledge.

Meyer-Drawe, K. (2001). *Leiblichkeit und Sozialität. Phänomenologische Beiträge zu einer pädagogischen Theorie der Inter-Subjektivität*. Fink.

Mörgen, R. (2014). verKörperte Ungleichheiten und Soziale Arbeit. In N. Langsdorff von (Ed.), *Jugendhilfe und Intersektionalität* (pp. 74–93). Budrich.

Peiffer, L. (1993). "Soldatische Haltung in Auftreten und Sprache ist beim Turnunterricht selbstverständlich". Die Militarisierung und Disziplinierung des Schulsports. In U. Herrmann & U. Nassen (Eds.), *Formative Ästhetik im Nationalsozialismus. Intentionen,Medien und Praxisformen totalitärer ästhetischer Herrschaft und Beherrschung. Zeitschrift für Pädagogik* (Vol. 31, pp. 181–196). Beltz Juventa.

Plato. (2012). *Republic*. Penguin.

Polanyi, M. (1966). *966. The Tacit Dimension*. Routledge.

Ruhs, A. (2010). *Lacan. Eine Einführung in die strukturale Psychoanalyse*. Löcker.

Scheffel, M. (2006). Wer spricht? In A. Blödorn, D. Langer, & M. Scheffel (Eds.), *Stimme(n) im Text. Narratologische Positionsbestimmungen* (pp. 83–100). De Gruyter.

Schindler, L. (2011). Teaching by Doing: Zur körperlichen Vermittlung von Wissen. In R. Keller & M. Meuser (Eds.), *Körperwissen* (pp. 335–350). Springer VS.

Schmitt, J.-C. (2000). *Die Logik der Gesten im europäischen Mittelalter*. Klett Cotta.

Schmitz, H. (1997). *Höhlengänge. Über die gegenwärtige Aufgabe der Philosophie*. Akademie Verlag.

Schöpfs-Potthoff, M. (1984). Die veranstaltete Masse. Nürnberger Reichsparteitage der NSDAP. In H. Pross & E. Buß (Eds.), *Soziologie der Masse* (pp. 148–170). UTB.

Silverstone, R. (2008). *Mediapolis. Die Moral der Massenmedien*. Suhrkamp.

Tillmann, A., & Weßel, A. (2018). Das digitale Spiel als Ermöglichungsraum für Bildungsprozesse. In M. Pietraß, J. Fromme, P. Grell, & T. Hug (Eds.), *Jahrbuch Medienpädagogik 14. Der digitale Raum—Medienpädagogische Untersuchungen und Perspektiven* (pp. 111–132). Springer VS.

Volkelt, J. (1920). *Das ästhetische Bewusstsein. Prinzipienfragen der Ästhetik*. Beck.

Volkelt, J. (1922). *Die Gefühlsgewissheit. Eine erkenntnistheoretische Untersuchung*. Beck.

Waldenfels, B. (2000). *Das leibliche Selbst. Vorlesungen zur Phänomenologie des Leibes*. Suhrkamp.

Wulf, C. (1994). Mimesis in der Erziehung. In C. Wulf (Ed.), *Einführung in die pädagogische Anthropologie* (pp. 22–44). Beltz.

Wulf, C. (1997a). Geste. In C. Wulf (Ed.), *Vom Menschen. Handbuch Historische Anthropologie* (pp. 516–524). Beltz.

Wulf, C. (1997b). Mimesis. In C. Wulf (Ed.), *Vom Menschen. Handbuch Historische Anthropologie* (pp. 1015–1029). Beltz.

Wulf, C. (2002). Globalisierung und kulturelle Vielfalt. Der Andere und die Notwendigkeit anthropologischer Reflexion. In C. Merkel & C. Wulf (Eds.), *Globalisierung als Herausforderung der Erziehung. Theorien, Grundlagen, Fallstudien. European Studies in Education* (Vol. 15, pp. 75–100). Waxmann.

Wulf, C. (2008). Rituale. In H. Willems (Ed.), *Lehr(er)buch Soziologie. Für die pädagogischen und soziologischen Studiengänge* (Vol. 1, pp. 331–349). VS Verlag.

Wulf, C. (2014). Mimetisches Lernen. In M. Göhlich, C. Wulf, & J. Zirfas (Eds.), *Pädagogische Theorien des Lernens* (pp. 91–101). Beltz.

Wulff, H. J. (2005). Moral und Empathie im Kino: Vom Moralisieren als einem Element der Rezeption. In M. Brütsch, V. llcdigcr, U. von Keitz, A. Schneider, & M. Tröhler (Eds.), *Kinogefühle. Emotionalität und Film* (pp. 377–394). Schüren.

The Embodiment of Gender in Childhood

Anja Tervooren

With respect to childhoods in late modernity, two contrasting observations can be made regarding gender. On the one hand, gender difference is arguably being enacted even more dramatically now than it was in the 1980s or 1990s. In the interplay between merchandising and gender marketing that has become increasingly established since the turn of the millennium, products such as toys, food, and school supplies are now offered in versions for boys and for girls. Aimed to appeal to children's tastes, these products address children as boys or girls. The children, in turn, learn through their engagement with these products to present themselves as boys or girls and to embody these genders.

On the other hand, there are signs of greater latitude in children's enactment of gender in both private and public spheres. For example, the topic "My Child is Transsexual" is discussed in digital parenting forums and in parenting advice literature, and the topic of intersexuality is also making its way into political debates. A reorganization of gender relations can also be seen at the legislative level, such as in 2017, when Germany's Federal Constitutional Court decided that too great an emphasis had been placed on the assignment of an individual to one gender or the other, and that those who did not accept or desire categorization according to the adjectives "female" or "male" suffered discrimination as a result. This led to the

---

A. Tervooren (✉)
University Duisburg-Essen, Essen, Germany
e-mail: anja.tervooren@uni-due.de

© The Author(s), under exclusive license to Springer Nature Switzerland AG 2022
A. Kraus, C. Wulf (eds.), *The Palgrave Handbook of Embodiment and Learning*,
https://doi.org/10.1007/978-3-030-93001-1_15

introduction of a third gender category: "diverse". The multifaceted nature of gender embodiment and the ways in which people learn to represent binary conceptions of gender are thus very topical issues.

Theories of gender and embodiment should therefore permit the shedding of light on both dichotomous and ambiguous enactments of gender and the analysis of gender hierarchies in society while bearing in mind the characteristics specific to each phase of life and the transformation of social gender relations.

The following explains in four steps how the embodiment of gender in childhood has been theoretically conceived and empirically investigated since the 1970s. The first step introduces the theory of approaches to gender socialization as well as ethnomethodology. It can be seen from these approaches that too little attention was paid to the body and embodiment. It is only with the introduction of deconstructive approaches in gender studies that focus on the performativity of gender and the materialization of bodies that gender and embodiment in childhood have become understood as a cultural act—a point which is elaborated in the second step. The third step introduces debates about intersectionality that include criticism of approaches focusing on only one social category and identify the interweaving of different social categories as a desideratum of current research on embodiment and gender. The fourth step concludes the article by pointing out new perspectives in research on gender as embodiment and by addressing the topic of children's vulnerability and care relationships connected to them.

1 Beyond Embodiment: Socialization as Boys or Girls

A distinction between sex and gender was first proposed in the 1950s by U.S. psychiatrists who treated children born with ambiguous genitalia. Their parents were advised to select one of the sexes, to have their child undergo the relevant surgical procedure, and to raise the child unambiguously as the chosen sex thereafter. This distinction between biological and cultural gender, which had been developed with regard to the phenomenon of intersexuality in childhood, was soon taken up by women's studies, which was then emerging internationally, in order to denote that a person's gender identity could not be inferred by his or her corporality, but that it was instead acquired in the process of socialization (Dausien & Thon, 2009). Thus, two things were inscribed into the discussion of gender in childhood from its outset, namely, the question of how gender is to be thought of as embodied, and the proposed division into body or nature on the one hand, and culture on the other.

The sociological and educational debate on the topic of "gender and childhood" began in the 1970s, when attention was drawn to the fact that belonging above all to the female gender was systematically associated with disadvantage beginning in childhood and continuing throughout the life course. Against the backdrop of Talcott Parsons's structural functionalism, a teleological model formed a basis from which it was assumed that gender roles are acquired primarily during childhood and adolescence and can then be completed in adulthood. Early psychoanalytical and feminist research, by contrast, followed Freud's model of sexual development in childhood in explaining binary gender development in terms of the cultural conditions of early childhood in which women are primarily responsible for childrearing. That research focused on the mother and child dyad and, later, on the primary caregiver and child (Chodorow, 1978; Benjamin, 1988). There was not yet explicit treatment of the body or of the embodiment of gender; it disappeared behind an emphasis on structure in the first approach, and behind the triad of parents and child in the second.

As early as the 1980s, there was criticism that these theories of gender socialization lent from the outset greater significance to gender-specific differences in socialization *between* gender groups (i.e., between boys as one group and girls as another) than to differences *within* each gender group. Their assertion that the achievement of a coherent identity was a self-evident goal of all children and adolescents also drew critique (Bilden, 1998, orig. 1991). Carol Hagemann-White points out that neither gender nor sexuality is a "fact of nature" that develops from corporality, but rather that the gender binary is appropriated as a settlement specific to each culture (Hagemann-White, 1984). Children therefore learn firstly to recognize the gender binary and, second, to present themselves in accordance with it. Thus, in stark contrast to classical socialization theories' strong emphasis on social structures, these approaches grant children active participation in the process of socialization.

Empirical research in the narrower sense, focused on children's growing up and understanding children as active participants in the learning of gender, was lacking at the beginning of this debate and has been developing since the late 1980s (Thorne, 1993). Early empirical research examined girls' lived realities with the aim of reducing their disadvantage and thus proposing, for example, appropriate ideas for advancing girls' education. Gender was thus defined as a category of social inequality which systematically produced a disadvantage for girls and women in the educational system and in the sphere of work in educational institutions, as well as in social relations of reproduction and production. The viewpoint of disadvantage remained fundamental to this research approach, even when boys were identified as the actually vulnerable group, as happened in the 1990s and was later extended by the PISA studies since the turn of the millennium. The emerging boyhood studies focused primarily on their experiences in school, asking how and by what means boys become educational losers in educational institutions (e.g., Budde & Mammes, 2009). Studying boys exclusively makes it possible to elaborate the different enactments of masculinity within a group of boys or to compare the enactments of hegemonic masculinity in different groups of boys.

However, those in girlhood and boyhood studies who see their work as research on differences always have to master a balancing act: on the one hand, they have to take seriously the social and cultural peculiarities of girls' and boys' everyday lives and lifeworlds and examine them in detail, and on the other hand, they have to avoid producing the gender difference qua method. Even today, the concept of socialization that is used to describe the socialization of girls and boys in relation to the category of gender includes within it a bundle of theoretical and empirical approaches that engage with the study of children and adolescents as they grow up—albeit from different and even partly contradictory theoretical viewpoints (Bilden & Dausien, 2006). The strength of the concept of socialization lies in its description of the reproduction of two genders that are understood to be distinct, whereby the disadvantage connected with one or the other gender is understood as rooted in culture and is not seen as explained by the nature of the gendered bodies themselves. Body and embodiment are thus explicitly outside the focus of these concepts of how gender is learned. Childhood studies research, too, has long been based on a separation of culture and nature, and has rarely addressed embodiment in order to prevent children from being equated with nature and thereby with the immediacy and innocence often associated with it.

2 Generating Gender in Everyday Interactions

In the early 1990s, an extended theoretical and methodological debate developed in what has since become known as interdisciplinary studies around the category of gender, in which there was vehement criticism of the reification of the category that necessarily occurs when talking about female or male socialization. The core of the critique was that gender studies participate in the reification of the differentiation of genders in their presupposition of the category they claim to study. To avoid this, the critique allied itself above all with those theories which specifically do *not* assume that gender is always already there, and which show that and how gender is "made" in the context of inter-actions and institutions.

This process was described by Candace West and Don Zimmerman (1991) in what they call their ethnomethodologically informed approach to doing gender as the "socially organized achievement" of participants in interactions (ibid., p. 14): "Doing gender involves a complex of socially guided percep-tional, interactional, and micropolitical activities that casts particular pursuits as expressions of masculine or feminine 'natures'" (West & Zimmerman, 1991, p. 14). They explicitly criticized the concept of gender roles for down-playing the active participation of subjects and emphasize that all action must be understood as situated, as occurring in the context of virtual or real others and of institutions in particular. Thus, gender does not emerge from the actions of a subject, but is produced in a social arrangement and continually performed anew and made present by all concerned.

Georg Breidenstein and Helge Kelle (1998) start from this theoretical basis, combine it with an ethnographic research strategy, and elaborate practices of gender differentiation among children in a primary school. Among other things, they show how interactions in a purposefully pedagogically progres-sive and gender-conscious school—such as when children are asked to call upon each other and a girl always chooses a boy and a boy always chooses a girl—actually reinforce dichotomous gender distinctions rather than weaken them. Melanie Kubandt (2016) analyzes how "processes of gender *differentia-tion* are carried out in the daily routines of child day care centers" (Kubandt, 2016, p. 48), both by the children and by professionals and parents. On the level of the children, she elaborates a complex, variable, and flexible use of gender grouping, for example, in processes of group division (ibid., p. 53), and focuses on social practices in which the gender dichotomy is broken down. One example is that of five-year-old Mia, who describes herself as a "fan of boys", behaves similarly to the boys, and whose status within the group of children is acknowledged (ibid., pp. 53–54). Both studies flesh out how gender is learned and how it is represented in everyday life. However, they do not explicitly focus on how gender is embodied, and their emphasis on the social construction of gender brings with it the danger of ignoring the mate-rial side of embodiment.

The doing gender approach is still widely used in educational science, although the catchiness of its name is in fact part of its problem, for the approach, which is actually very well elaborated methodologically and theo-retically, can be reduced to a catch-all term used to describe all social catego-ries (such as "doing disability") and pedagogical orders (as in "doing pupil") as well. But even if studies adequately take into account the complexity of this approach, they are criticized for focusing on the "how" of producing gender and for paying too little attention to societal level and the significance of gender norms. This micro-sociological orientation of the oft-employed ethnomethodologically oriented doing gender approach can explain the gender binary as produced in interactions, and can also reconstruct it in empirical studies without taking a given body or even psychosocial identities as a reference point. That makes it possible to explain the embedding of gender enactments in their immediate, everyday contexts, but does not permit the reconstruction of the relationship to social rules and norms to the same extent. In addition, it fails to address the materiality of the body, its specificity at different ages, and the changes in it throughout the process of growing up. These are pivotal, however, especially for a theory of embodiment as a process that takes place differently at different ages.

3 Embodiment of Gender Norms and Their Transgression

In the 1990s, the issue of transgressing gender boundaries became one of the central topics of gender studies. On the one hand, research on the gender transition of adult transsexuals reconstructed how they belatedly learn to embody the gender with which they identify (Hirschauer, 1993; Lindemann, 1993). On the other hand, comparative cultural analyses found that many cultures have gender models that go beyond dichotomies. For example, traditional Albanian cultures envisage a third gender, so that if no boy is born into a family, one of the girls can assume a position from childhood on in which she performs the traditional activities of a son and dresses accordingly. Sexual desire, however, is denied to these "sworn virgins", as it would be at odds with a heterosexual order (Schrödter, 2002, pp. 128–129).

During this period, the works of the philosopher Judith Butler were widely received in international and German-speaking contexts. She takes phenomena of urban subcultures, such as drag, as her starting point to develop her concept of the "performativity of gender identity" (Butler, 1990, 1993) and also to make it possible to describe the transgression of gender boundaries. Borrowing from phenomenology, performance studies, and approaches to the performative rooted in the philosophy of language, Butler conceives of the subject not as voluntaristically designing itself, but also as affected by circumstances.

The Embodiment of Gender in Childhood 251

In this context, Butler assigns central importance to what she later calls gender norms (Butler, 2004). The subject is understood to relate to these iteratively and—as poststructuralism would have it—in a way which is necessarily always shifting. In this approach, the performative is situated in the field of tension between material practices and logics of representation, and a surplus of meaning is always produced anew. The repetition, which has an inherent surplus of meaning, thus points to the possibility of constituting gender identities that are different from what societal norms expect.

In order to describe the enactment of gender in late childhood and also to focus on the change of the enactment from one generation to the next, Anja Tervooren draws on this Butlerian concept of the performativity of gender, conceives of "human action as performing cultural action" (Wulf & Zirfas, 2014, p. 515), and presents an ethnographic study of the enactment of gender and desire in late childhood (Tervooren, 2006). On the empirical basis of the rituals, games, and dances studied, she shows how such rehearsal takes place in a three-step process that culminates in the embodiment of gender and desire. First, the children are connected to cultural knowledge and body knowledge in an iterative and changing way. Next, rehearsals of the body are tested and shown in the context of the peer group. Third, if this performance in front of an audience consisting primarily of peers is found to be good, this way of moving the body is then enacted repeatedly in a stylized way and is eventually embodied through this constant iteration (Tervooren, 2007).

From this perspective, Tervooren is able to analyze both the body and the gradual materialization of gender in late childhood. Moreover, she focuses on practices of crossing gender boundaries as "passing" between the sexes and considers sexuality as a category in its own right. The point here is decidedly not to impute sexual desire to children, but rather to understand the concept of sexual desire "as an urgent desire to belong to each other, which can but need not include physicality or the imagination of one's first sexual acts" (Tervooren, 2006, p. 174). This describes a relationship to a best friend and one's first time "being together" with a boyfriend or girlfriend; thus, desire in this sense is not derived from understandings of desire in adulthood as it is in talk of "homosexual children". As a result, the question of the embodiment of gender and the greater importance of a society's (gender) norms are accentuated more than in the ethnomethodologically influenced empirical works. In addition, Tervooren's work points out the transgression of gender norms and gives greater attention to social discourses. As developed for the study of childhood, this deconstructive approach to gender research has been taken up for the study of the identities of adolescents who do not fit into the heteronormative order (Kleiner, 2015).

4 Embodying Multiple Differences and Debates About Intersectionality

The doing gender approach was soon developed further in response to criticism. One critique held that gender could not be the one central social category in the study of difference and the social inequality that emerges over it; another was that the intersection of social categories needed to be the focus. As Fenstermaker and West argued: "when we move from a description of the reified *categories* of race or class or gender to a framework that reveals *joint action* in *specific situations*, we can see how the doing of difference actually happens, and how it might change" (2002, p. 214, emphasis in original). Theoretical debates in interdisciplinary gender studies are now turning overall to the topic of intersectionality (McCall, 2005; Walgenbach et al., 2007), but often continue to take the category of gender and its complex scientific theorization as a starting point for grasping the entanglements of categories both theoretically and methodologically. The question now being asked is: "What comes after gender studies?" (Casale & Rendtorff, 2007).

In childhood studies, theoretical and methodological findings from gender research are increasingly being applied to other social categories. This is especially true in research done in the aftermath of the PISA studies, some of it with qualitative designs, which interview children themselves in order to study the effects of social class on children's educational trajectories and their experiences with migration. An intensive engagement with the category of disability in childhood, which should also follow here, is still in its infancy in the German-speaking world despite the fact that it has already reached considerable sophistication in the international sphere (Runswick-Cole et al., 2018). There are as yet few empirical works focusing on the entanglement of lines of difference in childhood and adolescence, as the theoretical complexity of such a perspective often cannot be realized on the methodological level (Pfaff & Tervooren, 2022).

In his recent methodologically oriented works, Stefan Hirschauer rejects the fact that certain differences are selected in advance, and thus that one thinks in terms of structure theory instead of praxeologically reconstructing the process of social differences becoming relevant or irrelevant. For Hirschauer, the central question is which difference is in effect when, where, and how. He criticizes theoretical approaches, such as that of Judith Butler, in which there is no undoing gender. Ethnomethodology and poststructuralism highlight the contingency of gender classification but insist on its omnirelevance. Instead, every concrete case of doing difference is "always a meaningful selection from a series of competing differentiations. Only this selection creates a difference that also makes a difference. It is not enough whether a categorization is perceptually or linguistically accomplished once: what is crucial is whether it is connected to this point of contact in social processes—in interactions, biographies, procedures, discourses, etc." (Hirschauer & Boll, 2017, p. 12). It is still rare to find work in childhood and youth studies in which a decision is not made in advance as to which are the relevant social categories to be investigated, and so studies using the approach of un/doing differences in childhood and adolescence are a current desideratum for research.

The 2006 study "Impossible Bodies, Impossible Selves: Exclusions and Student Subjectivities" by Deborah Youdell is an ethnography of one British and one Australian secondary school. Youdell focuses on school processes of inclusion and, based on interpretations of observation protocols and interviews, she is able to show the mechanisms by which identity as a more or less good student systematically depends on several other categories of identity (Youdell, 2006, p. 163). By looking at identities as constellations from the outset, Youdell can also address the interaction of different categories in the processes she focuses on.

For research on childhood, an interweaving of deconstructive and reconstructive perspectives on gender could shed light on both the current present-making of the category and, with critical intent, on practices of transgressing gender boundaries. In my view, however, it would make sense in the debate on intersectionality to revisit the now rather marginalized discussion of the category of gender, to connect it with the complexity of the debate already achieved at the end of the last millennium, and, above all, to focus on the question of the embodiment of differences as "complex embodiment" (Siebers, 2008).

5 New and Old Dimensions of Gender, Body and Embodiment: Vulnerability and Care in Childhood

In the German-speaking and in the Anglo-American and Scandinavian contexts, childhood studies is seen primarily as social scientific research on childhood. In many cases it ties in with sociological debates, only sometimes with anthropological and philosophical ones. It primarily reconstructs social orders in which the life phase of childhood is historically constituted in different ways; the learning of gender is taken into account, but its embodiment is less so. In as much as the establishment of childhood studies in the German-speaking world began in the mid-1970s in an interdisciplinary manner, and the historical, philosophical, sociological, and educational approaches were noticed outside of the field and by the public at large, it is the social scientific component that can assert itself most strongly in the context of the empirical turn in educational science for the analysis of childhoods (Tervooren, 2016). After a long period in which childhood was studied as a life stage and in a diachronic perspective on the lifespan predominated, this new childhood research considers childhood under the mantle of a social structural category. This leads to the taking of a synchronic perspective, asking how children generate meaning in their activities moment by moment and how they position themselves in the generational order. As in gender studies, the idea that the difference—here between children and adults, there between girls and boys—is a natural, that is, "biological" difference, has been sharply rejected right from the beginning, and the concept of generational order has been explicitly developed with reference to the relationality between generations (Alanen, 2001). Leena Alanen explicitly borrows the concept of generational order from gender research that examines the mutual conditionality of genders (Alanen, 1994).

In order to understand children as "participants in practices" (Bollig & Kelle, 2016) and to understand their position within the generational order, the level of children among themselves has been examined very closely; however, children's fundamental dependence on care, especially from their primary caregivers, has received much less attention. Yet the central question of educational research on childhood is how the task of educating and caring for children and their bodies is organized in different cultures and at different points in history. More strongly anthropologically oriented research on childhood (Blaschke-Nacak et al., 2018) places its particular emphasis on vulnerability in general (Burghardt et al., 2017) and includes child vulnerability in particular much more extensively in its analysis of children's social productivity, albeit so far without referring to the category of gender. This would have to be based on a reciprocal interdependence of children's vulnerability and agency, without rehabilitating earlier paternalistic or maternalistic positions via the topos of vulnerability (Heinze, 2017).

Vulnerability has not yet been systematically elaborated from the perspective of research on childhood and current gender research in relation to the practices of care—the latter including the physical dependency of children not only in their early lives, but later on as well. One opportunity for further development is to take a closer look, empirically and otherwise, at the category of gender in care relationships, to reconstruct the care work that parents, and especially mothers, still, take on in early childhood, and to analyze it with regard to the relationship between the autonomy and dependence of all participants. Against the background of a relational concept of generations, this would mean making the mutual interdependence of generations the focus of analysis, and examining both sides of the care relationship. Discussions about the interdependencies in the dyad of primary caregiver and child, as were had at the beginning of the debate about gender in psychoanalysis (Benjamin, 1988), could advance this work. This is equally true for bringing the topic of the body more fully into the debate, where embodiment should be conceived of as a cultural phenomenon that is constituted in action as a cultural performance and that continues to evolve and change throughout the life course.

References

Alanen, L. (1994). Gender and Generation: Feminism and the "Child Question". In J. Qvortrup, M. Bardy, G. Sgritta, & H. Wintersberg (Eds.), *Childhood Matters: Social Theory, Practice and Politics* (pp. 27–42). Avebury.

Alanen, L. (2001). Childhood as a Generational Condition: Children's Daily Lives in a Central Finland Town. In L. Alanen & B. Mayall (Eds.), *Conceptualizing Child-Adult Relations* (pp. 129–143). RoutledgeFalmer.

Benjamin, J. (1988). *The Bonds of Love. Psychoanalysis, Feminism, and the Problem of Domination*. Pantheon Books.

Bilden, H. (1998/1991). Geschlechtsspezifische Sozialisation. In K. Hurrelmann & D. Ulich (Eds.), *Handbuch der Sozialisationsforschung* (pp. 279–301). Beltz.

Bilden, H., & Dausien, B. (Eds.). (2006). *Sozialisation und Geschlecht. Theoretische und methodologische Aspekte*. Barbara Budrich.

Blaschke-Nacak, G., Stenger, U., & Zirfas, J. (Eds.). (2018). *Pädagogische Anthropologie der Kinder. Geschichte, Kultur und Theorie*. Beltz Juventa.

Bollig, S., & Kelle, H. (2016). Children as Actors or as Participants of Practices? The Challenges of Practice Theories to an Actor-Centered Sociology of Childhood. In F. Esser, M.-S. Baader, T. Betz, & B. Hungerland (Eds.), *Reconceptualising Agency and Childhood: New Perspectives in Childhood Studies* (pp. 34–47). Routledge.

Breidenstein, G., & Kelle, H. (1998). *Geschlechteralltag in der Schulklasse. Ethnographische Studien zur Gleichaltrigenkultur*. Juventa.

Budde, J., & Mammes, I. (Eds.). (2009). *Jungenforschung empirisch. Zwischen Schule, männlichem Habitus und Peerkultur*. Springer VS.

Burghardt, D., Dederich, M., Dziabel, N., Höhne, T., Lohwasser, D., Stöhr, R., & Zirfas, J. (2017). *Vulnerabilität. Pädagogische Herausforderungen*. Kohlhammer.

Butler, J. (1990). *Gender Trouble: Feminism and the Subversion of Identity*. Routledge Chapman & Hall, Inc.

Butler, J. (1993). *Bodies That Matter. On the Discursive Limits of "Sex"*. Routledge.

Butler, J. (2004). *Undoing Gender*. Routledge.

Casale, R., & Rendtorff, B. (Eds.). (2007). *Was kommt nach der Genderforschung? Die Zukunft der feministischen Theoriebildung*. transcript.

Chodorow, N. (1978). *The Reproduction of Mothering: Psychoanalysis and the Sociology of Gender*. University of California Press.

Dausien, B., & Thon, C. (2009). Gender. In S. Andresen, R. Casale, T. Gabriel, R. Horlacher, S. Larcher Klee, & J. Oelkers (Eds.), *Handwörterbuch Erziehungswissenschaft* (pp. 336–349). Beltz.

Fenstermaker, S., & West, C. (2002). "Doing Difference" Revisited: Problems, Prospects, and the Dialogue in Feminist Theory. In S. Fenstermaker & C. West (Eds.), *Doing Gender, Going Difference. Inequality, Power and Institutional Change* (pp. 205–216). Routledge.

Hagemann-White, C. (1984). *Sozialisation: Weiblich—männlich?* Leske + Budrich.

Heinze, C. (2017). Verletzlichkeit und Teilhabe. In I. Miethe, A. Tervooren, & N. Ricken (Eds.), *Bildung und Teilhabe. Zwischen Inklusionsforderung und Exklusionsdrohung* (pp. 47–63). Springer VS.

Hirschauer, S. (1993). *Die soziale Konstruktion von Transsexualität*. Suhrkamp.

Hirschauer, S., & Boll, T. (2017). Un/doing Differences. Zur Theorie und Empirie eines Forschungsprogramms. In S. Hirschauer (Ed.), *Un/doing Differences. Praktiken der Humandifferenzierung* (pp. 7–26). Velbrück Wissenschaft.

Kleiner, B. (2015). *subjekt bildung heteronormativität: Rekonstruktion schulischer Differenzerfahrungen lesbischer, schwuler, bisexueller und Trans*Jugendlicher*. Barbara Budrich.

Kubandt, M. (2016). Relevanzsetzungen von Geschlecht in der Kindertageseinrichtung—theoretische und empirische Perspektiven. *Gender, 8*(3), 46–60.

Lindemann, G. (1993). *Das paradoxe Geschlecht. Transsexualität im Spannungsfeld von Körper, Leib und Gefühl*. Fischer.

McCall, L. (2005). The Complexity of Intersectionality. *Signs: Journal of Women in Culture and Society, 30*(3), 1771–1800.

Pfaff, N., & Tervooren, A. (2022). Differenztheoretische Ansätze. In H.-H. Krüger, C. Grunert, & K. Ludwig (Eds.), *Handbuch Kindheits- und Jugendforschung*. Springer VS.

Runswick-Cole, K., Curran, T., & Liddiard, K. (Eds.). (2018). *The Palgrave Handbook of Disabled Children's Childhood Studies*. Palgrave Macmillan.

Schrödter, S. (2002). *FeMale. Über Grenzverläufe zwischen den Geschlechtern*. Fischer.

Siebers, T. (2008). *Disability Theory*. The University of Michigan Press.

Tervooren, A. (2006). *Im Spielraum von Geschlecht und Begehren. Ethnographie der ausgehenden Kindheit*. Juventa.

Tervooren, A. (2007). Einüben von Geschlecht und Begehren. Plädoyer für eine rekonstruktive Sozialisationstheorie. *Feministische Studien, 25*(1), 40–56.

Tervooren, A. (2016). Erziehungswissenschaftliche Kindheitsforschung als interdisziplinäres Projekt. Traditionslinien und Herausforderungen. In S. Blömeke, M. Caruso, S. Reh, U. Salaschek, & J. Stiller (Eds.), *Traditionen und Zukünfte. Beiträge zum 24. Kongress der Deutschen Gesellschaft für Erziehungswissenschaft* (pp. 233–244). Barbara Budrich.

Thorne, B. (1993). *Gender Play. Girls and Boys in School.* Rutgers University Press.

Walgenbach, K., Dietze, G., Hornscheidt, L., & Palm, K. (Eds.). (2007). *Gender als interdependente Kategorie: Neue Perspektiven auf Intersektionalität, Diversität und Heterogenität.* Barbara Budrich.

West, C., & Zimmerman, D. H. (1991). Doing Gender. In J. Lorber & S. A. Farrell (Eds.), *The Social Construction of Gender* (pp. 13–37). Sage.

Wulf, C., & Zirfas, J. (2014). Performativität. In C. Wulf & J. Zirfas (Eds.), *Handbuch Pädagogische Anthropologie* (pp. 515–524). Springer VS.

Youdell, D. (2006). *Impossible Bodies, Impossible Selves. Exclusions and Students Subjectivities.* Springer.

The Adult-Child Co-existence: Asymmetry, Emotions, Upbringing

Tatiana Shchyttsova

1 Introduction: Intergenerational Asymmetry and Overcoming the Subject-Centered Thinking

The adult-child relation is asymmetric due to the irreducible difference between their respective life horizons and life positions. Such an intergenerational asymmetry belongs to basic characteristics of *conditio humana*. It irrevocably implies that the adult *has to* bring the child up. Being thus a fundamental feature (structure) of human social life, the intergenerational asymmetry has been interpreted and experienced in different ways depending on historical-cultural and social contexts. The classical Modernity (Enlightenment), by elaborating and advancing the concept of the autonomous rational subject, had introduced a new paradigm of the adult-centered thinking built on the idea of maturity (Kant). Within this paradigm, the child had been conceived of as a not-yet-a-subject. Correspondingly, the adult-child co-existence had been understood in terms of the moral and cognitive subordination which meant that the adult subject had to help the immature human entity to become a full-fledged (autonomous and rational) subject. It is noteworthy that along with this subordinating vision there had been developed another one which interpreted the child as a symbol of spontaneous

---

T. Shchyttsova (✉)
University of Vilnius, Vilnius, Lithuania
e-mail: Tatiana.shchyttsova@ehu.it

© The Author(s), under exclusive license to Springer Nature Switzerland AG 2022
A. Kraus, C. Wulf (eds.), *The Palgrave Handbook of Embodiment and Learning*,
https://doi.org/10.1007/978-3-030-93001-1_16

natural creativity free from conventional social normativity (Jean Jacques Rousseau). However, regardless their seeming polarity, both these visions—the subordinating and the idealizing—were dialectically complementary within the classical modern paradigm of the adult-centered thinking, because each of them, in approaching the otherness of the child, presupposed a particular mode of appropriation of the child's perspective.

The two abovementioned attitudes toward the otherness of the child were reflected then in corresponding pedagogical approaches. German philosopher E. Fink defines them as the authoritative pedagogy and the sentimental one, respectively (Fink, 1970, p. 222). The polarity of these approaches is clearly articulated in the laconic antithesis between 'leading' (*Führen*) and 'letting growing' (*Wachsen lassen*) as definitions of respective adult's stance on the core principle of pedagogical relation. Fink highlights that despite their opposition both alternatives are characterized by one and the same logic, namely, that "in the first case the freedom of the educator is thought irrelational, in the second case the nature of the pupil is thought irrelational" (Fink, 1970, p. 222). In other words, the difference between the seemingly alternative types of pedagogy is not truly paradigmatic, since each of them presents a kind of subject-centered education. They differ only in terms of a 'regulative idea'. Whereas at the forefront of the former is rationality, at the forefront of the latter is spontaneous creativity. The 'irrelationality' at issue—both in the case of authoritative pedagogy and in the case of sentimental one—indicates that both approaches rely upon the concept of the subject developed in the classical Modernity. Their difference is merely ideological since they differ on whether the present adult subject or the future one (the newborn one) is preferred.

The chapter is motivated by the necessity of overcoming such subject-centered thinking—be it performed from the adult-centered perspective or the child-centered one, since neither allows to approach a genuine field of the mutual interpersonal relatedness constituted by vivid asymmetry of the adult-child co-existence. It follows, the very way how I am going to approach asymmetry in this chapter is built on the theoretical premise of the intergenerational decentration of the subject understood by me not merely as an attempt to go beyond the homogenizing dictate of the adult rationality for the sake of authentic articulation of the child's perspective on the world, but as an attempt to make a shift from the subject-centered approach as such to that one which will concentrate on the asymmetrical correlation peculiar to the adult-child co-existence (Shchyttsova, 2016). Trying to further elaborate this approach in the given chapter, I follow the general lines of the Finkean new philosophical-anthropological and pedagogical paradigm based on the idea of the intergenerational *sharing* the world (Fink, 1987, 1992, 1995). The paradigm is

The Adult-Child Co-existence: Asymmetry, Emotions, Upbringing   261

innovative with regard to the modern, both classical and very recent, approaches in the humanities and social sciences aimed at clarification of the unique value of the otherness of the child (the child's perception and rationality) (Merleau-Ponty, 2010; Meyer-Drawe, 1987; Meyer-Drawe & Waldenfels, 1988; Welsh, 2013) and, consequently, at interpretation of the world, social practices and cultural meanings *from the perspective of the child*, given the perspective is irreducible to that of the adult (Corsaro, 2005; Hausendorf, 2001; Heinzel, 2000)[1]. Fink outlines a pedagogy which arises from the intuition that the old and the young can learn from each other and that the intergenerational asymmetry inherently has a co-operative and con-creative potential so that educational co-existence can be practiced as a mutual relation of the different periods of life ('old and young') where none has an absolute advantage (Shchyttsova, 2019)[2].

In this chapter, I will concentrate on the emotional dimension of the asymmetrical being-with-one-another of adult and child. The general purpose of the chapter is to elaborate some basics of the phenomenology of *affective asymmetry* in the adult-child co-existence and to show communicative-educational implications of such asymmetry. Educational relation will be considered as an elemental (basic) phenomenon of human being and human social life. Indeed, the adult-child co-existence is educative (that is contributes to child's becoming), even if the adult does not develop special pedagogical reflections characteristic of pedagogy as a scientific discipline. Pedagogy as a science arises out of the adults' primary, pre-scientific being concerned about how to bring up children. The chapter deals with this pre-scientific everyday experience of the adult-child co-existence *as* an asymmetric interpersonal relation genuinely implying an educative meaning. The analysis to be further realized is philosophical-anthropological as for its theoretical framework and phenomenological as for its method. There is a rich tradition of the phenomenologically oriented pedagogy (Brinkmann, 2016; Kraus, 2019; Lippitz, 2019; Meyer-Drawe, 2012) with which this chapter correlates. At the same time, the philosophical phenomenological perspective to be developed here differs from the perspective of the phenomenological pedagogy in that regard that the former seeks to clarify constitutive conditions of upbringing as a pre-scientific intergenerational experience whereas the latter focuses on pedagogical experience and learning process as a special practical field that already

---

[1] Patryck J. Ryan (2008) discussing the recently introduced trend called *the new social study of childhood* expresses serious doubts about the newness of the new trend and stresses that the childhood-centered thinking is not yet per se "a paradigm shift".

[2] Friederike Heinzel seems to be much more closer to Fink when she suggests to replace the research *about* children with a research *with* children (Heinzel, 2000). To this topic see also Christensen and James (2000).

presupposes corresponding theoretical reflections and didactic stance. By revealing a certain affective asymmetry as a constitutive principle of the adult-child educational co-existence, this chapter aims to contribute to philosophical rethinking of intergenerational experience in terms of mutual interpersonal relatedness and open complementarity that lie beyond the subject-centered ontology.

I'll start with one routine dialogue between mother and her child that indicates certain crucial aspects of the intergenerational asymmetry. The first section will be devoted to preliminary phenomenological analysis of this talk aimed at revealing its particular emotional implications. In the second section, I will clarify a fundamental difference between the existential anxiety experienced by adult human being and the existential anxiety experienced by child. I will argue then (in the third section) that this very difference defines a primary existential task of upbringing and will tackle the problem of communicative fulfillment of this task. The fourth section will be devoted to clarification of the essential complementarity between the child's existential anxiety and the adult's patience. In conclusion, it will be shown that and why the adult-child educational co-existence can be characterized by a shared joy.

2 An Intriguing Talk: The Mutual Relatedness and the Asymmetric Concerns

I begin with a conversation of a two-and-half-year-old boy (Buddy) and his mother published in the book *The Sociology of Childhood* by W. A. Corsaro. As he clarifies a context of this communicative situation mother and her son talked every weekday at this time as she prepared lunch. The day before the boy had cut his finger. In the talk entitled *Do Chips Have Blood on Them?* (Corsaro, 2005, pp. 20–22), Buddy is still curious about 'blood' from his cut finger.

> *Do Chips Have Blood on Them?*
> Mother: What?
> Buddy: Chips [potato chips] have blood on them? Do they have blood on 'em?
> Mother: No, I don't believe so.
> Buddy: Kids and people do.
> Mother: Um-hum.
> Buddy: And monsters.
> Mother: Yeah.
> Buddy: Like Grover has blood on him.

The Adult-Child Co-existence: Asymmetry, Emotions, Upbringing 263

Mother: Well, Grove's a pretend monster. He's really a puppet, you know?
Buddy: Yeah.
Mother: So he wouldn't have any blood on him.
Buddy: But Harry does.
Mother: Well, they're just like your puppets. Your Big Bird and your Cookie Monster.
Buddy: Yeah.
Mother: They're made out of cloth and furry things.
Buddy: Yeah, like—
Mother: Somebody made them—
Buddy: Harry has blood.
Mother: I don't think so. Pretend blood maybe.
Buddy: Yeah, maybe—maybe Grover and Cookie Monster and Harry have pretend blood. Maybe they do—maybe they have real blood.
Buddy: Mommy, someday I wanna go to Sesame Street and we can see if those monsters have blood.
Mother: You do?
Buddy: Yeah.
Mother: I don't know. We'll have to see about that. But you know what? Sesame Street is really a make-believe land.
Buddy: Oh, I didn't notice that.
Mother: You can pretend a lot of things about Sesame Street.

I have called this talk an intriguing one because it indicates certain affective and structural correlations in this mother-son communicative interaction that appear important for the purposes of the chapter and are likely to have far-reaching implications. In this section, I will set out, by means of phenomenological description, an elemental heuristics of the conversation, paying a particular attention to mutual relatedness of what is expressed by mother and son, respectively, that is to relational nature of each phenomenon which shows itself in course of the dialogue.

First of all, we see that the child is deeply concerned about the very reality of blood. What he insistently tries to find out is whether all beings around him 'have blood on them'. He shows an affective pre-disposition to make sure that they do. Communication with mother is a way for him to receive a confirmation in this regard. Given his previous having been affected by cutting the finger his curiosity manifested in the series of questions is not just a cognitive intention (willing to know something new about the 'objective world'), but truly an existential one deeply rooted in his previous experience. He is intrigued by the fact of having blood. On the one hand, this fact is inevitably (even if only unconsciously) associated with violation of the bodily boundaries and thereby with a possibility of destruction of his body. On the other hand, the same fact motivates him to curiously examine various co-beings in the world with regard to the same quality he just discovered in himself. Thus, even if it's an anxious curiosity, it manifests itself through an insistent exploration of the world. Communication with mother serves as a channel for such exploration. Furthermore, his communication with mother is built on pre-reflexive trust in relation to her as his primary care person. Describing the mother's perspective in this communicative situation, Corsaro says:

> She takes the opportunity to display openness to his curiosity and concerns. In fact, this routine of 'talking at lunch' may have been created by Buddy's mother for this very reason. (Corsaro, 2005, p. 23)

By this comment he highlights the primordial ethical asymmetry in the adult-child relation which is an asymmetry of the adult's absolute (irreplaceable) responsibility in relation to the child on the one hand and the child's pre-reflexive trust in relation to the adult care person on the other hand. The asymmetrical pair trust—responsibility[3] reveals the original mutual relatedness of the generations that define the primary ethics connecting the adult and the child as the ethics of support. However, the ethics of support (taken in itself) implies a moral inequality of the child and the adult and stresses a leading role of the adult. The same emphasis on the leading role of the mother is made also in the Corsaro's abovementioned comment. At the same time, the presented talk indicates more than a supportive attitude of the care person with regard to the child's curiosity and concerns. Mother's mode of communication is rather playful. She does not dictate and does not insist on anything constantly avoiding such a communicative tactics as asserting an 'objective knowledge'. What is at issue thus is an intriguing mutual relatedness of the child's existential curiosity and the adult's playful-careful attitude. In order to clarify further emotional and communicative implications of this intriguing relatedness I will address in the next section phenomenological interpretations of existential anxiety elaborated by Heidegger and Kierkegaard. Taking my bearings from the theories of these two thinkers, I will show that the child's existential anxiety essentially differs from the adult's one and will argue then (in the third section) that this very difference conditions a primary task of upbringing.

---

[3] Comp. with H. Nohl's asymmetrical pair of the adult's love for the child and the child's loyalty to the adult (Nohl, 2020).

3 Existential Anxiety: Care and Curiosity

We will approach anxiety as a fundamental existential feeling to be taken into consideration in order to understand (co-)existential tasks and asymmetrical constitution of upbringing. Kierkegaard and Heidegger are thinkers whom we have to address in order to reconsider the question of existential anxiety from the intergenerational perspective. My general thesis in this regard is that their conceptions of anxiety are related to different life-stages of human being: Heidegger's conception relates to adult's existence, Kierkegaard's one—to the child's existence. In what follows, I will reconstruct a principal difference between their descriptions of anxiety and, after this, clarify its fundamental pedagogical implications[4].

Heidegger analyzes existential anxiety in the context of his systematic phenomenological account of mood or state-of-mind (*Befindlichkeit*) as a primary mode of how single individual as being-in-the-world is disclosed to itself. The phenomenon of mood is conceptualized by him as an existential disposition and affective force that thoroughly attunes human existence in its totality, that is attunes the individual's relation to itself and to all what is encountered in the world. Anxiety is singled out in this connection as a distinctive state-of-mind (Heidegger, 1962, p. 226). It must be stressed that Heidegger's interpretation of anxiety follows in many aspects the Kierkegaard's analysis of anxiety developed in his famous work *The Concept of Anxiety*. Both thinkers thematize anxiety as an affective experience that in some exceptional manner reveals the very constitution of human existence. According to both of them, anxiety originates from that the existing self is related to itself as a capability of Being and is individuated (singularized) due to (by) this very relation. This general thesis is an existential apriori valid regardless the age of human being. However there is a significant difference in their interpretations of the relation mentioned above and, correspondingly, in their concrete phenomenological descriptions of anxiety as the individual's distinctive affective disposition. The difference at issue is precisely about the existential difference between adult and child. As it will be shown further Heidegger's and Kierkegaard's descriptions of anxiety presuppose respectively two fundamentally different modes of self-relation—namely, care and curiosity.

According to Heidegger, person becomes anxious due to facing the necessity to take over her existence as a potentiality-for-Being that has been merely thrown in the world. That is, in experiencing anxiety, human being is

---

[4] This and next section partly draw on my paper *Anxiety and Upbringing: Rethinking existential anthropology from the intergenerational perspective* (Shchyttsova, 2021).

disclosed to itself as a thrown potentiality-for-Being (Heidegger, 1962, p. 233). Anxiety reveals thus to the existing individual his/her ontological constitution. Heidegger designates this constitution by the word 'care'. It is noteworthy that the notion of *care* while designating a structure of human existence (Heidegger, 1962, p. 241) belongs at the same time to a dictionary of emotions. 'Care' means a non-indifferent relation of the existing self to itself. This non-indifference is captured in the basic formula of Heidegger's existential ontology: human there-being (*Dasein*) is an entity which is distinguished by the fact that "in its very Being, that Being is an issue for it" (Heidegger, 1962, p. 32). Anxiety is conceived of as an affect which disposes human being toward facing—realizing—this basic existential fact. Thus, anxiety and care *as affects* are shown in Heidegger's description as pushed into each other and as mutually grounding. That they appear essentially complementary is peculiar to the adult human being and is connected with the phenomenon of guilt (a being-guilty)—to speak more precisely, with a role this phenomenon plays in constitution of the individual's existing. Taking adult human being as a human 'norm' Heidegger shows that and why—due to what ontological structure—the existing individual can experience her own existence as a burden to be taken over. One of the constitutive elements of this experience is the fundamental being-guilty which means that the existing individual is 'always already' responsible for both her past and her present and her future. Thus, in case of the adult human being there is an essential connection between anxiety, being-guilty and care. This trio forms an affective dimension of the structural wholeness of the human existence of the adult person.

In order to approach existential anxiety that belongs to child we have to switch to Kierkegaard's analysis of this phenomenon. It is noteworthy that both Heidegger and Kierkegaard investigate a phenomenon of primordial being-guilty as the basis (as the condition of possibility) for the very distinction of morally good and evil, for morality in general (Heidegger, 1962, p. 332; Kierkegaard, 1980, p. 44). However, unlike Heidegger, the primary interest of the Danish thinker is transformations of human spirit[5] which happen due to its transition from innocence to the primordial being-guilty (the last one is considered by him on the basis of its mythological portraying as the original sin within the Biblical theological context). Anxiety is addressed by Kierkegaard as a phenomenon playing pivotal role in these

---

[5] Kierkegaard means by spirit a distinctive constitution of human existence which is defined by him also as self (Kierkegaard, 1941, p. 17). Spirit or self is thought of by him not metaphysically-substantially, but rather in terms of an open dynamics conditioned by a unique dialectical structure of self-relation.

transformations. Thus, contrary to Heidegger, Kierkegaard describes the phenomenon of anxiety that is characteristic of the human self (spirit) in state of innocence. In *The Concept of Anxiety*, innocence as a special mode (stage) of existence is analyzed by Kierkegaard predominantly on the example of the Biblical Adam—Adam *before the Fall*. However Adam, although being a paradigmatic figure for Kierkegaard's analysis of anxiety peculiar to the spirit (the existing self) in the state of innocence, is not the only example he explicitly discusses. Kierkegaard highlights that the phenomenon of anxiety he described in the abovementioned work "belongs so essentially to the child" (Kierkegaard, 1980, p. 42). Child (being-a-child) is viewed thus as an embodiment of the innocent mode of existence mythologically symbolized by Adam. In what follows, I will briefly reconstruct his core description of anxiety stressing its relevance to the child's existence.

Child's innocence as a particular existential condition is defined by Kierkegaard as "an ignorance qualified by spirit" (Kierkegaard, 1980, p. 44). Like in the adult's human existence, anxiety arises in the child's existence out of the relation of the self to its own possibility of being able. However, unlike the situation with the adult, this possibility is initially completely obscure to the child. As Kierkegaard puts it: child "has no conception of what he is able to do" (Kierkegaard, 1980, p. 44). Thus, anxiety is an affect that manifests the relation of the child's spirit to nothing. Innocence, says Kierkegaard, is anxiety "because its ignorance is about nothing" (Kierkegaard, 1980, p. 44). Therefore the child's innocent self (spirit) cannot be burdened with the being-guilty described by Heidegger[6]. As Kierkegaard formulates it: "The anxiety that is posited in innocence is in the first place no guilt, and in the second place it is no troublesome burden" (Kierkegaard, 1980, p. 42).

It follows that Heidegger's existential dialectics built on the opposition of the pole of authenticity and that of inauthenticity cannot be valid as well if we address the child's innocent mode of existence. Instead of the dramatic dilemma described in Heidegger's *Being and Time* (the existing individual, in being faced with anxiety, either resolutely takes her own being over or escapes this task, dissolving into anonymous everydayness), Kierkegaard shows that the child's existential condition is characterized by an existential dialectics of different kind. He defines anxiety as "a sympathetic antipathy and an antipathetic sympathy" (Kierkegaard, 1980, p. 42). This definition describes the relation of the innocent spirit to nothing, namely "to the enormous nothing

---

[6] Heidegger builds his phenomenology of anxiety on the relation of the existing self to certain 'nothingness'. He shows namely that Dasein is essentially guilty due to the irrevocable nullity (*Nichtigkeit*) of its factical existence (Heidegger, 1962, p. 330). It differs from the way how Kierkegaard interprets the very place or existential function of *nothing* in the innocent spirit.

of ignorance" (Kierkegaard, 1980, p. 44). Thus, anxiety peculiar to the child's existence combines two opposite affective aspirations: affective turning away from and being-attracted to the "anxious possibility of being able". In other words, that which fills with anxiety (the possibility of being able) is at the same time a subject of passionate interest or curiosity. In Russian everyday language, there is a very good expression that grasps such a controversial state-of-mind: 'uzhasno liubopytno'—'anxiously curiously'. The expression seems to be the most accurate description of the primordial affective disposition of the innocent self. Child's spirit in facing 'the enormous nothing of ignorance' is anxiously curious about its being-in-the-world. Kierkegaard mentions in this regard: "In observing children, one will discover this anxiety intimated more particularly as a seeking for the adventurous, the monstrous, and the enigmatic" (Kierkegaard, 1980, p. 42).

By having differentiated the anxiety of the child from that of the adult, we clarified an affective dimension of that primordial existential difference between being-an-adult and being-a-child that was very well indicated by Mollenhauer when he pointed out that for the young, "that which is possible outweighs that which is real" (Mollenhauer, 2014, p. 17). The phenomenon of upbringing is to be considered now from the point of view of the affective asymmetry in the adult-child co-existence described above. In particular, we have to ask: How should upbringing look like in order to correspond to the child's existential anxiety?

4   A Primary Existential Task of Upbringing and Fairy Stories

This section will be concentrated on what is required from adults insofar as they have to do with children whose existence is characterized by the state-of-mind 'anxiously curious'. What is at issue thus is a primary task of upbringing implied in the difference between the adult's anxiety and the child's anxiety. Speaking more generally: What are the pedagogical implications of this asymmetry?

The state-of-mind 'anxiously curious' is an existential a priori which implies the child's existential need to have such experiences that will tranquilize his/her anxiety. Correspondingly, a primary task of upbringing is to satisfy this existential need. We consider thus upbringing as a relational phenomenon that is to be rooted in the adult's having to respond to child's existential anxiety. Whether the adult succeeds in fulfilling the primary task of upbringing depends on a quality of response. It follows, the fundamental question of the adult-child co-existence is how to respond—how to communicate with the child—in order to cor-respond to his/her primordial affective disposition? This question shall help understand the difference of the children's curiosity analysis developed in this chapter from elaboration of this topic in pedagogical theories. It is obvious that children's passionate searching for both new and pedagogical ways of nourishing that search have been among the central issues of systematic pedagogy starting at least from Montessori (Montessori, 2009). In the contemporary pedagogical discourse some authors focus on positive meaning of children's ignorance and inability as constitutive elements of learning (Benner, 2005; English, 2012), others inquire into the ways of cultivating and promoting curiosity (Clark, 2017; Lindholm, 2018; Lucas & Spencer, 2020). This chapter helps to reveal (co-)existential affective preconditions of upbringing as a pre-scientific educational relation. It adds a new perspective on the phenomenon of upbringing by grounding adult-child communication in structures and basic emotions of the existing self. Kierkegaard appears in this context as a highly significant author because, in addition to his work *The Concept of Anxiety*, he outlines in *Journals and Papers* some basic ideas as for a way of communication that might be relevant to the abovementioned primary task of upbringing. In what follows, I suggest a kind of actualizing rereading—including interpretation and further development—of his fragments on this topic.

Kierkegaard provides us with a very simple notion that describes what upbringing should be in order to correspond to the child's primordial state-of-mind. It is the notion of *intellectual-emotional nourishment*. This notion, which might seem a commonplace idea in today's pedagogy, implies that adult's communication with child can only fulfill the primary existential task of upbringing if it addresses child's existence *in toto*—not some particular (separated) faculties. From the existential-phenomenological point of view upbringing is a communication between two freedoms that essentially differ with regard to their association with anxiety. In the child's existence, actuality of freedom is experienced anxiously curiously as a 'possibility of possibility'. It allows us to add a new interpretation to the very word 'upbringing'. To bring up means to help the child to be and to become oneself while having this anxiously curious relation to oneself as a possibility of possibility. This meaning is implied in the tranquilizing function of the nourishment of child's anxious curiosity to be provided by the adult. In other words, 'bringing-up' is about helping the child to keep up his/her state-of-mind in certain balance, that is in a condition that will enable the child's further exploration-and-manifestation of his/her own being-in-the-world.

All said above explains why Kierkegaard says that to bring up human beings is a very rare gift. Indeed, in order to address—to approach—child's anxiety, (a bringing-up) communication must cor-respond to the dialectics of anxiety. In this connection, Kierkegaard pays special attention to children's deeply rooted desire to hear 'fairy' stories (Kierkegaard, 1967, p. 113) and, more generally, to the art of telling stories to children. A masterful storytelling is considered, thus, a significant mode of providing children with that intellectual-emotional nourishment which is required in order to support children's existential constitution. Kierkegaard warns in this concern:

> Not to tell children such exciting imaginative stories and tales leaves an unfilled space for an anxiety which, when not moderated by such stories, returns again all the stronger. (Kierkegaard, 1967, p. 118)

'Exciting' and 'imaginative' seem to be decisive qualities of the stories supposed to correspond to the child's primordial existential need. At issue is thus a mode of communication that opens to the child a possibility to be touched by the *poetic*, to exercise a power of enchantment (Kierkegaard, 1967, p. 114). It is the child's being-in-touch with the poetic that allows the child not to lose existential balance and productive openness in his/her anxiously curious state-of-mind.

It is obvious that telling fairy stories as a way of upbringing (taken in the existential meaning clarified above) is relevant only for a certain age of child. Relying on developmental psychology, we can indicate some minimal, albeit schematic, definition of the child's age that might be recognized corresponding to the idea of intellectual-emotional nourishment of the child's existential anxiety. I suppose that the lowest boundary in this sense can be set around the second year of life. At this age, the individuation of the child is already manifest in many aspects. Above all, I would like to emphasize a child's mastery of the 'No' (in gesture and word). According to René Spitz, "this is perhaps the most important turning point in the development of the individual /.../ with the appearance of semantic symbols it becomes the origin of verbal communication" (Spitz, 1967, p. 204). The child's mastery of the 'No' indicates not only his/her primary acquaintance with the medium of language, but also a particular intensity of existential anxiety. I mean that although what the child is able to do still remains obscure for him/her such 'No-s', in being said many times every day, already project latent unstable (temporary) outlines of the child's self-understanding.

5 Child's Anxiety and Adult's Patience

Given upbringing is to be understood in terms of the adult's communicative cor-respondance to the child's existential constitution—that is to the child's primordial state-of-mind—the question arises: What is an adult's affective disposition cor-responding to this communicative task? Indeed, there must be a kind of *asymmetric complementarity* between the affective dispositions of adult and child whose communication performs upbringing of the child. An affective complementarity to be explored in this section will be considered as a phenomenon of irreducible mutual relationality in the adult-child co-existence. It means that we will proceed from that factical apriori that adults always-already *have to* care about children or, as Mollenhauer formulates it: "task of upbringing and Bildung ... is a debt owed by the adult generation to children" (Mollenhauer, 2014, p. 7). The co-existential structure 'have to bring up' presupposes that interpersonal relations of adult and child are rooted in emotionally attuned responsivity (Waldenfels) that by its very nature is a kind of affective circle since the child is always already in need (i.e. being entrusted to adult) and adult is always already in debt (i.e. charged with responsibility). It follows it would be wrong to approach the adult-child co-existence so as if there were first two separate subjects and then there must be raised the question about their relation (Meyer-Drawe, 1987). On the contrary, respective subjectifications of the old and the young are to be considered against the background of their being-with-one-another-in-the-world. Thus, given the adult-child mutual relationality I would like to clarify what affective disposition (moral emotion) is required for supporting—nourishing—the child's primordial state-of-mind 'anxiously curious'? I claim, it is a patience. My general thesis in this regard is that child's anxiety and adult's patience are essentially complementary affects in the intergenerational co-existence due to its irreducibly asymmetric character.

Phenomenon of patience can be understood differently. For the purposes of this chapter, I suggest to differ two meanings of patience—hierarchical and co-operative. By the hierarchical patience is meant a popular interpretation of patience according to which adult has to be patient in communication with child because of child's intellectual and moral deficiency. Such interpretation is grounded on the adult-centered vision of child as not yet a full-fledged subject. Within the frame of this vision, adult is expected to be patient while explaining something to a child due to child's temporary difficulties in understanding the messages conveyed by the adult. Although the hierarchical concept of patience is justified to some extent and in certain aspects, it must be emphasized that it is based on the reductionist vision of child's existence. Within the framework of this approach, patience's immediate correlate is child's behavior perceived as manifestation of his/her constitutive deficiency (like a constant repetition of the same questions, mis- and non-understandings, failures to follow general rules etc.). To be patient means thus to show tolerance of child's deficiency (resp. of natural delay in child's becoming-an-adult). What is crucial here is that adult's patience entails a willingness (a goodwill) to endure communication with the deficient subject 'for a good cause' so to say while by 'good cause' is meant a successful child's becoming a full-fledged subject. In other words, hierarchical patience is peculiar to instructive (top-down, didactic) communication of this or that knowledge recognized as 'valid' and 'objective' in "the world of adult people" (Husserl, 2006, p. 243).

Co-operative patience, in its turn, is peculiar to the poetic communication used by the adult in order to fulfill the primary existential task of upbringing. As we saw earlier, masterful poetic communication has another 'good cause'— the keeping up the balance and openness of the child's existential constitution. It occurs by virtue of the child's being touched and excited by the poetic performed through various aesthetical forms (narratives, metaphors, images etc.). Like in top-down instruction, in the poetic communication with child an adult has to be patient as well. Yet the experiential field of the patience underpinning the poetic communication has another structure. What is crucial here it is that the poetic is at the same time content and *medium* of the adult-child communication. Being a medium implies that the poetic is approached and shared co-operatively by adult and child. It is an essentially asymmetrical experience, but not a hierarchical one since to communicate the poetic is only possible by performing it that is by co-participating in it together with the child. Adult and child are engaged in the medium of the poetic as irreducibly asymmetrical and nevertheless equally constituting participants. Therefore to be patient in the masterful poetic communication does not mean to show tolerance of delay in child's becoming-an-adult. Patience is rather an affective element necessary for creating a poetic medium that will be able to captivate the child. In this regard patience is originally intertwined with a hopeful anticipation of fulfillment of the poetic as an event shared by the child and the adult. To sum up, both child's anxiety and adult's patience—as essentially complementary affects—are to be thought of from the perspective of their relation to the poetic which appears the most relevant medium for the primary existential task of upbringing discussed in this chapter.

6 Conclusion: A Shared Joy—From Routine Talks to Teaching Settings

From what was said above follows that the adult-child educational co-existence can be characterized by a shared joy deeply rooted in its asymmetric constitution. Indeed, co-participation in the medium of the poetic (be it reading a fair story or visit to the theater or something else of this kind) is an *enjoyment* for both, child and adult. Bilateral joy appears as a genuine mood of the co-participative sharing the poetic by the adult and the child. What is crucial here: it is the very way of the intergenerational sharing of the joy, given the latter is experienced both by the adult and by the child due to their respective relation to the poetic. To put it laconically: a shared joy does not mean at all a common—one and the same—joy. On the contrary, upbringing performed by means of the poetic communication is joyful insofar as the joy concerned is not about unification (totalization), but proceeds from the experience of irreducible difference—from the asymmetric relatedness to one another in the given communicative situation. Thus, the phenomenon of shared joy at issue is possible insofar as the adult-child difference is displayed as a vivid interplay of the mutually related positions. The sharing of the joy occurs (takes place as an embodied co-existential experience) due to the asymmetric performative sharing of the medium of the poetic by the adult and the child, respectively. It follows the very feeling of sharing the joy arises as a kind of 'added value' that can be neither planned in advance nor controlled by any of the participants engaged. A joyful atmosphere shared by the adult and the child, respectively, is related ultimately to what happens in/to their 'togetherness'. At issue is thus an intergenerational experience in which there is no subject in the classical sense, that is subject as an instance which might *underly* the experience as a principle of its (total) conceivability. The shared joy is thus a unique phenomenon that overcomes the subject-centered optic regarding the adult-child educational co-existence.

In the routine talk we started with, the mother is far from insisting on the 'objective knowledge' about the things in question. Instead of a direct top-down instruction, she carefully and at the same time playfully avoids representation of the objective (ultimately valid) point of view using the relativizing sentences *I don't believe so, I don't think so, maybe*. By so doing she allows for the child's question about the reality of monsters and their blood to remain open—open not only for the child's further investigations and inquiries, but also for a possibility of shared intergenerational co-participation in the medium of the poetic, that is in the realm of fantasy able to deal with any anxious images and ideas in a very delicate manner.

Adult's masterful poetic communication and performative intergenerational sharing the medium of the poetic are the upbringing options open and, undoubtedly, well known for 'good parents'. However these options are not easily cultivated within the institutional framework of scientific pedagogy since it always implies a danger of what Meyer-Drawe and Waldenfels call "Pädagogisierung"—pedagogization (Meyer-Drawe & Waldenfels, 1988, p. 278)—an attitude which suppresses the otherness of the child. Given such systemic danger in pedagogy, the efforts aimed at elaboration of this or that kind of synthesis of phenomenological research of childhood and didactics should be very welcomed[7]. Yet even such efforts concentrate as a rule on doing justice to the specifics of children's exploration of the world and on revealing an essentially participatory and not merely receptive manner of this exploration. What I have tried to achieve with this chapter is to indicate a possibility to think of the adult-child co-existence in terms of the nonhierarchical asymmetry that, being deeply rooted in emotional dimension, implies a very particular ethos of sharing the world.

References

Benner, D. (ed.) (2005). *Zeitschrift für Pädagogik*. 49. Beiheft: Erziehung - Bildung - Negativität. Theoretische Annäherungen. Analysen zum Verhältnis von Macht und Negativität. Exemplarische Studien. Beltz.

Brinkmann, M. (2016). Phenomenological research in education: A systematic overview of German phenomenological pedagogy from the beginnings up to today. In M. Dallari (ed.), Encyclopaideia. *Journal of Phenomenology and Education, 20*(45), 96–114.

Christensen, P., & James, A. (Eds.). (2000). *Research with Children: Perspectives and Practices*. Falmer Press.

Clark, E. Sh. (2017). *Cultivating Classroom Curiosity: a quasi-experimental, longitudinal study investigating the impact of the question formulation technique on adolescent intellectual curiosity*. Dissertation, Boston University, School of Education. Retrieved from: https://open.bu.edu/handle/2144/26473.

Corsaro, A. W. (2005). *The Sociology of Childhood*. Pine Forge Press.

English, A. (2012). Negativity, Experience and Transformation: Educational Possibilities at the Margins of Experience - Insights from the German Traditions

---

[7] I would like to mention in particular Kraus' elaboration of such a didactic setting as *performative play* (Kraus, 2012).

of Philosophy of Education. In P. Standish & N. Saito (Eds.), *Education and the Kyoto School of Philosophy. Contemporary Philosophies and Theories in Education* (Vol. 1, pp. 203–220). Springer.

Fink, E. (1970). *Erziehungswissenschaft und Lebenslehre*. Rombach.

Fink, E. (1987). *Existenz und Coexistenz: Grundprobleme der menschlichen Gemeinschaft*. Königshausen, & Neumann.

Fink, E. (1992). *Natur, Freiheit, Welt. Philosophie der Erziehung*. Würzburg: Königshausen, & Neumann.

Fink, E. (1995). *Pädagogische Kategorienlehre*. Königshausen, and Neumann.

Hausendorf, H. (2001). Was ist 'altersgemäßes Sprechen'? Empirische Anmerkungen am Beispiel des Erzählens und Zuhörens zwischen Kindern und Erwachsenen. *Osnabrücker Beiträge zur Sprachtheorie, 61*, 11–33.

Heidegger, M. (1962). *Being and Time*. Trans. John Macquarrie and Edward Robinson. Blackwell.

Heinzel, F. (2000). Einleitung. In F. Heinzel (Ed.), *Methoden der Kindheitsforschung. Ein Überblick über Forschungszugänge zur kindlichen Perspektive* (pp. 21–36). Beltz Juventa.

Husserl, E. (2006). *Späte Texte über Zeitkonstitution (1929–1934). Die C-Manuskripte* (*Husserliana Materialien*, vol. VIII).

Kierkegaard, S. (1941). *The Sickness Unto Death*. Transl. with an Introduction by Walter Lowrie. Princeton University Press.

Kierkegaard, S. (1967). *Journals and Papers*, 1, A-E. ed. and Trans. Hovard V. Hong, & Edna H. Hong, assist. By Gregor Malantschuk. Indiana University Press.

Kierkegaard, S. (1980). *The Concept of Anxiety*. ed. and transl. with Introduction and Notes by Reidar Thome in collaboration with Albert B. Anderson. Princeton University Press.

Kraus, A. (2012). Das "performative Spiel" als ein didaktischer Weg "zu den Sachen selbst" – Zum Zusammenhang von phänomenologischer Kindheitsforschung und Didaktik. In T. Shchyttsova (Ed.), *Geborensein und intergenerative Dimension des menschlichen Miteinanderseins* (pp. 231–252). Traugott Bautz.

Kraus, A. (2019). A Pedagogy of Cultural Awareness – A Phenomenological Approach to Knowledge and Learning. In B. von Carlsburg (Ed.), *Transkulturelle Perspektiven in der Bildung – Transcultural Perspectives in Education. Reihe: Baltic Studies* (pp. 127–135). Peter Lang.

Lindholm, M. (2018). Promoting Curiosity? Possibilities and Pitfalls in Science Education. *Science & Education, 27*, 987–1002.

Lippitz, W. (2019). *Phänomene der Erziehung und Bildung. Phänomenologisch-pädagogische Studien*. Springer.

Lucas, B., & Spencer, E. (2020). *Zest for Learning: Developing Curious Learners Who Relish Real-world Challenges*. Crown House Publishing.

Merleau-Ponty, M. (2010). *Child Psychology and Pedagogy: The Sorbonne Lectures 1949–1952*. Trans. Welsh, T. Northwestern University Press.

Meyer-Drawe, K. (1987). *Leiblichkeit und Sozialität: Phänomenologische Beiträge zu einer pädagogischen Theorie der Inter-Subjektivität.* Wilhelm Fink Verlag.

Meyer-Drawe, K., & Waldenfels, B. (1988). Das Kind als Fremder. *Vierteljahrsschrift für wissenschaftliche Pädagogik, 3*(88), 271–287.

Meyer-Drawe, K. (2012). Zur Erfahrung des Lernens. Eine phänomenologische Skizze. In T. Shchyttsova (Ed.), *Geborensein und intergenerative Dimension des menschlichen Miteinanderseins* (pp. 187–204). Traugott Bautz.

Montessori, M. (2009). *Grundlagen meiner Pädagogik* (10 Auflage ed.). Quelle & Meyer Verlag.

Mollenhauer, K. (2014). *Forgotten Connections: On Culture and Upbringing.* Routledge.

Nohl, H. (2020 [1933]). Der pädagogische Bezug und die Bildungsgeminschaft. *Handbuch der Pädagogik.* Beltz.

Ryan, P. J. (2008). How New Is the "New" Social Study of Childhood? The Myth of a Paradigm Shift. *Journal of Interdisciplinary History, xxxviii*(4), 553–576.

Shchyttsova, T. (2016). *Jenseits der Unbezüglichkeit. Geborensein und intergenerative Erfahrung.* Buchreihe Orbis Phaenomenologicus. Königshausen und Neumann.

Shchyttsova, T. (2019). Poetics of Intergenerational Relations. To the Importance of Eugen Fink's Cosmological Substantiation of Educational Coexistence. In M. Brinkmann et al. (eds.), *Leib – Leiblichkeit – Embodiment.* Phänomenologische Erziehungswissenschaft, 8, pp. 267-278. Springer VS.

Shchyttsova, T. (2021). Anxiety and Upbringing: Rethinking existential anthropology from the intergenerational perspective. (in print)

Spitz, A. R. (1967). *Vom Säugling zum Kleinkind. Naturgeschichte der Mutter-Kind-Beziehungen im ersten Lebensjahr,* Trans. G. Theusner-Stampa, Stuttgart: Klett-Cotta.

Alterity and Emotions: Heterogeneous Learning Conditions and Embodiment

Anja Kraus

1 Pedagogy, Culture and Equal Freedom

Education is a human right, applying equally to all. In this regard, equality is central to all pedagogy. Equality embraces social recognition (cp. Honneth, 1992). How can social recognition be qualified for the context of pedagogy?

While there is controversy about what is pedagogically desirable, there is a broad consensus about the adult being responsible for the personal relationship with the learner at its center. In the European humanistic tradition, a pedagogical relationship is regarded as a natural component of education. The pedagogical relationship is interpersonal, asymmetrical and, in principle, intergenerational. However, the ultimate goal of pedagogy is—what else?—to enable the learner to act independently, taking increasing ownership of his or her own learning and life. Strictly speaking, pedagogy is about rendering itself obsolete. The principal pedagogical means are the transmission of knowledge, encouragement and guidance, as well the contestation of the learner's endeavors of independence.

Consequently, the right of all human beings to make their own decisions as an equal right is arguably the main focus of social recognition in educational contexts. Of central importance for pedagogy is, thus, to examine the options

---

A. Kraus (✉)
Department of Teaching and Learning (Ämnesdidaktik), Stockholms universitet, Stockholm, Sweden
e-mail: anja.kraus@su.se

© The Author(s), under exclusive license to Springer Nature Switzerland AG 2022
A. Kraus, C. Wulf (eds.), *The Palgrave Handbook of Embodiment and Learning*,
https://doi.org/10.1007/978-3-030-93001-1_17

for this in a learning situation, for example in a classroom. In this chapter, this will be envisaged with an education of emotions perspective.

Equal freedom principally relates to the uniqueness of a pupil. Pupils in a classroom differ in terms of their bodily dispositions, social skills and cultural and transcultural imprint; they usually do not even share the same motivation and background knowledge. However, collective happenings are customarily in the foreground at school, and the personal and social disparities are usually largely hidden, overshadowed, repressed or tacit. Nonetheless, the uniqueness of each pupil is constantly triggered during the school day in terms of a broad variety of emotions, and it is displayed foremost in embodied and vital terms. Examples of this not least include the pupils' individual, bodily and emotional comportments toward going into breaks; e.g. during the school day, the pupils follow their private dreams and daydreams. Pupils experience boredom, or moments of passion, and they act expansively in many different ways. Any of these actions could serve as approach to the individuality of a pupil and his/her freedom. Before one approach is chosen, however, we must briefly consider pupils' uniqueness and heterogeneity in the classroom in its whole.

One can trace the idea of an inclusive classroom back to the tradition of designing the classroom according to what benefits society, or a certain community. The students are then, for the most part, addressed as a collective. The individual pupil is encouraged to align with a common project. Basically, norms and comportments exist on the one side, and the individual's adaptation to them in the individual's own terms exists on the other. In the foreground of classroom education is, thus, whether and how an individual comes to terms with the authoritative social norms and comportments. If addressed in the classroom, personal and social differences are normally taken merely as the pupils' heterogeneous learning conditions. Attention is being paid to gender, age, nationality, ethnic background, skin color, political opinion, gender, religious belief or physical constitution. Attempts to meet the pupils' uniqueness and heterogeneity are related to learning objectives, approaches, content, pace and tools that are in the best case tailored and optimized for each learner. Pape and Vander Ark (2018) would speak here of 'personalized learning' as "a path to actively engage, motivate, and inspire all learners to embrace difference, overcome challenges, and demonstrate mastery" (p. 8). 'Personalized learning', in terms of taking the heterogeneous learning conditions of the pupils into account, counts as a progressive and appropriate approach.

Seen from teacher's side, respect for the learners' particularity and individuality is then more or less understood in negative terms. That is, the teacher prevents the hierarchization of the pupil-based factors of social and cultural difference. At first glance, there is nothing problematic about being mindful of the pupils' heterogeneous learning conditions.

However, a second glance on research in this field reveals that as pupils' participation is mostly restricted to given options, while their freedom to make their own decisions is hardly noticeable in the school (Helsper & Lingkost, 2013). Seen from the pupils' side, their heterogeneous learning conditions typically appear in terms of adaption, e.g. like 'you are met as a migrant now and, once, you will become like everybody else here'. Thus, personalized learning usually does not come anywhere near to providing the freedom to act without constraint. We, thus, do not know for certain that the pupils will be enabled to gradually take ownership of their own lives exclusively by a pedagogy that is mindful of their heterogeneous learning conditions and make provisions for meeting those. It can be reasonably assumed that the pupils can see this inconsistency. Hence, in the following, the negative aspects of freedom will be scrutinized in order to prepare the ground for refining the idea of 'meeting the learners where they are'.

2   Egalitarian Difference and Uniqueness

Honneth (1992) associates the development of a personal identity with social recognition, arguing that self-confidence is generated and stabilized in love, self-respect stabilized in law and self-esteem stabilized in solidarity. In his concept of egalitarian difference, he combines the equality of freedom perspective with social recognition of difference. The right to equality and the right to difference are not seen as contrasts, but as mutually dependent on each other. Their interplay is supposed to underlie all social development. Egalitarian difference therefore describes a desirable status quo, norm or standard, and a category for the understanding of social situations, cultural features, ideas, actions or relationships between people.

It was Prengel (2006) who adopted the concept of egalitarian difference in the educational discourse. To her, it describes the equality of freedom, as well as difference and diversity as educative resources. The latter are differences between different social groups and subgroups and between individuals, as well as the intrapsychic and even intra-somatic heterogeneity of different personality components. Thus, Prengel assumes that humans differ not only in terms of social and cultural features, but also regarding emotions, hidden talents and abilities, and not least in their private interests and the thoughts each one expresses or withholds. As we all undergo permanent change, 'no one is ever the same as before, and, thus, we become even less equal to any other' (from a non-political point of view).

> The pedagogy of diversity is based on the 'indeterminability of human beings', so it cannot diagnose 'what someone is', nor 'what should become of him or her'. [...]. People can be adequately described only in terms of processuality and environmental interdependence. (Prengel, 2006, p. 191, author's transl.)

Thus, education is a matter of "transcending oneself into the unknown" (Peukert, 2004, p. 382, own transl.). Consequently, it comprises freedom in many more ways than those being balanced with the social recognition of the heterogeneous learning conditions. The principle of egalitarian difference incorporates the expression of the desire and will to see life in all its variety; Prengel (2001, p. 93, author's transl.) writes:

> Life in all its variety is valuable, because suppression and hierarchization of the expressions of life are experienced as loss, limitation, disruption, or even destruction of the riches of life opportunities, as 'tort'. (Lyotard)

We will come back to Lyotard. Here, we note that factors of social difference cannot be clearly ascribed, nor can egalitarian difference be reached once and for all. As a means of pedagogically supporting the pupils in taking the ownership of their own lives, egalitarian difference is less a status quo and more a process feature. According to Prengel, it is essential to educational practice.

This chapter hypothesizes that how a teacher fathoms a learner's uniqueness is of central importance for the ultimate goal of pedagogy, that is for enabling the learner to take ownership of his/her own learning and life. In what follows, pupils' freedom to make their own decisions in a classroom situation will be approached from an education of emotions perspective. From this perspective, as we will see, practice comes into view as enacted via embodiment.

3 Uniqueness and Alterity

A short example may serve to illustrate the variety of pupils' life expressions at school.

> A class of 6th grade pupils (12-year-olds) were asked to bring a toy to school for their art lesson. Their task was, with reference to the artist Jeff Wall, to stage the

toy in the schoolhouse in terms of what would happen to it at school, and take a photo of their arrangement. The results were narrative assemblages, a scene like a cabinet of wonder, or a still life. However, the majority of the pupils created a scenario of violence.

Generally, a toy represents the playful side of a child. If there is some authenticity in the pupils' toy arrangements, and if the arrangements represented some aspects of the pupils' personal, social and cultural preconditions of learning, then their photos would represent what school does to the pupil-photographers' playful side. Not a few pupils staged their toy at school in a violence scenario, that is threatened, and as a victim. The reason for this could lie in the pupils' age, as many 12-year-olds certainly say a bitter farewell to their childhood; this also depends on other conditions in their private lives. In any case, violence scenarios express the perception and experience of alterity, that is of radical otherness, either as social experiences or as the experience a person has within him-/herself. Thus, one can read such violence arrangements as expressions of not being able to make the voice heard in a social context—perhaps even in the school.

Lyotard (1993) raises his philosophy on humanity in referring to the experience of marginalization and of not being heard. He provocatively reformulates the question of what forms the uniquely human as "what if what is 'proper' to humankind were to be inhabited by the inhuman?" (p. 2) He sees humanity in a person's "struggle constantly to assure his or her conformity to institutions and even to arrange them with a view to a better living-together" (p. 4); however, he does not regard noble goals as decisive for humanity:

> [O]ne can take pride in the title humanity for exactly opposite reasons. Shorn of speech, incapable of standing upright, hesitating over the objects of its interest, not able to calculate its advantages, not sensitive to common reason, the child is eminently the human, because its distress heralds and promises things possible. Its initial delay in humanity, which makes it the hostage of the adult community, is also what manifests to this community the lack of humanity it is suffering from, and which calls on it to become more human. (Lyotard, 1993, p. 4)

Humanity is explained here as the sensitivity for the not-yet, as struggling, as difficulties and faults, a status for which the child is highlighted as an example. At once, the attention is drawn to hegemonic discourses that silence the voices that are not written into their scripts and that are not well-established.

In this regard, the perception and experience of ultimate alterity can come up. Lyotard creates his own term for this: 'the differend'.

4   Hegemonic Discourses and 'the Differend'

Lyotard (1993) takes in a linguistic perspective, when developing his concept of alterity. Linguistically seen, one and the same thing changes its quality when put into different phrases: There is a difference between something being ciphered out, or being known, of being described, or being recounted, questioned, shown or ordered. For example, depending on the context, the utterance 'Water!' could be the answer to a question, an order or some other form of communication (cp. Wittgenstein, 1958, §27). This is due to each phrase following a set of rules, that is a phrase regimen, according to which the phrase and its meaning are constituted. "A phrase 'happens'" (Lyotard, 2002, p. xii). The phrase regimens, discourses or language games correspond to phenomenologies; an event escorts, so to speak, a phrase regimen. The differing connotations of the phrases are linked to corresponding life scenarios, which even derive from the differing connotations themselves. Seen from this linguistic angle, all facts and all knowledge, thus, depend on the rules of language. Lyotard (2002) refers to the "disentanglement of language games in Wittgenstein" (p. xiii) when pointing at the phrase regimens being heterogeneous, and not translatable into one another. The phrase regimens themselves cannot be expressed. Connotation, thus, happens in the face of what is not presentable.

To take ownership of one's own learning and life, it appears as important to know about the heterogeneity of the phrase regimens, or language games, as this plays an important role in a person's aligning with and committing to a community. One could easily draw didactic conclusions from that (cp. Kraus, 2016), but lesson planning is not the focus of the present discussion. Here, it is expected that exploring the dynamics, strategies and power relations that are related to the phrase regimens allows one—at least to some extent—to define pupils' freedom to make their own decisions in a classroom situation and to take ownership of their own learning and lives.

First of all, Lyotard (2002) warns against universal discourses that seek to ground themselves hierarchically and to place themselves above all others. A universal, hegemonic discourse or grand narrative is a *meta-narrative* on current affairs, creating some kind of interconnection between singular events; 'class struggle', 'capitalism' and 'inclusion' are examples. In daily contexts, hegemonic discourses pre-program how certain phrase regimens are linked together or how this is supposed to be done. Mimetic processes make one join a hegemonic discourse and act accordingly (Wulf, 2011). How the phrase regimens are linked together is a "problem of politics" (Lyotard, 2002, p. xiii).

In reading Horkheimer and Adorno's *Dialectic of Enlightenment* with Rocco (1994), we can, for example, identify instrumental thinking in education and society as hegemonic. Horkheimer and Adorno ([1944] 2002) point out the symbolic violence that accompanies the Enlightenment's postulate of reason as ciphered out in terms of logical formalism. They criticize a "reduction of thought to a mathematical apparatus" and contend that "the machinery of thought subjugates existence" (p. 20). They explain their point as follows: The discourse of Enlightenment confronts

> the abstract self, which alone confers the legal right to record and systematize
> [...] by nothing but abstract material, which has no other property than to be
> the substrate of that right. The equation of mind and world is finally resolved,
> but only in the sense that both sides cancel out. The reduction of thought to a
> mathematical apparatus condemns the world to be its own measure. What
> appears as the triumph of subjectivity, the subjection of all existing things to
> logical formalism, is bought with the obedient subordination of reason to what
> is immediately at hand. (p. 20)

Various mechanisms of deception hide the reduction of thought as it is unfolded here. A reduction of thought can be experienced as loss, a limitation, a disruption or even as the destruction of the riches of life opportunities (cp. Prengel, 2001, above).

Regarding pedagogy's goal of enabling the students to take ownership of their own learning and life, Horkheimer and Adorno (2002) and Lyotard would say that this is dependent at first glance on the compatibility of an individual pupil's approach with the corresponding hegemonic discourses. However, when attention is placed on a pupil's uniqueness, the incommensurability of phrase regimens comes into relief. Lyotard (2002) calls attention to the fact that the domination of 'one' way of understanding the world structurally does injustice to other such options and other opinions by putting them into the position of differends:

> [A] differend would be a case of conflict, between (at least) two parties, that
> cannot be resolved for lack of a rule of judgement applicable to both of the argu-
> ments. One side's legitimacy does not imply the other's lack of legitimacy.
> However, applying a single rule of judgement to both in order to settle their
> differend as though it were merely a litigation would wrong (at least) one of
> them (and both of them if neither side admits this rule). (p. xi)

A differend is a clash, an incompatibility, incongruency and incommensurateness. As we have learnt above, the child can be put in the position of being differend in relation to the adult. Being differend means counting as incommensurable, not equal, powerless and even as negligible. Lyotard likewise gives the example of the colonized in relation to the colonizer, the proletarian in relation to the ruling classes. What a child, a colonized person, a proletarian says is not heard. How does such voicelessness come into being? Lyotard (2002) explains it by relating to the statement of a professor of French literature, Robert Faurisson, who claimed in the 1970s that the only testimony of the Holocaust he would accept would be that of someone who had actually gone through the gas chambers. Since those who have seen the gas chambers in operation are those who have died, this criterion for reliability in fact silences all possible testimonies. Faurisson's statement sets the victims of the Holocaust off as differend. The example is quite extreme.

However, the phrase regimen that is put into effect brings a group of persons into the position of being subordinated, passive, victims, the differend, without giving them the possibility to defend themselves. Being set into the position of not being heard in a social context brings about the perception and experience of alterity, that is of radical otherness. This can be a social experience or even an experience that one has within oneself. In any case, it does a person or group wrong. "A wrong results from the fact that the rules of the genre of discourse by which one judges are not those of the judged genre or genres of discourse" (Lyotard, 2002, p. xi). Thus, a plaintiff is divested of his/her voice in a merely structural way. There is no position from which s/he can prove that s/he has been done wrong. Lyotard (2002) describes this in many variants: There will be no understanding of the plaintiff's idea of justice by the ruling, if their understandings about justice differ. A victim will not even be able to prove that s/he has been done wrong, "if the author of the damages turns out directly or indirectly to be one's judge" (p. 8), or if the judge is already convinced of the guilt of the victim or "when no presentation is possible of the wrong he or she [the victim] says he or she has suffered" (p. 8). Lyotard calls it a tort, when one's suffering is regarded as not existing as long as it remains inexpressible.

'Tort' usually lasts until the wrong is put in understandable phrases according to ruling discourses. Due to his conviction that it is language that makes us fit to share in communal life, adult consciousness and reason" (Lyotard, 1993, p. 3), Lyotard stresses the significance of an appeal to a third party to give a voice to the one who is put into the position of the differend. An authorized advocate who is able to hear the victim and who can speak for him/her/ it. Besides that, the enforced silence can also become a transit situation, in which new discourses are developed.—What does the possibility and circumstances of the differend mean for education and pedagogy?

There is already a trace of the exclusion of the 'other' running through the discourse of education theory, especially insofar as postcolonial perspectives are taken as "not only an intellectual fashion, but the only access to world and national history appropriate to the age of globalization" (Brumlik, 2016 in Jörissen, 2019, own transl.). However, the agenda connected to a pedagogy of the 'other' seems to make the mistake of taking the categories of social difference (ethnic background, gender etc.) for a respect for the uniqueness of the pupils. Then, the possibility of being positioned as differend, ultimate alterity and tort seems to not be considered to an adequate degree.

The pupils who experience ultimate alterity in the classroom may take the on them enforced silence in the school context as a transit situation, in which new discourses are developed. However, e.g. their teachers can also be potential advocates for them, giving a voice to the silenced. The urgency of the problem of alterity and differend for the pupils, and the teacher's potential role in this, become obvious in a case study (Kraus, 2010), the result of which is sketched in the following: In this study, the first 20 minutes of an art lesson with ninth graders has been documented by film and analyzed with the 'documentary method' (Bohnsack et al., 2011) and with Lyotard's terminology:

Light was shed on the attempt of all pupils in the classroom to provoke their teacher in different ways to dismiss, or to turn them away. In direct and indirect ways, the pupils display a whole spectrum of affronts, forms of disrespect, outrage and offense. In this way, they address their teacher's position of power; in addition, the hegemonic discourses of school regulations regarding general conduct are marked and accentuated. The rules envisage sending those who disturb a lesson to a school helper. However, instead of reacting in the expected way, the teacher masterly withstands the situation. By not punishing the pupils who are provoking her, she avoids setting them up as differend, even if she is in the position to do so. By not acting, the teacher becomes a victim. The power passes to the unruly pupils; their rebellious phrase regimens put her into the position of the differend. What follows next may appear as contra-intuitive: After a while of setting the teacher into the position of ultimate alterity, the pupils finally calm down and the teacher gains back control over the class, giving the lesson, in which the pupils now participate in a constructive and friendly manner. An apparently quite significant stage in this process of appeasement is the teacher's attempt to convince the pupils that the lesson is a common endeavor, demonstrating the attitude of egalitarian difference as she does so.

The teacher seems to be tested by the pupils, in the end giving them the proof that she will not use her power and perform the 'one' way of understanding the world by setting the pupils into the position of differends. In this way, she may, at least temporarily, have won against the violence of a collectively shaped form of compulsion. In this regard, the actions of the teacher were in a way proactive and not as passive as they may have appeared. It is difficult to imagine that this teacher has given the pupils any reason to behave as they did; one cannot even think of any other unequivocal reason for their affronts. At the same time, the result of the teacher not acting according to the hegemonic discourses was in this case obviously equivalent to 'meeting the learners where they are', and led to the restitution of conversation. She succeeded by creating mutual consent about the lesson being a common undertaking to their all's best. She seems to have a silent understanding about that the pupils will accept the offer.

What seems to come into effect here is what Krämer (2010, p. 32) describes: "Violence turns out as the condition of the possibility of language and conversation". At the same time, Krämer describes violence as a break in the intersubjective processes of making sense together and the disallowance of responses to violence in the medium of language. Waldenfels (2002) elucidates the difficulty of determining the origin of violence: "Violence cannot be traced back to the initiative or property of individuals or groups, nor to a mediating authority, nor to encoded rules" (p. 174). Violence acts in a manner of its own, degrading all, those in the leading role as well as the passively affected to its statists. Even if the offenders are the visible initiators and bear the social guilt for it, violence is bottomless, so to speak. Nobody will ever win over violence in its own terms. According to Waldenfels (2002), one must instead respond to this stripping out of all authority and the limited sphere of influence over violence in order to be able to return to a dialogue. Non-violent action is, thus, not just a question of exercising the will to suppress somebody's urge to perform aggressions but might be the possibility to fight a differend.

The art education example, as well as the case study, conveys violence. Nevertheless, the pupils seem to have come quite close to the goal of pedagogy in terms of taking ownership of their own learning and lives. They convey a differend, an enforced uniqueness, incompatibility, oddness that is related to voicelessness and powerlessness. In so doing, they show general protest against any disrespect of distinctiveness and thereby claim ownership of their own learning and lives. In this regard, they de facto take for themselves the freedom to make decisions for their own lives.

At the same time, their behavior is only reactive. We may therefore recognize here that "in speaking one does not basically practice autonomy but in fact experiences heteronomy" (Krämer, 2010, p. 41, own transl.). The disentanglement of language games and the incompatibility of different phrase regimens seem to effectively be bridged less by language than by practices and embodiment—those of the teacher in the case study. In correspondence to this, Krämer (2010) complements Honneth's social recognition concept with her concept of intercorporeal existence. The teacher shows us that one can respond to the creation of a differend by being alert to whether and how it is created, and also by being aware of the conditions under which the differend becomes effective, true, valid and/or common sense—at the same time, proposing an alternative to this, a shared classroom culture.

This chapter sought to scrutinize the negative concept of freedom in order to prepare the ground for refining the idea of 'meeting the learners where they are'. An answer to the question of how a pupil's uniqueness in the classroom can be fathomed in terms of the ownership of the own learning and life, is still pending, however.

5 Conclusions and Outlook

The aforementioned examples from everyday school life drew our attention to concrete challenges and, concomitantly, to the fact that the body cannot be relieved from its being located. It became clear that being alive means being vulnerable (cp. Butler, 2004) and, potentially, being exposed to alterity, or to being positioned as the differend. Alterity, violence and the differend appeared as a sort of litmus test of personal freedom, as they seem to make visible some neuralgic points, at which taking ownership of one's own learning and life is at stake. Egalitarian difference was identified as a way to pedagogically react to alterity, violence and the differend, potentially disarming it. According to Lyotard, the uniqueness of a person as the freedom to make one's own decisions is urgently faced with incompatible phrase regimens and easily ends up in the state of differend.

However, drawing upon Geertz (1973), we can identify another possible track for further research also on proactive decision-making, even if this will stay rather abstract here. The anthropologist explains being human as becoming a cultural being, linking this to becoming individual.

To be human here is [...] not to be Everyman; it is to be a particular kind of [hu]man, and of course [hu]men differ. (p. 53)

Becoming human is becoming individual, and we become individual under the guidance of cultural patterns, historically created systems of meaning in terms of which we give form, order, point, and direction to our lives. [… Hu]Man is to be defined neither by [her]his innate capacities alone, as the Enlightenment sought to do, nor by [her]his actual behaviors alone, as much of contemporary social science seeks to do, but rather by the link between them, by the way in which the first is transformed into the second, [her]his generic potentialities focused into [her]his specific performances. (p. 52)

Culture shapes communities, as well as it forms individuality. What is more, Geertz describes culture as the link between the innate dispositions of a person and his/her outer personality, and, thus, in terms of generic potentialities and specific performances. Even if the use of the term culture usually stresses historically developed commonality, the similarities of a particular group of people and shared narratives, the display of cultural parameters is, to a certain extent, dependent on the individuals. Culture is conveyed by persons, and it is up to each individual with his/her unique blend of experiences, perspectives and backgrounds to be the recipient and the agent of a culture. The individual perceives culture as part of his/her identity. On these points, even the founder of Cultural Anthropology, Edward Tylor (2010), agrees:

Culture, or civilization, taken in its wide ethnographic sense, is that complex whole which includes knowledge, belief, art, morals, law, custom, and any other capabilities and habits acquired by [hu]man as a member of society. (p. 1)

In cultural contexts, one faces the fact that everybody is unique, and reacts to cultural features in a unique way. At the same time, culture is learned, exercised and practiced. It is imparted and developed. In order to enable the young to eventually take ownership of their learning and lives, pedagogy introduces culture to the next generation as, for example, the historically created systems of meaning. Culture provides for some third party and may even advocate for a differend, as well as it may enact it. Culture also offers specific possibilities of a transit in silence in which new discourses are developed, or practices and embodiment that effectively bridge different phrase regimens. The freedom of pupils to make their own decisions in a classroom situation is, thus, directed to culture. Future empirical studies of corresponding enacted practice and embodiment may provide a clearer picture of a cultural determination of the differends and options for change.

References

Bohnsack, B., Pfaff, N., & Weller, W. (2011). *Qualitative Analysis and Documentary Method in International Educational Research*. Barbara Budrich.

Butler, J. (2004). *Precarious Life: The Powers of Mourning and Violence*. Verso.

Geertz, C. (1973). *The Interpretation of Cultures. Selected Essays*. Basic Books.

Helsper, W., & Lingkost, A. (2013). Schülerpartizipation in den Antinomien von Autonomie und Zwang sowie Organisation und Interaktion—exemplarische Rekonstruktionen im Horizont einer Theorie der Anerkennung. In B. Hafeneger, P. Henkenborg, & A. Scherr (Eds.), *Pädagogik der Anerkennung, Grundlagen, Konzepte, Praxisfelder* (pp. 132–156). Debus Pädagogik.

Honneth, A. (1992). *Kampf um Anerkennung. Zur moralischen Grammatik sozialer Konflikte*. Suhrkamp.

Horkheimer, M., & Adorno, Th. W. (2002 [1944]). *Dialectic of Enlightenment*. Stanford University Press.

Jörissen, B. (2019). *Territories of Theory: Post-Colonial Irritations of My Theoretical Practice*. https://joerissen.name/en/territories-of-theory-post-colonial-irritations-of-my-educational-theoretical-practice/

Krämer, S. (2010). 'Humane Dimensionen' sprachlicher Gewalt oder: Warum symbolische und körperliche Gewalt wohl zu unterscheiden sind. In S. Krämer & E. Koch (Eds.), *Gewalt in der Sprache* (pp. 21–42). Wilhelm Fink.

Kraus, A. (2010). Die Ausgrenzung von Schülerinnen und Schülern als Falle für Schulunterricht—Aspekte nicht-formal angeeigneten Wissens. In N. Wenning & M. Spetsmann-Kunkel (Eds.), *Strategien der Ausgrenzung—Exkludierende Effekte staatlicher Politik und alltäglicher Praktiken in Bildung und Gesellschaft. Perspektiven der Erziehungswissenschaft und der Sozialwissenschaften auf Integration und Segregation* (pp. 151–169). Waxmann.

Kraus, A. (2016). What Do the Things Show Us? Learning as Displacement. *Culture, Biography and Lifelong Learning, 2*(2), 17–30. http://www.cbll.org/index.php/cbll/chapter/view/56

Lyotard, J.-F. (1993 [1988]). *The Inhuman: Reflections on Time*. Stanford University Press.

Lyotard, J.-F. (2002 [1983]). *Le Différend*. University of Minnesota Press.

Pape, B., & Vander Ark, T. (2018). *Practices That Meet Learners Where They Are*. http://digitalpromise.org/wp-content/uploads/2018/01/lps-policies_practices-r3.pdf

Peukert, H. (2004). Bildung und Religion. Reflexionen zu einem bildungstheoretischen Religionsbegriff. In K. Dethloff, R. Langthaler, H. Nagl-Docekal, & F. Wolfram (Eds.), *Orte der Religion im philosophischen Diskurs der Gegenwart* (pp. 363–386). Parerga.

Prengel, A. (2001). Egalitäre Differenz in der Bildung. In H. Lutz & N. Wenning (Eds.), *Unterschiedlich verschieden. Differenz in der Erziehungswissenschaft* (pp. 93–107). Leske + Budrich.

Prengel, A. (2006 [1993]). *Pädagogik der Vielfalt. Verschiedenheit und Gleichberechtigung in Interkultureller, Feministischer und Integrativer Pädagogik*: VS Verlag für Sozialwissenschaften.

Rocco, C. (1994). Between Modernity and Postmodernity: Reading Dialectic of Enlightenment against the Grain. *Political Theory, 22*(1), 71–79.

Tylor, E. B. (2010 [1871]). *Primitive Culture: Researches into the Development of Mythology, Philosophy, Religion, Art, and Custom*. Cambridge University Press.

Waldenfels, B. (2002). *Bruchlinien der Erfahrung*. Suhrkamp.

Wittgenstein, L. (1958 [1953]). *Philosophical Investigations* (G. E. M. Anscombe, Trans.): Basil Blackwell Ltd.. https://static1.squarespace.com/static/54889e73e4b0a2c1f9891289/t/564b61a4e4b04eca59c4d232/1447780772744/Ludwig.Wittgenstein.-.Philosophical.Investigations.pdf

Wulf, C. (2011). Die Unhintergehbarkeit der Gewalt. *Paragrana, 20*(1), 111–117. https://doi.org/10.1524/para.2011.0018

Part IV

Body, Space and Learning

Pedagogical activities focus on fostering the independence of young people by supporting their learning and development, and enabling them to meet various intellectual and real-life challenges. The task of education (*Bildung*) is to enable individuals to comprehend, dispute and reshape their own existence and the features of the world. Pedagogical practices aim to convey learning content and to spark the child's desire for the pursuit of knowledge as a life-long endeavour.

According to the concept of embodiment, the involvement of the body in thinking, sensing and acting conveys educational content. In a learning situation, always only certain knowledge, skills and attitudes are brought to the fore while others are overshadowed; certain tools are used and other impulses are avoided; certain structures and features are highlighted whereas others are suppressed. Such profiling usually also involves the preferment of certain conceptions of the human being to others. Gender, cultural background and class play a role in such a profiling, providing criteria for the creation of social structures, of a structure of knowledge, values, administration and so on. The social structures are conveyed and mediated discursively, visually, materially, spatially or bodily. They play a central role in our comprehension of the world and our own existence and, thus, in processes of embodiment and learning.

However, constellations of space, objects and bodies emerge foremost in a material way. They affect life and education primarily without being expressed in words—they are simply implied or indicated. Tacit knowledge serves here as an umbrella concept. Examples of space-related tacit knowledge are environments formed by architecture, cultural-symbolic constructs, socially constructed space, as well as the impact of materials, technologies, virtual and real-life connections. These real-life connections mingle with body-related tacit knowledge, such as those of habitus, non-discursive practices, nonverbal communication and interaction, forms of social agreement and contextual influences on human behaviour. The classification of tacit knowledge creates a backdrop for systematic and empirical research on forms of understanding and practices. Knowledge about the impact of the tacit dimensions of life on learning may allow for modelling supportive learning environments and learning scenarios that foster the independence of young people by supporting them to meet various intellectual and real-life challenges.

The chapters in this section describe specific, explicit and tacit space- and body-related knowledge that is important for initiating learning and for enabling the learner to meet intellectual and real-life challenges. The focus is on how subject matters and learning practices participate in the constellations of space, objects and bodies, and how the learning is influenced by these constellations. They also deal with related questions of power, hegemony and exclusion.

In Chap. 18 that opens this section *Gabriele Klein* investigates the connection between movement and touch. Her basic premise is that bodily practices and experiences are important in the formation of communities and cultures. What are the consequences of the social distancing brought about by COVID-19 for the way we use our bodies? In any event it is important to rediscover and to live 'movement' as a key element of personal freedom, a central characteristic of the modern age which, since the 1970s, has led to powerful new bodily experiences. This presents the health service with important challenges. Connections between the body and education have not only been important historically—for example, in the early to mid-twentieth century Swiss and German 'Lebensreform', 'Rhythmusbewegung' and 'Wandervogel' movements. Even today it is very important to be aware of the reciprocal relationship between educating the body and developing a sensitivity towards differences in cultural and social life. The author then looks at the systems of the body as systems of touch. She examines how important movement and touch are for a fruitful way of understanding the world and ourselves. Questions of embodiment are central not only in education but also in the way we live our everyday lives in society.

In Chap. 19 on 'Like Water Between One's Hands', *Gabriele Brandstetter* describes the fluidity, transience and momentariness of contemporary dance and performance as an 'aesthetic of the ephemeral'. She contributes to the concept of embodiment and learning by relating these spatial modes of somatic experience to social terms, such as interaction and synchronization, memory, identity and transformation. Concepts of the embodiment of time and temporality are examined by means of metaphors of the ephemeral and vanitas, questioning how these ideas affect the phenomenology of body and memory, identity and transformation. The idea of ephemerality is linked to the social and aesthetic discourse of modernity. The chapter analyses the practices of somatic experience, of interaction and synchronization, and outlines an 'aesthetic of the ephemeral'.

In Chap. 20 on the 'Materiality and Spatiality of Bodily Learning' *Arnd-Michael Nohl* and *Morvarid Götz-Dehnavi* examine the material and spatial aspects of learning and the significance of material things for processes of learning. With the 'material turn', new theoretical opportunities arise for grasping the complex process of learning. First, this chapter challenges the anthropocentricity of conceiving human beings as subjects and material things as objects. Second, it examines the constitution of spatially based bodily learning. Spatiality is here conceived as the result of transactional practices between human beings and physical things. In an example of a videography-based inquiry into educational interaction in a preschool, the authors differentiate between the children relying on habituated space and their coping with emergent space.

Chapter 21 by *Bernd Wagner* on 'Body-Related Learning Processes in Museums' concerns tangible cultural heritage, and here, body-related learning in the museum. The author argues that museums and universities display or preserve a vast part of our tangible cultural heritage that is still only rudimentarily accessible to preschool and primary school children. The material turn in cultural studies has led to an increased interest in object-related learning processes in educational science. The study gives an overview of research that focuses on children's sensory confrontations with objects in collections and on children's performing with objects. The author describes body-related historical learning processes in the German Historical Museum (DHM) in Berlin and considers further perspectives on learning processes in museum collections, based on educational anthropology.

Movement and Touch: Why Bodies Matter

Gabriele Klein

One of the basic premises of the sociology of the body is that bodies, bodily practices and physical sensations and experiences are important and necessary for the formation of sociality and culturality. This premise has been called into question by the COVID-19 pandemic which, in 2020, sparked a global social crisis of epic proportions. The pandemic has helped to speed up a greater process of social transformation that had already been taking place for some time, namely the digitalisation of society. It has also given rise to a number of epistemic crises that have called former certainties into question, including the increasing amount of attention being paid to the societal and cultural significance of bodies and bodily practices, as well as the social relevance of social fields relating to the body, like sport, dance and care work. Since the 1970s, bodies have increasingly become the focus of public and academic interest, but they have gained new meaning since the beginning of the pandemic: now, they are both, dangers and in danger.

What kind of impact has social distancing, which is at its core physical distancing (Klein & Liebsch, 2020), had on the body and bodily practices in light of the digital society (Nassehi, 2019) that we live in? We should not view the COVID-19 pandemic as a disruption, as a state of exception after which we will be able to return to an 'old normal'. Rather, there will be a 'new normal'—and this will also be the case for the changed status of interaction

---

G. Klein (✉)
Hamburg University, Hamburg, Germany
e-mail: gabriele.klein@uni-hamburg.de

© The Author(s), under exclusive license to Springer Nature Switzerland AG 2022
A. Kraus, C. Wulf (eds.), *The Palgrave Handbook of Embodiment and Learning*,
https://doi.org/10.1007/978-3-030-93001-1_18

between bodies, which is generated through orders of touch that, in turn, have led to changes in the formation of subjects. What do established theories in the sociology of the body have to say about the societal relevance of bodies, and what kinds of eruptions and confusions have been unleashed by the COVID-19 crisis?

1 Movement: One of Modernity's Leading Concepts

Movement is good for you! Movement strengthens your immune system! Movement promotes resilience! Movement keeps you young! Movement is slimming! Movement makes you happy! In recent years and decades—more or less since the 1970s and the birth of the fitness movement in the US and Europe—we have encountered these kinds of sentences in all kinds of places. Health advisors and nutritionists, fitness magazines, doctors' practices and gyms, health insurance providers and public health authorities have all been promulgating these guiding principles. They seem to incite each individual to take action—and they also address the individual explicitly. As verbalisations of a practice of self-care, the responsibility for which is shouldered by the individual, these principles are another component of a fundamental process of social transformation.

Since the 1960s and 1970s, a process of *restructuring* has been taking place, during which society has transformed *from an industrial society into a post-industrial society* and therefore into a society with a growing loss of industrial physical labour (with the decline of the mining and steel industries), accompanied by a rise in the number of people working in the service industry. At the same time, unions have fought to reduce working hours, creating more free time for the individual. This increase in free time led to the establishment of a leisure market in the 1970s that has been increasingly commercialised and eventified. Movement and physical activity have thus become important economic factors in this new leisure market in post-industrial society.

The rise of the post-industrial society has led to the transformation of cities from the functional cities of modernity to theatralised, museified and eventified urban landscapes. Here, it is above all the inner cities that have been increasingly adorned with festivals, cultural, dance and sporting events, above all in the field of popular sports like marathon, triathlon and bicycle racing. All of these events have become important economic factors in the urban tourism that is expanding with the theatralisation of the city.

Relevant to the changes that have occurred to the status of the body is the paradigm shift that has taken place in *public health policy* towards preventative action strategies. Preventative healthcare is taking up more and more space, and public health programmes that aim to get people to take preventative steps and to take care of their own health are increasing in importance. The neoliberal, governmental concept of self-care in post-industrial societies is thus also asserting itself in the field of healthcare, which is reflected in the incitements to physical activity described at the beginning of this chapter.

Related to these developments is the *body boom*, as it was referred to in Germany, that began in the 1970s with the fitness and bodybuilding movements. It has led to the Americanisation of European cultural traditions of movement and, with it, the establishment of the commercialised exercise sector. At the same time, with martial arts, with popular dance cultures like tango (Klein, 2009), salsa and lambada, with disco dancing and pop dances like hip-hop (Klein & Friedrich, 2003) and techno (Klein, 2004), and with meditation techniques like yoga, tai chi and aikido, alternative practices of movement from Asian, South American and African cultures have conquered the new leisure and fitness markets of the global North. In the 1990s, the wellness movement injected established fitness culture with its own postulates of mental health and inner balance. Awareness, mindfulness, resonance and resilience—these are the essential terms that have also gradually found their way into academic debates.

The new surge in attention being paid to the body has also led to the increasing significance of social fields that are essentially body-based—like *dance*. Be it contemporary stage dance, performance art (which is based on bodily and choreographic practices), dance-education projects (such as community dance) or dance therapy—dance is now considered a bodily practice that can be used to clearly illustrate just what kind of contribution physical movement can make to processes of knowledge and education, sociality and culturality, perception and experience. For, unlike sport, where aesthetic movement can be present (e.g., in an elegant run) but is not constitutive of the aims and purposes of the activity, in dance, movement itself is, in Giorgio Agamben's words, 'pure mediality' (Agamben, 2000, p. 58). From a microsociological perspective, dance is a medium that can be used to show that bodily communication is an independent action that shapes reality and allows alternative bodies of knowledge to become apparent and visible (Klein, 2004). This position is formulated in opposition to Jürgen Habermas, who, in his 'Theory of Communicative Action', characterises bodily movements as 'non-independent actions' (Habermas, 1984, p. 97). In dance studies, dance is considered an ephemeral art form and therefore a symbol of liquid modernity

(Bauman, 2000). It is viewed as a model of social and cultural reality (Klein & Noeth, 2011), as it shows how people use bodily practices—gestures, poses, movements and touch—to virtually 'dance' their way into conventions (like in the conventional bourgeois dance form, the waltz) (Klein, 1994); or to question, break and subvert patterns of everyday perception and experience (Klein, 2020), as is the case in some forms of contemporary and modern dance (Brandstetter & Klein, 2013).

Simultaneous with these developments was the 'return of the body' (Kamper & Wulf, 1989) to cultural studies and the social sciences in the 1970s, spearheaded in the German-speaking world by sociologist Dietmar Kamper and pedagogue Christoph Wulf. Historically speaking, this was not the first time that the body was making a return, as it had been a key element in modern debates on the theory of education. As early as at the turn of the nineteenth century, as the circulation of goods, people and information was accelerating, Johann Heinrich Pestalozzi introduced to the public debate on education the idea that movement invigorates people 'in mind and soul' (Meusel, 1973). He had been influenced by the pedagogue Johann Christoph Friedrich GutsMuths who, in one of his main works, the much-discussed 1793 *Gymnastics for Youth* (GutsMuths, 1800), laid the theoretical foundations for adolescent physical education. GutsMuths understood physical education as an essential component of a bourgeois upbringing and therefore as something with clear goals of affective and self-control, which was also the case regarding the premilitary training associated with apparatuses of self-constraint. It was the age of burgeoning modernity, which Norbert Elias, in his two-volume 'On the Process of Civilisation' (Elias, 2012), would later describe as the decisive phase in the establishment of the psychological structure that characterises the modern subject.

The relationship between the body and the formation of the subject was then taken up once more during a renewed surge in the critique of civilisation at the beginning of the twentieth century: while movement was seen as a driving force—of the colonial circulation of goods, information and people as well—physical movement became a credo for alternative lifestyles and a medium that made it possible to escape the hectic pace of industrial society, for example, in the German *Lebensreform* (life reform) movement and the alternative movements that accompanied it, such as the *Rhythmusbewegung* (rhythm movement), the expressionist dance movement and the *Wandervogel* movement (akin to the Scouts movement). Movement, above all in the 'great outdoors' and the 'fresh air', offered an alternative to life in sooty, congested industrial cities and became the epitome of self-reflection and holistic bourgeois lifestyles.

With the return of the body in the 1970s, the sociological and pedagogical relevance of the body once again stepped into the academic spotlight. A number of German pedagogues developed new school concepts that were also realised in the 1970s, such as the Laborschule Bielefeld (Laboratory School Bielefeld). But they also developed new physical education concepts, which were now understood as lessons in which children could experience their bodies (Funke-Wieneke, 1983). The bedrock of these concepts was above all the idea that the physical development of children and adolescents plays a very essential role in education and human development.

But the body returned to academic debates in the fields of sociology, philosophy and cultural studies as well. Scholars turned to theoretical concepts of which the academy had lost sight, such as those in Norbert Elias' 'On the Process of Civilisation', which had been published by a German Jew in England in 1939. They also formulated a sociology of the body using the writings of anthropologists and phenomenologists Arnold Gehlen (1993), Helmuth Plessner (2019) and Maurice Merleau-Ponty (2012), as well as sociological writings by Pierre Bourdieu (1984) and Michel Foucault (1979). The sociology of the body sees the body as an essential component of sociality and culturality—even as the foundation of social and cultural processes, practices, techniques and orders, as Marcel Mauss argues (1973). To this day, it is considered self-evident in the sociology of the body that the body is a social instrument, intermediary, medium, actor, symbol and representative all at once, and that bodily practices are fundamentally at the heart of sociality (Gugutzer et al., 2022).

In summary, we can say that certainties regarding the social and cultural relevance of bodies and the essential role that they play in society have become objects of discourse in the fields of education theory, cultural studies and the social sciences when societal developments have led to the radical transformation of social *dispositifs*: during the societal confusion at the time of the Enlightenment; with the rise of modernity, colonialism and imperialism, and the outbreaks of war at the beginning of the twentieth century; and with society's transition towards becoming a post-industrial, global and, ultimately, digital society.

Even if the approaches taken in different theories of the body vary, they have always been based on several main arguments:

- that physical and corporeal practices provide elementary access to the world;
- that interactions and complexes of interaction, as Maurice Merleau-Ponty and Erving Goffman (1967) have shown, are intercorporeal, that is, the

corporeal entanglement of subjects is not an effect of communication, but its precondition and basis;

- that action does not, as in Max Weber's conceptualisation, primarily take social effect through its intentionality and rationality, but in and through bodily practices (Klein, 2004);
- that the presence of bodies is a guarantee for the creation of intimacy and trust, of recognition and affection; and, finally,
- that touch constitutes an essential component of orders of interaction, which means that the latter are not just based on orders of the body, but that orders of the body make orders of touch possible (Lindemann, 2020).

The COVID-19 pandemic and the ensuing restrictions to interpersonal contact have called these certainties into question. What are the implications for the theory that bodies have an essential societal and cultural impact and that they are fundamental to the generation of cultural formations and practices? Why do bodies matter? And how has our understanding of the body and our relationship to the body (our own and the body of the other) changed during the COVID-19 pandemic?

2 Bodies in Crisis: Orders of the Body as Orders of Touch

The policy of 'social distancing' affects bodies: keeping a 'safe distance', wearing face masks, working from home, learning online in schools and universities; the closure of all sites of leisure and physical encounter: pubs and clubs, bistros and beer gardens, playgrounds and pools, football stadiums and golf courses, churches and mosques, theatres and cinemas; the cancellation of festivals, private celebrations, culture and art festivals and sporting events; isolating the elderly; sick people and dead people; the invisibility of refugees, street people and people affected by domestic violence, above all women and children. Lockdowns and their social effects address the body, and do so paradoxically, for they have been enacted against the body and, at the same time, for its own protection (for more detail, see Klein & Liebsch, 2021). During this social crisis, which was sparked by a virus, it has become possible to see and experience the fact that sociality is enacted physically and materially—and that this has consequences that are becoming apparent, but that we still cannot grasp to their full extent. For the imperative of distance, the prohibition against touch, our ongoing worry about clean hands and hygiene standards in shops, the suspicions we harbour against other people as potential threats—all of this is changing us, but we do not yet know how and whether these changes will be permanent.

As of April 2021, there were only a few reliable studies available, but here were a few figures from Germany relating to the situation of children and adolescents, who had been hit particularly hard by the effects of social distancing. It was becoming apparent that the number of young people suffering from anxiety, sleep and eating disorders, drug and tablet abuse, and depression was growing. The number of people being admitted to psychiatric emergency departments was on the rise. Numbers from Germany showed that before the COVID-19 pandemic, about 20% of children and teenagers had psychiatric problems; the figures reveal that this proportion has climbed to one-third. The German Federal Association of Contract Psychotherapists had said that this is because children had lost social contact to their peers as well as their access to music and exercise in clubs. In 2021, the German Catholic Church alone had 4000 children's and youth choirs that were no longer singing. In sports clubs, too, there had been significant declines in membership and increasing numbers of above all children and adolescents cancelling their memberships; the figures were as high as 60% in club sports for children and adolescents (as of March 2021). Clubs and sports associations were justifiably worried that they will lose these members in the long run.

Although there are not yet any reliable studies available on child abuse and sexual abuse in lockdown, outpatient child protection clinics, social workers and doctors suspect that even if statistical data suggests that there has been a decline in sexual offences, this is probably because they have become even more invisible than they were to begin with. The Outpatient Clinic for Protection against Violence at the Charité Hospital in Berlin, for example, registered 30% more cases of domestic violence and child abuse in June 2020 year on year. The closures of childcare centres and schools have played a major role here, as this is where domestic violence against children is usually discovered.

While the prevalence of violent touch has increased during the pandemic, not being allowed to touch loved ones and the loss of the intimacy and affection that are expressed in touch are important factors that indicate that a change is taking place in bodily practices. This is because separation, bans on contact and quarantine have not just created social distance, they have also changed how our facial expressions, gestures, body language and movement express practices of touching and being touched (in both the literal and figurative sense)—leading to what we might refer to as 'distant socialising'. When bodies are kept at a distance, when touch becomes threatening, and harmful contagion is a potential consequence of that touch, everyday routines and rituals and, with them, systems of figuration that are of major significance to the formation of identity begin to unravel. In developmental psychology, touch is considered fundamental to the constitution of the self, because it is physical contact that forms the core of the experiences that inscribe themselves into the subject's habitual dispositions and form their basis. It is, as Carl-Eduard Scheidt, Professor of Psychosomatic Medicine and Psychotherapy at the University of Freiburg, has said, 'ultimately our early bodily experiences that help us to judge the emotional significance of the sound of a voice, the rhythm of language, the contour of a movement, a smell or a glance in a matter of milliseconds' (Scheidt, 2020, p. 48).

The German phenomenologist Bernhard Waldenfels has shown how the tactile, the haptic and feeling converge in touch (Waldenfels, 2002, p. 64). Touching is a motor, sensory and affective act all at once. This view is nothing new in cultural history. Even Aristotle ascribed the tactile sense a special quality of meaning, as it takes effect not through a medium, but together with the skin, the largest sensory organ in the body, as a medium itself (Aristotle, 1968). Touching and being touched in the twofold sense are bound to the body and to physical movement. Touch takes place in (barely definable) worlds between interacting bodies, whose boundaries and intersections, degree of proximity and distance, affection and resistance, separation and gaps become tangible in the act of touching.

The sociology of the body views touch as intercorporeal, that is, it foregrounds the bodily based complex of interaction in the act of touch and not individual bodies. This is a perspective that is also shared by Brian Massumi when he posits that it is the situated, relational entanglement of bodies that is primary and not the feeling and thinking individual. For Massumi, the embodied mode of human existence is 'never entirely personal […]. [I]t's not just about us, in isolation. In affect, we are never alone' (Massumi, 2015, p. 6). Touch is thus also how we relate to the world; it requires contact—with people, animals, things and objects. It is generated in and through interactions, in intercorporeal figurations.

Just as touch requires bodily based complexes of interaction and acquires connective, mediative and translative, that is, medial functions, touch can also convey the cultural meaning of interactions and their orders, for example, in greetings—through the now forbidden handshake or kiss on the cheek. However, it is not just the COVID-19 pandemic, but the digitalisation of society that has once more made touch and the tactile sense subjects of discussion in media studies, medicine, the social sciences, technology and cultural studies (e.g., El Saddik et al., 2011; Harrasser, 2017; Schmidgen, 2018; von

Thadden, 2018). The Corona crisis and its distancing requirements have forced both cultural studies debates and societal discourses in which touch is ascribed a special significance to take place, for instance, in sport, dance and acting, but also in nursing, care work and sex work. As conferences take place by video and telephone due to the pandemic, once more taking centre stage are media debates about how gestures are being transformed into standardised emojis and clapping hands, and how changes are taking place in the way that we touch devices—for example, how we have gone from performing writing movements on paper or pressing movements on the touch telephone and TV to swiping movements on the smartphone (e.g., Kaerlein, 2018), which Marshall McLuhan was already addressing as early as in the 1960s (McLuhan, 1994).

Moreover, the situations in which bodies are present that have accompanied social digitalisation and that rely on touch—for example, the boom of gentle, non-invasive healing methods and self-care practices that utilise the techniques of touch and aim to improve how the body feels, like wellness, chilling and cuddle parties—have been pushed to the sidelines during the COVID-19 crisis.

The sense-making significance of art and theatre as sites of touch have also been called into question, places that are not considered essential in the pandemic and that have been forced to close. A few more figures show that, in Germany—like in all other countries in lockdown—people are singing, dancing, making music and theatre less than almost ever before. The German cultural sector, which employs approx. 1.8 million people—550,000 of them in precarious work—generated about EUR 170 billion in 2019, meaning that it created more added value than the chemical industry. It is now receiving aid from the Neustart Kultur (New Start Culture) programme to the tune of EUR 2 billion. This will indeed be a new start, as the performing arts alone, after one year of closures, have recorded a sales collapse of 85% (as of April 2021). However, aside from these figures, it is above all vilification and the loss of social significance that are plaguing culture. Art is the glue holding society together, as politicians were wont to claim in their speeches before the pandemic. Now this sense-making social bonding agent has been moved into the same category as swimming pools and brothels in some state regulations.

But people working in the cultural sector are fighting to legitimise their (by all means considerable) relevance. They are utilising an argument that was established within the scope of the 'performative turn' in the 1990s as digitalisation was taking off, namely that theatre and artistic spaces foster something that stands in opposition to digitalisation: proximity, uniqueness, unrepeatability and co-presence. Accordingly, discussions in art theory, theatre studies and, above all, dance studies have emphasised the role played by touch in co-presence and stressed that art targets our perception and challenges our senses synaesthetically (e.g., Klein & Haller, 2006; Brandstetter et al., 2013; Egert, 2019; Fluhrer & Waszynski, 2020; Marek & Meister, 2021). They thus consider theatre and artistic spaces to be sites of touch in a positive sense: they *aim* to contaminate, affect. Above all participative theatre forms have asserted the potential of the tactile and its special capacity for getting us to reflect upon the relationship between culture, the environment and the world of things. They have maintained that this quality is characteristic of contemporary theatre and essential to the functioning of society during the COVID-19 debate as well. However, the way that we are affected in modern bourgeois artistic spaces is generally by maintaining distance—which is perhaps why cultural sites have not been hotspots of infection. Whether at the theatre or at an exhibition, we are left to our visual sense; in order to be affected, we keep at a distance that is already inscribed into the space through the architecture and arrangements; the audience sits or stands—disciplined and silent. This sensory experience, which—unlike at the sports stadium—leads to the dispersion of little aerosol, is still something that is drilled into our bodies in bourgeois cultural institutions and controlled socially. And it is secured by technical means with, for example, the infiltration of technological touch media and interactive exhibition formats in artistic spaces.

But even outside of theatre, dance and art, sites of touch have become rare during the COVID-19 pandemic. It is evident that bodily communication is being increasingly formalised, for example, due to face mask requirements and social distancing rules. Moreover, the importance of visual communication in everyday interactions is growing, for example, due to video conferences, and in portals and formats for virtual sexual communication. Both changes—the formalisation and virtualisation of body-based communication—are reinforcing the experience of the 'homo clausus', a social figure that Norbert Elias saw as one manifestation of modern sociation, where the We-I balance shifts to one side in favour of monadic self-perception (Elias, 2010). However, today's monadic pandemic life is not taking place in social isolation. Digitalisation and virtual worlds are making it possible for people to 'meet', 'dial in' and exchange views. But online interaction is reduced to affective touch: for example, we perceive an interesting discussion to be less exciting during a video conference, jokes seldom relieve tension and comedy is more difficult to generate and less contagious (Kühl, 2020, p. 398).

The formalisation and virtualisation of body-based communication are changing the micro levels of social interaction and their vitalising foundation. Joy, empathy, arousal, touch and awareness are words that become subjects of discussion when bodily experience, the proximity to other bodies and the act of sensorily experiencing (smelling, tasting and seeing) the other change, and when alterity, a basal component of identity, is increasingly generated through social distance and the digital image. The current pandemic and the ensuing social distancing are thus not the first time that the issues relating to the entanglements between the real and the virtual (Baudrillard, 1988), the physical and the imaginary (Kamper, 1986), the anthropological and iconographic (Benthien, 2002) have been broached.

3   Conclusion

We could view the restructuring and changes that have taken place to the social significance of bodies cultural-pessimistically as one more episode in the history of the loss of corporeality. This interpretation would be another chapter in an illustrious history of sociological thought about the body: for example, Theodor W. Adorno and Max Horkheimer, who write in the *Dialectics of the Enlightenment*: 'The body cannot be turned back into the envelope of the soul. It remains a cadaver, no matter how trained and fit it may be' (Horkheimer & Adorno, 2002, p. 194). This cultural-critical theory, which posits an irreversible loss of bodily experience, was given a media theoretical twist in the 1990s by, for example, Dietmar Kamper and Christoph Wulf in allusion to Jean Baudrillard and accentuated in the theory of the disappearance of the body in the image (Kamper & Wulf, 1989, p. 3) and as a simulacrum (Baudrillard, 1988). The body that has been driven back by the COVID-19 crisis can be described in a similar way: as contact has been reduced and people have been required to stay home, the digital image has grown in importance. This has also changed orders of touch: trust, proximity, compassion, optimism, consolation, fear and care are now generated in and through images—thus also changing their performative strategies of authentication.

As figurations of touch become images, we see 'new bodies' being created using digital techniques of bodily communication. We are increasingly taking it for granted that we communicate with and through digital bodies—video conferences, Zoom yoga, Instagram fitness—which is forcing the practical implementation of a concept of the body that has been in the works for some time now: the 'hybrid body', whose bodily experiences can be localised on a spectrum between the real and the virtual, the representative and the imaginary. According to media sociology, this development harbours the potential to expand our realm of experience with new hybrids of real and virtual (e.g., Fuhse, 2010; Krotz & Hepp, 2012). It therefore seems likely that hybridity as a mode of sociality is being normalised, and that sensations, perceptions and sensitivities are productively are being organised into a flexible constellation of bodily feeling, media expression and virtual communication, as well as representative and imagined forms (May et al., 2009), which many people seem to find satisfying.

In all these developments, the contours of new orders of the body are becoming visible: they are not individualised, insular 'homines clausi' (Elias, 1998) whose purpose is individual sense-making and self-staging. Rather, they are relational bodies that are always conceived of in connection to others: to other people, to the environment, to the climate, to the economic community.

Overall, we can say that the COVID-19 crisis has set society the task of redefining when bodies are dangerous or in need of protection and when their physical presence is seen as necessary. This has led to discussions about the relevance of the corresponding societal subsystems (such as art, sport, religion, education and health), which have increasingly become the subject of public debate. But it is not just the comparative significance of the individual societal subsystems that is being rearranged, as the sociologist Rudolf Stichweh has claimed. In March 2020 (Stichweh, 2020, p. 198), he said that religion, culture and sport would be the societal fields that would come out on the losing side of the COVID-19 crisis, as they were not essential in the fight against the pandemic. Religion, culture and sport—these are genuinely bodily fields for which corporeal practices, in groups and masses as well, are constitutive.

The COVID-19 crisis has thus made it clear that bodies are the battlefield on which the struggle to define the relationship between the subsystems and their power structures is being staged. The disappearance of the collective body in public space—like the mass body in sport, religion and culture—indicates just how much significance these subsystems have lost. At the same time, new forms of digital collectivisation are taking effect, changing the individual's opportunities to experience themselves corporeally as part of a collective: the digital society.

References

Agamben, G. (2000 [1996]). Notes on Gesture. In G. Agamben, *Means without End: Notes on Politics*, trans. V. Binetti & C. Casarino (pp. 48–59). University of Minnesota.

Aristotle. (1968). *De Anima, Books II and III (with Passages from Book I)* (D. W. Hamlyn, Trans.). Clarendon Press.

Baudrillard, J. (1988 [1981]). Simulacra and Simulation. In M. Poster (Ed.), *Jean Baudrillard: Selected Writings*, trans. P. Foss & P. Patton (pp. 166–184). Stanford University Press.

Bauman, Z. (2000). *Liquid Modernity*. Polity Press.

Benthien, C. (2002). *Skin: On the Cultural Border between Self and World* (Dunlap, Trans.). Columbia University Press.

Bourdieu, P. (1984 [1979]). *Distinction: A Social Critique of the Judgement of Taste* (R. Nice, Trans.). Harvard University Press.

Brandstetter, G., Egert, G., & Zubarik, S. (Eds.). (2013). *Touching and Being Touched: Kinesthesia and Empathy in Dance and Movement*. De Gruyter.

Brandstetter, G., & Klein, G. (Eds.). (2013). *Dance [and] Theory*. transcript.

Egert, G. (2019 [2016]). *Moving Relation: Touch in Contemporary Dance* (R. Rossi, Trans.). Routledge.

El Saddik, A., Orozco, M., Eid, M., & Cha, J. (Eds.). (2011). *Haptics Technologies: Bringing Touch to Multimedia*. Springer.

Elias, N. (1998 [1995]). Die Entstehung des homo clausus. In H. Keupp (Ed.), *Lust an der Erkenntnis: Der Mensch als soziales Wesen; Ein Lesebuch* (2nd ed.). R. Piper.

Elias, N. (2010 [1939]). *The Society of Individuals* (M. Schröter, Ed., E. Jephcott, Trans.). In R. van Krieken (Ed.), *The Collected Works of Norbert Elias*, 2. University College Dublin Press.

Elias, N. (2012 [1939]). *On the Process of Civilisation: Sociogenetic and Psychogenetic Investigations* (Jephcott, Trans., S. Mennell, E. Dunning, J. Goudsblom, & R. Kilminster). In R. van Krieken (Ed.), *The Collected Works of Norbert Elias*, 3. University College Dublin Press.

Fluhrer, S., & Waszynski, A. (Eds.). (2020). *Tangieren—Szenen des Berührens*. Rombach.

Foucault, M. (1979 [1975]). *Discipline and Punish: The Birth of the Prison* (A. Sheridan, Trans.). Vintage Books.

Fuhse, J. (2010). Welche kulturellen Formationen entstehen in mediatisierten Kommunikationsnetzwerken? In J. Fuhse & C. Stegbauer (Eds.), *Kultur und mediale Kommunikation in sozialen Netzwerken* (pp. 31–54). Springer VS.

Funke-Wieneke, J. (1983). *Sportunterricht als Körpererfahrung*. Rowohlt.

Gehlen, A. (1993). Ein Bild des Menschen. In A. Gehlen (Ed.), *Anthropologische und sozialpsychologische Untersuchungen* (pp. 44–54). Rowohlt.

Goffman, E. (1967). *Interaction Ritual: Essays on Face-to-Face Behavior*. Pantheon Books.

Gugutzer, R., Klein, G., & Meuser, M. (Eds.). (2022). *Handbuch Körpersoziologie* (2nd ed.). Springer VS.

GutsMuths, J. C. F. (1800 [1793]). *Gymnastics for Youth: Or a Practical Guide to Healthful and Amusing Exercises for the Use of Schools; an Essay Toward the Necessary Improvement of Education, Chiefly as it Relates to the Body* (C. G. Salzmann, Trans.). Joseph Johnson.

Habermas, J. (1984 [1981]). *The Theory of Communicative Action: Reason and the Rationalization of Society* (T. McCarthy, Trans.). Polity Press.

Harrasser, K. (Ed.). (2017). *Auf Tuchfühlung: Eine Wissensgeschichte des Tastsinns*. Campus.

Horkheimer, M., & Adorno, T. W. (2002 [1947]). *Dialectic of Enlightenment: Philosophical Fragments* (E. Jephcott, Trans., G. Schmid, Ed.). Stanford University Press.

Kaerlein, T. (2018). *Smartphones als digitale Nahkörpertechnologien: Zur Kybernetisierung des Alltags*. transcript.

Kamper, D. (1986). *Zur Soziologie der Imagination*. Carl Hanser.

Kamper, D., & Wulf, C. (1989). *Transfigurationen des Körpers: Spuren der Gewalt in der Geschichte*. Reimer.

Klein, G. (1994). *Frauen Körper Tanz: Eine Zivilisationsgeschichte des Tanzes*. Heine.

Klein, G. (2004). *Electronic Vibration: Pop Kultur Theorie*. VS.

Klein, G. (Ed.). (2009). *Tango in Translation. Tanz zwischen Medien, Kulturen, Kunst und Politik*. transcript.

Klein, G. (2020). *Pina Bausch's Dance Theater: Company, Artistic Practices and Reception* (E. Poelzer, Trans.). transcript.

Klein, G., & Friedrich, M. (2003). *Is This Real? Die Kultur des HipHop*. Suhrkamp.

Klein, G., & Haller, M. (2006). Bewegung, Bewegtheit und Beweglichkeit: Subjektivität im Tango Argentino. In M. Bischoff, C. Feest, & C. Rosiny (Eds.), *e_motion in motion. Jahrbuch Tanzforschung* (Vol. 16, pp. 157–173). Lit.

Klein, G., & Liebsch, K. (2020). Herden unter Kontrolle: Körper in Corona-Zeiten. In M. Volkmer & K. Werner (Eds.), *Die Corona-Gesellschaft: Analysen zur Lage und Perspektiven für die Zukunft* (pp. 57–65). transcript.

Klein, G., & Liebsch, K. (2021). Ansteckende Berührungen: Körperordnungen in der Krise. In J. Beuerbach, S. Gülker, U. Karstein, & R. Rösener (Eds.), *Sinn in der Krise: Kulturwissenschaftliche Beobachtungen zur Covid-19-Pandemie*. Praesens (forthcoming).

Klein, G., & Noeth, S. (2011). *Emerging Bodies: The Performance of Worldmaking in Dance and Choreography*. transcript.

Krotz, F., & Hepp, A. (Eds.). (2012). *Mediatisierte Welten: Forschungsfelder und Beschreibungsansätze*, 6. Springer VS.

Kühl, S. (2020). Jeder lacht für sich allein: Zum Unterschied von Interaktion unter Anwesenden und unter Abwesenden. *Forschung & Lehre, 5*, 398–399.

Lindemann, G. (2020). *Die Ordnung der Berührung: Staat, Gewalt und Kritik in Zeiten der Corona-Krise*. Velbrück.

Marek, K., & Meister, C. (Eds.). (2021). *Berührung: Taktiles in Kunst und Theorie*. Wilhelm Fink.

Massumi, B. (2015). *Politics of Affect*. Polity Press.

Mauss, M. (1973 [1935]). Techniques of the Body. *Economy and Society, 2*(1), 70–88.

May, C. R., Mair, F., & Finch, T. (2009). Development of a Theory of Implementation and Integration: Normalization Process Theory. *Implementation Science, 4*, 29. https://doi.org/10.1186/1748-5908-4-29

McLuhan, M. (1994). *Understanding Media: The Extension of Man*. Routledge.

Merleau-Ponty, M. (2012 [1945]). *Phenomenology of Perception* (D. A. Landes, Trans.). Routledge.

Meusel, H. (1973). *Johann Heinrich Pestalozzi über Körperbildung: Studientexte zur Leibeserziehung*, 10, Limpert.

Nassehi, A. (2019). *Muster: Theorie der digitalen Gesellschaft*. C. H. Beck.

Plessner, H. (2019 [1928]). *Level of Organic Life and the Human: An Introduction to Philosophical Anthropology* (M. Hyatt, Trans.). Fordham University Press.

Scheidt, C.-E. (2020). Abschied vom Handschlag. In B. Kortmann & G. Schulze (Eds.), *Jenseits von Corona: Unsere Welt nach der Pandemie: Perspektiven aus der Wissenschaft* (pp. 43–50). transcript.

Schmidgen, H. (2018). *Horn oder Die Gegenseite der Medien*. Matthes & Seitz.

Stichweh, R. (2020). Simplifikation des Sozialen. In M. Volkmer & K. Werner (Eds.), *Die Corona-Gesellschaft: Analysen zur Lage und Perspektiven für die Zukunft* (pp. 197–206). transcript.

von Thadden, E. (2018). *Die berührungslose Gesellschaft*. C. H. Beck.

Waldenfels, B. (2002). *Bruchlinien der Erfahrung* (pp. 64–97). Suhrkamp.

Like Water Between One's Hands: Embodiment of Time and the Ephemeral of Dance

Gabriele Brandstetter

1   Introduction

Today, the familiar and established essentialist and naturalist view of the objectified body is questioned by scholars pursuing diverse discursive lines and utilising ethnographic, phenomenological, poststructuralist and dialogical approaches. Traditional physicalist and biological trajectories are increasingly being replaced by dynamic conceptualisations that take into account difference, hybridity, dissemination, interaction and multimodality. Inherited and adopted habitus also comes into play, as do diverse tacit modes of the constitution of practices, such as emergence, reinterpretation, differentiation and consolidation in somatic trainings and dance techniques; together, these form social and educational relations and dispositions. The ephemeral of movement and interactive performance is entangled within these concepts and discourses of dance and transformative aesthetics.

The word 'ephemer' has its origins in the Greek *ephēmeros* and means short-lived, alive for a single day, transient. For entomologists, mayflies fall under the order of Ephemeroptera—reflecting the short lifespan of the insects. Similarly, the term ephemerides originally referred to astronomical tables in which the daily movement of the stars was tabulated. The format of the desk calendar, where every day a page is ripped off to reveal the next day's

---

G. Brandstetter (✉)
Free University of Berlin, Berlin, Germany
e-mail: theater-tanz@fu-berlin.de

© The Author(s), under exclusive license to Springer Nature Switzerland AG 2022   **311**
A. Kraus, C. Wulf (eds.), *The Palgrave Handbook of Embodiment and Learning*,
https://doi.org/10.1007/978-3-030-93001-1_19

entry, is also derived from this practice of recording day-to-day changes. Likewise, notes, events and memories were retained as *hypomnemata*, creating the earliest forms of the diary. Crucial for these ephemerides, logbooks and diaries—and later also for periodicals—is the temporal structure of the transient, which protocols the moment as a strategy for ordering events. Complementary to this daily record keeping of the ephemeral is the ontological and aesthetic experience of the transience of time and the transience of life as a whole.

In early modern times and during the baroque period, the ephemeral was linked to the topos of Vanitas (Benthien & von Fleming, 2018), which encompasses the experience and the metaphor-rich lament about the transient nature of life. Vanitas is associated with notions of "nothingness, appearance, futility, dream, uselessness, senselessness, idolatry—but also of the void, the ephemeral, the transitory, the fleeting" (Benthien & von Fleming, 2018, p. 13). In the tension between a 'memento mori' and 'carpe diem', a rich iconography unfolds in art, wherein decay is reflected in wilting flowers and rotting fruit, skulls represent the subject of mortality and fragility and volatility are mirrored in wafer-thin glasses and soap bubbles.

In literature, visual art, music and dance (the danse macabre), the complex time structure of Vanitas becomes the subject of various means of representation inherent to each medium: in the celebration of the here and now (carpe diem) as a response to and consequence of transience; in the lament about the fleeting nature of youth and beauty; and in the reflection of irretrievability—in the intrinsic repetition and contradiction of repetition. Goethe's couplet on the transience of beauty thematises the aesthetic experience of the ephemeral and its associated melancholy:

> "Warum bin ich vergänglich, o Zeus?", so fragte die Schönheit.
> "Macht' ich doch", sagte der Gott, "nur das Vergängliche schön."
> Und die Liebe, die Blumen, der Tau und die Jugend vernahmen's:
> "Alle gingen sie weg, weinend, von Jupiters Thron." (Goethe, 1998, p. 563f)

(Why am I mortal, o Zeus? was Beauty's question./Answered the God: because I only made mortal things beautiful./And Love, the flowers, the dew and youth understood./Then departed, crying, from Jupiter's throne.)

2 The Ephemeral, Embodiment and Modern Arts

By 1900, the experience of the ephemeral had increasingly become a theme in the arts—now within the context of symbolism, both, in terms of decadence and in the celebration of youth. Hugo von Hofmannsthal's terza rima 'Über Vergänglichkeit' (On transience) (1894) uses fragments of the Vanitas theme: "Dies ist ein Ding, das keiner voll aussinnt,/Und viel zu grauenvoll, als daß man klage:/Daß alles gleitet und vorüberrinnt" (Hofmannsthal, 1984, p. 45). (This is a thing that no one thinks out fully,/and much too dreadful to complain about/That everything slips and flows away.) In her famous complaint in Richard Straus' '*Rosenkavalier*' (1911) about the inexorable dwindling of time and the transience of youth, the Marschallin interweaves melancholy and a reflection of the ephemeral: "Die Zeit ist ein sonderbar Ding [...]. Sie ist um uns herum, sie ist auch in uns drinnen. In den Gesichtern rieselt sie, im Spiegel da rieselt sie, in meinen Schläfen fließt sie. Und zwischen mir und dir da fließt sie wieder, lautlos, wie eine Sanduhr" (Hofmannsthal, 1986, p. 40). (Time is a strange thing [...]. It is around us, it is also inside us. It trickles over our faces, it trickles over the mirror there, it flows over my temples. And between me and you, it flows again, silently, like an hourglass.) Although the ephemeral has been thematised in art and in the self-perception of individuals since antiquity, only with the advent of modernity has the term and its relevance within aesthetics become central to the theory and perception of temporality and being in time. With the rise of certain new dynamics—the advent of traffic, industrialisation, the press and changes in fashion, the experience of the ephemeral has become both intrinsic to and synonymous with the idea of modernity. In his famous essay 'Le Peintre de la vie moderne' (The Painter of Modern Life) (1863), the French poet Charles Baudelaire describes the experience and the art of portraying the ephemeral as the very signature of modernity. Art is no longer defined by that which endures and bridges time; instead, "La modernité, c'est le transitoire, le fugitif, le contingent" (Baudelaire, 1976, vol. 2, p. 691). (Modernity—it's the transitory, the fleeting, the contingent.) In the aesthetics of modernity, the transitory, the fleeting and the contingent become key categories for understanding not only the acceleration of daily life in the city but also the experiences of social and political change (Simmel, 1995). The fleeting nature of movement in the rhythm of the big city characterises the time-experience of the ephemeral: consider the figure of the flâneur, highlighted by Walter Benjamin in his 'Passagenwerk' with reference to Baudelaire (Benjamin, 1982, vol. V, pp. 60–77), and the transformation of the cityscape portrayed by Louis Aragon in his novel 'Le Paysan de Paris' (The peasant of Paris) (1926). Aragon was the first to use the term 'The Ephemeral' as a nominalised adjective, in reference to the veritable cult of the ephemeral in the early twentieth century, sparking the term's eventual establishment in the discourse on modernity and its aesthetics. Joachim Krausse distinguishes three areas in which the ephemeral plays a central role in the theoretical discourse of the twentieth and twenty-first centuries: "one, the acceleration of change and the temporalisation of the spatial; two, the dematerialisation and devaluation of the physical; three, medialisation and communicative networking" (1990, p. 241). In so doing, Krausse emphasises the importance of the work of the US-American architect Richard Buckminster Fuller, who first outlined a concept of ephemeralisation in his book *Nine Chains to the Moon* (1938). In *Nine Chains*, the synergies of interwoven processes of acceleration, dematerialisation and interconnectedness are linked to a new model of architecture that is no longer conceived of as the enduring oeuvre of building-creation, but as construction following the principles of lightness, "ephemeralisation" and "tensegrity" (Krausse, 1990, p. 254). For the arts as well as for the aesthetic discourses of the twentieth and twenty-first centuries, this created new impulses, placing the temporality and dynamics of fluid and volatile processes at the centre. Since the 1970s, theorists of all stripes have addressed particular aspects of ephemeralism—Paul Virilio, for example, on speed and disappearance (Virilio, 1986, 1997); Jean François Lyotard on the fleeting, *Les immatériaux* (1996); Elizabeth Grosz on the volatility of a globalised, networked world (Grosz, 1994); and Hartmut Rosa on acceleration and deceleration (Rosa, 2013) as forms of the everyday experience of time. With the development of media such as photography, film, radio, television and electronic networks, social communication and aesthetic experience are changing in specific ways: according to Ralf Schnell and Georg Stanitzek (2005), the ephemeral is crucial for the perception and the time structures of media disruptions. Inasmuch aspects such as acceleration, disappearance and synchronisation are relevant to the perception of the ephemeral, so too are fractures, distortions, cuts, cracks, blanks or tears (in the tape) of the passage of time—all characteristic of the aesthetics of the ephemerality of modernity.

Correspondingly, aesthetic theories of the ephemeral highlight questions about time structures in relation to both art and the body of the viewer. This leads to strategies of dissolution of the concept of work all the way to the destruction of the 'works' themselves—in action art, for example, in order to highlight the event (John Cage, Yves Klein) or the 'happenings' (Goldberg, 2001; Schimmel, 1998), in the US-American painter Allan Kaprow's *18*

Happenings in 6 Parts (1959), for example, an 'event', in which those aspects noted by Baudelaire dominate: what happens is transitory, bound to a place and a situation; the structures of the event are contingent on those present and have no further meaning beyond what happens in the here and now.

An aesthetic of the ephemeral is by no means limited to the temporal arts—music, theatre, dance and performance—even though these disciplines have played a decisive role, since the avant-garde, in the dissolution of boundaries between all forms of artistic expression and between art and life. Within aesthetic theory, the opposition between permanence and the fleeting in relation to works of art dissolves in the context of discourses on the ephemeral and its associated economies of work, property and their capitalisation—especially in regard to those art forms and pieces that are (ostensibly) permanent. Thus, in his *Aesthetic Theory* (2002), Theodor W. Adorno describes the category of the permanent, canonical, enduring of works of art and their ownership as a fetishisation under the sign of capital:

> As soon as artworks make a fetish of their hope for their duration, they begin to suffer from their sickness unto death: The veneer of inalienability that they draw over themselves at the same time suffocates them. (Adorno, 2002, p. 28)

Of course, a cultural and art history of the ephemeral and its associated experience of time cannot focus solely on Western philosophies and aesthetics concepts. The manner in which transience is perceived and addressed in different cultures—for example, in Japan during the cherry blossom festival (sakura), in which the viewing (hanami) of the short-lived flowers conveys both beauty/blossoming and mortality—would have to be part of any comparative study on the aesthetics and embodiment of the ephemeral. The philosopher François Jullien, in his study *Du temps »* (2004), compares the conjugations of temporal structures between Western thought, influenced by antiquity, with Chinese philosophy, which did not develop a transcendental concept of time, and therefore understands the relationship between moment and duration and processes of the decay (such as ageing bodies) in a different way.

Diverse concepts of the ephemeral have developed not only within different philosophies of time and within the diversity of artistic expression (and their materiality), but the epistemic dimension of the fleeting is also embedded in the temporal structure of momentariness and duration, the fluidity of phenomena and strategies of preservation: the transience of temporal phenomena and their materiality (such as clouds, smoke and liquids), their aesthetic and/or experimental scientific observation, and the documentation thereof describes a circle in which the temporal tension between event and history, between material artefact and its transience must itself be part of the perception and its reflection. Thus, a "topography of the fleeting" (Brandstetter, 2020) between movement and objectivity is always confronted with the moment of withdrawal—the cloudy place—in the moment of recording, retaining and preserving.

As an example for this constellation of the fleeting nature of phenomena—their fundamental 'untenability'—and strategies for fixing knowledge, let the cloud be the tangible manifestation of the transitory. Goethe's analysis of the scientist Luke Howard's 1815 *Theory of Clouds* points to this double-sided phenomenon, reflected in the morphology of the cloud. Phenomenology and epistemology work together to define the fleeting changing form, the 'irregular nature' of these structures as a 'perforated continuum', and to describe the coincidental creation of these forms and states of matter as "limit conditions [Gränz-Zustände]" (Vogl, 2005, p. 72). The purpose lies in sparking in the viewer a notion of clouds as spectacular, dramatic theatre of the sky. As dynamic bodies, unfinished, constantly in the act of becoming, singular and unrepeatable in form, they convey the aesthetic experience of the "transitory" (Ibid.) and envelop the viewer in a paradox of seeing: the closer one gets to these volatile bodies, the more they dissolve. On closer inspection, writes Goethe, this 'object' can no (longer) be observed: in the act of observation, the thing, the body, becomes a 'happening'—a fleeting, dissolving event. Such a configuration of withdrawing, 'cloudy' make these 'bodies' 'hypothetical objects': "An aesthetics of form, of shapes and figures is thus overtaken by an aesthetics of occurrence" [Ästhetik des Erscheinens] (Vogl, 2005, p. 78). The elastic and the mobile, the 'floating' inherent to the clouds indicate a method of observation and analysis that sees itself as hypothetical and processual.

Fleeting is thus the relation of the object—transformational morphology of bodies—and the viewer: a constellation that implies not only the viewer's involvement but also their kinaesthetic experience as an element of ephemerality. Clouds are, in this sense, a kind of placeholder; they are 'allegories of reading' for art forms, events, processes of embodying the ephemeral. They are 'difficult objects' because, as bodies without definite limitations and forms, they challenge both the representation of the arts and the discourses of epistemology: they even occupy the place of an "epistemological emblem", marking the limits of knowledge and of representability (Vogl, 2005, p. 70).

3 Ephemeral Bodies and Memory

Within the context of the paradox already inherent to the concept of the ephemeral exists the space within which the cultural techniques of preserving and losing, remembering and forgetting, as well as their various storage mediums, move: ephemera by definition embrace processes and things that are transitory and determined for short-term use, such as tickets, daily calendars, postcards and ad mail. The short-lived nature of these momentary media, as well as the length of time collections and collectors (ephemerists) bestow upon them (Richards, 2000), deftly mark this contradiction. The idea of the ephemeral and the predetermined expectation that it will disappear is reversed by an 'Encyclopaedia of the Ephemeral', which preserves the limited temporality of momentary existence in an archive for the future. A theory of the archive and its structures of knowledge, a critique of "archive fever" (Derrida, 1997) and the canon, begins here in order to bend the temporality of the ephemeral, long sedimented in collections and archives, back into the path of movement, of disappearance, and finally into the transience, the ephemerality of the archive itself.

Since the advent of postmodernism, the relationship between art, the viewer and positionality [Situativität]/the event has been discussed in depth in art and theory—as well as being critically analysed in terms of its politics of historical documentation and the processuality of appropriation. In contrast to the aesthetics of the artwork in art and performance, questions of an "aesthetics of the performative" (Fischer-Lichte, 2008) are now coming to the fore. Simultaneously, questions of vitality and decay, liveness and media documentation, transformation and the transitory nature of media changes as well as critiques of the institutions of preservation (museums and archives) and practices of curating are being discussed in the context of the theory and the practice of art. One example is the work of artists who stage the theme of transience in their work as a process—in a contemporary revision of 'Vanitas', by exhibiting the remnants of events or performances, displaying the waste and its temporality and the relation between human-animal bodies (Brandstetter, 2019).

In his installation *Untilled* (2012) at dOCUMENTA 13, Pierre Huyghe addresses the circulation between garbage and the museum, as well as the unpredictable and uncontrollable dissolution of the boundaries between art, exhibition and nature or, more specifically, the processes of life. In order to do so, he exchanges the exhibition spaces of the museum for open gardens. And, as the artist, he busies himself with the processes of transformation between nature and culture: the creation and degeneration of a compost heap; bee-keeping (and thus with the art of bees: honeycomb construction and bee swarms/dance), which colonises the classical sculptures in the garden and makes the artist appear not as Pygmalion with a female statue, but as a bee-keeper. And finally, there is the albino dog named 'Human', whose pink-painted leg looks like a play on the boundaries and transitions of human-animal relationships: these components of what is usually called an art 'installation', point in *Untilled*—it is already in the title—to a temporality that is not clearly delimited—distinctly *not* 'un-til'. It is instead overflowing, transient, accidental and dissolving. In a different way, the Swiss artists Dieter Roth and Daniel Spoerri deal with the theme of transience, the ephemeral and the conditions of art and the museum, by staging those processes of decay and chance in which culture and nature are intimately interwoven: food and the perishability of organic matter, intertwined with a fundamental questioning of the relationship between art and life, of the aesthetic boundaries between beauty and waste/apostasy, the philosophical differentiations between the actual (*res*) and the rest (*akzidens*), and with the economic themes of consumption and conservation. Roth explicitly designed his installation *Selbstturm/Löwenturm* (1989) in and for the museum, as an artwork of decay, in order to directly call into question the mission and the basic definition of the museum and the storage magazine, namely, to preserve works of visual art and to exhibit them, again and again. How then to store and exhibit objects and their material disintegration (such as mouldy cheese or chocolate busts chewed up by insects)? (Bohlmann, 2018). In contrast, the artist Daniel Spoerri developed his *trap pictures* (*Tableau piège*, 1960) from the transience of a meal, by fixing the remains and hanging them with the tabletop on the wall as a picture. The *Eat Art* happening thus became an arrangement of remnants, wherein the restoration and preservation for posterity is exposed as a practice of "substitute immortality" (Groys, 1997, p. 198). With different emphases, artists and historiographers both work on the challenges presented by the materiality of things (objects) and events, as well as the preservation of the vestiges (processuality) of their transmission. The challenge of these relationships between event, history and performativity is illuminated in the act of dealing with the works of artists who consciously depict the 'remnants', the materiality of remnants, of garbage and of the organic—as well as its decay—during their transfer to the archive, and thereby during their inexorable advance into history. In so doing, these artists simultaneously trigger a critique of the institutions and discourses of the ephemeral as well as memory and its storage media.

4 Movement and Embodiment: The Ephemeral of Dance

Among the artistic disciplines, dance is traditionally considered the most volatile art form—although this topos too must be questioned. How does processuality—temporality as a structured sequence of movements—differ from other performative arts? Is dance therefore considered more fleeting, because the modes of memory, the methods and techniques of recording and transmitting are less standardised than musical notations? And, at least in Western culture, because (body) knowledge about dance is more marginal, incomplete and less discursively powerful? The question here is not only about the tension between the fleeting nature of a (dance) performance and the persistence of diverse, medially and historically changing forms of recording (Brandstetter, 2004), but also about how the transitory nature of movement and contingencies in the process of perceiving and remembering also mark the specific aesthetic-temporality of the ephemeral. The time-experience of the ephemeral is in the perception of the period, of the moment and its situativity, interlinked with the reflexive mode of the gaze. An aesthetic experience of suddenness (Bohrer, 1981) is sparked (often illustrated with lightning or fireworks) in the now of the moment, while simultaneously being erased and recursively retrieved and repeated in the temporality of an afterthought. This characteristic aesthetic self-temporality connects the temporal structure of the ephemeral to the spatially defined aesthetics of atmosphere (Böhme, 1995). The respective subject's perception is decisive for the sensory experience of a situation and for the sense of its temporal dimension: its condensation or extension in durational experiences of eternity in that moment. This aesthetic experience of the ephemeral cannot be assigned to just single sensory organs; instead, the quality of these time perceptions is multimodal. Time-forms and time structures—their movement, periodicity and the quality of their materiality (in sound, corporeality or spatiality)—are physical, simultaneously and embodied experienced through a kinaesthetic "listening" (Brandstetter, 2013) and through a reflexive dimension, inherently linked to the ephemeral (and the melancholy of transience), that reverberates with the afterimage and the aftersound of the (just) past. This peculiar mode of perception, attention and sensual resonance between a fleeting phenomenon and its perceiving subject is also a fundamental characteristic of embodied aesthetic experience (Waldenfels, 2010; Mersch, 2015). The ephemeral thus not only encompasses the now of an already vanishing moment, but is also intertwined with spatial experience, the situativity and positionality, as well as the material and sensory qualities, of perception. The experience of lightness and "dematerialisation effects" (Krausse, 1990, p. 250) in modern architecture or the effects of immersion through virtual time-space experiences correspond to those perceptions that Roland Barthes in 1964 called "coenesthetic" (Barthes, 1990, p. 301): the fundamentally self-specific and self-temporal experiences of space, of the position and gravity of the body, of its gravitational awareness and equilibrium in regard to the momentary situation—in short, the moment of feeling and emotional and cognitive processes associated with it.

5 Movement, Fluidity of Time and (Physical) Transformation

After all, it is dance that brings together these experiences of aesthetic and temporality in movement, in the temporal and material condensation of ephemerality, in bodily and temporal transience.

In a scene by Lebanese choreographer and performer Rabih Mroué, from the piece *Water Between Three Hands* (2016),[1] the dancer Jone San Martin steps into a bright circle lit by a spotlight and begins to tell a story in which she transforms the ephemerality of the performance into a particular act of conservation of her dance work: at the end of each performance, she says laconically, she always ran immediately into the dressing room, where she wrung out her clothes and collected her sweat in a bottle. She did this for over 20 years; she observed the changes in the secretions of her body in the bottles: the colour nuances, the gradual evaporation and the thickening of the fluid, the sedimentation of the liquid: "I collected the remains of all the bottles/and put them in a little nylon bag./I weighed it/and there were about 11 grams of 'sweat powder'." San Martin goes on to explain how she came up with the idea of returning this extract, this sediment of 20-years' embodied (dance) work, back into her body. She sniffs; she inhales the sweat powder like a drug; then she restitutes this outflow/abundance of her enduring dance practice back into her body in a mere instant. San Martin refers to this moment of self-transubstantiation as occurring 'like a flash'—a metaphor for a lightning-fast incident. It is that metaphor of the lightning-fast occurrence that frequently (see, e.g., W. Benjamin, Th. W. Adorno) frames the auratic, energetic moment of stopping or condensing time and time perception. In San Martin's mind's eye, precisely such a time-moment of the highest time-density occurs, in

---

[1] Rabih Mroué: Water between Three Hands, UA Kampnagel/Hamburg, 23.04.2016, as the second production of the Dance On/First Edition project; here: Scene No. 13.

which the memories of all her previous performances rise and are superimposed in a single image: "all in one image;/one big sublime image/holding different years and different performances [...]/an image that lasted for a few seconds/before it disappeared" (ibid. Scene 13). The magic of this experience drives her: she drinks the rest of the powder dissolved in water—and now she does not *see* the performances as a single *image* all at once—they are instead re-embodied. Re-embodied in a single moment—not in a dance of hours and years, but a memory-move of "lost time", condensed in "this moment", in one instant: "in an instant, it (my body) was dancing all the dances/that I had ever performed in my whole life" (ibid., Scene 13). It is also the moment of collapse: "Immediately, I died"—just as in the mythical dances during which the dancers dance to death (in *Giselle*, in *The Red Shoes*, as in the poets H. von Hofmannsthal's *Elektra* or Paul Valery's *L'Âme et la Danse*). The utmost and most extreme moment of the dance is that particular intoxicated state in which time and memory coincide, in 'one shot'. Cardiac arrest and the stoppage of time—a 'Now', a 'Shot'—in that moment, they are one, embodied and dissolved simultaneously. However, even this is not deliverable to posterity. The trace of time—the movement—continues. The stopping of time (the *shot*—of the photo or the rifle) is a leap across the fabric of perception. Or, as dancer Amy Shulman in the same performance says, "I decided to stand still and not to move at all./But that's impossible. (She turns around)/because if I'm still,/time is not."[2] These parts of the performance *Water between Three Hands* are displaying and interweaving basic concepts of the ephemeral in dance and performance: the tension between long duration (lifelong work on the body and body techniques) and the density of time in the experience of 'stand still'; the experience of the time passing and the transformation of the (ageing) body (which was a motor of the dance-project of 'dance on'); and the experience of fluidity and ephemerality of movement in contrast with the hard work of the dancing body with sweat and the power of physical energy.

In his interview on the question of *Stop making art*, Mroué refers to the topos of the ephemerality of the performing arts: like the volatility and the tangibility of a performance that flows like water between one's hands, "we can't grasp the now in our hands. It is a moment that always flees" (Mroué, 2014, p. 23). Holding a performance in this now would, according to Mroué, mean that this present would have to be put on hold indefinitely, "by keeping it as a work in progress and unfinished" (ibid., p. 24). In a sense, Mroué's own work as an artist pursues this concept of an ongoing progress and a process of constant re-appropriation, while also deconstructing the dichotomy, the strict

---

[2] Script, Scene 10, Graph 3/'No Face'.

either/or of presence and representation. He implicates, indeed interweaves, the temporality and the evidentiary potential of the performative present in the processes and mediums of representation. In so doing, he corrodes, even corrupts and traverses—in theory (which, in his opinion, belongs to the work of the artist) and in performative practice—the opposition between presence (performance) and representation, which has by now become a topos within performance theory.

Across cultures and eras, the image of flowing water—in the flow of time as well as in the paradox of *Water between Three Hands*—has characterised the experience of the simultaneity of embodiment and untenability of the ephemeral. It is an inherent dimension of embodiment and the tacit knowledge not only in dance but of any performative interaction. The parameters on 'aesthetics of the ephemeral' (which is not yet written) could provide impulses and new settings of exploration for a future research on embodiment, body and memory, social interaction and practises of transformation.

References

Adorno, T. W. (2002 [1970]). Ästhetische Theorie. In G. Adorno & R. Tiedemann, *Gesammelte Schriften in 20 Bänden*, 7. Suhrkamp.

Aragon, L. (1926). *Le Paysan de Paris*. Editions Gallimard.

Barthes, R. (1990 [1964]). La Tour Eiffel. In *Œvres Completes. Éric Marty*, 1, pp. 1379–1400.

Baudelaire, C. (1976 [1863]). Le peintre de la vie modern. In C. Pichois (Ed.), *Œvres Complètes*. Dossiê.

Benjamin, W. (1982). Das Passagen-Werk. In T. Rolf, H. Schweppenhäuser, T. W. Adorno, & S. Gershom (Eds.), *Gesammelte Schriften* (Vol. 1). Suhrkamp.

Benthien, C., & von Fleming, V. (Eds.). (2018). Paragrana. In *Zeitschrift für Historische Anthropologie*, 27(2). Reflexionen über Vergänglichkeit in Literatur, bildender Kunst und theoretischen Diskursen der Gegenwart. Vanitas.

Bohlmann, C. (2018). Vergänglichkeit für die Ewigkeit? Zur musealen Konservierung des Ephemeren. In C. Benthien & V. von Flemming (Eds.), *Zeitschrift für Historische Anthropologie* (27(2), pp. 99–114). Paragrana.

Böhme, G. (1995). Atmosphäre. In *Essays zur neuen Ästhetik*. Suhrkamp.

Bohrer, K. H. (1981). *Plötzlichkeit. Zum Augenblick des ästhetischen Seins*. Suhrkamp.

Brandstetter, G. (2004). Aufführung und Aufzeichnung—Kunst der Wissenschaft? In E. Fischer-Lichte, C. Risi, & J. Roselt (Eds.), *Kunst der Aufführung. Aufführung der Kunst* (pp. 40–50). Theater der Zeit.

Brandstetter, G. (2013). Listening—Kinesthetic Awareness in Contemporary Dance. In G. Egert & S. Zubarik (Eds.), *Touching and Being Touched. Kinesthesia and Empathy in Dance and Movement* (pp. 136–179). De Gruyter.

Brandstetter, G. (2019). On the Margins of HiStories: Transfusions between Document and Performance. In S. Foellmer, M. K. Schmidt, & C. Schmitz (Eds.), *Performing Arts in Transition. Moving between Media* (pp. 169–181). Routledge.

Brandstetter, G. (2020). Topographien des Flüchtigen. Bewegung und Objekthaftigkeit im Tanz. In P. M. Meyer (Ed.), *Ephemer*. Wilhelm Fink.

Derrida, J. (1997). *Dem Archiv verschrieben. Eine Freudsche Impression* (H. Gondek & H. Naumann, Trans.). Brinkmann u. Bose.

Fischer-Lichte, E. (2008). *The Transformative Power of Performance. A New Aesthetics*. Routledge.

Fuller, R. M. (1938). *Nine Chains to the Moon*. J.B. Lippincott Company.

Goethe, J. W. von. (1998). *Sämtliche Werke. Briefe, Tagebücher und Gespräche. Gedichte 1756–1799*, I(1) (K. Eibl, Ed.). Suhrkamp.

Goldberg, R. (2001). 18 Happenings in 6 Parts / More New York Happenings / Yam and You / The Element of Place. In R. Goldberg (Ed.), *Performance Art. From Futurism to the Present* (pp. 128–138). Thames & Hudson.

Grosz, E. (1994). *Volatile Bodies. Toward a Corporeal Feminism*. Indiana University Press.

Groys, B. (1997). Die Restaurierung des Zerfalls. In *Logik der Sammlung. Am Ende des musealen Zeitalters* (pp. 197–204). Hanser.

Hofmannsthal, H. (1984). Über Vergänglichkeit. In E. Weber (Ed.), *Sämtliche Werke. Kritische Ausgabe*, 1(45). De Gruyter.

Hofmannsthal, H. (1986). Der Rosenkavalier. In D. Hoffmann & W. Schuh (Eds.), *Sämtliche Werke. Kritische Ausgabe, 23: Operndichtungen* (Vol. 1). Fischer.

Jullien, F. (2004). *Über die ›Zeit‹. Elemente einer Philosophie des Lebens*. Diaphenes.

Krausse, J. (1990). Art. *Ephemer*. In K. Barck (Ed.), *Ästhetische Grundbegriffe* (Vol. 2, pp. 240–260). Springer.

Lyotard, J. (1996 [1985]). Les immatériaux. Marquard, Odo: Finalisierung und Mortalität. In K. Stierle & R. Warning (Eds.), *Das Ende. Figuren einer Denkform* (pp. 467–475). Fink.

Mersch, D. (2015). *Epistemologien des Ästhetischen*. Diaphenes.

Mroué, R. (2014). *Like Water between Two Palms of One's Hands*. https://www.kumquatperformingarts.com/danceon-water

Mroué, R. (2016). *Skript zu Water between Three Hands, zweite Produktion des Projekts Dance On/First Edition*. Kampnagel.

Richards, M. (2000). *The Encyclopedia of Ephemera: A Guide to the Fragmentary Documents of Everyday Life for the Collector, Curator, and Historian*. Routledge.

Rosa, H. (2013). *Beschleunigung und Entfremdung. Entwurf einer kritischen Theorie spätmoderner Zeitlichkeit*. Suhrkamp.

Schimmel, P. (1998). *Out of Actions. Zwischen Performance und Objekt. 1949–1979, Ausstellungskatalog*. Peter Noever.

Schnell, R., & Stanitzek, G. (2005). Ephemeres. Mediale Innovationen 1900/2000. In *Ephemeres. Mediale Innovationen* (pp. 7–12). Transcript.

Simmel, G. (1995 [1903]). Die Großstädte und das Geistesleben. In R. Kramme, A. Rammstedt, & O. Rammstedt (Eds.), *Gesamtausgabe, 7: Aufsätze und Ab-handlungen 1901–1908* (pp. 116–131). Suhrkamp.

Virilio, P. (1986 [1980]). *Ästhetik des Verschwindens* (M. Karbe & G. Roßler, Trans.). Springer.

Virilio, P. (1997 [1990]). *Rasender Stillstand* (B. Wilczek, Trans.). Fischer.

Vogl, J. (2005). Wolkenbotschaft. In L. Engell, B. Siegert, & J. Vogl (Eds.), *Wolken* (pp. 69–81). Archiv für Mediengeschichte.

Waldenfels, B. (2010). *Sinne und Künste im Wechselspiel. Modi ästhetischer Erfahrung*. Suhrkamp.

Materiality and Spatiality of Bodily Learning

Arnd-Michael Nohl and Morvarid Götz-Dehnavi

Bodily learning is, eo ipso, a matter of materiality and space. How can human beings learn anything relevant to their body without getting in touch with material things? And how can we understand 'getting in touch with material things' as a process without taking into account the space that is its very basis? Educational science, however, has only recently started to pay due attention to the significance of the material and spatial dimensions of learning. The 'material turn' that has overwhelmed social sciences in recent years, created new theoretical opportunities to grasp the materiality of learning (cf. Fenwick & Edwards, 2010). However, spatiality, as a highly complex theoretical problem, is still not included in a systematic way in educational thinking. While acknowledging that there exist various theoretical approaches that take into account the materiality *and* spatiality of bodily learning, this chapter proposes to view this subject from the angle of Pragmatism. The chapter will draw mainly on the thinking of John Dewey and George Herbert Mead, who were strongly influenced by Charles Sanders Peirce.

To answer the main question of this chapter, that is how can we conceive of the materiality and spatiality of bodily learning, we begin by challenging the anthropocentricity of conceiving human beings as subjects and material things as objects. As an alternative, we use Dewey and Bentley's 'trans-action' perspective to rethink learning as a process that inseparably involves both

A.-M. Nohl (✉) • M. Götz-Dehnavi
Helmut Schmidt University, Hamburg, Germany
e-mail: nohl@hsu-hh.de; dehnavi@hsu-hh.de

© The Author(s), under exclusive license to Springer Nature Switzerland AG 2022
A. Kraus, C. Wulf (eds.), *The Palgrave Handbook of Embodiment and Learning*,
https://doi.org/10.1007/978-3-030-93001-1_20

human beings and material things. Key concepts of Peirce's semiology will help us to understand the significance of the direct embodied nature of learning (Sect. 1).

Next, in line with Mead's thoughts on spatiality we elaborate further on learning via the body. According to Mead, spatiality is the result of transactional practices between human beings and physical things. Spatiality is thus constituted by the (temporal) opposition of things which we touch directly, and distant things, whose essence we anticipate—like the taking over of the perspective of the human other—as an impulse for action based on previous experiences of manipulation. A possible discrepancy between experiences of anticipation and experiences of contact then constitutes an opportunity for bodily learning (Sect. 2).

Based on this theoretical argumentation we then, in a third step, demonstrate its usefulness with an empirical example that we take from an inquiry into educational interaction in child care centres. As the materiality and spatiality of bodily learning is a genuinely multimodal process, videography of children's everyday practices would appear to be the most valid source of empirical data. After some notes on the interpretation of videography, we focus on the analysis of an intriguing scene: a group of children carry chairs through a narrow door and are advised by their teachers to hold the chairs so that they point in a specific direction (Sect. 3).

1 'Transaction' and the Materiality of Learning

Advocators of the material turn in social and educational sciences often refer to the influential works of Bruno Latour (1999) who, in *Pandora's Hope*, not only challenged the Cartesian dichotomy of the cognizant human subject and the recognized material object but elaborated on the intermingling of things and humans from which so-called hybrid actors (ibid., p. 180), such as a driver-and-a-car or a lecturer-and-a-beamer, emerge. Such an epistemological perspective, however, was already developed half a century earlier by John Dewey and his co-author, Arthur F. Bentley, with the concept of "transaction". Introducing their main point, Dewey and Bentley challenge the readers' habits of perceiving and thinking by giving a new account of the notion of 'hunter' and 'rabbit':

> If we watch a hunter with his gun go into a field where he sees a small animal already known to him by name as a rabbit, then, within the framework of half an hour and an acre of land, it is easy—and for immediate purposes satisfactory

enough—to report the shooting that follows in an interactional form in which rabbit and hunter and gun enter as separates and come together by way of cause and effect. If, however, we take enough of the earth and enough thousands of years, and watch the identification of rabbit gradually taking place, arising first in the sub-naming processes of gesture, cry, and attentive movement, wherein both rabbit and hunter participate, and continuing on various levels of description and naming, we shall soon see the transactional account as the one that best covers the ground. This will hold not only for the naming of hunter, but also for accounts of his history back into the pre-human and for his appliances and techniques. No one would be able successfully to speak of the hun*ter* and the hun*ted* as isolated with respect to hun*ting*. Yet it is just as absurd to set up hunt*ing* as an event in isolation from the spatio-temporal connection of all the components. (Dewey & Bentley, 1989, p. 125; italics in original)

Whereas from the epistemological perspective of "interaction" (ibid.) the hunter and the rabbit are conceived of as *given* entities, a focus on "transaction" (ibid, p. 101) means refraining from pre-defining any entities and epistemologically suspending the dichotomy between humans and nonhumans. This enables the inquirer to observe the "common system" (ibid., p. 114) of practices (e.g. of hunting) in which actions and operations emerge that eventually shape the entities involved. As Dewey and Bentley demonstrate with their example, this "common system" unfolds in space and time.

The notion of a "common system" reminds us of Latour's (1999, pp. 66 and 180) concept of the "network" of "actants" (as he calls the human and non-human agents). To "describe the strange situation" (such as hunting or experimenting) "in which an actor emerges out of its trials", Latour (1999, p. 308) proposed the term "name of action". In this situation, the human and non-human actants do not yet "have an essence" but are "defined only as a list of effects—or performances—" (Latour, 1999, p. 308). At this point, Latour explicitly refers to Pragmatist thinking. As he acknowledges, the "term 'name of action' allows one to remember the pragmatic original of all matters of fact" (ibid.).

Indeed, the founder of Pragmatism, Charles Sanders Peirce, proposed that our concepts are genuinely connected with practices and their effects:

Consider what effects, that might conceivably have practical bearings, we conceive the object of our conception to have. Then, our conception of these effects is the whole of our conception of the object.[1] (CP, 5.402)

---

[1] We cite Peirce's Collected Papers (Peirce, 1931–1935) by volume followed by paragraph number.

If we assume that the object of our conception is a "trans-action", a "common system" (Dewey and Bentley), or, in the words of Latour, a "network" of "actants", its naming combines both (human) constructions and real consequences. Peirce argues that the connection between a material object and its concept is based on the entire previous experience of humanity. These previous experiences, all the already-accomplished practical exchange processes between humans and the world, suggest specific qualities of material things or at least they suggest their possibility. Hence, we connect to a physical thing, for example a train, such that if we were to board it, "a certain kind of sensible result *would* ensue, according to our experiences hitherto" (CP, 5.457), for example that the train brings us to another city. Hence, when we relate to physical things (or other living creatures) we anticipate the probable outcomes by leaning on the past as the "storehouse of all our knowledge" (CP, 5.460). At the same time, this grasp of the material object is open to the future. The Pragmatist maxim includes the future in which new experience may emerge and may induce us to change our conception of the qualities of the material object.

These theoretical considerations have a great bearing on learning theory. Basing our approach on Dewey and Bentley's trans-action perspective and Peirce's Pragmatist maxim, the following questions regarding the theory of learning guide our inquiry: How do human beings become competent parts of a 'common system' of 'trans-actions'? How do their bodies relate to other human and non-human entities so that a proper 'hybrid actor' (Latour) emerges? A 'hybrid actor' is a composition through which human and nonhuman components interact, exchange properties, support each other, etc.—Furthermore, during such (bodily) learning processes, the following questions emerge: How do human beings learn what effects must be ascribed to the respective hybrid actor or its parts, which may have a practical implication? How do human beings connect these effects to the conception of the object?

As regards human learning,[2] we find important answers to these questions in Peirce's semiology, especially in his trichotomy in which he occasionally refers to learning. Peirce differentiates three categories of consciousness:

First, feeling, the consciousness which can be included with an instant of time, passive consciousness of quality, without recognition or analysis; second, consciousness of an interruption into the field of consciousness, sense of resistance, of an external fact, of another something; third, synthetic consciousness, binding time together, sense of learning, thought. (CP, 1.377)

---

[2] A more symmetrical approach to learning in trans-action would also have to consider non-human learning.

With this trichotomy we can capture several processes of bodily learning in which material things are related to human beings in various ways. We will use practical examples to explain this.

Although it is difficult to imagine a situation in which one has a pure 'feeling' in the sense of Peirce, a boy's first attempts at riding a bicycle might give an impression of what this 'feeling' is about. The moment in which the boy, released from his parents, who previously guided him, experiences the combination of horizontal balance and forward motion, a "passive consciousness of quality, without recognition or analysis" (CP, 1.377), comes into being. Peirce would conceive of such an experience (e.g. of the combination of horizontal balance and forward motion) as *Firstness*, that is "the idea of that which is such as it is regardless of anything else" (CP, 5.66). This "simple positive character" (CP, 5.44) refers to the possibly most immediate contact with things that lie ahead of any symbolically structured constructions. If the boy pushes down on the right pedal while simultaneously leaning his body to the left of the bike, he notices that these transactions with the bike maintain the simultaneity of balance and forward movement. This intersection of "action and reaction" (CP, 5.45)—the movements of the boy and the resistance of the bike—is a manifestation of *Secondness*: it is specific, existential and without any generalization. But if these movements are repeated, step by step a certain expectation arises (which, in this case, is tacit and embedded in practices). This practical expectation is what Peirce calls *Thirdness*. Thirdness concerns the practical and theoretical convictions of human beings. These may be verbally expressed in propositions but more often than not they exist as habits. As a proposition, we would express the conviction of the boy as "if one presses the pedal and leans his body to the other side, both balance and forward motion are secured". We suggest calling this first form of bodily learning '*Constituting Thirdness*'.

This Thirdness is soon differentiated. The boy, when pedalling, encounters things that offer resistance, such as when he simultaneously turns the handlebars too much in one direction. In this situation, after a short moment of Firstness, already overlapped and reshaped by the tacit expectation (in the sense of Thirdness) of being able to keep one's balance, Secondness follows. This time Secondness offers a modification of experience—a reaction to the initial action, which turns out to be different than expected. Thus, the unexpected arises—the combination of balance and forward motion is interrupted when the handlebars get jammed, followed by a crash. According to Peirce, in Secondness reality enforces itself on cognition. The trans-action of one's body and a bicycle, previously experienced as combining forward motion and balance, is fundamentally altered when one abruptly turns the handlebars. As

Peirce reminds his readers, "it is by surprises that experience teaches all she deigns to teach us" (CP, 5.51). In this moment of surprise, "the real is that which insists upon forcing its way to recognition as something *other* than the mind's creation" (CP, 1.325). Secondness, in this sense, is then pivotal for bodily learning because it is the moment in which bodily movements and cognition intersect. This Secondness, after being repeated, is again turned into a Thirdness: the initial expectation of the boy that he can push down on the pedals and thereby guarantee balance and forward motion is now differentiated in the sense that a sharp turn of the handlebars will immediately bring this down.

This second form of bodily learning with things may be called '*Extending Thirdness*'. The new expectation is directly connected to the previous expectation (that one can combine balance and forward motion by pushing down on the pedals and leaning to the opposite side) and differentiates the latter. In the end, both expectations are merged, and a synthesis evolves (cf. CP, 1.381). If we imagine how constituting and extending Thirdness goes on and on, practical expectations and convictions come into being during these learning processes, which spin the "thread of life" and provide it with "continuity" (CP, 1.337). In this sense, Peirce describes 'Thirdness' as a "synthetic consciousness" and a "sense of learning" (CP, 1.377).

Inasmuch as learning is concerned with appropriating propositions, that is a language-based statement with a claim to truth (e.g. learning the theory of bicycling), this refers to the *acquisition of explicit knowledge*. If the learning process involves the body and leads to appropriating habits of action (e.g. actually riding a bike), this refers to the *acquisition of capabilities*. As propositions always refer to other propositions (e.g. if one is not to turn the handlebars too far in one direction one may not know what 'too far' is), Peirce argues that the "real and living logical conclusion" is the "habit" (CP, 5.491).

Moreover, propositions usually imply a cognizing human being and a recognized other. In contrast, habits connect human beings to the regularities of the world. Habits are repertoires of actions which have been constituted in the "trans-action" (Dewey & Bentley, 1989, p. 125) between human beings and the world and which have finally been stabilized. These habits endow life with continuity and, as in the example of the hunter and the rabbit, constitute a connection of human beings and the world in time and space. Learning in general and bodily learning in particular means to grow into these habitualized trans-actions.[3]

---

[3] At this point, another rather complex mode of learning that one could describe as 'altering Thirdness' and that is often referred to as 'transformative learning' must be mentioned but cannot be elaborated on here (see Nohl, 2009).

2 Spatiality and Temporality: A Multimodal Process

Time and space play a major role in all those bodily learning processes in which people encounter the world. It is, therefore, necessary to complement the argumentation for a learning theory based on Dewey, Bentley and Peirce with a theory of space and time. Albeit not referring to learning, George Herbert Mead's thinking is ground-breaking in this regard.[4] In short, Mead argues that space is constituted by the temporal and ontological antagonism between contact and distance experience, whereby experience here, in the sense of Pragmatism, refers to the encounter of organism and world—not, or not only that is, to a level of consciousness anchored in the human subject. Starting with Mead's complex reflections on the constitution of things[5] we now elaborate on his ideas including learning-theoretical issues.

According to Mead, and to put it simply, at the beginning of ontogenesis the newborn still lives in a complete "trans-action" (to use Dewey and Bentley's term) with the elements of its environment, without being able to distinguish them from itself. Only in the processes of exchange with the closest reference persons, which Mead interpreted as gradually becoming significant interactions, does a person learn to distinguish him or herself from other people and to take over their perspective (cf. Mead, 1913). This ability to take over the perspective of others, developed during socialization, is then also the prerequisite for the baby not only to perceive a surface in things but also to attribute to them a resistant inner being. Mead assumes "that the organism in grasping and pushing things is identifying its own effort with the contact experience of the thing" (1932, pp. 120–121). Quite analogously to the significant interaction with human beings, he writes: "One arouses in himself an action which comes also from the inside of the thing" (ibid., p. 121).

Of course, this only works as far as a contact experience occurs at all, that is as far as a human being and a thing get in direct touch. In the distance experience, on the other hand, the resistant inner being can only be anticipated against the background of previous experiences, that is hypothetically. Mead explains this with the example of a book:

---

[4] Although first published in 1980, Hans Joas' (1997) work continues to provide the authoritative reconstruction of Mead's extensive but scattered published work. Sons (2017) is also helpful for understanding Mead's thoughts on spatiality.

[5] See Joas (1997, pp. 145–166) and Nohl (2011, pp. 141–160).

> If I see a distant book an indefinite number of manipulatory responses are aroused, such as grasping it in a number of ways, opening, tearing its leaves, pressing upon it, rubbing it, and a host of others. One, picking up the book, is prepotent and organizes the whole act. It therefore inhibits all others. (Mead, 1932, p. 127)

As far as previous experiences of contact and ways of using the object are available, the object triggers (in a similar way to an interaction partner) dominant as well as marginalized impulses for action. To use Peirce's terms, each of these impulses refers to a respective Thirdness as a way of relating to the book. The person will then approach the book and do what they want with it—according to the dominant impulse. Only now, in this contact experience following the distance experience, can the thing be grasped as such, whereas before it was a hypothetical anticipation. According to Joas' interpretation of Mead, a "permanent space ... is constituted through relating all distance experiences to contact experience" (Joas, 1997, p. 150).

However, the contrast between distance and contact experience is not only space-constituting but also temporal. A person can make a contact experience, that is a trans-action based on direct contact, only with a finite number of things at any given time. In contrast, this person perceives the majority of things and people from a distance. Because of this distance, the person can only reach these distant things with a time delay. In this person's view there is indeed a simultaneity of all visual perceptions, but only with those things with which he is directly connected (such as the chair on which he sits, the floor on which he stands) does a co-presence take place (cf. Joas, 1997, p. 193).

Distance experiences, on the other hand, draw on past contact experiences and refer to contacts that are still in the future. "One can remain unaware of this [expectational character; the authors] as long as the interplay of expectations and the subsequent perceptions function smoothly, with no problems" (Joas, 1997, p. 193). For example, one enters a classroom, sees a chair opposite the door, perceives it as a seating device and approaches it to sit down. Where the anticipation of distance perception corresponds to the subsequent contact experience, where the distant things, as soon as they have moved closer, can be used in the same way as anticipated (for example, if one can sit down on the chair), the temporal character of this experience is overshadowed. But if this does not work, that is if the distance things are falsely anticipated (if, for example, the chair was only a dummy chair), it becomes apparent that these things are "in an immediate sense both spatially and temporally distant" (Joas, 1997, p. 189; emphasis in original). Moreover, as Sons (2017) shows, one must imagine this contrast between contact and distance experience against the background of a whole ensemble of things (and people) that can be included in the practices, but also can be 'left out', for example when a person walks through a room—past chairs, table and cupboard—to the window to open it. In such "temporal-spatial chains of actions" all participants then get into a "spatial sequence relationship" (ibid., p. 249).

Where space is constituted based on stabilized and habituated human-thing connections the way we anticipate distant things and the way we treat them are largely identical. Here, one could say, a continuous presence is reproduced in the habituated space; the human being lives in what Mead calls the "undifferentiated now" (1967, p. 351). If we transfer these thoughts to the trichotomy of Peirce (see Sect. 1), we could speak of a spatio-temporal Thirdness based on habits. But at the moment when the way we anticipate the distant thing and the way we eventually react with it fall apart, that is when space is no longer habituated, something new appears, an event that makes a difference in the connections between people and things. At this moment, a more or less new space emerges. Then a new spatio-temporal Thirdness needs to be acquired or an old one to be extended. The spatial learning process that is prompted by the emergent space may involve cognitive perception (the acquisition of new knowledge), but it is certainly based on a new practical relation of the body and the world in which, eventually, new habits are constituted.

Where the practical anticipations of distance experiences do not correspond to the subsequent contact experiences, where the distant things, as soon as they have moved closer, cannot be manipulated in the same way as anticipated, previous habits are going nowhere. Then the body has to learn new ways of dealing with the things that were previously distant. Spontaneous impulses, as well as reflective thinking, may inspire new modes of manipulation (cf. Nohl, 2009). Trial and error, mimesis (Gebauer & Wulf, 1995), and, as we will see in the next section, teaching and education help to tune into the right way of handling things. As soon as a new way of manipulating things has emerged and has been turned into a routine, a new habit, in the sense of Thirdness, will then guide the practical expectations with which the human being approaches such distant things. Bodily learning, therefore, in a way that is complementary to a new consciousness of spatiality (and temporality) caused by cognitive learning, leads to practical expectations towards the objects (be they human or non-human) in time and space. It is by bodily learning that the body is readjusted in space and time.

We have introduced this distinction between the space we are used to and newly emerging space here with analytical intent. Space and time, however, are not constituted in this stringent absoluteness; rather, one must assume that our anticipation of the distant things always correspond more or less to what we do with them when we reach them (cf. Joas, 1997, p. 193). Also, because space is usually formed by a multitude of relations between humans and things (cf. Sons, 2017, p. 249), the habituated space and the newly emerging space are always in a mixed relationship, to be empirically identified in each case. For this reason, the habituation of space and the need for (bodily) learning are always present.

Similar to Dewey and Bentley's 'trans-action' perspective as well as Peirce's Pragmatist maxim, Mead's considerations do not refer to a solipsistic individual, but to social practice. The fact that we live at the same time and in the same space is connected with "the construction of the world not from every individual perspective separately, but rather in a common praxis as a common world" (Joas, 1997, p. 181). As far as the constitution of space is concerned, Joas also points out that Mead did not understand sociality solely as an interaction between people, but proceeded from a "general sociality also in the domain of the relationships of such physical objects among themselves" (Joas, 1997, p. 185).

Although human beings are by and large socialized collectively in time and space and although the world is a shared one, as Joas says, there are issues for which socialization, as the natural process of growing into the collectively shared time and space, does not suffice. In the next section, we will inquire into how small children learn to adjust their bodies to each other and to physical things and are also guided by their caregivers to do so.

3   A Bodily Learning Task: Manoeuvring Chairs Through a Door

The materiality and spatiality of bodily learning are not only complex theoretical issues but also present a challenge to empirical research. A close account of bodily practices in space and time needs to be combined with a longitudinal perspective on changes in the capabilities and knowledge of the learners. Far from meeting these requirements (especially that of a longitudinal inquiry), in this section, we only wish to give a brief insight into the intricacies of bodily learning. We will inquire into how teachers educate infants to collectively manoeuvre chairs through a door. Before we turn to our empirical analysis of bodily learning, we briefly mention the empirical methods used.

3.1 Multimodality and Videography Research

To empirically investigate the bodily learning of infants and their interaction with teachers in a child care centre, we follow up on the approach proposed by Asbrand and Martens (2018) for video-based classroom analysis. Such videography enables a "multimodal interaction analysis" (Asbrand & Martens, 2018, p. 109) that does not only consider the verbal components of the interaction but also the bodily movements and material things involved.

In 2019 a student assistant spent two mornings in a child care centre located in a village in Saxony, Germany, videotaping the interaction in a group of about 15 children, aged 3–5 years, and their teachers almost continuously. Using a thematic log, we then identified sequences (of approximately one and a half minute) that seemed particularly useful to interpret due to what the children were doing (eating, playing, etc.), their interactive density and theoretical considerations. Our main research goal was to empirically analyse how educating and teaching were accomplished and how they intermingled. The verbal interactions of the selected sequences were subsequently transcribed.[6]

For the interpretation of videographies with the Documentary Method (see Bohnsack, 2020), Asbrand and Martens (2018) proposed taking into account the sequentiality of the videographed interactions. In a 'formulating interpretation' the non-verbal events (bodily movements and material things), separated from the (previously transcribed) verbal interaction, are put into words in such detail that the sequence and the mutual relationship of the individual movements become evident even below complete (institutionalized) actions. In the 'reflective interpretation', it is then a matter of analysing how the participants manipulate things and interact verbally and non-verbally with one another (cf. Asbrand & Martens, 2018, p. 121; see also Nohl et al., 2021).

3.2 The Empirical Example: Bodily Learning in the Child Care Centre

The video recording starts when the children have already lifted the chairs and are about to walk towards the door. It remains unclear what they have done before and whether the teachers have asked them to carry the chairs (which is very likely).

---

[6] In addition to the child care centre in the Saxonian village, we have also videographed five mornings in a child care centre in Hamburg. This project was financed by the Helmut Schmidt University. Members of the project group were Susann Schmidt, Steffen Amling and the authors.

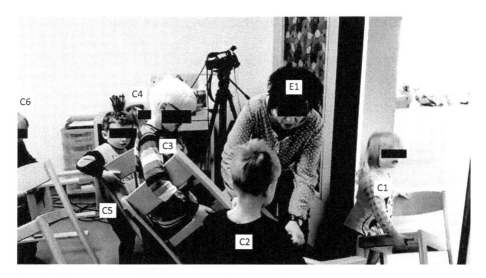

Fig. 1 Photogram at 00:01 (copyright: the authors)

The following photogram (Fig. 1) gives an idea of the complexity of the tasks the children are confronted with: They have to lift and carry their chairs, they have to manoeuvre their chairs through the door to the second room and, last but not least, while doing so, they have to coordinate with the other children. Whereas the first task brings to the fore the materiality of learning, the latter tasks are concerned with spatiality, too. All three tasks, however, involve bodily learning, either already accomplished previously or to be performed in this very situation.[7]

In the first five seconds, the following interactions take place:

> Child C1, who at the beginning of the shot passes through the door frame and has her gaze directed forward towards the second room, holds her chair by the backrest and the seat while the chair's legs are pointing down. The wooden chair, like all other chairs carried by children, consists of a square seat with an approximately 5 cm rim, to the front of which two round chair legs are attached. At the back, the chair legs continue about 30 cm above the seat. The right and left struts are connected by a backrest which is conically bent backward and slightly conical at the top and bottom and is about 10 cm wide. When teacher E1 asks C2 to hold his chair differently, C1 turns her head to E1, looks at the hands of C2, turns back again, continues walking and steps out of view of the camera.

---

[7] Admittedly, the following analysis is subject to an 'interactive' perspective in the sense of Dewey and Bentley (1989). A 'transactional' perspective should not be based on given "children" and "chairs," but should, in particular, put our knowledge of these fixed concepts in the background and describe objects and people in detail (see Nohl, 2018).

At the same time, C2 holds his chair with its legs pointing upwards at about 80°. E1, while talking to C2 (saying: "not forward like that if you bump you (…) put it right in your stomach"), bends forward and grabs the foot of C2's chair with her left hand, with her right hand she touches C3's chair briefly and then pulls the back of C2's chair towards her with her right hand, so that the chair is turned and its feet point downwards at about 45°. C2 holds his chair firmly and lifts it a little further. As he now continues towards the door, E1 briefly touches his left upper arm.

C3 stands in the funnel-shaped queue before C2 and observes how E1 corrects C2. To this he adds, echoing E1, "not forward". C3 holds his chair to the backrest and seat so that the chair legs are directed downwards, and he looks down too. E1 reaches briefly for C3's chair with her left hand, while C3 continues walking towards the door and finally enters the second room.

Behind and slightly to the left of C3, C5 follows him slowly, holding his chair by the backrest and its seat, while its legs are pointing down. Whereas C6, who just enters into view of the camera and holds his chair similarly, is positioned behind and slightly to the left of C5, C4 stands just to the left of C5 so that she is almost out of view of the camera.

The very fact that the teacher stands at the doorway and observes the children, intervening in their handling of the chairs every once in a while, shows that she perceives them as persons who still need to learn. However, these five seconds of video recording reveal that the majority of these children have already acquired two important 'Thirdnesses' that help them to accomplish their tasks:

First of all, without any guidance from their teacher, the children have positioned themselves in a funnel-shaped queue that allows them to walk collectively through the bottleneck of the door. Each child moves forward by following the preceding child, walking slightly to its left or right and slowly but surely heading for the middle of the door (zipper principle). This is not, or not only, an individual capability but reveals a collective appropriation of the space in which the movements of most children are adjusted to each other. The main point of this adjustment is to correctly anticipate the moving distant objects (the other children and their chairs) while one is moving in the space oneself and to keep the right distance to them. That this habituation of a spatio-temporal Thirdness is not a matter of course can be seen both in the warning of the teacher ("if you bump") and in the fact that C4 falls out of this collective appropriation of space. Later it will take E1 some effort to get C4 to carry her chair through the door. The other children, however, have apparently performed this bodily learning task before. Whereas C4 is confronted with an emergent space, for the other children this space is already habituated.

Secondly, all children have already learned to carry a chair, that is, they have established a 'Thirdness' that relates their body to this piece of furniture. While they are not faced with any practical obstacles that would make them learn to hold the chair differently (as they do not bump into each other), further bodily learning here is initiated by the teacher's warning to point the legs of the chair downwards. The verbal warning is, however, not sufficient: the teacher changes the direction of C2's chair in the space, touches C3's chair and, later, also realigns C6's chair. Apparently, the teacher does not trust that her verbal warning is enough and, therefore, resorts to these bodily interventions. By doing so, she instigates bodily learning on the part of the children who begin to extend their previous Thirdness (their previous way of carrying a chair).

4   Outlook

If we wish to understand bodily learning, we must take account of its material and spatial dimensions. As this chapter argued, Pragmatism, and especially the works of Peirce, Mead, Dewey and Bentley, offers congenial basic theoretical concepts that help us to grasp the phenomena with which we are presented. Videography, then, is a suitable method of producing data on the multimodality of bodily learning.

The videography-based research on educational interaction in the child care centre may have given an idea of the usefulness of the theoretical perspective outlined in this chapter. However, more research is needed. There is a broad range of subject matter that is awaiting further research, for example the habituation and emergence of space during the transition to primary school, the material and spatial dimensions of digital learning, the interrelatedness of spatiality and temporality in adult learning, or issues of bodily learning in adventure education. Such empirical analyses will not only shed light on aspects of the educational field that are as yet unknown. They will also help us to further develop the basic theoretical concepts with which we try to understand the intricacies of bodily learning and its material as well as spatial dimensions.

References

Asbrand, B., & Martens, M. (2018). *Dokumentarische Unterrichtsforschung*. Springer.

Bohnsack, R. (2020). Iconology and Documentary Method in the Interpretation of Divergent Types of Visual Materials. In L. Pauwels & D. Mannay (Eds.), *The Sage Handbook of Visual Methods* (pp. 397–412). Sage.

Dewey, J., & Bentley, A. F. (1989). Knowing and the Known. In J. A. Boydston (Ed.), *J. Dewey—The Later Works, 1925–1953, 16: 1949–1952* (pp. 1–294). SUP.

Fenwick, T., & Edwards, R. (2010). *Actor-Network Theory in Education*. Routledge.

Gebauer, G., & Wulf, C. (1995). *Mimesis. Culture, Art, Society*. University of California Press.

Joas, H. (1997). *G. H. Mead: A Contemporary Re-examination of His Thought*. MIT Press and Polity Press.

Latour, B. (1999). *Pandora's Hope*. Harvard University Press.

Mead, G. H. (1913). The Social Self. *Journal of Philosophy, Psychology and Scientific Methods, 10*, 374–380.

Mead, G. H. (1932). "The Physical Thing" Supplementary Essay 2. In A. E. Murphy (Ed.), *The Philosophy of the Present* (pp. 119–139). Open Court.

Mead, G. H. (1967). The Biological Individual. In *Mind, Self, and Society* (pp. 347–353). CUP.

Nohl, A.-M. (2009). Spontaneous Action and Transformative Learning. *Educational Philosophy and Theory, 41*(3), 287–306.

Nohl, A.-M. (2011). *Pädagogik der Dinge*. Klinkhardt.

Nohl, A.-M. (2018). Die empirische Rekonstruktion materieller Artefakte mit der Dokumentarischen Methode. In A. Tervooren & R. Kreitz (Eds.), *Dinge und Raum in der qualitativen Bildungs- und Biographieforschung* (pp. 37–53). Budrich.

Nohl, A.-M., Dehnavi, M., & Amling, S. (2021). VInteraktionsmodi und pädagogische Prozesse: Zur videographiebasierten dokumentarischen Interpretation von Interaktionen in Kindertagesstätten. In A. Geimer, D. Klinge, S. Rundel & S. Thomsen (Hrsg.), *Jahrbuch Dokumentarische Methode, 4*, (pp. 77–101). centrum für qualitative evaluations- und sozialforschung e.V.

Peirce, C. S. (1931–1935). *Collected Papers of Charles Sanders Peirce, Volumes 1–6* (C. Hartshorne & P. Weiss, Eds.). Harvard University Press.

Sons, E. (2017). *Interaktivität und Dinge in der kulturellen Bildung*. Springer.

Body-Related Learning Processes in Museums

Bernd Wagner

Educational science research indicates that children from preschool to primary school age create meanings in terms of their personal relationships and interactions in their physical surroundings that they often express through bodily postures. This can be observed in museum visits that are the subject of video-ethnographic research (Amann & Hirschauer, 1997; Wagner, 2013). Young children initiate subjective practices and relationships both within their peer groups and with collection objects.[1] For those creative activities that are connected to forms, senses and emotions, objects with concrete and tangible properties are needed so that preschool and primary school children can create meaning through artistic expression and play (Isenberg & Jalongo, 2000). Developing an exploratory relationship with objects in a museum exhibition can be described as a form of learning process. Early social science education in Germany, founded on the discipline and teaching methods of *Sachunterricht*, is processual and based on the way preschool and primary school children interact with different materials (Pech, 2009; Pech & Rauterberg, 2007, p. 3). Within these learning processes, educational strategies that focus on the discursive dimensions of learning with objects in school,

---

[1] "Up to primary school age children live in a world of relationships and develop theories to understand their place in the world, some are more useful than others. The discussion of these theories and paying attention to their function is tangible early childhood learning" (Scholz, 2010, p. 39).

B. Wagner (✉)
University of Leipzig, Leipzig, Germany
e-mail: bernd.wagner@uni-leipzig.de

© The Author(s), under exclusive license to Springer Nature Switzerland AG 2022
A. Kraus, C. Wulf (eds.), *The Palgrave Handbook of Embodiment and Learning*,
https://doi.org/10.1007/978-3-030-93001-1_21

especially in the primary school subject (*Sachunterricht*), are highlighted (Pech & Rauterberg, 2008). The approach sees the interests and questions of children as a starting point of learning and relates this to the childhood educational science known in German as *Kindheitsforschung* (Heinzel, 2010)[2]. The approach places less emphasis on particular skills and formal knowledge, and instead stresses the need to facilitate the individual child's processes of figuring out and interacting with objects.

First, the following chapter describes the research field: children and their physical access to objects in collections (Sect. 1). Then learning processes of preschool and primary school children in museums, with reference to anthropological studies and the concept of contact zones, are described (Sect. 2). As an example, research in performative play stations for preschool children in the permanent exhibition *German History in Images and Artefacts* of the German Historical Museum (DHM) in Berlin is presented (Sect. 3). Finally, results from the research project are shown in the context of body-related learning processes of preschool and primary school children (Sect. 4).

1 The Research Field: Children and Their Physical Access to Collection Objects

A short overview of educational research based on publications in the field with an emphasis on preschool and primary school children in museums is given in this section. First, we look at the discourse in English-language publications. This discourse is dominated by many authors who criticize learning theories for their strict cognitive focus, thereby neglecting learning approaches with the body. Richard Jordi (2011), for example, describes body and mind interactions in his article 'Reframing the Concept of Reflection: Consciousness, Experiential Learning, and Reflective Learning Practices'. This is based on a theoretical approach. From Jordi's point of view, these interactions can lead to more holistic learning experiences. He postulates that the use of all human senses enriches the learning experience, and that inclusive learning environments benefit from physical activity and the spirit of discovery. Joanne Yoo and Sarah Loch (2016), in 'Learning Bodies: What Do Teachers Learn from Embodied Practice?', reflect on the *Sky High* program for teachers, which was designed to raise the awareness of body language and to show ways of

---

[2] "That's why education processes are perceived as subjective genesis processes only when answers to questions are given that the subject, from a need to find things out and to understand the world, has discovered for him or herself" (Schäfer, 1999, p. 119).

increasing the learning motivation of socioeconomically disadvantaged students. In their ethnographic research, Yoo and Loch find that a visit to a museum can be a motivating experience with experiential learning approaches. These experiences can help to diminish prejudices, for example that museums are only accessible for intellectuals. Because of long distances or small budgets in some rural areas, museum visits are almost impossible. An alternative is to offer a museum experience in school, for example by ordering selected collection items in what is called a museum carrying case, or by collecting objects which provide a special learning experience. In 'Beyond the Walls with Object-Based Learning', Cassandra Barnett (2019) outlines how collections and exhibits can be moved around in order to offer a museum experience to remote schools. This requires professional networks and training for teachers to enable them to discuss the provenances and properties of objects with a school class and create mind-opening experiences. Studies of learning materials and environments show that interventions are open to historical, artistic as well as physical and chemical elements. Steven Murow and Arnold Chavez (2017), in 'Exploring Matter: An Interactive, Inexpensive Chemistry Exhibit for Museums', reflect on field reports about a modest college exhibition. Through interactive activities and learning through examples, students are challenged and can become enthusiastic about chemistry: an area in which large museums often fail.

Body-related learning processes integrating experiences and the senses are not limited to analog learning arrangements; digitalization and digital culture require new competences and perspectives too. In 'The Interactive Museum: Video Games as History Lessons Through Lore and Affective Design', Sky Anderson (2019) deals with the controversial topic of integrating computer games into educational contexts. Even though most computer games have a commercial background, their interactive potential and the emotional involvement of the players can be used in pedagogical contexts. The author analyzes contents of computer games and compares players' experiences to analog learning methods. He finds that some give the impression of being an interactive museum. Also, combinations of digital and analog elements are thought to expand educational value and learning. Maria Dardanou (2019) focuses ethnographically on that point in 'From Foot to Pencil, from Pencil to Finger: Children as Digital Wayfarers' by describing how children can intensify the museum experience with digital devices during and after their visit. Like an interactive computer game, they can use their photos, videos and notes/drawings to develop a story with their tablet that involves them emotionally and leads to connections between the different things they are learning. It is not only that the children experience the museum through interacting with their bodies, but the fact that they document it via digital devices and develop stories which can be experienced even after the museum visit.

Different kinds of involvement and perspectives during learning processes are the subject of Amy Chou and Janet Shih's article 'Show Me What You See: An Exploration of Learning in Museums and Learning in Theatre' (Chou & Shih, 2010). The authors' qualitative research, based on semi-structured questionnaires, focuses on individual learning strategies. The authors argue that performance techniques and storytelling in museums and theaters are suitable in contexts of individual learning strategies. They find that, through narrative approaches and personal involvement, the impact of museum visits is intensified. Ran Peleg and Ayelet Baram-Tsabari (2017) discuss in their qualitative- and quantitative-based research (391 questionnaires and 67 interviews) the performances that are put on in museums to create a learning environment. Personal involvement in a story can help and hinder learning at the same time. On the one hand, clear and explicit information is absorbed easily through the personal link with the audience; on the other hand, some information or aesthetic elements are interpreted by audience members, opening up the possibility of facts being misinterpreted. That is why a play put on in a museum must be directed in a way that is more than just entertainment; it must provide educational value too. Nevertheless, playing and performance are thought to be central elements in museum education. Pamela Krakowski (2012) observes in 'Museum Superheroes: The Role of Play in Young Children's Lives' how children who are still in kindergarten can benefit from a visit to an art museum when they experience the exhibition by playing. In particular, connecting children's personal environment and interests, for example superheroes, to a museum's topic will motivate the children and the experience may enrich their knowledge.

Another way for children in kindergarten or preschool to connect with museum educational offers is through role-play, in which the children create their own exhibition and guide the visitors. Alice Hope's case studies in 'Young Children as Curators' (Hope, 2018) raise the idea that, in contrast to a passive reception, children give meanings to objects or displays when they create their own scenarios. When they have experienced that perspective, children are better prepared to visit a museum and understand other concepts. Because the possibilities in one's own exhibition are almost endless, children can use their imagination and give objects fantastic meanings, what stimulates them to play with all the senses. In contrast to Cassandra Barnett's (2019) approach, not just the collection objects are introduced in school, but rather the idea of creating museum scenarios and presenting collections. Recently, reactions to nationalism and learning experiences that relate to a complicated globalized world have become more important. Museums with a multicultural orientation can provide learning environments that support transcultural awareness. In her article 'Black Museums and Experiential Learning', Cheylon Woods (2018) describes the history of exclusion in museums. She argues that more space should be given to the initiatives of Black communities and other minority groups to enable them to show their culture in appropriate ways. According to the author, this approach ontributes to the idea of a *democratic museum.*

In Germany there is not a great deal of research on museum education for children. Early childhood education studies in Germany address children's negotiation processes with objects. They show that testing out and exploring objects, even if they irritate children or result in failure, is vitally important for the acquisition of knowledge and problem-solving skills (Nentwig-Gesemann, Fröhlich-Gildhoff & Pietsch, 2011a). This can also be seen in the context of personal experiences, in which mimetic self-formation processes are created (Gebauer & Wulf, 1992; Schäfer, 2011; Nentwig-Gesemann, Fröhlich-Gildhoff, & Pietsch, 2011a). Mimetic activity is defined as the ability to use one's senses to creatively and physically imitate cultural expressions. Subjective perceptions are stored as internal images and then reproduced physically. This process is not just simple imitation but involves imaginative expression and interpretation. Mimetic processes are a necessary part of the informal conditions that foster development and learning. They characterize an environment in which children are dynamically involved in their surroundings and can familiarize themselves with collection objects.

The Swedish model of integrating preschool and primary school shows that it is not beneficial that professionals in social science teaching methods (Sachunterrichtsdidaktik) bring concepts from primary school into early years learning. Instead, issues of early years learning should also be considered as the task of primary schools; comprehensive coordination is needed between preschools and primary schools (Scholz, 2010, p. 34). However, transitions between kindergarten and primary school are non-linear and thus require coping strategies and transitional phases. Exactly how such transitional phases can succeed and how procedural knowledge about them can be expanded may have important implications for future research. Further studies of the experience horizons of preschool children dealing with collections can be applied to this field of research (Duncker & Kremling, 2010). Educational Science conceptions of early years education, such as the importance of mimetic learning, offer insights into concepts and methods of learning in the social sciences. In particular, early years education can be considered as the focal point of social sciences teaching methods. Tangible learning opportunities can mediate children valuable impressions of history, social change, different actors and stakeholders. These impressions are based on relevant objects—for example a piece of the Berlin Wall as a source of contemporary history—that can be incorporated into social science teaching. A focus in social sciences teaching is the participative role of the child actively developing and presenting ideas—more detail will be given in the empirical material of the following chapter. For preschool and kindergarten children, historical changes can be explained less by conceptual arguments than by physical respectively hands-on processes in which emotional connections are created (Wulf et al., 2001). In the following chapter, early childhood educational practices such as the development of experience horizons are shown in the context of the *German History in Images and Artefacts* exhibition. Connections are drawn between the scientific discipline of early childhood education and the methods used in social science teaching.

2 Contact Zones with Collection Objects

The learning processes of preschool and primary school children are tied to personal interpretations of situations as well as affective creations. Possible meanings are tested out through subjective experiences and performative self-portraits (Wagner, 2013; Stauber, 2004, 2006).[3] The performativity of this process is seen in spontaneous interactions with museum objects.[4] For example Marie Louise Pratt (1996) develops the idea that contact zones in a museum establish a distance from everyday interpretations of things and encourage situations of negotiation and testing. This idea calls for interactive spaces in museums to add experiential dimensions to exhibits. Pratt points out that a contact zone provides visitors with insights into unknown or past worlds; as such a zone 'is an attempt to invoke the spatial and temporal copresence of subjects previously separated by geographic and historical disjunctures, and whose trajectories now intersect' (Pratt, 1992, p. 7).

Reflections on the performative nature of contact zones in museums expand and fundamentally challenge our approaches to teaching in primary schools;

---

[3] Stauber (2004) emphasizes the interactive body-related aspect of self-dramatization in peer groups. She sees the importance of the production of action communities, embodying meanings and opening up spaces. In addition, Stauber addresses presentation of the self, forms of recognition and membership of groups.

[4] "If human action is perceived as cultural acting and cultural performance, changes in understanding of social and educational processes arise. In this case the physicality of the actors, the event and directorial character of the actors deserve greater attention" (Wulf et al., 2001 p. 9).

they also challenge current educational concepts for non-formal education, which revolve around models of concentric circles, original movements and conceptual change. Pratt favors a performative concept of learning in museums as part of an interactive process that can lead to students' broader understanding of content. Performative forms of learning as directorial, active social practices can be understood within Judith Butler's (1990) framework—for example in negotiating the meaning of museum objects. These practices help describe the activity of children where they express themselves through body-related mimetic actions. Contact zones, as described by Pratt, are designed as a kind of performance-like museum visit for primary school children. Contact zones in a museum should have flexible arrangements of objects to allow groups of children to move and act with them. This gives children room to playfully approach objects in the exhibition whose materiality arouses curiosity (Nohl, 2011). Performative games support viewers in negotiating asymmetric meanings, which Pratt considers as constitutive for contact zones[5]. Spontaneous moments of play in the museum can be analysed from a pedagogical perspective and can be made fruitful for educational purposes, such as creating a multi-perspective understanding of objects.

For several years there have been efforts to welcome children more in museums and exhibitions. This includes providing educational materials for learning purposes. Several prominent Berlin museums, such as the Ethnological Museum of the Prussian Cultural Heritage Foundation, have a children's museum with activities tailored to primary school classes. There are hands-on play and experimentation stations. But many of our museums' educational activities for children are only installed for short-term projects and do not have sufficient space. In the next section we will look at research with a long-term learning environment, linked to a permanent collection in the German Historic Museum and based on the anthropological concept of contact zones. The learning environment with several stations allows small, accompanied groups of children to explore objects for themselves, as accompanying researchers observe the way children learn as they are confronted with these objects. The resulting stations are tailored to explorative learning and offer thus predominantly sensory experiences. When children try things out and negotiate at the stations, even when they get annoyed or fail, these are considered to be vital stages in the acquisition of procedural knowledge and problem-solving skills.

---

[5] A previous research project developed contact zones for groups of children in the exhibition *American Indians* in the Ethnological Museum in Berlin. The study focused on pupils' intercultural dialogues at the museum and in its storage rooms (Wagner, 2010).

3 Example: Contact Zones in the Permanent Exhibition *German History in Images and Artefacts* at the German Historical Museum (DHM)

The empirical examples presented here show that stimulating objects encourage physical and sensual exploration among preschool children (Koester, 2006). Generally, children first observe the tangibility of an object in an exploratory phase followed by conceptual contemplation. Accompanying adults often offer conceptual classifications and contexts too early and disrupt children while they are testing out objects. The route through the exhibition has interactive stations which are intended to be places where children can have both an aesthetic and a hands-on experience. Questions as to how children learn can be answered here. The preschool children participating, for whom this is often their first visit at the DHM, have contributed to formulating these educational principles. Some parts of the exhibition, intended for adults, have been adjusted or altered for children's sections. For example a large painting from the turn of the nineteenth and twentieth centuries from the DHM that was considered important in the design of the exhibition was hardly noticed by the visiting children. However a car prototype, not originally intended to be included, has been met with broad interest. The stations are designed as contact zones where the objects' materiality lends itself to historical learning.

The contact zones promote discovery and learning by drawing attention to selected objects from the collection and by opening up certain niche showrooms for small groups. In the resulting spatial contact zones, the children can intensively examine the exhibition objects and then relate them to things from their everyday lives (Treptow, 2005). The visiting preschoolers compare what they experience here with things they know from everyday contexts, as observed in the discussions about the lyre, the car prototype and a model of Berlin tenements. The empirical material shows that exhibits that encourage comparing to and contrasting with life-worlds by means of familiar objects are of particular interest. For example the station that focuses on children's fashion in 1900 based on two sailor suits stimulates a playful exchange. Children can try on the clothes and compare themselves with a large mural and the items in the showcases. Preschoolers produce play structures with reference to their living environment and find historical traces in the present. Change and continuity is experienced in relation to historical objects, helping children to mediate themselves the contexts and usage patterns of things they see.

4 Prospects for Body-Based Processes of Learning About Objects in Museums

Striking about the video-ethnographic material is that the extra-curricular learning center of the museum could be a valuable space for the informal education of five-year-old children, in contrast to processes that often are preoccupied by instruction and interactions that are part of the school as an institution. Throughout the film material, there are scenes that can be identified as group formations related to the home or to childcare facilities. It seems that productive learning situations cannot be produced by explanatory remarks or the question-answer games that are often played in schools but through non-formal group interactions in the five-year-olds' physical surroundings. This type of learning is not necessarily led by the guides in the museum, though this obviously depends on the group's learning stage. The visiting children are expecting to learn about the things on display. This reflects what they are used to when they engage in educational activities. Preparatory work with children groups can provide suggestions how object-oriented disputes about meaning are reconciled. In addition to the school-related learning processes described, there are other developments to be seen in the following encodings.

4.1 Open Coding: Physically Testing Out and Selecting Unfamiliar Objects According to Their Use

Passing through the route of contact zones, the groups of children repeat ways of dealing with objects in the collection. The footage shows that in the negotiation processes, children show that they can work and act independently and demonstrate subjective learning strategies (in German: *Selbsttätigkeit*: Klafki, 1998) inspired by the objects in the exhibition. Particularly impressive in this regard are the sequences at the *Hunting* station (Picture 2). Museum staff offers children stick figures of humans and animals (some of which can be seen in historical paintings in the collection room) before they reenact hunting stories. The stick figures are used for historical and present-day hunting scenes. In these sequences, all seven groups displayed the same forms of interaction: the children listen attentively to the museum guides, move together in a tight circle in order to participate in the activity, view the material and await the stick puppets. While the museum guides point out representations in the subject area and describe the various roles of the figures, the children grow increasingly restless. The children of the sample groups appear to be particularly interested in animal figures. Many children become active immediately and test out the didactic material. They want a closer look at the stick puppets straight away and express wishes about the roles they would like to perform in the play. The museum guides respond to these pleas and start the game phase. In that performative acting phase the comparison of multiple groups of children shows some differences at this point. There are nonetheless the following similarities: the children involved listen to the introduction by the museum educator and there are few signs of spontaneity or the wish to develop new forms. As preschool children, they demand that play material is provided at an early point. The aim of the station, a comparison of historical and contemporary hunting forms, is not a priority and does not capture the attention of the children.

Other footage shows that unusual objects in games (e.g. the stick puppets) trigger bodily impulses and the need to conduct body-based experiments in children's groups. In practice, particular objects that point to possible ways they might be used, but still seem strange and elude categorization, attract children and lead to physical interactions (Serrell, 1996; Norman, 1999). These objects are not totally extraneous, but they cannot be compared directly to a familiar object or to everyday contexts. The objects are unfamiliar and lead to explorations and tests. This is in particularly evident at the *Living* station. In addition to the model of a Berlin apartment building, which is displayed in a showcase, there are two kettles hidden inside covered boxes, with porcelain and enamel cups and pieces of coal. All the children see the covered boxes and then reach in without being able to view the contents. They make immediate guesses about what they can feel. Often they look to the adults, seemingly seeking confirmation. Once the covers of the kettles, cups and coal are removed, the children reach out to feel the objects in order to examine what they are made of. In four out of seven videos taken at the station, children visibly and spontaneously try to drink from the cups, but also smell and test the weight of the objects, such as the piece of coal. The concrete objects provoke body-related investigations about what they were used for and similarities in the living environment of children are discussed.

4.2 Open Coding: Approaching the Meanings of Objects via Everyday Experience

The children involved in the sample tap into the meanings of unfamiliar objects. The objects are found in everyday contexts and scenes that are associated with known worlds. At the play stations, the children initiate their own re-creations of things used in daily life, regardless of the intentions of the museum guides—only in rare cases they are instigated by accompanying teachers. A very good example is the comparison made by one preschool child, when he feels a piece of coal at the *Housing* station. The child describes a family experience where the use of coal is of great importance. He tells of a family barbecue on the Tempelhof field, a Berlin city park. The child develops spontaneous associations with the everyday use of this particular object and moves away from what the museum intended it to signify. Through using their bodily senses, the children manage to figure out the everyday uses of objects. Many children imitate drinking from the porcelain or enamel cup. A film sequence shows one child who, in the context of testing cups, offers a cup of coffee to his teacher. Habits of acquaintance, including those of adults, are connected to objects that are unfamiliar. In the context of testing out objects, children create connections between objects and arrange them in relational object environments. This aspect gains more importance when a series of interactive stations is designed, as the objects displayed are linked to the activities of collecting in order to produce object relationships (Duncker, 2007). The children of the sample groups also have the opportunity to present their own collecting activities in the structured game *Collecting*[6]. Their own understanding of the way objects relate to each other helps them to understand the collections of the museum.

Although communication is largely guided by the museum staff, communicative interactions also develop among the children. In the footage we can see that these interactions cause disputes about property. Four selected video segments show that the way children communicate in small groups involves physical exploration, which strengthens their understanding of objects. In the sequences, very many children try out the shapes of objects and comment on their own experiences of what the items are used for. These situations are observed by other children, who are then encouraged to relate the objects to their own bodies or to other objects in the room. In addition to the usual behavior of children in a group, for example playful self-representations, these games that involve moving around, the body, clothing and language, also involve unusual things in the exhibition. Preschool children gain an awareness of social reality and learn to test out spaces physically by, for example, moving around the photomontage of a forest to test out what their body movements mean. A result is that educational events that the children organize themselves

---

[6] "However, what emerges here is a highly differentiated picture of childlike world appropriation. Children become interested in things through a methodical process of acquiring knowledge, and they maintain and strengthen these interests through collecting things as a means of social integration and developing social relations" (Duncker & Kremling, 2010, p. 63).

pave the way to experiencing the exhibits. For these performative experiments to take place, children need a space where they are free of the interpretations of adults (Foucault, 2001; Stieve, 2012). This gives children the opportunity: 'to wrest a new order of the things' (Treptow, 2005, p. 803), and allows them to make their experiences of things more tangible as well as gain a belief in their own ability to do things (*Selbstwirksamkeitsüberzeugungen*) (Nentwig-Gesemann, Fröhlich-Gildhoff, Harms & Richter, 2011b) in non-school environments. The collaborative study designed a research field of interactive stations in which the observation and analysis of video ethnography-based data interpretation gives hints on the vital importance of mimetic, body-related learning processes. The objects from the collections of the DHM challenge children and cause performative interactions which can be thematized in following more formal learning courses.

The performative practices in museum collections point to the disciplinary links between early years education and social science education, which have been reflected in this research. These practices can be anchored in the concept of early years social science teaching (*Frühe Sachbildung*) and used in the development of concepts that assist the transition from preschool to primary school. In several European countries, such as Switzerland, initial trials with joint modules and study phases for preschool and primary school teachers have been launched. The use of educational spaces with physical access to collection objects is beneficial for such a joint training of the two professions. Museums, which are open to both preschool and primary school groups, offer object-based, body-related learning experiences, combined with approaches to cultural heritage. These experiences can be reflected in both educational institutions and can serve as a common ground of further projects.

References

Amann, K. & Hirschauer, S. (1997). Die Befremdung der eigenen Kultur. Ein Programm. In S. Hirschauer & K. Amann (Eds.), *Die Befremdung der eigenen Kultur. Zur ethnographischen Herausforderung soziologischer Empirie* (pp. 7–52). Suhrkamp.

Anderson, S. (2019). The Interactive Museum: Video Games as History Lessons through Lore and Affective Design. *E-Learning and Digital Media, 16*(3), 177–195.

Barnett, C. (2019). Beyond the Walls with Object-Based Learning. *Knowledge Quest, 47*(4), 44–49.

Butler, J. (1990). *Gender Trouble. Feminism and the Subversion of Identity*. Routledge.

Chou, A., & Shih, J. (2010). Show Me What You See: An Exploration of Learning in Museums and Learning in Theatre. *Journal for Learning through the Arts, 6*(1). http://escholarship.org/uc/item/2h473935

Dardanou, M. (2019). From Foot to Pencil, From Pencil to Finger: Children as Digital Wayfarers. *Global Studies of Childhood, 9*(4), 348–359.

Duncker, L. (2007). Kindliches Sammelverhalten. *Sache-Wort-Zahl, 87,* 7–14.

Duncker, L., & Kremling, C. (2010). Sammeln als Form frühkindlicher Weltaneignung—Explorative Beobachtungen und Befragungen von Vorschulkindern. In H.-J. Fischer, P. Gansen, & K. Michalik (Eds.), *Sachunterricht und frühe Bildung* (pp. 53–65). Klinkhardt.

Foucault, M. (2001). *The Order of Things. An Archaeology of the Human Sciences.* Routledge.

Gebauer, G., & Wulf, Ch. (1992). *Mimesis.* Kultur—Kunst—Gesellschaft. Rowohlt.

Heinzel, F. (ed.) (2010). *Kinder in Gesellschaft. Was wissen wir über aktuelle Kindheiten?* Grundschulverband.

Hope, A. (2018). Young Children as Curators. *The International Journal of Art & Design Education, 37,* 29–40.

Isenberg, J., & Jalongo, M. (2000). *Creative Expression and Play in Early Childhood* (3rd ed.). Prentice Hall.

Jordi, R. (2011). Reframing the Concept of Reflection: Consciousness, Experiential Learning, and Reflective Learning Practices. *Adult Education Quarterly, 61*(2), 181–197.

Klafki, W. (1998). Selbsttätigkeit als Grundprinzip des Lernens in der Schule. In W. Klafki (Ed.), *Erziehung—Humanität—Demokratie* (pp. 111–134). Universitätsbibliothek. Marburg.

Koester, H. (2006). *Freies Explorieren und Experimentieren—eine Untersuchung zur selbstbestimmten Gewinnung von Erfahrungen mit physikalischen Phänomenen im Sachunterricht.* Logos.

Krakowski, P. (2012). Museum Superheroes: The Role of Play in Young Children's Lives. *The Journal of Museum Education, 37*(1), 49–58.

Murow, S., & Chavez, A. (2017). Exploring Matter: An Interactive, Inexpensive Chemistry Exhibit for Museums. *Journal of Chemical Education, 94,* 1571–1579.

Nentwig-Gesemann, I., Fröhlich-Gildhoff, K., & Pietsch, S. (2011a). *Kompetenzorientierung in der Qualifizierung frühpädagogischer Fachkräfte. Eine Expertise der Weiterbildungsinitiative Frühpädagogischer Fachkräfte.* Deutsches Jugendinstitut e. V.

Nentwig-Gesemann, I., Fröhlich-Gildhoff, K., Harms, H., & Richter, S. (2011b). *Professionelle Haltung—Identität der Fachkraft für die Arbeit mit Kindern in den ersten drei Lebensjahren.* Deutsches Jugendinstitut e. V.

Nohl, A. (2011). *Pädagogik der Dinge.* Klinkhardt

Norman, D.-A. (1999). Affordance, Conventions and Design. *Interactions, 6*(3), 38–43. ACM Press.

Pech, D. (2009). Sachunterricht—Didaktik und Disziplin. Annäherungen an ein Sachlernverständnis im Kontext der Fachentwicklung des Sachunterrichts und seiner Didaktik. In www.widerstreit-sachunterricht.de, 2009, Nr. 13.

Pech, D., & Rauterberg, M. (2007). Sachunterricht als wissenschaftliche Disziplin. In www.widerstreit-sachunterricht.de, 2007, extra beiheft.

Pech, D., & Rauterberg, M. (2008). Auf den Umgang kommt es an. 'Umgangsweisen' als Ausgangspunkt einer Strukturierung des Sachunterrichts—Skizze der Entwicklung eines 'Bildungsrahmens Sachlernen'. In www.widerstreit-sachunterricht.de, 2008, Beiheft 5.

Peleg, R., & Baram-Tsabari, A. (2017). Learning Robotics in a Science Museum Theatre Play: Investigation of Learning Outcomes, Contexts and Experiences. *Journal of Science Education and Technology, 26*(6), 561–581.

Pratt, M.-L. (1992). *Imperial Eyes: Travel Writing and Transculturation*. Routledge.

Pratt, M.-L. (1996). Arts of the Contact Zone. In D. Bartholomae & A. Petroksky (Eds.), *Ways of Reading* (pp. 582–596). St Martin's.

Schäfer, G. (1999). Fallstudien in der frühpädagogischen Bildungsforschung. In M.-S. Honig, A. Lange, & H. R. Leu (Eds.), *Aus der Perspektive von Kindern? Zur Methodologie der Kindheitsforschung* (pp. 113–133). Beltz.

Schäfer, G. (2011). *Was ist frühkindliche Bildung? Kindlicher Anfängergeist in einer Kultur des Lernens*, 2. Beltz.

Scholz, G. (2010). Die Frühe Bildung als Herausforderung an das Sachlernen. In H.-J. Fischer (Ed.), *Sachunterricht und frühe Bildung* (pp. 29–42). Klinkhardt.

Serrell, B. (1996). *Exhibit Labels: An Interpretive Approach*. Altamira.

Stauber, B. (2004). *Junge Frauen und Männer in Jugendkulturen. Selbstinszenierungen und Handlungspotentiale*. Leske + Budrich.

Stauber, B. (2006). Mediale Selbstinszenierungen von Mädchen und Jungen. *Diskurs Kindheits- und Jugendforschung, 1*(3), 417–432.

Stieve, C. (2012). Inszenierte Bildung. Dinge und Kind des Kindergartens. In A. Dörpinghaus & A. Nießeler (Eds.), *Dinge in der Welt der Bildung. Bildung in der Welt der Dinge* (pp. 57–86). Neumann.

Treptow, R. (2005). Vor den Dingen sind alle Besucher gleich. Kulturelle Bildungsprozesse in der musealen Ordnung. *Zeitschrift für Pädagogik, 51*(6), 797–809.

Wagner, B. (2010). Kontaktzonen im Museum—Kindergruppen in der Ausstellung 'Indianer Nordamerikas'. *Paragrana, 19*(2), 192–203.

Wagner, B. (2013). Informelles Sachlernen von Kindern im Museum der Dinge. In A. Nohl & C. Wulf (Eds.), Mensch und Ding. Die Materialität pädagogischer Prozesse. *Zeitschrift für Erziehungswissenschaft, 16*(2), 203–218.

Woods, C. (2018). Black Museums and Experiential Learning. *Research Issues in Contemporary Education, 3*(1), 57–66.

Wulf, C., Göhlich, M., & Zirfas, J. (Eds.). (2001). *Grundlagen des Performativen: Eine Einführung in die Zusammenhänge von Sprache, Macht und Handeln*. Beltz.

Yoo, J., & Loch, S. (2016). Learning Bodies: What Do Teachers Learn from Embodied Practice? *Issues in Educational Research, 26*(3), 528–542.

Part V

Body, Virtual Reality and Mindfulness

This section examines the processes of embodiment that have arisen as part of the digital transformation of society as well as the extent to which mindfulness can help us to deal critically with virtual reality. To a large degree, the traditional division between online and offline has become irrelevant in the lives of young people. Both forms of being and acting are equally familiar to them and are essential in their everyday lives. A life that is not ready to communicate online is almost inconceivable for the young. Through being both users and producers, the digital natives and other users develop new forms of digital productivity and creativity. They are comfortable with sending screenshots and selfies and using the diverse forms of digital communication, etc. It is hard to say what the potential and also the limitations of these new forms of communication, information and entertainment may be. New connections between distance and traditional classroom learning are constantly being developed. Many of these developments have come about or have been accelerated as a result of the coronavirus crisis.

Michalis Kontopodis and *Kristiina Kumpulainen* in Chap. 22 describe "a radical shift in the lives of children and young people" in the new media era. The 'internet' or 'App generation' share ever more ideas, thoughts and information within virtual *networks* and communities, and also engage in e-learning. They play games and use digital collaborative work spaces with virtual reality tools, thus co-creating, locating, filtering, editing and re-using media content. The boundaries between 'being online' and ways of life that are 'not directly technical' are increasingly blurred. Multiple interrelations between technical devices and human actors shape, transform and diffuse the actions by means of technical mediation. Engagement, completeness and coherence are replaced by confused entanglement, multimodality and speed.

356   Body, Virtual Reality and Mindfulness

As a consequence, Kontopodis and Kumpulainen see education today as enabling multiple connections between various types of media, as well as between different spheres of life and diverse cultural and socio-economic milieus. Two case studies show that habitual users find it natural that programmes of action and 'compositions' of life settings and interfaces deprive them of control and agency.

This leads into Chap. 23 by *Benjamin Jörissen, Martha K. Schröder* and *Anna Carnap* in the field of aesthetic and arts education. The authors describe the use of the 'OpenSpace method' in the frame of s.c. *BarCamps*, i.e. participative conferences, to investigate young people's activities in post-digital cultures. Their wide-ranging quantitative and qualitative study shows that temporary forms of "networking and expressive articulation, play and work, individuality and collectivity, remix and originality" are combined with "the externalization of memory practices, sociality as a networked attention economy, creativity imperatives or hyper-individualized information and communication styles". They describe how bodily practices are intertwined with technology. 'Traditional' theatrical and musical performances are adapted to forms of digital and post-digital creativity and new digital-aesthetic practices emerge. Non-digital practices are restaged and new value is given to the forms of real-life physical action that once have been quite prosaic. Digital transcultural countercultures arise.

Another angle is to be found in Chap. 24 by *Andreas Nehring* on mindfulness, a practice that is beginning to play an increasingly important role in education and therapeutic processes. Mindfulness is a metacognitive state of awareness that is reached by purposely refraining from judgement and by bringing one's attention to the present moment. The aim is to attain self-perception through introspection and increased awareness of the body through the interweaving of thought processes with physical states. There is an assumption that "the body is able to adapt to its environment in a reactive and self-organizing (autopoiesis) way which connects all systems with each other". With its roots in Buddhism, mindfulness training is directed towards the deficiencies of the Western lifestyles, especially in the business world. It aims to compensate for adverse effects of civilization, such as burn-out, painful relationships, poor concentration and mindless distraction. Furthermore, in mindfulness approaches, finding meaning in one's life as an individual and self-management is linked to popular culture, lifestyle and to a clear narrative dramaturgy. Nehring reminds us of the need to "develop a systematic cultural-analytical understanding of mindfulness", also of the reception of mindfulness from a historico-cultural-comparative perspective.

Technical Mediation of Children's Onlife Worlds

Michalis Kontopodis and Kristiina Kumpulainen

1 Blurring Children's On- and Offline Worlds

Increasing numbers of children and young people from across the world are engaging in speedy communication which takes place through interactive media devices. Present-day technologies enable the distributed production and peer-to-peer circulation of advanced audio-visual designs and bits of information across different geographical areas—the prediction being that by 2025 every child and young person in the planet will have daily access to the Internet at a speed of 1 MB per second (ITU, 2019). Numerous digital solutions have also been taken into use across the world, as to mitigate the problems created by school closures during the recent COVID-19 outbreak.

Much research has explored the role media and digital technologies play in everyday lives and learning of children and young people, inside and outside of school (cf. Kontopodis et al., 2019; Kumpulainen & Sefton-Green, 2014; Pachler et al., 2010; Selwyn, 2013). Terms such as the 'net generation' (Tapscott, 2009), the 'App generation' (Gardner & Davis, 2013) and

---

M. Kontopodis (✉)
University of Leeds/GB, Leeds, UK
e-mail: m.kontopodis@leeds.ac.uk

K. Kumpulainen
University of Helsinki, Helsinki, Finland
e-mail: kristiina.kumpulainen@helsinki.fi

© The Author(s), under exclusive license to Springer Nature Switzerland AG 2022
A. Kraus, C. Wulf (eds.), *The Palgrave Handbook of Embodiment and Learning*,
https://doi.org/10.1007/978-3-030-93001-1_22

'networked teens' (Boyd, 2014) have been introduced to describe a radical shift in the lives of the children and young people in the new media era.

While the first wave of relevant scholarship mostly explored online learning, communication and gaming, a second wave of research argues that the boundaries between life online and life offline are increasingly blurred, to an extent that the original meanings of the words online and offline seem to be diffused, both in theory and in practice. Luciano Floridi (2014) introduced, in this frame, the term 'onlife' to account for the contemporary ways of living in which humans are endlessly surrounded by smart, responsive objects when they play, shop, learn, entertain themselves and conduct relationships or even wars. Being 'onlife' is indeed a fundamental dimension of the everyday lives of children and young people—particularly of those in North-Western urban settings, as doing things online and offline is merely a matter of swiftly switching between the different modalities of everydayness. At the same time, it seems that media scholars are moving from a focus on so-called new media to exploring how older and newer forms and means of communication and learning may be intertwined (Debray, 2000; Jenkins, 2006; Leander, 2008).

Central in understanding how new media operate and how they may affect children's everyday lives and learning is the notion of 'technical mediation' (Latour, 1994). While the concept of 'technical mediation' has often been used in a rather generic way, Bruno Latour (1994, pp. 32–29) identifies four distinct modes of 'technical mediation' in his analysis of the multiple interrelations between technical devices (so-called actants) and human 'actors':

- 'black-boxing', which renders invisible the role of technical devices
- 'translation' of a programme of action to another one
- 'composition', that is relating of things that were previously different or unrelated
- 'delegation' of action from a certain actor to another one (e.g. from a developer team to software)

According to Latour, all these modes of technical mediation work through human actors and technical devices symmetrically, that is without that human actors always have the central role, as other paradigms would presume. Latour argues that technical mediation shapes, transforms and diffuses action, so that understanding who or what is acting is not always straightforward.

The work by Bruno Latour did not refer originally to interactive, fast and mobile audio-visual media designs—nor did it refer to children's and young people's learning and corporeality. We propose that this analytical concept can be useful when trying to understand how children's bodies, media and digital technologies and other devices relate to each other as to produce the blurred, contemporary, 'onlife' worlds, which children and young people inhabit. In this frame, we will employ below Latour's concept of 'technical mediation' in order to analyse two empirical examples from our recent research projects. The first example explores various forms of technical mediation between a two-year-old girl and a music-making App in a home setting. The second example highlights the interrelations between a five-year-old boy and virtual reality technologies in a Makerspace workshop associated with the FabLab Berlin. The analysis of the two empirical examples leads into a broader discussion about learning and education in the contemporary 'onlife' worlds.

2   Emilia with a Music-Making App

During one of our recent European projects, Kristiina, the second author, studied a home setting in a suburban metropolitan area in southern Finland, with a Finnish-speaking family consisting of a mother, father and one two-year-old child Emilia.[1] The child's name has of course been replaced with a pseudonym to ensure anonymity. The empirical data collection followed the principles of the 'day-in-the-life' methodology developed by Julia Gillen and her team (Gillen et al., 2007; Gillen & Cameron, 2010), and combined interviews with parents, photography, video recordings and field notes of children's digital literacy practices at home (Kumpulainen et al., 2020).

Emilia was sitting on a sofa using a music-making App that she had independently located online, while she was glancing through the different applications, which her parents had allowed her to search on a tablet. In this App, different pictures make different sounds. At first, Emilia was just going through the pictures, tapping them one by one and listening to different sounds. The sounds made her laugh, and she became interested in tapping different sounds. Her father then joined in to see what she was doing, and for a while, they together explored the functions of the App and how it worked. In doing so, Emilia and the father engaged, to some extent, in unpacking the 'black box' of the invisible ways in which the technology worked. They explored the various options of the App interface; however, they could not intervene in the design of the App or the mechanics of the tablet, which remained 'black-boxed' in Bruno Latour's (1994) terms.

---

[1] We refer here to the 'Digital Literacy and Multimodal Practices of Young Children' COST Action (Nr. IS1410) led by Prof. Jackie Marsh (University of Sheffield).

Eventually the dad left Emilia and she continued to produce sounds with the App on her own. Emilia's engagement was in this case mediated by the App, that is followed programmes of actions and rules, which the App developers created as well as rules, which her parents have set for her usage of the tablet and technology, in general. These rules—that is her parents giving her a certain amount of freedom in using the tablet—allowed her to explore different applications and resulted in Emilia locating and using a music-making App that attracted her attention. Neither the App developers nor the parents needed to be constantly present for Emilia to follow the rules, as the initial programme of action set by developers was 'delegated' to other actors, that is parents, Emilia and the device itself and then to the device and Emilia alone.

Soon Emilia became distracted, and she changed places from the sofa to the floor. After this, her mother joined her to see what she was doing. Emilia started to play the sounds to her mother, and together, they got seemingly excited about tapping the pictures and creating the sounds, and they shook their bodies to the rhythm of the sounds that they had created. Here, both Emilia's and mother's online/onscreen activity became blurred with their offline/offscreen body movements. This could be the beginning of a 'composition' in Latour's terms, that is of a specific combination of previously unrelated App sounds and Emilia's and her mother's body movements. These findings also evidence, in Latour's terms, how a programme of action, that is music-making with the App, that is onscreen, was 'translated' into another programme of action, in which Emilia and her mother were no longer making music on the tablet but moving and dancing to the sounds, which the App was playing back in the 'onlife' space emerging out of the 'composition' of the sitting room (offline/offscreen) and the App interface (online/onscreen). If repeated, this composition could eventually turn in the future into a trivial family dance or become part of some wider ritualised family activity, such as dancing in front of guests, dancing as a way to begin the day in the morning and so on (Wulf et al., 2001).

3 Jörg in Engagement with Virtual Reality and Immersive Technologies

During another recent European research project,[2] Michalis, the first author, followed ethnographically Jörg (pseudonym), a five-year-old boy, who participated in a virtual reality workshop, one form of Makerspace associated with the FabLab Berlin (cf. Kontopodis & Kumpulainen, 2020). A fab lab, that is

---

[2] We refer here to the project *Makerspaces in the Early Years: Enhancing Digital Literacy and Creativity* (MakEY) led by Prof. Jackie Marsh (University of Sheffield, Marie Skłodowska-Curie Grant Nr 734720).

Technical Mediation of Children's Onlife Worlds   361

fabrication laboratory, is an open digital fabrication studio where one can learn how to use 3D printers, laser cutters, computer numerical control (CNC) routers, design software and electronics. The FabLab Berlin consisted of so-called Makerspaces, that is collaborative work spaces for making, learning, exploring and knowledge sharing with the available tools and technologies. It also offered access to a professional Do-It-Yourself studio and was not only open to children and young people but also to adults and, in some cases, to professional entrepreneurs.

In one of FabLab's collaborative working spaces, a female facilitator, who was about 30 years old, asked Jörg to create with cardboard and a variety of other tools such as scissors, paint, pencils that were provided a world for a wooden doll, which she had brought to the FabLab. After Jörg created the world of the doll with cardboard and painted it, he was asked to also create a similar environment for the doll by means of virtual reality tools. Other children were present, including Jörg's older brother, who was producing his own version of the virtual environment for the same doll. Jörg could see the doll (offscreen) on a desk alongside the painting materials as well as the doll's virtual replication on a 2D laptop screen. For 3D vision he was required to wear the HTC VIVE headset, which was connected through cables to two controllers, one for each hand as well as a set of sensors and a data processing unit. When he did that, he could no longer see anything offscreen.

While Jörg tried the HTC VIVE headset, he stepped on the (offline/offscreen) cable connecting it to the processing unit and almost fell on the floor. The facilitator quickly supported him so that he didn't fall and moved the cable further away, so that Jörg could focus on the virtual environment as it appeared through the HTC VIVE headset. Then the facilitator invited Jörg to use the mouse, select a virtual brush and move it in a certain direction so as to further paint, modify and design the doll's virtual environment. The facilitator explained to Jörg that he could move his whole body and even walk around, if needed, during the painting, but within the provided virtual room space, which was marked by virtual walls. Two minutes later, Jörg was crossing the virtual wall, which meant that he also moved out of the offline/offscreen marked workshop area; without realising it, he slightly touched a (real) chair with his back, which he couldn't have seen as he was wearing the HTC VIVE headset. This was unexpected for him and created some confusion; the facilitator intervened again, Jörg removed the headset, with everybody—him and the other boys—bursting into laughter.

How virtual reality and immersive technologies work is not of importance to the average modern-day user, it is usually 'black-boxed', as also had been the case in the previous example with Emilia. Little is known on how the processing unit processes the recorded data, the coding behind the rather user-friendly painting interface or the multiple connections between all different parts (cables, sensors, controllers, PC and VR headset). When Jörg stepped literally *on* the cable and metaphorically *out of* the virtual reality environment some of this 'black-boxing' was reversed—but not for long (Latour, 1994). If Jörg, as it often happens in FabLabs, would engage for a longer period of time in the coding of the software and/or in the production and design of the hardware, this black-boxing could be entirely reversed and re-programming could take place.

The 'composition' of software + PC + virtual reality headset + cables + sensors + controllers + chairs did not just do *more* or *better* of what Jörg would anyway do, it did *different* things: Jörg spent a while walking around and moving his hands offline/offscreen, an action which was 'translated' through the sensors into online/onscreen brushing, painting, deleting and finally into designing a virtual 3D environment for the doll in ways that neither Jörg *nor* the software programme (and its developers) would have necessarily envisaged in advance. The environment initially designed for the doll on cardboard with standard (offline/offscreen) painting tools was then 'translated' into something quite different: a 3D space on screen, mediated through software as well as through a series of offscreen cables, sensors, controllers and other devices. Jörg could after a certain point leave the space and 'delegate' (in Latour's sense) his programme of action to the software, which would continue providing the 3D-designed/immersive environment for the doll in Jörg's absence.

4   Outlook: Learning, Teaching and Schooling in Contemporary 'Onlife' Worlds

As the two cases in these brief extracts evidence, children's bodies and everyday lives are nowadays becoming more and more intertwined with technical devices. Different modes of technical mediation ('translation' of a programme of action to another one; 'composition'; 'black-boxing' and 'delegation' of action from humans to software and vice-versa) are continuously at work, so that the boundaries between life 'online' and life 'offline' are becoming increasingly blurred. Contemporary children's and young people 'onlives' unfold within complex on-/offline/ on-/offscreen, technically mediated environments. Ever more frequently, children and young people move across multiple technical interfaces, devices and designs—sometimes they even create new ones—as to share with others their knowledge, feelings, dreams, phantasies and concerns. As opposed to listening to commercial music or to watching mass TV programmes, they thereby often become 'digital makers', that is to say co-productive and transformative in co-creating, locating, filtering, editing and re-using media contents. They sometimes even (re-) programme soft- and hardware and create new platforms and interfaces (Kajamaa & Kumpulainen, 2019; Kontopodis et al., 2019).

When considering the relevant research findings and the two aforementioned examples from our studies of children's everyday lives and learning, it becomes evident that formal education can no longer remain a secluded space. The technical devices and communicative resources that teachers and students use inside and outside the classroom mediate the communication and learning between teachers and students in quite different ways than classic school curricula, textbooks and notebooks did. Images have always, of course, played an important role in education as they can shape and transfer human imagination to other places and times (Wulf, 2022). The new element in contemporary *Bildung*, that is enculturation and formation through images (in German: *Bilder*), is speed and multimodality, as Arnd-Michael Nohl and Morvarid Götz-Dehnavi (this volume) also argue. Images with multi-sensory effects, often in 3D formats, are technically mediated, edited and circulated in speedy ways, thereby capturing children's and young people's attention, imagination and learning. To respond to and build on the technical mediation of children's everyday lives, it is important that contemporary schooling and its teaching and learning practices will similarly transcend online and offline spaces and, when relevant and possible, enable multiple connections between various types of media and literacies, as well as between different (on-)life spheres and diverse cultural and socio-economic milieus.

Even if children and young people are often offered more possibilities to engage creatively with technology today than with the commercial music or TV programmes in the past, technical mediation is not as neutral as digital industry suggests that it may be: it enables certain actions to happen and prevents others from happening. Much attention is given in the relevant literature to the various layers of knowledge-power relations incorporated in 'black-boxed' technology—be it racial, gendered, age-related, capitalist and/ or geo-political (Banaji, 2015; Selwyn, 2013; Taylor & Hughes, 2016). Seen from such a perspective, there is a need to move away from learning existing ways of doing things with technology; rather, the emphasis can be placed on how children may experiment with the mediating technologies and the various 'onlife' environments, which children, researchers, programmers, facilitators and various non-human actors co-create and co-inhabit, so that plural, inclusive and sustainable virtual realities emerge (Hasse, 2015; Kontopodis, 2019).

It is clear that education today should recognise the different forms of technical mediation, as part of (trans-) literacies that create opportunities for children's and young people's communication and learning in and across their onlife worlds. This equally applies to assessing learning achievements that clearly can no longer rest on narrow and pre-defined assessments that by large rely on the notion of completeness and coherence in learning (Kumpulainen & Sefton-Green, 2014). Instead, here, we should cherish unpredictability and possibilities that arise both for teaching and for learning. Hopefully, in this way, formal education can support children and young people in their (learning) 'onlives' while further co-designing and even transforming the contemporary, messy and unstable, technically mediated environments, in which they find themselves entangled.

References

Banaji, S. (2015). Behind the High-Tech Fetish: Children, Work and Media Use Across Classes in India. *International Communication Gazette, 77*(6), 519–532.

Boyd, D. (2014). *It's Complicated: The Social Lives of Networked Teens*. Yale University Press.

Debray, R. (2000). *Introduction à la médiologie*. Presses Universitaires de France.

Floridi, L. (2014). *The Fourth Revolution: How the Infosphere Is Reshaping Human Reality*. Oxford University Press.

Gardner, H., & Davis, K. (2013). *The App Generation: How Today's Youth Navigate Identity, Intimacy, and Imagination in a Digital World*. Yale University Press.

Gillen, J., & Cameron, C. A. (Eds.). (2010). *International Perspectives on Early Childhood Research: A Day in the Life*. Palgrave Macmillan.

Gillen, J., Cameron, C. A., Tapanya, S., Pinto, G., Hancock, R., Young, S., & Gamannossi, B. A. (2007). A Day in the Life: Advancing a Methodology for the Cultural Study of Development and Learning in Early Childhood. *Early Child Development & Care, 177*(2), 207–218.

Hasse, C. (2015). *An Anthropology of Learning: On Nested Frictions in Cultural Ecologies*. Springer.

ITU [International Telecommunication Union]. (2019). *ICT Facts and Figures*. Online Report. Retrieved September 3, 2020, from https://www.itu.int/en/ITU-D/Statistics/Documents/facts/FactsFigures2019.pdf

Jenkins, H. (2006). *Convergence Culture: Where Old and New Media Collide*. New York University Press.

Kajamaa, A., & Kumpulainen, K. (2019). Agency in the Making: Analyzing Students' Transformative Agency in a School-Based Makerspace. *Mind, Culture & Activity, 26*(3), 266–281.

Kontopodis, M. (2019). The Fluid Classroom: Book Narratives, YouTube Videos & Other Metaphorical Devices. *Paragrana, 28*(2), 101–105.

Kontopodis, M., & Kumpulainen, K. (2020). Researching Young Children's Engagement and Learning in Makerspaces: Insights from Post-Vygotskian and Post-human Perspectives. In A. Blum-Ross, K. Kumpulainen, & J. Marsh (Eds.), *Enhancing Digital Literacy and Creativity: Makerspaces in the Early Years* (pp. 11–23). Routledge.

Kontopodis, M., Varvantakis C., & Wulf, C. (eds.) (2019). *Global Youth in Digital Trajectories*. Routledge.

Kumpulainen, K., Sairanen, H., & Nordström, A. (2020). Young Children's Digital Literacy Practices in the Sociocultural Contexts of their Homes. *Journal of Early Childhood Literacy, 20*(3), 472–499.

Kumpulainen, K., & Sefton-Green, J. (2014). What Is Connected Learning and How to Research It? *International Journal of Learning and Media, 4*(2), 7–18.

Latour, B. (1994). On Technical Mediation: Philosophy, Sociology. *Genealogy. Common Knowledge, 3*(2), 29–64.

Leander, K. (2008). Toward a Connective Ethnography of Online/Offline Literacy Networks. In J. Coiro, M. Knobel, C. Lankshear, & D. Leu (Eds.), *Handbook of Research on New Literacies* (pp. 33–65). Routledge.

Pachler, N., Bachmair, B., Cook, J., & Kress, G. (2010). *Mobile Learning: Structures, Agency, Practices*. Springer.

Selwyn, N. (2013). *Education in a Digital World: Global Perspectives on Technology and Education*. Routledge.

Tapscott, D. (2009). *Grown Up Digital. How the Net Generation Is Changing Your World*. McGraw-Hill.

Taylor, C., & Hughes, C. (Eds.). (2016). *Posthuman Research Practices in Education*. Palgrave Macmillan.

Wulf, C. (2022). *Human Beings and Their Images. Imagination, Mimesis, Performativity*. Bloomsbury.

Wulf, C., Althans, B., Audehm, K., Bausch, C., Göhlich, M., Sting, S., Tervooren, A., Wagner Willi, M., & Zirfas, J. (2001). *Das Soziale als Ritual. Zur performativen Bildung von Gemeinschaften*. Leske & Budrich.

Creative and Artistic Learning in Post-digital Youth Culture: Results of a Qualitative Study on Transformations of Aesthetic Practices

Benjamin Jörissen, Martha Karoline Schröder, and Anna Carnap

1 Introduction

Digitalization and mobile networking have changed our lives and the lives of children and young people enormously (Hugger et al., 2013; Aufenanger, 2015; Calmbach et al., 2016; Kontopodis et al., 2017; Feierabend et al., 2018; Albert et al., 2019). Digital networks, apps, and algorithms permeate the lives of children and young people. In both, systematical and historical perspective, genuine digital or 'online cultures' (see, e.g., Rheingold, 1994; Turkle, 1995; Sandbothe & Marotzki, 2000; Marotzki, 2003; Boellstorff, 2008), which arise from specifically structured socio-technological contexts and platforms located 'on' the Internet, can be distinguished from the cultural effects of digitalization that take place outside the online sphere, respectively (and nowadays in particular), in hybrid environments permeated by digital

---

B. Jörissen (✉)
Universität Erlangen-Nuremberg, Erlangen, Germany
e-mail: benjamin.joerissen@fau.de

M. K. Schröder
Institute for School Quality and Teacher Education, Leipzig, Germany

A. Carnap
Humboldt University of Berlin, Berlin, Germany
e-mail: anna.carnap@hu-berlin.de

© The Author(s), under exclusive license to Springer Nature Switzerland AG 2022
A. Kraus, C. Wulf (eds.), *The Palgrave Handbook of Embodiment and Learning*,
https://doi.org/10.1007/978-3-030-93001-1_23

technology. If we speak of a 'post-digital' state or 'post-digital culture' in the latter sense (Cramer, 2015; Jörissen, 2019; Stalder, 2016), then this refers to the fact that structures resulting from digitalization dynamics—such as the externalization of memory practices, sociality as a networked attention economy, creativity imperatives or hyper-individualized information, and communication styles—have begun to structure or restructure even 'non-digital', that is, not directly technical, ways of life. The 'non-digital' realm suddenly not only needs a name of its own for the first time, but increasingly it can no longer be explained without referring to digital terms such as software (Kitchin & Dodge, 2011), algorithms (Pasquale, 2015), and platforms (Srnicek, 2016).

In this contribution, we refer to aesthetic and arts education as a paradigmatic field with regard to the complex relations of bodies, embodiment, and learning practices. Under post-digital conditions, as we will demonstrate, the conditions of aesthetic and arts education are changing significantly for children and young people. Digital social network platforms such as *Instagram*, *Snapchat*, and *TikTok* have significantly transformed aesthetic and artistic practices. Paradigmatically, this had already become apparent in the ephemeral creative and collective design practices on the *Minecraft* game platform, where a considerable number of children and young people create often highly elaborate structures that are constantly being built over and thus exist on the platforms for only a limited time. Networking and expressive articulation, play and work, individuality and collectivity, remix and original appear to be intertwined.

In the period 2016–2019 the research project "Post-digital Cultural Youth Worlds—Development of New Methodological Instruments for the Further Development of Research on Cultural Education in the Digital and Post-digital World" investigated how digital change has affected the current artistic-creative practice, cultural education, and participation of young people.[1]

2 Research Design and Core Results

In two sub-projects, changes in aesthetic and creative practices have been studied in an intertwined mixed-methodological research design that encompasses extensive qualitative as well as quantitative data collection. The quantitative-representative part of our study covered 2067 face-to-face interviews with young people between 14 and 24 years (Keuchel & Riske, 2020),

---

[1] Funded by the German Ministry of Research and Education; Reference number: 01JK1605B; Acronym: DiKuJu.

whereas the qualitative part covered online-ethnographies, expert interviews with professionals in the field of arts and cultural education, group discussions with young people, as well as a series of case studies. Additionally, a methodological conceptualization of the innovative, OpenSpace-inspired method of an explorative *Research BarCamp* bringing together young experts and professionals was developed and realized. In the following, we will provide an overview of core results of the qualitative part of the project.

2.1 Ethnographic Research in Online Networks: Levels of Post-digital Transformations of Creative Practices

Our ethnographic research on online platforms, such as *YouTube, Instagram*, and in the (still existing) informal network of weblogs formerly called the *blogosphere* (Herring et al., 2005), brought to light different practices of digital and post-digital creativity.[2]

1. 'Post-digital transformations of expressive articulation and experience' can be found online on different levels of reference:

   (a) In relation to traditional, that is, 'pre-digital', aesthetic, and artistic-creative practices, we find a 'transfer into digital environments', where, for example, theater performances take place in virtual worlds or traditional practices of music making take place in the digital sphere—for example, in the context of virtual choirs.

   (b) 'Emergent new digital-aesthetic practices', such as independent game programming, performative practices of live-coding, circuit bending, generative algorithm-based artistic practices, can be distinguished from these.

   (c) The nature of 'post-digital creative activities' becomes particularly evident in distinctly non-digital practices that exhibit a 'vintage' character (explorations of mechanical, electro-mechanical, or analog-technical creative practices such as analog photography, instant photography, instrument crafting, rediscovery of old analog synthesizers, etc.) but which are nevertheless always (re-)staged in digital networks and thus relate to digitally networked forms of visibility, presumably also sub-

---

[2] We have prepared a continuously updated YouTube playlist on the topic of (post-) digital aesthetics and creative practices (Jörissen, 2019) and refer below to the list position of the respective linked videos. Cf., for example, for (a) Jörissen (2019), nos 54, 61, 62, 64, 70; for (b) Jörissen (2019), nos 14, 16, 20, 26, 30, 40, 65, 67; for (c) Jörissen (2019), nos 63, 66, 71.

stantially made known through networking platforms and thus even may be part of viral (retro-analog) trends.

2. 'Post-digital transformations of forms of communication and performative enactment'

   The dissemination and visualization of creative practices already played a significant role in the 'digital cultures' of the early Internet and World Wide Web. In contrast to such digital or online-centered contexts, such as those that took place within online communities (Turkle, 1995), gaming communities (Jörissen, 2004), and virtual worlds (Boellstorff, 2008), post-digital transformations of forms of communication and staging of aesthetic and artistic-creative practices are characterized by seamless integration as well as by the elimination of the difference between 'online' and 'offline'. Since the spreading of affordable mobile devices, mobile data plans, and cloud computing solutions, the state of 'being online' deeply embedded in everyday life and in particular plays a special role in youth's peer cultures (cf. phenomena like *Lets play*, *Vlogger*, *Hauls*, *Memes*, *Foodies*, *do-it-yourself*, etc.) as well as on the level of informal cultural peer education (tutorial videos and other 'HowTo' offerings). Here, online networking platforms based on user-generated content such as *Instagram*, *Twitch*, and above all *YouTube* are of considerable importance (see also Rat für Kulturelle Bildung, 2019).

3. Finally, a third aspect is the post-digital transformation on the level of social forms and cultural orientations of aesthetic and artistic-creative practices. The transcultural and also transculturalizing effects of the globally networked cultural space of the Internet were already emphasized in the early phases of its development and dissemination (see, e.g., Sandbothe & Marotzki, 2000; Poster, 2001, 2006; Jörissen, 2003). Accordingly, in our online research we found numerous transcultural creative practices, ranging from aesthetic-artistic practices with specific cultural references (e.g., *furry*, *quilting*, *manga*, and *cosplay*) to forms of globally oriented creative activism, digital countercultures, and other aestheticized forms of political-actionist practices, such as *flashmobs/smartmobs*.

2.2 Group Discussions with Young People and Interviews with Experts in Cultural Education: The Digital as a Challenge

A total of seven group discussions (Loos & Schäffer, 2013) with young people were conducted with the goal to gain first insights into digital or post-digital creative practices in current youth culture. Furthermore, we conducted 26 interviews of experts with professional teachers, cultural workers, and youth leaders in various fields and institutions of cultural youth education. The expertise of the interviewees results from their work-related familiarity with the peer-cultural, digital practices of the young people, their aesthetic work with the target group itself or (on the management and program planning level) from their industry-specific knowledge and their knowledge bases based on 'insider experience' (cf. Meuser & Nagel, 2009). The core results of both surveys can be summarized as follows:

1. Post-digital 'background noise': For young people today, digitality is largely not a subject of discussion, but rather a constitutive, 'inescapable' background to the world in which they live (Baym, 2015). Consequently, it is difficult to ask young people directly about digital transformations of their creative practices—on the one hand, because of the 'naturalisation' of digital transformation due to its seamless embedding in everyday life, and on the other hand, because of the limited experience of children and young people with regard to the rapid pace of digitalization that has been taking place since the 1990s.
2. Visibility in digital networks: Issues of visibility, media exposure, as well as effects of power and surveillance that come along with digitalization processes are addressed as problematic. Techniques of limited persistence and tactics of limited visibility to selective publics in network platforms are strategically used by young people to gain more control over their own visibility (e.g., the platform Snapchat with its ephemeral images or the Instagram Stories, which are automatically deleted after 24 hours; see also Engel & Jörissen, 2019). At the same time, however, visibility is an identity-relevant currency in the digital attention economy (also in the 'star system' of today's networked worlds; see Reckwitz, 2017).
3. Complexity and contingency: Both young people and experts consider the effects of digitalization to be quite contingent and therefore hardly foreseeable; at the same time, however, they are dealt with by young people in everyday creative activities. In both groups (young people and experts) the

'micro-generational' differences are only addressed implicitly; moreover, we found no explicit engagement with somewhat invisible and difficult to understand phenomena such as algorithmicity and artificial intelligence.

4. Critique and encouragement: While negative effects like 'hatespeech' on the net are clearly addressed as a problem, the potential for inspiration, on the other hand, especially with regard to practical knowledge and skills, is emphasized. On the one hand, the digital availability of foreign-language content helps language learning in schools, while at the same time encouraging participation in a wide range of models and models of creative activities (*how to*, *life hacks*, etc.). For example, in a group discussion with three teenagers aged between 14 and 16 growing up in an urban environment (our translation):

[A]: Yes, it's generally the case with me, I've noticed that lately, everything I do with my cell phone is mostly in English, that is, me, most of the videos I watch are in English, and most of the time I also watch tips for handicrafts and ideas, because I often like to do that when I have time. And as I said, this also helps with school and it certainly determines, in—it's already a big part of my free time, Youtube, unfortunately [A and B grin]. [B]: Yes, but you can also get inspired somehow, for example, if you want to do something, for example, yes, as A already said, like making something or presents for family or friends [nods and shrugs his shoulders]. (Student, PG270717_G2; lines 126–137)

2.3   The *BarCamp* as a Network-Based Research Instrument: Performative Transgressions of Traditional Genre Boundaries in Digital and Post-digital Settings

The *BarCamp* we conducted, which was at the center of the explorative method development already announced in our project title, was originally a conference method from technology research. As a participatory format it was adapted in the context of the US-American 'Web 2.0' scene in the 2000s; from here it has established itself first in net-savvy scenes, then in educational scenes (*Educamps*), in the context of digital (youth) media culture, in economic and non-profit innovation areas and other fields. As a so-called 'unconference', the *BarCamp* has no predefined lectures and workshop topics, but is rather designed in a participatory manner by the participants (who by definition participate in the *BarCamp* as experts) in the form of topic-centered 'sessions'. Clearly, *BarCamps* are all about collective, networked, and non-hierarchical ways of imparting knowledge, but also the *BarCamp* itself, as a whole, can be understood as a collective learning process where unexpected developments, questions, and insights are already laid out in the temporal and spatial structure. The session topics are proposed on site by the participants and chosen in (different) selection procedures, so that the topics or actions that are of greatest interest finally reach the panels. From a methodological point of view, the *BarCamp* can be understood as a "transformative large group process" (Weber, 2009), which is characterized by processes of collective negotiation and, above all, collective relevance-setting. The conducted sessions can be regarded as the result of a group dynamic validation and, to this extent, as collective "focusing metaphors" (Bohnsack, 2017, p. 92), even outside of the interactions within the sessions. This selectivity is further condensed in successive session phases of the *BarCamp*, so that topics, questions, and insights from previous sessions can lead to further, more in-depth, or (transformatively) differently positioned thematic settings. Our preliminary explorative methodological assumption was that *BarCamps* should therefore express collective layers of experience in a condensed form which can be interpreted through reconstruction, whereby the underlying social form is essentially based on the principle of the social network (White, 2008; Fuhse & Mützel, 2010).

In our case, our project partner, the Academy for Arts and Cultural Education of the Federal German Government and the State of North Rhine-Westphalia in Remscheid, served as a very well-established and visible network hub in terms of cultural activities and topics. A *BarCamp* topic chosen by the participants (*Who are we?*) offered, in line with a group discussion that delivered the original idea for this, a balanced amount of participation (in terms of the interest of the intended target groups) on the one hand and minimal exertion of influence on the topics to be raised on the other hand. The three-day *BarCamp* was conducted with 46 young people from different regions of Germany (North Rhine-Westphalia, Berlin, and Bavaria). The young people were aged between 13 and 27, with the majority between 13 and 17 and still attending school (29 persons). With regard to age, formal educational qualifications or types of school attended, gender and migration experiences, the aim was to achieve a diverse mix of participants in order to bring together as many different perspectives as possible. In the following we summarize our evaluation results firstly with regard to the session topics and secondly with regard to the implicit collective (post-) digital positions within the sessions.

2.3.1 Session Topics as Focus Metaphors: Transgressions of Traditional Boundaries of Cultural and Cultural Education Genres

In the session planning phase of our *BarCamp*, aesthetic practices became detached from their traditional institutional settings. Classical genre designations of creative and leisure activities, such as dance, target shooting, and cooking, were initially proposed, but were not chosen to be realized as session topics by the participants. Instead of the topic 'target shooting', for example, games are categorized as *eSports*. The proposed and chosen session topic *OnStage* refers to any kind of performance, such as theater, comedy, musical, and dance, but also *standup comedy*, *poetry slams*, and *pechakucha*. English terms that probably have been mainly acquired on the Internet are often preferred to German terms, especially to institutionally established genre designations (e.g., 'Performance im Haus' instead of 'Aufführung im Haus', 'Poetry' instead of 'Dichtung', 'Storytelling' instead of 'Geschichten erzählen'). The *OnStage* session particularly caught our attention, since it signifies a transformation and transgression of the traditional concept of a stage (in the sense of a tangible, spatially delimited stage of a theater) to an imagined, open, improvised stage that corresponds to the situation of media presence and loss of control over one's own visibility that we already found in our group discussions. Shared imagination and performative practice are suffice to be (or feel to be) 'on stage'. Formerly indispensable roles such as 'the director' or 'the actress' are replaced by an artistic-creative hybrid subject. This rather spontaneous form of staging oneself as part of a shared social experience contrasts with the painstaking preparation and performance of a classical (e.g., theater) production at the end of an arduous rehearsal phase. Following a similar logic, the keyword *#poetry* proposed (in English, in the place of traditional German terms like 'Poesie', 'Dichtung', or 'Lyrik') for another *BarCamp* session stands for the performative, situational performance in the sense of a 'poetry slam'. In its stage-like, public and improvisational character, it is juxtaposed with the 'poetry' as a matter of written or printed constellations of text, as well as juxtaposed with the more intimate connotations of 'poetry' in traditional youth culture, such as poems written into an autograph book or poems written as a part of love letters—poetry album.

Although it is worth noting that such practices are not necessarily accompanied by a break with more traditional forms of expression, what we find here is a shift from creative practices and the subject configurations that accompany them to more spontaneous, collective, and performative logics.

Classical artistic and creative activities such as acting, painting, making music, and dancing, which follow the traditional model of artistic subjectivity which is individually developed and 'educated' in the sense of the German term 'Bildung', are practiced and also discussed by some of the participants. However, in the collective process of choosing the *BarCamp* topics of highest interest, traditional formats were dismissed as topics in favor of the new and emergent formats of a networked era. Instead or in addition to traditional forms of creative (individual) subjectivity, these practices correspond to community-oriented and emancipatory creative processes, and also to hybrid, networked, and collective forms of creative subjectivity.

2.3.2 Four (Ideal) Types of Implicit Collective (Post-) Digital Orientations

The whole session schedule of our *BarCamps* can be seen as a range of the situated interests of the *BarCamp* participants. We used a reconstructive comparative analysis of the session plannings with regard to the media-structural logic of the individual sessions in order to distinguish differing media- and technology-related modes of sense-making and learning. We discovered collective forms of practice that range from the traditional to the new, among which we identify four different 'ideal types' (in a Weberian sense, cf. Swedberg & Agevall, 2005, p. 120):

1. Predigital mass media practices are characterized by sessions with a classical media orientation, such as television formats or chart or popular music, as well as by a tool-like access to media. These practices can be digital but do not have to be. The session 'Listening to Music and Painting' (the music was streamed, but could also have come from an analog medium) or the session 'Talk Show Love' with its explicit mass media reference falls into this category.
2. Digital technology-centered practices have an explicit focus on digitality. Sessions such as 'E-Sports', 'Artstyle and Storytelling in Video Games', or 'Net Activism' focus on digital-cultural expertise, digitally situated creative practices or forms of reflexivity related to digitality.
3. Post-digital spill-over practices introduce (whether implicitly digital or explicitly digitality-related) action into non-digital, material, and physical action contexts. These sessions, in which the structural embeddedness of digitally related gaming and performance formats in everyday life can be clearly seen, are modeled on Internet or digitally based formats, such as

(*adventure* and *jump'n'run*) video games or digital interactive storytelling. But they transfer their fascination into performances that are bodily co-present and thereby expand them, as in the sessions *Exitroom*, *creepypasta*, and *#poetry*.

4. Post-digital, partly inverse hybridizations were shown in sessions that are action-, space-, and body-oriented while at the same time situative and transient. In the post-digital state, the explicitly 'analog' element and the emphasis on the body receive special attention (again) and must be named, distinguished, and thus delimited from digitalized or, so to say, 'digitally contaminated' practices. At the same time, visibility, hybridity (e.g., also remix aesthetics), and affectivity are central points of reference, as they are in the culture of digitality. The sessions 'On Stage', 'Performance in the House', and 'Laughter Yoga in the Forest' can be categorized as such.

2.4 Case Studies: In-depth Analyses of Hybrid Creative Practices

In our study, we discovered a discrepancy between our observations on online platforms and teenage live environments. Whereas our online-based research uncovered a broad range of digital and post-digital creative practices, the group discussions we conducted as well as our quantitative data show that those kinds of active creative practice (as opposed to receptive practices) are much less frequent and much less common in (at least German) youth cultures. In order to better understand the nature of those active practices, we conducted case studies on digitalized and post-digitalized creative practices within teenage live environments. In the process, we specifically targeted participants of a local 'digital festival' organized by the city of Nuremberg in 2019.

Using the method of 'transactional interviews' and respective group settings, which is sensitized to the role of material and media artifacts for educational and social processes (Nohl, 2011; Nohl & Wulf, 2013), we researched the interconnectedness of subjects, media, spaces, and temporalities. The case studies show how digital, socio-technical architectures of computer applications (such as social media platforms) shape or preform aesthetic practices.

Figure 1 shows an exemplary process sequence for hybrid creative practices. Lara and Lara (names are pseudonyms; both girls have the same first name), two 12-year-old neighbors whom we met in the context of a so-called *coder-dojos*, presented to us in the interview, among other things, their short videos produced on and with the social media platform *TikTok* (about 12 seconds long). In some of these videos, humanoid cat figures appear that move

Creative and Artistic Learning in Post-digital Youth Culture... 377

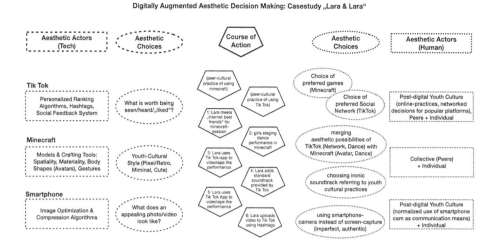

Fig. 1 Hybrid creative practices using the example of the case vignette 'Lara and Lara'

synchronously to music or spoken dialogues in the computer world of the online multiplayer game *Minecraft*. The videos flicker and abruptly change brightness and color. Lara and Lara staged them in collaboration with their *Internet Best-Friends* on *Minecraft* and took a video of this in-game performance directly off their computer's screen using their smartphones. The shortest videos are part of a hybrid creative practice in which "human and non-human actors" (Nohl, 2014, p. 29) are significantly involved as follows:

1. The multiplayer online platform *Minecraft*, on whose servers the filmed events are interactively staged, has a specific affordance character that is attractive to young people due to its combination of manageable, reduced (retro) pixel aesthetics on the one hand and highly developed but easy-to-use crafting tools on the other hand (Niemeyer & Gerber, 2015). Creative actions can already be understood on this level as a socio-technically distributed process (implicit aesthetics and encoded action possibilities).
2. A socio-technical network emerges centered around the *hashtag Minecraft* on the platform *TikTok* in the form of a diffusely delimited collective that tends to be globally connected. From an ontological point of view, such a hashtag network consists, among other things, of actant-actor interactions of network protocols, data formats, and (prod-) user interactions (Galloway & Thacker, 2007), as well as 'memes' that possess both an aesthetic connectivity and a performative challenge character and are thus an essential

characteristic of distributed creative processes in social networks (Shifman, 2014).

3. With its audio-visually centered interface structure, which is internally strongly based on Artificial Intelligence and personalizing ranking algorithms, *TikTok* itself represents a platform-specific field of appearance, which, even before any active interaction or selection, offers users specific videos and sound tracks for imitation or further use.

4. The chosen interface or hardware, the computer on which *Minecraft* is played, and the smartphone used to film the computer screen, trim the video, link it to the soundtrack and hashtag, and upload it to *TikTok*, are all essential to the creative process.

5. Within these interconnected socio-technical constellations, Lara and Lara bring in aesthetic and staging decisions that correspond to a habitus marked by youth culture, playfulness, and the love of games, while at the same time testifying to a high level of reflexivity marked by (self-)ironical elements of their stagings.

3   Conclusion

In post-digital culture, the familiar, institutionalized, and established boundaries, for example, between disciplines such as dance, music, or theater, but also between audience and creators, the subjects of experts and lay people, between the activities of making, marketing (sharing), and receiving, are increasingly dissolving—or else they are being reframed and acquiring new meanings in networked practices.

Staging, performativity, and enactment—a life *OnStage*—become basic elements of a post-digital dispositive, and thus may often serve as a purpose and motivating factor, for creative activities. Against this background, the long-term build-up of expertise with relatively steep learning curves, as is usual in the context of classical cultural pedagogical learning fields (such as in the music, art, or dance school paradigm), seems to be replaced or at least supplemented by temporary, project-like, more flexible network logics with flatter learning curves.

Material and traditional aesthetic-creative and artistic practices are intertwined in different ways with digital technologies and applications. An application in the sense of hybrid creativity arises where algorithms actively incorporate aesthetic knowledge into design processes; a collective and collaborative creativity arises where networking technologies merge with net-cultural practices (hashtags, memes, and channels). Overall, algorithmically organized commercial platforms such as *TikTok*, *Instagram*, *YouTube*, *Snapchat*, or *Twitter* play a central, practically ineluctable role in this process. This indicates a significant shift. In classical (Western) forms of individualized creative practice, the creative subject appears at the same time as the expert subject of a specific (aesthetic) knowledge, ability, and judgment. The creative process then appears as an inner-subjective process of decision making, which is articulated in the efficacious engagement and effort put into the artistic work. Knowledge and ability thereby refer to historical, institutionalized, discursive aesthetic practices (e.g., 'the arts').

In post-digital forms of creative practice, aesthetic expertise seems to be increasingly hybridized (implicit aesthetic knowledge of software, apps, and gadgets); the incentive to create seems to be governmentalized (creativity imperative and attention economy); institutional practices give way to far more fluid forms: memes, remix materials, and platform trends (e.g., influencers). Post-digital artistic authorship refers (increasingly with the new generations) to post-anthropocene, socio-technical hybrid subjects (collective, networked, and algorithmized). This implies that learning (at least with regard to aesthetic practices) should be observed not only as an individual but as a collective process that includes also non-human actors (such as observing and learning algorithms, observing and learning digital and material designs). When bodily practices become ever more, and in ever more complex ways, not only intertwined with technological designs and interfaces but also *defined by* the technical and logical conditions involved in those processes, in the sense that those processes contribute to the formation and habitualization of bodily practices in general—and especially with regard to young people—than the question of which actors have the power to define those conditions, and thus define the bodies and subjects we may learn to be(come), is a crucial one.

References

Albert, M., Hurrelmann, K., Quenzel, G., Schneekloth, U., Leven, I., Utzmann, H., & Wolfert, S. (2019). *Jugend 2018–19. Shell Jugendstudie: Eine Generation meldet sich zu Wort*. Beltz.

Aufenanger, S. (2015). Wie die neuen Medien Kindheit verändern. Kommunikative, kognitive und soziale Einflüsse der Mediennutzung. *merz - medien + erziehung*, 2015, 2.

Baym, N. K. (2015). *Personal Connections in the Digital Age*. John Wiley & Sons.

Boellstorff, T. (2008). *Coming of Age in Second Life: An Anthropologist Explores the Virtually Human*. Princeton University Press.

Bohnsack, R. (2017). *Praxeologische Wissenssoziologie*. UTB.

Calmbach, M., Borgstedt, S., Borchard, I., Thomas, P. M., & Flaig, B. B. (2016). *Wie ticken Jugendliche 2016? Lebenswelten von Jugendlichen im Alter von 14 bis 17 Jahren in Deutschland*. Springer-Verlag.

Cramer, F. (2015). What Is 'Post-digital'? *A Peer-Reviewed Journal About*. Retrieved from http://www.aprja.net/?p=1318

Engel, J., & Jörissen, B. (2019). Unsichtbare Sichtbarkeiten. Kontrollverlust und Kontrollphantasmen in öffentlichen und jugendkulturellen Digitalisierungsdiagnosen. In T. Alkemeyer, N. Buschmann, & T. Etzemüller (Eds.), *Gegenwartsdiagnosen. Kulturelle Formen gesellschaftlicher Selbstproblematisierung in der Moderne* (pp. 549–568). Transcript.

Feierabend, S., Plankenhorn, T., & Rathgeb, T. (2018). *JIM 2018. Jugend, Information, (Multi-) Media. Basisstudie zum Medienumgang 12- bis 19-Jähriger in Deutschland*. Medienpädagogischer Forschungsverbund Südwest.

Fuhse, J. A., & Mützel, S. (2010). *Relationale Soziologie: Zur Kulturellen Wende der Netzwerkforschung*. VS Verlag.

Galloway, A. R., & Thacker, E. (2007). *The Exploit: A Theory of Networks*. University of Minnesota Press.

Herring, S. C., Kouper, I., Paolillo, J. C., Scheidt, L. A., Tyworth, M., Welsch, P., Wright, E., & Ning Yu. (2005). Conversations in the Blogosphere: An Analysis 'From the Bottom Up'. *Proceedings of the 38th Annual Hawaii International Conference on System Sciences*, pp. 107b–107b. https://doi.org/10.1109/HICSS.2005.167

Hugger, K., Tillmann, A., Bader, J., Cwielong, I., & Kratzer, V. (2013). Kids Mobile Gaming: Mobiles Spielen bei Kindern im Alter von 6 bis 13 Jahren. *Diskurs Kindheits- und Jugendforschung, 8*(2), 13–14.

Jörissen, B. (2003). Who's Online? Anthropological Remarks on the Construction of Self and Other in Computer-Mediated Communication. In B. Qvarsell & C. Wulf (Eds.), *Culture and Education*. Waxmann.

Jörissen, B. (2004). Virtual Reality on the Stage. Performing Community at a LAN-Party. In P. Hernwall (Ed.), *Envision. The New Media Age and Everyday Life*. Stockholm University. Retrieved from http://www.uni-magdeburg.de/iew/joerissen/web/material/joerissen_virtualrealityonthestage.pdf

Jörissen, B. (2019). *Postdigital Transformation of Aesthetics & Aesthetic Education*. YouTube-Playlist. Retrieved from https://www.youtube.com/playlist?list=PLhXEPPnT87bzAUEuPZvXy4vC6xuIH8hoZ

Keuchel, S., & Riske, S. (2020). Postdigitale kulturelle Jugendwelten. Zentrale Ergebnisse der quantitativen Erhebung. In A. Scheunpflug & S. Timm (Eds.), *Forschung zur kulturellen Bildung* (pp. S79–S98). Springer VS.

Kitchin, R., & Dodge, M. (2011). *Code/Space: Software and Everyday Life*. MIT Press.

Kontopodis, M., Varvantakis, C., & Wulf, C. (Eds.). (2017). *Global Youth in Digital Trajectories*. Routledge.

Loos, P., & Schäffer, B. (2013). *Das Gruppendiskussionsverfahren: Theoretische Grundlagen und empirische Anwendung*. Springer-Verlag.

Marotzki, W. (2003). Online-Ethnographie—Wege und Ergebnisse zur Forschung im Kulturraum Internet. In B. Bachmair, P. Diepold, & C. de Witt (Eds.), *Jahrbuch Medienpädagogik 3* (pp. 149–165). Leske + Budrich.

Meuser, M., & Nagel, U. (2009). The Expert Interview and Changes in Knowledge Production. In A. Bogner, B. Littig, & W. Menz (Hrsg.), *Interviewing Experts* (pp. 17–42). Palgrave Macmillan UK. https://doi.org/10.1057/9780230244276_2

Niemeyer, D. J., & Gerber, H. R. (2015). Maker Culture and Minecraft: Implications for the Future of Learning. *Educational Media International, 52*(3), 216–226. https://doi.org/10.1080/09523987.2015.1075103

Nohl, A.-M. (2011). *Pädagogik der Dinge*. Klinkhardt.

Nohl, A.-M. (2014). Bildung und konjunktive Transaktionsräume. In F. von Rosenberg & A. Geimer (Hrsg.), *Bildung unter Bedingungen kultureller Pluralität* (pp. 27–40). Springer Fachmedien. https://doi.org/10.1007/978-3-531-19038-9_3

Nohl, A.-M., & Wulf, C. (Eds.). (2013). *Mensch und Ding: Die Materialität pädagogischer Prozesse*. VS Verlag für Sozialwissenschaften. Retrieved from https://www.springer.com/de/book/9783658035006

Pasquale, F. (2015). *The Black Box Society: The Secret Algorithms That Control Money and Information*. Harvard University Press.

Poster, M. (2001). *What's the Matter with the Internet?* University of Minnesota Press.

Poster, M. (2006). *Information Please: Culture and Politics in the Age of Digital Machines*. Duke University Press.

Rat für Kulturelle Bildung. (2019). *JUGEND / YOUTUBE/ KULTURELLE BILDUNG. HORIZONT 2019*. Rat für Kulturelle Bildung. Retrieved from https://www.rat-kulturelle-bildung.de/fileadmin/user_upload/pdf/Studie_YouTube_Webversion_final.pdf

Reckwitz, A. (2017). *The Invention of Creativity: Modern Society and the Culture of the New*. John Wiley & Sons.

Rheingold, H. (1994). *The Virtual Community: Finding Connection in a Computerized World*. Minerva.

Sandbothe, M., & Marotzki, W. (Eds.). (2000). *Subjektivität und Öffentlichkeit. Kulturwissenschaftliche Grundlagenprobleme virtueller Welten*. Herbert von Halem.

Shifman, L. (2014). *Memes in Digital Culture*. MIT Press.

Srnicek, N. (2016). *Platform Capitalism*. John Wiley & Sons.

Stalder, F. (2016). *Kultur der Digitalität*. Suhrkamp.

Swedberg, R., & Agevall, O. (2005). *The Max Weber Dictionary: Key Words and Central Concepts*. Stanford University Press.

Turkle, S. (1995). *Life on the Screen: Identity in the Age of the Internet*. Simon & Schuster.

Weber, S. M. (2009). Großgruppenverfahren als Methoden transformativer Organisationsforschung. In S. Kühl, P. Strodtholz, & A. Taffertshofer (Eds.), *Handbuch Methoden der Organisationsforschung* (pp. 145–179). VS Verlag für Sozialwissenschaften. https://doi.org/10.1007/978-3-531-91570-8_8

White, H. C. (2008). *Identity and Control: How Social Formations Emerge*. Princeton University Press.

Mind the Body: Mindfulness Meditation as a Spiritual Practice Between Neuroscience, Therapy and Self-awareness

Andreas Nehring

The Buddhist concept of mindfulness meditation (Conze, 1969; Anālayo, 2017; Williams & Kabat-Zinn, 2013; Bhikkhu Sujato, 2012; Cousins, 1994–1996; Crosby, 2013; Gethin, 2011; Jordt, 2007) is currently being met with broad receptivity in various social functional areas. Understood by its advocates as a non-denominational practice of self-awareness, mindfulness meditation is one of the most important phenomena of what various socio-theoretical approaches call 'spirituality', as distinguished from 'religion'. Against this background, mindfulness meditation can be seen as a magnifying glass for the socio-cultural figurations of 'spirituality' in Western societies (Nehring & Ernst, 2013). Oscillating between therapy and religious experience, scientific subject matter and pedagogical concept, mindfulness meditation offers a way to ask how the added value of an implicit 'spiritual'[1] certainty, practised and transformed in meditation, is expressed discursively in different social functional areas.

---

[1] John Welwood has coined the term 'spiritual bypassing' (Welwood, 2002). See also: Sherrell & Simmer-Brown, 2017; Fossella, 2011).

A. Nehring (✉)
University of Erlangen, Erlangen, Germany

© The Author(s), under exclusive license to Springer Nature Switzerland AG 2022
A. Kraus, C. Wulf (eds.), *The Palgrave Handbook of Embodiment and Learning*,
https://doi.org/10.1007/978-3-030-93001-1_24

1 General Aspects of Mindfulness

The term 'mindfulness' describes a self-reflexive form of attention control in which one's own experience of a situation is reflected upon from the perspective of a second-order observation within the framework of a meditative practice. The aim is a non-judgemental, neutral attitude in which thoughts and feelings are observed in the process of their coming into being and passing away.

As an attitude of emotional and rational acceptance of a given state, mindfulness results in insight into the dynamics of conscious thought processes and a deeper awareness of the interweaving of thought processes with physical constitutions (psychosomatic feedback).

Through its connection with the experiential situation of a meditative practice, that is a ritualized technique, the concept of mindfulness represents the possibility of a conscious experience of the interweaving of habitualized and automatized evaluational and emotional patterns with an implicit knowledge of the body. This experience is supposed to open up scope for shaping and changing them in everyday experience.

Borrowed to a large extent from the Buddhist tradition of Vipassanā (Anālayo, 2006), these qualities of mindfulness have been made available for therapeutic purposes in medicine and psychology by the American molecular biologist Jon Kabat-Zinn, among others. Since the late 1970s, these qualities have formed a therapeutic programme called 'Mindfulness-Based-Stress-Reduction' (MBSR) and have been used with great success in the treatment of a wide range of psychosomatic and physical illnesses (Kabat-Zinn, 1990; Badham & King, 2019; Hickey, 2010).

Although the exercises used today are derived from the Buddhist meditation techniques, they have only found their present form through encounter with Western culture and its understanding of individual experience (McMahan, 2008; King, 2019; Husgafvel, 2016). Both a philosophical concept and a meditation practice, mindfulness has been appropriated in the West since the early twentieth century and is currently receiving considerable attention in science, religion, the educational system and popular culture, far beyond medicine and psychotherapy. It is no exaggeration to say that mindfulness is currently the most popular buzzword when it comes to the training of consciousness.

In the business world, mindfulness meditation is recommended to stressed employees and managers as a means of burn-out prevention. In medicine, psychology and cognitive neuroscience, research is being conducted into the health-promoting effects of mindfulness meditation. Philosophers such as Thomas Metzinger call for mindfulness meditation at schools to familiarize children with the dynamics of their own consciousness and its physical effects (Metzinger, 2017; Metzinger, 2009). In pedagogy, mindfulness is discussed as a practice of self-care and a tool for preserving the joy of learning (Bache, 2008; Flores, 2017). In conferences between Buddhists and neuroscientists, the effects of mindfulness meditation on the brain are debated,[2] and in the media landscape, where the increased public attention towards mental illness is translated into questions of personal lifestyle, mindfulness meditation is presented reflexively as a contemporary offer of meaning to life. This area can be described as 'popular mindfulness discourses'.

In order to adequately assess the variety of references to mindfulness in science and society, it is necessary to focus on the interaction between the various socio-cultural receptions and applications of mindfulness. This focus, which is missing from some of the previous research, is necessary not only to deepen our knowledge of the (empirically validated) psychological effectiveness of mindfulness (Sauer, 2011), but also to better understand the social and cultural prerequisites of the concept.

The acceptance and effectiveness of mindfulness overlap in the therapeutic, religious and educational functional areas. Acceptance, in turn, can only be explained by highlighting the cultural prerequisites. An approach into this discursive field from the perspective of cultural studies can, to my mind, show more than just the crispness of empirical research. Therefore, I attempt to look at the enormous amount of research that has been done in this field in recent decades from an abstract perspective by taking into account the interactions of psycho-social dynamics. The question of why mindfulness meditation in particular is so popular at present is thus seen as highly relevant in its apparent simplicity. As a step towards an understanding of what makes this meditation practice so attractive in contemporary culture, I will address a few key considerations.

2 Cultural Studies Approaches

A cultural studies approach considers the concept of mindfulness under contemporary conditions. Mindfulness as a practice is interwoven with discourses of its legitimation and interpretation, that is with explicit semantics. It is an

---

[2] See a critical review of the Mind & Life conferences with the Dalai Lama (Samuel, 2014; Lopez Jr., 2008).

epistemological triviality, but in contrast to positivist attempts that empirically confirm the often unquestioned 'effectiveness' of mindfulness, it should be emphasized that these semantics are not only derived from interpretations of what is 'experienced' in meditative practice, but they also structure the experiential dimension of an engaged meditation practice in the form of expectations and pre-settings. In a way, albeit from a different perspective, this has also been highlighted by David Chalmers (Chalmers, 1997) in his discussion on the methodological problems of the neuro-phenomenological approach suggested by Francisco Varela, Evan Thompson and Eleanor Rosch in their book *The Embodied Mind* (Varela et al., 1991). In this highly influential publication, they argue for an 'enactive approach' which could bridge the third-person perspective of science and the first-person perspective of individual experience. The authors explicitly refer to Buddhism as a means to overcome the gap "between the human mind as studied by science and the mind as personally experienced" (Rosch, 2017, p. 1). Chalmers argues,

> Of course, there are deep methodological problems here. The first is the old problem that the mere act of attention to one's experience transforms that experience. As we become more patient and careful, we may find that we are studying data that are transformed in subtle ways. This is not too much of a problem at the start of investigation—we have a long way to go until this degree of subtlety even comes into play—but it may eventually lead to deep paradoxes of observership. (Chalmers, 1997, p. 39)

I will argue from a different perspective. What makes the phenomenon of the multidimensional reception of mindfulness so exciting is that in the discussion on mindfulness, we can recognize the application of a superordinate social and cultural studies question. That is the question of how, in a given historical situation, the boundary between an experience accessible only to the individual consciousness (from the perspective of the first person) and its re-presentation in communication, i.e. externalized, stabilized and objectifiable for reflective observation (from the perspective of the third person), is drawn by means of media such as language, visual media and bodily practices. The question is whether mindfulness as a sensory experience (consciousness) that can only be experienced privately has something to do with public forms of negotiating mindfulness in social discourses (communication). This relates to one of the core questions of methodology in Religious Studies with regard to the analysis of religious experience (Proudfoot, 1985; Taves, 2009; Sharf, 1998).

Every cultural studies approach to mindfulness must develop not only a systematic cultural-analytical understanding of mindfulness but also a historico-cultural-comparative analysis of the reception of mindfulness in 'Western' and 'Eastern' discourses.

The contemporary reception of mindfulness in North America and Europe is, in many ways, layered by cultural exchange and transfer relations. One recalls, for example, the great line of reception of Buddhism since the nineteenth century (Prebish & Baumann, 2002; Batchelor, 1994; Coleman, 2001; Prebish & Tanaka, 1998; Tweed, 1992). But this is only one dimension of the phenomenon. For not only are the sources of the respective Buddhist interpretation of mindfulness itself extremely heterogeneous; mindfulness is not even necessarily Buddhist, and therefore it only fits to a limited extent into the stereotypes of a West-East cultural transfer. The reception of mindfulness in Europe is not directly 'Asian' in its essential parts, it is moreover mediated through discourses from the cultural area of North America (which is different from Europe).

Similarly, in a systematic cultural-analytical perspective, the reception of mindfulness cannot be reduced to the functional area of the religious sphere and its discourse on the quality of religious experience. Rather, mindfulness stands for a subsystem-wide offer of meaning that can be addressed as 'spirituality' (Carrette & King, 2005). In the background here is a term borrowed from the sociological research of knowledge: 'spirituality' (Knoblauch, 2009). Spirituality in a sociological understanding describes various forms of searching for personal meaning that are not bound to organizations and that can be defined as 'religious' but do not have to be.

Following Thomas Luckmann (Luckmann, 1967), Hubert Knoblauch has argued that the plausibility of the term 'spirituality' lies in the offer of a deep existential personal experience to the individual. This happens within the framework of a popular form of communication, that is a highly generalized, broadly connectable cultural form open to various interpretations, which is easy to learn, does not require any special prerequisites for participation and can be applied to almost all areas of life.

The concept of spirituality can epistemologically be conceived as an experiential dimension of implicit certainty, which is experienced and brought to life as the basis of a process of interpretation based on meaning.

Mindfulness aims at the development of the first-person perspective and thus at a self-perception through introspection. Introspection, however, is considered an inescapably subjective phenomenon that is not valid in scientific argumentation because it is not subject to observation and intersubjective comparison. This becomes very clear in a conversation between Mattieu Ricard and Wolf Singer. Ricard argues:

It is not enough to think hard about how the mind might function and then come up with complex theories, as Freud did, for example. Such intellectual adventures cannot replace 2000 years of direct exploration of the workings of the mind through thorough introspection by experienced practitioners who have already achieved stability and clarity. Even the most sophisticated theory of a brilliant thinker, if it is not based on empirical evidence, cannot be compared to the accumulated experience of hundreds of people, each of whom has spent dozens of years exploring the most subtle aspects of the mind through direct experience. (Singer & Ricard, 2008, p. 11f.)

This statement shows that it is not appropriate to speak of a lack of observability, but one has to focus on the positions of observation, since the phenomenologically interesting potency of human consciousness consists in being able to observe itself self-reflectively. Consciousness is always consciousness of something and therefore of oneself as well. The problem that arises is the insertion of subject and object of observation. How can people cognitively perceive, classify and symbolically transform the world, and at the same time apply these processes, which let reality come into being, to themselves? The human being draws a picture of him/herself as a subject equipped with a consciousness. These basic assumptions of phenomenology are now reactivated in various ways in the mindfulness discourse: For example human beings transcend themselves through this ego-centrism, or in the conception of the 'mind' as a counterpart to the 'brain', as is discussed in detail in the debates on the philosophy of mind and for the freedom of will.

3 Meditation as a Body Technique, Connection to Neuroscience

In mindfulness meditation, however, introspection takes place on two reciprocally restricted levels, the physical and the mental. As already mentioned, it is a physical technique that seeks to influence consciousness through the body by first placing the body in the focus of attention, that is in the meditation terminology 'experiencing mindfulness'. The two central techniques are respiration and body scanning, somatically comprehensible for example in the measurement of heart rate and oxygen consumption. In this revitalization of the body-mind relationship, a closure to the inside is carried out in such a way that an interruption of the continuity of constant further differentiation of the self through new experiences is carried out through the interaction of body and mind, which is usually associated with the charged concept of the 'holistic'.

A central assumption in the popular discourse on modernity is now that a new quality of a claim to self-location within one's biography is emerging for individuals, within the framework of differentiation processes on a social level. Due to the demands of contingency compensation, the decision-making processes become more complex, etc. it becomes more difficult to maintain the unity of the self or of 'wholeness' postulated as existential. Pathologies such as depression and burn-out emerge and are attested to as symptoms of social change, especially in working conditions. Meditation is supposed to offer a problem-solving strategy as well as a preventive measure at this very point.

Of course, the functionality of introducing meditation practices into everyday life can be questioned. As a social practice, mindfulness, despite its supposed distancing from all claims and dogmatic positions, is far from being a non-normative practice. In every discourse in which mindfulness meditation is received, this meditation practice is ideologically enriched according to the rules and guidelines of the respective discourse; that is it is placed under the conditions of that discourse. As mentioned above, this can include a definite reference to Buddhism but does not have to. Accordingly, the high adaptability of mindfulness is a socio-cultural indicator, namely an indicator for not least being attractive for various ideological enrichments in contemporary society.

A central prerequisite for the highly discursive adaptability of mindfulness seems to be that mindfulness as a practice of reflexive self-correction can be applied in everyday life. Whether in a medical, psychological or pedagogical understanding of therapy and education or as a philosophical-ideological concept, the tenor is that mindfulness increases the distance to 'faulty' states of consciousness, such as those caused by illness, painful relationships or attentiveness disorder.

Popular culture helps to control processes of individual self-management, that is to make offers in relation to lifestyles and so on, which are a special form of communication because they usually have a very clear narrative dramaturgy. In mindfulness meditation, for example, one finds above all a semantics of benefit for health, the psyche, but also for the individual meaning of life. As a form of spirituality, the successful model of mindfulness meditation consists of making a promise within the framework of one's own individualization, one's own 'personality development' and one's own 'bio-graphy', which refers to the function of the 'popular' (Knoblauch, 2009, p. 152).

This theoretical framework—that is understanding spirituality as a popular form of semantization and explication of individual experiences—allows us to elaborate the special nature of mindfulness meditation between religion, therapy, education and 'technologies of the self' (Foucault et al., 1988). The reference to Buddhist traditions of self-liberation or self-redemption is obvious here.

Significantly, Buddhism is understood to promote a subjectivist approach, something which is reinforced in interpretations intended for Western readers. The subject, it is emphasized, is the ultimate foundation of Buddhist religion, both the starting point of the perception of reality, which is understood as suffering, and the potential for salvation from it (Wallace, 2004; Reddy & Roy, 2019). According to Nyanaponika Thera (Nyanaponika, 1965), whose works were fundamental to the reception of mindfulness meditation in the USA, the subjectivist perspective of Buddhism culminates in its self-understanding as "the doctrine of mind" (Nyanaponika, 2007, p. 14f.), which is about recognizing, forming and liberating the mind—which Nyanaponika synonymously describes as 'consciousness'—through the practice of mindfulness. In discourses on mindfulness meditation, this subjectivistic character of the teachings of the Buddha is emphasized in a specific way by referring to the personal-individual character of the knowledge acquired through meditation. Nyanaponika speaks of mindfulness meditation as the 'path of self-help', which he considers to be the actually real help.

However, that this is already a normative construction becomes clear not only from Nyanaponika's resolute dismissal of teachings "which claim that human beings can only be redeemed by the grace of a God" (Nyanaponika, 2007, p. 165), but rather from the fact that the 'path of self-help' requires explicit legitimation, which consists in seeing mindfulness meditation as one of the remedies against the 'degeneration of humanity', against the 'catastrophes' of self-destruction that were to be observed in Christian Europe in the twentieth century, as well as against the 'mindless distractions'. Mindfulness, on the other hand, promotes the "unfolding of a high and supreme humanity, the true superhuman, of whom so many spirits have dreamed and to whom so many misdirected efforts have been made" (Nyanaponika, 2007, p. 21f.). It would therefore be naïve to believe that mindfulness meditation is only about the subjective path of self-liberation. Mindfulness meditation is a collective practice that aims to train a form of certainty that is socially predetermined and thus also under ideological assumptions. Mindfulness is a state of certainty.

4   Thich Nhat Hanh: Mindfulness and Interbeing

In the broad reception of the writings of the Vietnamese monk Thich Nhat Hanh, a 'spiritual' interpretation of mindfulness in the religious sense prevails, whereby the boundaries between the therapeutic scene and the esoteric scene that refer to him must be described as fluid. Thich Nhat Hanh adapts practices and teachings from the Theravāda tradition as well as from Mahāyāna, both of which are represented in his country. Known as expressions of a politicized 'engaged Buddhism', his books are dedicated to the connection of the concept of mindfulness with the holistic philosophy of 'inter-being', a mystically accentuated theory of conditional emergence. 'Interbeing' is an artificial term coined by Nhat Hanh himself and is meant to express the mutual connectedness of all beings. Nhat Hanh's claim is to rehearse the experience of that connectedness through mindfulness meditation. As early as 1966 he founded his own order, the Tiep Hien Order (Order of Interbeing), which can be considered an important nucleus of mindfulness centres throughout the world today.

Through the writings of Thich Nhat Hanh, alongside those of authors such as Alan Watts, Jack Kornfield, Joseph Goldstein or Jon Kabat-Zinn, mindfulness has become so popular that in the meantime it does not seem possible to identify clear lines of reception, nor does it seem sensible to assign it to one religious tradition. For it is precisely in mindfulness centres that the concept of mindfulness has been decontextualized in such a way that it can be developed into a unified doctrine of contemplation that combines Western and Eastern mystical traditions. A well-known example of this in Germany is the former Benedictine monk Willigis Jäger, who represented a mystical form of spirituality based on a universalistic concept of religious experience (Nehring, 2005). Mindfulness centres are thus places where therapeutic and religious practice overlap to such an extent that it seems more appropriate to speak of 'popularized spirituality' (Knoblauch, 2009) than of Buddhist tradition in the narrower sense.

With the concept of mindfulness, Nhat Hanh tries to fructify the practice of meditation for positive change in everyday life, especially in social relations. He argues that, as a form of emotional and rational concentration on a given state, mindfulness results in insights into the dynamics of one's own thought processes. The aim is to achieve a deeper awareness of the interweaving of thought processes with the object world and the social environment. Accordingly, mindfulness not only causes fundamental changes in the perception of one's own self and its relationship to reality, but also a changed practice of relating to the world resulting from this perception. With the help of the observer position, which can be taken up in meditation through introspection, the unity of reality should be realized/experienced.

The decisive factor for Nhat Hanh is that this experience is an intentionally aspired-to state within the meditation practice, a state which on the one hand was promised in advance in the mediation of the technique, and on the other hand is intended to evoke the living connection with reality as an ethical attitude. One can therefore speak of an initiated translation process from explicit to implicit knowledge. The propagated All-unity is to be internalized to the extent that it becomes physically manifest:

> You are conscious of the presence of bodily form, feeling, perception, mental functionings, and consciousness. You observe these 'objects' until you see that each of them has intimate connection with the world outside yourself: if the world did not exist then the assembly of the five aggregates could not exist either [...]. You meditate on them until you are able to see the presence of the reality of one-ness in your own self, and can see that your own life and the life of the universe are one. (Nhat Hanh, 1976, p. 47f.)

Nhat Hanh develops mindfulness meditation, which focuses on the emergence in interdependence and the interrelation of reality, as a method of introspection. "It is a penetration of mind into mind itself" (Nhat Hanh, 1976, p. 45). This penetration is decidedly delimited from rational approaches: "Meditation is not a discursive reflection on a philosophy of interdependence, but rather one's own powers of concentration should be developed to reveal the real nature of the object being contemplated" (Nhat Hanh, 1976, p. 45). In this way the first-person perspective, self-perception through introspection, becomes the starting point for the perception of reality. Introspection—as an inescapably subjective method of observation—is thus removed from scientific observation from the third-person perspective and thus also from intersubjective discourse. It aims at an experience that can only be undergone by oneself or at a qualitative 'perception'. Nhat Hanh spuds in at the interface of the observer position in the first-person perspective and the second-person perspective. Consciousness is, as mentioned above, always consciousness of something and also of oneself. Starting from a certainty of reference to one's own thinking and consciousness, Nhat Hanh sees meditation as a method to guide human consciousness to reflexively observe itself and connect to one's bodily experience.

> Breath is the bridge which connects life to consciousness, which unites your body to your thoughts. Whenever your mind becomes scattered, use your breath as the means to take hold of your mind again. (Nhat Hanh, 1976, p. 15)

The unity of body and thought cannot be achieved in conceptual reflection, but in the holistic meditative practice of perception and experience, which interweaves the perspectives of the first and second person. The meditator creates a self-image as a subject endowed with consciousness. This consciousness can reflexively refer to the subject as well as to the world as an object in such a way that the meditator transcends them through meditative self-reference—that is, that reflection is suspended in self-reflection.

Nhat Hanh has formulated this process in the theses of the 'Seven Miracles of Mindfulness', which have become basic articles on the websites of numerous mindfulness centres throughout Europe:[3]

1. Mindfulness is about bringing out our authentic presence, making us alive in the here and now and getting in touch with things.
2. Mindfulness makes us realize that life is already there. We can really be in contact with it and give it meaning and depth.
3. Mindfulness gives life force to the object of our contemplation, touches and embraces it. This makes ourselves alive and life becomes more real.
4. Mindfulness mediates concentration. When we concentrate in our everyday life, we will be able to look at everything more deeply and understand it better.
5. Mindfulness enables us to look deeply and allows us to better recognize the object of our observation outside and inside ourselves.
6. Mindfulness leads to understanding that comes from deep within ourselves. We gain clarity and thus the readiness for acceptance is encouraged.
7. Mindfulness leads to liberation through the insights thus gained. Wherever we practice mindfulness there is life, understanding and compassion.

What is interesting about these statements is that the experience itself is made a guarantor of presence and co-presence against an observer position from outside, which Nhat Hanh attributes to the natural sciences. The semantics of 'presence' takes on a central function in Nhat Hanh and in the further reception of his approach. Mindfulness is supposed to enable a sense of self as

---

[3] Since formulations differ and there are several versions of the seven theses on the web, I offer a summarized version here. Cf. http://www.intersein-zentrum.de/thich.html.

release from ego-centrism and, at the same time, a higher degree of empathy and social competence.

The Seven Miracles of Mindfulness describe a state that is supposed to be achieved through meditation practice using certain techniques. The aim is not so much the classical liberation from the karmic process of coming into being and passing away through insight into the nature of the dhammas, but rather a change in everyday practice in dealing with oneself and one's environment—increased self-perception becomes a guarantee of increased self-awareness in one's own social relations. The promise is well known: The difference between subject and object is to be overcome through this interaction of body and mind. This state of perception is described in the texts on mindfulness meditation under the label 'holistic', a term which at first sight can hardly be conveyed with the ideas of transience, suffering and non-self-ness from the texts of the Pali Canon. Nhat Hanh sees in this the special contribution of Mahāyāna:

> When reality is perceived in its nature of ultimate perfection, the practitioner has reached a level of wisdom called non-discrimination mind—a wondrous communion in which there is no longer any distinction made between subject and object. This isn't some far-off, unattainable state. Any one of us—by persisting in practicing even a little—can at least taste of it. (Nhat Hanh, 1976, p. 57)

5 Jon Kabat-Zinn: Mindfulness as Therapeutic Buddhism

Mindfulness meditation has become widely known in recent years, especially in therapeutic contexts. In particular, the method of *Mindfulness Based Stress-Reduction* (MBSR) developed in the USA by the American molecular biologist and physician Jon Kabat-Zinn has advertised this type of meditation as effective method for treating a wide range of diseases. From stress-induced mental illnesses, such as depression, anxiety disorders and somatoform pain disorders such as fibromyalgia and burn-out, to pain caused by illness, mindfulness meditation is praised as being successfully used to build greater tolerance for illness and improve pain management strategies.

Mindfulness Based Stress-Reduction is conceptualized as an eight-week course that combines elements from different meditation techniques. Kabat-Zinn has presented his approach in his book *Full Catastrophe Living* (Kabat-Zinn, 1990), which was published in Germany under the (somewhat more mundane) title *Gesund durch Meditation* (Kabat-Zinn, 2006). If one follows the instructions of this book, then mindfulness is seen by Kabat-Zinn as an exercise or path that should lead to inner peace and to insights. "Cultivating mindfulness can lead to the discovery of deep realms of relaxation, calmness, and insight within yourself" (Kabat-Zinn, 1990, p. 12).

A 'new territory, previously unknown to you or only vaguely suspected' is to be opened up to patients through mindfulness meditation. The path to a 'real self-understanding' promises healing. "The path to it in any moment lies no farther than your own body and mind and your own breathing" (Kabat-Zinn, 1990, p. 12). With the MBSR method, Kabat-Zinn decidedly refers to the Buddhist tradition and to Vipassanā meditation in particular, and emphasizes that he is thus taking up a practice which "has flourished over the past 2,500 years", and was not only practised in monasteries and among laypeople, but which is particularly widespread among the Western youth today "drawn by the remarkable interest in this country [US] in meditative practices" (Kabat-Zinn, 1990, p. 12).

While the reception of the concept of mindfulness in psychology focuses on the description of an attentive state of consciousness, Kabat-Zinn is aiming at more than that: Mindfulness is a 'path' or 'life path' that one has to follow. Kabat-Zinn sees himself as influenced by ideas of Buddhist ethics, but emphasizes that mindfulness meditation is an approach of universal validity.

> It can be learned and practiced, as we do in the stress clinic, without appealing to Oriental culture or Buddhist authority to enrich it or authenticate it […]. In fact one of its major strengths is that it is not dependent on any belief system or ideology, so that its benefits are therefore accessible for anyone to test for himself or herself. (Kabat-Zinn, 1990, p. 12)

As I already pointed out, the universalization and especially the decontextualization of Buddhist meditation practice by American meditation teachers such as Kabat-Zinn, or Jack Kornfield, Joseph Goldstein and Sharon Salzberg prepared the ground for the adaptation of the practice into the therapeutic context.

There are various interesting aspects of Kabat-Zinn and his reception of the meditation practice. The discrepancy between Buddhist religious and non-Buddhist scientific contextualization of the programme is obvious. In analysing MBSR, one can investigate the borderlines between religion and science. MBSR is the key phenomenon of what might be called 'therapeutic Buddhism'.

Mindfulness is described by Kabat-Zinn as a holistic body experience that differs from a state of 'dis-attention', whereby, according to the (controversial) parapsychologist Gary Schwartz, inattention—thinkably vague—is defined as "not attending to the relevant feedback messages of our body and our mind that are necessary for their harmonious functioning" (Kabat-Zinn, 1990, p. 228). Kabat-Zinn sees the disregard of physical signals to the psyche as the cause of most diseases and therefore conceives of MBSR as an attempt to sensitize the patient to interactions between psyche and body. As a central insight, Kabat-Zinn teaches an 'interconnectedness' not only of body and mind but, by means of 'feedback loops', of all individual systems in the body and the environment, which leads him to a theory of the embedding of the body in the environment and to the definition of health as a 'dynamic process'.

> If connectedness is crucial for physical integration and health, it is equally important psychologically and socially [...]. The web of interconnectedness goes beyond our individual psychological self. While we are whole ourselves as individual beings, we are also part of a larger whole, interconnected through our family and our friends and acquaintances to the larger society and ultimately to the whole of humanity and life on the planet. (Kabat-Zinn, 1990, p. 157)

The personal-individual disposition is seen as an activating potential for self-healing powers. A prerequisite for this is the perception of the body as a "universe in itself" that organizes itself and is equipped with cells that have the ability to

> regulate itself as a whole to maintain the internal balance and order [...]. The body accomplishes this inner balance through finely tuned feedback loops that interconnect all aspects of the organism. (Kabat-Zinn, 1990, p. 155)

With the help of a scientific superstructure, Kabat-Zinn designs an image of a human being as an entropy-producing system and establishes the 'holistic' perspective with the help of an analogy between the Buddhist concept of emergence in dependence (Pali: paticca-samuppāda; Skt: pratītya-samutpāda) and the so-called Gaia-hypothesis from systematic ecology, which is based on a systems-theoretical understanding of life. According to Kabat-Zinn, the body is able to adapt to its environment in a reactive and self-organizing (autopoiesis) way by means of the 'feedback loops' which connect all systems with each other. Kabat-Zinn thus ties in with approaches that have been developed in the environment of structural-functional and constructivist concepts in biology, anthropology and cognitive psychology by Gregory Bateson, Humberto Maturana, Francisco Varela and Eleanor Rosch. The Dutch scholar of religious studies Wouter J. Hanegraaff has aptly described this field of theory as New Age Science (Hanegraaff, 1996).

The central concept of Kabat-Zinn is, as already mentioned, 'interconnectedness', which marks the connection of mind and body and thus the 'wholeness' as well as the connection to all living beings. According to him, these idealistic, natural-philosophical speculations about 'being whole' make the difference between mindfulness meditation and other stress management techniques. (Kabat-Zinn, 1990, p. 164)

What is striking is not the attempt to scientifically enrich the MBSR concept, but that the MBSR programme combines the life form of mindfulness with a very strong concept of individuality. On the one hand, it uses the affirmation of stereotypical 'Eastern' ideas and practices to distance itself from stereotypical 'Western' concepts of individuality, but on the other hand, it formulates nothing but a promise of salvation for the individual, in so far as the individual has to "walk the path of mindfulness" (Kabat-Zinn, 1990, p. 441) in order to reach the state of 'being whole' with him- or herself.

6   Mind and Body

Three aspects I would like to highlight as results from the reflections above.

Deepened everyday experience—mindfulness as reframing of everyday experiences: Whether it is interpreted as 'just being' or as a radical acceptance of one's own existential 'Geworfen-Sein' into existence, mindfulness always carries with it the promise of an experience that is 'purer' precisely because it is 'unconditional'. It is interesting to note that it is not the moment of experience itself that is conceived as something 'deeper' (e.g. as in mysticism), but that the results of meditation should allow for a 'deeper' way of life. It is not the practice itself that is the plunge into a deeper layer of experience, but the results of the practice that lead to a changed and 'deeper' insight. Mindfulness does not refer to elevated or transcendental experiences of presence, but it promises a new framing of everyday presence, that is new perspectives on everyday life, which is to be achieved above all by training greater tolerance towards everyday states of consciousness.

Embodied consciousness—mindfulness as a consciousness technique of embodied experience: Meditation practice promises the prospect of a changed life practice through the perception of consciousness as embodied consciousness. Mindfulness is intended to provide the individual with ways and strategies for dealing with the states of consciousness on the basis of his/her implicit knowledge that is initially explicitly learned and then habitualized. For this purpose the embodiment of these states is made tangible, that is presented in meditation practice.

Difference-knowledge—body/mind—mindfulness as an insight into the transience of conscious states: Mindfulness meditation can be seen as a practice that provides the late modern subject with a difference-knowledge of the interaction of consciousness and body through the technique of consciousness conveyed in it. Consciousness is experienced as somatic consciousness. The sense and purpose of this practice seems to be to practice the phenomenal transience of states of consciousness and in this way to achieve a higher tolerance of affects and knowledge of dysfunctional states of consciousness. The existential self-presentation of motives such as transience is seen as an antidote to such dysfunctional states. What dysfunction is, however, is highly dependent on the respective discursive appropriation of mindfulness.

7   Conclusion

From the point of view of cultural studies, what is remarkable about mindfulness and its reception is that and how it is adapted in various discourses. Mindfulness obviously hits not only one but several nerves of Western lifestyle, it also carries an implicit normativity. As a social practice, mindfulness is, as mentioned before, anything but a non-normative practice despite its distancing from all claims and dogmatic positions. Mindfulness discourses take on a non-normative character that can be reflected upon precisely in its promise of purity, that is in the suppositional experience of 'pure perception', 'mere existence', 'immediate presence'.

The normative tenor is that mindfulness enables distancing from 'faulty' states of consciousness. Faulty attitudes and convictions must—in order to be recognized as faults—deviate from a norm. The obvious question, of course, is: Who defines the norm? Who defines what is 'dysfunctional'? In other words, the problem here is not that mindfulness as a social practice is necessarily normative, but the explicit attribution that mindfulness as a practice is 'neutral'. It is also striking that the correction achieved through mindfulness as practice is designed as a self-correction. As a popular form of spirituality, mindfulness can be read as a practice of self-care, which—like all conceptions of the self—is subject to historical-contingent conditions. Mindfulness is at the centre of the concepts of how individual self-care is normatively conveyed and conceived in late modern Western society.

Mindfulness meditation, as a physical practice, is a technique of consciousness that has undoubtedly therapeutic value. From an ideology-critical point of view, however, it presents itself as something like a problematic self-interpretation of today's Western societies, and especially of the demands that arise for the individual.

References

Anālayo. (2006). *Satipaṭṭhāna: The Direct Path to Realization*. Windhorse Publications.
Anālayo. (2017). *Early Buddhist Meditation Studies*. Barre Center for Buddhist Studies.
Bache, C. M. (2008). *The Living Classroom: Teaching and Collective Consciousness*. State University of New York Press.
Badham, R., & King, E. (2019). Mindfulness at Work: A Critical Review. *Organization*, 1–24.
Batchelor, S. (1994). *The Awakening of the West. The Encounter of Buddhism and Western Culture*. Paralax Press.
Bhikkhu Sujato (2012). *A History of Mindfulness. How Insight Worsted Tranquillity in the Satipaṭṭhāna Sutta*. .
Carrette, J., & King, R. (2005). *Selling Spirituality. The Silent Takeover of Religion*. Routledge.
Chalmers, D. (1997). Moving Forward on the Problem of Consciousness. *Journal of Consciousness, 4*(1), 3–46.
Coleman, J. W. (2001). *The New Buddhism. The Western Transformation of an Ancient Tradition*. Oxford University Press.
Conze, E. (1969). *Buddhist Meditation*. Harper & Row.
Cousins, L. S. (1994–1996). The Origin of Insight Meditation. *The Buddhist Forum, IV*, 35–58.
Crosby, K. (2013). *Traditional Theravada Meditation and Its Modern-Era Suppression*. Buddha Dharma Centre.
Flores, S. A. (2017). Contemplative Pedagogy: Mindfulness Methodology in Education & Human Development. *Journal of Education and Human Development, 6*(3), 65–69.
Fossella, T. (2011). Human Nature, Buddha Nature: On Spiritual Bypassing, Relationship, and the Dharma: An Interview with John Welwood. *Tricycle Magazine*.
Foucault, M., Martin, L. H., Gutman, H., & Hutton, P. H. (1988). *Technologies of the Self: A Seminar with Michel Foucault*. University of Massachusetts Press.
Gethin, R. (2011). On Some Definitions of Mindfulness. *Contemporary Buddhism, 12*(1), 263–279.
Hanegraaff, W. J. (1996). *New Age Religion and Western Culture. Esotericism in the Mirror of Secular Thought*. .

Hickey, W. S. (2010). Meditation as Medicine. A Critique. *CrossCurrents, 60*, 168–184.

Husgafvel, V. (2016). On the Buddhist Roots of Contemporary Non-Religious Mindfulness Practice: Moving Beyond Sectarian and Essentialist Approaches. *Temenos, 52*(1), 87–126.

Jordt, I. (2007). *Burma's Mass Lay Meditation Movement: Buddhism and the Cultural Construction of Power.* Ohio University Press.

Kabat-Zinn, J. (1990). *Full Catastrophe Living.* Dell Publishing.

Kabat-Zinn, J. (2006). *Gesund durch Meditation. Das große Buch der Selbstheilung.* Fischer.

King, R. (2019). Meditation and the Modern Encounter Between Asia and the West. In M. Farias, D. Brazier, & M. Lalljee (Eds.), *The Oxford Handbook of Meditation.* Oxford University Press.

Knoblauch, H. (2009). *Populäre Religion. Auf dem Weg in eine spirituelle Gesellschaft.* .

Lopez, D. S., Jr. (2008). *Buddhism & Science. A Guide for the Perplexed.* The University of Chicago Press.

Luckmann, T. (1967). *The Invisible Religion. The Problem of Religion in Modern Society.* .

McMahan, D. J. (2008). *The Making of Buddhist Modernism.* Oxford University Press.

Metzinger, T. (2009). *The Ego-Tunnel. The Science of the Mind and the Myth of the Self.* Basic Books.

Metzinger, T. (2017). Autonomie durch Achtsamkeit und Argumentationstheorie. *Bundesprüfstelle für jugendgefährdende Medien AKTUELL, 4*, 13–14.

Nehring, A. (2005). Die Erfindung der religiösen Erfahrung. In C. Strecker (Ed.), *Kontexte der Schrift, Kultur, Politik, Religion, Sprache, 2* (pp. 301–322). Kohlhammer.

Nehring, A., & Ernst, C. (2013). Populäre Achtsamkeit. Aspekte einer Meditationspraxis zwischen Präsenzerfahrung und implizitem Wissen. In C. Ernst & H. Paul (Eds.), *Präsenz und implizites Wissen. Zur Interdependenz zweier Schlüsselbegriffe der Kultur- und Sozialwissenschaften* (pp. 373–401). Transcript.

Nyanaponika Thera. (1965). *The Heart of Buddhist Meditation. A Handbook of Mental Training Based on Buddha's Way of Mindfulness.* Weiser Books.

Nyanaponika Thera. (2007). *Geistestraining durch Achtsamkeit. Die buddhistische Satipaṭṭhāna-Methode.* .

Prebish, C., & Baumann, M. (Eds.). (2002). *Westward Dharma. Buddhism Beyond Asia.* University of California Press.

Prebish, C., & Tanaka, K. K. (Eds.). (1998). *The Faces of Buddhism in America.* University of California Press.

Proudfoot, W. (1985). *Religious Experience.* University of California Press.

Reddy, J. S. K., & Roy, S. (2019). Understanding Meditation Based on the Subjective Experience and Traditional Goal: Implications for Current Meditation Research. *Frontiers in Psychology.* https://doi.org/10.3389/fpsyg.2019.01827

Rosch, E. (2017). *Introduction to The Embodied Mind* (2nd ed.). MIT Press.

Samuel, G. (2014). Between Buddhism and Science, Between Mind and Body. *Religions, 5*, 560–579.

Sauer, S. (2011), *Wirkfaktoren von Achtsamkeit. Wirkt Achtsamkeit durch Verringerung der affektiven Reaktivität?* .

Sharf, R. H. (1998). Experience. In M. C. Taylor (Ed.), *Critical Terms for Religious Studies* (pp. 94–116). The University of Chicago Press.

Sherrell, C., & Simmer-Brown, J. (2017). Spiritual Bypassing in the Contemporary Mindfulness Movement. *ICEA Journal, 1*(1).

Singer, W., & Ricard, M. (2008). *Hirnforschung und Meditation. Ein Dialog.* Suhrkamp.

Taves, A. (2009). *Religious Experience Reconsidered. A Building-Block Approach to the Study of Religion and Other Special Things.* Princeton University Press.

Thich Nhat Hanh. (1976). *The Miracle of Mindfulness: An Introduction to the Practice of Meditation.* Beacon Press.

Tweed, T. (1992). *The American Encounter with Buddhism 1844–1912. Victorian Culture and the Limits of Dissent.* .

Varela, F., Thompson, E., & Rosch, E. (1991). *The Embodied Mind: Cognitive Science and the Human Experience.* MIT Press.

Wallace, A. B. (2004). *The Taboo of Subjectivity. Toward a Science of Consciousness.* Oxford University Press.

Welwood, J. (2002). *Toward a Psychology of Awakening.* Shambhala Publications.

Williams, J. M. G., & Kabat-Zinn, J. (Eds.). (2013). *Mindfulness. Diverse Perspectives on its Meaning, Origins and Applications.* Routledge.

Part VI

Classroom Practices

When entering a classroom during a break, we see many different activities going on: pupils talking to each other, or interacting in other ways, playing games on their mobile phones, reading, preparing for the next lesson; the teacher opens a window, starts the PC and rushes around getting teaching equipment ready. In the 'liminal situation' of a school break, bodies 'act' on their own, introducing thoughts, agency and personality to the social situation, playing with things and identities. In the liminal state, even the 'turbulent noise' of one's body and the body's 'subliminal murmurs' may be perceived. The primacy of the senses, the multifaceted mixture of sensations and the authenticity of the experiential are expressed, before control and observation shall bring about organized school-based learning processes. Before 'nature is catalogued', and before technology, prevailing forms of knowledge and social organization annex the sensing bodies, before marginalization of singularity is brought about, a veiling and taking over of experience occurs. In the classroom, this take-over happens by means of analysis and observation, the sciences and technology. The world of the senses is then transformed, e.g. by the sciences, as they establish what counts as truth: by an administration that rules social and cultural processes, and by media that are exercising influence through their seductive power.

Indeed, when the school bell rings, this signifies that the classroom rules, that is waiting for one's turn, power relationships and codes of behaviour, are to be established. However, even if the well-organized classroom is declared to be an optimal arrangement for learning, usually, there are also clear signs that the pupils want to revert to the exciting conditions of the liminal situation. The more fluid, malleable state is thus not completely replaced by the orderly classroom situation. The liminal situation continues, at least in the minds, ruling the everyday world as classroom settings, as a constant dream scenario.

During the lessons, this dream scenario may reveal itself as 'revolt', i.e. in disruptive behaviour, in pupils covertly talking to their neighbours, in distracting activities, in cheating and so on. The hidden, unobserved space is a 'backstage' in which the pupils interact peer-to-peer. Here, their individuality comes into play; sensory perception, words and community join. Sometimes, on the 'backstage' even an intense focus develops, and complete immersion in an activity takes place. Diverse practices, symbolic fights and negotiations between the individual, their peers and the norms of the institution occur. If we look at the impact of these 'backstage' happenings on the education taking place in the classroom it turns out that the subversive happenings play 'an active part in the institutionalisation of the pupils into schooling'. It makes sense to talk about a 'pedagogy of the third space' (Gutiérrez), which builds on learners' participation in the construction of learning activities through multiple voices, that is not only institutional ones. The pedagogy of the third space envisages a dialectic between the individual and the social, between the world as it is and the world as it could be.

In educational research, the endeavour to harmonize classroom education with the polyphony, diversity and contrast of its 'backstage' happenings is not new. Most discussion concerns here the ambiguous relationship between theory and practice. There is a well-established consciousness that educational practice derives from a broad range of imaginative, intuitive and rational elements. It requires a practical knowledge to grasp them; for richer and more inclusive practice, aspects of learning in the classroom need to be drawn from various sources and diverse instances. Classroom education is dependent on how the above-described fleeting experiences are linked to official teaching and learning. Is there any room left for imagination, for random thoughts, agency and personality in the classroom, playing with identities and so on, or is a pupil's relationship to his or her own experiences marginalized or veiled?

In Chap. 25 *Staffan Selander* starts with the observation that in education and in most studies on education the body has been perceived as a prerequisite for the development of theoretical knowledge. Practical knowledge with a focus on sport, art, music and vocational education has been considered less important. In this chapter this division between theory and practice is discussed in order to develop a more satisfactory understanding of learning, based on the importance of bodily experiences for learning. Learning is understood as a complex multimodal social practice. It is often characterized by mimetic, performative and emotional aspects. Since it takes place in this way, learning contributes to the personal development of young people, in which meaning making is of central importance.

Nathalie Sinclair and *Eva Jablonka* in Chap. 26, in their investigation of the material aspects of mathematical practice in the classroom, connect mathematical activity with gestures and movements of the body. They investigate how mathematical, 'abstract, static and disembodied thought' is applied, structured and developed by operations in which embodiment, bodily actions and tools play a central role. They draw consequences for mathematics education and acquisition of knowledge that happens through oral transmission and mental operations. They employ three examples of mathematical activities—counting, cubing and computing—using these to show the importance of physical activities in different mathematical practices.

Cornelie Dietrich and *Valerie Riepe* in Chap. 27 show that when children learn in school their experience becomes concrete through a process of embodiment. This is why staging and repeating the performance of teaching in social choreographies is of central importance for school learning. These choreographies structure the movements of groups of pupils in time and space. Firstly, therefore, the authors elaborate on the concept of social choreography, a term that is commonly used in the teaching of dance. Secondly, they use two examples from primary school lessons to clarify the concept of social choreography. The first of these is circle time, which demands equal, participatory communication between pupils and teacher. The second is the choreographic arrangement of the hierarchical order that exists between the teacher and the pupils in terms of space. The task of circle time is to create order through a disciplinary choreography, through the inter-responsiveness between order and disorder, between rule-governed behaviour and vitalistic dynamics. In the third and final part the authors reflect upon the results of the empirical research in conjunction with theoretical observations.

Juliane Engel and *Cristina Diz Muñoz* in Chap. 28, both theoretically and empirically, address the question of how (postcolonial) subjectivation processes take place in glocalized classrooms, that is in classrooms where both local and worldwide perspectives play a role. By focusing on socially asymmetrical, powerful classroom relations, they investigate the physical negotiation of experiences of difference that cannot be expressed verbally. They examine the strengths and weaknesses of videographic research in this area: first, by discussing how embodied learning can be made accessible through videography (1), then by exploring the implications of postcolonial cultural theories on the epistemological potential of videography when it comes to embodied learning processes (2), and finally by explaining how the embodiment of social norms can be understood as subaltern processes of subjectivation (3).

Chapter 29 by *Tiago de Oliveira Pinto* is based on the hypothesis that playing a musical instrument naturally leads to increased physical activity, while the results of the music played vanish in time. Instrumental music also reveals extensive possibilities of expression, learning and experiencing, whereas it does not have an obvious semantic content. Thus, in terms of embodiment and learning, organized sound relates to the physical body, to transience and to social attributions. When it comes to performance or to the process of learning musical skills, the sensual spectrum necessarily expands from sound and hearing to embodiment, revealing more extensive possibilities of expression, all associated with the phenomenon of music. Indeed, the process of learning and experiencing music, regardless of its social and cultural context, is essentially one that relates to physical practice. Music expresses itself in a social context and in the physical body at the same time, that is music lives as a social activity, while certain instrumental techniques also depend directly on physical skills. Musical practices are always grounded in an embodied learning experience.

The Role of Bodily Experience for Learning Designs

Staffan Selander

1 The Role of the Body for Learning

The understanding of the role of the body for learning entails many possible aspects in a spectrum from the training of the body itself to the role of the body for all kinds of learning, from the body as a ground for phenomenological experiences to its social role in terms of how we communicate and position ourselves in the situated, social room (Merleau-Ponty, 1999; Werler & Wulf, 2006). And to understand the brain, lots of metaphors have been used, based on dominant technologies at the time: for example, a clock, a machine, or a computer. But the brain is not anything like this: it is not a mechanical thing, nor a time-coded computer; it is an organ within a biological body. And it is an active organ, not a passive receiver of stimuli, which over time develops stable patterns in relation to the environment by way of iterative network connections (Changeux & Ricœur, 2002).

In this chapter, I would like to focus on one of the contemporary challenges concerning learning in a hybrid, complex society (Brooks et al., 2021; Gee, 2004; Kress et al., 2021; Morin, 2008; Selander, 2008b; Selander, 2015). This discussion needs to, as I see it, embrace a multifaceted, multimodal understanding of knowledge representations and learning, but also the performative aspects of learning in different micro-arenas, as well as a critical view on the

---

S. Selander (✉)
Stockholm University, Stockholm, Sweden
e-mail: staffan.selander@dsv.su.se

© The Author(s), under exclusive license to Springer Nature Switzerland AG 2022
A. Kraus, C. Wulf (eds.), *The Palgrave Handbook of Embodiment and Learning*,
https://doi.org/10.1007/978-3-030-93001-1_25

(often taken for granted) dichotomy between theoretic and practical knowledge. I will do so out of a design-theoretic, multimodal perspective.

1.1 The Body and the Soul—And the Question of Social and Individual Discipline

Ever since the Greek philosophers, we can notice a deep interest in the question of the soul, either as a part of the body (Epicurus) or as an entity of itself (Plato). This divide of body and soul has ever since had a strong influence in the thinking about learning in schools, not the least in terms of a need to discipline the body in the formal, compulsory educational system from the end of the nineteenth century.

The understanding of the upbuilding of formal, compulsory education could start with the following question: Why did our societies build schools at the end of the nineteenth century? A common answer is that this was because of the industrialization. The problem with this explanation is that industrialization came much later in most of our societies. Another possible answer is that this was a way to create social order in the bigger cities, where hordes of young people who went around and created troubles of different kinds (Sandin, 1986). To create social discipline was a strong first argument for the building up of schools. Still another answer, of course, is that technological development makes life more complicated, and it will take longer and longer time to train young generations. However, this will also lead to another question: If more and more people today will be out of the labour market or only do simple work, and more and more people will have more leisure time, why would they need a longer education? An answer to this would be: because of our democratic intentions to involve everyone in the organization and maintaining of our societies and cultures. If working conditions change, more time would also be available for meaningful work (Hägglund, 2019).

The existing educational system in the midst of the nineteenth century in Europe was the Lancaster system, where older children educated the younger at different work-stations, and the role of the teacher more or less was to walk around and keep the order. With the beginning of formal schooling, the architectonic panopticon became an ideal, for schools as for prisons. From a central place, the teacher—or the guard—could see what everyone was doing. The school panopticon—the classroom—had a somewhat elevated teacher's desk and benches for the pupils. From this central position, the teacher could see everything that happened in the room, and he (or she) could steer all activities in terms of content (the book), time (lessons), working space (the classroom), and discipline. In this environment, the pointer was important. It was a tool for pointing at the central aspects of for example a map or of what was written on the blackboard—and a symbol for the right to speak (the sceptre). However, it was also the tool for punishment and keeping order.

Today, much is different, since much teaching is digitally based and possible to carry out as distance education (not the least during the years of COVID-19). Furthermore, content is based on digitally distributed sources of information (not one central book) and we can see an increasing interest in simulation programs and (serious) games of different kinds, as well as in out-of-school activities (like maker-spaces) and outdoor learning (Graeske et al., 2020; Kress, 2010; Nouri, 2014; Selander et al., 2019). In our late modern, hybrid society, teachers do not control the time, the content, and the learning space the way his or her predecessors did. And he or she is not any longer (in most countries) allowed to physically punish youngsters. Instead, teachers develop a new capacity to orchestrate digitally based schoolwork, with a focus on both epistemic and social dimensions. And we can notice a shift from the teacher in the centre to the pupil in the centre (Collins & Halverson, 2008).

The social discipline in schools went hand in hand with the discipline of individual bodies. In the panopticon-school, discipline was explicit and hard. It was important for the pupils to sit still with the hands on the bench (we can here get a hint of the undertones of sexual discipline). There was also a special kind of work-oriented body-discipline. As for example, when Pestalozzi talked about drawing, he emphasized the importance of training how to depict things correctly, as the stove at the end of the classroom. And even if it took a semester to learn this, the pupil had at least been disciplined, since he had been sitting still and worked (Pestalozzi & Buss, 1803; Johnsen et al., 1997). Pestalozzi and Buss (1803) also describe the explicit social training, for example how pupils should sit in line and loudly, in chorus, say what they were doing: 'I draw a straight line,' and then, 'Under the first line I draw a second straight line,' and so on.

Another example could be seen in writing in early schooling. It was important to learn how to write elegantly (without any ink plumps) and perfect (in the same kind of style). Why so? Well, mainly because this was the way that society could store its collective memory in such a format so that everyone else could read it. With new technologies, this special skill disappeared. Now we can notice a renewed interest in handwriting, but from a totally different point of view, namely that it is good for the training of the brain. Taking notes by hand helps (most) individuals to remember better than only listening is the argument.

Social and individual discipline seems today to be a bit of a different character, and in many of our social practices more incapsulated and inherent. So is the case with a growing, centralized control of educational content and testing, where the steering and control mechanisms are built into digital, educational programs. And this is done with arguments like the more impersonal the teaching and testing is, the more objective and just it would be (as if knowledge was a specific entity that could be measured objectively, see further arguments below). This kind of 'impersonalization' can also be noticed in many other relations between a social/political institution or an enterprise and the individual users/clients/customers/pupils, and so on, who are supposed to manage most of the communication themselves, by way of computer programs, and where it in many cases is almost impossible to get a personal contact by way of for example a visit or a telephone call.

In line with this, we can notice a new emphasis on self-control, with arguments like young children should be trained for being able to collaborate, being responsible, chevaleresque, and being creative individuals who can take initiative—in other words, trained for a late-capitalist society in flux, where they are supposed to act as entrepreneurs (Lindstrand et al., 2016). It seems like automatic subordination in relation to AI (Artificial Intelligence) goes hand in hand with individual self-regulation. However, this contradiction does not mean that AI could not be a help for individual development and support learning based on individual variations and interests. It is rather the opposite, but it takes a democratic political leadership to develop this aspect, which also would entail a clearer trust in professional competence and communication.

Thus, new ideals do not mean that the discipline of the body—in its social and individual meaning—has disappeared. It has only changed and become more internalized. Already Jackson (1990) talks about 'the hidden curriculum,' by which he meant the kind of social discipline that was incorporated and not overtly seen in symbolic control and the classroom rituals (see Bernstein, 1996 on symbolic control and Wulf et al., 2010 on rituals). To these aspects, we could also add the social and cultural mechanisms for dominance, control, and subordination (which Bourdieu, 1977, 2010, talked about in terms of habitus).

1.2 Knowledge and Knowing

Let us for a moment reflect on what it means to learn and to know something. For example,

- I learnt a new word in Portuguese.
- I learnt to play the clarinet.
- I learnt a new profession.

Obviously, learning here refers to very different kinds of capacities and activities. But let us add something more:

- I leant to how to use the Portuguese word correctly in a conversation.
- I learnt to play the clarinet with modulation—together with others.
- I learnt a new profession and have worked in this profession for a couple of years.

In the first case, learning a new word here also entails a deeper understanding of its possible nuances and its social and cultural connotations. In the second case, learning an instrument is not only about playing the right tone, but to coordinate the playing with others and being able to express variations—an aesthetic judgement. And in the third case, learning a profession in formal education is not really the same as to learn to coordinate all different professional aspects in relation to a specific case in situ.

These examples point at the fact that words/terms like 'learning' and 'knowing' do not refer to fix entities or things. Rather, they refer to culturally specific ways of talking about, and recognizing, learning in different settings (Kress et al., 2021; Lim, 2015; Selander & Kress, 2017; Selander, 2017). We can for example make distinctions between scientifically based knowledge, procedural knowledge, and knowledge based on reflected experience (Rolf, 2015). Aspects of knowledge entail facts and scientific knowledge (Greek: *episteme*) and knowing how to do things (Greek: *techne*). However, learning also entails vaguer, but still essential, aspects like identity building and the development of self-regulation (Nussbaum, 2011), judgement (Greek: *phronesis* and *phronimus*; Ricœur, 2005), *Bildung* or perspective on the world and understanding the frontlines of knowledge, a capacity to seeing things in their context, self-understanding, and cultivating of oneself (Gadamer, 1975), collaborative work and co-creativity (Hansen et al., 2015), and (in more modern terms) to meta-reflect and develop a personal way to constantly learn anew (*generic* learning). Learning can therefore also mean to re-learn, as when you go from playing the flute in the compulsory school to playing it at the musical academy. More seldom we talk about the 'shadows of education' or the 'black learning'—'the Lucifer effect'—as when people are educated to be grim or to torture, or are indoctrinated to believe only in a certain ideology (Selander, 2017; Teistler, 2006; Weizer, 2007; Zimbardo, 2007).

412　S. Selander

All in all, these different aspects on learning see learning as a capacity that is rooted in our biological body and carried out by using or exploring material and semiotic resources in the environment. Thus, learning can be seen as an increasing capacity to use (and elaborate) these cultural resources and technologies (for good or bad). To know more is to know more variations, to develop more elaborated stories and explanations, techniques, and methodologies. And this is the (only) way we can understand learning, by way of its material and semiotic manifestations, since we can never see what is going on inside the head of the learner (Säljö, 2005). It also opens up for an understanding of learning as a result of contextual, mimetic, and sequenced practices over time. This is, as I see it, a far more dynamic understanding of learning than seeing learning as a result of the capacity to remember facts (Kress et al., 2021).

2　Theoretic and Practical Knowledge

An often taken for granted division is that between theoretic and practical knowledge. For example, you learn theoretic knowledge in school, but practical knowledge at the working place. The first problem here is that 'knowledge' and 'learning' are not very well-defined concepts. As we have seen above, learning and knowledge can be defined or specified in many ways.

To say that theoretic knowledge is learnt in schools (or universities), and practical knowledge outside these institutions, is a misleading dichotomy. Every kind of learning (however most obviously so in professional education) entails both theoretic and practical aspects (even if we analytically can separate them), and it would be more to correct to say that theoretic and practical knowledge are intertwined. Every theoretic knowledge entails a practical side, and every practice has more or less conscious connection to a theoretic paradigm or model.

Let us just mention one example. A traditional sheet of music entails tones and semitones, as well as different clefs, and so on. And most of us learn this in school, at least on a basic level. But how shall we interpret dasia-notes, neumes from the Medieval Ages, Japanese shamisen-note, or modern serious music with 'carpets' of tones, where the precise tone is not clear, rather the interval in which the tone could be played? And so is the case in all knowledge domains: we 'know' how to interpret information when we have an interpretative practice to relate it to. This also points at the performative aspect of learning, not only in music and arts, but in all possible knowledge domains. Information-linking and action-linking goes hand in hand in learning and meaning-making (Selander, 2019; Wickman, 2006; Østern & Knudsen, 2019). This also leads us to the next step: designs for and in learning.

3 Designs for and in Learning

The design-perspective entails a multimodal understanding of knowledge representations, sign-making, and signs of learning in different formal (e.g. schools), semi-formal (museums), or non-formal (as learning at home) settings. It focuses on situated sequences over time (see Learning Design Sequences: Selander, 2008a; Selander & Kress, 2017; Selander et al., 2021), and how signs are transformed and transducted in the making of sketches and new representations (Kress, 2010; Selander, 2013). It also focuses on institutional and individual framings and interests. Furthermore, we can add an interest in taking part in different processes to change and develop teaching and learning—design as function and meaning, and collaborative design and design patterns as an elaborated methodology (however, still with different roles, where the researcher is the critical partner for discussion, who can introduce new concepts and transgress taking-for-granted explanation or ideas of how things should be) (Dorst, 2015; Glawe & Selander, 2021; Knutsson et al., 2021).

3.1 Designs in Learning

'Designs in learning' is a conceptualization of individual learning paths, ways to think and solve problems. Learning can (metaphorically) be seen as an activity that develops alongside different, rhizomatic threads, depending on interests and choices in relation to material and semiotic resources (Lindstrand & Selander, 2022). Thus, if we see learning in this way, we can see a difference in how things are learnt and in what ways learning about something has been transformed and shaped anew (or re-designed) into a new knowledge representation. I would also argue that this way of looking at learning goes deeper than the idea of a fixed knowledge entity that could be objectively measured.

A sensitivity for how things are learnt and represented also gives more interesting clues for a teacher to think of in what ways he or she could support and challenge a pupil/student to develop further. If, for example, a group of students learn about X by way of school textbooks and pen and paper, and another group of students learn X by way of dynamic, digital programs, they would be able to show their learning in different ways, with an emphasis on different aspect. This will be noticed in terms of how different modes are used and how different multimodal resources are orchestrated (Bezemer & Kress, 2016; Kjällander, 2011).

I would like to give two different examples of this. The first one is a study about learning music by way of composing with the help of the program GarageBand and iPads (Bandlien & Selander, 2019). Different 'stop moments' in the learning process were here in focus, where both risks and opportunities could be detected, in other words significant moments in the learning-design-sequence (Selander, 2008a). In a creative, learning design process, it is not clear—from the beginning—which choices the learners will make and which routes they will take. In this case, the technology made it possible to track these choices and routes, and thereby get a clearer picture of the pupils' knowledge and what they have learnt compared to earlier sequences.

The other example is a project where pupils were asked to interpret a poem and represent their new understanding by way of making a film (Höglund, 2017). This transduction (changes of representations by way of different media; Kress, 2010) and the ways the students represented their new understanding became, of course, also a challenge for the teacher's interpretation of their new knowledge and their learning (Kress & Selander, 2012). What for example would be able to explicitly argue for in an essay will in the film rather be presented as a narrative. To be able to follow the learning, the teachers have to be able to follow the arguments and choices that were taken during the process (also see Lindstrand, 2006). As I see it, both these examples point at an understanding of learning as a multifaceted and multimodal communicative activity, where the richness of information about the learning that has taken place and the new knowledge that the participants have acquired could not be tracked by a standard test.

3.2 Sketching as Transformation and Transduction of Information

Sketching is here understood as a (bodily and epistemologically based) process of choices and the creation of tentative fixing points within a learning sequence. I would like to make a difference between *sketching as exploration* and *sketching as formation of knowledge*. The first one is characterized by curious exploration of phenomena, the second by adapting the new findings to possible forms for finalizing and representing the findings of the explorative process—as in the form of an essay, a film, a PowerPoint presentation, a dance, or for example an exhibition.

Sketching is used in different ways in different areas. In dance courses, sketching is as an assemblage of possible dance elements to create and try out a reconfiguration of signs in order to express an attitude, a feeling, or a mood. In filmmaking, sketching is used in the work to present the script, in the tentative draft of scenes. In writing, the sketch is the first draft, the first configuration of the structure or the tentative formulation.

The sketch is used to fix certain aspects, but also to elaborate on possible variants and expressions. Sketches are seen as assemblages of modes within a selected medium. The sketch is here understood as the vehicle in the motivated action to select signs and transform (and transduct; Kress, 2010[1]) and re-configure or re-design them into full representations. Thus, the sketch is an important tool in a design process for shaping, negotiating, and making choices. It is an important tool in the learning process for elaborating possible meanings.

4   Designs for Learning—Conclusive Remarks

Learning (from a design-theoretic perspective) is a perspective with a focus on designs *for* and *in* learning, where learning could be understood as an increasing capacity to incorporate, make meaning and use of a rich variation of material and semiotic resources (Selander, 2017; Selander et al., 2021). This perspective combines a socio-cultural understanding of knowledge representations with a multimodal understanding of sign-making, within formal, semi-formal, and non-formal institutional framings. It is a perspective that can be used to analyse conditions for research, teaching, and learning (Björklund Boistrup & Selander, 2022).

This perspective is a clear epistemological standpoint, coupled to a methodological approach—Learning Design Sequences. But it is also based on an ontological understanding of learning as incorporated and performative acting, intertwined with theoretic insights and reflections in processes of change.

---

[1] 'Transformation' is a change of representations within the same modes and medium (as text to text), whilst 'transduction' is a change of representation between modes and media (as text to film; Kress, 2010).

References

Bandlien, B. T., & Selander, S. (2019). Designing as Composing Music with iPads: A Performative Perspective. In A. L. Østern & K. N. Knudsen (Eds.), *Performative Approaches in Arts Education. Artful Teaching, Learning and Research* (pp. 81–96). Routledge.

Bernstein, B. (1996). *Pedagogy—Symbolic Control and Identity. Theory, Research, Practice*. Taylor, & Francis.

Bezemer, J., & Kress, G. (2016). *Multimodality, Learning and Communication: A Social Semiotic Frame*. Routledge.

Björklund Boistrup, L., & Selander, S. (Eds.) (2022). *Designs for Research, Teaching and Learning. A Framework for Future Education*. Routledge.

Bourdieu, P. (1977). *Outline of a Theory of Practice*. Cambridge University Press.

Bourdieu, P. (2010). *Distinction. A Social Critique of the Judgement of taste*. Routledge.

Brooks, D., Dau, S., & Selander, S. (Eds.). (2021). *Digital Learning and Collaborative Practices—Lessons from Inclusive and Empowering Participation in Emerging Technologies*. Routledge.

Changeux, J.-P., & Ricœur, P. (2002). *What Makes Us Think?* Princeton University Press.

Collins, A., & Halverson, R. (2008). *Rethinking Education in the Age of Technology*. Teachers College Press.

Dorst, K. (2015). *Frame Innovation. Create New Thinking by Design*. The MIT Press.

Gadamer, H.-G. (1975). *Truth and Method*. Sheed & Ward.

Gee, J. P. (2004). *What Video Games Have to Teach Us About Learning and Literacy*. Palgrave Macmillan.

Glawe, M., & Selander, S. (2021). *Innovativ design för lärande*. Liber.

Graeske, C., Lundström, S., Thunberg, S., & Vallin, H. (2020). Spawn 2.0—Att spela sig till läsning. In Y. Lindberg & A. Svensson (Eds.), *Litteraturdidaktik: Språkämnen i samverkan* (pp. 42–63). Natur, & Kultur.

Hägglund, M. (2019). *Vårt enda liv. Sekulär tro och andlig frihet*. Volante.

Hansen, P., Shah, C., & Klas, C.-P. (2015). *Collaborative Information Seeking. Best Practices, New Domains and New Thoughts*. Springer.

Höglund, H. (2017). *Video Poetry: Negotiating Literary Interpretations. Students' Multimodal Designing in Response to Literature*. Dissertation. Åbo Academy University Press.

Jackson, P. W. (1990). *Life in Classrooms*. Holt, Rinehart and Winston.

Johnsen, E. B., Lorentzen, S., Selander, S., & Skyum-Nielsen, P. (1997). *Kunskapens texter. Jakten på den goda läroboken*. Oslo Universitetsforlaget.

Kjällander, S. (2011). *Designs for Learning in an Extended Digital Environment. Case Studies of Social Interaction in the Social Science Classroom*. Dissertation. Stockholm University.

Knutsson, O., Ramberg, R., & Selander, S. (2021). Designs for Learning and Knowledge Representations in Collaborative Settings. In E. Brooks, S. Dau, & S. Selander (Eds.), *Digital Learning and Collaborative Practices—Lessons from Inclusive and Empowering Participation in Emerging Technologies* (pp. 12–21). Routledge.

Kress, G. (2010). *Multimodality. A Social Semiotic Approach to Contemporary Communication*. Routledge.

Kress, G., & Selander, S. (2012). Multimodal Design, Learning and Cultures of Recognition. *The Internet and Higher Education*. https://doi.org/10.1016/j.iheduc.2011.12.003

Kress, G., Selander, S., Säljö, R., & Wulf, C. (Eds.). (2021). *Learning as Social Practice. Beyond Education as an Individual Enterprise*. Routledge.

Lim, K. Y. T. (2015). *Disciplinary Intuitions and Designs of Learning Environments*. Springer.

Lindstrand, F. (2006). *Att skapa skillnad. Representation, identitet och lärande i ungdomars arbete och berättande med film*. Dissertation. HLS Förlag.

Lindstrand, F., & Selander, S. (2022). Designs in learning and rhizomatic webs. In L. Björklund Boistrup & S. Selander (Eds.), *Designs for Research, Teaching and Learning. A Framework for Future Education*, (23–33). Routledge.

Lindstrand, F., Insulander, E., & Selander, S. (2016). Mike the Knight in the Neo-Liberal Era. A Multimodal Approach to Children's Multi-Media Entertainment. *Journal of Language and Politics, 15*(3), 337–351.

Merleau-Ponty, M. (1999). Kroppens fenomenologi. Daidalos. [Phénoménologie de la perception, 1945].

Morin, E. (2008). *On Complexity*. Hampton Press.

Nouri, J. (2014). *Orchestrating Scaffolded Outdoor Mobile Learning Activities*. Dissertation. Stockholm University.

Nussbaum, M. (2011). *Creating Capabilities. The Human Development Approach*. The Belknap Press of Harvard University.

Østern, A.-L., & Knudsen, K. N. (Eds.). (2019). *Performative Approaches in Arts Education. Artful Teaching, Learning and Research*. Routledge.

Pestalozzi, J. H., & Buss, C. (1803). *ABC der Anschauung oder Anschauungs-Lehre der Massverhältnisse*. J.G. Cotta.

Ricœur, P. (2005). *The Course of Recognition*. Harvard University Press.

Rolf, B. (2015). Tre kunskapsmodeller. In A. Bronäs & S. Selander (Eds.), *Verklighet, verklighet. Teori och praktik I lärarutbildning*. Studentlitteratur.

Säljö, R. (2005). *Lärande och kulturella redskap. Om lärprocesser och det kollektiva minnet*. Norstedts Akademiska Förlag.

Sandin, B. (1986). *Hemmet, gatan, fabriken eller skolan? Folkundervisning och barnupfostran i svenska städer 1600–1850*. Dissertation. Arkiv Förlag.

Selander, S. (2008a). Designs for Learning—A Theoretical Perspective. *Designs for learning, 1*(1), 10–24.

Selander, S. (2008b). Designs for Learning and the Formation and Transformation of Knowledge in an Era of Globalization. In Roth, K., & Selander, S. (eds.). Identity, Communication and Learning in an Age of Globalization, Studies in Philosophy and Education. Springer. 27(4), 267–283.

Selander, S. (2013). Transformation and Sign-Making: The Principles of Sketching in Designs for Learning. In M. Böck & N. Pachler (Eds.), *Multimodality and Social Semiotics* (pp. 121–130). Routledge.

Selander, S. (2015). Conceptualization of Multimodal and Distributed Designs for Learning. In B. Gros & Kinshuk, & Maina, M. (Eds.), *The Futures of Ubiquitous Learning: Learning Designs for Emerging Pedagogies* (pp. 97–113). Springer.

Selander, S. (2017). *Didaktiken efter Vygotskij—Design för lärande.* Liber.

Selander, S. (2019). Can a Sign Reveal Its Meaning? On the Question of Interpretation and Epistemic Context. In S. Zhao, E. Djonov, A. Björkvall, & M. Boeriis (Eds.), *Advancing Multimodal and Critical Discourse Studies* (pp. 67–79). Routledge.

Selander, S., Insulander, E., Kempe, A.-L., Lindstrand, F., & West, T. (2021). Designs for Learning—Designs in Learning. In G. Kress, S. Selander, R. Säljö, & C. Wulf (Eds.), *Learning as Social Practice. Beyond Education as an Individual Enterprise* (pp. 30–70). Routledge.

Selander, S., & Kress, G. (2017 [2010]). *Design för lärande—ett multimodalt perspektiv.* Studentlitteratur.

Selander, S., Lim, F. V., Wiklund, M., & Fors, U. (2019). Digital Games and Simulations for Learning. In H. C. Arnseth, T. Hanghøj, T. D. Henriksen, M. Misfeldt, R. Ramberg, & S. Selander (Eds.), *Games and Education: Designs in and for Learning* (pp. 17–29). Brill/Sense.

Teistler, G. (ed.) (2006). *Lesen lernen in Diktaturen der 1930er und 1940er Jahre. Fibeln in Deutschland, Italien und Spanien.* Studien zur Internationalen Schulbuchsforschung, Schriftenreihe des Georg-Eckert-Instituts, Band 116. Hahnsche Buchhandlung.

Weizer, H. (2007). *Gärningsmän. Hur helt vanliga människor blir massmördare.* Daidalos.

Werler, T., & Wulf, C. (Eds.). (2006). *Hidden Dimensions of Education* (Vol. 23). European Studies in Education. Waxmann.

Wickman, P.-O. (2006). *Aesthetic Experience in Science Education. Learning and Meaning-Making in Situated Talk and Action.* Lawrence Erlbaum Associated Publishers.

Wulf, C., Althans, B., Audehm, K., Bausch, C., Göhlich, M., Sting, S., Tervooren, A., Wagner-Willi, M., & Zirfas, J. (Eds.). (2010). *Rituals and Identity. The Staging and Performing of Rituals in the Lives of Young People.* The Tufnell Press.

Zimbardo, P. (2007). *The Lucifer Effect. How Good People Turn Evil.* Ryder.

Mathematics Learning: Structured Ways of Moving *With*

Nathalie Sinclair and Eva Jablonka

1 Introduction

We open with three examples of mathematical activity from a range of contexts. As you read through them, consider how they compare with your own experiences of mathematics, particularly in relation to the various ways in which the body—the senses and various body parts—are at play in the mathematical activity. We will use these to highlight some of the material aspects of mathematical practice, aspects that are sometimes overlooked when, in pedagogical contexts, attention is focused on knowledge acquisition through oral transmission and mental operations. In the following sections, we use these and further examples to structure our discussion of mathematical embodiment.

1.1 Counting

> [...] The meanings
> a language must have are the meanings
> it lacks: located outside it, like sunlight

N. Sinclair (✉)
Simon Fraser University, Burnaby, BC, Canada
e-mail: nathsinc@sfu.ca

E. Jablonka
Freie Universität Berlin, Berlin, Germany

© The Author(s), under exclusive license to Springer Nature Switzerland AG 2022
A. Kraus, C. Wulf (eds.), *The Palgrave Handbook of Embodiment and Learning*,
https://doi.org/10.1007/978-3-030-93001-1_26

and grass. So together with meaning
there has to be pointing at meaning.
Excerpt from Language Poem (1). (Bringhurst, 2013, p. 173)

A four-year-old child is sitting on the floor in front of a bunch of marbles. She is asked how many there are. We know what to listen for: 'one, two, three' and so on. We know that some children will peter out after saying 'three' or 'four' and that others will not say the number words in the right order, or decide to count just some of the marbles or not match the number of the number words with the number of the marbles. But we also know that a significant quality of the counting can involve the child pointing to the marbles, one at a time, sometimes even touching the marble as the number word is uttered. In this mathematical practice, the finger both draws attention to the marble and helps track the passage from one marble to another. We know this moving of the finger becomes more reliable over time—early on, the finger may point more than once at the same marble; it may skip some marbles along the way; it may even point without having a detectable target. Learning to count thereby involves both saying number words in a certain order and moving the finger in a certain way, as well as co-ordinating the two. Recent research has shown that this finger-speech practice of counting persists into adulthood. When asked to count a large number of dots, adults will perform better when they count using their fingers to point at the dots; and if they are prevented from doing so, they will move other parts of their bodies instead, such as a chin or a foot, in rhythmic accompaniment to their speech (Carlson et al., 2008).

1.2 Cubing

[…] there is nothing in knowledge which has not been first in the entire body, whose gestural metamorphoses, mobile postures, very evolution imitate all that surrounds it. (Serres, 2011, p. 70)

The Romanticist Froebel developed a box with a cube composed of eight smaller wooden cubes. With reference to this box, Froebel depicted 71 'forms of beauty' [*Schönheitsformen*] and 22 'forms of knowledge' [*Erkenntnisformen*], in addition to 100 'forms of life' [*Lebensformen*] (Reimers, 2014). According to Froebel, the 'forms of knowledge' (as depicted in Fig. 1a) are actualised by pulling apart the whole cube, rearranging the parts and creating the original whole. As such, the whole and its parts, form and size, relative position and combination emerge as

Mathematics Learning: Structured Ways of Moving *With*

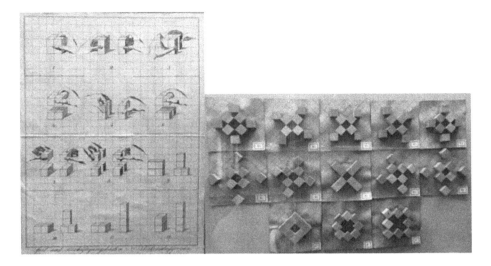

Fig. 1 Exhibits in the Friedrich-Froebel-Museum in the Thuringian town Bad Blankenburg, in the house that the practitioner and theorist of early pedagogy used for his first kindergarten. The images refer to the *Spiel und Beschäftigungskasten No. 3* (play and activity box No 3). (a) Some of the forms of knowledge and gestures used to interact with the cubes; (b) some of the forms of beauty. (Source: Authors' own photos)

'perceptible facts' (Froebel, 1897, p. 119). The symmetric 'forms of beauty' are created by systematically moving and turning to the right or the left some cubes from one initial position around a centre of cubes in a fixed position, in a 'dance of shapes', as shown in Fig. 1b (Froebel, 1897, p. 134).

In terms of these variations of 'forms of beauty', it is not unjustified to associate Froebel with experimentation in geometric forms as found in concrete art. Indeed, Cross (1983) traces the educational influence of some principles of the Bauhaus Basic Course in design to the Froebelian tradition amongst other developments in progressive education, in particular via the Bauhaus' teacher Johannes Itten's background in childhood education.

Childhood education in the romantic era, avant-garde art in the twentieth century and mathematics, all share the intention of exploring properties in structures and compositions. The example shows the recognition (both by Froebel and by the artists) that engaging in bodily activity shapes perceptual interaction. The cubes themselves are important, so is the way that the hand manoeuvres as it grabs the cube by its flat faces, slides it into place to align with other cubes along edges and vertices and turns the cube to expose different orientations (see Fig. 1a). The example also hints at a double foundation

1.3 Computing

> Of course, these algorithms 'work', they can be useful, but there is also something more to them, something enjoyable beyond the mere reach of an arithmetical solution. [...] Algorithmic play excites the kind of challenging pleasure essential to gaming. (Maheaux, 2019, pp. 419–420)

Computational tools (such as sets of counting tokens, rods, sandboxes, abaci, tables and diagrams) have a long and culturally diverse history. The evolution of methods for computation and their conceptualisation in different mathematical activities is associated with the evolution of material devices; the inferred mental scheme is tied to the observable physical operation in handling the tool. Another interplay concerns the operations performed with a particular device and their records on a writing medium, which in turn might become a tool not only for recording but also for producing results (e.g. Freiman & Volkov, 2018).

These mutual relations can be seen in the use of Chinese counting rods. These are sticks made of varying material. Volkov's (2018) account of their history reveals that the oldest rods are from tombs of the second or first century BCE and their usage evolved over a couple of centuries, until the counting rods disappeared in the second half of the second millennium CE. The length and diameter of the rods changed; the older versions were comparatively longer. In the seventeenth century, the counting rods were used in Japan with (modified) Chinese procedures (Fig. 2).

The numbers or coefficients of equations were represented on a counting surface (or board), often with some grid-like structure, in the form of configurations of rods in particular 'cells'; pictured in mathematical treatises, the rods were represented as lines.

A place-value system with base 10 was chosen. Colours were used for distinguishing positive and negative numbers (black rods for positive, red or white rods for negative numbers). For each digit, a configuration of horizontal and vertical rods is placed in a cell on the counting surface. The horizontal/vertical orientation alternates for each digit (possibly for visually separating these, even without a visible underlying grid). So, there are different configurations depending on whether the digit is in positions for 10^{2n} or for 10^{2n+1}.

Fig. 2 Picture of a master and disciples using counting rods from the Seijutsu Sangaku Zue 1795; according to Volkov (2018, p. 152) a collection of pictures related to computation methods by Miyake Katataka (1663–1746). (Source: Public domain, Wikimedia Commons (https://upload.wikimedia.org/wikipedia/commons/4/47/Counting_board.jpg))

Table 1 Counting rods used for digits in different positions in a place-value system with base 10

	1	2	3	4	5	6	7	8	9
Position 10^{2n}	$\vert$	$\vert\vert$	$\vert\vert\vert$	$\vert\vert\vert\vert$	$\vert\vert\vert\vert\vert$	T	⊤	⊤	⊤
Position 10^{2n+1}	—	=	≡	≣	≣	⊥	⊥	⊥	⊥

A rod perpendicular to the convention for the respective position stands for five rods if the digit is in the interval between 6 and 9 (Table 1).

Algorithms are performed through shifting and turning rods (for some examples of arithmetic operations, see Volkov, 2018). Notably, if there is some carry over, the representation of a digit in a higher position can be easily changed (by putting additional rods into the 'cell' and by substituting five rods by a perpendicular rod). The tabular format of the counting surface, which allowed for two-dimensional representations, together with the simplicity and flexibility of the device enabled the development of some mathematical methods that are easy to apply also in learning contexts: not only were algorithms for arithmetic operations (including common fractions) performed with the counting rods, but also procedures for solving quadratic and cubic equations and simultaneous linear equations with up to five unknowns (Volkov, 2018; Pollet, 2018).

2 From Tool to Body to Tool–Body

In the examples provided above, a shared feature of the mathematical activity was the specific ways in which the body acted *on* or *with* physical tools. In broad terms, the Cartesian insistence on isolating the human subject as separate from the environment, and isolating the cognising mind as separate from the body, has had the effect of diminishing the perceived relevance both of the environment and of the body—both in thinking and in learning. This is particularly true in mathematics, which has, since the advent of modern mathematics in the nineteenth century, pursued the fantasy of total abstraction (which, as Gray, 2004, shows, produced much anxiety, even amongst mathematicians).

Interestingly, while attention to the role of tools in learning, as well as to the embodied nature of knowing, has grown in the educational research literature, these have often been pursued as separate strands of research. We will briefly discuss each strand and then propose that a more complex, combined attention to tools and the body may provide insight into issues such as the role of affect and memory in mathematics learning, as well as production of mathematical inscriptions. Moreover, we argue that the independent interest in tools and in the body reflects analytic tendencies in mathematics education research that work against the *mangle of practice*, as Pickering (1995) describes it, which is the intertwining of individual, material and disciplinary agencies of mathematical activity.

2.1 Tools and Manipulatives in Mathematics Education

As chronicled by Kidwell et al. (2008) in their book, *Tools of American Mathematics Teaching, 1800–2000*, 'tools' have long been an important aspect of the material culture of mathematics classrooms. These tools included ones that mathematicians also used, such as compasses and tables, tools used in everyday settings (abaci and calculators) and also tools of explicit pedagogical design, such as Caleb Gattegno's geoboards. Physical objects such as Froebel's so called 'gifts' were of great pedagogical significance to their inventors and to kindergarten activists in Europe and USA. But, arguably, this did not occur until the post-war era of the twentieth century, when pedagogical tools were called 'manipulatives', and became of widespread use in elementary school classrooms. Their perceived value was linked to the 'hands-on learning' advocated by progressive educators such as Piaget and Dewey.

As research on the use of manipulatives grew, in the 1980s and 1990s (and continues today, with a particular focus on so-called virtual manipulatives), attention narrowed in on the manipulatives themselves, often locating the mathematics within them—manipulatives became seen as concrete instantiations of concepts. While some studies have pointed to the positive benefits of the use of physical manipulatives such as Dienes blocks (for place value), geoboards (for geometric explorations) and Cuisenaire rods (for number relations) in the mathematics classroom, provided they are used intentionally by teachers, over an extended period of time (Laski et al., 2015), there have also been critiques, particularly in relation to the time it takes to learn how to use the manipulative and the questionable effectiveness of transferring from a manipulative setting to a paper-and-pencil one (Uttal et al., 1997).

For the past two decades, researchers have studied the additional affordances that virtual manipulatives may have for learning (Sarama & Clements, 2009; Moyer-Packenham et al., 2015), particularly in terms of providing links between visual models and their associated mathematical symbols. More recently, the concept of a 'duo of artefacts' has been introduced into the research literature, which involves the use of co-ordinated physical and virtual manipulatives that not only help teachers build upon their existing practices with physical manipulatives but also provide learners with non-overlapping affordances that can help them develop deeper understandings of a school subject (Soury-Lavergne & Maschietto, 2015).

In all these studies, which gain in sophistication in terms of identifying increasingly effective ways of supporting students' mathematical learning, the research focus remains on the pedagogical tools. In terms of our examples in the previous section, this would amount to studying the marbles, the cubes and the rods as potential mediators of mathematical meaning. The question of how the body takes up these tools remains implicit.

2.2　The Body in Mathematics Education Research

With the publication in 2000 of Lakoff and Núñez's book *Where Mathematics Comes From*, attention to the particular role played by the body in mathematics learning became a central focus of research. The authors emphasise the sensorimotor experiences that can give rise, through s.c. 'metaphoric mapping' (creating a basic schema of mathematical thought), to the development of certain mathematical concepts. For examples, actions such as gathering a bunch of things together or walking along a path can entail bodily experiences that act as metaphors for the concept of addition. The authors sought to account for the emergence of mathematical ideas, but also managed to motivate research on the design of particular bodily experiences that could be metaphorically mapped, as well as other concepts, such as an arithmetic as motion along a path, or fractions as containers (Wood, 2010).

A particular class of body movements has gained even more attention, which is the movement of the hand and in particular movements of hands, i.e. gestures. For example, Sinclair and Pimm (2015) take the pinching gesture as an instantiation of the grounding metaphor of object collection. The role of gestures in mathematics thinking has been studied extensively, with many results of improved performance of students who are encouraged to use gestures (Cook et al., 2008), and by teachers who use gestures in the classroom (Singer & Goldin-Meadow, 2005). Gestures offer a complementary, spatial and temporal means of communication to language, and can thus supplement and enrichen linguistic meanings (Núñez, 2003).

While acknowledging the important role that the body plays in shaping mathematical understanding, this research treats the body as if it were an intransitive verb, that is by focusing more on its movements alone than on its movements *with* or *on* things. Most of the research on gestures, for example, treats them as an accompaniment to speech and as a movement that occurs 'in-the-air', and thus at a distance from the material world.

2.3 The Body–Tool in Mathematics Education

This sub-section explores the shift from isolating the body or the tool to considering the body–tool interaction. Some researchers, for example, have studied gestures not just for their communicative potential but also for their manipulative or epistemic value (Streeck, 2009). When a child uses Froebel's box to manipulate a cube, she is using her hand as a tool to operate on the world, and not necessarily to communicate meanings to others. The fingers and hand become tools, in the same way they do when we count on our fingers. Yet these hand movements on the cube, particularly as they are repeated over time, can become communicative, either as part of an imaginative replaying of the event or in order to describe or recount events to others. The gesture used to indicate the opening of a jar has become a gesture after repeated performances of opening actual jars. The gesture of many quick finger-pointings has become a gesture after repeated counting experiences.

With new touchscreen technologies, these types of gestures have changed, not only in terms of the particular movements that are enabled by the interface, but by the fact that they are often encountered and repeated, as in the zooming-in gesture of a smart phone. Here too the gesture can be seen as a tool—but a special tool that is part of the body yet operates on the tablet. For example, Sinclair and de Freitas (2014) describe the new gestures that arise when a young learner interacts with *TouchCounts*, a multi-touch learning application, gestures that begin as movements of the finger on the screen, but can then turn into gestures 'in-the-air'. Such situations help draw attention to the trace of the structured movement with/on objects that give rise to gestures, and may help explain their relevance to learning.

Before the advent of touchscreen technologies, the work led by Ferdinando Arzarello on the different ways patterns of dragging geometric objects on the screen helped to crystallise this manipulation-communication function. In Arzarello et al. (2002), the authors identified several different operations of the computer mouse—called drag modalities—that seemed to matter to the cognitive experience of solving problems in a dynamic geometry environment. For example, 'wandering dragging', which involves dragging an object haphazardly on the screen, was used when no hypothesis had been made about the relationships between geometric objects. But 'dummy locus dragging', where the mouse followed a certain path, was used when a hypothesis had been made. Although these findings were offered within the context of research on the use of dynamic geometry environments, the relevance of theories of embodiment is hard to overlook, since each of these drag modalities relates to not only constraints of the tool but also the structured ways of moving the body.

The focus on manipulatives as concrete representations could thus be seen as shifting, with the main reason for their use being "more to do with *structured acts of moving* than with *acts of moving structures*" (Ng et al., 2018, p. 568, emphasis in original). As these authors state,

> the main purpose of a manipulative is not to (re)present mathematical concepts, but to mould the learner's motions, in the process occasioning opportunities for learners to expand and interweave their repertoires of mathematically relevant structures. (p. 569)

As movement becomes more and more structured, the environment becomes more orderly and perhaps more mathematical. At the same time, the body becomes more and more integrated into the structured tool environment in such a way that it becomes difficult to separate these three components. Instead of the emergence of an autonomous mathematics learner, we might instead talk about the individuation of a body–tool–mathematics assemblage, which not only refuses to position the tool as being exclusively instrumental but also imagines a more permeable body–tool dyad. As in Merleau-Ponty's (1945) conception of the blind man and the cane, it becomes difficult to see where the body–tool interface lies—is it where the hand touches the cane, or at the tip of the cane, which 'sees' the ground it touches?

3   Motion and Inscription in the Mangle of Tool–Body–Mathematics

Motion in the three introductory examples means performing, observing and sensing tool–body relations in ways that stabilise into some pattern that becomes an operational template, such as counting or algorithmic calculations. Executing operational templates supports and often precedes conceptualisation (as the Serres quotation cited above suggests).

For example, in a study by Johnson et al. (2019), children were asked to count an unstructured pile of 31 pennies. About 40% counted farther in the number sequence when asked to count this larger collection than when just asked to count out loud and to go as high as they could. Some children started with an inconsistent co-ordination of numerals and objects, but then, presumably due to the rhythm of sliding pennies across the table while saying each number word, swung into a successful pattern. A similar phenomenon has also been observed in children's use of *TouchCounts*, as they tap the screen repeatedly to generate successive ordinal numbers (shown symbolically and stated verbally)—with the added phenomenon of changes in speed accentuating a shift of attention from units to tens places (Sinclair & de Freitas, 2014).

In educational research, Palatnik and Abrahamson (2018) stress the epistemic function of

> temporal-spatial movement patterns and sustaining the learner's attention to these patterns [...] as a means of alerting the learner's attention to latent irregularities in the enactment that result from encountering in the workspace unfamiliar information structures. (p. 306)

Temporality has been explored as well through the concept of rhythm. For example, Ingold (2011) has argued that rhythm is a "dynamic coupling of movement" (p. 60) that provides an accessible accounting of the interfacing of human and material. In mathematics education research, Bautista and Roth (2012) have suggested that "it is precisely in rhythm that we find the inseparability of affect and cognition" (p. 93). Indeed, Sinclair et al. (2016) showed how rhythm could be used to study not only cognitive and affective aspects of learning but also social ones, and found how the changes in rhythms over time related to new mathematical understandings.

We want to point out that when subprocesses enacted in the operational template become incorporated into symbolic tools (i.e. mathematical notation), which then can be manipulated on a writing medium, mental operations evolve from the template and the concomitant visual and motoric sensations. The example of the Chinese counting rods shows that their use led to a particular mathematics that could not have emerged without them. A more contemporary example that was studied by Menz (2015) shows how this also occurred amongst a group of topologists working at a blackboard to compile a list of obstructions for the projective plane and to classify these obstructions for 2-regular directed graphs. The gestural template they developed as they drew, re-drew and mimed the embedding of an octahedron in a torus eventually became a symbolic tool. While the visual and motoric sensations of the published diagrams (Fig. 3a) may be difficult to appreciate, its traces are easier to follow and even mimic in any one of the 122 diagrams drawn in chalk on the blackboard during the nine hours of collective mathematical activity (Fig. 3b).

Some notations in the context of permutations offer a more accessible example of how the traces of an operational template on a drawing medium become a tool not only for recording a process but also for producing new templates, new routines and new concepts. A permutation can be seen as the process of rearranging a set of different objects. For example, when looking for anagrams or playing Scrabble with the letters e v l i (four different permutations of these produce meaningful English words), one may immediately see that exchanging the last two letters l and i produces the word e v i l. To keep track of this pair-switching that leaves the rest of the arrangement untouched (a type of permutation that is called a transposition) one can, for example, write (3, 4) where the numbers here refer to the previous position of the symbols of the switched objects. Another way of keeping track of the movement is to compare the original with the new arrangement, symbolised as a form of mapping, by writing the new below the initial arrangement (Fig. 4). In this notation, the import of bodily action in the form of spatial arrangements and exchange of two objects is obvious.

To keep track of a sequence of transpositions a diagram such as in Fig. 5 can be produced. It shows all six permutations of the three letters *a*, *e* and *r* (four of which make meaningful words). The six vertices (the dots) of this graph are the permutations; edges (the lines) are drawn between the vertices when one 'word' can be formed by a pair-switch from the adjacent word as shown by the labels of these edges (see Clark, 2005). Starting with the 'word'

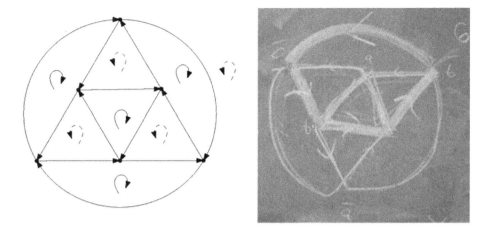

Fig. 3 (a) A 2-regular orientations of C^2_6 in their stylised form; (b) the drawing on the backboard. (Source: diagram by graduate student Finn, Menz (2015), Figs. 6–18 (left) p. 199; Fred's diagram, Menz (2015), Figs. 6–16 (right), p. 196)

Fig. 4 A permutation of four letters achieved by swapping the last two. (Source: Authors' own diagram)

aer at the top, one arrives at the 'words' in the second 'row' by one transposition and at the ones in the last 'row' by two transpositions. This notation has features both of an array and of a graph. Clark (2005) calls it a 'transposition graph' and uses it to proof the *parity theorem* in a "pictorial, constructive, and immediate way" (p. 124). There are many ways to arrive, through a series of swaps, at a particular permutation. In the diagram, this can be explored by moving along the edges and taking different paths from the initial word to the target permutation (including some 'detours', going up and down or moving in a zig-zag). While these paths consist of different numbers of swaps, they have something in common, which is expressed in the parity theorem. It states that either all such paths (sequences of transpositions) consist of an even number of swaps or all such paths consist of an odd number of swaps. When trying some different paths in the diagram (e.g. by moving along with a finger

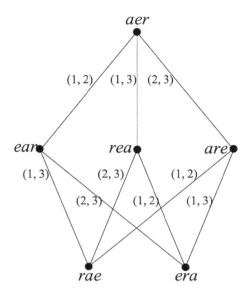

Fig. 5 A diagram showing all six permutations of the letters *a, e* and *r* in a transposition graph. (Source: Authors' own diagram)

while counting on when moving between 'rows'), it becomes obvious that it is impossible that one path would consist of an odd number of steps and another of an even number.

Similar pictorial, constructive and immediate approaches can be found e.g. in the Cayley diagrams used in abstract algebra (group theory), where the reasoning occurs not only visually through the graph, but temporally, as the eyes or the finger move along edges from vertex to vertex. With these images, mathematicians (and students) can perform complex mathematical procedures even the absence of a visual stimulus. In such cases, the manipulative operations of the hand, which moves along actual edges, become gestures used to perform (for oneself or for others).

4 Some Futures of Embodiment in Mathematics Education

In considering embodiment in relation to body–tool–mathematics, we have come across a few interesting new areas of research. For example, in relation to the discussion on rhythm, we have become interested in considering the affective, perhaps even psychodynamic, dimensions of the kinds of operational templates we have been discussing. There could be, on the one hand, the comfort and power of carrying out these structured routines, where the hand seems to know where to go, as when one multiplies two three-digit numbers on paper. Alternatively, and perhaps intensified around the tool itself, it might be worth exploring the affective relations that arise from body–tool interactions. Four decades ago, Papert (1980) was already talking about objects-to-think-and-feel with, when discussing his own attachments to gears as a young child. Turkle (2011) explored this idea further, studying the relationships that people developed with various types of tools, relationships she terms 'evocative', and that were far from being merely instrumental or cognitive. What tools and objects do we offer children in the mathematics classroom? Do they stand a chance of being similarly evocative? Certainly, the aesthetic considerations of Froebel's 'gifts'—not only in terms of their beautiful design but also in terms of the attention to sensory knowing—are rarely discussed in contemporary mathematics education literature on manipulatives or digital tools, but perhaps they could be.

From a more psychoanalytic point of view, Donald Winnicott's (1953) concept of a transitional object may also provide a fruitful avenue of research. At the very least, it would challenge the customary assumption that manipulatives and digital tools are discardable after the required learning has taken place. But it could also offer another image of the relationship that learners and teachers might develop with mathematical materials, not only as providing physical and symbolic structures, but also as offering affective ones. At a very basic level, for example, what are the affective structures at play when children are asked to interact with very big objects, like the straight-edges and compasses that teachers often use at the backboard, compared with the much smaller versions of these tools? In the former, the whole body would be involved in drawing the circle; the torso would be called upon to draw the line; the eyes would have to move along the line and around the circle instead of seeing it all at once. Gerofsky (2011) has conducted explorations in this vein, studying how the size of students' gestures relates to their own comfort with and understanding of the graph of a function. While the causal links are difficult to establish, it seems that gesturing a function with your whole body can improve conceptual understanding. While Froebel's 'gifts' tend to be quite small, we are interested in the body-size rods of our third example and what they entail in terms of large-scale operational templates.

Recognising the significance of performing and sensing patterned tool–body relations also has implications for the way in which we might conceptualise (cultural and individual) memory in mathematical practice. For example, as Kiesow (2016) has observed, the extensive use of gestures in structuring mathematical work with symbolic representations reveals the moving hands' function as part of a 'processor'. Further, we can think of (some) mathematical concepts as emerging from a reconstruction of a (cultural) repertoire of gestural templates in the form of the mimetic memory of a practical activity involving touch and a co-ordination of the movement of hand and eyes (e.g. counting, or the concept of a circle from making pottery on a potter's wheel while keeping the same distance from the centre, as well as getting rid of 'edges'). Then the function of manipulatives or mathematical tools for re-activating these templates and their aesthetic effect can be explored—aesthetic because they constitute part of mathematical sensing. This has political repercussions as well; as per Rancière's (2004) work, the aesthetic operates through the conjunction of sensing and of 'common' sense, conditioning our modes of perception, as well as our social institutions.

References

Arzarello, F., Olivero, F., Paola, D., & Robutti, O. (2002). A Cognitive Analysis of Dragging Practises in Cabri Environments. *ZDM: The International Journal on Mathematics Education, 34*(3), 66–72.

Bautista, A., & Roth, W.-M. (2012). The Incarnate Rhythm of Geometrical Knowing. *The Journal of Mathematical Behavior, 31*, 91–104.

Bringhurst, R. (2013). Six Poems with One Title. *Manoa, 25*(1), 173–181.

Carlson, R., Cary, M., Avraamides, M., & Strasberg, S. (2008). What Do the Hands Externalize in Simple Arithmetic? *Journal of Experimental Psychology, 33*(4), 747–756.

Clark, D. (2005). Transposition Graphs: An Intuitive Approach to the Parity Theorem for Permutations. *Mathematics Magazine, 78*(2), 124–130.

Cook, S., Mitchell, Z., & Goldin-Meadow, S. (2008). Gesturing Makes Learning Last. *Cognition, 106*, 1047–1058.

Cross, A. (1983). The Educational Background to the Bauhaus. *Design Studies, 4*(1), 43–52.

Freiman, V., & Volkov, A. (2018). History of Computations, Computing Devices, and Mathematics Education from the Teaching and Learning Perspective: Looking for New Paths of Investigation. In V. Freiman & A. Volkov (Eds.), *Computations and Computing Devices in Mathematics Education Before the Advent of Electronic Calculators* (pp. 3–21). Springer Nature.

Froebel, F. (1897). *Friedrich Froebel's Pedagogics of the Kindergarten or His Ideas Concerning the Play and Playthings of the Child.* A Compilation of Froebel's Essays Selected by Wichard Lange and Published in Berlin 1861. Translated by Josephine Jarvis & Edward Arnold.

Gerofsky, S. (2011). 'Seeing' the Graph vs. 'Being' the Graph: Gesture, Engagement and Awareness in School Mathematics. In G. Stam (Ed.), *Integrating Gesture*. John Benjamins.

Gray, J. (2004). Anxiety and Abstraction in Nineteenth-Century Mathematics. *Science in Context, 17*(2), 23–47.

Ingold, T. (2011). *Being Alive: Essays on Movement, Knowledge and Description*. Routledge.

Johnson, N., Turrou, A., McMillan, B., Raygoza, M., & Franke, M. (2019). 'Can You Help Me Count These Pennies?': Surfacing Preschoolers' Understandings of Counting. *Mathematical Thinking and Learning, 21*(4), 237–264.

Kidwell, P., Ackerberg-Hastings, A., & Roberts, D. (2008). *Tools of American Mathematics Teaching* (pp. 1800–2000). Johns Hopkins University Press.

Kiesow, C. (2016). *Die Mathematik als Denkwerk—Eine Studie zur kommunikativen und visuellen Performanz mathematischen Wissens*. Springer VS.

Laski, E., Jor'dan, J., Daoust, C., & Murray, A. (2015). What Makes Mathematics Manipulatives Effective? Lessons from Cognitive Science and Montessori Education. *SAGE Open*. April 2015. https://doi.org/10.1177/2158244015589588

Maheaux, J.-F. (2019). The Unsettling Playfulness of Computing. In A. Volkov, V. Freiman, (Eds.), *Computations and Computing Devices in Mathematics Education Before the Advent of Electronic Calculators. Mathematics Education in the Digital Era*, Vol. 11. Springer, Cham. https://doi.org/10.1007/978-3-319-73396-8_16

Menz, P. (2015). *Unfolding of Diagramming and Gesturing between Mathematics Graduate Student and Supervisor During Research Meetings*. PhD Dissertation, Department of Mathematics, Simon Fraser University. Retrieved from http://summit.sfu.ca/item/15503

Merleau-Ponty, M. (1945). *Phénoménologie de la perception*. Gallimard.

Moyer-Packenham, P., Shumway, J. F., Bullock, E., Tucker, S. I., Anderson-Pence, K. L., Westenskow, A., Boyer-Thurgood, J., Maahs-Fladung, C., Symanzik, J., Mahamane, S., MacDonald, B., & Jordan, K. (2015). Young Children's Learning Performance and Efficiency When Using Virtual Manipulative Mathematics iPad Apps. *Journal of Computers in Mathematics and Science Teaching, 34*(1), 41–69.

Ng, O., Sinclair, N., & Davis, B. (2018). Drawing Off the Page: How New 3D Technologies Provide Insight into Cognitive and Pedagogical Assumptions about Mathematics. *The Mathematics Enthusiast, 15*(3), Article 14. https://scholarworks.umt.edu/tme/vol15/iss3/14

Núñez, R. (2003). Do Real Numbers Really Move? Language, Thought, and Gesture: The Embodied Cognitive Foundations of Mathematics. In R. Hersh (Ed.), *18 Unconventional Essays on the Nature of Mathematics* (pp. 160–181). Springer.

Palatnik, A., & Abrahamson, D. (2018). Rhythmic Movement as a Tacit Enactment Goal Mobilizes the Emergence of Mathematical Structures. *Educational Studies in Mathematics, 99*(3), 293–309.

Papert, S. (1980). *Mindstorms: Children, Computers and Powerful Ideas*. Basic Books.

Pickering, A. (1995). *The Mangle of Practice: Time, Agency, and Science*. The University of Chicago Press.

Pollet, C.-V. (2018). Interpreting Algorithms Written in Chinese and Attempting the Reconstitution of Tabular Setting: Some Elements of Comparative History. In V. Freiman & A. Volkov (Eds.), *Computations and Computing Devices in Mathematics Education Before the Advent of Electronic Calculators* (pp. 189–214). Springer Nature.

Rancière, J. (2004). *The Politics of Aesthetics: The Distribution of the Sensible* (G. Rockhill, Trans). Continuum.

Reimers, B. (2014). Ein unerforschter Schatz. Verborgenes Archivmaterial auf Ausstellungsreise. Talk at the Opening of the Exhibition 'FRÖBEL 2020'. Museum der Wahrnehmung (MUWA), Graz, Austria.

Sarama, J., & Clements, D. H. (2009). 'Concrete' Computer Manipulatives in Mathematics Education. *Child Development Perspectives, 3*(3), 145–150.

Serres, M. (2011 [1999]). *Variations on the Body* (R. Burks, Trans.). Univocal Publishing.

Sinclair, N., & de Freitas, E. (2014). The Haptic Nature of Gesture: Rethinking Gesture with New Multitouch Digital Technologies. *Gesture, 14*(3), 351–374.

Sinclair, N., & Pimm, D. (2015). Whatever Be Their Number: Counting on the Visible, the Audible and the Tangible. In M. Meletiou-Mavrotheris, M. Mavrou, & E. Paparistodemou (Eds.), *Integrating Touch Enabled and Mobile Devices into Contemporary Mathematics Education* (pp. 50–80). IBI Global.

Sinclair, N., Chorney, S., & Rodney, S. (2016). Rhythm in Number: Exploring the Affective, Social and Mathematical Dimensions of Using *TouchCounts. Mathematics Education Research Journal, 28*, 31–51.

Singer, M., & Goldin-Meadow, S. (2005). Children Learn When Their Teacher's Gestures and Speech Differ. *Psychological Science, 16*(2), 85–89.

Soury-Lavergne, S., & Maschietto, M. (2015). Number System and Computation with a Duo of Artefacts: The Pascaline and the E-Pascaline. In X. Sun, B. Kaur, & J. Novotna (Eds.), *The Twenty-Third ICMI Study: Primary Mathematics Study on Whole Numbers* (pp. 371–378). ICMI.

Streeck, J. (2009). *Gesturecraft: The Manu-Facturing of Meaning.* John Benjamins.

Turkle, S. (2011). *Evocative Objects: Things We Think With.* MIT Press.

Uttal, D., Scudder, K., & DeLoache, J. (1997). Manipulatives as Symbols: A New Perspective in the Use of Concrete Objects to Teach Mathematics. *Journal of Applied Developmental Psychology, 18*, 37–54.

Volkov, A. (2018). Chinese Counting Rods: Their History, Arithmetic Operations, and Didactic Repercussions. In V. Freiman & A. Volkov (Eds.), *Computations and Computing Devices in Mathematics Education Before the Advent of Electronic Calculators* (pp. 137–188). Springer Nature.

Winnicott, D. (1953). Transitional Objects and Transitional Phenomena: A Study of the First Not-Me Possession. *The International Journal of Psycho-Analysis, 34*(2), 89–97.

Wood, M. (2010). Not Understanding Andy: A Metaphorical Analysis of Students' Resistance to Learning. *For the Learning of Mathematics, 30*(3), 17–22.

Social Choreographies in Primary School Education

Cornelie Dietrich and Valerie Riepe

Scholastic and classroom instruction, with its specific social forms and forms of communication, is, on the one hand, produced and shaped by the bodies of the actors involved and, on the other hand, itself produces the latter precisely in their corporeality as scholastic actors. The becoming of the body in and through school can be described as a "materialization of experience" (Butler, 1993), in which, however, "bodies never quite comply with the norms by which their materialization is impelled" (ibid., 2). The tension displayed here between materialization, materialized experience and the dynamics and resistance inherent to the process is the subject of this contribution. Living human bodies are always bodies in movement: even during work requiring great concentration, even during sleep. These movements—as an expression of the human ability and need for movement—are given a scholastically condensed form that is suitable for teaching and that we will discuss in what follows as social choreography. The aim is to make the dual significance of the moving body for everyday life in the classroom comprehensible and susceptible to empirical research: as both formative and formed, as both implementing pedagogical orders and commenting upon them (Hewitt, 2005; Klein, 2010; Dietrich & Riepe, 2019; Riepe, 2021). What we called social

---

C. Dietrich (✉)
Humboldt Universität of Berlin, Berlin, Germany
e-mail: dietricc@hu-berlin.de

V. Riepe
University of Applied Science Europe, Hamburg, Germany

© The Author(s), under exclusive license to Springer Nature Switzerland AG 2022
A. Kraus, C. Wulf (eds.), *The Palgrave Handbook of Embodiment and Learning*,
https://doi.org/10.1007/978-3-030-93001-1_27

choreographies are regularly occurring forms of movement that are (by virtue of having become) self-evident for all participants. As dependable orders, they structure the movements of a group in space according to certain rules, and as such, they are also significant for each social order in the pedagogical domain. We discuss the connection between the two aspects: the rule-governed movement and what it says about the pedagogical setting or how it helps to bring the latter into being. We proceed in three steps in what follows.

We first present the theoretical concept of social choreography, as it is used in dance studies and the social sciences (Sect. 1). We then elucidate this concept by way of two empirical examples: firstly, that of circle time in primary school, a configuration that is widespread in many pedagogical settings (Sect. 2.1); and, secondly, that of the choreographic treatment of the hierarchical order between teacher and pupils by virtue of their positioning in space (Sect. 2.2). What interests us here is not only the creation of order by a disciplining choreography but also the inter-responsiveness between order and disorder, between rule-governed behaviour and vitalistic dynamics, out of which a being-in-movement that is proper to schooling emerges in turn. Finally, we will summarize the results of the theoretical and empirical investigations (Sect. 3).

1 Social Choreographies

Choreography is colloquially understood as the conception, notation and study of patterns of movement. Within dance studies, on the other hand, there is constant debate about what choreography actually is (cf., e.g., Siegmund, 2010; Quinten & Schroedter, 2016). From the very start, what is at issue here is the tension between the notation-centred, prescriptive aspect and the performative, process-oriented aspect of choreography. The term choreography was introduced at the court of Louis XIV and, starting in the late seventeenth century, it was understood and used as synonymous for "dance notation" (Brandstetter, 2005, p. 54). The emergence of the term can thus be understood as an attempt to record the practice of dance at the royal court using the medium of written language. Furthermore, the "art of dancing according to choreography and writing dances" (Feldtenstein, 1972) served—in the context of choreography treatises—as instruction for fitting courtly behaviour in the public space (Brandstetter, 2005). Thus, since the beginning of the history of choreography, there has been a connection between educational aims and the objective of giving the fleeting quality of dance a fixed form and making it permanently visible.

If, for dance studies, choreographies thus represent "the basic material for studying concepts and practices of movement" (ibid., p. 53), Andrew Hewitt tries to bring about an interweaving of aesthetic and sociological interpretive models in his concept of "social choreography" (Hewitt, 2005). In so doing, Hewitt opposes the one-sided reference to two different 'body ideologies.' One of these he calls a materialistic ideology, which regards the body as material for the implementation of pre-scripted discourses and social orders. Starting from a materialistic concept of the body of this sort, one would try to explain how a given social order would be inscribed in bodies, which then reproduce and reify this order on a daily basis. Hewitt refers to the other ideology as that of physical immanence, within which the body forms the final point of resistance against social and discursive determinants. The point of departure is a vitalistic view of the body, which, in following its own impulses, is continuously deciding for or against a social order. According to Hewitt, the challenge would consist of resisting these two competing ideologies of body politics:

> We need a semiotic that articulates their interactions and collisions. The critical challenge is to marry text-based analysis to the analysis of performance; a challenge that is not simply for dance historians but also for those cultural historians who wish to learn from dance and who are dissatisfied with their discipline's tendency to reduce aesthetic phenomena to the status of document, to its simple sociological determinants. (ibid., p. 10)

He treats social choreographies here not as a metaphor, but rather as the aesthetic medium for rehearsing social order:

> This study differs in substance from the writings on the dance metaphor cited in an earlier note by stressing the social and political function of choreography—its disposition and manipulation of bodies in relation to each other—over the metaphysical resolution that dance offers. Rather than being interested in questions of how the metaphor, or even the practice, of choreography resolves problems of metaphysical subjectivity, this study will concern itself instead with the historical emergence of choreography (within modernism broadly defined) as a medium for rehearsing a social order in the realm of the aesthetic. Particularly when dealing with performative genre, moreover, that constantly demarcates its own artistic borders even as it acknowledges what its material (the body) has in common with the extraaesthetic—"metaphor" is an inadequate model for understanding the relationship of aesthetics to politics. (ibid., pp. 11–12)

He thus also opposes the view that performativity does not follow a script, but rather first emerges in doing: "you think you are acting spontaneously, but look, let me show you the script" (Hewitt, 2005, p. 46). What is at issue for him is not dissolving the dichotomy between determined script and freedom, but rather uniting the two poles: "Bodies are not writing. This being said however, they clearly do signify; the challenge is to understand how they do it" (Hewitt, 2005, p. 8). For what we say about a movement should also express the mobility of the movement and thus open up as wide an array of interpretive models as possible.

The dance scholar and sociologist Gabriele Klein further develops Hewitt's concept in relation to the public space and, using examples drawn from everyday culture, illustrates "how the social as a choreographic order is already inscribed in the public space" (Klein, 2010, p. 97). According to Klein, the concept of social choreography "thus does not primarily relate to the social aspect of choreography in the sense of a social aspect of the aesthetics of dance. Rather social choreography relates to the aesthetics of the social as a performative order of space, body, movement and subjects" (ibid., p. 101). Drawing on Hewitt, she assumes that social choreographies create reality: a reality that comes into being in the process of giving order to bodies in movement, following predetermined rules or rules that they have themselves created. For Klein, social choreography could thus become an

> analytical category that allows us to think the spatiality and temporality of the social as a mobile, but in its mobility still structured pattern of inclusion and exclusion, of marginalization and power, but also of subversion, transformation or revolution. (ibid., p. 101)

In what follows, we want now to look more closely at the aesthetic-analytical category within social choreography that Hewitt and Klein emphasize. Social choreography can thus become an analytical category that aims to uncover the aesthetic in the social. We follow Hewitt here and look for moments of interaction and collision between the vitalistic and materialistic dimensions: we take the mobility of movement particularly seriously even where it eludes unambiguous ascriptions of meaning.

2 Studying Social Choreographies in Primary School

We now present two phenomena in which pedagogical order, social choreography and the vitalistic obstinacy of children are intertwined: on the one hand, the choreography of the circle, which is extremely popular in German primary schools, and, on the other hand, the regulation of the relationship of above and below in the classroom, which is played out both at the blackboard and physically and in the visual axes to which the physical movements give rise. The following analyses were developed in the context of ethnographic studies that were carried out in four primary schools (Dietrich & Riepe, 2019).

2.1 Circle Time

Since the 1970s and 1980s, the strict seating arrangement in classrooms, in which children sit in rows at single or double desks, has gradually become more varied. Thus, group tables (with four to six children) were introduced, and the circular formation has been introduced more and more frequently as well. All more recent choreographies involve the same programmatic objective of allowing children to see (and look at) one another better and promoting discussion-based activities and cooperation among the pupils. Circle time, in particular, favours equal, participatory communication among pupils and between pupils and teachers. Thus, Peterßen's *Kleines Methodenlexicon* notes that in circle time [*Kreisgespräch*: literally 'circle talk']:

> [C]hildren and teacher sit together in an open circle of chairs …, so that *everyone can look as one another*. […] It should always be used when *genuine discussion* is sought, in order to translate what has been learned or even merely thought into words, in order to gain mutual familiarity with different views, etc. (Peterßen, 2001, p. 168 [our emphasis—C.D./V.R.])

In the presentation, we focus here on those dimensions of circle time that have coalesced into key categories (Breidenstein et al., 2013, p. 157) in the course of the material analyses:

(a) the circle as a geometric figure in Euclidean space,
(b) the circle as a moving line in the practical space of the actors and
(c) the circle as a figure enclosing a middle or an object (of learning).

Whereas the first dimension, as the imagining of an ideal equality, is particularly frequently mentioned and invoked in the linguistic and visual documents, the two latter dimensions first emerge from the ethnographic studies of the concrete practical approaches to and ways of thematizing circular seating.

2.2 The Circle as a Geometric Figure in Euclidean Space

As a geometric figure formed from the children's bodies, we encounter the circle in all sorts of pedagogical contexts, from pre-school and primary school to adult education: as circular seating or a morning circle, a discussion circle, singing in a circle or a circle for reflection. Heinzel (2001, 2016) mentions the symbolic significations of the circle: community, connectedness, a wholeness that is greater than its parts and equality. She interprets the "triumphal march" of circular seating in the primary school of the 1990s as a form in which hierarchies can be dismantled and in which democratic learning processes, as well as conflict mediation and problem-solving, can succeed. According to Peterßen (2001), circular seating was transferred from the family table to school in reform pedagogy and has been regarded ever since as a stable complement to individualized and competitively organized scholastic learning (Fig. 1).

In the ethnographic study of everyday school life, however, this equality in the circle appears to be far less complete than the discussed programmatic

Fig. 1 Source: Authors' own picture

writings suggest. In their ethnographic research, both de Boer (2006) and Kellermann (2008) have noted how merely by way of the organization of speaking turns, the asymmetrical generational and role difference between teacher and pupils is constantly maintained and the claim to an "egalitarian exchange among children and with the teacher" (Kellermann, 2008, p. 190) is thus belied. Whereas previous research usually examines the speech acts within the circle, but assumes the circle itself as a given, in what follows, in addition to looking at the linguistic level, we will undertake corporeally based, choreographic analyses of movements.

From an observation record, school A:

> Then Ms. Schuhmann announces that the children should sit in a circle. But she says that the circle has to look a little different than usual: "the circle has [to be] less circular," "more like a rectangle," "no one is permitted to sit here," "there has to be place here for a line of people," she instructs and indicates a gap with her arms, like a flight attendant, making large movements—arms outstretched and hands held straight at almost a 90 degree angle from the elbow—while the children sit down on the floor [...]. Using additional slow arm movements—arms and hands held parallel and close to each other in front of each child and standing with legs and feet parallel to one another—she assigns the children at the openings of the circle a kind of 'parking space' on the circular line.

The teacher's instructions about 'a circle, but less circular, more like a rectangle' must seem contradictory to the children. She thus starts to get the children organized using bodily gestures to make clear what she wants. Her movements are reminiscent of those of a flight line marshaller at an airport or a parking lot attendant, who direct the arriving planes or cars to their places. The large arm movements first serve to demarcate a (restricted) area, where the children are not allowed to be. Using language and bodily gestures, she thus establishes her position as a possessor of knowledge, while, at the same time, addressing the children as unknowing tools to carry out her conception. Within the process of producing the circle, she has thus again displayed the asymmetrical difference in roles between the children and her.

2.3 The Circle as Moving Line in the Children's Space of Action

Further interpretive horizons are opened up when we look at the circle as the arena for the children's action. The children themselves first create the circle by forming its outer line and turning towards the interior. If we focus our attention on how such circles come into being, how they are dissolved again and everything that happens on the line of the circle during circle time, we find interactive movements between two or three neighbours, playful horsing around in 'make-believe' mode, pensive interactions with one's own body or its accessories (watch, bracelet, shoes, hair, face, shoulders and legs) as well as with what is outside the line of the circle: desks, pens, folders, books and so on. The children know the choreographic rules: you are not supposed to have anything in your hands, knapsacks are put behind the chairs and you do not touch your neighbour. But, at the same time, the children are constantly playing with these precepts of circle time at the border between inside and outside that they themselves form. In its mobility, this line appears fragile and highly demanding (Fig. 2).

The circular seating can be grasped as a dynamic process in this dimension, inasmuch as both the circular line, by virtue of comings and goings, and the circle as a whole—say, due to the formation of pairs—is repeatedly commented on, called into question or even negated. For the children, the circle is not only a *geometric figure*, which is imposed on them as ordering structure, but rather it is also and perhaps above all a *moving line*, which first emerges from the children's bodies.

The following excerpt from the observation record describes how the circular seating arrangement comes into being in a third primary school class:

Fig. 2 Source: Authors' own picture

T.: "So, I'd like you now to sit in a circle" […]. The children react in very different ways. Some push desks toward the walls to create an open space in the middle. Two children sit on one of the tables and begin to talk to each another and to horse around playfully, while keeping an eye on what is going on in the emerging middle of the circle […]. Other children take their chair, put it somewhere in the open space […], take another chair, and so on. Still others push three or four of the chairs that are jumbled together in the middle toward the imaginary line, one next to the other; then they sit down. While this collective work is happening, there are many brief encounters between two or three children who look at each other, touch each other, talk and coordinate. […] This goes on for 90 seconds and then all of them sit down in a circle on their chairs and—little by little—turn their heads toward the middle. In the meanwhile, the teacher has taken several objects from a canvas bag and placed them on the floor in the middle; she wants then to show and discuss them in the circle. As she marks the end of the transitional situation by saying "So, I've brought you different things here," the way in which the children move changes. They are now sitting one by one on their chairs. Their movements and physical interactions can all be situated on the depth axis (front/back), but hardly any more on the breadth axis (right/left). It is striking how often the children touch *themselves* on legs, shoulders, head and hair. Their upper body tilts forward or they lean backwards, sometimes with the chair rocking back and forth a little. They scrape their feet, back and forth, on the floor and cross them."

In the 90 seconds that it takes to form the circle—the liminal, weakly structured transitional phase between two lesson sequences (Göhlich & Wagner-Willi, 2001)—the space of the children's action is more open and multidirectional than in the situation of the established circle. The task of together forming a circle gives an impetus to move in the group of children. Phenomenologically, a collective circle subject, in the sense of an intercorporeality (Waldenfels, 2015, p. 215), can be assumed. The movement-events that result from the intermediate spaces between the children, from the "intertwining of one's own and the other's movements" (ibid., p. 216), form a special field of forces, in which there is a collision between what is one's own and what is in common; we would otherwise be dealing with a "frictionless process of assembly line work" in the classroom (ibid., p. 215). The individual is here a point in a common line; it is only possible to understand and experience the line, however, by expanding the boundaries of one's own body towards one's neighbours, so that the line can be closed. This is easier to understand on the background of the children's experience, which includes not only circular seating in the form of a circle of chairs (which is already known from pre-school) but also *circle games*, in which children play both with the fragility of the circular line and with alternating between a radially centred and decentred focus of their attention: this alternation is often what makes the game interesting.

> For example, in 'Plumpsack' (a German game similar to 'Duck, Duck, Goose'), all the children stand in a circle, except for one who walks around the outside of the circle, drops an object behind one of the children as discreetly as possible, and then runs once around the circle. The child who has thus been marked has to catch the runner in time; otherwise, he or she is the next one who has to run around the circle and try to become part of it again. "Don't turn around, because the Plumpsack is going around. Whoever turns around or laughs, gets a knock on the back."

There is a tension between the prohibition on turning around and the need to do just that, if you do not want to be the loser or, in other words, excluded from the circle. Each current movement in these games arises out of the inherent choreography, which is the product of various fields of tension: between inside and outside (front and back), closed and open circle (right and left), staying still and moving (standing and running), touching and not touching one another. In every circle game, this necessarily gives rise to permanent micro-movements, which transcend and comment on the order of the geometric figure shown in the first section. Considered from the point of view of the phenomenology of the body, a circle can thus only arise and be maintained, if the breadth axis (right/left) is continually secured; but the pedagogical order, on the other hand, requires an orientation to the radial depth axis that is as rapid and exclusive as possible.

2.4 The Circle as Figure Enclosing a Middle

The circle always encloses objects: for example, playthings in discussion time or objects that the teacher brings to illustrate something she wants to talk about (Fig. 3). But there are also invisible objects in the middle: for example, topics that the class council wants to discuss, contentious points or stories that are being presented.

This still from a teaching video shows a religion lesson about the foods that, in the Jewish tradition, form part of the Passover meal, which, from the point of view of religious history, exhibits a close relationship to the Christian

Fig. 3 Source: Authors' own picture

Eucharist. The teacher has placed the foods, which are unfamiliar to the children, in the middle of the circle. They include salt water, unleavened bread, a dark brown apple mash, bitter herbs and so on. In the first part of the circle time, she discusses the symbolic meaning of each of the foods with the children. As the lesson continues, the children are encouraged to taste the foods in the middle and to share them with others. The lesson thus runs, in the spirit of practically oriented teaching, from discussion of the object to be understood, by way of the remote sense of vision (looking at it), to direct contact with the object in the form of touch and taste. The children's reactions are highly varied. Some of them are seemingly unreservedly open to what is new and alien. The boy raising his hand at the back left of the picture has even slid forward on his chair, and his eyes, arms, torso and even his legs are open towards the middle: he has put himself in a kind of starting position, as if he wanted to get going into the middle of the circle right away. And he is in fact the child who first takes a piece of bread afterwards. Other children also raise their hand, but with the other hand they encircle their own body: they maintain a balance between reserve, trying to reassure themselves, and their curiosity. And, finally, children can also be seen who—at least at this point still—are crossing feet and hands, arms and legs, and who thus maintain a more closed posture towards the foods, which are addressing them here in a materiality that is both familiar and unfamiliar.

In terms of cultural history, however, the circular arrangement around an object has much deeper roots. Sachs (1933) traces it back to the basic human need "to measure and shape spaces with the body" (ibid., p. 100). Precisely in early circle dances, the dancers do not only frequently encircle (imaginary) centres, but also objects or persons to be found there. To encircle an object here means "to take possession of it, to incorporate it, to bind and exorcise it ('spell circle')" (ibid.). On the one hand, the dangerousness of what is danced around is exorcized; on the other hand, it is brought into the community of the dancers.

In circles that are organized for pedagogical purposes, the stimulation and tension created by the alien object in the (thematic) middle are preserved inasmuch as what is discussed in the circle always has a certain novelty. This is also the case in the scene shown above. The objects that the teacher brought with her were already mentioned in the story that the children heard previously, but in their sensory reality, they are new. In a group discussion, the children said that they found what was discussed 'exciting,' 'unusual,' 'cool' or 'funny.' The alien object in the middle of the circle appeals to the children to move towards it and to enter into communication with it. This centring movement does not only occur mentally, however, but also has a corporeal side, which can readily come into conflict with the conversational rules: one of the most remarkable findings from the group discussions was that in responding to the question about the rules of conduct during the story circle, all the children mentioned *keeping their feet still*. You are not allowed to create 'a disturbance with your feet' when someone is talking. It is evidently hard for the children to respect this keeping of their feet still when reacting to the unsettlingly new and alien object in the middle of the circle.

2.5 Choreographic Height Axes and Hierarchical Rank

If up to now we have considered the breadth (right/left) and depth (front/back) axes, we want now to supplement the latter by the dimensions of the (power) axes *above* and *below* (Riepe, 2021). The regulation of heights in the classroom here reveals a choreography that defines 'permitted' and 'prohibited' levels:

> Hylia seems absent. She rests her upper body on her thighs, so that her long, dark hair falls forward, and she is shaking her hands, arms, upper body and head. She carefully sits up while making this slow shaking movement, rounding her shoulders and her hair falling over her face. When she is sitting upright again, she now lets herself slowly slide backwards over the bench. First her hair touches the floor and then her head. Her hands remain on her hips. Alessandro, who is sitting next to her to the left, leans down toward her and smiles. No one

Social Choreographies in Primary School Education 449

else pays attention to her. She looks at me—I am sitting behind the rows of seating on a single chair—and laughs. Then she also puts her hands on the floor, next to her head. Ms. Knapper now asks the children to count the syllables in the words on the blackboard. Hylia then sits up straight again on the bench and participates. Alessandro also counts, first kneeling on the bench; he then stands up behind it and rocks back and forth from one leg to the other. He raises his hand and is also called on by Ms. Knapper. Then Hylia stands up on the bench. After just a few seconds, Ms. Knapper screams "Hylia sit down!" and she moves her name down on the blackboard. "Where am I?" she whispers to Alessandro. "You're slipping further and further down!" he answers. "You're at ready to learn!" Ardi whispers. "Ah ok," Hylia replies with a dismissive wave of the hand. Hylia sets herself apart from the static formation by being one height line different from the other pupils. She rests her upper body on her thighs, so that her long, dark hair falls forward, she closes her hair-curtain to the scene in front of her or opens up contents that are all her own to the observer: Hylia deprives herself of the view of the blackboard and all her surroundings, veiling her eyes and forming a self-enclosed unit unto herself, in a kind of 'introspection.' In terms of the overall picture, from the observer perspective, she clearly sets herself apart physically from the group. From the teacher's perspective, she simply disappears behind the backs of the people in the rows in front of her. As the sliding-forward movement becomes a shaking articulation of hands, arms, upper body and head, she is, moreover, the only dynamic aspect in the picture. The vigorous gestures make her isolation now seem more aggressive and like a form of tense refusal of her surroundings. She carefully sits up while making this slow shaking movement, rounding her shoulders and her hair falling over her face. She thus cautiously and tensely approximates the position of the other pupils, but—in terms of her view—still remains shut off. She now repeats her movement from above, forwards and downwards and then back to the starting position, but in the other direction, backwards and downwards (Figs. 4, 5, 6, and 7). When she is sitting upright again, she thus lets herself slowly slide backwards over the bench. First her hair touches the floor and then her head. Her hands stay loosely on her hips. Her arms are not placed on the hips with fingers visible from the front, so that the gesture takes up less space or appears less aggressive, but rather as maintaining contact with the requisite bench (Fig. 4). The connection to the floor and the simultaneous revealing of her face now bring her back into the overall picture, also because Alessandro leans down over her and smiles at her. The rest of the situation continues to be unaffected by her activity. The tension involved in Hylia's movement reaches its highpoint when her gaze is now clearly directed at the observer and she laughs. Her focus on herself, seemingly inwards, is thus turned outwards again. By addressing the observer, a person who is not directly involved in the scene, via eye contact and the laughter that follows it, she presents herself not as caught-in-the-act and abashed, but rather as defiant and motivated.

Fig. 4 Source: Authors' own picture

Fig. 5 Source: Authors' own picture

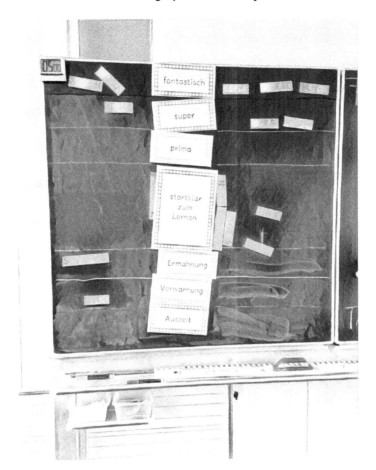

Fig. 6 Source: Authors' own picture

The moment is interrupted by the teacher, who asks Hylia to count the syllables in the words on the blackboard and thus to put herself back into the overall picture. Hylia then sits up properly on her bench and, actively cooperating, disappears within the homogeneous formation. A common rhythm of all the students is restored and yet each of them acts for him- or herself. Alessandro, who up to now has been the only pupil to respond to Hylia's movements, also actively counts the syllables. Now, he becomes the dynamic corporeal focus, first kneeling on the stool, then standing up behind it—thus opening up what is so far the highest level beneath the standing teacher—and rocking from one leg to the other, back and forth in rhythm with the syllable-counting class. He raises his hand and is also called on. His departure from the overall arrangement is thus marked as 'seen' and acceptable, since his body is in uniform rhythm with the situation.

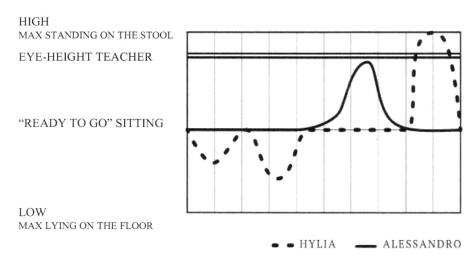

Fig. 7 Source: Authors' own diagram

As if she had to surpass his 'height,' Hylia now stands up on the bench, thus constituting the corporeal and dramaturgical apex of the arrangement. This is underscored by the teacher's screaming "Hylia sit down!" and then moving her name down on a list on the blackboard (Fig. 6). Her highest point is thus followed by the steepest fall: physically, from standing up on the stool to sitting and as evaluated by the teacher on a hierarchical measuring rod on the blackboard. Hylia's corporeal uprising is interpreted as provocation or crossing of a line by Ms Knapper. But why did she get up on the stool? Did she want to provoke Ms Knapper? Did she want to have a better view of the board? Did she want to outdo Alessandro? Or did the tension simply burst out of her at this point?

If, up to now, all the other movements in the class were tolerated by Ms Knapper, she clearly marks standing on the stool as breaking the rules. The sharp disciplinary reaction can thus clearly be attributed to the teacher's eye level. Her eyes are above those of all the children (including those who are squatting or standing; Fig. 4). The highest height and power axis in the class is reserved exclusively for her or is exclusively embodied by her.

The 'list' that is used in the class also alludes to the hierarchical height axis in the room. It can be understood as the changing of a traffic light in which the children start at green (ready to learn) and could slip down to yellow (warning, reprimand) and red (time out) or, alternately, move up to more intense green (good, super, fantastic). As invocation of a "doing equality"

Social Choreographies in Primary School Education   453

(Dietrich, 2017), in the sense of a (supposedly) homogeneous starting position, all the children begin each day at 'ready to learn' and move 'up' or 'down' from there. At the end of the school day, the children in the 'fantastic' and 'super' range then receive a sticker on a special index card. There are only consequences in the lower part of the list in the lowest, red 'time-out' category, since the child is then brought to the so-called island: a room with monitor, in which the child has to read the class rules again and write down which rule he or she has broken.

The relative terms 'above' and 'below' prove to be particularly relevant in communication, which makes Hylia's corporeal dialogue with the height levels even more plausible.

> "Where am I?" Hylia whispers to Allesandro, thus returning to the self-involved, introspective picture from the beginning of the scene and simultaneously, by virtue of the low voice in which she speaks, resubmitting to the rules of her surroundings—and the disciplining of the list. "You're slipping further and further down!" the latter replies, thus summing up the curve of her movement. If, at first, Hylia only moved her body 'downward' (and later 'upward'), she is now 'pushed down' the blackboard in front of everyone by Ms. Knapper. A parallel could be made here between the expressions 'slipping down' and 'getting on the wrong track': as the taking of an undesirable 'bad turn' or as a moral fall. "At ready to learn!" Ardi whispers from the row in front of her. "Ah ok," Hylia replies with a dismissive wave of the hand, since "ready to learn" is the zero-line from which all curves of movement, both upwards and downwards, are possible again.

In the other material as well (Riepe, 2021, p. 161f), the body levels between above and below become apparent as a permanent controlling instance of the hierarchical distribution of the situations and thus, on the one hand, include lying, sitting and standing postures. On the other hand, it is constantly reproducing both the homogeneous (zero-)line of the targeted mean of the normal distribution—as seated pupils—and the power axis of the teacher's line of sight, which is always (physically) superior to the children.

As against the participatory ideal of a 'pedagogy of equals,' which is also repeatedly mentioned as goal in such discussions with the teachers:

> T: So, I always try (--) how can I say it (-) at the same level, eye-to-eye; (-) it's important to me (.) that I have a good relationship with the children- (-) that they (.) so, I take the children as (.) they are ....

It is, nonetheless, apparent here that the line of sight of the—above all, standing—teacher is a non-negotiable upper limit of the height and power axis.

3 The Organization of Equality and Hierarchy as Two Examples of a Corporeal Pedagogical Dynamic

Using the examples of the corporeal order of the circle and the exploration of new (lesson) objects in 'the middle' and the axes between 'above and below' in rehearsing and reflecting on linguistic phenomena, the focus on social choreography serves here to broaden our perspective on the production of order via space and time in a pedagogical setting.

Thus, the body formations discussed and their pedagogical intentions are characterized by different either tightly meshed or loose systems of (corporeal) rules; it is apparent in them, however, that considerably more than just an arrangement of children's bodies for the purpose of facilitating orderly or instructive discussion is realized in practice.

The circle is not simply the contours, comprising children's bodies, of a stage for social interactions, but is itself a form of interaction and brings its own dimensions of meaning into play. In circle time, a series of axes of movement are created, which call, in varied and ambivalent ways, on the children involved to move between inside and outside, between centre and periphery, as individual body and simultaneously as an intercorporeal subject amidst the other children, to position themselves and thus to behave as being-positioned by the teacher and the things. This ambivalent variety of movement axes and possibilities is inherent to the choreography of the circle. From the point of view of cultural history, it was possible to illuminate not only the sense of community and the idea of equality and wholeness, but also the fascination of the alien object in the middle, which wants to be incorporated, but to which, at the same time, a certain distance must be maintained. Thus, scenes of movement and contact (between one another) arise in every chair circle, discussion circle, morning circle, even though precisely these two things, movement and contact, cannot be permitted. A 'semiotics of collision' (Hewitt, 2005) comes into being here: a fabric of meanings in which very heterogeneous elements are brought into relation with one another.

Thus, on the one hand, the symbolic order of equal participation in the sense of a 'doing equality' was apparent. This order can best be grasped by the Euclidean figure of the circle, which gives expression both to cultural symbolics of equality and, in the scholastic context, to symbolics of the child-friendly opportunity to contribute one's own topics and standpoints. On the other hand, the corporeal-intellectual order of behavioural dispositions towards productive discussion in the sense of a 'doing sameness' also became apparent

(Dietrich & Riepe, 2019; Riepe, 2021). The latter includes the rules, which apply in the circle, of speaking in turns and of keeping quiet, in linguistic terms, and, above all, still in physical terms. This demands restraining spontaneous ideas, as well as minimizing body movements: in particular, sideways movements and movements towards the exterior. But it also includes the expectation that all children should relate in a similarly engaged, interested and curious way to the alien object (of learning) in the middle of the circle.

If these dimensions appear in the circle primarily in relation to the physical *spatial* level, the guided exercise on the blackboard can be assigned to the level of *temporal* rhythming. Thus, variations in the movement of the students' bodies continue to be accepted by the teacher, as long as they, on the one hand, fit into the rhythm of the situation and, on the other, remain subordinate to the height axis of the teacher's line of vision.

Finally, all the dimensions of pedagogical order are met by vitalistic-spontaneous responses of the children. Here, instead of speaking of a '*doing* something,' we need to speak of a '*being* my lived and answering body.' Whereas the children are engaged in the production of—two, in themselves, contradictory—equalities in the above-mentioned dimensions, they are always already corporeal beings in their dual form of having a body and being a body. Whereas the explicit pedagogical intention addresses the child's body as an instrument for creating and maintaining pedagogical orders, the impetus to move that is inherent to the process stimulates the children in expressive and corporeal terms. This can also be read, with Butler (1990), as the reiteration of a resistance that is inevitably contained in the process: as the redirecting of the norm that is always inherent to every repetition of the norm.

References

Brandstetter, G. (2005). Choreographie. In E. Fischer-Lichte, D. Kolesch, & M. Warstat (Eds.), *Metzler Lexikon Theatertheorie* (pp. 52–55). Metzler.

Breidenstein, G., Hirschhauer, S., Kalthoff, H., & Nieswand, B. (Eds.). (2013). *Ethnografie. Eine Praxis der Feldforschung*. UVK.

Butler, J. (1990). *Gender Trouble*. Routledge.

Butler, J. (1993). *Bodies that Matter: On the Discursive Limits of "Sex"*. Routledge.

De Boer, H. (2006). *Der Klassenrat als interaktive Praxis. Auseinandersetzung Kooperation Imagepflege*. VS Verlag für Sozialwissenschaften.

Dietrich, C. (2017). Im Schatten des Vielfaltdiskurses: Homogenität als kulturelle Fiktion und empirische Herausforderung. In I. Diehm, M. Kuhn, & C. Machold (Eds.), *Differenz—Ungleichheit—Erziehungswissenschaft. Verhältnisbestimmungen im (Inter-)Disziplinären* (pp. 123–138) Springer VS.

Dietrich, C., & Riepe, V. (2019). Praktiken der Homogenisierung. Soziale Choreographien im Schulalltag. *Zeitschrift für Pädagogik, 5,* 669–691.

Feldtenstein, C. J. (1972). *Die Kunst nach der Choreographie zu Tanzen und Tänze zu schreiben.* Verlag der Schröderschen Buchhandlung.

Göhlich, M., & Wagner-Willi, M. (2001). Rituelle Übergänge im Schulalltag. In C. Wulf, B. Althans, K. Audehm, C. Bausch, M. Göhlich, S. Kersting, A. Tervooren, M. Wagner-Willi, & J. Zirfas (Eds.), *Das Soziale als Ritual. Zur performativen Bildung von Gemeinschaften* (pp. 119–204). Leske+Budrich.

Heinzel, F. (2001). *Kinder im Kreis. Kreisgespräche in der Grundschule als Sozialisationssituationen.* Universitäts-Habil-Schrift.

Heinzel, F. (2016). *Der Morgenkreis—Klassenöffentlicher Unterricht zwischen schulischen und peerkulturellen Herausforderungen* (Pädagogische Fallanthologie, 13). Verlag Barbara Budrich.

Hewitt, A. (2005). *Social Choreography: Ideology as Performance in Dance and Everyday Movement.* Duke University Press.

Kellermann, I. (2008). *Vom Kind zum Schulkind. Die rituelle Gestaltung der Schuleingangsphase. Eine ethnografische Studie.* Budrich University Press.

Klein, G. (2010). Das Soziale choreographieren. Tanz und Performance als urbanes Theater. In N. Haitzinger & K. Fenböck (Eds.), *Denkfiguren. Performatives zwischen Bewegen, Schreiben und Erfinden* (pp. 94–103). epodium.

Peterßen, W. H. (2001). *Kleines Methodenlexikon* (2nd updated ed.). Oldenbourg.

Quinten, S., & Schroedter, S. (Eds.). (2016). *Tanzpraxis in der Forschung—Tanz als Forschungspraxis: Choreographie, Improvisation, Exploration.* transcript Verlag.

Riepe, V. (2021). *Choreographien der Homogenisierung. Zur Verkörperung von Gleichheiten in der Grundschule.* transcript.

Sachs, C. (1933). *Eine Weltgeschichte des Tanzes* (3rd printing of the Berlin 1933 ed.). Olms.

Siegmund, G. (2010). Choreographie und Gesetz: Zur Notwendigkeit des Widerstands. In N. Haitzinger & K. Fenböck (Eds.), *Denkfiguren. Performatives zwischen Bewegen, Schreiben und Erfinden* (pp. 118–129). epodium.

Waldenfels, B. (2015). *Sinne und Künste im Wechselspiel. Modi ästhetischer Erfahrung, 2.* Suhrkamp.

On the (In)Visibility of Postcolonial Subjectivation: Educational Videography Research in Glocalised Classrooms

Juliane Engel and Cristina Diz Muñoz

Based on the results of an interdisciplinary project on glocalised living environments[1] this contribution discusses how students locate themselves relationally in the face of new relational possibilities. In accordance with current demands, which emphasise that the image-like (and already existing, finished) subject can no longer be used as the starting point for education theories (cf. Thompson et al., 2017; Tervooren & Kreitz, 2018), it addresses the question of how (postcolonial) subjectivations take place—how the pupils' subjecthood in glocalised classrooms is performatively assumed as an ongoing process (Butler, 2015). In this perspective it can be analysed how the unspeakable is articulated relationally, for example physically, and how the ambivalence between the undermining and the recognition of globalising norms of one's own and of others, for example as relations of domination, as powerful, productive, optimising, and submissive positioning of the pupils, is also physically negotiated. It can be understood in terms of the (subaltern) subject's

---

[1] Funded by the German Research Foundation, DFG: 'Glocalised Environment: Reconstructing the Modes of Ethical Judgement in Geography Lessons'. (Prof. Dr. Juliane Engel, University of Bamberg; Partners: Prof. Dr. Rainer Mehren, University of Gießen, PD Dr. Stefan Applis, University of Erlangen-Nuremberg), Term: 2015–2019. "The term 'glocalization' […] describes this increasing complexity of potential interrelations as a dynamic process of local and global developments. By indicating complexity or rather by showing the multi-directionality of the globalization concept itself, locality and globality can be understood in their syncratization, and thereby counter widespread notions of globalization created by a mostly eurocentric perspective." (https://www.paedagogik.phil.fau.de/dfg-research-project-glocalized-living-environments/)

J. Engel (✉) • C. Diz Muñoz
University Frankfurt, Frankfurt, Germany
e-mail: j.engel@em.uni-frankfurt.de; c.diz@em.uni-frankfurt.de

© The Author(s), under exclusive license to Springer Nature Switzerland AG 2022
A. Kraus, C. Wulf (eds.), *The Palgrave Handbook of Embodiment and Learning*,
https://doi.org/10.1007/978-3-030-93001-1_28

agency (Spivak, 2012): what is mostly discussed within discourses on achievement's optimisation as a lack of competence of individual students could be then thought and revised in its postcolonial dimension.

Whose bodies are being taught and sustained in the classroom arises at this point as a central aspect to be considered in our investigation. The basis for this shift is a relational praxeology which, as an innovation in education theory, opens up new access to the physical level of subjectivation processes in glocalised classrooms.

The insight into the relativity and materiality of educational processes is based on empirical observations. It in turn creates a need for a corresponding systematic further development of educational-qualitative methodology (Althans & Engel, 2016; Engel et al., 2021). If one looks, for example, at current discourses of video-based learning and teaching research, it is surprising how the visualisation procedure of videography is attributed an objectifying character in many places—both in quantitative and in qualitative studies—and how the constructional achievements of videographies for the innovation of educational science objects are often neglected (Engel, 2015). With Hall (1997), practices of representation always implicate the positions from which we speak or write. In our work we therefore start from the question of how something is made visible through educational videographies and how structural invisibilisations (must) therefore occur (Engel, 2016a, 2016b). We aim to interrogate the particular understanding of what a coherent image construction is—which goes back to Greek antiquity and has been increasingly conventionalised. Against this cultural-historical background and in view of their (methodologically mostly unquestioned) dominant subject positioning, methodological and practical definitions in discourses of videography research can therefore be critically interrogated and reformulated. We will demonstrate this in three steps in the following: First, by discussing how embodied learning can be made accessible through videography (1), then by exploring the implications of postcolonial cultural theories on the epistemological potential of videography when it comes to embodied learning processes (2), and finally by explaining how the embodiment of social norms can be understood as subaltern processes of subjectification (3).

1 On the (In-)Visibility of Learning Processes: Videography as a Way of Seeing in Education Research

What do we *see* when we talk about learning, educational processes, or teaching? How do identify the active parties in these processes? And how do we define the beginning and end of the processes we observe? These questions have been debated since the dawn of research on learning and education; they come up again in the context of classroom videographies when the researchers' analytical attitude is to be destabilised and the various entities are not fixed from the outset. Researching body-related learning and educational processes means going beyond considering them solely on the level of student-teacher interaction and as something that can be easily captured on camera. Instead, the research takes a broader perspective and examines these processes in their spatial dimension, in the relationship between human and object, in the performativity and materiality of the event (cf. Engel, 2019). But to avoid centring anthropocentric epistemological logic as a given, we must reexamine the methods of data collection and evaluation of classroom research focused on educational investigation on "qualitative meaning-understanding methods" (Proske & Rabenstein, 2018, p. 7)[2] insofar as, in keeping with the performative, practical, and material turn, learning practices are conceptualised as processes of relationalisation rather than as exclusive attributes of a 'strong' subject, in the sense of an anthropocentric logic of knowledge (Jörissen, 2015; Rabenstein, 2018a).

In German-speaking education science, the concept of *subjectivation* is primarily discussed in connection with Butler's and Austin's theories on processes of discursive invocations (e.g. Rose & Ricken, 2017).[3] In contrast, the term *subjectification* is used more in connection with investigations of socio-material dimensions (e.g. Gelhardt et al., 2013; Alkemeyer & Buschmann, 2016; Rabenstein, 2018a, 2018b). The present text interrelates these two approaches; that is it discusses how things or spaces can be modalities of invocation and how they too have the potential to subjectivise. In order to operationalise both epistemic qualities in our analysis, we trace the interplay and relationality of processes of subjectivation or subjectification in their performative, socio-material, and spatial levels.

In European iconography, the golden ratio has been tied to anthropological or subject-theoretical positionings of normative provenance since the Ancient Greek statues and even more so since the Renaissance (cf. Belting, 2011 for a discussion of the golden ratio in relation to bodies and de Campos et al., 2015 in relation to bodies and space). To expand this historico-cultural

---

[2] All translations of hitherto untranslated quotes from sources in German are by the authors. Please compare the information in the bibliography.

[3] In *The Psychic Life of Power: Theories in Subjection* (1997), Judith Butler summarises this argumentation scheme, which is relevant for education theory, as follows: "no subject emerges without a 'passionate attachment' to those on whom he or she is fundamentally dependent (even if that passion is 'negative' in the psychoanalytic sense). It is the formation of this unconscious attachment through dependency that leaves the subject open to 'subordination' and 'exploitation' and which supports the order of power" (1997a, p. 7).

argumentation we should note that the idea of optimisability qua media-based observation was established in pedagogy from an early stage, since it can already be found in the time of panoptism (Jörissen, 2011, 2014). The Meritentafel (honour roll plaque) for example can be interpreted as a technology to visually objectify inner moral states (ibid., 2014). This also means that in the European cultural sphere, a basic panoptic structure has been inherent in pedagogy since its (modern) emergence and informs certain discourses on classroom videography research.

From the perspective of subjectification theory, our text reflects on this (very condensed) historico-cultural analysis of the discursive connections between imaging procedures in pedagogy and the phantasms and semantics of subject-centred optimisation and related practices of disciplining bodies.

In the following, we ask how "in our culture, human beings are made subjects" (Foucault, 1983). With attention to the dynamics of power, we analyse the sociocultural conditions and possibilities (Gomolla & Radtke, 2002) that produce people as unequal subjects through processes of invocation and disciplinary practices of governance (Keller, 2017; Bosančić & Keller, 2019; Alkemeyer & Brümmer, 2019). From an education theory perspective, we are interested in how unequal subjects are produced and how they are "integrated into discourses and power relations" (Keller et al., 2012). For some time now, there has been a new surge of interest in educational theories of subjectivation/subjectification[4] (Ricken et al., 2019b; Fritzsche, 2012; Tervooren, 2006). In both school pedagogy (Reh & Rabenstein, 2013; Rabenstein, 2018a, 2018b) and general pedagogy (Rose & Ricken, 2017; Ricken et al., 2017), research has been conducted that focuses on the phenomenon of subjectification from the perspective of education theory (Rieger-Ladich, 2004, 2012; Kleiner & Rose, 2014). Compared to approaches in cultural studies and sociology (cf. Amling & Geimer, 2016, 2017; Traue et al., 2018; Spies, 2019), which can empirically show how practices of bodily (self-)government are entangled in social discourses (Bröckling, 2007), the perspectives of education science raise awareness of transformational potentials and open up space to reflect on changing bodily practices of subjectification, or on how pedagogical processes are made possible by practices of subjectification. Hence, thinking with Foucault, 'being made a subject' goes hand in hand with the idea of

---

[4] Butler uses the term subjectivation to analyse the discursive production of the subject, while Foucault uses the term subjectification. Both of these traditions are relevant to our approach. In this text, we are mostly using the term subjectification, as we are concerned with the dynamics of power at play in processes of discursive production of the subject.

fashioning oneself into a subject—but it is also precisely the intersection of these two aspects that constitutes a particular challenge that calls for further inquiry that is not only categorical and theoretical but also empirical and methodological. (Ricken et al., 2019a)

Based on this genetic approach to analysis that calls attention to the bodily processes of subject formation, our text builds on empirical studies that focus on how practices of (unequal) subjectification through placement in space have been transformed and transmitted.

We are interested in these signifying placements in space as (re)addressing, from the perspective of education theory, as this allows for an analytical perspective on the questions:

> As *whom* is someone addressed, *how* is that person addressed as someone specific, and *whom* does this addressing turn them into? And to whom do they turn themselves into in response to that addressing? (Ricken & Kuhlmann, 2019, p. 3)

Our reconstructions of subjectivising practices of bodily signifying are based on videography studies and are particularly attentive to the dynamics of addressing. On that basis, we have developed videography research that attends to how looking through the camera is itself an event marked by power relations. We discuss it as a sociocultural practice of rendering visible (Kolbe et al., 2008; Kravagna et al., 1997). From a postcolonial perspective, rendering visible vulnerable groups or groups that are othered is particularly important (cf. Spies, 2018; Traue et al., 2019). This is because relations of recognition are based on visibilities in which visuality itself is given an epistemic status, as Traue et al. (2019) explain:

> In other words, our analytical task is not a matter of looking harder or more closely, but of seeing what frames our seeing—spaces of constructed visibility and incitements to see which constitute power/knowledge. (Traue et al., 2019, p. 327)

From a perspective of postcolonial analysis, practices of (self-)designation are key here because they allow for (bodily) educational processes through acts of (re)addressing and recognition. Considering this in the context of video, in the following we will discuss the epistemological potential of videography research that attends to dynamics of power (2) on the one hand, and object-related epistemological potentials using the example of videographic approaches to subaltern processes of subjectification (3) on the other hand.

2 On the Epistemological Potential of a Videographic Focus on Embodied Learning Processes

In her epistemological reflections, Spivak exposes the epistemic violence of scientific politics of epistemology and their claims to validity (Spivak, 2012; Castro Varela & Dhawan, 2010). In education science as well, engaging with the epistemological implications of research approaches and methodologies shows that

> knowledge and cognition not only cannot be separated from social, i.e. political and societal contexts, but that this is precisely where they are found, which is why they (can) never exist in a 'pure' form. (Reichenbach et al., 2011, p. 12)

This is how we understand the methodological and research angle of our videography as an act of seeing and focusing on embodied learning and educational processes. While reconstructing the (re)addressing in the classroom as everyday practices of subjectification, we reflect on the epistemic violence inherent in our research methodology of videography as an act of knowledge politics. Understanding the camera's gaze as a focus on embodied learning and educational processes entails paying close attention to their performative power. Hence, by exploring new fields of research and research perspectives in an approach that is critical of hegemonic power, the camera allows for a sharper awareness of (critical) social contexts of method development (Bachmann-Medick & Kugele, 2018; Göttlich et al., 2001). This sharpening occurred particularly at the level of developing new research methodologies following the critique of cultural representations of familiar research subjects and methods (Hall, 1997). It has shaped our videography research insofar as the crisis of representation can be considered an important momentum for education research on the body-related emergence of subjects and associated educational figures. It stresses the importance of critical perspectives on familiar phenomena and cultural representations of (eurocentric) representations of bodies (ibid.).

In *The Spectacle of the 'Other'* (Hall, 1997), Stuart Hall discusses how hurtful photographic depictions of the body (seen here in the context of advertisement) can be when they represent the vulnerability of subject positionings.

Consequently, we have experimented with new possibilities of representation in our work, in order to, for example, productively destabilise the trained, conventional view of subject-centred educational processes and the associated representations of embodied learning and educational processes, thereby opening them up to the relationality of subjectification (Engel, 2020a, 2020b).

Unlike the high-angle shot (Seidel et al., 2003), which usually represents the students' bodies (relatively passively) sitting at tables as part of a disciplined complete system of interaction and which focuses primarily on cognitive learning processes, the following photographs show bodies participating in learning processes and educational processes that make it possible to study subjectification processes in a way that is attentive to the dynamics of power at play.

All photographs reproduced here are stills from videography-based studies conducted as part of the DFG research project on *Glocalized Lifeworlds*. They offer the potential to critically examine how bodies participate in educational processes at school and to analyse subjectification in this context also on its non-verbal, performative level (Fig. 1).

Photographic representation of subjectification in the context of overstepping boundaries (Fig. 2).

Photographic representation of subjectification through technology and media, showing subjectificating practices of mise-en-scène and interaction with the audio recorder and the camera (Fig. 3).

Photographic representation of subjectification in the context of (sexualised) violence (Figs. 4 and 5).

Fig. 1 Physical learning and education processes in the classroom's world trade game are here portrayed from a high-angle camera shot: wide shot of the classroom from above. (Source: Authors' own picture)

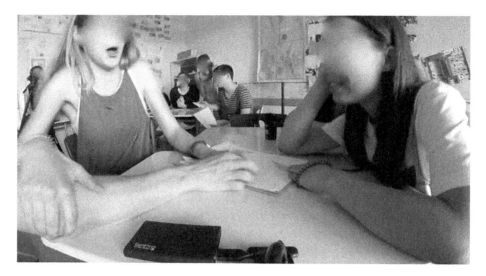

Fig. 2 Touch: A student is holding her breath while trying to stop a hand reaching for a piece of paper. (Source: Authors' own picture)

Fig. 3 Body and technology: An isolated, lonely student interacts with the audio recorder and then addresses the camera directly. (Source: Authors' own picture)

Thus, the relevance of relationality of body-related educational processes to education science can be affirmed on two levels: First, they shed light on how education theory can build on cultural studies insights about processes of subjectification in the interplay of bodies, spaces, and objects (Engel, 2020a,

On the (In)Visibility of Postcolonial Subjectivation... 465

Fig. 4 Wanting to participate in class activities, a student reaches for a pair of scissors. Another student wants to push the first one out of her territory; her hand gestures express distancing attempts. (Source: Authors' own picture)

Fig. 5 A student holds another in a headlock while looking at a girl. Neither of the girls at the table looks at what the other students are doing; they smile and keep on working. (Source: Authors' own picture)

2020b). Second, the example of vulnerable and marginalised subject positionings outlines the socio-critical dimension of these insights (Engel, 2017; Engel et al., 2019a).

> The question that comes to the fore in the current debate about education—a rather tense debate largely based on supposedly obvious self-understandings—is what is 'constructed' as educational reality by whom with what means and to what end. (Reichenbach et al., 2011, p. 7)

Thus, following the work of Sabine Reh (2012) and Bina Mohn (2002) on (self-)reflexive videography research, we ask: What is it about our focusing gaze through the camera, looking at embodied practices of signifying, that can recognise, acknowledge, and show appreciation, while also possibly having a subjugating effect? This approach to videography research allows us to think about the way we look at someone through the camera as marked by both recognition and subjugation (Tsang, 2020).[5] How, then, can we use the camera to look at, for example, embodied processes of learning and education, which on the one hand are validated in this way but also subjected to our gaze on the other hand? We recognised that unequal subject positionings are brought forth not only by practices of body-related designation, which also occur on the level of language, but that placement in space also operates as a form of addressing, as that socio-material relationalisations, in short, the entanglement of bodies, things, and spaces are crucial factors (Engel, 2019). Certain subject positions reveal themselves to be particularly vulnerable in light of the interplay of bodies, materialities, and relationalities. Therefore, videography research that incorporates postcolonial insights focuses not only on linguistic practices of signifying and being signified but also on where subjects are placed in space or in relation to space, on spatial processes of invocation, and on the entanglements of people and things, that is on the socio-material dimension of invocations and of these entanglements.

Reconstructing implicit structures of invocation (as is commonly done in documentary subjectification analysis) has proven to be particularly insightful, as it constitutes the groundwork for showing how bodies are addressed and produced as specific and unequal subjects on an implicit level, even if

---

[5] According to Wu Tsang, this is the case particularly in the context of migration and flight, because these vulnerable groups of people, Tsang explains, are particularly dependent on relations of visual recognition: "Documenting within this context, Wu Tsang employs a magical realist approach, allowing the boundaries between fact, fiction and surreal narrative to be intentionally fluid. What has commonly been referred to as a 'refugee crisis' is structurally encountered in the film as a crisis of representation" (https://www.berlinerfestspiele.de/en/berliner-festspiele/programm/bfs-gesamtprogramm/programmdetail_277205.html).

there is no explicit invocation to that effect. This raises critical questions about power relations that a research approach inspired by postcolonialism engages with: Who is seen and how? To what extent do hegemonic structures of perception determine the field of what can be seen and put into words?

> If research in the fields of the sociology of knowledge and sociology of culture that explores (audio-)visual phenomena wants to engage with the state of contemporary media relations, it should also engage with the fundamental levels of the socio-techno-symbolic process. It should begin by developing interpretive analytics for describing the relationalities of what can be seen and what can be said, concerning the alliances of image, text, sound, and materiality. (Traue, 2013)

A self-critical reflection on the interplay of mediality and aesthetics in this context requires taking decisions on how to sift through, sort, and edit the material. For example, are we showing the system(s) of interaction between students and teachers and discussing it as 'teaching'? Does our camera angle emphasise certain things? Are our questions and approach in keeping with subject-relevant didactics? Hence, the central methodological question is how to use the medium of videography to aesthetically represent research objects in such a way that they open up new possibilities for thinking about embodied learning and processes of subjectification. A postcolonial angle further explores how videography as a medium offers representational possibilities that allow it to develop an aesthetic that includes diverse cultural representations of embodied learning processes while allowing for self-critical awareness of the epistemic violence tied to these learning processes. In terms of visual regimes, this means investigating how practices of making visible and making invisible emerge. In this context, Santos (2007) refers to hegemonic thinking as 'abyssal thinking':

> Modern Western thinking is an abyssal thinking. It consists of a system of visible and invisible distinctions, the invisible ones being the foundation of the visible ones. The invisible distinctions are established through radical lines that divide social reality into two realms, the realm of 'this side of the line' and the realm of 'the other side of the line'. (Ibid., p. 45)

Our seeing is also overlooking, blocking out, looking away; our line of sight also obscures things. Seeing, then, emerges from the conflict between the visible and invisible aspects of embodied learning and educational processes, a conflict that is inherent in all seeing—even through the camera—as we have demonstrated in our empirical studies (Engel, 2019, 2020a, 2020b;

Engel & Diz Muñoz, 2021). This allows for (self-)critical reflection, at the level of methodology, on the sociocultural form of *looking* at practices of bodily signifying, placement, and entanglements.

3   Whose Bodies Are Taught

Theorist Sylvia Wynter (2003; Wynter & McKittrick, 2015) explores the concept of 'the human' and the epistemological establishment of its meaning. She notes that some subject positionings are excluded from this category through discourse. In an exchange with Katherine McKrittick (2015), Wynter defines the Western concept of 'human' as "the measuring stick through which all other forms of being are measured" (ibid., p. 3)—resulting in certain bodies not being produced as bodies, but as something 'other'. In the course of our analysis, we have explored how the bodies of students are constructed (Engel & Diz Muñoz, 2021) as "less-than-human" (Wynter, 2003) or "something other than human" (Snaza, 2018, p. 343) by practices of signifying, placement, and entanglement. They are marginalised in the social life of the classroom and are dehumanised and minoritised in verbal addresses (Engel et al., 2019; Engel, 2020a, 2020b).

Our work echoes Wynter's as well as Mignolo's: "The Human is therefore the product of a particular epistemology, yet it appears to be (and is accepted as) a natural independent entity existing in the world" (Mignolo, 2015, p. 108). Whose bodies, then, are taught? Whose bodies are addressed and how (respectfully or disparagingly)? How are they thus (re)presented or (re)signified, that is given validity and charged with meaning, in the context of seating arrangements, systems of interaction, discussions in class, and didactic models? And which bodies are neither seen nor heard in the process? Wynter's project is one of cognitive transformation towards a new understanding of the human origin story—a reading that has been characterised as decolonial by authors such as Mignolo (cf. Mignolo, 2015).

4   Videography and Subaltern Subjectification

We compared 27 group discussions before the treatment (a course module we developed as part of our research project) and 27 group discussions after. These insights, combined with a triangulated video-based investigation of the performative level (Engel, 2015) of judgement logics (Engel, 2020b; Rabenstein, 2018a), allowed us to critically discuss changes in bodily positioning of self and other in the context of the students' global networking processes (Engel, 2020a, 2020b; Thompson, 2019).[6] The typification that emerged points to the correlation between implicit attitudes about value and the students' spaces of experience (Engel et al., 2020).

This made it easier to understand that, for example, some students' attitudes and body postures expressing powerlessness, resignation, or anger are rooted in concrete everyday experiences.

This analysis of perspectives is in line with current demands that have been stressing how outdated it is to develop body-based education theories around the notion of a malleable (and already existing, complete) subject (cf. Jörissen, 2015; Thompson et al., 2017; Rieger-Ladich, 2012; Nohl, 2017; Tervooren & Kreitz, 2018).

Asking how (postcolonial) subjectifications—that is specific practices of bodily signifying, placing, and entanglement—emerge and how they operate, in short, how people and their bodies are in a process of continually becoming what they are (Engel, 2020a, 2020b), can open up wider critical reflection at the intersection of education science and cultural studies. By paying attention to the various perspectives, it is easier to understand how that which cannot be said in words is articulated in terms of relationality[7] as well as how the tension between recognising globalising norms of self and other and subverting them, for instance as relations of dominance, are negotiated in terms of powerful, productive, and/or subordinated bodily positionings (Engel & Fritzsche, 2019). By focusing on the relationality that comes to the fore in this process as an emphasis on the wider fact of the 'entanglement' of educational processes (Ricken, 2013, p. 35), it becomes possible to explore—using video as a tool—bodily processes of subjectification even beyond anthropocentric epistemological logics (Engel, 2015, 2020b).

The epistemological and pedagogical arguments involved in this process can be connected to Judith Butler's cultural theories on the matrix of intelligibility and Michel Foucault's on the archaeology of knowledge.

---

[6] Christiane Thompson (2019) for example points out that "a new form of subjectification had emerged under the rubric of 'global expertise' that increasingly binds addressees in education to using output-based data sources that are made available digitally" (p. 299). Our research project also traced the close link between issues of globalisation and competitive and performance-oriented forms of subjectification of students and teachers (Engel, 2019).

[7] It is crucial to note that the relationality of subjectification processes does not operate on the level of linguistic or non-linguistic utterances, but is rather determined by whether the articulations in the discourse are or can be heard. "In terms of the concept of conflict, reinventing discourse thereby implies an ethical position at the same time, insofar as it is about acknowledging the conflict by keeping it open. As much as possible and for it to attend to plurality it should be about 'expressing what was previously unsayable' (Koller, 1999, p. 150)" (von Rosenberg, 2011).

Elaborating on their concept of a cultural matrix of intelligibility, Butler highlights the interplay between phenomena that, being recognised by society, are (hegemonically) perceivable and how they materialise in discourse in the process of (re)citing social norms (Butler, 1991, 1997b). In *The Archaeology of Knowledge* (1972), Michel Foucault emphasises how crucial it is to critically reflect one's own methodological positionality and the inevitable (re)production of knowledge and (powerlessness) it entails. He stresses how important it is, with regard to research methodology, to "uncover cultural facts that, as 'conditions of our rationality' (DE I, 776), shape our contemporary thinking and language. Hence the point is also to question our thinking and our language" (Kammler et al., 2014, p. 51). As we also have explained in our work, it is therefore not only possible but necessary to nurture open spaces where the findings of research methodology on embodied learning and pedagogical processes and their already socially accepted norms can not only be 'cited' and repeated but where they can also be subverted and rethought. In our work we have discussed this process as a crisis of representations of education science approaches to how learning and pedagogical processes are embodied and how they are (re)signified (Hall, 1997). Analysing (re)signification in terms of the dynamics of power and difference at play yields insights about how body-related pedagogical processes are given meaning or granted validity (Engel et al., 2021), pointing the way for how researchers can focus more on how familiar (hegemonic) categories are reproduced and consolidated or indicating ways of analysing change and development of diverse or pluralising research objects. These questions have been central for researchers whose work is about vulnerable groups and hence draws on postcolonial, gender-sensitive, and/or queer perspectives. This opens the way for a "persistent critique" (Spivak et al., 1996) that does not produce a "coherent narrative" (ibid.), but rather recognises "that networks of power/desire/interest are so heterogeneous" and attempts "to disclose and know the discourse of society's Other" (Spivak, 1988). In the course of our research, we have developed a relational methodology—an innovative approach in terms of education theory—based on new (video-based) approaches to embodied processes of subjectification. Because vulnerable, precarious subject positions are not due to individual cases of certain students (Engel, 2019) but could be traced as structurally identical in cross-case studies (Engel et al., 2020), our research pays particular attention to practices of marginalisation and subalternity (Engel, 2020b). Students who cannot be classified into familiar categories of difference according to their physical appearance are excluded, marginalised, and minoritised by their classmates and teachers on a daily basis. Their bodies are addressed violently (Butler, 1997a). Triangulated analyses of the videographies and the questionnaires show that the othering of certain students in the classroom (understood as a space of interaction or as a sub-organisation) was also related to their collective affiliations, which the other students and the teacher seemed unable to neatly classify into their usual social categories of difference:[8] These students do not fit in into their group. The typifications we have developed show that students often have multiple collective affiliations.

In a relational analysis of subjectification, implicit normalisation processes and how they are embodied in the context of learning processes are taken into account, allowing for structures and relations of inequality that emerge in this process to be recognised more clearly. Espousing a postcolonial perspective, it pays attention to "the different starting conditions in plural societies to reflect global interconnections and interdependencies rather than identifying otherness" (Messerschmidt, 2018, p. 573). In this sense, Sylvia Wynter interprets being human as a praxis (Wynter & McKittrick, 2015) and calls for a new worldview that would produce other social bodies and other social imaginaries (cf. Wynter, 2003). In this context, and following Judith Butler's epistemology, it is crucial to note that something can only be perceived and recognised if it is socially intelligible, that is if it already exists as a cultural imaginary construct. It is at the level of reflection on a given structure that discourse or regimes of looking can be critically shifted. However, it is not only discourses that regulate zones of intelligibility by themselves; they "also produce spaces of exclusion by identifying and recognising certain subject types" (Rieger-Ladich, 2012, p. 63). This is because, as discussed in theories about inequality, subjects are positioned within contexts of empowerment and/or disempowerment (Engel et al., 2019b; Beach, 2017; Beach & Johansson, 2017; Rose & Ricken, 2017).

References

Alkemeyer, T., & Brümmer, K. (2019). Die Körperlichkeit des Lernens. In B. Dippelhofer-Stiem & S. Dippelhofer (Eds.), *Enzyklopädie Erziehungswissenschaft Online. Rubrik: Erziehungs- und Bildungssoziologie* (pp. 1–27). Beltz Juventa.

Alkemeyer, T., & Buschmann, N. (2016). Praktiken der Subjektivierung— Subjektivierung als Praxis. In H. Schäfer (Ed.), *Praxistheorie. Ein soziologisches Forschungsprogramm* (pp. 115–136). Transcript.

Althans, B., & Engel, J. (2016). Responsive Studien als ästhetische Resonanzräume. In B. Althans & J. Engel (Eds.), *Responsive Organisationsforschung. Methodologien und*

---

[8] This area is characterised by ambiguous or non-binary categories of classification, such as transgender aspects or transcultural affiliations.

institutionelle Rahmungen von Übergängen (pp. 179–206). Springer VS. Volume in an Anthology: Göhlich, M. (ed.). (2004–2020). *Organisation und Pädagogik*, 14.

Amling, S., & Geimer, A. (2016). Techniken des Selbst in der Politik—Ansatzpunkte einer dokumentarischen Subjektivierungsanalyse. *FQS. Forum Qualitative Sozialforschung, 17*(3). https://doi.org/10.17169/fqs-17.3.2630

Amling, S., & Geimer, A. (2017). Muster und Aporien der Subjektivierung in der professionellen Politik. In T. Spies & E. Tuider (Eds.), *Biographie und Diskurs. Methodisches Vorgehen und Methodologische Verbindungen* (pp. 151–167). Springer VS.

Bachmann-Medick, D., & Kugele, J. (2018). *Migration: Changing Concepts, Critical Approaches*. De Gruyter.

Beach, D. (2017). Whose Justice is This! Capitalism, Class and Education Justice and Inclusion in the Nordic Countries: Race, Space and Class History. *Educational Review, 69*(5), 620–637. https://doi.org/10.1080/00131911.2017.1288609

Beach, D., & Johansson, M. (2017). The Challenges and Response of Location: Transnational Migration in Six Different Rural Areas in Sweden. *XXVVI European Society for Rural Sociology Congress*, 24–27.

Belting, H. (2011). *Bild-Anthropologie. Entwürfe für eine Bildwissenschaft*. Fink.

Bosančić, S., & Keller, R. (2019). *Diskursive Konstruktionen. Kritik, Materialität und Subjektivierung in der wissenssoziologischen Diskursforschung*. VS.

Bröckling, U. (2007). *Das unternehmerische Selbst. Soziologie einer Subjektivierungsform*. Suhrkamp.

Butler, J. (1991). *Gender Trouble: Feminism and the Subversion of Identity*. Routledge.

Butler, J. (1997a). *The Psychic Life of Power: Theories in Subjection*. Stanford University Press.

Butler, J. (1997b). *Excitable Speech. A Politics of the Performative*. Routledge.

Butler, J. (2015). *Senses of the Subject*. Fordham University Press.

Castro Varela, M. d. M., & Dhawan, N. (2010). Mission Impossible: Postkoloniale Theorie im deutschsprachigen Raum? In J. Reuter & P.-I. Villa (Eds.), *Postkoloniale Soziologie. Empirische Befunde, theoretische Anschlüsse, politische Intervention* (pp. 303–329) transcript.

de Campos, D., Malysz, T., Bonatto-Costa, J., Pereira Jotz, G., de Oliveira Junior, L. P., & da Rocha, A. (2015). More Than a Neuroanatomical Representation in the Creation of Adam by Michelangelo Buonarroti, a Representation of the Golden Ratio. *Clinical Anatomy, 15*(6), 702–705. https://doi.org/10.1002/ca.22580

Engel, J. (2015). Image Language and the Language of Images. *Research in Comparative and International Education, 10*(3), 383–393. https://doi.org/10.1177/1745499915580636

Engel, J. (2016a). Pädagogische Blicke zwischen inneren und äußeren Bildern. In G. Graßhoff, F. Schmidt, & M. Schulz (Eds.), *Pädagogische Blicke* (pp. 164–192). Beltz Juventa.

Engel, J. (2016b). Zur (Un-)Sichtbarkeit organisationalen Lernens. Theoretische Überlegungen. In A. Schröer, M. Göhlich, S. Weber, & H. Pätzold (Eds.),

Organisation und Theorie. Beiträge der Kommission Organisationspädagogik (pp. 199–207). Springer VS.

Engel, J. (2017). Pädagogische Blicke zwischen inneren und äußeren Bildern. In G. Graßhoff, F. Schmidt, & M. Schulz (Eds.), *Pädagogische Blicke* (pp. 164–192). Juventa.

Engel, J. (2019). Diskurse der (Nicht-)Präsenz. Artikulationen—Materialitäten—Fremdheiten. In J. Engel, M. Gebhardt, & K. Kirchmann (Eds.), *Zeitlichkeit und Materialität* (pp. 195–204). transcript.

Engel, J. (2020a). Relational Practices of Subjectivisation. In G. Kress, S. Selander, R. Säljö, & C. Wulf (Eds.), *Education as Social Practice*. Routledge. (Forthcoming).

Engel, J. (2020b). Zum sichtbar Unsichtbaren. Relationale Praktiken der Subjektivation in der Videographieforschung. In C. Demmer, T. Fuchs, F. Kreitz, & C. Wiezorek (Eds.), *Das Erziehungswissenschaftliche qualitativer Forschung* (Schriftenreihe der DGfE-Kommission Qualitative Bildungs- und Biographieforschun, 3) (pp. 61–85). Springer VS.

Engel, J., Applis, S., & Mehren, R. (2020). Zu glokalisierenden Praktiken ethischen Urteilens in Schule und Unterricht. *The Policy Environment for Development Education and Global Learning, Zeitschrift für internationale Bildungsforschung (ZEP), 43*(4), 13–24.

Engel, J., Beach, D., & Jörissen, B. (2019a). Special Issue: Cultural Sedimentations—Ethnography on the Materiality and Historicity of Aesthetic Practices. *Ethnography and Education, 15*(3), 267–269. https://doi.org/10.1080/17457823.2020.1738255

Engel, J., & Diz Muñoz, C. (2021). Erziehungswissenschaftliche Ansätze einer post-kolonialen Subjektivierungsforschung. In S. Bosančić, F. Brodersen, L. Pfahl, L. Schürmann, T. Spies, & B. Traue (Eds.), *Following the Subject: Grundlagen und Zugänge enpirischer Subjektivierungsforschung (Subjektivierung und Gesellschaft)*. Springer VS.

Engel, J., Epp, A., Lipkina, J., Schinkel, S., Terhart, H., & Wischmann, A. (2021). Gesellschaftlicher Wandel und die Entwicklung qualitativer Forschung im Feld der Bildung: Repräsentationskritiken, diskursive Verschiebungen, methodologische Wagnisse und methodische Innovationen. *Schwerpunkt der Zeitschrift für qualitative Forschung (ZQF), 22*(1).

Engel, J., & Fritzsche, B. (2019). Introduction—Cultural Identity in Multilocal Spaces. *Journal Diaspora, Indigenous, and Minority Education (DIME), 13*(1), 1–12.

Engel, J., Gebhardt, M., & Kirchmann, K. (Eds.). (2019b). *Zeitlichkeit und Materialität. Interdisziplinäre Perspektiven auf Theorien und Phänomene der Präsenz* (pp. 195–205). transcript.

Foucault, M. (1972). *The Archeology of Knowledge*. Tavistock Publications.

Foucault, M. (1983). The Subject of Power. In H. Dreyfus & P. Rabinow (Eds.), *Michel Foucault: Beyond Structuralism and Hermeneutics*. Harvester.

Fritzsche, B. (2012). Subjektivationsprozesse in Domänen des Sagens und Zeigens Butlers Theorie als Inspiration für qualitative Untersuchungen des Heranwachsens von Kindern und Jugendlichen. In N. Ricken & N. Balzer (Eds.), *Judith Butler: Pädagogische Lektüren* (pp. 181–205). Springer VS.

Gelhardt, A., Alkemeyer, T., & Ricken, N. (Eds.). (2013). *Techniken der Subjektivierung*. Wilhelm Fink.

Gomolla, M., & Radtke, F. O. (2002). *Institutionelle Diskriminierung: Die Herstellung ethnischer Differenz in der Schule*. VS.

Göttlich, U., Mikos, L., & Winter, R. (2001). *Die Werkzeugkiste der Cultural Studies. Perspektiven, Anschlüsse und Interventionen, 2.* transcript.

Hall, S. (1997). The Spectacle of the 'Other'. In S. Hall & Open University (Eds.), *Cultural Representations and Signifying Practices* (pp. 223–291). SAGE in association with the Open University.

Jörissen, B. (2011). Bildung, Visualität, Subjektivierung—Sichtbarkeiten und Selbstverhältnisse in medialen Strukturen. In T. Meyer, K. Mayrberger, S. Münte-Goussar, & C. Schwalbe (Eds.), *Kontrolle und Selbstkontrolle. Zur Ambivalenz von E-Portfolios in Bildungsprozessen* (pp. 57–73). VS Verlag.

Jörissen, B. (2014). *Medialität und Subjektivation. Strukturale Medienbildung unter besonderer Berücksichtigung einer Historischen Anthropologie des Subjekts.* Habilitationsschrift. http://joerissen.name/wp-content/uploads/2014/07/Jörissen-Benjamin-2014.-Medialität-und-Subjektivation-Habilitationsschrift.pdf

Jörissen, B. (2015). Bildung der Dinge: Design und Subjektivation. In B. Jörissen & T. Meyer (Eds.), *Subjekt Medium Bildung* (pp. 215–233). VS.

Kammler, C., Parr, R., Johannes, U., Schneider, E., & Schneider, U. (2014). *Foucault-Handbuch, Sonderausgabe. Leben—Werk—Wirkung*. J. B. Metzler.

Keller, R. (2017). Neuer Materialismus und Neuer Spiritualismus? Diskursforschung und die Herausforderung der Materialitäten. *Österreichische Zeitschrift für Volkskunde, LXXXI*(120), 5–31.

Keller, R., Schneider, W., & Viehöfer, W. (Eds.). (2012). *Diskurs—Macht—Subjekt. Theorie und Empirie von Subjektivierung in der Diskursforschung.*

Kleiner, B., & Rose, N. (Eds.). (2014). *(Re-)Produktion von Ungleichheiten im Schulalltag. Judith Butlers Konzept der Subjektivation in der erziehungswissenschaftlichen Forschung*. Barbara Budrich.

Kolbe, F., Reh, S., & Fritzsche, B. (2008). Lernkultur: Überlegungen zu einer kulturwissenschaftlichen Grundlegung qualitativer Unterrichtsforschung. *Zeitschrift für Erziehungswissenschaft, 11*(1), 125–143. https://doi.org/10.1007/s11618-008-0007-5

Koller, H.-C. (1999). *Bildung und Widerstreit. Zur Struktur biographischer Bildungsprozesse in der (Post-)Moderne*. Fink.

Kravagna, C., Graw, I., Silverman, K., Williams, L. K., De Lauretis, T., Stabile, C. A., Jay, M., Tagg, J., & Colomina, B. (1997). In A. Solomon-Godeau (Ed.), *Privileg Blick. Kritik der visuellen Kultur*. Ed. ID-Archiv.

McKrittick, K. (2015). Yours in the Intellectual Struggle: Sylvia Wynter and the Realization of the Living. In K. McKrittick (Ed.), *Sylvia Wynter. On Being Human as a Praxis* (pp. 1–8). Duke University Press.

Messerschmidt, A. (2018). Bildung und globalisierte Ungleichheit. In A. Bernhard, L. Rothermel, & M. Rühle (Eds.), *Handbuch Kritische Pädagogik. Eine Einführung in die Erziehungs- und Bildungswissenschaft* (pp. 568–581). Beltz Juventa.

Mignolo, W. (2015). Sylvia Wynter. What Does It Mean to be Human? In K. McKrittick (Ed.), *Sylvia Wynter. On Being Human as a Praxis* (pp. 106–123). Duke University Press.

Mohn, B. (2002). Realismus als nützliche Fiktion. Instrumentelles Dokumentieren. In B. Mohn (Ed.), *Filming Culture. Spielarten des Dokumentierens nach der Repräsentationskrise* (pp. 199–228). Lucius & Lucius.

Nohl, A.-M. (2017). *Interview und Dokumentarische Methode. Anleitungen für die Forschungspraxis.* VS.

Proske, M., & Rabenstein, K. (2018). *Kompendium Qualitative Unterrichtsforschung Unterricht beobachten—beschreiben—rekonstruieren.* Klinkhardt.

Rabenstein, K. (2018a). Ding-Praktiken. Zur sozio-materiellen Dimension von Unterricht. In M. Proske & K. Rabenstein (Eds.), *Kompendium Qualitative Unterrichtsforschung. Unterricht beobachten—beschreiben—rekonstruieren* (pp. 319–347). Klinkhardt.

Rabenstein, K. (2018b). Wie schaffen Dinge Unterschiede? Methodologische Überlegungen zur Materialität von Subjektivationsprozessen im Unterricht. In A. Tervooren & R. Kreitz (Eds.), *Dinge und Raum in der qualitativen Bildungs- und Biographieforschung* (pp. 15–35). Barbara Budrich.

Reh, S. (2012). Mit der Videokamera beobachten. Möglichkeiten qualitativer Unterrichtsforschung. In H. Boer & S. Reh (Eds.), *Beobachtung in der Schule— Beobachten lernen* (pp. 151–169). Springer VS.

Reh, S., & Rabenstein, K. (2013). Die soziale Konstitution des Unterrichts in pädagogischen Praktiken und die Potentiale qualitativer Unterrichtsforschung. Rekonstruktionen des Zeigens und Adressierens. *Zeitschrift für Pädagogik, 59*(3), 291–307.

Reichenbach, R., Ricken, N., & Koller, H.-C. (2011). *Erkenntnispolitik und die Konstruktion pädagogischer Wirklichkeiten (Schriftenreihe der Kommission Bildungs- und Erziehungsphilosophie in der Deutschen Gesellschaft für Erziehungswissenschaft).* Schöningh.

Ricken, N. (2013). Zur Logik der Subjektivierung Überlegungen an den Rändern eines Konzepts. In Ricken, N. (Ed.). *Techniken der Subjektivierung* (29–47). Brill Fink.

Ricken, N., & Kuhlmann, N. (2019). *Pädagogische Professionalität— Anerkennungstheoretische und adressierungsanalytische Perspektiven.* Jahrestagung der DGfE-Kommission "Professionsforschung und Lehrerbildung".

Ricken, N., Rose, N., Kuhlmann, N., & Otzen, A. (2017). Die Sprachlichkeit der Anerkennung. Eine theoretische und methodologische Perspektive auf die Erforschung von "Anerkennung". *Vierteljahrsschrift für wissenschaftliche Pädagogik, 93*(2), 193–235. https://doi.org/10.1163/25890581-093-02-90000002

Ricken, N., Thompson, C., & Casale, R. (2019a). Vorwort der Herausgeberinnen und Herausgeber. In N. Ricken, R. Casale, & C. Thompson (Eds.), *Subjektivierung. Erziehungswissenschaftliche Theorieperspektiven* (p. 7ff) Beltz Juventa.

Ricken, N., Thompson, C., & Casale, R. (2019b). *Subjektivierung. Erziehungswissenschaftliche Theorieperspektiven.* Beltz Juventa.

Rieger-Ladich, M. (2004). Unterwerfung und Überschreitung: Michel Foucaults Theorie der Subjektivierung. In N. Ricken & M. Rieger-Ladich (Eds.), *Michel Foucault: Pädagogische Lektüren* (pp. 203–223). VS.

Rieger-Ladich, M. (2012). Judith Butlers Rede von Subjektivierung. Kleine Fallstudie zur "Arbeit am Begriff". In N. Ricken & N. Balzer (Eds.), *Judith Butler: Pädagogische Lektüren* (pp. 57–73). VS.

Rose, N., & Ricken, N. (2017). Interaktionsanalyse als Adressierungsanalyse. Eine Perspektive der Subjektivationsforschung. In M. Heinrich & A. Wernet (Eds.), *Rekonstruktive Bildungsforschung. Zugänge und Methoden* (pp. 159–175). VS.

Santos, B. d. S. (2007). Beyond Abyssal Thinking: From Global Lines to Ecologies of Knowledges. *Review (Fernand Braudel Center), 30*(1), 45–89.

Seidel, T., Prenzel, M., Duit, R., & Lehrke, M. (2003). *Technischer Bericht zur Videostudie "Lehr-Lernprozesse im Physikunterricht".* Leibniz-Institut für die Pädagogik der Naturwissenschaften, IPN.

Snaza, N. (2018). The Earth is Not 'Ours' to Save: Bewildering Education and (In)human Agency. In J. Jagodzinski (Ed.), *Interrogating the Anthropocene: Ecology, Pedagogy, and The Future in Question.* Palgrave Macmillan.

Spies, T. (2018). Postkoloniale Perspektiven auf sexualisierte Gewalt. In A. Retkowski, A. Treibel, & E. Tuider (Eds.), *Handbuch Sexualisierte Gewalt und pädagogische Kontexte. Theorie, Forschung, Praxis* (pp. 222–230). Beltz Juventa.

Spies, T. (2019). Subjekt und Subjektivierung. Perspektiven (in) der Biographieforschung. In A. Geimer, S. Amling, & S. Bosančić (Eds.), *Subjekt und Subjektivierung. Empirische und theoretische Perspektiven auf Subjektivierungsprozesse* (pp. 87–110). Springer Fachmedien.

Spivak, G. C. (1988). Can the Subaltern Speak? In C. Nelson & L. Grossberg (Eds.), *Marxism and the Interpretation of Culture* (pp. 271–313). University of Illinois Press.

Spivak, G. C. (2012). *An Aesthetic Education in the Era of Globalisation.* Harvard University Press.

Spivak, G. C., Landry, D., & MacLean, G. M. (1996). *The Spivak Reader: Selected Works of Gayatri Chakravorty Spivak.* Routledge.

Tervooren, A. (2006). *Im Spielraum von Geschlecht und Begehren. Ethnographie der ausgehenden Kindheit.* Beltz Juventa.

Tervooren, A., & Kreitz, R. (2018) (eds.). *Dinge und Raum in der qualitativen Bildungs- und Biografieforschung.* Barbara Budrich.

Thompson, C. (2019). Bildung in Zeiten globaler Expertise. In N. Ricken, R. Casale, & C. Thompson (Eds.), *Subjektivierung. Erziehungswissenschaftliche Theorieperspektiven, pp. 281–300.* Beltz Juventa.

Thompson, C., Casale, R., & Ricken, N. (2017). *Die Sache(n) der Bildung. Publikation der Kommission Bildungs- und Erziehungsphilosophie.* Schöningh.

Traue, B. (2013). Visuelle Diskursanalyse. Ein programmatischer Vorschlag zur Untersuchung von Sicht– und Sagbarkeiten im Medienwandel. *Zeitschrift für Diskursforschung, 1*(2), 117–136. https://doi.org/10.1007/978-3-658-13610-9_5

Traue, B., Blanc, M., & Cambre, C. (2019). Visibilities and Visual Discourses: Rethinking the Social with the Image. *Qualitative Inquiry, 25*(4), 327–337. https://doi.org/10.1177/1077800418792946

Traue, B., Pfahl, L., & Globisch, C. (2018). Potentiale und Herausforderungen einer empirischen Subjektivierungsforschung. In S. Lessenich (Ed.), *Geschlossene Gesellschaft. Verhandlungen des 38. Kongresses der Deutschen Gesellschaft für Soziologie* (pp. 1–5). VS.

Tsang, W. (2020). *There is no Nonviolent Way to Look at Somebody.* Einzelausstellung Martin Gropius Bau (9/4/2019 until 01/12/2020). https://www.berlinerfestspiele.de/en/berliner-festspiele/programm/bfs-gesamtprogramm/programmdetail_277205.html

Von Rosenberg, F. (2011). *Bildung und Habitustransformation. Empirische Rekonstruktionen und bildungstheoretische Reflexionen.* transcript.

Wynter, S. (2003). Unsettling the Coloniality of Being: Power, Truth, Freedom: Towards the Human, After Man, is Overrepresentation. An Argument. *CR: The New Centennial Review, 3*(3), 257–337. https://doi.org/10.1353/ncr.2004.0015

Wynter, S., & McKittrick, K. (2015). Unparalleled Catastrophe for Our Species? Or, to Give Humanness a Different Future: A Conversation. In K. McKittrick (Ed.), *Sylvia Wynter. On Being Human as a Praxis* (pp. 8–89). Duke University Press.

Music as an Embodied Learning Experience

Tiago de Oliveira Pinto

To the memory of
Anna Kerekes Wittmann (1900–1984), my first music teacher

1 Introduction

Ludwig van Beethoven (1770–1827) was completely deaf in the last decade of his life and is still considered one of the greatest musicians who ever existed. Throughout his life he searched for new sounds and sound combinations, explored what is special in the intermingling of different melody lines, and created a music that was previously 'unheard of'. In addition, he constantly tried out new technical possibilities on the piano. Beethoven's tragic fate as a musician—because deafness seems to be fundamentally opposed to music—already indicates two aspects that must be considered when defining music: Music is not limited to the dimension of sound, nor is music something to be experienced simply and exclusively by listening. Although the acoustic dimension is central, "even if music is necessarily organized sound, it is plain that this is not sufficient for something's being music" (Davis, 2003, p. 491). If that were different, at some point there would have been no more composing

---

T. de Oliveira Pinto (✉)
University of Music Franz Liszt, Weimar, Germany
e-mail: tiago.oliveira@hfm-weimar.de

© The Author(s), under exclusive license to Springer Nature Switzerland AG 2022
A. Kraus, C. Wulf (eds.), *The Palgrave Handbook of Embodiment and Learning*,
https://doi.org/10.1007/978-3-030-93001-1_29

Beethoven, we would not be able to enjoy his *9th Symphony* today, for example, because he himself conceived his last three symphonies in almost complete deafness and could no longer hear them in concert.

While a certain physical materiality had let him down with his deafness, Beethoven was able to create his works with the help of another material aspect, namely thanks to the Western practice of writing music, which captures the fleeting sound on a material level. Beethoven himself had brought musical notation to the greatest possible perfection in his time. In this context, the written form seems particularly removed from the fundamental physicality of the body, when producing music. In other words, music notation is itself materialized music, which allows a purely intellectual comprehension of the same. This musical materiality of the writing, in its way remote from direct relationship to the bodily senses, was the 'salvation' for the deaf Beethoven, whose body had lost the ability to express music directly. Only his intellect had to express itself through his musical writing. At this stage, nothing else was possible for him.

At the moment when it comes to sound implementation and to performance, especially to the process of learning musical skills, the sensual spectrum necessarily expands and reveals those much more extensive possibilities of expression that are associated with the phenomenon of music.[1] Indeed, the process of learning and experiencing music, regardless of its social and cultural context, is essentially one that relates to physical practice. It is the combination of physical experience with a specially trained hearing that comes to life in music as a universally existent but always distinct phenomenon that can be recognized, interpreted, and thus also lived. In this sense, music practice is always accompanied by a physically supported learning experience. This chapter is about that particular learning experience.

2 Music as an Intangible Human Manifestation

The first problem that arises is understanding the immateriality that music represents. An intangible nature of something like music and physical corporeality seem to be two dimensions that initially are opposed one to another, as body is first of all matter. But music proves that it only exists based on an indirect immateriality, because it always needs something tangible in order to arise and to be passed on. Listening to music alone may seem immaterial, as

---

[1] A selection of introductory papers on musical performance can be found in Rink, 2002.

it is about a process that is exhausted in time, is neither visible nor palpable, and always comes to an end, which is expressed in its silencing. However, making music sound on an instrument is simultaneously a physical act, as is singing, which is ultimately the basis of the comprehensive physical dimension that characterizes learning and teaching of music, and its ultimate mastership. In a study on music as living heritage, I summarized the somehow paradoxical musical phenomenon in one short sentence: "Therefore, music is 'undetectably material' and, simultaneously and in apparently contradictory terms, 'substantially intangible'" (de Oliveira Pinto, 2018, p. 50).

3   The Formal and Its Context—Body and Mind

What about the identity of music if it is understood as 'musical art'? In Western tradition a musical piece is already present in its written representation:

> According to the formalist, one piece of music is distinguished from another in terms of its pattern alone. When we are acquainted with a work's sound structure, there is nothing more to be known about the basis for its identity. (Davis, 2003, p. 492)

This identity will of course always be connected with the context in which music is created and in which it is played. In such a juxtaposition of formalism and contextualism, the duality of mind and body that is expressed in music becomes recognizable. However, some music aestheticians see it differently. For them the context is a music-historical one in which the musical work is initially embedded in its 'disembodied' form (Hindrichs, 2014). However, it can be argued against this that if music-historical epochs include certain traditions, practices, and conventions, physical aspects also gain importance. Context refers to spatiality, not only the temporal but also the local, and living bodies are always located and moving in both. In a historical musical context understood in this way, embodiment plays an important role.

Singing, listening, and rhythmic movements are universal musical abilities of humans. All three presuppose physical actions, justify the physicality of music, and above all form the basis of its learning process (Busch, 2016). The human body and embodiment are subjected to a constantly changing use of body and corporeality in connection with cultural expressions, especially with performing arts. Both—the body itself and the embodiment—adapt to the given circumstances and contexts. 'The body making music' always tells us a lot about this music.[2]

---

[2] "The body obviously has vast potential as a source of information on music" (Grupe, 2010, p. 74)

While in the Brazilian province of Bahia, in the town of Santo Amaro in the region of Recôncavo, on a certain occasion with the musician and long-term research partner Vavá (Evilásio de Andrade), we approached the city's central market place. From quite a distance we saw a group of people gathered around a *capoeira* event. In the middle of the performing group, three *berimbau* musical bows could clearly be seen in action. They protruded from the crowd in a coordinated, that is joint up and down, movement, which Vavá immediately recognized: "Look, there they are playing São Bento Grande. And how wild they play it! It's sure to be a tough *capoeira* fight." Nothing could be heard of the so-called São Bento Grande *berimbau* pattern yet, we were too far away, but the movement sequences of the musical bows were enough for the connoisseur to identify the musical repertoire, especially that it was already at an advanced stage. An experienced instrumentalist can see how something is being played from the physical use of the instrument. In addition, she or he will also be able to judge whether the musician observed is competent, plays correctly and well, even if without hearing anything. Music is thus primarily produced physically and can also be assessed in relation to it, by observing this physical action.

4 Movement Sequences as Musical Activity

It can be assumed that any kind of music writing derives from a physical action in performance. Pre-forms of European musical notation and also notations in other written musical cultures gave priority to the articulations that are performed on the instrument: guitar and lute tablatures, Chinese musical notation, transcriptions, and so on. European music notation began in the ninth century with the fixing of melodic configurations with so-called neumes, by the use of short lines, arcs, and signals. These graphical symbols of the Gregorian chant were noted directly above the biblical text. These signs represent the conducting movements by which an ensembles leader directed his *Schola Cantorum*. So, music notation is first of all the graphic implementation of a physical sequence of movement patterns. It illustrates how music is fundamentally controlled by the body's actions. It has therefore always been very useful for music teaching and has supported the musical learning process.

Beethoven always related the possibilities of the notation to the greatest possible perfection of musical expression. Perhaps his deafness was partly to blame for the obsession with trying to capture the sound of the music as precisely as possible.[3] To a certain extent, he transferred the inaudible to the visual; that is he moved from the lost physical to the spiritual-mental. Ultimately, he transferred the immaterial hearing to the equally immaterial inner sound experience of his 'spiritual eye', supported by what was materialized in music writing, since the specifically physical (the hearing organ) which could no longer be used. In the end, the material serves the immaterial.

An example from African music research corroborates the importance of physical action as departing point for musical sound. Attempts to transcribe musical phenomena from Africa, in particular percussive music in conventional staff notation, had to fail gloomily again and again. Not only in musicological treatises, especially in school books of music education, one consistently encounters completely inadequate representations of African and other music.[4] This continuing misunderstanding is contrasted with the musical transcriptions by musician and cultural scientist Gerhard Kubik, who in his research was able to make musical transcriptions from silent films based on his own learning of African musical instruments, such as the xylophones from Uganda *amadinda* and *akadinda*. Kubik had filmed the musicians in such a way that one can exactly follow the movements, especially the impacts of the beater on the xylophone plates, in the sequence of the movie picture. With a so-called frame-to-frame analysis of the film strip, Kubik (1984) was able to create a precise and complete transcription of the music. The transcribed piece can then easily be played from this notation. It was not the sound of the music, absent in the silent film, but only the sequence of movements of the instrumental performance that gave rise to this kind of musical notation (Fig. 1).

Captions to Fig. 1:

1, 2, 3, and so on = different movements patterns (as in Kubik, 1984, p. 213)
x = hand clapping
o = silent movement
,_____, = duration of metric circles

Music results from sequences of movements, while, at the same time, it stimulates further movements again. It brings together the motoric skills of different bodies (in rowing, military marches, etc.), its rhythm coordinates complex collective actions (in ballet), and so on. Basically, only music or acoustically rhythmic processes enable the movements of a larger amount of

---

[3] With the invention of the metronome in 1815 by Johann Nepomuk Mälzel, which Beethoven promoted quite intensely, he was able to specify a precise definition of the tempo for his works and prescribe it for future interpreters.
[4] See my critical remarks on this behalf in Tiago de Oliveira Pinto, 2011.

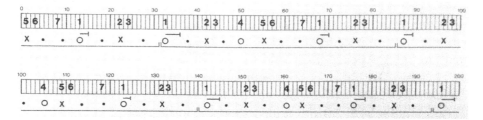

Fig. 1 Short extract of a transcription of a drumming piece sequence from a silent film, based on a 'frame-to-frame' analysis (Kubik, 1984, p. 216)

different participants to be synchronized. This is to say that the actions of the body are responsible for making a collective music-gathering possible: in the string quartet it is the body sign as 'visual signaling' (Grupe, 2010) of the first violinist, in the orchestra that of the conductor, which warrant an exact collective start of the piece. With the conducting, the question sometimes even arises who goes ahead of whom: are the musicians just following the conductor visually, or isn't he also driven by the development of the music by controlling the musical flow with his feedback?

Additional examples from all over the world prove that constant feedback between musical sound and movement sequences is essential. Furthermore, when expanded to gestures, these movement sequences built the bridge between music and narrative art, as I witnessed in Amazonia among the Aparai indigenous people:

> In 1993, I had the opportunity to copy and to archive the sound collection of German technician Manfred Rauschert, who had spent almost 25 years among the Aparai-Wayana people in Northern Brazil. The objective was to return these cultural documents to the people, presenting them some samples of the songs and instrumental music that Rauschert had collected decades before. Thus, I travelled together with Manfred Rauschert, who at this stage was almost 80 years of age, to the Aparai-Wayana in the Bona village, Tumucumaque National Park, close to the Brazil-Surinam border. Trials made with a number of music cassettes from the Rauschert collection played in the village on a tape recorder proved instructive. The original intention was to find out whether there still existed, among the present generation of Aparai-Wayana, reservations in the sense of ancient taboos, in particular regarding mentioning the names of deceased persons. This was no longer the case. But listeners did object to the imperfect nature of several recorded presentations of even the best story tellers of the generation next to the last. The reason was quickly found: what were missing were the explanatory gestures, e.g., round, curved, far, very high, from

east to west, and so on. Rauschert then imitated the gestures during the presentation of the tape, e.g., in rendering the myth of the wind-born creator. He completed the sound from the tapes, with the missing gestures and movements. From this moment on the spectacle was received by all with much enthusiasm. Sound and movement proved to be indissoluble for this people. (cp. de Oliveira Pinto, 1995, pp. 127–130)

From the twelfth century onward, European musical notation passed over to neglecting the physical articulations, fixing the sound phenomenon alone, away from the motion sequences, and primarily moving the fixed pitches into the main focus of the notation.[5] This form of music notation neglects the body making the music. This separation of practice and intellect, of body and mind, followed by that of emotion and the rational conception of music, of technical execution and expression of feelings, and so on, is what distinguishes so-called Western art music culture from others.[6] And the musical parameter 'harmony' seems to be even the furthest away from the human body. Tonality and the functional harmony of Western music have been intellectually drained in such a way that the only consequence of this linear and progressive historical development was the path to a completely 'disembodied' atonality.

But let's get back to certain types of music in Africa. Here the separation between the musical, intellectually conceived work and the pure musical-practical exercise is constantly bridged and summarized in the course of the performance. If, from the point of view of research, there is a mental-spiritual distance from musical practice, then this can only relate to the functions assigned to its representation: religion, ritual, festival, and so on. But here, too, a unity is sought in the performance. A holistic musical system is revealed, which is always about the entirety of a sound-body-movement-collective action. In contrast, European art music, which from the sixteenth century onward was gradually based on written form, is progress-oriented. It seems to be backed on a formally linear pattern of development, whereas music in Africa tends to obey a cyclical principle:

<u>Differing views on Music</u>

in Africa
- Holistic Musical Systems(sound-body-movement-collective)-based

---

[5] Only with the possibilities of sound software can the tonal musical events be visualized even more comprehensively.

[6] The music critic and musicologist Eduard Hanslick (1825–1904) goes so far as to recognize the beautiful in music alone in its abstract configuration, independent of performance and emotion (*Vom Musikalisch-Schönen*, 1852).

- Cyclic perception of music

./.

in Europe
- Written and progress-oriented music
- Linear perception of music

Seen in this way, it is misleading if one very often ascribes a disproportionate amount of 'rhythm' to the music in Africa and its outcomes in Latin America and the Caribbean. The reality is different: music is not primarily played rhythmically in Africa, but in Europe this element, which was strongly represented in the past, has withered more and more in the course of history, especially in its 'art music' format. This development can be observed in the notation and the related musical conception. It was not until the twentieth century that lack of rhythm was somewhat overcome in Europe. Composers like Stravinsky or Bartók have given more space to the rhythmic component in their instrumental works. However, it is above all the most important musical phenomenon of the twentieth century, the worldwide disseminated pop music, that brought rhythmic elements from Africa into the global musical panorama via the North American continent.

In general, one can say that the rhythmic component is emphatically physical, the harmonic component more conceptual.[7] The physical part of pop music in particular leads to its smooth adoption and dissemination. The physical perception is more immediate than the abstractly intellectual one. The ability to move collectively to the music is crucial here. Nevertheless, this categorization is not absolute, because ideally the body-mind balance is established with pure music-making. Ultimately, it shows itself in all music-making, in its mediation, as in its reception, with different weightings. The importance of musical embodiment as a distinct learning mode lies in this balance.

5   Body in Anthropology

The human body was a central subject already of early social anthropology (Mauss, 1936, and others). Ethnologists and social scientists observed that the body not only provides support for habits and customs, but is also changed, adorned, and repurposed for special activities and modeled anew. In short, the use of the body is always characterized by symbolic behavior and social role ascriptions.

---

[7] Harmonics is an element closer related to space, rhythm is closer to time. Movement occurs in space + time.

The anthropologist Mary Douglas investigated this emphatically social role of the human body. In the chapter 'The two bodies' of her epochal book *Natural Symbols. Explorations in Cosmology* (Douglas, 1970), Mary Douglas comes to different evaluations of the human body by dividing it into two distinct units: the social and the physical body:

> The social body constrains the way the physical body is perceived. The physical experience of the body, always modified by the social categories through which it is known, sustains a particular view of society. There is a continual exchange of meanings between the two kinds of bodily experience so that each reinforces the categories of the other. As a result of this interaction the body itself is a highly restricted medium of expression. (Douglas, 1970, p. 69)

This conception of the bodies' role initially fits well with the definition of the body in the area of the musical learning process. However, music plays a special role here, doing it possibly better than most forms of cultural expression, namely by connecting the two bodies that Douglas particularly emphasized. Music expresses itself in the social and in the physical body at the same time. On the one hand, music lives from its social attributions, but certain instrumental techniques also depend directly on the physical skills of a body. The lesser a portion of physical ability is present, the more instrumental techniques must be learned and practiced with great effort. This very culture-dependent physical learning process leads Mary Douglas to criticize other authors of her time. Especially she disagrees with the Structural Anthropology of Claude Levi-Strauss (1958), because of its apparent lack of concern for cultural variants. This reluctance must also be observed in music research since, on the one hand, music is a universal phenomenon, while, on the other hand, distinct musical cultures deal with music very differently.

6   Embodiment and/as Music

The embodiment's perspective demands that psychological processes are explicitly seen and examined with reference to the body. It is assumed that psychological processes always correlate with physical reactions (Storch et al., 2010). On closer inspection, embodiment concerns a fundamental question of both philosophy and psychology: the so-called body-soul problem. The question of how one should grasp the connection between 'body' (i.e., body, matter, brain) and 'soul' (i.e., cognition, psyche, thinking) is a fundamental one that runs through the entire history of philosophy.[8] The focus of current social-scientific interest in the body is the relationship between socio-cultural structures and the self-education of people as social persons or subjects. The theoretical instruments used to analyze these relationships are diverse, because the body is still viewed as a platform for identity representations, self-expression, and self-staging that communicates context-specific signs (Stangl, 2021). Early research on music-related bodily behavior was undertaken in German-speaking countries as early as at the turn of the twentieth century.

After his death in 1895, Joseph Rutz, a German singing teacher, left behind a comprehensive musical 'type theory' without ever having fully recorded this theoretical structure. His son Ottmar Rutz made this his life's work. In 1908 he made his father's teachings on the physiological determination of the sound character of the human voice public under the title of *New Discoveries of the Human Voice*. In the following 40 years, Ottmar Rutz presented numerous other monographs and essays in which he further differentiated the 'Rutz typology' and developed theories of expression and physiognomy that went beyond music. Rutz' theory was based on the discovery that when singing and speaking, not only the organs of speech come into action, but other parts of the body as well, such as the core muscles, all working together. As a tenor, Rutz Senior noticed that he could sing certain works better in certain postures than in other poses of the body. He recognized that the entire physical effort is required to do justice to music performance. Therefore, Rutz proposed a systematization of the body's basic posture while performing (singing):

As the four 'types' (Typen), Rutz distinguishes between the following body postures during the singing act:

1. Push the abdomen horizontally forward and keep this curvature. This gives the voice a dark and soft sound. Breath deep.
2. Push the abdominal muscles just above the hips horizontally backwards and arch your chest. The voice sound light and soft.
3. Push the muscles on the sides of the torso at an angle, either downwards forwards or downwards backwards. Voice light and harsh.
4. Slant the muscles on the sides of the torso, either forward upward or backward upward. Voice sound dark and hard. (Rutz, 1911, 8, 9)

It is important to note that Rutz used famous personalities from history to illustrate three of his four types of body posture: type 1 corresponds to Caesar, Goethe, Napoleon, among other personalities; type 2 is best represented by

---

[8] Gallagher, 2011. On the dynamics of body cognition, see also Shapiro, 2011, p. 124.

Frederic the Great, Schiller, and Beethoven; type 3 reminds one of statues of the old Greeks and of Franz Liszt; while type 4 has "not been observed so far in real life".[9]

An opposite pole to the body holistic postures in order to better express music, is the hands of musicians, especially of instrumentalists. According to the psychologist G. Révész, hands are of utmost importance in any instrumental performance. They have created entire civilizations and cultures, as Révész observed in 1944 (Révész, 1944). However, hands also express thoughts and feelings with gestures. So, here the coexistence of the material and the spiritual applies, materialized and expressed with the hands. The scope becomes even broader if we don't limit the hands' role to playing alone and include the craftsmanship of musical instruments, where highly skilled manual techniques are likewise required.

In the past, instrumentalists believed that the hand had to be better prepared for technical use in playing an instrument. In the nineteenth century, special devices for strengthening and agility, or for the extraordinary stretching of the full palm—in a sense a 'balancing act' of the hand—were developed. The devices produced for this purpose were Dactylion, Chiroplast, or simply the 'finger supporting device' by Atkins.

In 1881 Benjamin Atkins patented this "new and useful device for supporting and exercising the fingers of players on keyboard instruments". Essentially, it is a series of rings suspended from springs, "so as to compel the user to put forth unwonted strength" in depressing her or his fingers. In time this would foster "a superior decision of touch with greater flexibility and rapidity of motion".[10]

But Chiroplast, Dactylion, and other devices for exercising pianist's hands could not accomplish what sports equipment can do for the fitness of its users. In the long run, these devices proved to be unusable for instrumental play. The young Robert Schumann (1810–1856), who absolutely wanted to become a piano virtuoso, ruined the index and middle fingers of his right hand with excessive physical exercise with devices, similar to the ones mentioned above.

Even if the hand-training devices are no longer in use nowadays, many instrumental and vocal teachers regard almost everything that happens on the instrument to produce music as technology or 'technical ability'. This has to

---

[9] It is probably no coincidence that Rutz' physiological studies on the human body as a cultural instrument would bring him later close to nationalistic and even antisemitic ideologies (in *Menschheitstypen und Kunst*, Jena 1921).

[10] https://www.sciencesource.com/archive/Atkins%2D%2DFinger-Supporting-Device%2D%2D1881-SS2607561.html

be learned and often comes before the final work on the musical piece as such. The ability to overcome instrumental difficulties stays in the foreground, or, to come straight to the point, the ability to accurately reproduce many, even uncomfortable notes and fingering sequences in a short time is paramount. And this short time makes pure mental remembrance in music almost impossible. The renowned Portuguese pianist Maria João Pires is quite clear about it:

> I don't believe in the head so much as I believe in the body's ability to remember. I don't care much about what my fingers do! If you only practice with your brain and fingers, it is very one-sided and makes you vulnerable in precisely such situations.[11] The connection is too simple and takes up too much space in the brain! You have to literally wake up the memory with your body, because only it remembers all gestures and movements. (Pires, 2014)

The training of pure instrumental technical skills remains an individual practice. One of my colleagues from a course in brass instrument performance at the University of Music Franz Liszt in Weimar once mentioned to me: "What I expect from my students is that 95% what they do in their studies is 'sport'. Only the remaining 5% of their activity on the instrument can be expected as 'art'."

In fact, sport and musical performance are driven by the unspoken similarity between the mechanical (physical training) and the individual musical rehearsal. In both cases the body is in the core of the musical activity, and practicing is a rather 'body-driven' than embodied learning process. Both, training in sport and practicing in music, are directed toward the perfect preparation for specific and outstanding goals, with much outcome for the public and empowered with exceptional professional excellence. Both rely on high emotional input and mental control at the same time, both attract the attention of an audience, who expect a great show, without ever foreseeing the real outcome of it, until the 'performance' has not come to a complete end.

Unlike most professions, but similar to sport, the learning process in music cannot start as an adult. This illustrates the long-term body relatedness in musical practice. It is the same with cycling or swimming, for example: both are ideally learned in childhood, not as a grown up. In the case of music, this is paired with the cognitive perception that is also prevalent in languages: music must be learned and practiced from an early age. Interestingly enough,

---

[11] Mrs. Pires refers to a situation in which she had to play a different Mozart piano concerto than that she had prepared for the occasion, because of a previous lack of communication with conductor Ricardo Chailly. On stage she had to switch and play a concerto, she had played in the past, but not expecting to perform it in that concert night. She managed to do it completely by heart.

this applies to both technical ability (body) and musicality (mind). It means that if you had never touched a piano key before the age of 20, you won't ever be able to master Beethoven's *Appassionata* or Liszt's *B minor Sonata*. "Manual skills" (cf. Révész, 1944) are based on both, on training that is decoupled from the music and on intensive music-making.

If the hand is of central importance from a technical point of view, the entire body is necessary for making music in its full sense. Watching the musician performing you can literally hear the music, since body movements are also transmitted to the audience. After all, dance is the immediate physical reflex of music—but this opens up a new topic, going beyond the scope of this chapter.

7 Rehearsal, Education, and Music-Making

Where, however, does music begin to disconnect itself from sport, and where is practicing and rehearsing no physical or mechanical activity by itself any longer? The Swiss cellist and instrumental pedagogue Rudolf von Tobel commented on this in 1969:

> We only master a work when we can actually play it, i.e. reproduce it without noticeable effort. So we have to achieve the greatest impact with the least amount of effort and avoid any unnecessary effort. Pablo Casals on this: "Ce n'est pas un effort, c'est un plaisir". "Relaxation and suppleness are my only tricks." We achieve this with those energy factors that do not cost us any effort, and even offer opportunities to rest: with the weight of our limbs and their fall, as well as with sweeping movements. (von Tobel, 1969, pp. 4–5)

Rudolf von Tobel's instrumental pedagogical approach therefore focuses on the elements of its own weight and the fall, an arm, for example, and then also the swinging movements that go with it. He insists that "swing movements are never broken down, but always holistic, flowing" (von Tobel, 1969, 5). The use of these three economic energy factors—dead weight, uninhibited fall, and swinging movements—moves the entire body of the musician. In the end, this will lead to learning to sing and play correctly, promoting self-control, as well as "accuracy and concentration, perseverance, balance and devotion". Tobel is certain that this is a path to human perfection, we would say a process, in which body and mind are perfectly coordinated.

While the dilemma in Western academic music education is the lack of consensus on essential basic issues such as the balance between artistic standards and educational excellence, as well as in dealing with current social challenges (inclusion, cultural diversity, making music with everyone, new media), this is a conflict hardly manifest in other musical cultures, because practicing and making music do not necessarily represent different or even opposing activities. If they are assessed differently, then not on the stage, because it goes without saying that due to the close teacher-student relationship in traditional Indian music, for example, the student may sit next to his or her master on stage when having reached a certain level of proficiency.

To make music and to practice an instrument (or the voice) are two different approaches to music, although both belong to a process which must be considered and learned within the broad scope of music education. Practicing can be defined as turning away from the ritual, based on the remarks by Mary Douglas, whereas playing on stage for an audience rather represents a genuine ritual—the concert 'ritual' itself.

In a musical exchange project involving Germany and Afghanistan which lasted for several years between the *Afghan National Institute of Music* Kabul and the *University of Music Franz Liszt* Weimar, different music masters from Kabul, invited for a tour and workshops to Germany, came accompanied with two 12- and 13-year-old students. The *rubab* lute player and musical leader of the ensemble would position his young pupil right at his side on stage. This was an extraordinary recognition and reward, given to the young musician by his master in public and even in a performance abroad (photo). What was going on in this musical setting on a very high level was what Christoph Wulf has called "cultural learning as mimetic learning" (Wulf, 2016, p. 374) (Fig. 2).[12]

8 *Musizieren*/'Making' Music

If we combine what has been said above, we come to a dimension that is beyond the written scores: the act of making music. In German there is a term clearly expressing these concepts, the word 'Musizieren'. Because of the lack of such a term in English, the musicologist Christopher Small coined the verb 'musicking'. Small argues that the essence of music lies not in musical works but in taking part in performance, in social action (Small, 1999). For him music is thus not so much a noun as a verb, 'to music'. It is the action of 'music', the action of performing or setting to music. Furthermore, according to Small, the meaning of 'musicking', as he likes to put it, also lies in the relationships that are established between the participants and the performers.

---

[12] A few of the public presentations of the Afghan ensemble of the Safar-Project (Weimar-Kabul) can be found in the YouTube Chanel of the University of Music Franz Liszt. See, for example, http://www.amrc-music.org/mediathek/videos-safar-2012/

Fig. 2 Photo: Rubab master Ustad Ghulam Hussein with pupil, from Kabul: the master and his student on stage in Weimar (University of Music Franz Liszt, 2015)

Making music in groups and ensembles is the rule worldwide, despite the occasions for solo performances (e.g., by a pianist or by an organ player). As a largely collective event, the aforementioned anthropological approach by Margret Mead comes into play, because the music-making body simultaneously determines the spatial demarcation from others within the same event. The human body is itself an instrument that confronts the social world of and with people. In a figurative way, each individual instrument in the larger group of a symphony orchestra relates to many different musical instruments in use and being sounded. In such a group, the musical self-determination of each of the instrumentalists leads to an exchange with the ensemble and at the same time to the development of an awareness of the whole, in contrast to their own sounding world. The reflection taking place in this social context leads to the establishment of a unique collective musical body.

9 *Musizieren* as an Educational Cultural Practice

Intergenerational transmission of cultural practices and of tacit knowledge through mimesis and other forms of learning by direct participation[13] is one of the most important elements of musical learning and also of cultural

---

[13] See, among others, Gebauer & Wulf, 1998; Wulf, 2014, 2016.

maintenance, contributing essentially to its social relevance. How this can develop to true musical mastery has briefly been mentioned with the example from Afghanistan above.

We have emphasized previously that playing musical instruments requires expertise. Learning and teaching are closely linked to musical expertise. Expertise, learning, and teaching are essential in cultural heritage. The dynamics of cultural transmission rely on different forms of educational strategies within the community or the social context of informal education. These strategies of passing musical and performing skills and techniques to the younger generation demonstrate much about the cultural practice itself. Studying the methods and practices of transmitting cultural knowledge gives insights into the culture itself.[14]

Intergenerational transmission is therefore an important issue in the UNESCO Convention on the Safeguarding of the Intangible Cultural Heritage (2003). Safeguarding measures in general are very much focused on cultural transmission. Transmitting musical skills goes far beyond technical details of instrumental performance, for instance, because it encompasses basic cultural knowledge, aesthetic principles, and a great deal of social information. Research on educational aspects of a musical culture will contribute to formal music education and lead to increased interest in the diversity of educational systems in the world for the benefit of the research itself and for a more global-oriented discipline of musical pedagogy.[15]

Therefore, music educationists in schools and institutions of higher learning in Western and other countries have stressed the importance of fostering a deeper understanding not only of musical structures but also of the need to pay attention to the implications in music from a global perspective. Globalization is seldom so clearly perceptible as through musical diversity. Music educator and ethnomusicologist from Seattle, Patricia Campbell, is convinced that "it is vital for (music) teachers to teach musically and culturally" (Campbell, 2005, p. 36). This approach is well on the way to being widely recognized.

Music taught in a community and anchored in a traditional setting, however, without being bound by an official and formal curriculum, can allow the study of music to play an integral part in a broader pattern of education, bringing about an in-depth immersion in a whole tradition or life style. In Bahia, Brazil, for example, this can be found in the *candomblé* religion or in

---

[14] The importance of performance for musical transmission and educational purposes has been discussed for a long time from the most different angles in music research. Regarding musical pedagogical research in contemporary traditional Southeast Asian context, see Ramón Pagayon Santos, 2012, p. 53.

[15] In this regard, cf. Dargie, 1996.

samba de roda. In the Bahian tradition, a young *candomblé* drummer will not restrict his learning to specific sound patterns and to playing techniques alone, but must also learn about the right way to react to dance movements. Above all the neophyte drummer will gain an understanding of the entire complex of religious foundations. This educational process is holistic, in the end giving the pupil a proper place in society, providing him/her with a profound awareness of a specific cultural heritage and the world view associated with it. In the broad sense, such a traditional music education is the pathway to social achievements that will distinguish him as an educated person.

Ideally a socially grounded music education is focused on a total involvement of the pupils through different forms of learning, practices, and performance. To act and to think as a performer will also be important in academic music studies in contexts of living heritage. Music research closely involved with educational concepts and skills has the potential to become an endeavor that directly refers to questions of basic social relevance (Bleibinger, 2018, p. 273).

A more specific focus of our research is located in the field of performance studies, covering approaches within the social and art sciences, as well as in anthropology and global history.[16] Musical practices are considered as social phenomena to be studied in any geographical and/or economic environment. The approach is a transcultural one, trusting in the plurality of cultures, rather than in the authenticity of any absolute nature or single cultural existence. Thus, Western musical theory, for instance, is not seen as a main or autonomous research subject but as part of the general global musical diversity, like any other musical tradition. Therefore, a primary concern is focused on human beings as performers holding and transmitting cultural knowledge. Furthermore, transculturation clearly embraces a non-segregationally approach in cultural theory. This is why music, as a phenomenon that most outstandingly covers both material and intangible cultural aspects, relates in almost every way to transcultural processes, independently of specific societies or of any time period or stylistic epoch.

10 The Musical Instrument as Extension of the Body

A musical instrument can be understood as the extension of a musician's body (de Oliveira Pinto, 2004). To play on it and to express one's own ideas, skills, and sentiments through music is a strong embodied experience, much closer

---

[16] I'm referring here to the program of the UNESCO Chair on Transcultural Music Studies, University of Music Weimar, Germany. See, for instance, Tiago de Oliveira Pinto, 2016, 2018.

496 T. de Oliveira Pinto

to one's own body than using any other device—a typing or a drilling machine, a computer, and so on. The musician's body resonates in the instruments' sound and voice.

In many cases this instrument is so intimately related to the personality of its player, that the instrument keeps his or her name, even decades and centuries after the musician's lifetime—this is the case with famous Stradivari violins and other instruments named after one of their former owners or players.[17] Also, when an instrumental teacher chooses one of his or her preferred pupils to hand over the musical instrument, a part of the body of this teacher is being transferred, symbolically substantiating all the learnings and musical skills internalized during the previous learning process. And when being played afterward, this instrument will be part of a new body, that of the former pupil, keeping its attributes from the previous musical generation to which it had belonged before. The musical instrument becomes a cultural body, transcending wood, metal, and so on, the specific matter it is constituted of. To learn how to handle it is a most enduring and enormously rewarding experience that reunites human body and mind alike.

At the end, a personal recount:

By the age of eight I started studying violin with a Hungarian teacher, Dona Ana (Ana Kerekes Wittman), from Budapest, who emigrated to São Paulo, Brazil, in 1956 to escape from the Soviet occupation of her home country. I realized later that much of my career as a musician, anthropologist, and cultural producer goes back to the foundations Dona Ana gave me as a child and teenager until my 18th year of life.

The perception I had was that my teacher's instrument was intimately related to her. I remember when giving classes and holding her violin in her hands, Dona Ana would illustrate what she just had said before by playing. Especially in moments of verbal restriction, when her Portuguese language skills were not enough to express what she intended to say, she would communicate with her instrument. These are unforgotten remembrances of an early stage of my musical learning experiences.

Later, when I was already studying at university, and shortly before her passing, Dona Ana handed on her instrument to me, an absolutely unexpected, enormous honor! This violin, which since then is in my possession, was made by the Austrian *Hof Lauten und Geigenbauer Johann Joseph Stadlmann, Wien* in 1776: a precious old instrument, which has certainly experienced much wonderful music. Ludwig van Beethoven was only six years old when Stadlmann completed it. This luthier probably delivered it to the Habsburg court, where

---

[17] For instance, Israeli-French violinist Ivry Gitlis (1922–2020) owned Sancy, a Stradivarius violin made in 1713. It was named after its first-known owner from the Leloup family of Sancy in the Auvergne, France, in the first half of the nineteenth century.

the Vienna court orchestra was officially supplied with his stringed instruments (as stated in the inner label of most of Stadlmann's instruments). Or it might even be that Stadlmann sent the violin to the court of Prince Esterhazy, Bratislava/Pressburg/Pozsony, who also ordered Stadlmann's instruments for his orchestra, which in those days was directed by Josef Haydn. In this latter case, the violin would already have started its musical life in Hungary or at least in a Hungarian context. It would leave the country involuntarily almost 200 years later, as the only piece of luggage Dona Ana could take with during a precipitous night getaway from Budapest in 1956.

My teacher studied with the internationally renowned Jenö Hubay (1856–1938), violin virtuoso, composer, and rector of the Liszt Ferenc Academia in Budapest. Dona Ana graduated from this Music Academy in the 1920s. Most probably Hubay, her teacher, had also taken the instrument in his hands. There are certainly many stories around my violin made by Stadlmann, as with any other historical musical instrument. Unfortunately, we can only imagine that these stories exist, without ever being able to unearth them all.

Today, when making music, I perceive my instrument as a part of my own inner feelings. As it probably always did for generations of musicians, this violin continues playing its role as an extension of a body: not as a prosthesis, in order to overcome some physical incapability, but to give strength to emotions, to self-fulfillment and to the pure joy of an aesthetical outcome. Above all, though, 'my Stadlmann' supports me today by becoming a 'musical self', with the same strength and brightness of a sounding moment, as it did before, with my teacher and with so many previous musicians. To play an instrument is a sensitive emotion-based expression of mutual commitment, a very special and unique one between a human and a musical being, and a most vibrant living evidence that music in fact is an embodied experience for life.

References

Bleibinger, B. (2018). Making Music and Musical Instruments: Making Society? Thoughts Based on Personal Experiences in the Field. In J. Marti & S. R. Gutiez (Eds.), *Making Music, Making Society*. Cambridge Scholars Publishing.

Busch, B. (Ed.). (2016). *Grundwissen Instrumentalpädagogik. Ein Wegweiser für Studium und Beruf*. Breitkopf & Härtel.

Campbell, P. S. (2005). *Teaching Music Globally. Experiencing Music, Expressing Culture*. Oxford University Press.

Davis, S. (2003). Music. In J. Levinson (Ed.), *The Oxford Handbook of Aesthetics* (pp. 489–514).

Dargie, D. (1996). African methods of music education – some reflections. *African Music, 7*(3), 30–43.

Douglas, M. (1970). *Natural Symbols. Explorations in Cosmology*. Barrie & Rockliff.

Gallagher, S. (2011). Interpretations of embodied cognition. In W. Tschacher & C. Bergomi (Eds.), *The implications of embodiment: Cognition and communication* (pp. 59–71). Exeter.

Gebauer, G., & Wulf, C. (1998). *Spiel, Ritual, Geste. Mimetischen Handeln in der sozialen Welt*. Rowohlt.

Grupe, G. (2010). Between Introspection and Exhibition: Body-Related Aspects of Musical Performances. Visual Signaling, Motional Patterns, Tactility, and the Significance of Playing a Guitar Behind One's Head. In B. Muszkalska & R. Allgeyer-Kaufmann (Eds.), *BodyMusicEvent. Proceedings from the International Musicological Conference Wroclaw (Poland)* (pp. 65–76). Phaidra.

Hindrichs, G. (2014). *Die Autonomie des Klangs. Eine Philosophie der Musik*. Oxford University Press.

Kubik, G. (1984). Transkription afrikanischer Musik vom Stummfilm: Methoden und Probleme. In A. Simon (Ed.), *Musik in Afrika. Mit 20 Beiträgen zur Kenntnis traditioneller afrikanischer Musikkulturen* (pp. 202–216). Museum für Völkerkunde.

Levi-Strauss, C. (1958). *Anthropologie structurale*. Plon.

Mauss, M. (1936). *Les techniques du corps*. In M. Mauss (Ed.), *Sociologie et anthropologie*. Les Presses universitaires de France.

Oliveira Pinto, T. d. (1995). Aparai-Wayana. Cultural support of the Carib people in the Northwestern Amazon region. *The World of Music, 33*(2), 127–130.

Oliveira Pinto, T. d. (2004). Instrumentos Musicais. In P. Junge (Ed.), *África. Arte de um Continente*. CCBB.

Oliveira Pinto, T. d. (2011). Mehr als Polyrhythmen und Lebensfreude: Vom Umgang mit afrikanischer Musik in der Schule. *Musik und Unterricht, 102*, 28–35.

Oliveira Pinto, T. d. (2016). Musik als Kultur. Eine Standortsuche im immateriellen Kulturerbe. *Die Tonkunst. Magazin für klassische Musik und Musikwissenschaft, 10*(4), 378–389.

Oliveira Pinto, T. d. (2018). *Music as Living Heritage. An Essay on Intangible Culture*. EMVAS.

Révész, G. (1944). *Die menschliche Hand. Eine psychologische Studie*. S. Karger.

Rink, J. (2002). *Musical Performance. A Guide to Understanding*. Cambridge University Press.

Rutz, O. (1911). *Musik. Wort und Körper als Gemütsausdruck*. Breitkopf & Härtel.

Shapiro, L. (2011). *Embodied Cognition*. Routledge.

Small, C. (1999). Musicking – the meanings of performing and listening. A lecture. *Music Education Research, 1*(1), 9–22.

Stangl, W. (2021). Keyword: Embodiment. *Online Lexikon für Psychologie und Pädagogik*: https://lexikon.stangl.eu/2175/embodiment/ (Accessed 2021-01-03).

Storch, M., Cantieni, B., Hüther, G., & Tschacher, W. (2010). *Embodiment. Die Wechselwirkung von Körper und Psyche verstehen und nutzen* (p. 2). Huber.

von Tobel, R. (1969). *Musizieren, Übern und Erziehung*. Gstaad.

Wulf, C. (2014). Geste. In C. Wulf & J. Zirfas (Eds.), *Handbuch Pädagogische Anthropologie* (pp. 177–188). Springer VS.

Wulf, C. (2016). Immaterielles Kulturerbe. Aktuelle Entwicklungen und grundlegende Strukturelemente. *Die Tonkunst. Magazin für klassische Musik und Musikwissenschaft, 10*, 1.

Part VII

Bodies in Times of Glocalizations

In the many different processes of embodiment and of learning we find universal elements that are characteristic of *Homo sapiens* and, at the same time, elements that are particular to different regions and cultures. There are effects of religion, colonialism, racism, violence, poverty and many other frameworks of life that become inscribed into our bodies as we are social beings. An example of the huge diversity of cultures and different ways of understanding the body is Sub-Saharan Africa where there are almost 2000 languages and 3000 ethnic groups. Many of the body features which are characteristic of these ethnic groups are the result of complex social processes and are unknown outside of the particular region or locality. There is often a clash between local and global or Western forms of learning. Conflicts are inevitable. In Africa, the Islamic world, Latin America, India and China, concepts of the body and embodiment have emerged, in which commonalities and differences to Western ideas and practices are interwoven. For example, for the Yoruba who live predominantly in Nigeria, Benin and Togo, the word *omoluwabi* denotes an embodiment of values (integrity, courtesy and discipline), of a sense of justice, craftsmanship, tolerance and sensitivity, that is essential for 'an education of the heart, mind and hands' in which different elements are integrated (*Michael Omolewa* and *Adetola Adejo*). Chapter 30 shows us how the body is a key medium of education in the indigenous society and culture of the Yoruba, and it reflects the impacts of religious and other cultural aspects on embodiment and bodily processes of learning.

Whereas the case study of the Yoruba showed the importance of embodiment in cultures of Sub-Saharan Africa, Chap. 31 approaches our topic from a different angle (*Reza Arjmand*). This chapter analyses the key importance of

Islam for the conceptions of the body in many African and Asian cultures, at the same time as there are diverse cultural practices. As far as Islam is not only a religion but a way of life, the conceptions of the human body in the Qur'an have a powerful influence on people's everyday lives and the realm of education in the Islam world. The body is a sign of God; in the words of the Prophet Muhammad: "God created Adam upon His image". The human body has two spheres: the first consists of the physical parts of the body such as ears, eyes, mouth, heart and so on; the second includes anatomical experiences such as speaking, listening and dying. The interconnectedness of body and spirituality is central. The chapter also shows how the microcosm of the human body relates to the macrocosm, which leads to the discipline and control of bodies in the everyday lives of Moslems. Finally, Sufism serves as an example and illustration for the significance of embodiment for education.

Chapter 32 examines the effects of slavery, colonialism and racism on how human bodies and body images are formed in Brazil and Latin America (*Karina Limonta Vieira*). From a phenomenological viewpoint, the bodies of the indigenous population can still be distinguished from those of the descendants of the three million African slaves and from the people whose ancestors once emigrated from Portugal and Spain. The complex make-up of the body or bodies in Latin America is due to their commonalities and their differences. The way children are taught in schools, particularly in their sports lessons, shows how in Brazil an attempt is made to standardize the many diverse forms of bodiliness. Here the aims and values of liberalism and capitalism play an important role. The various body types and conceptions of the body are important for creation of a national identity, and all the more so since the physical differences are associated with social differences which are used for the creation of social hierarchies. Normative body images are not least important in the fields of sexual attraction and gender differences. The form and appearance of the female body, under the rule of machismo, to a large degree still determines female identity and attractiveness.

Chapter 33 uses a historical case study to consider the characteristics of the body in Ancient China and the importance of embodiment for human development and education. In the view of *Hongyan Chen* there are substantial differences between the Western and the Chinese conception of the body. Whereas the West was governed for a long time by mind-body dualism, she argues that one can find the tradition of a holistic view of the human being and the relationship of the body to the mind in China. On both sides we see an increasing interest in the body, and scholars from different language and culture areas attempt to construct a paradigm shift of body studies. This chapter focuses on the anthropological aspect of the body in traditional Chinese discourse. A historical-cultural approach has been applied to trace back the influence of Ancient China on the conception of the body and to identify the differences to Western understanding. In this case, time (*Shi*), repetitive exercise (*yangsheng, Li*) and harmony (*yin* and *yang, Qi*) are essential for the nurture and development of an energetic body, without the need for strength. In the field of Chinese pedagogy and education there is a growing interest in a consciously body-based learning in which our attention is drawn to the influence of Chinese traditions.

The last chapter (Chap. 34), concluding this section of the handbook, examines Hindu education in India (*Srajana Kaikini*). It shows that crucial for learning to act and to behave in a way that is ethically correct is the embodiment of aims and values and the attainment of practical knowledge. The chapter shows that the abasement of the body, of the Dalits for example, serves to create working bodies and (hu)manpower for in terms of social recognition 'low', yet necessary social jobs. The article shows that in large sections of Indian society the dignity of the human being and a person's social status is controlled by valuing or devaluing the body. Colonialism and caste, the gender and class system have led to the discrimination of large sections of the population. This has resulted in a differentiation between several body forms, such as the suffering body, the labouring body and the discriminated body. There have also been efforts to develop the concept of a sensing, thinking and acting body, which has met with a great deal of opposition. In this process Kaikini sees a relationship between embodiment, metaphysics and the social framing of learning, which she regards of central importance for the quality of education in Indian democracy.

Embodiment of the Values System in Indigenous African Society

Michael Omolewa and Adetola Adejo

1 Introduction

It is important to state from the outset that there is no uniformity in the cultural or traditional practices of the Africans, although there may be similarities. This is because Africa, as a region, comprises such vastness in size and cultural differences, even in sub-Saharan Africa with an estimation of 2000 languages and 3000 peoples. It is, of course, also true that there are some broad similarities in cultural practices, especially South of the Sahara Desert where intangible cultural traditions and practices are most common. In the entire region, however, there is a commonality in the use of the body as conveyor of information, values and attitudes and in being groomed to adopt specific measures of transforming the individual, the community and the wider society.

In African countries such as Nigeria, Ghana, Tanzania and Malawi, among others, traditional education of youngsters involves intellectual, physical and attitudinal training in order to develop fully into acceptable adults in the society. In addition, different kinds of games, including wrestling and running, training for healthy living, cooking, dressing, hunting, farming, carpentry, training to become a smith, drumming, dancing, marriage counselling

---

M. Omolewa (✉)
University of Ibadan, Ibadan, Nigeria

A. Adejo
Babcock University, Ilishan-Remo, Nigeria

© The Author(s), under exclusive license to Springer Nature Switzerland AG 2022
A. Kraus, C. Wulf (eds.), *The Palgrave Handbook of Embodiment and Learning*,
https://doi.org/10.1007/978-3-030-93001-1_30

and critical thinking, form part of the traditional curriculum at different stages of the life of the youth. Even on becoming an adult, and after the usual rites of passage, the average African continues to learn from traditional education through a lifelong process. This process fosters unity and citizenship in the African man's or woman's immediate environment (Adeyemi & Adeyinka, 2002).

The interactions of Africans with Islamic and Western worlds introduced literacy and the knowledge of reading, writing and arithmetic. The injection of literacy into the indigenous African system has led to a general disappointment that many of the core African values have been eroded by the indiscriminate response of Africans to the external systems that are found more attractive. Therefore, this study aims at examining how the body is used both in the training and in the transmission of African values, from one generation to another. It will also identify the parts of the body that are involved in the process of the teaching and imparting of knowledge, and the cultivation of core African values.

We shall use the Yoruba as a case study for our discourse. One reason for this choice is that the Yoruba are among the most widely dispersed peoples in Africa, as their presence continues to be evident even in Europe, the United Kingdom, the United States, Brazil, El Salvador, Cuba and, of course, in African countries including Togo, Benin, Sierra Leone, the Gambia, Liberia and Nigeria, where they are domiciled in the South West (Akintoye, 2010). A further attraction for the choice of the Yoruba is in the availability of ample literature and resources by scholars such as Ayo Bamgbose, Olabiyi Yai, Akinwumi Isola and many other researchers on aspects of the Yoruba language and culture. It must be noted that Wole Soyinka, the first African Nobel Laureate in Literature, is Yoruba.

In addition, we have relied on interviews with persons who we regard as custodians of the indigenous traditions in the absence of written evidence. These custodians have served as informants who have benefited from the wealth of oral traditions passed on through generations. Our selection of informants has considered the differences in age, religious affiliation and gender. Moreover, the evidence from interviews has been supplemented by ample materials in form of articles and books published by African scholars of different faith and persuasions.

We have also used materials in the form of written comments and observations of foreigners who visited Africa and who keep in touch with the local practices in the communities visited. An example of these foreigners was J. D. Y. Peel, an English person who specialised in the study of Yoruba and became Professor of Sociology at the School of Oriental and African Studies at the University of London (Marchand, 2016). Another example was Ulli

Beier, a German, who was recruited to the Department of Extramural Studies of the University College, Ibadan, (UCI), in Nigeria (Ogundele, 2003, 1998; Abiodun, 2011; Breitinger, 2011). UCI was Nigeria's first and oldest University, founded by the British colonial government. Peel lived among the Ijesa people, a branch of the Yoruba of Western Nigeria, and taught at the University of Ife founded in the city of Ile Ife, considered the cradle of Yoruba civilisation. Beier arrived in Nigeria on 1 October 1950, and it is interesting to note that the country was later to be granted political independence by the British government exactly ten years later, 1 October 1960. Both Peel and Beier became close friends of the key traditional rulers among the Yoruba of Western Nigeria who in turn began to give them their trust and confidence. Both Europeans identified with the culture of the Yoruba people. Beier went deeper in his relationship with the core cultural group of the Yoruba. Thus, after his arrival, he chose to be initiated into the traditional cults. Ulli Beier's decision demonstrated his respect for the traditional system and made him a total insider, with unlimited access to "the mundane and celestial worlds of the Yoruba ... ritual performances and traditional festivals to 'orisa' (deity) tradition and worship, poetry, local priests and everyday ordinary peoples" (Raheem, 2019). He, in particular, "had the singular honour of being trusted by the diverse cultural agencies with even the smallest of details handed down from their forebears" (Raheem, 2019).

Both Peel and Beier were also physically and emotionally connected with the local people and visited Yoruba towns where they mingled with people from all social classes. Their observations of the practices of the Yoruba were, therefore, intimate and reliable. However, it is important to note that the practices of the people have not been static. Thus, Jacob Ade Ajayi, a leading scholar in African historiography, in his seminal study of change and continuity, observed that there has been a consistent evolution of the several features and elements of the use of the body (Ade Ajayi, 1969).

This discourse about the body in Africa is arranged chronologically, comprising the pre-literate, industrial and technological periods. The pre-literate educational provision was done wholly in the non-formal setting. The discussion on the status in Africa in the pre-literate setting is followed by the description of the change which was introduced by the coming of foreign cultures and practices and led to cosmopolitanism and the attraction of the Arabic and Western culture through the Islamic and Western education. Even at this time, the education in the non-formal setting continued. Finally, we explore the post literate, industrial and technological phase of the embodiment of the African culture or value system, which was again dominated by non-formal education components.

2 The Mission of the Body

Broadly, the body has remained the key instrument used by Africans in many directions and for a variety of purposes. The body of the African, in its physical form, in colonial times was reported as strong and virile, and this would explain why Africans were preferred as slaves when there was competition with other 'races' for access to powerful workers on the farms and industries in America and the Caribbean (Horton, 2003). Africans were found to be resilient, powerful and adaptable, and that is why they have been acclaimed as being capable of both simultaneously suffering and smiling in many parts of the world, including their own homeland Africa.

The body, however, transcends the physical form and is used through the process of learning to convey a message, develop some competence and be used for more lasting goals. Basically, therefore, the use of the entire body has been geared ultimately to produce an 'omoluwabi', an embodiment of values, the person of integrity, a perfect gentleman, well bred, courteous, disciplined and endowed with competence, compassion and character—the 3Cs.

The 'omoluwabi' is groomed to possess an independent spirit, defiance of inequity and social injustice; demonstration of aptitude in craftsmanship, integrity, valour, honour, knowledge of traditional history, traditional medicine, norms and practices, and investment of the talent, as well as skill for the advancement of the individual and the wider community. The 'omoluwabi' was predictably known for tolerance and sensitivity to differences.

Competence, compassion and character were the core values of the 'omoluwabi'. Money or the accumulation of wealth was not the priority or preoccupation of the noble Yoruba person. The 'omoluwabi' was particularly expected to possess character. The development of character is, therefore, mandatory. As the elders of Africa put it, "if there is no character, beauty becomes ugliness" (Olagunju, 2020). Similarly, it is strongly argued that a person's character will always expose his or her identity. The attribute of a steady and dependable character was appreciated by Heraclitus the Greek philosopher, who was credited to have argued that character is destiny. The Yoruba contend that 'iwa', character, is 'ewa', beauty, thus the emergence of the word, 'iwalewa', character is beauty.

Ulli Beier observed that character, 'iwa', is the key product of sound training, and that its possession is the source of beauty, victorious living and success in every undertaking. This philosophy about the value of character was summarised in the saying, 'iwalewa', or character is unquantifiable beauty. On his return to Germany, Beier founded the unit for the propagation of African culture, which he named Iwalewa House at the University of Bayreuth. It is interesting that Beier became so intensely attracted by the concept and practice of 'iwalewa', thus sharing the profound faith in the quality of character (Ogundele, 1998). For as the Yoruba put it, "It is your character and character alone, that will make your life happy or unhappy", and "If you have a good head but lack character, the head will soon lose its goodness" (Olagunju, 2020).

The story of Ulli Beier is interesting. Attracted by the Yoruba philosophy of the development of the person, he was ardently fascinated by the ancient Yoruba culture and its powerful agencies. He was disturbed by the threats posed to the Yoruba rich traditions by the new religious movements, Westernisation and colonial rule. He was particularly disappointed by the ardent admiration the emergent educated elites had for Westernisation, while at the same time showing less concern for local traditions and cultures (Beier, 1957). His mission to give the deserved respect and recognition to the rich African culture was already being pursued by the Yoruba cultural reawakening and rebirth that had begun around the early decades of the twentieth century. This was the time of the *Egbe Omo Oduduwa*, a cultural group composed of Western educated elites of Yoruba extraction, which later led to the formation of the Action Group, a political party which was led by Chief Obafemi Awolowo, the Premier of Western Nigeria (Arifalo, 2001).

Another significant core value of the 'omoluwabi' is compassion. Compassion is a deeply ingrained value in the African worldview, practiced in every social, economic, political and religious structure of a community. Compassion gives the community its identity. It is an ethical duty, a way of life. This virtue of compassion is so deeply rooted that it withstands the pressures of modernity, even among the youth. Because of the deeply ingrained community value in Africans, compassion seems to have survived the onslaught of individualism as well. For instance, there is no limit to the sacrifices the 'omoluwabi' can make for a visitor. African elders have a saying that: 'The hen with chicks does not swallow the worm'. This means that an African would rather cater to the needs of the guest first before meeting own needs. According to Chief Abiodun Adejo (personal communication, 21 November 2020), if a guest were to visit and there was only a plate of food available, the 'omoluwabi' is expected to share the food with guest or give up the food so that the guest is fed first before any other person. He added that the best parts of anything—clothing, food and shelter—were to be offered to the guest first and then the 'omoluwabi' will make do with whatever is left.

3 The Process

The body is used both in the training and in the transmission of the values of 'omoluwabi' from one generation to the other. Thus, the purpose for which the Yoruba is weaned from birth is to bring the 'omoluwabi' out of the baby, by bringing the beauty out of the baby through the stage of acculturation and sustained teaching and learning. This process of weaning is also made the duty of all stakeholders, the parents, the peers and the wider community, charged with bringing up the next generation through inspiration, guiding and instilling values. Of course, while bringing up the child and younger adult, there could be some scolding, in which corporal punishment is administered. However, the end product has been noted as salutary as the standards of ethics, integrity and sensitivity to differences have been successfully transmitted (Omolewa, 2007). Parts of the body are identified as part of the process of the teaching and imparting of knowledge and cultivation of the values of the 'omoluwabi'. For example, the head is a major component of the components for successful living: the use of the Head, the Hand and the Heart, the 3Hs.

3.1 The Head

The head, 'ori', is the first instrument for learning the basic value of integrity. The head is accepted as the first and leading part of the body. It is believed that the head determines the destiny of the individual. The Yoruba, in their prayer 'ori mi gbe mi lo siibi ire mi', confess that it is the head that can support their dreams and translate their vision to a mission and progress: 'ori mi'. Thus, special attention is paid to the nurturing of the head, taking care of it and investing in its nourishment. The head is adorned with care and attention. Likewise, the husband and father is accepted as the head of the family with the responsibility to guide and guard other members of the family. The head is venerated. In similar ways, the elders in the society are venerated and accepted as ancestors at death. The masquerades are believed to be spirits of the ancestors who are on a visit to the earth. Thus, no disrespect is to be accepted. The head is given special greetings in the form of poetry known as the 'oriki'. The 'oriki' is chanted or sung to welcome a person of all ages, social class or professional choice. It is usually in the form of praise, ascribing to the recipient of the 'oriki' some past noble deeds of the individual or the family. 'Oriki' is also a form of exaltation and encouragement. Sometimes, it takes the form of prophetic declaration. When you praise a person from a town, they get happier and closer to you. People will be friendly with you if you know their 'oriki'. It has been observed that crying children stop crying when someone sings their 'oriki' (Oyedele, personal communication, 27 November 2020).

The head, so appreciated and given due recognition, is expected to strive to attract the best to the entire body: good deeds of kindness, sacrifice, love, compassion and sensitivity. Another part of the body that is often invoked in the learning process is the hand.

3.2   The Hand

The Yoruba take special interest in the development of the interest of the young ones in their use of their hands, accepted as special gifts of the Supreme Being. Learning to do something with the hands is vital. To this end, serves an apprenticeship system in which a young person is attached to a trade, a profession or business such as such as hunting, building, traditional medical practice or knowledge of the herbs. The master craftsman supervises the apprentice over the period of learning the craft or profession. Beginning from the lowest level of attachment, the apprentice is supposed to perform menial jobs in obedience and humility and surrender. In learning by doing, simultaneously, the apprentice is actively taught to use the hands. This is much unlike the system of Western education where 'book knowledge' precedes the hands-on, that is the doing of the work. In the Yoruba context, there is flexibility in the duration of the apprenticeship. Basically, however, learner performance is determined by aptitude, skill and ability.

In the indigenous system, there is no question of first learning and later getting prepared for employment. Learning and working happens simultaneously. This arrangement ensures that there is always some job to be performed. Therefore, no question of unemployment arises. Laziness and indolence are seen as unacceptable to the society.

3.3   The Heart

The heart, 'okan', with its intangible mind, 'emi', is recognised as perhaps the most important part of the body that dominates the other parts. It is believed that once the mind is touched, all other parts are affected by the touch. It is, therefore, assumed that the mind can be used as the medium with which to reach other parts: hence, the decision to give prior attention to the mind. The mind is to be cultivated to learn about the virtues of purity, nobility, holiness, sacredness, love, mercy, compassion, dedication and personal sacrifice to which it must dedicate itself never to desecrate. The mind also remains at the centre of use for the cultivation of values, and the grooming for acceptance of goodness and righteousness. During the training of the mind, there is a deliberate rejection of those temptations and pressures such as sin, immorality, corruption, wickedness and other possible prevailing iniquities of the age.

3.4 The Body Language: The Eye and the Nose as Non-verbal Communicators

In addition to the focus on the separate parts of the body, there is body language, which is not verbal; it does not involve talking but includes the instrumentality of the movement of a part of the body, mostly the eye and the nose, and the face, in such a way that it communicates a message to the onlooker, without making a sound. One's thinking, positive or negative, is reflected in his or her emotions, moody or excited, and a smile says that one is happy.

The interpretation of the unspoken message by the person involved leads to a response required by the sender of the message. For example, a frown would be used for expressing displeasure, quiet for insisting on silence. When a question is asked, or a shaking of the head an objection to a request is indicated. Mothers are often associated with the use of body language, e.g. gestures to be silent, by this, conveying a message, taught or developed naturally.

Through body language, communication is carried out and one is able to talk without sound. We can instruct, direct, inform and address an individual using body language, as well as communicate to the target what is required to do. If the person to whom the message is sent fails to respond or react, in Yoruba the recipient is mocked as 'Ko m'oju', one who is deficient in the knowledge of body language.

3.5 Learning Through Music and Dance

Almost all the parts of the body are used in the body movements, which involve music and dance. The art of dancing is used to instil values that are fundamental to the African ways of life. Music and dance are introduced to equip the learners with the ability to function effectively in other areas of learning such as language acquisition, speech, literacy, numeracy and other related themes. They are given to learners to enjoy, thus providing them with an artistic outlet and a way to relax. Learners often anticipate the music and dance sessions with excitement because compassion and choice are usually encouraged and nurtured. Through carefully planned music and dance programmes, learning takes place during initiation, festivities, the age-grade system, home education and community education where everyone is encouraged to learn the norms and values of the society (Omolewa, 2007).

3.6   Integrated Learning

It is important to note that learning in the indigenous system does not leave room for compartmentalisation in the sense of separating learning into branches of science and arts. The child gets exposed to all branches of learning. Similarly, the separation of learning into the primary, secondary and tertiary levels is not known, as education is considered to be lifelong, unbroken and continuing throughout life. Indeed, there is a curriculum available even after life on the requirements for successful living after death, as the dead are reminded, 'a j'okun, ma jekolo, nkanti won ban je lohunni ko ma ba won je': don't eat worms, nor millipedes, get to know what the requirements are there yonder and adapt (Adesegun A. personal communication, 27 November 2020).

Another characteristic of the indigenous education is the community-focused system. The upbringing of the child is not exclusive responsibility of the parents, but of everyone in the community. Everyone is involved in bringing up the child: communal system, interaction. The welfare of others is important, and individuality was discouraged. This is different from the arrangement of examination preparation and 'rat-race competition' in Western education.

3.7   Learning in the Indigenous Society

The body parts are supposed to convey the message of the values acceptable to the Yoruba society, the goal of the Yoruba knowledge system is the cultivation of basic values for the benefit of the individual and the wider society, as stated earlier. The question can be asked about why Africa has been able to sustain the tradition of producing a people like Yoruba who, until today and despite of colonialism, have remained rich in culture, facing the struggles of life with determination and strength and ensuring the continuity of the life that is founded on communal living? Many African communities have sustained the culture of caring for one another, not allowing government to take on the role, as is done in the technologically and industrially developed parts of the world, consciously and by education avoiding being too self-centred or thinking only about one's self instead of the collective population. Africans have also been found to enjoy living a simple life, being contented with sharing the little each one has with others, compassionate and filled with love. It is amazing and often inexplicable how the ordinary and usually extremely poor people choose to offer services to neighbours, shunning the temptations of accumulating material possession.

The explanation is found in the inculcation of the basic discipline of faith in the afterlife, the home of the ancestors where rewards are given to those who have lived a good life of service to others and sacrifice involving denial of self. At the centre of the process of acquiring this discipline is the invocation of the knowledge of the Supreme Being, given several names such as God, and descriptions such as the Almighty, and recognised as the Maker and Creator of the universe who knows all things because He has made them all. He is believed to be capable of doing all things because His authority is unlimited and unstoppable. The efficacy of the belief in the power of the spirit world has been noted by Ulli Beier from the vantage position of his initiation. The knowledge of the Supreme Being is, however, accompanied by sanctions for failing to adhere strictly to the demands for living a life of decency, fairness and firmness. The instruments for enforcing these sanctions included appeals to the spirit world sometimes in the form of masquerades who were believed to be visitors from the outer space who have come to ensure that social justice and equity were practised. Those found wanting were compelled to face the prescribed punishments, some of which were as humiliating as ostracism from the wider society of individuals or families that were deviants. Again, Ulli Beier ensured that he had adequate knowledge of the forces which held the people together. To this end, he got initiated into the secret society, the Ogboni cult (Morton-Williams, 1960). The implication was that by becoming a member of the Ogboni cult, and a devotee, he had unlimited access to the priests, priestesses, healers, traditional rulers and devotees of several Yoruba religious cults from which he learnt about deeper issues or "the categories that embody the macrocosmic world of the Yoruba" (Raheem, 2019).

The potency of the indigenous African culture may be explained by the system of sanctions that were put in place. For example, in the process of the choice of a marriage partner, each family of the proposed couple would conduct an in-depth search of the antecedents of the individuals concerned. Questions would be asked about the antecedents of the parents, and if there had been incidents of criminality, insubordination and related anti-social behaviour, and if any family had been associated with stealing, there would be an opposition to the association with such a family. It is the cultivation of the tradition of transparency and nobility of character that would explain why homes were built in the indigenous community without the modern burglar-proof windows and doors, as well as walls that now look like prison houses. It was inconceivable to allow a lady to be married into any family where there was indolence or laziness, as everyone was expected to have cultivated the tradition for hard work and industry. There were objections to homes with any trace of cowardly behaviour, as courage and chivalry were applauded by the society. The society was groomed to appreciate nobility of character involving selflessness and dedication, accountability and transparency, and to shun materialism and the pursuit of personal interests, which are often associated with corruption. In later years, the society had been transformed into a corruption-infested, acquisitive, materialistic community where self-interest prevails over the collective interest of the indigenous society.

Later in the history of Africa, the interaction with the Islamic and Western worlds introduced literacy and thus the knowledge of the 3Rs involving reading, arithmetic and writing. It has been argued that the injection of the 3Rs into the indigenous system of the 3Cs did not necessarily lead to an improved performance of the expectations of the indigenous society. Rather, it has been noted that products of the 3R became arrogant and disrespectful of their illiterate elders. Consequently, there has been a general disappointment that many of the core values have been eroded by the often indiscriminated responses of Africans to the external systems that are found more attractive, and subsequently the adoption of European modes of dress, language, eating style and greetings. It has been observed that many of these African traditionists have continued to live the indigenous way with the long greetings, dress codes and the showing of respect to elders by acknowledging their wisdom and experience and bowing to salute them.

There are some Africans who have continued to resist the foreign incursion and who lament the wholesale adoption of the foreign dress codes, such as the Arab purdah and shawl, the European suit and ties, the greetings of 'hi' instead of the longer version of asking for the state of the health of the neighbour and how he slept and whether he dreamt or not.

Many of these Africans attracted by the Western cultural practices have been tempted to look down on the illiterate population as unfortunate human beings robbed of the light of civilisation. Arrogant and self-conceited, they are known to show off their knowledge in an arrogant manner (Ayandele, 1974).

However, the 'omoluwabi' traits of character, compassion and competence have substantially remained. Thus, among the Yoruba, it was common for the community to accommodate the religious differences introduced by the coming of Islam and Christianity. For example, during Muslim celebrations, Christians joined in the celebration of the festivities and shared in the joy that accompanied the slaughter of rams. Similarly, Muslims joined in the celebration of Christian festivals including the Christmas and Easter celebrations. The gulf and hostility experienced in other societies were generally unknown among the Yoruba and certainly were not acceptable.

It should also be noted that in spite of the glorification of the changes brought by the connection of Africans with the Arab and European civilisations, it is clear that the culture and values of hard work, industry and honesty was eroded by the contact with the foreign influences.

In contemporary society, many of the basic expectations of the indigenous system remain in the society to varying degrees. The body continues to remain a composite of tangible things, which display physically some potent messages that are systematically intangible and represent something that is abstract. The body serves as the conveyor of the values of the society, which rejects anti-social values and practices of cruelty, ignorance, corruption, incompetence, carelessness and disloyalty, while extolling the values of strong character where character continues to matter and be considered a desirable end of a person's destiny. For any learning among the children and younger adults to be sustainable and efficient, the indigenous education systems must be constantly taken into consideration.

References

Abiodun, R. (2011). The Elephant Lies Down Like a Hill: Tribute to Ulli Beier 1922–2011. *African Arts., 44*(4), 4–7.

Ade Ajayi, J. F. (1969). The Continuity of African Institutions under Colonialism. In T. O. Ranger (Ed.), *Emerging Themes of African History* (pp. 196–197). Heinemann Educational Books.

Adeyemi, M. B., & Adeyinka, A. A. (2002). Some Key Issues in African Traditional Education. *McGill Journal of Education/Revue des sciences de l'éducation de McGill, 37*(2), 223–240.

Akintoye, S. A. (2010). *A History of the Yoruba Nation*. Amalion Publishing.

Arifalo, S. (2001). *Egbe Omo Oduduwa: A Study in Ethnic and Cultural Nationalism (1945–1965)*. Stebak Books.

Ayandele, E. (1974). *Educated Elite in Nigerian Society*. Ibadan University Press.

Beier, U. (1957). The Attitude of the Educated African to his Traditional Art. *The Phylon Quarterly, 18*(2), 162–165.

Breitinger, E. (2011). In Memory of Ulli Beier. *African Studies Bulletin, 73*, 67–69.

Horton, J. (2003). Race: The Power of an Illusion. https://www.pbs.org/race/000_About/002_04-background-02-04.htm

Marchand, T. (2016). JDY PEEL, 1941–2015. Obituaries. Royal Anthropological Institute. http://www.therai.org.uk/archives-and-manuscripts/obituaries/jdy-peel

Morton-Williams, P. (1960). The Yoruba Ogboni Cult in Oyo. *Africa: Journal of the International African Institute., 30*(4), 362–374.

Ogundele, W. (1998). Rereading Beier. *African Quarterly on the Arts, 2*(3), 61–65.

Ogundele, W. (2003). Omoluabi. Ulli Beier, Yoruba Society and Culture. *African Studies, 66*, 302.

Olagunju, L. (2020). Trump: Not Until He is Disgraced. *Nigerian Tribune*.

Omolewa, M. (2007). Traditional African Modes of Education. *International Journal Review of Education, 53* (5&6), 593–612. UNESCO Institute for Lifelong Learning.

Raheem, O. (2019). The Ulli Beier Archives at the Centre for Black Culture and International Understanding (CBCIU), Nigeria and a Summary of Holdings. *Africa Bibliography, 2018*, vii–xxii.

Embodiment in Education in the Islamic World

Reza Arjmand

Have We not lay open thy breast. (Qurʾān[1], XCIV, 1)

Islam is perceived not only as a religion but as a way of life with detailed directions for its adherents, and the human body is among the areas that are explored and discussed extensively. While the body is certainly an essential aspect of human existence, treating it as an object of study is no easy matter. Despite the wealth of literature on the body in Islam, embodiment in education is a rather neglected topic and, except sporadically in various texts, is not properly addressed. Indeed, the body as a physical and conceptual tool is implicated in all human attempts to construct knowledge, which means that it can be intrusively ever present or frustratingly transparent depending on the epistemological vantage point one chooses to employ in discussing a topic (Bashir, 2010).

This chapter begins with a brief account on the body and embodiment in Islam based on the Qurʾān as the common denominator for all Muslims and on which, despite variations in exegesis, all Muslim doctrines rest. The chapter then continues with the discussion on the notion of embodiment and education in Islam by examining some of the theories underpinning it from

---

[1] The terms in other languages are usually Arabic or Persian. The transliteration of Arabic and Persian terms in this chapter is based on *ALA-LC Romanization Schemes for Non-Roman Scripts* (1997). Familiar variant names, however, follow the official spelling of the individuals or sites, even though they may not fully comply with the ALA-LC system.

R. Arjmand (✉)
Linnaeus University, Växjö, Sweden
e-mail: reza.arjmand@lnu.se

© The Author(s), under exclusive license to Springer Nature Switzerland AG 2022
A. Kraus, C. Wulf (eds.), *The Palgrave Handbook of Embodiment and Learning*,
https://doi.org/10.1007/978-3-030-93001-1_31

various perspectives. Evidently, given the heterogeneous contextual characteristics of Muslim cultures and societies, both temporally and geographically, it is impossible to achieve a coherent and comprehensive theory of embodiment from an educational perspective. This account, hence, is an attempt to show clearly and concisely the diverse theoretical views that exist across the Muslim intellectual world on the notion of embodiment and education. The chapter therefore discusses various dominant philosophical and educational schools.

1 Body and Embodiment in Islam: An Ontological Account

Qurʾān as the primary source of religious knowledge in Islam contains the term 'nafs' to denote the human person in their entirety, usually without specifically differentiating between soul and body (Calverley & Netton, 2012), while likewise there are exclusive references to the physical corpus as well. This is specifically more discernible in verses where the Qurʾān mentions the creation of human beings from dust or clay or various human organs. An important feature of the Qurʾānic view of the human body is that it is put forth as 'ayah' (sign of God), "It is among His Signs that He created you from dust" (Qur'an XXX, 20). It also addresses creation and physical constitution ('khalq') (The Qurʾān, XLV, 3–4). Moreover, it is stated that God has created man "in the best of moulds" (XCV, 4). The Islamic version of the concept of 'imago dei', expressed by the saying of the Prophet Muhammad, 'God created Adam upon His image' should be seen and understood in this light (Shahzad, 2007). The Qurʾān mentions different body parts many times, spread throughout the text and particular terms do not always convey the same meaning in different contexts. In some parts of the Qurʾān the human body is treated as a functional element and in a metaphorical sense aimed at encouraging the pursuit of an ethical and pious life. The body parts in the Qurʾān are cited in conjunction with the faith of believers to ensure that there is a complete understanding of the harmony between the workings of the body and the message of the Qurʾān. In the Qurʾān, the human body can be seen as two divided spheres. The first consists of the various physical elements, such as the flesh, fluids, eyes, ears, head and heart. The second includes anatomical experience, such as speaking, weeping, eating, fasting, listening and dying, and what the body experiences in the light of religious faith (Huda, 2017).

The wellbeing of the physical body is deemed significant for Muslims who recognize it as a vessel of spirituality. According to Islamic tenets, the human body in its physicality is made of clay, completed by a process of ensoulment, not earlier than four months after conception.[2] The flesh is not seen as evil, and its needs and desires should be fulfilled in reasonable moderation. The Islamic tradition insists overwhelmingly on the connectedness of the human body and spirituality (Hoffman, 1995). As Bashir (2010) puts it, the body appears as a lynchpin within Islamic cosmological thought, holding the cosmos together by mediating between its physical, metaphysical and social aspects.

The body in Islam is seen as a microcosm which reflects the cosmos in its entirety. This notion, which is more pronounced among Sufi scholars, has resulted in a Muslim cosmological scheme and affects various social as well as epistemological domains. If we consider the physical quality of corporeality, however, the theory of microcosm and macrocosm forms the basis of two sets of correspondences: (1) the equivalence between the different components of the material world and the various elements of the human body, which often amount to seven—hence the link with the astrological seven planets; and (2) the way in which the four cosmic elements (water, fire, air and earth) correspond to the four bodily humours (blood, phlegm, red bile and black bile); the elements of both groups have contrasting qualities—humidity, dryness, heat and cold (Gignoux, 2004) which correspond to the body as a complete whole. The Muslim philosophers al-Kindi, Avicenna and Fakhr al-Din al-Razi, all of whom are known for their distinctive approach to education, connected the four elements with the four qualities ('ṭabāʾiʿ') heat and cold (the active force), and dryness and moisture (the recipients) (Rafati, 2002), which affect not only the physical body but also the intellect and habits of learning.

There is a large amount of material on the taxonomy of the body and its respective terminology within the Islamic philosophy and subsequently education and this is beyond the scope of this concise chapter; however, a brief reference to human body typology in Islam seems necessary. The Islamic metaphysical body is composed of 'jirm' (mass), a higher component of the celestial bodies,[3] while mundane bodies are composed of the four classical cosmic elements ('al-basāʾiṭ'). 'Badan' and 'jasad' are used as synonyms of 'jism' (anatomical body); whereas the former is also used for the bodies of animals, the latter is reserved for the bodies of higher beings. In addition,

---

[2] Among other implications, this means that from a Muslim juridical perspective (except for the Mālikī school among Sunnīs) contraception is not murder and abortion is permissible during the first four months of pregnancy.

[3] The idea is originally attributed to Pythagoras and his notion of the 'harmony of the spheres', which maintained that informed by their *jirm*s, the celestial bodies move according to mathematical equations. *Jirmiyyūn* are philosophers who, as followers of Pythagoras, argue that in the same vein as the celestial bodies, the human soul is the harmony of its body (the doctrine of *iʾtilāf* or *ittiḥād*).

'haykal' is a gnostic term to connote the physical world as a whole to include planets, since the world-soul and the spirits of the stars dwell in them like the human soul in its body (Nicholson, 1998).

Muslim scholars have often discussed the notion of the body in dichotomic conjunction with the soul—a subtle form or substance infused within or inhabiting a physical body. The significance of corporeality and the way the human body is fashioned has resulted in an ontological perspective among a group of Muslims who followed the literal meanings of passages in the Qur'ān that likened God to humans. Utilizing such Qur'ānic verses which suggest that "God is seated on a throne" (II, 255) and others that suggest "God has hands" (III, 73; V, 64; XLVIII, 10) and "eyes" (XX, 39; LII, 48; LIV, 14), the school of 'Mushabbihūn' (anthropomorphists) was formed who believe in 'tajsīm' (Corporealism) (Martin, 2018). The philosophical foundation of Corporealism is based on the premise that only that which has a physical extension can exist and thus, as the Qur'ānic descriptions suggest, God must have a 'jism' (physical body) to exist. Studies based on such anthropomorphism form a large part of Muslim literature on corporeality and embodiment, and Muslim scholars across various disciplines are divided on this. In point of fact, most of the speculative theologians and their opponents who disputed this doctrine found ways to hedge extreme positions of totally affirming or totally denying the human attributes of God. 'Tashbīh' and 'taʿṭīl' became terms of opprobrium used ascriptively, rather than descriptively, as accusations against theological opponents (Martin, 2018). The outcome of the contentious polemics regarding Islamic anthropomorphism on epistemology also highlights the similarity between divine knowledge and scholastic or mundane knowledge, between which there is a clear division. The latter is subordinate to the former. Divine knowledge is present and solely accessible through 'waḥy' (revelation), while mundane knowledge is acquired by scholastic means. Divine knowledge is also of a higher order, both quantitatively and qualitatively, but nevertheless ultimately identical with human knowledge (Arjmand, 2008). Thus, there are different ways of attaining the same knowledge and hence various approaches to knowledge acquisition are required: through direct divine illumination, a prophetic approach for which human spiritual development is required, or alternatively through philosophical inductive methods. While the latter moves from the imagination upwards to the theoretical intellect, the prophetic illumination approach goes in the reverse direction, from the theoretical intellect to the imagination.

The Muslim body is heavily regulated, and there is a long line of corporeal rules and regulations which stipulate various aspect of embodiment both in private and in public domains. In certain schools of thought within Islam,

Shiism and Sufism for instance, the body of certain figures becomes a source of grace and bounty even after death. This explains the abundance of shrines across parts of the Muslim world. The graves are perceived as the

> sites where divine favour and blessing occur, where mercy and grace descend; they are a refuge for the distressed, a shelter for the despondent, a haven for the oppressed, and a place of consolation for weary hearts, and will ever remain so until resurrection. (Qomī, 1961, p. 562)

As beings mired down in the material world, humans cannot but think with and through the body. This fact, a truism in the modern study of corpo-reality, can be illustrated in the Islamic context by considering God's anthropomorphically corporeal description of himself in the Qur'ān that amounts, from the internal Muslim perspective, to a self-portrait (Bashir, 2010). The extensive use of corporeal metaphors in the works of Muslim scholars underscores the comportment of the body as an a priori fact of life. The variation of perspectives and the association of the body and its taxonomy as a means for understanding the cosmos, from celestial beings to society, deserve a systematic approach to its understanding.

2   A Functionalist Approach to Embodiment in Islam

Apart from the widely debated theological doctrine of 'tashbīh' (anthropomorphism) and the notion of ascribing human attributes to the divine body, which is more pronounced among some schools, for instance Ash'arīes,[4] al-Farabi's (872–950) theory of functionalism is one of the earliest endeavours to utilize embodiment to explain the role of social and political institutions. In a similar vein to its Western equivalent, which appeared much later in nineteenth-century Europe, al-Farabi employs organic analogy as a method to decipher and explain how certain social practices or institutions serve to further the survival of the social system in its entirety. In his magnum opus, *The Perfect State* (1985, p. 23), al-Farabi notes that

---

[4] The Ash'arī is a school of Muslim theology whose main ideas, mostly concerning the notion of divine corporeality, are formulated as a response to the theological doctrines of the Mu'atazilī (rationalist school of Islamic theology who emphasize the supremacy of human reason and free-will) (Watt, 2008). Whereas the Mu'atazilīs endeavoured to apply reason and rational argumentation as a methodological tool to religious knowledge, Ash'arīs maintained an orthodox and literal approach to the interpretation of the Scripture. The difference between the two schools of thought is more pronounced in the notion of corporeality and *divine* anthropomorphism.

the excellent city[5] resembles the perfect and healthy body, all of whose limbs cooperate to make the life of the animal [man] perfect and to preserve it in this state.

Using the corporeal metaphors, al-Farabi provides a detailed argument for the theoretical underpinning of functionalism: differentiation, (secondary) socialization and social solidarity:

The city and the household may be compared with the body of a man. Just as the body is composed of different parts of a determinate number, some more, some less excellent adjacent to each other and graded, each doing a certain work, and there is combined from all their actions mutual help towards the perfection of the aim in the man's body.—Yet there is combined from these different aims, when they are perfected and combined, mutual help towards the perfection of the aim of the city. This again may be compared with the body, since the head, breast, belly, back, arms and legs are related to the body as the households of the city to the city. The work of each of the principal members is different from the work of the other, and the parts of each one of these principal members help one another by their different actions towards the perfection of the aim in that principal member. Then there is combined from the different aims of the principal members, when they are perfected, and from their different actions, mutual help towards the perfection of the aim of the whole body (Farabi, 1961, p. 37).

Al-Farabi's functionalist view defines education as a route towards the realization of 'al-insān al-kāmil' (the perfect human being) who has obtained theoretical virtue through intellectual knowledge and mores through practices. Similar to Western functionalism, 'al-insān al-kāmil' is a building bloc of 'al-madīna al-fādilah' (the perfect society) and defines the aim of education as the attainment of 'sa'ādah' (happiness).[6] 'Sa'ādah' is the ultimate aim of

---

[5] Although it implies state, the 'city' or 'polis' was used for such city-states as Athens and Sparta which were relatively small and cohesive units, in which political, religious and cultural concerns were intertwined (Aristotle, 1984). Despite the functional resemblances, the extent of their similarity to modern nation-states is controversial.

[6] Often translated literally as 'happiness', sa'ādah (the highest aim of human striving) is a comprehensive concept including happiness, bliss, wellbeing, prosperity, success, perfection, blessedness and beatitude (Ansari, 1963). Sa'ādah can be achieved through ethical perfection and education. Thus, sa'ādah somehow becomes close to the notion of Platonic 'Good'. Seen in such a way, Sa'āda could be translated as 'political happiness' or the public good. An educational perspective, however, bestows a unique attribute to the term, making it closer to the notion of 'education as a public good'. Given such an inclusive definition of sa'ādah, the investment in education benefits both the society and the individual, economically and otherwise. While a wide array of interpretations is provided for sa'ādah by Muslim scholars, some, such as for instance Miskawyah in his treatise Kitāb al-Sa'āah (The Book of Happiness) (1928), consider sa'ādah to be a moral condition which may be achieved through tahdhīb (moral cleansing).

al-Farabi's utopia where the sole distinction between inhabitants comes from their function including the meritocracy. Al-Farabi's Neo-Platonic epistemology, which is still in practice throughout the Muslim world, sometimes in combination with other schools or intellectual trends, endeavours to reconcile "aql' (reason) with Islamic dogma. Informed by the Muslim 'kalāmī' frame of reference, al-Farabi's epistemic functionalism produced a practical result. Throughout his trilogy[7] he formulated and presented the first comprehensive taxonomy of knowledge in Islam (Arjmand, 2008). Intriguingly, 'kalām' (the science of the word of God) discusses the content of faith and prophecy, in order to block the doors of falsification ('taḥrīf'), and deviation is another instance of the use of organic allegory and anthropomorphism in which the corporeal attribute of the divine as the form of utterance is emphasized. Al-Farabi's functionalist theory and the role of education and its respective institutions are a reminder of contemporary social psychological theories of education such as discursive institutionalism, development theory and its subsidiary modernization theory, which maintain that in order to build an ideal society, modern institutions with specific functions are required and education and its institutions bear the task of moulding the ideal human being functional in social arenas.

3 A Peripatetic Perspective on Embodiment and Education

The Peripatetic approach to embodiment as suggested by Avicenna (980–1037) and Averroes (1126–1198) sees the body as a pyscho-philosophical composition of matter ('hayūlā') and form ('ṣūrat'). From a cosmogonic view, the birth of the body from an active male principle (form) and a receptive female principle (matter)[8] posed a substantial problem for Neo-Platonist Muslim philosophers in their attempts to derive the material, corporeal world from the incorporeal and effect a reconciliation with the absolute doctrine of creation (de Boer, 2012). The Aristotelian expression 'forma corporeitatis' ('ṣūrat jismīyyah') suggests that the form of the body is one of the five continuous magnitudes (along with line, surface, space and time). This means that conti-

---

[7] The trilogy consists of: *Kitāb iḥṣā' al-'Ulum (The Book of Taxonomy of Sciences)*, *Risla fī al-'Aql (Treatise on Reason)* and *Kitāb al-Ḥurouf (The book of Letters)*.

[8] Similarly, theories about gender difference in cosmological accounts portray the earthly hierarchy between male and female as a reflection of grander cosmic principles. According to Bashir (2010), the contrast between male and female bodies in such schemes indicates, simultaneously, a complementarity and a hierarchy between the two types of bodies.

nuity ('ittiṣāl') is perceived as the form of the body (de Boer, 2012). The dichotomy of form and matter is also an important issue in Avicenna's theory of knowledge, one of the dominant schools of education and acquisition of knowledge in Islam. Avicenna elaborates that knowledge comes about by abstraction (Avicenna & Rahman, 1952), through a process of sense-perception in which the matter of the perceived object is left out, while the form is perceived. The next step in the process of abstraction is reached in the imagination, which can preserve an image that is free of matter (Rahman, 2012). The process of abstraction is concluded in conception which makes the particular universal. Hence, knowledge acquisition is a multi-layered process beginning with sensory perception for which the various faculties within the human body are used. Avicenna's quintuple process of learning is initiated by 'sensus communis' which fuses information coming from different external senses into an object or a percept. Then 'khayāl' (memory-image) is set to work: a faculty which contains the image of the object perceived after that object is removed from direct perception. Third 'takhayyol' (lit. imagining) is a faculty which combines images retained in the memory and separates them from one another, thus making a distinction between the visual attributes of the specific thing perceived and others. Thanks to this faculty, eccentric images can be formed, for example, that of a golden mountain by combining the image of gold with that of a mountain. While much of the activity of this faculty is non-rational and, in fact, recalcitrant to the control of reason, it plays a fundamental role in rational activity because thinking never comes about without the interplay of image. The fourth faculty 'wahm' (estimation) helps the external perception to perceive the physical form of the thing, while its inner meaning is perceived by an internal sense (Avicenna, 1964). Lastly, fifth is a faculty which retains the forms of perceived things, and their meanings and ideas as perceived by 'wahm'. This faculty, which is a storehouse of ideas and meanings rather than that of externally perceived forms, is very important because it retains individual meanings, just as the faculty of memory preserves individual forms (Rahman, 2012). According to Avicenna sensory knowledge is acquired knowledge, its source being the sensed stimuli, and it means the external and internal faculties of the sense. The subject of intellectual knowledge is then the thing perceived, and its means is the human's speculative faculty entrusted to him by God, which is capable of acquiring that rational knowledge. In order that intellectual knowledge be effective, it must have a particular structure and an instrument to regulate its operation, and likewise to verify the soundness of the thought and reasoning, this instrument is logic. Logic is the theoretical art or the instrument which protects the intellect from making a mistake (Al-Naqib, 1993).

To Avicenna, the soul, which is different from the substance of the body and is intangible, and the faculties required for the acquisition of knowledge are merely different functions of the human soul (Avicenna, 1994), which is perfected in knowledge, wisdom and good deeds, and is drawn towards the divine light. For Avicenna education's goal is the development of the individual, not only morally but also physically and mentally. Bodily mundane practices such as nutrition, wellbeing, leisure and resting are considered important prerequisites for learning. Avicenna's views granted him the ability to develop his theories of learning from a pure philosophical to a social and psychological approach. Thus, in the Peripatetic tradition the body along with the psyche was considered the subject matter of learning and education.

4   A Sufi Approach to Embodiment and Education

Sufism as a philosophical school appeared as response and rival to Peripateticism. Its efforts were devoted to an alternative philosophical approach to replace Aristotelian and Neo-Platonic logics and metaphysics. The new approach was "based on the relationship between Light as the main principle of creation and knowledge, and that which is lit up—the rest of reality" (Leaman, 2000, p. 408). This tradition led to various theories by such Shiite philosophers as Mullā Ṣadrā, Mīr Dāmād and Mullā Hādī Sabzivārī, mainly in the Persianate world. It is referred to frequently as *Ḥikmat-i Muta'ālīya* (Transcendental Theosophy), a rather novel discipline within Islamic philosophy. Contemporary with the emergence of European rationalism by Grotius, Descartes and Spinoza, this intellectual movement left its imprint on the epistemological debate among Muslims. The 'new wisdom' as it is called, on the one hand, borrowed Mu'atazilī's position in 'kalāmī' debates, and on the other hand, the entire philosophical tradition from al-Kindi to Avicenna, and to these were added the elements of mysticism and the Sufi notion of 'direct vision' (Arjmand, 2008). This reintroduced such old intellectual debates as the dichotomy of body and soul among the Muslim philosophers and the essential question of the role of body as the vessel of soul in the process of receiving knowledge.

Sufism considers the human body as a doorway that connect the exterior and interior aspects of reality. In material terms, bodies are objects like any other, subject to generation and corruption and enmeshed in relationships with other material forms of the world of appearances. The less agitation the body shows during and after crossing over the threshold, the more the embodied person can be said to have mastered the transition. The classical Sufi notion of knowledge acquisition is based on the unveiling of truth to recipients who have developed the capacity, through both corporeal and spiritual means, to receive it. Sufi attention to the structure of the human body as a form is particularly cognizant of the body's double meaning: on the one hand, the body is seen as the ultimate source of most problems since its instinctive appetites restrict human beings from thinking beyond their immediate desires; on the other hand, the body is a seat of the human capacity to theorize and explore because it enables human beings to transcend materiality. The contrast between the two functions endows the body with a complete ambiguity that makes corporeality an advantageous lens through which to appraise Sufi ideas and social patterns (Bashir, 2011, p. 28).

The 'Ishrāqī' (Illuminationist) epistemology, as one of the instances of Sufism, is formed after the notion of 'knowledge by presence', a kind of knowledge that takes place within its own framework, such that the whole anatomy of the notion can hold true without any need to an external objective reference calling for an exterior relation. It is "the knowledge of Truth" to which the criterion of truth or falsehood is not applicable (Ha'iri Yazdi, 1992, p. 43). Although the notion of 'presence' has a specific connotation, meaning a cleansing of the soul, preparing it to stay connected to the host of knowledge, the body is concealed as a vessel in order to receive it. It is a reminder of the Socrates analogy on the role of educator as a midwife where the body is used to allegorically evince the process,

> My art of midwifery is in general like theirs [midwives] [...] and my concern is not with the body but with the soul that is in travail of birth. And the highest point of my art is the power to prove by every test whether the offspring of a young man's thought is a false phantom, or instinct with life and truth. (Plato, 1861)

This, in the Sufi tradition, is achieved through a 'murād' (master) and 'murīd' (disciple) relationship, based on a confined apprenticeship. Although the soul is the recipient and the host of knowledge by presence, it exists through bodily practices. The spiritual experience of receiving knowledge, however, requires a process of analysis and systematization for it to ensue from the sensory experience. The approach reveals "the distinction between knowledge by 'conception' and knowledge by 'belief'" (Ha'iri Yazdi, 1992, p. 46). Thus, embodiment lies at the core of the cultivation and refinement of the soul, which is made possible with the extensive Illuminationist symbolic anecdotal approach of Suhravardi. There are "guides to the kind of experiences to be encountered by the seeker and to their interpretation; indeed, a central figure in these narratives is often a guide" (Cooper, 1998); sometimes a master and sometimes a Muse, they often symbolize the Angel Gabriel who mediated the revelation of divine knowledge through 'wahy' (intuition). Whereas the Peripatetic notion of knowledge is based on a move from known components towards unknown ones, just as a mental process in the human mind relied on sensory perception, for Illuminationists such knowledge merely guarantees certainty. Suhravardi argues that there exists a more fundamental kind of knowledge that does not depend on form and which is, like the experience of pain, unmediated and undeniable. In this, Suhravardi challenges the Avicennian inherent form of knowledge which maintains that the knowledge as it is held by the knower is true only when it corresponds to reality.

Ibn Arabi (1165–1240) develops a systematic 'irfānī' (Gnostic) approach to ontology and epistemology. In his *al-Futūḥāt al-Makkīyya* (*The Meccan Illuminations*) Ibn Arabi argues that the body constitutes the medium between the self and the outer world (Shahzad, 2007). Likewise, Ibn Arabi's doctrine of 'waḥdat al-wujūd' (the unity of existence) focuses on the 'bāṭin', the esoteric reality of creatures instead of 'ẓāhir', the exoteric dimension. Thus, in the unity of existence realities are 'tajallī' (mere appearances) of the One, or the essence of the original. Therefore, nature and all that is in it is only a shadow of the One who has 'wujūd' that is intrinsic, absolute, unlimited and infinite, that is God (Sumbulah, 2016). In Ibn Arabi's own words (1974, p. 88),

O Thou Who hast created all things in Thyself,
Thou unitest that which Thou createst.
Thou createst that which existeth infinitely
In Thee, for Thou art the narrow and all-embracing.

Using the theological attributes 'tashbīh' and 'tanzīh' (distance and transcendence) as philosophical devices, Ibn Arabi portrays his unique view of the human body and its venerability. Despite the centrality of soul in Ibn Arabi's works, there is an abundance of allegorical allusions to the body in its physicality: "God created man's body in the form of the scale. He made the two panes his right hand and his left hand, while He made the tongue the pillar of himself. So, man belongs to whichever side he inclines" (Ibn al-Arabi, 1994, p. 3). Ibn Arabi likens the world-Perfect Man relationship with various states of human body and maintains that the state of the world before its appearance was like a proportioned body, before the soul was breathed into it (Shahzad,

2007). Like other Sufi scholars, the notion of the human body as a microcosm of the macrocosm (the universe) which fashions the foundations of his theory of 'waḥdat al-wujūd' is significant in two ways, as a hierarchy of existence and as a divine form and theomorphic entity. There are three basic worlds of the macrocosm—the spiritual, imaginal and corporeal, which are represented in humans by the spirit ('rūh'), soul ('nafs') and body ('jism'). That the spirit should be spiritual and the body corporeal presents no difficulties (Chittick, 1989). However, as Bashir (2010, p. 77) puts it, since the general pattern is that God is said to have created the human being simultaneously in the image of the world and as its centrepiece, the body is seen as a blueprint for the cosmos as well as society. The scope of this perspective is enlarged further by reference to the statement, found in 'hadīth' literature, which states that Adam was created in God's image. Here too, what is most significant is the body's mediating function since it both represents God and constitutes the human being, the species situated at the centre of the created world.

For Ibn Arabi, therefore, knowledge acquisition is a process of increasing illumination, gradually

> raising the possibilities eternally latent to a state of luminescence, for which 'qalb' (the heart) is the organ which produces true knowledge, comprehensive intuition, the gnosis ('ma'rifa') and everything connoted by ''ilm al-bāṭin' (esoteric science). It is the organ of a perception which is both experience and intimate taste ('dhawq').

Nevertheless,

> we are reminded at every turn, this 'heart' is not the conical organ of flesh, situated on the left side of the chest, although there is a certain connection, the modality of which, however, is essentially unknown. (Corbin, 1969, pp. 234–235)

Corbin (ibid.) maintains that

> this 'mystic physiology' operates with a 'subtile body' composed of psycho-spiritual organs (the centres, or Chakras, *lotus blossoms*) which must be distinguished from the bodily organs.

The very pillar of 'true knowledge' is imagination and the type of knowledge acquired is the knowledge that is 'ma'rifa' (gnosis), without which there would be only knowledge without consistency. Imagination enables human beings to understand the meaning of words, in the esoteric as well as the physical sense. Ibn Arabi argues that, by giving an objective body to intentions of the heart, this creativity of the imagination fulfils the first aspect of its function, which comprises a large number of phenomena designated as extrasensory perception.

Through the representational faculty ('wahm') every person executes Active Imagination to 'create'. Such creative operation implies the manifestation of an outward existence that is conferred upon something which already possessed a latent existence. Seen in this light, thus, in the process of learning and knowledge acquisition, the organ of creativity (the Active Imagination) serves to enable the process of creating objects and introducing changes to the outside world. Ibn Arabi presents the 'subtile body' as an exact non-material counterpart tethered to the physical body.

> This body cannot be apprehended by the physical human senses; however, it does have definite reality to it, which is felt during dreams and visions. These experiences are not mere mental projections but real encounters with other corporeous rather than corporeal bodies. (Bashir, 2011, p. 38)

Albeit practiced among vast groups of Muslims in various ways, the Sufi approach to embodiment and learning remains much at an abstract theoretical level and was never afforded the chance to find real application.

5   A Kalāmī Approach to Embodiment and Learning

Al-Ghāzali or as he is known in Western Latin literature, Algazelus (1058–1111) is regarded as one of the most influential Muslim philosophers (although he rejected his affiliation to philosophy[9]) who attempted to make the Sufi tradition of mysticism more recognized within scholastic and scientific circles. Through his magnum opus, *Iḥyāʾ Ulūm al-Dīn* (*The Revival of the Religious Sciences*), al-Ghāzali embarked on a new methodology based on a synthesis of various modes of Islamic thought reconciling Sufism and theology in an endeavour to make Islamic mysticism an acceptable part of the Sunni orthodoxy.

---

[9] Al-Ghāzali considered philosophy to be foreign knowledge and thus problematic for Muslims, due to its affiliation to the Greeks. For al-Ghāzali, philosophy is acceptable to the extent that it is in agreement with Islam. He summarized the philosophical polemics of his age in *Maqāṣid al-Falāsifa* (*The Aims of the Philosophers*). Following this demonstration of his intellectual mastery over philosophical questions, he composed his famous work *Tahāfut al-Falāsifa* (*The Incoherences of the Philosophers*), where he discusses the notion of God as the Ultimate Knower of the universal as well as the particular.

Departing from such a premise, he defines the human being as

> a spiritual substance (jawhar rūḥānī) not confined in a body, nor imprinted on it, nor joined to it, nor separated from it. It possesses knowledge and perception, and is therefore not an accident. (Calverley & Netton, 2012)

Al-Ghāzali identifies the non-corporeal 'rūḥ' (soul) with 'al-nafs al-muṭma'inna' and 'al-rūḥ al-amīn' of the Qur'ān and then uses the term 'nafs' also for the 'flesh' or lower nature, which must be disciplined in the interests of ethics (Calverley & Netton, 2012). In his *Al-Risālat al-Laduniyya* (1938) al-Ghāzali explains that the terms 'nafs', 'rūḥ' and 'qalb' (heart) are names for his simple substance which is the seat of the intellectual processes; he differentiates these from the animal 'rūḥ', a refined but mortal body in which reside the senses. In his *Kimīyā-yi Sa'ādat* (*The Alchemy of Happiness*), al-Ghāzali provides a description of the body as a cosmos that straddles theological and social concerns. He urges his readers to scrutinize the human body as a first step in exploring more distant realities. They are advised to go beyond their intuitive sense of how their limbs and sensory organs work in conjunction with the others to sustain life, and to come to know these is to know the world (Bashir, 2010). For al-Ghāzali the body as a microcosm prefaces his larger discussion where he proclaims the clearly natural basis for human conduct (Al-Ghāzali, 2008).

Al-Ghāzali's epistemology is not limited to the classic notion of Sufi attainment of knowledge based on the unveiling the truth to the recipients who have developed the capacity to receive it; rather it includes the means by which knowledge could be attained through the senses, reason and intuition. This results in a dichotomic line of philosophical abstraction in al-Ghāzali's notion of embodiment and his epistemology.

Al-Ghāzali divides knowledge into the science of transaction and the science of unveiling. While the former deals with behaviours and actions, the latter is knowledge of reality and the essence of things. It is the supreme, true knowledge which is not possible to attain through scholastic practices but needs a purification stage, both corporeal and spiritual, through which the soul reaches the phase where it receives the knowledge. Following this, the heart of the recipient of the light will be illuminated with divine knowledge.

As Bashir (2010) argues, al-Ghāzali's taxonomy of the body is noteworthy for intermixing physical and social aspects of experience. He thus relies on the body as a system to legitimize his conception of nature and society as structures that require the maintenance of a balance between their various parts. Al-Ghāzali's hybrid approach, as an amalgam of 'kalām' and mysticism, results in a social functionalist approach to embodiment in which all human activities are represented in the functions of the body's parts. Al-Ghāzali's works are prime instances of a connection between the body and society which can be seen in most Islamic cosmologies that invoke the body.

6   Islamic Didactics and Corporeal and Cognitive Development

Ibn Tufail's *Ḥayy ibn Yaqẓān* (*Philosophus Autodidactus*), a piece of philosophical and literary work and an allegorical novel inspired by Avicenna and Sufism, is a classic work in Islamic philosophy of education, its focus being the corporeal and cognitive development of human beings. The book is the story of Ḥayy, an autodidactic feral child, raised by a doe and living in isolation on a desert island, who, without contact with other human beings, discovers ultimate truth through a systematic process of reasoned inquiry (Ibn Tufayl & Goodman, 2009). Albeit concise, the book addresses various approaches to knowledge acquisition in Islam each of which is developed through a different school of thought. The significance of the book is that both forms of education, scholastic and experiential, are regarded as complementary. Training in one aids understanding the other.

In the 12th century, Ibn Tufail in his novel *Philosophus Autodidactus* elaborates Avicennian epistemology and gives a vivid example of the harmony of philosophy and religion, where Ḥayy, the sole inhabitant of an uninhabited island, a microcosm of the real world, encounters natural phenomena first through corporeal contacts and then sensory perceptions and moves beyond this to answer such complex questions as creation, soul and so on. His philosophical approach leads him to the knowledge which in the neighbouring island has been achieved through religious practices and scholastic education. The book emphasizes the role of the body in cognitive development and is the manifestation of the alternative paths to truth which otherwise is dominated by religious education. The deductive reasoning in *Philosophus Autodidactus* is fashioned around two axes. The first is the transition from the premises to logical argumentation and the arrival at a conclusion (using the example of Ḥayy and his surroundings as a microcosm of human history, social life and knowledge); the second is the progress from body to soul, that is from physics to metaphysics (where the body and all its physical features are described in order to discuss the soul, the animated component enclosed within it):

> Upon this [the death of the doe] the whole Body seem'd to him a very inconsiderable thing, and worth nothing in respect of that Being he believed once inhabited, and now had left it. Therefore, he applied himself wholly to the consideration of that Being. What it was and how it subsisted? What joyn'd it to this Body? Whither it went, and by what passage, when it left the Body? What was the Cause of its Departure, whether it were forc'd to leave its Mansion, or left the Body of its own accord? And in case it went away Voluntarily, what it was that render'd the Body so disagreeable to it, as to make it forsake it? And whilst he was perplext with such variety of Thoughts, he laid aside all concern for the Carcass, and banish'd it from his Mind; for now he perceiv'd that his Mother, which had Nurs'd him so Tenderly and had Suckled him, was that something which was departed; and from it proceeded all her Actions, and not from this unactive Body; but that all this Body was to it only as an Instrument, like his Cudgel which he had made for himself, with which he used to Fight with the Wild Beasts. So that now, all his regard to the Body was remov'd, and transferr'd to that by which the Body is govern'd, and by whose Power it moves. Nor had he any other desire but to make enquiry after that. (Ibn Tufayl & Goodman, 2009, p. 64)

The body lies at the heart of learning for Ḥayy through which Ibn Tufail engages in the classic debate on the Islamic notion of knowledge acquisition, its typology and the role of education throughout the human lifespan. His study moves from the outer world to the inner and from the observation of physicality towards invisible spirituality where corporeal development leads to cognitive progress. Ḥayy's development, as a representative of any person, and consequently any human society, is schematized in seven stages, each of seven years: an approach to education which was maintained in practice across the Muslim world. The first stage is childhood in which the approach to learning is based on intuition and physical imitation:

> [H]e went on, living only upon what he suck'd till he was two years old, and then he began to step a little and breed his teeth. He always followed the doe. ... By this time, he began to have the ideas of a great many things fix'd in his mind, so as to have a desire to some, and an aversion to others, even when they were absent. He saw that it must be like those bodies, which had a threefold dimension, length, breadth, and thickness and differ'd from them only in those acts which proceeded from it by means of animal or vegetable organs. [...] He proceeded to examine whether they did belong to Body quatenus Body, or else by reason of some property superadded to Corporeity. (Ibn Tufayl & Goodman, 2009, pp. 51–53)

At the age of seven, childhood is over and adolescence starts. From seven to twenty-one is the period of learning based on methods of practical reasoning, the kind that finds means to ends, first through experimentation and later through more complex deductive argumentation. The first signs of spiritualization appear around the time of puberty which develops throughout the next stage when the human being begins to think seriously about metaphysics. From twenty-one the age of wonder starts, when the soul addresses the abstract questions to which it cannot respond and struggles for their answer (Arjmand, 2018b) through new means. Then at twenty-eight the age of reason starts, when the paradoxical unity and diversity of the world is put into focus. This is a level beyond the abstraction which paves the way for the reason to develop into wisdom. At the age of thirty-five, when the soul begins to search deeper, wisdom awakes. The relation to metaphysics is not merely through knowledge, but through the emotions. The last stage, the spiritualization of wisdom, its growth from practice to experience, marks the end of tutelage and beginning of maturity, the fulfilment of self-awareness in the realization that all that has gone before is a 'ladder of love' towards union with God; for at the end of his seventh set of seven years, Ḥayy attains beatific experience (Ibn Tufayl & Goodman, 2009). The process of corporeal maturation and its resolution with the soul and the spiritual is the main tenet of the Islamic theory of human development; however, one can also see certain elements of Hellenistic philosophy, not least through the idea of the formation of various stages and the age of mental maturation. For Ibn Tufail the ultimate aim of education is the achievement of 'saʾādah' (happiness) which is defined as the goal of education in Islam, be it physical or spiritual, both on an individual and on a societal level.

7 Corporeal Practices in Islamic Education

Memorizing is often described as the main feature of Islamic education which as an educational method has provoked both criticism and praise from various scholars.[10] Known as 'dhikr', the practice of memorizing and subsequent remembering, often associated with certain corporeal movements, is recognized as a distinct practice among Sufis. This practice which involves repeating a piece of text accompanied by certain body positions or movements is

---

[10] As the central feature of Islamic education, memorizing is often criticized as a method which is said to weaken critical thinking and problem-solving and encourages obedience and the absence of participation in the society (Arjmand, 2018a). On the other hand, it is given credence by some scholars who argue that in the absence of an inclusive education system and where there is a dysfunctional infrastructure, memorizing has served as a method to make the education of students with disabilities and from disadvantaged groups possible. Abū al-ʿAlāʾ al-Maʿarrī the Muslim blind philosopher and Taha Hussein the blind Egyptian educator and minister of education are among instances of scholars who have praised memorizing as a didactic method to set the scene for their, otherwise unattainable, education.

common in elementary stages of education in such institutions as 'maktab' (in Persianate lands), 'kuttāb' (Arab countries) and 'mektephane' (Turkish/ Ottoman). Here Taha Hussein explains the practice in his village 'kuttāb' in Upper Egypt:

> 'Our Master' did not sing [The Alf īyyah[11]] with his voice and tongue alone, but with his head and body also. He used to nod his head up and down and waggle it from side to side. Moreover, he sang with his hands also, beating time upon the chests of his two companions with his fingers. Sometimes when the song was particularly agreeable to him, and he found that walking did not suit him, he would stop till it was finished. (Hussein, 2001, p. 43)

Body movements, while memorizing the text, often used to facilitate learning religious texts is not exclusively Islamic. Coming from Yiddish, 'shuckling' (to shake, to swing), the ritual swaying during Jewish prayer or study, usually back and forth but also from side to side, was also used in such educational institutions as the 'heder' (old-fashioned elementary school for teaching Judaism). As some historical evidence suggests, various studies (Arjmand, 2008; Goldziher, 1908; Landau, 2003; Pedersen & Makdisi, 2003) consider 'heder' to be the source of inspiration for Muslim 'kuttāb', where similar practices were tailored accordingly. While some scholars argue that historically the practice was performed "to afford the body exercise during study and prayer, which took up a large portion of the time" (Jacobs & Eisenstein, 2002), others (Karo et al., 1921) see it as an expression of the soul's desire to abandon the body and reunite itself with its source.

Despite this, the practice is widely ascribed to the Sufi practice of 'dhikr', the performance of which involved a body-based relationship with the outer world, explained by theories regarding the exterior-interior divide. The issue of how the body could represent internal states while acting in the external world is implicated in stories about masters' 'samā' (listening, performed as a mystic dance). When performed with religious sanction, Sufi 'samā' involved moving bodies as conduits between an interior world and an exterior cosmos that was filled with movement (Bashir, 2011). Bodily movement, be it in the form of ritual daily prayer ('ṣalāt') or 'dhikr', is perceived as an act of submission to God. When put in an educational context movement is seen as the facilitator of memorizing and learning, through concentration and devotion.

---

[11] The Alf īyyah is a rhyming book of Arabic grammar written by Ibn Mālik in the thirteenth century, still in use as a textbook for beginners in many Islamic educational institutions. The Alf īyyah is one of the first books to be memorized by students after learning the Qur'ān.

The dichotomy of body/soul, and the notion that chastising the body contributes to the purification and perfection of the soul, is shown clearly in the use of physical chastisement ('t'dīb') in education. As Ariés (1996) puts it, the concept originates from the separate nature of childhood, of its difference from the world of adults, and the elementary concept of its weakness, which brought it down to the level of the lowest social strata. The insistence on humiliating childhood in order to mark it out and improve it led to stricter discipline in education and hence to greater infliction of corporal punishment. In Islamic literature on education we find several attitudes towards corporal punishment approval, albeit with certain qualifications, proposals for alternatives to physical punishment and its integration into a more sophisticated method of dealing with children's behaviour, and criticism of excessive corporal punishment based on psychological insight (Gil'adi, 1992).

Al-Ghāzali is a proponent of corporal punishment as an educational method and argues for the moderate use of chastisement of the pupils with the argument that

> [j]ust as the believer will ultimately thank God for putting him to the test, so will the child, when he gets older, thank his teacher and his father for beating him and educating him because, in his maturity, he will be capable of discerning the fruits of such an education. (Al-Ghāzali, 1998, p. 162)

> Yet this does not prove that excessive beating is praiseworthy. This is also the case with [causing] fear [as an educational means]: it can be divided into [three grades, namely] little, excessive and balanced. The most commendable balance and the middle way (between the two extremes). (Al-Ghāzali, 1998, p. 194)

Conversely, Ibn Khaldun (1980, p. 305) disagrees, finding that

> severe punishment in the course of instruction does harm to the student, especially to little children, because it belongs among (the things that make for a) bad habit. [...] Their outward behaviour differs from what they are thinking [...] and they are taught deceit and trickery. [...] Indeed, their souls become too indolent to (attempt to) acquire the virtues and good character qualities. Thus, they fall short of their potentialities.

Analysis of the connection between concepts of childhood and corporal punishment in the medieval Islamic context shows that discipline and bodily punishment could coexist with the treating children and childhood in a positive way, both intellectually and emotionally (Gil'adi, 1992). Corporal punishment, even if applied with moderation as a recommended measure by some Muslim scholars, despite the diverse views for and against it, rests on the primacy of soul over the body and the (also puritanical) premise that chastising the body elevates the soul. Thus, the body as the vessel of the soul shall endure to safeguard the precious gift with which it has been entrusted.

References

Al-Ghāzali, A. H. M. (1998). *Al-Risālat al-Ladunīyya* (M. Smith, Trans.). Royal Asiatic Society of Great Britain and Ireland.

Al-Ghāzali, A. H. M. (2008). *Kimīyā-yi Saādat* [The Alchemy of Happiness]. Intishārāt-i Nigāh.

Al-Naqib, A. R. (1993). Avicenna. *Prospects: The Quarterly Review of. Comparative Education, XXIII*, 53–69.

Ansari, M. A. H. (1963). Miskawyah's Conception of Sa'ādah. *Islamic Studies, 2*(3), 317–335.

Ariés, P. (1996). *Centuries of Childhood*. Pimlico.

Aristotle. (1984). *The Complete Works of Aristotle* (B. Jowett, Trans. Jonathan Barnes Ed., Vol. 6). Princeton University Press.

Arjmand, R. (2008). *Inscription on Stone: Islam, State and Education in Iran and Turkey*. Stockholms Universitet.

Arjmand, R. (2018a). Ijāzah: Methods of Authorization and Assessment in Islamic Education. In H. Daun & R. Arjmand (Eds.), *Handbook of Islamic Education* (Vol. 7). Springer.

Arjmand, R. (2018b). Islamic Education: Historical Perspective, Origin, and Foundations. In H. Daun & R. Arjmand (Eds.), *Handbook of Islamic Education* (Vol. 7). Springer.

Avicenna. (1964). *De Anima* (J. Hispalensis and D. Gundisalvus, Trans.). Éditions Orientalistes.

Avicenna. (1994). Risalat fi Ma'rifat al-Nafs al-Natiqa. In *al-Shifa* (vol. 5, pp. 248–257). Ayatollah Marashi Najafi Library Press.

Avicenna, & Rahman, F. (1952). *Avicenna's Psychology*. Oxford University Press.

Bashir, S. (2010). Body. In J. J. Elias (Ed.), *Key Themes for the Study of Islam* (pp. 72–92). Oneworld.

Bashir, S. (2011). *Sufi Bodies: Religion and Society in Medieval Islam*. Columbia University Press.

Calverley, E. E., & Netton, I. R. (2012). Nafs. In P. Bearman, T. Bianquis, C. E. Bosworth, E. van Donzel, & W. P. Heinrichs (Eds.), *Encyclopaedia of Islam*. Brill.

Chittick, W. C. (1989). *The Sufi Path of Knowledge: Ibn al-Arabi's Metaphysics of Imagination*. State University of New York Press.

Cooper, J. (1998). al-Razi, Fakhr al-Din: Metaphysics. In E. Craig & T. Crane (Eds.), *Routledge Encyclopedia of Philosophy*. Taylor, & Francis.

Corbin, H. (1969). *Creative Imagination in the Sufism of Ibn Arabi.* Princeton University Press.

de Boer, T. (2012). Djism. In P. Bearman, T. Bianquis, C. E. Bosworth, E. van Donzel, & W. P. Heinrichs (Eds.), *Encyclopaedia of Islam.* Brill.

Farabi, A. N. (1961). *Fusul al-Madani (Aphorisms of the Statesman)* (D. M. Dunlop, Trans.). Cambridge University Press.

Farabi, A. N. (1985). *Al-Farabi on the Perfect State: Abu Nasr al-Farabi's Mabadiʾ Araʾ ahl al-Madina al-Fadila (The perfect state)* (R. Walzer, Trans.). Clarendon.

Gignoux, P. (2004). Microcosm and Macrocosm. In *Iranica.* Bedesta Mazda.

Gil'adi, A. (1992). *Children of Islam: Concepts of Childhood in Medieval Muslim Society.* Macmillan.

Goldziher, I. (1908). Education (Muslims). In J. Hastings (Ed.), *Encyclopaedia of Religion and Ethics* (Vol. 5). Clark.

Ha'iri Yazdi, M. (1992). *The Principles of Epistemology in Islamic Philosophy: Knowledge by Presence.* State University of New York Press.

Hoffman, V. J. (1995). Islamic Perspectives on the Human Body: Legal, Social and Spiritual Considerations. In L. S. Cahill & M. A. Farley (Eds.), *Embodiment, Morality, and Medicine.* Springer.

Huda, Q. (2017). Anatomy. In J. McAuliffe (Ed.), *Encyclopaedia of the Qurʾān.* Brill.

Hussein, T. (2001). *al-Ayyām (The Days).* The American University in Cairo Press.

Ibn al-Arabi, M. (1994). *Al-Futūḥāt al-Makkīyya.* Dar al-Fikr.

Ibn al-Arabi, M., & Burckhardt, T. (1974). *La Sagesse des Prophètes (Fusūs al-Ḥikam).* A. Michel.

Ibn Khaldun. (1980). *The Muqaddimah: An Introduction to History.* Princeton University Press.

Ibn Tufayl, Muhammad ibn Abd al-Malik, & Goodman, L. E. (eds.) (2009 [1927]). *Ḥayy ibn Yaqẓān: A Philosophical Tale.* University of Chicago Press.

Jacobs, J., & Eisenstein, J. D. (2002 [1906]). Swaying the Body. In I. Singer & C. Adler (eds.), *Jewish Encyclopedia.* Funk and Wagnalls.

Karo, J., Ashkenazi, J., Isserles, M., Openhaim, A., & Rivkes, M. (1921). *Shulchan Aruch's Orach Chaim.* Naftali Tsaylingold.

Landau, J. M. (2003). Kuttab. In P. Bearman, T. Bianquis, C. E. Bosworth, E. van Donzel, & W. P. Heinrichs (Eds.), *Encyclopaedia of Islam.* Brill.

Leaman, O. (2000). Islamic Philosophy. In E. Craig & E. Craig (Eds.), *Routledge Encyclopedia of Philosophy.* Routledge.

Martin, R. C. (2018). Anthropomorphism. In J. McAuliffe (Ed.), *Encyclopaedia of the Qurʾān.* Brill.

Miskawyah, A. (1928). *Kitāb al-Saʿāah* [*The Book of Happiness*]. Al-Matb'ah al-'Arabiyah.

Nicholson, R. A. (1998). *Studies in Islamic Mysticism.* Kegan Paul International.

Pedersen, J., & Makdisi, G. (2003). Madrasa. In P. Bearman, T. Bianquis, C. E. Bosworth, E. van Donzel, & W. P. Heinrichs (Eds.), *Encyclopaedia of Islam.* Brill.

Plato. (1861). *The Theætetus of Plato* (L. Campbell, Trans.). Oxford University Press.

Qomī, S. (1961). *Mafātīḥ al-Janān*. Islamiyeh.

The Qurʾān. (n.d.) (A. Y. Ali, Trans.). Leicester, UK: Islamic Foundation.

Rafati, V. (2002). Lawh-i-Hikmat: The Two Agents and the Two Patients. *Andalib, 5*(19), 29–38.

Rahman, F. (2012). Avicenna: Psychology. *In Encyclopædia Iranica, 3*, 83–84.

Shahzad, Q. (2007). Ibn ʿArabi's Metaphysics of the Human Body. *Islamic Studies, 46*(4), 499–525.

Sumbulah, U. (2016). Ibn ʿArabī's Thought on Waḥdah Al-Wujūd and its Relevance to Religious Diversity. *Ulumuna. Journal of Islamic Studies, 20*(1), 53–73.

Watt, W. M. (2008). Al-Ashari, Abu ʾl-Hasan ʿAli b. Ismail. In P. Bearman, T. Bianquis, C. E. Bosworth, E. van Donzel, & W. P. Heinrichs (Eds.), *Encyclopaedia of Islam* (Vol. 1, pp. 694–695). Brill.

The Body in Education: Conceptions and Dimensions in Brazil and Latin America

Karina Limonta Vieira

1 Introduction

Although the body has been a subject of study in the human and natural sciences for a long time this has been less the case in Brazil and Latin America. The challenge in studying conceptions of the body is mainly due to the new conditions in which human beings find themselves in the world. Against the background of the Anthropocene and current scientific knowledge, body studies require new approaches and new methods. Some authors working in groups in their own countries and even in collaboration with Brazilians and Latin Americans, or in interdisciplinary studies in areas such as education, anthropology, and sociology, are attempting to overcome epistemological obstacles and develop theoretical perspectives. Some are also attempting to research phenomena specific to Brazil and Latin America, but there are few studies devoted to the process of researching the body. On the other hand, there are great social, cultural, and symbolic differences that mark the history of Brazil and Latin America, such as the indigenous, African, and European influences. Colonization by the Spanish or Portuguese contributed to the constitution of the body on this continent. In Latin America there was a forceful, violent colonization process of the indigenous people; Brazil was marked by the enslavement of the Africans. Therefore, it is the aim of this

---

K. L. Vieira, Dr. (✉)
Brandenburg University of Technology Cottbus-Senftenberg, Cottbus, Germany
e-mail: vieirkar@b-tu.de

© The Author(s), under exclusive license to Springer Nature Switzerland AG 2022
A. Kraus, C. Wulf (eds.), *The Palgrave Handbook of Embodiment and Learning*,
https://doi.org/10.1007/978-3-030-93001-1_32

study to understand the conceptions of the body in Brazil and Latin America. There are two key questions: What are these conceptions? How do conceptions of the body in Latin America and particularly in Brazil differ from those of the rest of the world? Are these conceptions of the body of importance in the field of education? The subsequent aim is to understand the conceptions in the Latin American education system as well as differing body images in the Brazilian school system in particular. This chapter is divided into four sections: the body in Latin America, the body in Brazil in particular on the basis of Brazilian culture and education, the discussion of the 'corpus absconditus' in Brazil and Latin America, and the prospects for mimetic processes, embodiment, and cultural learning.

In Latin America, the conceptions of the body are understood from a biopolitical perspective, in which the body is shown to be resistant to colonization and to European influences. However, in the fields of education and in particular, it appears as a body that is rather more compliant. In Brazil there is a great diversity of body concepts. Studies note that in school the body appears as disciplined and conforming to norms. In the field of Physical Education, the understanding of the body is broader. Concepts from different cultural and ethnic backgrounds, that is from Afro-Brazilian or the indigenous traditions, influence Physical Education. The conceptualization of the body in Brazil shows many different traditions and approaches, which cannot be integrated in a single concept. Therefore, the concept of the 'corpus absconditus' is used to describe the complexity of the human body (Wulf, 2013).

2 The Body in Latin America: Differences in Conceptions in Social and Educational Contexts

The body of the learner in social and educational contexts shapes up in a biopolitical and aesthetic way, i.e. being homogenized and regulated; the educational context forms a disciplined normative body.

2.1 The Bio-political and Aesthetic Body: Homogenized and Regulated by Latin American Society

Body studies in Latin America present several diffuse and superficial perspectives involving historical processes, methodological orientations, theory, local reflections, and social and symbolic conditions. They broach identity and alterity, power and conflict, gender and sexuality, health and illness, art, and media (Pedraza, 2007a; Ramos, 2011). However, most researchers consider these body studies important. Thinking about the body in Latin America goes back to the sixteenth century, a period in which colonized bodies were convinced that identity is forged in a process that occurs in and with the body, built from the distinction between body and soul, influenced by Christian tradition in exposing dress code differences between the colonizers and the colonized. The colonizing project of the division of labor imposes a racial and sexual division that includes forming subordinate subjects and reproducing hierarchies through education, language, gender difference, work, catechization, humiliation, and cultural annihilation. During the nineteenth century, national identity is related to the social representation of the body. It is expressed in physiognomy, people's appearance, dress, physical expressions, gestures, words, and power relations. During the republican period and the first decades of the twentieth century, the social experience of the body is linked to the norms and values expressed in the constitutions of the national states (Pedraza, 2007b, 2014).

According to Rodas and Pedraza (2014), colonizers seek to homogenize the anatomical and physiological body of medicine, the process of individualization, privatization, sanitation, and the development of urban life and capitalism. It is a dichotomous body, built historically and socially on biological characteristics and shaped by the social order (Scribano, 2016). It is a biopolitical body, which involves science, medical knowledge and power practices that shape the colonized people through the advent of a bourgeois way of life with its schools, gymnastics, sports, and consumption. The conceptualization of the body is marked by two major trends. The first one shapes the modeling and imposition of order and discipline developed in the nation states in Latin America from the nineteenth century onward. The second one is created by aesthetic-political experiences related to the emergence of contemporary subjectivity (Pedraza, 2007a, 2014).

The concept of the body is based on subjective experience (taking in a phenomenological perspective), interaction (appearance, gesture, and rituals), body practices (the role of the body for the creation of practical knowledge), institutions (the body disciplined in institutions such as school, hospital, work), aesthetic and social representations (body images as being beautiful, healthy, useful, and competent), and affective bonds (Ramos, 2011). The body in Latin America is a mechanical, subjective, and bio-political organism. Its conceptualization and understanding are based on a variety of social discourses. These discourses also influence the way people understand their corporeality and influence how the body is dealt with in schools and educational institutions. Here control and discipline play an important role.

2.2 The Body in School Education and Physical Education in Latin America

School education and Physical Education at school are equally important. However, in each field there are different conceptions and dimensions of the body of the learner. In the school situation, the body has to be disciplined and standardized, mainly within the classroom. In Physical Education the body of the learner is conceived as a supporting factor of the modernization process.

2.2.1 The Body in the School Situation: From Being a Well-Disciplined Body to a Body Experiencing New Things

In Latin America, the body of the learner is supposed to contribute to the growth of the country and the consolidation of the nation state. It should contribute to the development of a democratic system, to the evolution of rationality, civilization, and citizenship. Since the European colonialization, disciplining and standardizing the body of the learner were important goals of education (Giménez, 2007). Education was, and is still linked to the principles of citizenship, liberalism and capitalism (Pedraza, 2011). The school is the most important place for the formation of citizens. It functions as a bio-political institution that realizes the principle of surveillance of the learners' bodies, according to Foucault. As Bourdieu has shown, it also incorporates the forms of symbolic violence implicit in the habitus and its formation (Pedraza, 2007b).

Many devices are used for the creation of social affirmation and body remodeling, such as gender relations, corporal punishment, rituals, gesture, sport, technology, school subjects (curriculum), teacher training, and teaching methods. The ways to remodel the body depart from eugenic theories, with the construction of school architecture (clarity, ventilation, furniture, workspaces, recreation, etc.), school time (rational distribution of materials, pauses, recreation, stay in school, etc.) (Oliveira, 2007), and the school matrix of presenting the human body (marches, uniforms, rhythm, voice command, rituals, the sacrosanct nature of a well-trained body) (Gómez, 2009). The social construction of the learning body in, through, and for school takes place throughout history and reinforces the conception of a disciplined body. School education becomes an institution that disciplines and standardizes the bodies of the learners; i.e. with the help of rules students must learn to control their bodies (Muñoz, 2005).

The field of education does not question its formation of the body (Crisorio, 2016). Body studies in Latin American education focus on anatomical-political concepts in relation to phenomena such as school and pedagogy, hygiene and medicine, sexuality and youth. Research focuses on the formation of nation states and the processes of their consolidation in the nineteenth and twentieth centuries, in other words, on the evolution of biopower mechanisms. The analyses focus on the school and its micropolitical competences in pedagogy, teaching, curriculum development, and instructional psychology (Pedraza, 2007b). This also means considering the body of the learner as an object of collective policy and examining the formation of subjectivities at the interface between body, politics, culture, and knowledge. However, there is growing criticism and critical stance toward the homogeneity of modern subjectivities (Gomes et al., 2019), and the investigation of interconnecting subjectivity, diversity, and interculturality (Palacio, 2015).

Galak and Gambarotta (2015) distinguish conceptions of the body in Latin America as follows: the body reduced to natural instance, to body techniques (Marcel Mauss), to representation (David Le Breton), to performance and discourse (Judith Butler), and to the concept of corporeality. These conceptions of the body intertwine education and politics as an application of power and consider the body to be a historical and social construction.

2.2.2   The Body in Latin American Physical Education

The body has five epistemological conceptions: (1) the biological or organic body, (2) the schooled and disciplined body, (3) the body as a social and cultural construction, (4) the phenomenological body, and (5) the somatic body.

The conception of the organic or biological body emerges from Physical Education as a discipline in the school curriculum. This discipline prepares people for a modern, urban, and industrial life, whose physiological and evolutionary theoretical approach proposes an anatomical-physiological intervention in the organic body (Giménez, 2007). Physical Education as a discipline aims at seeking a balance between intellectual work and physical training, in order to generate productive people, whose objective is to govern people by means of mechanical restraint. From the conception of the individual as a living organism (and regarding its reproduction, regeneration, and production), Physical Education develops a process of normalizing students and standardizing their movements (Aisenstein, 2007). This conception of the body has a political-anatomical bias involving the concepts of 'biopolitics' and 'biopower' to use Foucault's terminology (Galak et al., 2018), which leads to the school-based production of a disciplined body (Gambarrota & Galak, 2012).

However, a turnaround takes place in Physical Education with a critique of Foucault's perspective of the political body; the body is rediscovered and seen as part of culture. Bodily culture and motion culture lead to the creation of the term 'bodily education' (Varea & Galak, 2013; Galak et al., 2018). From an anthropological perspective the body as a social and cultural construction questions the universality of behaviors, emphasizes the relativity of its social representations, and accentuates the body-related networks of symbolic signification. This means that knowledge applied to body is first and foremost cultural and that everyone makes sense of the body according to the worldview of the society in which they live. In this sense, each society builds its body knowledge from ideas, concepts, ways of thinking, behaviors, meanings, and values (Hurtado, 2008). Paradoxically, in this conception everything is explained as based on culture.

The phenomenological point of view rescues the dimension of what has been lived, felt, enjoyed, thought of, and experienced and refers to ways of educating from the angle of the experience of one's own body through forms of teaching such as free exploration, problem-solving, experimentation, and 'livingness', or living our real selves (Gallo & Urrego, 2015). This conception relates to the use of the senses and somatic education, as it recognizes the subjective activities and the decolonial use of the senses (Pedraza, 2010). Action is understood as a subjective instance that links people through sensory, emotional, cognitive, and social ties to the world around them. However, currently the use of the senses in education serves to assure one's own perception and knowledge, correct understanding, or correct moral judgment, that is to assure the acquisition of knowledge. In the following, I will examine different conceptions of the body in Brazil. The fact that they are so varied is significant for the multidimensional character of Brazilian culture and its development in the field of school education and Physical Education. This will help us to better understand the body, bodily culture, and the way it is continually changing.

3 The Body in Brazil: Conceptions in Brazilian Culture and Education

Instead of talking about the body in Brazil it is more appropriate to talk about different concepts of the body that have come about in the course of the history of social and cultural development in Brazil. Understanding the body of the learner in Brazil involves multiple cultural and social conceptions of body images and concepts dealt with in education.

3.1 The Body in Brazilian Culture: From the Body as an Expression of Mixed Racial Heritage to the Body as Capital

As the Brazilian constitution reflects the different ethnic origins of Brazil, the concepts of the body in Brazil also have a variety of cultural and ethnic origins. The Brazilian is a mixture of diverse ethnic groups such as indigenous, Portuguese, Africans, Italians, Germans, Japanese, Poles, Lebanese, and Turks (Diégues Junior, 1954). According to Rocha (2012), the conception of the Brazilian body has their specific physical appearances, gestures, and mimetic processes from that ethnic mixture. Their specific character defines their ways of thinking, their cultural inventions, and manifold constructions of identity. The body in Brazil is understood as the result of miscegenation, as rascal, Dionysian, sacred, as capital, the origin of sin and pleasure, as well as being a social construction and having complex corporeality.

Initially, the understanding of the Brazilian body comes from its conception and historical origin. In the colonial period, in contrast to the Christian principles, the naked body of the indigenous people were seen as representing innocence and naturalism. This pure body image coexists with the image of the body of animal-like and uncivilized 'black' people (Del Priore & Amantino, 2011). In this sense, thinking about the Brazilian body is a matter of examining and recognizing Brazilian identity, for the Brazilian body is a racial mix; it is a mestizo body (Freyre, 1987). For example, the body of the Brazilian woman may seen as one of short stature, dark skin, long, black curly hair, thin waist, big bottom, and small breasts, as well as typified by the beautiful body of the actress Sônia Braga. For a mestizo body, Rocha (2012) conceives three Brazilian body images: the rascal ('malandro'), the Dionysian, and the sacralized. The 'first image', the rascal or bad-boy ('malandro') body, suggests the idea of a 'sensual gait', of a 'seducer', of 'tripping someone up', whose bodily hexis expresses virile sexuality, indolence, gestures of both game and fight, as in the Capoeira fight performance, symbolized by a swinging walk, in short in manners that symbolize a personal character (Rocha, 2012, p. 86).

The 'second image' refers to the body of a Brazilian woman—mulatto, sensual, mestizo, and vibrant, who is presented together with the body of the man, the rascal ('malandro'), in Dionysian dances, such as 'Umbigada', 'Maxixe', 'Pernada', 'Samba', 'Batuque', 'Candomblé', and 'Capoeira'. The 'third image' is the sacralized body, represented in soccer and carnival—the body in these cultural practices works as a transversal symbolic operator in the constitution of the imaginary of national identity (Rocha, 2012).

The body as a social construction questions whether the body is the image of a whole society. The 'carioca' body has a value for embodying an ideal of perfection. This body must be exhibited, molded, manipulated, worked, sewn, decorated, chosen, built, manufactured, and imitated. Brazilian society develops this type of a body as a standard to be followed; it is regulated by the values of dominant men and submissive women who define the ideal body for each one based on patterns represented in the man's virile body or in the woman's delicate body (Goldenberg, 2004). Another aspect here is the body as capital whose power is to standardize the aesthetic models of corporeal beauty of men and women according to the social models imposed by the fashion market. It has a high degree of control over the body's appearance (Goldenberg, 2010). The same applies to the sin body and pleasure body, split between bondage and freedom (Del Priore, 2019). Brazil is one of the world's biggest markets for cosmetic surgery; and the strongest motivation for this is the quest for a perfect body.

The essence of the Brazilian body is the pulsating body of miscegenation and it bears the marks of a construction process, in which the idealized body is transmuted into strategies of domination and control over the individual bodies through processes of hybridization as a show, where it reveals the Brazilian identity, memory, and subjectivity (Velloso et al., 2009). Finally, the conceptions of the body in Brazil see the body foremost as a cultural artifact, which involves biological and cultural aspects, and, as well an aesthetic quality, the body expresses biological unity and is a social construction (Queiroz, 2000).

3.2 The Body in Brazilian School Education

The body as an object of education is a challenge. Research in this area refers to care, leisure, and the cult of the body. I will examine to what degree the body is considered in education. The existing research focuses on disciplining and standardizing the body at school.

3.2.1 Conceptions of the Body in Brazilian Education: Corporeality as a Criticism of the Disciplinary Nature of School Culture

Understanding and giving attention to the body of the learner in Brazilian education is closely linked to the role of the body in school. Here the focus is on the school and classroom culture as something which involves discipline (Louro, 2000).

Brazilian schooling is based on the principles of individuality, rationality, and civilization that we find in European culture and education. The social function of the school consists in transmitting knowledge through reason; consequently, it leads to disciplined bodies. According to Tiriba (2008), this involves using forms of surveillance such as control of movements, schedules, rituals, hygiene measures, diet standardization, and so on to shape and control the body. The school undertakes the task of cleaning, training, correcting, qualifying, and preparing the body of the learner for work.

Control of the body refers to the conception of a body that submits, is trained, transforms, and is prepared for work (Probst & Kraemer, 2012). In this concept of education there is a distinction between body and mind. This leads to the expansion of science, education, and civilization as related to the urban-industrial model of knowledge (Soares, 2007; Ayoub & Soares, 2019). In the case of Brazil, body education was part of the project of 'civilizing' the Brazilian nation (Oliveira, 2006). However, some studies criticized the way the body was treated in school. They realized that a dialogue was missing between different areas of knowledge. Biological, psychological, social, anthropological, economic, and historical dimensions of a body-based education are interrelated (Farah, 2010; Mendes & Nóbrega, 2004). One recognized the need of better perception of the body and corporeality in its relationship to the subjectivity of young people (Nóbrega, 2005). Aesthetic experiences shall help to avoid the dichotomy of mind and body.

3.2.2 The Body in Physical Education: Body and Mind, Corporeality, the Indigenous and Afro-Brazilian Cultural Body

The aim of discipline at school is related to the development of the bourgeoisie in the nineteenth century with its interest in health education. For medical, biological, positivist, and hygienist sciences, Physical Education is one of the key issues in medical institutions during the nineteenth and twentieth centuries and the mainstay of the health of society (Silva, 2020). In Brazil, moral and social training of the body is performed (Soares, 1994, 2005). In Physical Education, the conception of the body has its origin in the physical and natural sciences and their anatomical and physiological models that were related to the model of the 'machine-body'. In accordance with the mechanistic and rational concept of the body, the body was manipulated, dominated, and objectified (Silva, 2020).

In Brazil, a quite different body concept was developed in Physical Education in the 1980s. During that time the debate focused on the body/mind dichotomy, criticized instrumental rationality and questioned policies that saw the most important thing as being generating knowledge on topics such as health, power, and language. Philosophical and sociological studies on the ethics, aesthetics, and politics of bodies were applied (Galak et al., 2020; Soares, 1999). Approaches to the relationship between nature and culture, as well as to biological/cultural aspects of the body, gained in importance, also referring to the epistemological perspective of phenomenology, post-structuralism, and complex thinking (Nóbrega, 2006).

Merleau-Ponty's phenomenological approach to the body departs from the problem of the human body/mind split and develops the idea that the phenomenon of consciousness is much closer to the concrete organic body than to abstractions and isolated considerations of spirit, mind, or soul. These ideas underpin the notion of a global human body that involves thinking, feeling, and movement (Medina, 1983). The body shall not be seen as a sum of the parts and the soul as something that controls this set but should rather be understood in its entirety (Moreira & Simões de Campos, 2017). As a result, the division between body and mind through power games, truth regimes, cultural symbols, and social imagination are criticized. This takes place not least in the field of Physical Education. The practices of conditioning minds, immobilizing and controlling the school environment, sport itself, as well as the biologization of Physical Education, human biologization, and the machine-man are fundamentally questioned. At the same time, the critique contributes to maintaining the system (truth regimes etc.) (Zoboli, 2012).

The human being is complex. The conception of the body considers human corporeality as 'physis', 'bios', and anthropo-social. According to Moreira and Simões de Campos (2017), corporeality relates to the body and its place in the world that can be examined from an objective perspective (matter) and a subjective perspective (spirit and soul). Corporeality has the following inseparable dimensions: physical (organic-biophysical-motor), emotional-affective (instinct-drive-affection), mental-spiritual (cognition, reason, thought, idea, conscience), and socio-historical-cultural (values, habits, customs, senses, meanings, symbolisms) (Brito & Bastos, 2004). Research on body and corporeality in Physical Education associates movement with intentionality and stresses the corporeal existentiality in time and space, as well as the biographical, historical, cultural, and social complexity of the body.

4   Body Culture: Indigenous and Afro-Brazilian Body Practices in Physical Education

Brazilian Physical Education makes use of indigenous and Afro-Brazilian body practices in formal school education as a way of expanding the conception of the body. In these practices, the conception of the body is seen as body culture and body in motion. Anthropological, sociological, historical, and philosophical knowledge is combined, based on an intercultural perspective. In the consequence, educational models are derived according to which Physical Education and the conception of body culture embraces the culturally shaped body of indigenous and Afro-Brazilian people in their customs, beliefs and rituals, habits and values, and their symbolic and sociocultural traditions in terms of an ethnic alterity that constitutes the manyfold Brazilian identity (Camargo et al., 2011).

The indigenous body is a body that jumps, dances, plays, runs, moves, walks, or swims. The games of the Kalapalo people form the identity of the indigenous person and are playful ways of capturing reality: 'Kopü Kopü', 'Ukigue Humitsutu', 'Heiné Kuputisu', 'Emusi', 'Oto', and 'Hagaka' (Corrêa, 2009). In the Baniwa ethnic group that lives in the Amazon, games such as 'tapuchuca' (blind man's bluff), 'esconde-esconde' (hide-and-seek), 'jogo do palito' (to draw lots using toothpicks), and others with no equivalent in English, as 'onça e cutia, caiu no poço, balanço de cipó, gato e rato, ciranda-cirandinha, brincadeira da abelha', and 'avião' are examples of these bodily practices (Grando et al., 2010). The indigenous person assumes certain roles in his or her social context when he or she plays games; thus body practices reflect traditions, behaviors, memories, knowledge, and identity (Castro & Neira, 2009).

In Afro-Brazilian culture dance and games are part of Physical Education as body culture in motion. Recognizing movement, dance and games contribute to the construction of racial identity, the cultural rescue, and interculturality of Afro-Brazilian culture. The most well-known Afro-Brazilian dances and games are 'Capoeira', 'Congada', 'Jongo', 'Maracatu', and 'Samba de Roda'. These cultural performances are linked to religion and resistance and are characterized by the variation of movements, inherited from African ancestors through oral tradition. For Africans, the body is supposed to be a place of memory in performances (Santos, 2002). 'Capoeira', for example, is a dance and the most common game for bodily exercise in Physical Education classes. The body in 'capoeira' is a dialogic body ('corpo-dialogia'), that is a body that performs dialogues; therefore, it is a social and multifactorial process of inter-action between a body and the bodies of others. 'Capoeira' involves 'ginga', 'negativas', 'meia lua de frente' (dodges, twists, related moves), where every-thing mixes in improvisation, in interaction with the partner, and creates a bodily dialogue (Silva, 2008).

This conception of the body as part of body culture supports transforma-tive bodily practices in Physical Education in school that offer students an environment where they learn to socialize and respect social differences. They consider the cultural background of the other, thus enabling those who take part in the practice to construct their reality; creativity and imagination are active elements in the dynamics of playing games (Neira & Nunes, 2006). Each gesture, each move has a language with different senses and meanings expressed through the different bodies and determined by the social and his-torical background (Silva, 2011).

5   Discussion: The 'Corpus Absconditum' in Brazil and Latin America

In Latin America great social, cultural, and symbolic differences have devel-oped during the history of the continent, coming from the direction of the indigenous people, the Africans, and the Europeans, either through the forced attempt to make Latin America a nation or through submission to keep Brazil as a Portuguese colony. The conceptions of the body in Latin America and Brazil are the result of this social and cultural development. Furthermore, these studies arise from theoretical debates, surveys, and the analysis of arti-cles, dissertations, and theses. Nowadays we are presented with the challenge of studying the body of the learner always also as a 'corpus absconditus' in Brazilian and Latin American education. Two aspects are important in this understanding of the body: firstly, the approaches presented in texts studied, and secondly, the body as an epistemic object.

The first point draws attention to texts on the body in Brazil and Latin America which criticize its image and standardization. There are several stud-ies examining the complexity of bio-political impacts, according to which the body of the learner at school is mainly seen as to be disciplined and standardized. Only in Brazilian Physical Education the body is conceived as part of a more complex body culture.

Bio-politically, the body in Brazil is understood as the result of miscegenation, as rascal, Dionysian, sacred, as capital, the origin of sin and pleasure, as well as being a social construction and having complex corporeality. This may be the case because of the crossbreeding between the bodies of the Europeans, Africans, and Indians in Brazil (Freyre, 1987; Rocha, 2012). At the same time, the imposition of images and norms of European approaches to the human body is problematic as there is a struggle to form a Latin American identity and corporal subjectivity by excluding or at least reducing the European influence (Pedraza, 2007a; Cabra & Escobar, 2014). In Latin America, the bio-political body is formed by power and values that regulate the actions of the people in the consolidation of the nation state and the modern capitalist society. The dichotomies, homogenization, disciplining, standardizing, and aestheticization of the body are, since some decennia, criticized from a Foucauldian, phenomenological, and somatic perspective. Criticized is also the disciplining, homogenizing, and standardizing of the body for the labor market in classroom, school, and education. This means that the docile and thought-to-be passive body of the learner at school coexists with the political, aesthetic, and miscegenated bio-political body. However, in education in Brazil some practices from the indigenous people and the Afro-Brazilian tradition enlarge the above described restricted concept of the body.

All perspectives presented here do not adequately consider the body as being both a producer and also a product of culture and society (Gugutzer, 2004), i.e. the body is seen as the interface between nature (biological aspects) and culture (constructions and sociocultural aspects). However, images of the human body are dynamic; they develop and change meanings according to the very historical situation (Wulf, 2013). As an amalgam between subject and object the body is idiosyncratic. A large number of fragmented and disjointed images and concepts of the body can be distinguished (Ternes, 2005). At the same time, the influx of the traditional images of the body annihilates the physicality and materiality of the body to a certain degree (Kamper, 1999). Since a long time, there has been a strive towards overcoming the distinction between the external bodily world and the internal bodily world (Plessner, 1983). The idea gains ground that 'Körper' (German for physical body) and the 'Leib' (German for lived body) are interwoven and form a unity. The 'Leib' (lived body) with its individual history and memory is the central dimension for the perception and understanding of the world.

Lately, in Brazil one can recognize a changing view of the school space, as a *locus* of rituals, knowledge, social action, imagination, learning to learn, human development, teaching, and cultural learning. To prepare a child for the labor market is not any more regarded as the only function of the school. As the body of the learner is transformed in line with the complex challenges of the society, developing it is complex and challenging.

The body is also an epistemic object. Most research is based on documentary sources, and theoretical reflections, without empirical research (Cabra & Escobar, 2014). How is a conception of the body based on reductionist, universalist, and representative perspectives to be avoided? What is the role of field work in the conception of the body? Too often there is an absence of empirical research and the use of a variety of methods to examine the constitution of the body. No forms of representation should be excluded in our efforts to comprehend the complexity of the body. There is a need for more empirical field studies. We need to consider the dynamics and many different types of body there are in school. These types may differ from those we find in Brazilian Physical Education based on the body practices in indigenous games and Afro-Brazilian dances and games. Considering the biological, social, and cultural dimensions of Brazilian and Latin American bodies, we must reconstruct the interdisciplinary and intercultural concept of the body. We need to consider the influence of the particular phenomena of each culture and society on social interactions. Otherwise, there will be a deterministic and non-dynamic concept of the body (Vieira & Queiroz, 2017).

6   Perspectives for Mimetic Processes, Embodiment, and Cultural Learning

Human beings learn by assimilating what is external to them in order to survive and find a place for themselves. This assimilation is a mimetic process, a process of creative imitation. Human beings take an imprint of the outside world and incorporate it in their imaginary. They also use the body to take on the context of the imitated person or object, and to incorporate their implicit knowledge, values, and norms. As soon as a human being is born, she or he engages in mimetic processes and continues these ways of learning during the whole course of their life. In these processes, gestures, emotions, and ritual actions are performed and an interwoven relationship between body, language, and imagination is established (Wulf, 2022, 2013). Some research on these matters is carried out in Latin America; it makes clear that no simple understanding of the body is possible. However, to a large degree, the body seems to be a 'corpus absconditus' which raises many unanswered questions.

New forms of knowledge, research perspectives, and methods are necessary to develop comprehensive body studies (Michaels, & Wulf, 2020; Arabatzis, 2019), to better understand the human body in the Anthropocene amidst phenomena such as globalization, digitalization, artificial intelligence, robotics, new media, genetic research, and environmental problems (Wulf, 2022; Wulf & Zirfas, 2020). There is a great need for the development of new research questions, and new research methods on practical knowledge, cultural learning, and mimetic processes in gestures, rituals, and performances studies.

References

Aisenstein, Á. (2007). La matriz discursiva de la Educación Física escolar. Una mirada desde los manuales. Argentina, 1880–1950 [The Discursive Matrix of the School Physical Education. A Look from the Manuals]. In Z. Pedraza (ed.) *Políticas y estéticas del cuerpo en América Latina* (pp. 103–129) [Policies and Aesthetics of Body in Latin America. Ediciones Uniandes.

Arabatzis, T. (2019). What Are Scientific Concepts? In K. McCain & K. Kampourakis (Eds.), *What Is Scientific Knowledge? An Introduction to Contemporary Epistemology of Science* (pp. 85–99). Routledge.

Ayoub, E., & Soares, C. (2019). Estudos e pesquisas do e sobre o corpo: a produção da Pro-Posições (1990–2018) [Studies and Research of and on the Body: The Production of Pro-Posições]. *Pro-Posições, 30*(e20190077), 1–25.

Brito, M., & Bastos, J. (2004). Pensando a corporeidade na prática pedagógica em educação física à luz do pensamento complexo [Thinking the Corporeality in Pedagogical Practice in Physical Education in Light of Complex Thinking]. *Revista Brasileira de Educação Física., 18*(3), 263–272.

Cabra, N., & Escobar, M. (eds.) (2014). *El cuerpo en Colombia. Estado del arte cuerpo y subjetividad* [The Body in Colombia. State of the Art Body and Subjectivity]. IESCO, IDEP.

Camargo, V., Ferreira, M., & Simson, O. (2011). *Jogo, celebração, memória e identidade: reconstrução da trajetória de criação, implementação e difusão dos Jogos Indígenas no Brasil (1996–2009)* [Game, Celebration, Memory and Identity: Reconstruction of the TRAJECTORY of Creation, Implementation and Diffusion of Indigenous Games in Brazil (1996–2009)]. Editora Nimuendajú.

Castro, D. d., & Neira, M. (2009). Cultura corporal e educação escolar indígena—um estudo de caso [Body Culture and Indigenous School Education—A Case Study]. *Revista HISTEDBR On-Line, 9*(34), 234–254.

Corrêa, D. (2009). Brincadeiras indígenas Kalapalo: a abordagem da diversidade etno-cultural na educação física escolar [Kalapalo Indigenous Games: Approach to Ethno-cultural Diversity in School Physical Education]. *Revista Digital, 14*(139) https://www.efdeportes.com/efd139/brincadeiras-indigenas-kalapalo-na-educacao-fisica.htm

Crisorio, R. (2016). Sujeto y Cuerpo em Educación [Subject and Body in Education]. *Didáskomai, Montevideo, 7,* 3–21.

Del Priore, M. (2019). Jovens, belos e saudáveis: do corpo 'pecado' ao corpo 'prazer' [Young, Beautiful and Healthy: FROM the 'sin' Body to the 'pleasure' Body]. In *Histórias da gente brasileira: República—Testemunhos (1951–2000)* (Vol. 4). LeYa.

Del Priore, M., & Amantino, M. (eds.) (2011). *História do corpo no Brasil* [History of Body in Brazil]. Editora Unesp.

Diégues Junior, M. (1954). *Estudos das Relações de Cultura no Brasil* [Studies of Cultural Relations in Brazil]. Ministério da Educação e Cultura.

Farah, M. (2010). O corpo na escola: mapeamentos necessários [The Body at School: Necessary Mappings]. *Paidéia, 20*(47), 401–410.

Freyre, G. (1987). *Modos de homem, modas de mulher* [Man Customs, Woman Fashions]. Record.

Galak, E., Athayde, P., & Lara, L. (eds.) (2020). *Por uma epistemologia da educação dos corpos e da educação física* [For an Epistemology of Bodies Education and Physical Education]. v. 3. EDUFRN.

Galak, E., & Gambarotta, E. (2015). *Cuerpo, Educación, Política. Tensiones epistémicas, históricas y prácticas* [Body, Education, Policy. Epistemic, Historical and Practical Tensions]. Biblos.

Galak, E., Zoboli, F., Gomes, I., & Almeida, F. (2018). O corpo no campo acadêmico da Educação Física na Argentina e no Brasil: crítica e renovação da disciplina [The Body in the Academic Field of Physical Education in Argentina and Brazil: Criticism and Renewal of the Discipline]. *Revista da ALESDE, 9*(2), 79–90.

Gallo, L., & Urrego, L. (2015). Estado de conocimiento de la Educación Física en la investigación educativa [State of Knowledge of Physical Education in Educational Research]. *Perfiles Educativos, 37*(150), 143–155.

Gambarrota, E., & Galak, E. (2012). Educación de los cuerpos: crítica de la reproducción social y de las potencialidades de su transformación en el marco de la Educación Física [Education of the Bodies: Criticism of Social Reproduction and the Potentialities of its Transformation within the Framework of Physical Education]. *Estudios Pedagógicos, 38*(especial), 67–87.

Giménez, R. (2007). Um Estado Moderno y sus razones para escolarizar el cuerpo: el sistema educativo Uruguayo [A Modern State and its Reasons for Schooling the Body: The Uruguayan Educational System]. In Z. Pedraza (ed.), *Políticas y estéticas del cuerpo en América Latina* (pp. 43–68) [Policies and Aesthetics of Body in Latin America]. Ediciones Uniandes.

Goldenberg, M. (2004). *Nu &vestido: dez antropólogos revelam a cultura do corpo carioca* [Naked & Dressed: Ten Anthropologists Reveal the Culture of the Carioca Body]. Record.

Goldenberg, M. (ed.) (2010). *O corpo como capital: estudos sobre gênero, sexualidade e moda na cultura brasileira* [The Body as Capital: Studies on Gender, Sexuality and Fashion in the Brazilian Culture] (2nd edn.). Estação das Letras e Cores.

Gomes, I., Galak, E., Almeida, F., & Gómez, W. (eds.) (2019). *Sentidos y prácticas sobre la educación y los usos del cuerpo. Intercambios académicos entre Argentina, Brasil, Colombia y Uruguai* [Senses and Practices on Education and the Uses of the Body. Academic Exchanges among Argentina, Brazil, Colombia and URUGUAY]. Universidad Nacional de La Plata. Facultad de Humanidades y Ciencias de la Educación; Espirito Santo: EDUFES.

Gómez, W. M. (2009). El cuerpo en la escuela: los dispositivos de la sujetación [The Body at School: Restraint Devices]. *Currículo sem Fronteiras, 9*(1), 159–179.

Grando, B., Xavante, S., & Campos, N. (2010). Jogos/Brincadeiras Indígenas: a memória lúdica de adultos e idosos de dezoito grupos étnicos [Indigenous Games/Play: The Playful Memory of Adults and the Elderly from Eighteen Ethnic Groups]. In B. Grando (ed.) *Jogos e Culturas Indígenas: possibilidades para a educação intercultural na escola* (pp. 89–122) [Indigenous Games and Cultures: Possibilities for Intercultural Education at School]. EdUFMT.

Gugutzer, R. (2004). *Soziologie des Körpers* [Sociology of Body]. Transcript Verlag.

Hurtado, D. (2008). Corporeidad y Motricidad. Una forma de mirar los saberes del cuerpo [Corporeality and Motricity. A Way of Looking at the Knowledge of the Body]. *Educação e Sociedade, 29*(102), 119–136.

Kamper, D. (1999). Corpus absconditum. Das Virtuelle als Spielart der Absenz [Corpus absconditum. The Virtual as a Variety of Absence]. In R. Maresch & N. Werber (eds.), *Kommunikation, Medien, Macht* (pp. 445–446) [Communication, Media, Power]. Suhrkamp.

Louro, G. (2000). Corpo, escola e identidade [Body, School and Identity]. *Educação e Realidade, 25*(2), 59–76.

Medina, J. (1983). *A educação física cuida do corpo... e 'mente': bases para a renovação e transformação da educação física* [Physical Education Takes Care of Body ... and "mind": Foundations for the Renovation and Transformation of Physical Education]. Papirus.

Mendes, M., & Nóbrega, T. (2004). Corpo, natureza e cultura: contribuições para a educação [Body, Nature and Culture: Contributions to Education]. *Revista Brasileira de Educação, 27*, 125–137.

Michaels, A., & Wulf, C. (2020). *Science and Scientification in South Asia and Europe.* Routledge.

Moreira, W., & Simões de Campos, M. (2017). Necessidades do Corpo Criança na Escola: Possíveis Contribuições da Corporeidade, da Motricidade e da Complexidade [Needs of the Child Body at School: Possible Contributions of

Corporeality, Motricity and Complexity]. *Revista Internacional de Filosofía Y Teoría Social. Utopía y Praxis Latino americana, 22*(79), 131–139.

Muñoz, C. C. (2005). Entre la educación corporal caótica y la escolarización corporal ordenada [Between Chaotic Bodily Education and Orderly Bodily Schooling]. *Revista Ibero americana de Educación, 39*, 91–106.

Neira, M., & Nunes, M. (2006). *Pedagogia da cultura corporal: crítica e alternativas* [Pedagogy of Body Culture: Criticism and Alternatives]. Phorte.

Nóbrega, T. (2005). Qual o lugar do corpo na educação? Notas sobre conhecimento, processos cognitivos e currículo [What is the Body's Place in Education? Notes on Knowledge, Cognitive Processes and Curriculum]. *Educação & Sociedade, 26*(91), 599–615.

Nóbrega, T. (2006). (ed.). *Epistemologia, saberes e práticas da educação física* [Epistemology, Knowledge and Practices of Physical Education]. EdUFPB.

Oliveira, M. (ed.) (2006). *Educação do corpo na escola brasileira* [Body Education at the Brazilian School]. Autores Associados.

Oliveira, M. (2007). Currículo e educação do corpo: história do currículo da instrução pública primária no Paraná (1882–1926) [Curriculum and Body Education: History of the Primary Public Education Curriculum in Paraná (1882–1926)]. In Z. Pedraza (ed.), *Políticas y estéticas del cuerpo en América Latina* (pp. 69–102) [Policies and Aesthetics of Body in Latin America]. Ediciones Uniandes.

Palacio, J. (ed) (2015). *Cuerpo y Educación Variaciones entorno a un mismo tema* [Body and Education Variations around the Same Theme]. IDEP—Instituto para la Investigación Educativa y el Desarrollo Pedagógico. Serie Investigación.

Pedraza, Z. (2007a). Perspectivas de los estúdios del cuerpo en América Latina [Perspectives of Body Studies in Latin America]. *Anais XXVI Congreso de la Asociación Latino americana de Sociología.* Asociación Latino americana de Sociología. https://cdsa.aacademica.org/000-066/1836.pdf

Pedraza, Z. (ed.) (2007b). *Políticas y estéticas del cuerpo en América Latina* [Policies and Aesthetics of body in Latin America]. Ediciones Uniandes.

Pedraza, Z. (2010). Saber, Cuerpo y Escuela: el uso de los sentidos y la educación somática [Knowledge, Body and School: The Use of the Senses and Somatic Education]. *Calle14—Revista de Investigaciónen el Campo del Arte, 4*(5), 44–56.

Pedraza, Z. (2011). *Em cuerpo y alma: Visiones del progreso y de la felicidad. Educación, cuerpo y orden social en Colombia (1830–1990)* [In Body and Soul: Visions of Progress and Happiness. Education, Body and Social Order in Colombia (1830–1990)]. Universidad de los Andes.

Pedraza, Z. (2014). Claves para una perspectiva histórica del cuerpo [Keys to a Historical Perspective of Body]. In N. Cabra, & M. Escobar (eds.). *El cuerpo en Colombia. Estado del arte cuerpo y subjetividad* (pp. 81–114) [The Body in Colombia. State of the art Body and Subjectivity]. IESCO, IDEP.

Plessner, H. (1983). *Homo absconditus.* In G. Dux, O. Marquard, & E. Ströker (eds.) *Gesammelte Schriften VIII—Conditio Humana* (pp. 353–366) [Collected Writings VIII—Conditio Humana]. Suhrkamp.

Probst, M., & Kraemer, C. (2012). Sentado e quieto: o lugar do corpo na escola [Sitting and Quiet: the Body's Place in School]. *Atos de Pesquisa em Educação*, *7*(2), 507–519.

Queiroz, R. (ed.) (2000). *O Corpo do brasileiro: estudos de estética e beleza* [The Body of the Brazilian: Studies of Aesthetics and Beauty]. Senac.

Ramos, O. (2011). El cuerpo y la afectividad como objetos de estúdio en América Latina: intereses temáticos y proceso de institucionalización reciente [The Body and Affectivity as Subjects of Study in Latin America: Thematic Interests and Recent Institutionalization process]. *Sociológica*, *26*(74), 33–78.

Rocha, G. (2012). Paisagens corporais na cultura brasileira [Body Landscapes in the Brazilian Culture]. *Revista de Ciências Sociais, Fortaleza, 43*(1), 80–93.

Rodas, H., & Pedraza, Z. (2014). *Al outro lado del cuerpo. Estudios biopolíticos en América Latina* [On the Other Side of the Body. Biopolitical Studies in Latin America]. Ediciones Uniandes.

Santos, I. (2002). *Corpo e ancestralidade. Uma proposta pluricultural de dança-arte-educação* [Body and Ancestry. A Pluricultural Proposal of Dance-art-Education]. EDUFBA.

Scribano, A. (2016). Cuerpos, Emociones y Sociedad em Latino América: Una mirada desde nuestras propias prácticas [Bodies, Emotions and Society in Latin America: A Look from our Own Practices]. *Revista Latino Americana de Estudios sobre Cuerpos, Emociones y Sociedad, 8*(20), 12–26.

Silva, E. (2008). *O corpo na capoeira: introdução ao estudo do corpo na capoeira* [The Body in Capoeira: Introduction to Study of Body in Capoeira]. Editora da Unicamp.

Silva, M. (2020). *Do corpo objeto ao sujeito histórico: perspectivas do corpo na história da educação brasileira* (2nd edn.) [From the Object Body to the Historical Subject: Perspectives of the Body in the History of Brazilian Education]. EDUFBA.

Silva, P. (2011). Capoeira nas aulas de educação física: alguns apontamentos sobre processos de ensino-aprendizado de professores [Capoeira in Physical Education Classes: Some Notes on Teachers' Teaching-Learning Processes]. *Revista Brasileira de Ciências do Esporte, 33*(4), 889–903.

Soares, C. (1994). *Educação Física: raízes européias e Brasil* [Physical Education: European Roots and Brazil]. Autores Associados.

Soares, C. (1999). Dossiê: Corpo e Educação—Apresentação [Dossier: Body and Education—Presentation]. *Caderno CEDES, 19*(48), 5–6.

Soares, C. (2005). *Imagens da educação no corpo: estudo a partir da ginástica francesa do século XIX* (3rd edn) [Images of Education in Body: A Study Based on 19th Century French Gymnastics]. Autores Associados.

Soares, C. (ed.) (2007). *Pesquisas sobre o Corpo: Ciências Humanas e Educação* [Body Research: Humanities and Education]. Editora Fapesp.

Ternes, B. (2005). *Marginal Man. Dietmar Kamper als Denker jenseits Von Differenz und Indifferenz* [Marginal Man. Dietmar Kamper as a Thinker Beyond Difference and Indifference]. Argo Books.

Tiriba, L. (2008). *Arquitetura e corpo na escola: Educação e vivência do espaço. Salto para o Futuro: O corpo na escola* [Architecture and Body at School: Education and Experience of Space. Leap into the Future: The Body at School]. TV Escola.

Varea, V., & Galak, E. (eds.) (2013). *Cuerpo y Educación Física. Perspectivas latino americanas para pensar la educación de los cuerpos* [Body and Physical Education. Latin American Perspectives to Think About the Education of Bodies]. Biblos.

Velloso, M., Rouchou, J., & Oliveira, C. (eds.) (2009). *Corpo: identidades, memórias e subjetividades* [Body: Identities, Memories, and Subjectivities]. Mauad.

Vieira, K., & Queiroz, G. (2017). O corpo como desafio na educação: abordagens alemãs [The Body as a Challenge in Education: German Approaches]. In M. Thesing; L. Soares, and M. Soares (eds.), *Temas em debate: diálogos e aprendizagens* (pp. 192–225) [Debating Topics: Dialogues and Learning]. DictioBrasil.

Wulf, C. (2013). *Anthropology. A Continental Perspective*. The University of Chicago Press.

Wulf, C. (2022). *Education as Human Knowledge in the Anthropocene. An Anthropological Perspective*. Routledge.

Wulf, C., & Zirfas, J. (eds.) (2020). Editorial: Den Menschen neu denken—Einsätzehistorischer Anthropologie [Editorial: Rethinking Man—Deployments of Historical Anthropology]. *Paragrana, 29*(1), 9.

Zoboli, F. (2012). *Cisão corpo/mente: espelhos e reflexos nas práxis da Educação Física* [Body/mind Split: Mirrors and Reflexes in the Praxis of Physical Education]. Editora UFS. https://cdsa.aacademica.org/000-066/1836.pdf

Cultivating a Gentle Body: A Chinese Perspective

Hongyan Chen

1 Introduction: A Forceful Re-discovery of the Body

The sudden outbreak and global spread of the new coronavirus forces us, worldwide, to revisit and reflect upon the human body as being 'a multiple one' (Mol, 2003): a fragile body, which can easily be attacked by the virus transmitted through small drops of saliva; a powerful body, which mirrors world politics; a quarantine body, which has been marked by an era of 'no-touch' (no kisses on the cheek, no handshakes or other bodily contact while greeting); a trackable body, where the location of the body can be easily 'traced' by the modern technology track and trace system; a sanitized body, which is often warned by the medical authorities to "wash your hands before, during and after preparing food for at least twenty seconds"; a suppressed and repressed body, which needs to learn how to live well with the virus. Given this developing crisis, human beings have and are bodies at risk.

In the period of post-COVID 19, when people tend to slow down the routine of their daily lives, it may be the occasion to reflect on what was going on before this viral outbreak, and how the relationship to the human body changed (Marder, 2020). For much of the history of western philosophy,

---

H. Chen (✉)
Institute of International and Comparative Education, East China Normal University, Shanghai, China
e-mail: chenhongyanup@126.com

© The Author(s), under exclusive license to Springer Nature Switzerland AG 2022
A. Kraus, C. Wulf (eds.), *The Palgrave Handbook of Embodiment and Learning*,
https://doi.org/10.1007/978-3-030-93001-1_33

there has been a sharp dichotomy between mind and body. Body has been conceptualized as biological object. It is only in the last century that the 'nature' of the body was questioned as being the main issue and systematically examined. Merleau-Ponty (1962), as the leading proponent of body-phenomenology, reminds us that the 'fundamental philosophical act' would be to 'return to the lived world beneath the objective world', where experience of the own lived body becomes a vital situation for understanding the 'phenomenal field'. For him, the relation between objective world and experienced world as expressed in language and art, history, politics and nature can only be properly interpreted and clarified by focusing on the issue of perception and embodiment.

Unlike the negative attitude towards to the body in classic western philosophy, Chinese ancient texts have clearly referred to the body as a way of thinking. The human body has been considered as the most basic point of departure of meaningfulness. As Zhang argued, while "the classic western philosophy which attempts to comprehend the world begins with 'think', traditional Chinese philosophy starts with 'body'" (张再林, 2018, p. 316). Unfortunately, as modern academic discourse is strongly based on western principles, the body aspect in China remains a more or less unspoken field. Also in China, it is only the last decades that there has been a re-discovery of the body by local scholars. Until now, in their studies of the body as a subject, Chinese scholars have depicted a very different picture from the western scholars. One of the radical differences is that traditional Chinese thought has never been governed by mind-body dualism as in the West; rather, there is always a holistic view of mind-body whereby the body is the dynamic of the mental processes (张再林, 2018). Uncontroversially, a holistic position can be found both in Daoism and in Confucianism, where it is also essential to acknowledge the body as secular and sacred.

To give a systematic view of the traditional Chinese conception of the body, this chapter develops a case study and focuses on the holistic aspect of the body. It firstly addresses how the body has been historically discussed in different dynasties and educational systems. We argue that the body in China can only be understood as the common bond between family and state. We then highlight three features of the Chinese body, namely regular and repetitive exercise (without considering the physical rigour as western philosophy might do)[1], time (seasonally appropriate, rhythms, namely *Shi*) and harmony

---

[1] Yangsheng, however, emphasizes not physical rigour, but regularity and repetition (Farquhar & Zhang, 2012, p. 66).

(this must be achieved rather than being a natural state[2]). Ultimately, we argue that all three aspects can only become effective when we include the element of ritual, which finally aims to shape a 'soft' or gentle body. It is also worth noting that there is a significant difference between Chinese views on body and the phenomenological views of western contemporary philosophy. In Chinese thought, the lived body is always in continuity with the collective body, the ritual body and the time body. In addition, in contrast with the prevailing western viewpoints, Chinese discourse about body is beyond having and being, but a 'doing body', a body which enacts and performs.

2 The Body in Early Chinese Texts

Unlike the hiding of the body in western philosophy, the ancient Chinese classics are rich in discussions of the body. An accurate idea of how the body was conceived in early China can be found in different philosophical schools. Regardless of their difference concerning human nature, both Daoism and Confucianism share a common interest in the body. In both schools, the body is not treated as an object that one 'has', but rather associated with the process of unfolding, that is something is doing and also being done. Such an idea is often associated with the pattern of the family-self-state collective structure. Some of the recent studies have even considered the body as the starting point for understanding Chinese philosophy. As Zhang (Zailin & Shaoqian, 2009) argued, Chinese philosophy does not focus on universal categories of consciousness—as it is proposed by Immanuel Kant; rather, it follows the dual path of family and clan. Zhang provides various discussion on how the body can manifest the philosophy of existence, in an ethical and transcendental way.

2.1 The Physical Body as a Site of Family Heritage

Holding a holistic view on the body is epitomized in the Chinese reference to the body as *zonghe ti*, namely a "composite or synthesized corpus" (Farquhar & Zhang, 2012, p. 280). The most significant feature of this synthesized corpus lies in its physical existence. In Ancient China people did not feel hatred towards the body because of bodily pleasures and satisfaction such as food, drink and sex. On the contrary, they considered this process to be an

---

[2] When harmonizing is understood as the weaving together of many streams of activity and as the management of a relation between yin and yang tendencies in the dynamics of life, it becomes quite a complex concept (Farquhar & Zhang, 2012, p. 153).

automatic happening (Wu, 2003). When hungry the body needs food and eats, it develops an understanding of taste; when tired the body falls asleep and knows the body's limitations; when amused the body laughs; it senses the interaction with the world and its social environment. As Confucius said, "there is no body but eats and drinks. But they are few who can distinguish flavors" (Legge, 2016). By this, Confucius was reflecting on the physical needs of body; however, he also attempts to seek an optimal level of bodily practice, so that the body is trained as an intelligent one. It articulates the fact that there is no human nature apart from the physical body and its needs (Confucius in Slingerland, 2003, Analects, P259).

Such an acknowledgement of the material aspect of body endowed it with a positive meaning. The essential of 'I' is nothing more than what the body is doing and has done, as is written in the ancient text 'Qin ji zhi qie, wu zhong yu shen' I feel deeply the existence of myself; nothing is more divine and closer than my own body (亲己之切, 无重于身, quoted by Zailin & Shaoqian, 2009, p. 346). Moreover, it would be naive to see the physical body as belonging to one individual person. The existence of the physical body is often associated with the family. As the classic of Filial Piety articulates,

> One's body, hair, and skin are a gift from one's parents—do not dare to allow them to be harmed, this is the beginning of xiao (filial). (The classic of Filial Piety, 8.3, Analects, P79; Ames & Rosemont, 2009)

Here, the body has been considered as the extension of one's parents. In this case, the individual is not the only owner of the body, and he or she is also prohibited from hurting the body. In the day of one's death a person must reflect on his body and whether he has made it through life without disrespecting his parents. In many cases, the body has been compared to a family, and it is the representation of the family. A linguistic observation can also provide a good way of understanding how the body shares the same purpose of family. In Chinese, the parents call their children their 'flesh and bones' (*Gu Rou*), and the children will practice 'regurgitation-feeding' on the parents as 'my birth body' (*Sheng shen*); hands and feet stand for brothers (*Shou Zu*), ears mean friends, thighs and upper arms stand for right-hand man, and the cells we have in common stand for brothers. Thus, since birth, the body has been inextricably entangled with the family and brothers. As we read in Confucius' writings,

> A gentleman is respectful and free of errors. He is reverent and ritually proper in his dealings with others. In this way, everyone with the Four Seas is his brother.

How could a gentleman be concerned about not having brothers. (Confucius in Slingerland, 2003, p. 127)

Thus, the body is not a private thing owned by an individual. The body is not at the disposal of the subject. A body born in brotherhood practices a culture of respect for the body, and even worships the living body. This is articulated by Slingerland when he interprets Confucian's Analects:

Respect for certain parts of the body is a metaphor for discipline. For instance, Master Zeng was gravely ill and called his disciples to his bedside: "Uncover my feet! Uncover my hands." (Confucius in Slingerland, 2003, Analects 8.3, P79)

Zeng was particularly known for his filial piety, one of the main principles of which was preserving one's body intact. It is only now, on his deathbed, that Master Zeng can be sure to have made it through life without disrespecting his parents in this fashion. (ibid.)

Another statement has a similar meaning:

We have had the imperishable Way, and yet there have never been imperishable people. Therefore, to allow one's body to die is not to necessarily to sacrifice the [true] self, while to keep oneself alive at any cost in fact involves losing oneself. (Confucius in Slingerland, 2003, Analects, p. 129)

Because of the understanding of body as a family category, it is not difficult to understand the statement 'Morality is body' (德也者，得于身也，《礼记.乡饮酒》). And such a pattern of exchanging and creating the body is analogous with the movement of the cosmos and also the flow of virtue or morality (Miller, 2001).

2.2 The 'Self-Cultivated' Body: From Qi to Xiushen—A Double Transformation: Xiushen Yang Xing

If the family shapes the whole body, where is the 'creation' of a body? If we look at the significance of the physical body in ancient Chinese texts, we find the existence of the body is often the objective part of the subject 'I/me' with the responsibility of self-cultivation. "The staging of the body as an extension of family directed to a large extent the performance of the body in daily personal and communal life.—The life of the human body is generated from the movement and development of Qi" (Farquhar & Zhang, 2012, p. 256):

Despite the high value placed on the physical body, it should not lead to the misunderstanding that the body is purely an object. Instead, ancient Chinese emphasized the unity between the physically existing body and the subject. How to 'take care of the body' has been a recurring public issue, as the body is not only the individual's responsibility. "Thus, the learning of gentleman is used to improve the person, while the learning of the petty man is used like gift" (Mei qi shen, Xunzi; Hutton, 2014).

In general, two aspects of the 'caring body' can be differentiated in accordance with Chinese ancient culture: one aspect regards the 'physical good shape of the body' (*Yangsheng, xiushen*), and the second is the 'self-cultivated' nature of the body (*Yangxing*). Often, the body is the basis of analysis. For instance, in Chinese traditional medicine, the basic physiological principle of keeping the body alive is the continuous exchange of vital energy (*Qi*) between *Yin* and *Yang*.

> In the human body there are the nine orifices of ears, eyes, nostrils, mouth, anus, and urethra; the five *zang* organs of kidneys, liver, heart, spleen, and lungs; and the twelve joints of elbows, wrists, knees, ankles, shoulders, and hips, which are all connected with the universe. (The Yellow Emperor's Classic of Medicine, 1995, p. 26)

In Chinese traditional medicine, the human body is regarded as a network of Qi (namely energy flow) which embraces two basic physiological dynamics: yin and yang system. The former's function is to 'store the potential energy to maintain the dynamic homeostasis of the body', and the latter is responsible for 'transmitting this energy'. For the Daoist, then it is the body, not just the heart-mind *(xin)*, that must be cultivated and imaged in order to realize the unity of humans and the cosmos (Miller, 2001). However, Confucius requires a 'transformative' change from heart and embodiment:

> When a man is rebuked with exemplary worlds after having made a mistake, he cannot help but agree with them. However, what is important is that he changes himself in order to accord with them. When a man is praised with words of respect, he cannot help but be pleased with them. However, what is important is that he actually live up to them. A person who finds respectful words pleasing but does not live up to them, or agrees with others' reproaches and yet does not change—there is nothing I can do with one such as this. (Confucius in Slingerland, 2003, Analects, 9.24, p 94)

Here, the Master criticized those who consent superficially but do not transform their hearts. Nominal assent to the Confucian way is insufficient—one must love the Way and strive to embody it in one's person. The Master effortlessly embodies "in his words, behaviour, and countenance the lessons imparted throughout the rest of the text" (Confucius in Slingerland, 2003, Analects, p 98).

2.2.1 The Collective and State-Owned Body: A Devoted Body in Different Dynasties

The body has further associations as described here:

> From the body to the family, from the family to the nation, from the nation to the whole world—the body, family, nation and the whole world are different representations, but they have the same essence. Broadly speaking, the affairs dealt with by the saints cover the whole universe; but to speak narrowly, these matters do not go beyond the human body. (Zailin & Shaoqian, 2009)

In the third century B.C.E. in the Springs and Autumns of Mr Lü (Lüshi Chunqiu) we find the following:

> Human beings have 360 joints, nine bodily openings, and five yin and six yang systems of function. In the flesh tightness is desirable; in the blood vessels free flow is desirable; in the sinews and bones solidity is desirable; in the operations of the heart and mind harmony is desirable; in the essential Qi regular motion is desirable. When [these desiderata] are realized, illness has nowhere to abide, and there is nothing from which pathology can develop. When illness lasts and pathology develops, it is because the essential *Qi* has become static. ... States too have their stases. When the ruler's virtue does not flow freely [i.e., if he does not appoint good officials to keep him and his subjects in touch], and the wishes of his people do not reach him, a hundred pathologies arise in concert, and a myriad catastrophes swarm in. (Miller, 2001)

As Miller put, "the free flow of virtue (*de*) is not to be understood in terms of moral philosophy but by analogy with what is necessary to keep the body alive. Just as the circulation of bodily fluids is necessary for human survival, so also the free flow of 'virtue' is necessary in the state" (ibid.).

In the medical text *Huangdi neijing suwen* (Simple Questions on the Yellow Emperor's Internal Classic) we find the following (Miller, 2001):

The cardiac system is the office of the monarch: consciousness issues from it. The pulmonary system is the office of the minister mentors: oversight and supervision issue from it. The hepatic system is the office of the General: planning issues from it. The gall bladder system is the office of the rectifiers: decisions issue from it. … [and so on for the twelve systems of body functions associated with internal organs]. It will not do for these twelve offices to lose their co-ordination.

As Miller says: 'Here we see how the physiology of the body was correlated with hierarchical configuration of the state' (Miller, 2008).

3   Nurturing the Body in the Chinese Educational Context: Time, Repetitive Exercise and Harmony

When we conceptualize the Chinese body in terms of family, collective and state, we must not confuse this by the fact that in China it is assumed that the body itself has an imitative, a mimetic power (Gebauer & Wulf, 1995). Overall, it is necessary to differentiate the body as an individual existence and the body of a family state. Only with such consciousness of the body as being something that belongs can we understand why the body in ancient texts has widely been seen as subject for 'deliberate cultivation and nurturing' (Farquhar & Zhang, 2012), in Chinese *Xiushen Yangxing* (cultivate the body/self, nurture one's nature). To attain the status of an educated human being, people need extra effort, regulation, discipline and also self-discipline. As we noted above, since the body in China is often conceived as rooted in the family and state framework, the criterion of family has great generative power for the next generation. In Chinese tradition, self-control/discipline is the best path to attain the being of an educated person.

Study this Inner Canon, savor this; under the guidance of sages, explore and attend to the secrets of the body and soul—in this way, we can again perfect human life and complete the central voyage of human life.—Qu Limin, The Yangsheng Wisdom of the Yellow Emperor's Inner Canon, savor this; under the guidance of sages, explore and attend to the secrets of the body and soul—in this way, we can again perfect human life and complete the central voyage of human life. (Farquhar & Zhang, 2012, p. 125)

3.1 Body and Time

No doubt time is a starting point of modern western philosophy. However, unlike the western emphasis on the linear aspects (three modes of time: the past, the present and the future), the Chinese discuss time in a cyclical and dynamic way. It is not measurable clock-time. Like all other agricultural countries ancient China tends to follow the rhythmic changes of the four seasons and is maintaining an intimate relationship between the activity of human beings and the natural environment. "The human body depends on the natural world for its nurturance and cultivation, in accord with the natural regularities of life" (Farquhar & Zhang, 2012, p. 256). As is advocated in the Yellow Emperor's Inner Canon,

> The three months of the spring season bring about the revitalization of all things in nature. It is the time of birth. This is when heaven and earth are reborn. During this season it is advisable to retire early. Arise early also and go walking in order to absorb the fresh, invigorating energy … on the physical level it is good to exercise more frequently and wear loose-fitting clothing. This is the time to do stretching exercises to loosen up the tendons and muscles. Emotionally, it is good to develop equanimity. This is because spring is the season of the liver … violating the natural order of spring will cause cold disease, illness inflicted by atmospheric cold during summer. (Ni, 2011)

In general, there are three dimensions of the Chinese conceptions of time and body. Firstly, the whole world is controlled by the change of time, especially the change of the seasons; secondly, the recovery of each body part has its time, such as the liver in spring, heart in summer, lung in autumn and kidney in winter; and[3] thirdly, there is a need of timing, to unite the change of heaven/season, adjusting the needs of each body part.

Time is something that shows 'changes' and 'dynamics' than measurement. For instance, "*Tianzhishi* (heavenly time), *Shixing* (act or move in accordance with time), *Shiming* (time and destiny), *Sishi* (four seasons), *Yushi xiexing* (to go along with time), and *Cheng Tian Er Shi Xing* (to comply with heaven to act or to move in accordance with time)" (Chen & Bu, 2019). The concept of time here can be generalized as "timeliness, timing, opportune moments, proper timing, and availing oneself of the gathered momentum" (ibid.). This kind of multidimensional quality of time is often emphasized in ancient Chinese texts.

---

[3] For details check pp 23–24.

Time adjusts the body's rhythm (Farquhar & Zhang, 2012—the four times of the year). There are two dimensions of time: (1) the time of the body and (2) the time of nature (environment). As for the time of the body, there is a need to "harmonize the numbers" (Farquhar & Zhang, 2012). People use the concept of 'demon time' to identify when the body is in a vulnerable time:

> The 'demon times' of each day: it is when you first wake up from dreaming in the morning that you enter on the first demon time of the day (6:00–9:00 a.m.). This is the point at which things like heart disease, stroke, bronchitis begin to act up in your body.

Such kind of thinking is analogous with the concept of the 'rhythm' of the body. As Farquhar and Zhang also argue, "even on the scale of a life, there is a 'demon time', middle age, when physiology is turning away from its youthful vigor, but the pressure of social responsibility is at its highest" (Farquhar & Zhang, 2012).

In Farquhar and Zhang's research on *Yangsheng*, they also refer to the importance of the adjustment between body and time:

> We Chinese have a saying, 'eat turnip in the winter, ginger in the summer, no need to get a doctor's scrip'. Why do people say this? In the summer, our yang qi rises and floats toward the surfaces of the body, so the inner parts of the body develop a pattern of cold-damp; [under these conditions], the spleen-stomach system is at its weakest, and our digestive functions are thus also at their weakest, so in the summer, we want to eat warming and heating, lightening and dispersing things such as ginger and can't eat moistening and tonifying things— our body's insides don't have the power to digest them. But when winter comes, our yang qi is entirely retreating, and the inner parts of the body develop a pattern of inward heat, so we can eat moistening and tonifying things. Thus, eating turnip can clear [heat] and cool [the inside], and make qi flow along its pathway [qingliang xunqi]; it can help our body maintain a condition of coolness, with easy and smooth circulation. (Farquhar & Zhang, 2012, p. 152)

> The relationship between yin and yang are so intimately interactive, their antinomies so complexly nested in rank of ever more finely differentiated lights and darks, potentials and actuals (every yang aspect incorporates yang and yin aspects, every state of initiating entails its imminent completion, every completed thing holds within it the seeds of a new initiation), that the achievement of harmony is far from natural. (ibid., p. 154)

Time enables the body to renew itself: when looking at time with respect to its endless change, we only see things constantly renewing themselves; yet that things ceaselessly renew themselves is the very nature of time.

The *yangsheng* of the seasons in one year, the *yangsheng* of the monthly phases of the moon, the *yangsheng* of the four temporal turning points of the day—these are all versions of one another. The general principle is that of following along with heaven's timing (tianshi 天时). Zhang Qicheng calls "the three treasures of human body: *Jing*-essence, *qi*-energy, and *shen*-spirit" (Farquhar & Zhang, 2012, p. 35).

3.2 Repetitive Exercise

While ritual is considered as symbolic activity in a religious context in Ancient Greece, ritual is considered as an activity which aims to cultivate the self in Chinese culture. "The form and meaning of ritual are determined by tradition; they are malleable according to the needs of any present situation, as long as the performers understand them as being traditional" (Wulf, 2022).[4] According to Confucius, education involves not only words but takes place most importantly through the medium of the body. Such ideas are often articulated in his Analects, as here: Confucius said, "[D]o you disciples imagine that I am being secretive? I hide nothing from you. I take no action, I make no move, without sharing it with you. This is the kind of person that I am" (Confucius in Slingerland, 2003, Analects, 7.24 p. 72). Confucius is often said to 'speak too little', and some of his students criticized that he may have hidden some sort of esoteric knowledge from them. The Master then claims that what he actually taught is not what has been said, but rather to 'do with learning from the ancients and putting this learning into practice'. Such kind of body-based practice has been summarized by Wang Yangming, an extraordinary later Confucius scholar[5]: *shenjiao*, literally body or personal teaching (it contrasts with *yanjiao*, namely teaching through words). According to Wang, compared to theoretical teaching delivered by words, body teaching can arouse and touch the deeper emotions, via how the Master behaves, with the Master acting as a model or example to emulate. The response given by the Master is a reminder to the student of the significance of the body in our perception of the world. As he also said, "I wish I did not have to speak (yan), what does Heaven ever say?" (Confucius in Slingerland, 2003, p. 24, p. 72.)

Such training of the body is often connected with *Li*. *Li* is an ambiguous word, although it is significant in the analysis of the body in Ancient China.

---

[4] cf. Christoph Wulf, *Education as Human Knowledge in the Anthropocene*, especially chapter 9 on Confucianism. (2022) Fritz Graf. https://doi.org/10.1093/acrefore/9780199381135.013.5600

[5] Ching, J. (1972). *The Philosophical Letters of Wang Yang-ming*. Canberra, Australia: Australian National University Press.

Primarily, *Li* referred to the practice of making sacrificial offerings to the spirits of the ancestors. Later, in Zhou, the scope of Li extended as far as "daily lives that we might to be tempted to" (Analects). It relates not only rites, ceremonies and decorum, but also regards to specific rules applied in certain social intercourse. "Training the body to be at peace, harmonizing the perceptions, making the self learn to respond to stimuli in certain way, and (for Confucians) 'straightening' it with ritual propriety are the immediate goals of these early practices of self-cultivation in China" (Judy, 2011).

At first glance, the illustration of ritual might seem to control the corporeal body within certain rules. However, it is worth noting that ritual has two meanings. Confucius' well-known statement about ritual can be found in Analects, as follows:

> Restraining yourself and returning to the rites (*keji fuli*) constitutes Goodness. If for one day you managed to restrain yourself and return to the rites, in this way you could lead the entire world back to Goodness. The key to achieving Goodness lies within yourself—how could it come from others? (Confucius in Slingerland, 2003, *Analects* 12, p 125)

Ritual here is a prescriptive set of bodily instructions used to shape and transform one's behaviour. In this sense, it can easily be misunderstood that the ritual is a way to restrain and regulate human nature. However, we find that Confucius' contemporaries tended to be extravagant and arrogant, exceeding the limits of ritual, which is why he mentioned the rites. When Confucius talks about ritual, it is to remind people to look within themselves rather than looking to others. He means the same when he says, "[D]o not look unless it is in accordance with ritual; do not listen unless it is in accordance with ritual; do not speak unless it is in accordance with ritual; do not move unless it is in accordance with ritual" (Confucius in Slingerland, 2003, *Analects* 12.1). In other words, looking, listening, speaking and moving are all things that come from oneself, not from others. While Confucius used ritual as a noun, Xunzi, one of his followers, used ritual in a developmental sense, as he claims in his Discourse on Ritual (Watson, 2003). And further,

> Ritual means to nourish. The flesh of grass-fed and grain-fed animals, rice and millet, properly blended to create the five flavours nourish the mouth. The aromas and fragrances of spice and orchids nourish the nose. ... Therefore, ritual means to nourish." Xunzi uses metaphor to show how we should treat ritual as serving human needs, as flavour for the mouth, aromas for the nose, embroidery for the eyes, ritual is a way to nourish the body. When we read Xunzi's

writings, we find that he attempts to show that "bodily transformation that leads a person to perceive the world differently is connected to the aesthetic quality of the ritual experience". (Tavor, 2013)

3.3   Harmony

It is only through the body that harmony can be produced. If the body is in a harmonious relationship with its environment, it will be filled with a harmony that pervades the whole person. Harmony is thought to spread through the body of the individual and connects with the body of the family and the body of the state. It is seen as the task of human beings to create harmony between the body of the individual, the family and the community, the world and the cosmos. Harmony is thought of as something physical, arising through the resonance of human bodies with the environment and with the cosmos, when being in the right place, fulfilling their tasks. The harmony of the body is expected to develop over time by expanding it. Education, embodiment and learning all strive to acquire the capacity of creating harmony and humanity. From early childhood on, this ability is supposed to be acquired in rituals. From childhood on, rituals are a way to connect individuals with one another and are capable of creating harmonious communities. In their embodied, performative character, rituals create a public space which they make their own through their adherence to rules and through repetition. This requires bodily practice, repetition and the acquisition of practical knowledge from childhood on.

4   Discussion and Conclusion: Towards a 'Gentle' Body

In the last two decades, the human body has gained its central position in the academic discourse of modern social sciences and the humanities. The issues such as the political body, the gender-based body, racial bodies, masculinity and sexuality, the sacred body and religion, consumption and beauty, technology and body and so on contribute to the debate. Unlike the 'discovery' of the body in the western world, Chinese scholars believe that it is time to 'return' to the body. Many scholars believe that in contrast to the formal and abstract thinking of the West, traditional Chinese thinking is based on concrete roots in the practice and needs of the body. For instance, by comparing the different attitudes in the East and West towards the body, the historian Kuang-ming

Wu articulates the fact that in Ancient China 'body thinking' was holistic. According to Wu (Wu, 2003), 'body thinking' has two meanings: firstly, it refers to thinking through the body, namely bodily thought. In this sense, the body is an instrument that represents thought, and expresses the thinking; secondly, the body itself is a thinking subject, namely bodily thinking. Both aspects are essential for understanding why the body can be considered as the a priori of all thinking (Wu, 2003, p. 309). Such body thinking relates not only to personal life but also to communal interaction and in the cultivation of the arts of civilization. Such kind of thinking is beyond 'the differences between having a body' and 'being a body'. Ancient Chinese texts present a perfect image of the body as being what we do in and through our daily actions. In and through our bodies we perform, enact and stage our thoughts. An educated person was often considered as somebody 'without any strength to truss a chicken'. To understand the meaning of this sentence, it is necessary to trace our understanding of the body back to the classics and use the discovery of the traditional knowledge for the creation of new perspectives for embodiment and learning in the future.

References

Ames, R. T., & Rosemont, H., Jr. (2009). *The Chinese Classic of Family Reverence: A Philosophical Translation of the Xiaojing*. University of Hawaii Press.

Chen, H. Y., & Bu, Y. H. (2019). Anthropocosmic Vision, Time, and Nature: Reconnecting Humanity and Nature. *Educational Philosophy and Theory, 51*(11), 1130–1140. https://doi.org/10.1080/00131857.2018.1564660

Ching, J. (1972). *The Philosophical Letters of Wang Yang-ming*. Australian National University Press.

Farquhar, J., & Zhang, Q. (2012). *Ten Thousand Things: Nurturing Life in Contemporary Beijing* (Qu Limin, Trans.). Zone Books.

Gebauer, G., & Wulf, C. (1995). *Mimesis. Art, Culture, Society*. University of California Press.

Hutton, E. L. (2014). *Xunzi: The Complete Text*. Princeton University Press.

Judy, R. (2011). The Cultivation of Mastery: Xiushen and the Hermeneutics of the Self. *Early Chinese Thought. Intertexts (Lubbock, Tex.), 15*(1), 1–19. https://doi.org/10.1353/itx.2011.0013

Legge, J. (2016), *Confucianism: The Four Books and Five Classics—Collected Works of Confucius*. Delphi Classics.

Marder, M. (Producer). (2020 [2021], April 18). Contagion: Before and Beyond COVID-19.

Merleau-Ponty, M. (1962). *Phenomenology of Perception* (C. Smith, Trans.). Motilal Banarsidass Publishers.

Miller, J. (2001). Envisioning the Daoist Body in the Economy of Cosmic Power. *Daedalus, 130*(4), 265–282.

Miller, J. (2008). *Daoism. A Beginner's Guidebooks*. Blackwell.

Mol, A. (2003). *The Body Multiple: Ontology in Medical Practice*. Duke University Press.

Ni, M. (2011). *The Yellow Emperor's Classic Of Medicine: A New Translation of the Neijing Suwen with Comentary*. Boston and London: Shambhala.

Slingerland, E. G. (2003). *Confucius Analects: With Selections from Traditional Commentaries*. Hackett Pub. Co.

Tavor, O. (2013). Xunzi's Theory of Ritual Revisited: Reading Ritual as Corporal Technology. *Dao: A Journal of Comparative Philosophy, 12*(3), 313–330. https://doi.org/10.1007/s11712-013-9331-4

Watson, B. (2003). *Xunzi. Basic Writings*. Columbia University Press.

Wu, K.-M. (2003 [1997]). *On Chinese Body Thinking: A Cultural Hermeneutic*. E.J. Brill.

Wulf, C. (2022). *Education as Human Knowledge in the Anthropocene*. Routledge.

Zailin, Z., & Shaoqian, Z. (2009). Theories of Family in Ancient Chinese Philosophy. *Frontiers of Philosophy in China, 4*(3), 343–359. https://doi.org/10.1007/s11466-009-0022-5

张再林. (2018). *作为身体哲学的中国古代哲学 Tending towards 'the Philosophy of the Body'—Transformation of Traditional Chinese Philosophical Research Paradigm*. 北京: 中国书籍出版社.

The Body and the Possibility of an Ethical Experience of Education: A Perspective from South Asia

Srajana Kaikini

The concept of education demands a balancing act between offering a stabilising environment in which the learner grows through knowing and at the same time necessitating a dynamic environment that must continually re-invent itself to push at the very boundaries of knowledge. This task is made even more complex when the question of education is entangled with embodiment. Embodiment as a concept is not new in the philosophies of education in the South Asian region. However, the role of embodiment and its status in education is wrought with several problems given the region's complex socio-historical constitution. Embodied education in the South Asian and particularly the Indian context is marked by colonial heritage. This has resulted in mainstream modern school education systems carrying forward these legacies and categorisations resulting from the syncretic influence of a Victorian education system, instituted in India during its colonisation, on the indigenous education systems existing in the region.

In this chapter, I articulate the relationship between embodiment and the process of learning in the Indian[1] context in an attempt to understand the

---

[1] I use 'Indian' in this chapter as an indexical geographic term to talk about certain situated traditions that have their socio-political histories entangled with India as a place. The term is not a representative index of the nation's identity which is constituted by various plural metaphysical frameworks from the Islamic, Zoroastrian, Atheistic and Indigenous traditions, which have not been addressed within the scope of this research.

S. Kaikini (✉)
SIAS, Krea University, Sri City, Andhra Pradesh, India
e-mail: srajana.kaikini@krea.edu.in

© The Author(s), under exclusive license to Springer Nature Switzerland AG 2022
A. Kraus, C. Wulf (eds.), *The Palgrave Handbook of Embodiment and Learning*,
https://doi.org/10.1007/978-3-030-93001-1_34

possibilities of offering an ethical experience of education to learners. In the context of Indian education, the body becomes a highly contested territory which is ridden with colonial histories as well as sociological inequalities. This has led several social reformers and philosophers to actively talk about new imaginations in education as a central goal for social life in India. Some of the foremost thinkers widely discussed in this regard include Gandhi, Tagore, Ambedkar, Phule and J Krishnamurti who were, in turn, informed by varied metaphysical frameworks in subtle or explicit ways (Baniwal & Sharma, 2020). These intersections between pre-modern and modern thinking resulted in the articulation of several contextually specific problems peculiar to the Indian sub-continent.

In the following sections, I first address the problems of embodied education in India by looking at the social process of learning and the purpose of the body in learning. I then explore the relationship between the body and the mind within various metaphysical frameworks, thereby articulating the learner in terms of a body-mind complex. The contemporary conceptualisation of the body, although diverse, is also deeply troubled. The troubled body in the form of the suffering, labouring and discriminated condition of a mere body—separated from the mind—is seen as a violation of the otherwise integrated body-mind ideal. When the capacity to affirm the body as a sensing, thinking, acting body is in the focus, which, once defined and recognised, can enable the pursuit of ethical ideals for the collective 'social'[2] through the experience of education; this does not foremost amounts to an education promising a good life to particular educated learners. The focus is instead on the obligation of education towards the weakest and most vulnerable learner whose integrity as a sensing, thinking and acting body is at stake—a body that has been consistently violated at the cost of education and one that education cannot afford to ignore if it must stay true to its intended purpose. These are living conditions of the lower castes (e.g. Shudras) in the hierarchy of the Indian caste system with quite hard job duties. I am interested in that social characteristic of non-substitutable and unique difference in learners that education often fails to address and yet is currently most required to address in the context of a very disparate nature of 'socials' in India. Before we address the ethical challenge of a person's unsafe social situation, it is helpful to understand the necessary conditions that enable learning.

---

[2] I employ the term 'social' as used by Guru and Sarukkai (2019) to refer to distinct collectives that emerge through various processes in society.

1   The Social Process of Learning

What happens when learning occurs? If we look at the ample literature on the teaching techniques, methodologies and tools employed in various educational practices, it is clear that there should be a focus on the process of learning and its relationship with the human body. Does the body have anything to do with the process of learning? What does it mean to conceptualize learning in terms of place? More fundamentally, is the mind synonymous with the body? Let us address these questions by first tackling certain foundational conditions, given by society and intended by learners with which education operates.

The first condition is that of difference or radical plurality, that is the inevitability of difference in each learner in the classroom space. In short, the condition of difference makes it imperative for the people in the learning environment to recognise each learner as unique, particular and distinct from the other. This means that the process of learning is an attempt at making certain kinds of universals possible from these particularities that come together in the classroom or any learning environment. The second condition is the potential for transformation, that is learning presupposes transformation and a possibility of change, growth and movement. This transformation, promised by learning, is not possible without a clear intention or purpose of learning. An articulation of the intention will help one understand what exactly does the process of learning do to the learner? Keeping in mind these necessary conditions of learning, I posit further two essential characteristic conditions without which learning cannot take place: one, that we cannot learn without the presence of others; and two, that we cannot learn if we do not know why it is that we must learn something, that is learning must have a purpose.

A possible objection to the first essential condition—the necessity of the presence of others—may be posed by auto-didacticism, wherein one claims to learn all by oneself. However, this objection is quickly defendable in terms of relationality of the learner, suggesting that the auto-didact is inherently dependent on various others as 'sources' of learning and therefore cannot claim to be able to learn in isolation. Auto-didacts often create their own systems of learning and evaluation from these network of recognised sources. In other words, auto-didacticism is only possible through an alteration of the self as multiple learners. This possibility of learning as an auto-didact can be found in the figure of Ekalavya in the *Mahabharata*, who, having been denied formal training in archery from the teacher Droṇa because of his caste, teaches himself archery by adopting the image of Droṇā as his teacher (Sarukkai, 2018). In this context, Sarukkai (2018) argues that the non-substitutability of the learning subject implies that the only way in which Ekalavya could have learnt anything is by becoming his own teacher and adopting a symbolic image of Droṇā, thereby finding agency of learning in the possibility of becoming an alterity or another self.

A possible objection to the second essential condition, the purposefulness of learning, may come from those who argue for 'learning for the sake of learning'.[3] In the age of innumerable online courses and degrees on offer at the click of a button, 'learning for the sake of learning' is a trend where knowledge is consumed much like in the entertainment industry—one shops around, signs up for a course, one learns something new and then one moves on. This learning, however, does little to transform us in any essential way. By this, I mean that learning which has no intended purpose and that is really not put into empirical practice or application, does little to contribute to an education that seeks to transform us as human beings. Such a lack of purposefulness finds addressal in the educational philosophy of Gandhi where vocation, practice and action play as big a role in the process of an education as textual and verbal knowledge. A purposefulness of learning in order to engage with the world, therefore, necessarily implies giving importance to theories of action and ways of acting in the world. A practice- or application-oriented education is one that uses these approaches as educational methodology. The irony of purposefulness in learning is that the purpose is often conflated with being job-oriented, which defeats the purpose of engaging with learning as a process rather than a commodity, as is often the case in contemporary contexts.

As is often seen across student population in India, learning is geared towards a pre-determined, mostly vocational purpose. Some commonplace examples in India include the straightjacketing of education tracks into disciplines such as engineering, medicine, banking, corporate sectors and so on. The irony of such an approach is that it becomes an instrumentalisation of education, furthering existing hierarchies in the social space. For example, students in India who are considered 'bright' often end up taking science-based courses whereas those deemed 'average' are often implicitly compelled to take up arts-based or humanities-based courses, both determined by a quantitative marking system that does not take any account of differences in the subjectivity of the learners. These strange systems of socially pervasive norms have been so deeply entrenched in the post-colonial Indian socials that

---

[3] See Bowden and Marton (1998) for an account of the shift in focus in pedagogical vocabulary from teaching and knowledge transmission towards learning and learning environments in education.

a break from these very norms is often considered a radical act, instead of being standard practice.

In response to this problem, various alternative schooling models were set up during Indian renaissance in the 19th century (Mehrotra, 2007; Baniwal & Sharma, 2020). Mehrotra (2007, p. 26) outlines certain common characteristics of the educational commitments of alternative schools in India. These include a focus on overall development of the human being, focussing on the relevance of education, ecological and aesthetic awareness in education, acquiring life skills and particularly paying attention to the needs of learners with different needs. Thus, experiential learning and an emphasis on acquiring creative skills are brought back into focus in these alternative schools. While current trends show a substantial change in students' interests and choices, these changes occur only in very specific niche classes and sections of society that are not representative of the plurality of the Indian social.

The curatorial turn in education signals a shift in focus of education from simply being a business of knowing to enabling experiences of education (Ruitenberg, 2015). This also posits the educator as one who caters and cares for the interest, abilities and possibilities of the learners, thereby being need-based and inherently interested in addressing the distinct differences and particular natures of the learners—something that is gaining currency in contemporary teaching vocabulary as the "student-centric" approach (McKinnon & Bacon, 2015). Acknowledging that student-centrism is a necessary condition and not an added asset of education, learning as a social process cannot ignore the body[4] alongside the mind as an integral constituent of the learning environment. Further, given that learning is dependent on an experiential transformation, it can occur only as an embodied process. This necessary relation between the body and the process of learning has been highlighted by several modern educational philosophers in India, informed by various metaphysical conceptual frameworks.

The history of education in the South Asian context is deeply entwined with the education of philosophy and various practices of thinking at large. This implies that all those who took an active interest in the practices of thinking were also deeply invested in educating others as part of their practice (Baindur, 2020). Given that philosophy as a practice is concerned with the nature of knowing about the world and is in pursuit of understanding the way

---

[4] I use the mere word 'body' in this context to refer to the corporeal, living, breathing, physical body of us as human beings which is defined by its subjective experiences and has the capacity to have knowledge. The mere body is distinct from the 'body-mind' as used further in the chapter, which is used as a complex concept to refer to the body that senses, thinks and acts.

things are, the purposes of learning often implicitly have overlaps with purposes of philosophies.

In the South Asian context, we can draw instances of purposefulness from various socio-historic trajectories. Philosophical traditions, be it the Vedic, Upanishadic, the 'Darsanas' or the Buddhist or Jaina, have clearly articulated soteriological goals. The ensuing/desired liberation or emancipation was enabled by the process of an education aimed towards enlightenment. While enlightenment also played a key role in post Copernican Europe, bringing about a general cultural renaissance, it is important to note that these two enlightenments were distinctly different in their contextual histories and philosophical presuppositions, each being informed by their own situated metaphysical frameworks (Nola, 2018). This is especially important to note in the context of India's colonial past and its heritage which is still present today.

The education bills established by the British in India were drafted in the hope of being a means for their own colonial ends. One such example is the Education Bill of 1835 articulated by Thomas Macaulay. The bill reflects the colonial interest in 'civilising' the 'natives' through an active education in not just "the poetry of Milton, the metaphysics of Locke, and the physics of Newton" but also English as a language citing that "the dialects commonly spoken among the natives of this part of India contain neither literary nor scientific information, and are moreover so poor and rude that, until they are enriched from some other quarter, it will not be easy to translate any valuable work into them" (Macaulay, 1835).[5] However, it is not just this colonialism that has pervaded the learning landscape in India. There has always also been a longstanding form of 'internal colonialism', given the social inheritance of inequality in the form of caste and gender, informed by the modern concept of class.[6] This in turn translates into subtle implicit biases that make education in India often a privilege as opposed to a necessity, even today. This form of internal colonialism is tougher to outgrow unless actively and consistently addressed over a long and consistent period of time by both government and social groups.

This complex entanglement between practices of thinking, metaphysical determination upon purposes of learning, effects of colonialism and the

---

[5] The colonial mission of educating the colonised natives was directly politically motivated with a goal of establishing power. "We must at present do our best to form a class who may be interpreters between us and the millions whom we govern—a class of persons Indian in blood and colour, but English in tastes, in opinions, in morals and in intellect" (Macaulay, 1835). The use of education as an instrumental political device, motivated by intentions that were far from caring in nature, has been recognised, challenged and subverted in the years to come through the innumerable social reformers and educationists that appeared in the small towns as well as big cities of the nation and continue to do so in contemporary times.

[6] See Pinderhughes (2011) for a recent reconceptualisation of internal colonialism.

experience of learning that systems of education offer to its learners are foundationally pinned upon the ways in which the immanent and the transcendent converge in the existence of the learner, his/her/their body and minds. The existence of the learner and education's ethics of engagement with the learner therefore must first be understood through various metaphysical perspectives that implicitly or explicitly have a role to play in how the body is recognised within the learning environment. In the following section, I articulate various metaphysical perspectives on the relationship between the mind and the body in order to make possible the ethical body of the learners in any learning environment.

2   The Body and the Learning Environment: Some Metaphysical Perspectives

One major point of distinction between the metaphysical frameworks from South Asia and Europe is the relationship between the mind and the body. The various ways in which the mind and the body are conceptualised within different paradigms point towards the complex centrality of the body in the discussion of learning. The mind is inherently entangled with the body, therefore learning is embodied. Furthermore, as some contemporary thinkers point out, the mind-body problem appears to have been resolved to a considerable extent with respect to its Cartesian bifurcation (Stoljar, 2017). Therefore, it is not in the restitution of the body in discourses on education but in our understanding of the various imaginations of the embodied mind that we must learn about learning processes as geared towards distinct experiences. This complex of mind and body, henceforth addressed as the 'body-mind',[7] then becomes the foundation for us to imagine an ethical body as the human learning subject and offers a way towards understanding learning as an ethical experience.

There are several stakes involved in scholarship on the body in its attempt to bring the body into the discursive space. The stakes involved include gender, race, caste, class, 'dis'abilities and so on—all of them deeply contingent on the physical body. Several feminist and socio-political theorists like Ásta (2018), Das (2015), Blackman (2008), Westley (2008), Damasio (1999),

---

[7] Here I refer to the body-mind as a distinct conceptual entity that attributes the mind's capacities to the body as much as it establishes the mind as experientially embodied. This is similar to the processual manner in which Holdrege (1998, p. 347, p. 358) refers to the 'body-mind complex' in the context of transcendence at work within soteriological philosophies but is distinctly different in the context of its usage, which is very much immanent and bound by this world.

Synnott (1993) and Scarry (1985) have theorised the body and its sociality with respect to race and gender as well as its afflictions and crises. In the Indian context, there is a large amount of sociological literature on the role of the body as a political provocateur. However, within Indian conceptualisation, the task becomes slightly complicated when it comes to philosophical thinking on the body, given the complicated syncretic history of India, whereby contemporary theories of the body consider it as a cultural concept while pre-modern theories of the body are radically deterministic.

However, what does metaphysics have to do with the body, if at all? It is necessary for this question to be understood as it is closely linked with the possibility of change and transformation. In other words, would any concept of change ever be possible without the presence of the body? Here I presuppose a radically empiricist idea of knowledge and experience as entangled, whereby it would be impossible to talk in purely epistemological or ontological terms. This lineage of the mind as an integral constitution of what one calls the body takes up various trajectories in different pre-modern metaphysical systems in South Asia.[8]

Some philosophers of the Nyaya-Vaiśeṣika tradition, for instance, consider the mind to be a material entity like an instrument that senses. Thus the presupposition that it is only the body that senses and the mind that reasons is already challenged through this conception. Similarly, the Upanishads considered the human being as a composite of psychological and physical elements, whereby there was an attempt to look at the "agent of normal phenomenal experience" as distinct from "the transcendental" (Laine, 1998). Holdrege (1998, p. 369) argues that the body as a concept within the philosophies of the "Hindu" religion can be either seen as an 'integral body' taking up forms of either "the divine body[9], the cosmos body, the social body and the human body", or a "processual body" taking the form of "the ritual body, the ascetic body, the purity (sic) body, the devotional body, the Tantric body and so on". Each of these taxonomies of bodies are intended to be ways in which the body becomes the ontological location of creation of systems, order or practices that have various purposes. For instance, the body in the Upanishadic framework is ascetic and a teleological object of liberation (Holdrege, 1998, pp. 357–363).

All these conceptualisations bring into the picture the necessary relation between the concept of the self with the body-mind. The concept of the self

---

[8] See Michaels and Wulf (2013) for an account of perspectives on the role of sense across South Asian philosophical traditions.

[9] See Colas (2007) for more on the imagination of the divine body in Sanskritic logical traditions.

as entwined within the body and the mind is conceptualised differently in Buddhist metaphysics. In Buddhist metaphysics, for instance, the idea of the self is conventional but not essential as encompassed in the concept of the *anātman* (which loosely can be translated the theory of no-self [10]), and therefore, the nature of experience is understood as a causal complex of mental and physical events playing out in relation to each other. Thus, the dualism that we see in these schools of thought is not the Cartesian duality of mind as distinct from the body but the dualism in the kinds of experiences that are registered by the body-mind as a complex (Baindur, 2015b; Gupta, 2009; Flood, 2006; Holdrege, 1998; Griffiths, 1986).

The monistic metaphysical schools imagine the body-mind complex with a particular teleological commitment towards a unification of the mind and body wherein the subject-object distinction collapses. The Sānkhya-Yoga and the Advaita schools imagine the body as kind of 'technology' committed to the well-being of the body-mind through the discourses on practices of Yoga and its associated systems of healing like Āyurveda (Brennen, 2002). Within this framework, the mind and the body are not dichotomous, but co-constitutive (Larson & Bhattacharya, 1987).[11]

For instance, in the Āyurvedic metaphysical system the onus of understanding the body in relation to the world comes from a particular way of looking at the body, whereby the presupposition is that each body is uniquely constituted and thereby it is the body's constitution that is understood in order to determine the nature of 'dis'-ease caused to the body. The threefold categorisation of the human body into 'vāta', 'pitta', 'kapha' bodies largely reflects an intention of imagining the body through certain universal properties. Essential to these systems of categorisation is the understanding that the human living body is defined by its capacity to sense, think and act. The systematic extrapolation of these categories into the ways in which they respond to the environment and conditions around the body points to very different ways in which the concept of disease, for instance, is looked at in comparison to modern medicine. Disease is not looked at as an objective state of discomfort symptomatic to the generic body but a specific case of imbalance between the relation between the body and its environment (Baindur, 2015a; Brennen, 2002; Zimmerman, 1987). In this framework, it is not the state of disease that is targeted for cure but the general condition of the body—thereby putting the onus of well-being on the sensing, thinking, acting body.

---

[10] This no-self theory does not imply the absence of self but is a theory that is not committed to a permanent unchanging concept of a singular self.

[11] I am grateful to Meera Baindur for her scholarly inputs on this subject.

Two overarching presuppositions can be extracted from such an attempt at determining the body and its relation to its environment within the framework of Yoga—first, that the body is deeply dictated by the metaphysical constructs governing its conceptualisation; and second, that the body and the mind are necessarily connected as a complex system. Given these two presuppositions, we see how the question of education must necessarily take into account metaphysical predeterminations often implicitly influencing the body-minds in any learning environment.

The conditions for learning as outlined in the previous section, requiring the presence of others and an intention to learn, present before us the sensitive task of understanding what makes for a good education. In the Indian context, recent work on pedagogical methods reflects an active interest in understanding how this metaphysical presupposition of the body-mind as a complex influences the kinds of learning traditions that evolved in the South Asian region. These include not just the Sanskritic and the Buddhist, Jaina, Āyurveda traditions as mentioned above but also music, theatre, subaltern performative traditions, tribal education cultures, as well as contemporary education thinkers including Gandhi, Ambedkar, Vivekananda, Tagore, Sri Aurobindo, J. Krishnamurti, Phule and many more who left behind legacies of educational institutions (Sarukkai & Akshara, 2020).

Baindur (2020) highlights how learning in the Vedic traditions took twofold forms where the learner was expected to learn through repetition of whatever the teacher taught 'him', and secondly the learner was expected to understand the meaning of the teaching. Dialogue played an important role in the process of learning. Similarly, residential schooling was the norm, with the student expected to imbibe education not merely as accumulated knowledge but through internalised lived everyday experience. Vedic educational systems were thus implicitly informed by the Vedic metaphysics. This included a particular conception of society as being one comprised of immutable caste hierarchies. The redundant elements of Vedic rituals were challenged by Buddhists by negating the notion of an essential self, logically discarding caste as a concept and thereby proposing a conception of a society that is made up of 'conventional' social bodies that are relational in nature. The Buddhist 'sangha' became the site of collective learning just like the 'gurukul' was the site of experiential learning in the Sanskritic traditions. Historically, the major work that Buddhist metaphysics did in its response to Vedic metaphysics was to dismantle the conceptual basis of caste,[12] thereby influencing the learning environment very differently.

---

[12] See Guru and Sarukkai (2019) for a compelling argument on the bearing of metaphysics on caste.

While these concerns belonged to the pre-modern social in India, the reason I am invoking these here is to point out how the metaphysics percolates over time and implicitly dictates the foundational social fabric of modern-day learning environments in India. For instance, the significance of metaphysics in self-recognition is reflected by Ambedkar when he called for all Dalits to adopt Buddhism in an attempt to annihilate their Vedic inheritance of caste as a concept. In other words, the learning body, when seen in the contemporary Indian context, ridden by such binding presuppositions and ontological determinations, is deeply conflicted. Its heritage dictates the access and experience of education far beyond the ideals of a promised ethical experience of education, further complicated by colonial inheritances.

The body of the learner in contemporary India is far from being an enabled body-mind. With the general decolonial turn (Maldonado-Torres, 2011) taking sway across the globe, the coloniality power matrix of exploitation of people by applying ideas like that of center and periphery and the related body-politics shall be overcome, this is the aim of decolonial education. Then, the need for an account of the ways in which the body-mind is troubled by its metaphysical inheritances is necessary in order to understand the obligation of education to the body in the Indian context. Thus, instead of considering embodiment as some form of distinct educational practice, I want to focus my attention on the need to reclaim the place of the body-mind and bring it back into the learning space by outlining the following three ways in which the body has been displaced from the learning space through contextual forces. I am not concerned here with the training of the body in performative and body-centric education but with mainstream learning environments where the role of the body is often subordinated to the potentials of the mind as well as subject to implicit violations, thereby making the experience of secular contemporary education very disembodied and fragmented and often a futile experience.

3 The Body in Trouble: The Suffering Body, The Labouring Body, The Discriminated Body

The idea of education has been at the heart of several modern and contemporary philosophers in India, especially through India's independence and renaissance. They were not just educationists, but also social reformers, poets, philosophers and political leaders. The emphasis of their philosophies of education addressed different concerns and pushed towards different urgencies and crises in education including the crises of the body and its presence in the learning environment.[13] The concept of the body-mind in its threefold articulation as a sensing, thinking and acting entity as idealised in the conceptualisation of the pre-modern metaphysical systems mentioned above, fails to translate into the modern social. Instead, the contemporary socials have succeeded more in deteriorating and diminishing the body-mind of the learner, turning it into a suffering, labouring and discriminated body. In other words, the irony of the learning environments is that they do little to address the violence of certain living conditions.

J. Krishnamurti's philosophy of alternative schooling conceptualises the learner as a sensing, feeling body that needs an education not to conform to societal constructs but to set the "mind" free. He gives precedence to processes of perception, observation and paying attention to the world as central to ways of educating oneself (Krishnamurti, 1974, p. 10). Education, according to Krishnamurti, is to "learn never to accept anything which you yourself do not see clearly, never to repeat what another has said" (Krishnamurti, 1974, p. 11). According to Krishnamurti, an education of the mind is geared towards freedom from the known, which comes about through the process of understanding the known (Krishnamurti, 1975). Krishnamurti's keenness on an aesthetically motivated education reflects the presupposition of the learning body-mind as a sensing body.

The attempt to actively encourage this sensing body despite its pre-given social determination also reflects his understanding of how the body, when it enters the learning environment, is already suffering—a condition which the self might not recognise until it learns about it. In a conversation with the physicist David Bohm on the question of psychological conflict, Krishnamurti wonders whether the root of such suffering stems from the recognition that while the brain can grasp physical time, the mind has a very unpredictable relationship with time: "the mind not being of time, and the brain being of time—is that the origin of conflict?" (Krishnamurti & Bohm, 2014, p. 21). Such a view reflects a dualist understanding of the experiences of the body-mind where the self senses the world physically through embodied cognition, while also being guided by free imagination through a mental grasp of experience. Thus, the suffering body is, in its unlearning, unmediated and metaphysically pre-determined state, unable to recognise, perceive or even

---

[13] In the fields of scientific and socio-scientific education, systematic efforts in addressing innovative methods of teaching and 'epistemic practices' only highlight the large gaps and incongruences that need to be addressed between lived experience of education as compared to education as knowledge-transaction. For more see Kelly and Licona (2018).

understand that it is in fact suffering. It is the task of education, as seen by Krishnamurti, to re-instate this suffering, i.e. the unmindful body so that it can recognise its condition and come to understand that it is in fact suffering in order to reclaim its body-mindfulness.

Gandhi's philosophy of education, on the other hand, is influenced by Thoreau, Rousseau and Tolstoy and their tenets of naturalist education (Kaikini, 2019). Gandhi's educational commitment is towards practical utilitarianism, laying emphasis on vocation-based learning, or learning by doing, aimed towards self-sustenance that can ultimately enable or empower self-rule (in Hindi 'swaraj'). However, Kaikini (2019, p. 329) observes certain shortcomings in this utilitarian system which placed emphasis on job-oriented learning by pointing out that this experiment was a failure given that schools risked turning into production units, a view acknowledged by Zakir Hussain of the Wardha Education Plan. In addition, Gandhi's 'Nai Tālim' philosophy of education is highly pragmatic where the only way out of colonial dependence was by finding ways to generate one's own revenue and making primary education self-reliant. This came with its own risks, namely possible exploitation of the students by the teacher and becoming an opportunity for vested interests by economic groups in the profits generated by the school. Thus, while Gandhi's philosophy of education is veered overall towards economy, of time and resources, being pragmatic in approach and aimed at "character building and discipline", it turned out to be a failure in practice, as it also harboured the risk of deepening the already pre-determined labouring body's crises by making it harder to emancipate from labour (Kaikini, 2019, p. 335).

This privilege that betrayed Gandhi's philosophy of education was countered by Ambedkar's philosophy of education that has as an educational ideal a promising balance of modernity and progress as well as 'presence' in the form of embodiment, thus making education accessible to the caste-oppressed labouring body who could then hope to emancipate themselves from the lifelong yoke of a caste-dictated life of labour as well as imagine learning as a collective social process where one educates oneself not just for one's own betterment but for the betterment of others (Valeskar, 2012). Thus the labouring body is the second degree diminished form of the reasoning body, one that cannot even hope to sense, let alone think. This desensitised, unreasoning body becomes the discriminated body that continues to bear the brunt of restricting socials.

The crisis of the thinking body is when it becomes pre-determined into the kinds of work it is 'allowed' to do, a case in point being that of the inheritance of the caste social. The caste social categorises bodies in a manner that relegates the labouring body to the lowest of social orders and thereby farthest from any access to an egalitarian experience of education, if at all (Guru & Sarukkai, 2012). This powerful metaphysical predetermination of the learning body that decides who is eligible to be educated at all and who is not, foregrounds a crater in the social fabric of modern-day India. The champions of a reformist vision that strived to address the caste-ridden cause in education like Ambedkar, therefore, had a distinct vision of educating in order to agitate and bring about social change.

This discrimination has been deeply ingrained in a manner that cannot be directly addressed through certain standardised teaching methods. Instead, there is a need for a complex persistent process of education that is geared towards re-instatement of the completely perceptive body that has rid itself of its discriminatory violence. This violence and discrimination has been carried by Dalit, women, queer communities over generations, resulting in a pinning down of the discriminated self to the sensual body, that is often reduced to the unthinking, unreasoning, grossly explicit body, pushing the mind component of these into oblivion. This reduced body directly affects the ability to be open to and imbibe experiences of learning that help the re-instatement of the body-mind.

Several nineteenth-century social reformers such as Rammohan Roy, Dayanand Saraswati, Pandita Ramabai, Narayan Guru, Iqbal, Periyar and many other leaders, activists and political thinkers of the freedom movement drew inspiration from canonical as well as indigenous philosophical traditions (Baniwal & Sharma, 2020). It is also significant to note that several women reformers played an active role in education reforms towards equality of access and enabling the presence of e.g. the female learner in the classroom space. Basu (2005, p. 184) observes that surveys of indigenous education in Governments of Bombay, Madras and Bengal presidencies in 1820s and 1830s showed a total absence of girl students from the village schools and schools of higher education. These figures, mostly for the lack of adequate records or documentation, are slowly coming to the fore with active archival and documentation work.[14]

Amongst these nineteenth-century reformers were Savitribai Phule and her husband Jyotirao Phule who extensively championed the cause of such gross violence done to the discriminated body in education. The Phules instituted dedicated schools for female students, and for the lower caste community, namely the Mahars and the Mangs, in response to the lack of 'indigenous schools' in and around Poona in West India (Deshpande, 2016, p. 102). An

---

[14] See Ray (2005).

avid advocate for equal rights for the oppressed, Phule's philosophy of education was actively geared towards bringing about radical change in the system by engaging in dialogue with the Government as well as creating schools in order to address the gross inadequacies of the existing educational mandate in colonial India.

In a memorial addressed to the Education Commission dated 19 October 1882, Phule argues that the Government's education was merely patronising a "virtual high class education" that was meant to cater only to the upper classes and which resulted in a "monopoly of all the higher offices under them by Brahmins" (Deshpande, 2016, p. 104). He further criticises the lack of attention paid to adequate primary education for the masses, urging that there be

> schools for the Shudras in every village; but away with all the Brahmin schoolmasters! The Shudras are the life and the sinews of the country, and it is to them alone and not to the Brahmins, that Government must ever look to tide over their difficulties, financial as well as political. (Deshpande, 2016, p. 105)

In another conversation, Phule draws out a critique of the Vedic monopoly over education from within the system as follows:

> If God had created the Vedic scriptures for the liberation of entire mankind, the 'bhat' brahmans would not have prohibited the 'shudras' and the 'atishudras' from studying the Vedas. The 'bhat' brahmans have thus violated God's commandment and are not the 'shudras' and the 'atishudras' suffering for that? (Deshpande, 2016, p. 188)

Phule poignantly traces the suffering of the discriminated body of the 'shudra' to the basic lack of education in his prologue to *Shetkaryacha Asuud* (1883) (Cultivator's Whipcord):

> Without knowledge, intelligence was lost, without intelligence morality was lost and without morality was lost all dynamism! Without dynamism money was lost and without money the 'shudras' sank. All this misery was caused by the lack of knowledge. (Deshpande, 2016, p. 117)

Phule's sharp thrust is towards a philosophy of education that empowers and enables the learner to be an active citizen of the State, who is able to partake of all his/her rights and to be able to live a life of dignity as an equal.

The philosophies of education discussed above either challenge the pre-given metaphysics marking the body or re-enforce a different kind of metaphysics binding it. Given this deeper relationship between metaphysics and the body and the recognition of the various ways in which we have seen the body in crisis in the context of Indian education, as a suffering, labouring and discriminated body, the foundation of a just education is imaginable only when we make possible an ethical recognition of the body-mind in the learning environment.

4 Education's Obligation to the Body

Having thus far seen how various metaphysical systems a direct bearing upon the perception and constitution of the body-mind within the learning environment have, it is clear that the task for contemporary education is to understand its obligation towards the body and more specifically towards restoring and re-enforcing the body-mind of the learning subjects, in a way that instils and fosters their abilities to sense, think and act in the world.

Speaking about the social context of intellectual hierarchies, Guru and Sarukkai (2012, p. 14) observe that the capacity of knowledge making and reflection—a privilege historically denied to the Dalit community—can be cultivated only in the right material condition motivated by the possibility of innovation and imagination. The Dalit self, historically, was denied the possibility of becoming a body-mind and instead consistently relegated to becoming a mere labouring body that had no freedom to think. Therefore, they argue that a certain kind of freedom from context was essential, particularly for the labouring body, in order to become a thinking body-mind. This was also recognised by Ambedkar who himself took time and detached himself from his constraining working-class context to learn abroad. Moving away from the empirical to the theoretical, according to Guru and Sarukkai (2012, p. 24), is a 'social necessity', as it reverses "the orientalism that treats Dalits, tribals, and the OBCs as the inferior empirical self" in a move towards resisting 'museumising' the Dalit and tribal communities as mere exotic bodies. Thus, a mediated reflective space and time offered to the labouring body, in the form of resources to simply be in order to resuscitate the body-mind, is an essential obligation of education to restore the labouring body into a thinking body-mind.

Similarly, the woman's body in the India has a longstanding history of always being subject to this spectrum of oppression—from being museumised into a deity figure (e.g. imagining the Indian nation as a mother—'bharatmāta'[15]) to being denigrated as a suffering body confined to the space of the household, thereby becoming a provocation to several women saints, philosophers and wandering 'Bhakti' poets[16] be it Akkamahadevi, Lal Ded or Avaiyyar who broke this mould in order to reclaim their sensing and thinking body-mind. Thus, in the absence of a formal learning environment that could enable this restoration, forms of art, singing, dancing, writing or simply indulging in leisure became radical learning environments for the suffering body to resuscitate itself into a sensing body-mind.

The complex history of caste as a pervasive kind of social particular to India makes the discriminated body the most prevalent kind of troubled body that desires to be restored through education. This discrimination occurs at the fundamental level of the self and its conceptualisation. The self or the individual in the Indian social, as argued by Guru and Sarukkai (2019), is a 'we-self' or a collective self—one which sociological and philosophical theories concerning the individual from Euro-American contexts fail to address in the Indian context. This discriminated self, informed by the metaphysical givenness of caste through certain 'authorless agencies', suffers from a loss of community and identity as well as from a loss of basic social recognition. The discriminated self in formal learning environments often gets marked by social signs like caste-specific surnames, archetyping the body based on colour, odour, dialect and so on (Guru & Sarukkai, 2019, p. 117). These metaphysically sanctioned violations create a deep sense of internalised humiliation in the learner, who, having internalised the discrimination, then assimilates the experience of education as a mere fossilising of his or her violated self as a discriminated body.[17] An example of this can be found in the violations faced by a young Ambedkar in his school where he faced blatant discrimination as an untouchable (Ambedkar, 1993). This discriminated body, in a learning environment, is marked by a lack of recognition and acknowledgement, a forced absence of the body that is further ensured by the overpowering learning environment.

Presence, therefore, becomes very significant for the discriminated body that aspires to a sense of restoration to being, acting and experiencing in a shared learning space with other body-minds. In other words, the obligation of education towards the discriminated body is to ensure and enable its presence and actively resist its erasure through subconscious or internalised social

---

[15] See Cheema, Zainab (2012) for a critique of the anthropomorphising of the Indian nation.

[16] See Prentiss (1999) for an account of embodiment in Bhakti traditions.

[17] See Guru (2009).

behaviour that pervades learning environments. This shared presencing, therefore, in the spirit of what Guru and Sarukkai (2019) call as 'maitri' makes it possible to recognise the subjects as acting, experiencing body-mind selves that, through sensing, thinking and acting in relation to each other, learn from each other and for each other, making the experience of education first and foremost an ethical experience.

5   Towards an Ethical Experience of Education

In this chapter, I have first articulated the conceptualisation of the body within various metaphysical traditions in India. I then looked at the various complications that, within any learning environment, make these ontologies of the body troubled, be it suffering, labouring or discriminated. The obligation of learning environments is then to work on the process of addressing these differences in a way that restores the learner's embodied constitution as a sensing, thinking and also acting body-mind. Various educationists who have thought about education in the Indian context have asserted the necessity of embodied experience in education while also addressing various problems with the kind of misplaced idealism pervading the education system that was transplanted to India during colonisation. This does not imply that the education system that preceded the period of colonisation which included residential and collective learning systems like the 'gurukul' or the 'sangha' did not have their own problems in terms of caste- or gender-based 'un'recognition of certain bodies.

The models of education proposed by the educational reformists such as Krishnamurti, Ambedkar, Gandhi and Phule strived to generate new syncretic models that addressed the problems, at both systemic social levels and individual levels. While they all had various motivations and commitments in their educational philosophies, what is evident is that the double diminution of the body-mind—firstly into a mere disembodied mind, and second into a mere suffering, labouring or discriminated body—makes the very foundation of the process of education morally dispensable. If education has to be indispensable to human life, then it implies that it cannot be party to prolonging such reductions of the body.

Further, the conceptualisation of the self in relation to the body-mind as a relational complex, thinking, sensing and acting in this world, in the South Asian context, does not necessarily correspond to the singular concept of the self within the Cartesian context.[18] Therefore, the self as an ethical relational

---

[18] For more on the notion of the 'we-self', see Sarukkai and Guru (2019).

complex must necessarily be addressed as an embodied sensing, thinking and acting body-mind. There is need to articulate and imagine the notion of the self and its relation to embodiment, which I have not addressed in this chapter but merits attention. In this chapter, I have focused only the question of the mind and its relation to embodiment and the place of the body-mind in learning environments. The question that remains to be taken up for further research from this argument is around the relationship between the self, the mind and the body and how learning environments impact the self. The first step in this regard is the articulation of the body and the mind in such environments. It is only when the presuppositions of the body-mind are completely acknowledged, theorised, realised and cared for as a matter of principle within philosophies of education that education can strive to become an ethical experience.

Acknowledgements: I would like to thank Christoph Wulf, Meera Baindur, Sundar Sarukkai, Jayant Kaikini, Vivek Radhakrishnan, Ritwik Kaikini and Rakshi Rath for their valuable insights and discussions that enriched the process of writing this chapter.

References

Ambedkar, B. R. (1993 [1936]). Waiting for a Visa. In V. Moon (Ed.), *Dr. Babasaheb Ambedkar: Writings and Speeches, Vol. 12, Part I* (pp. 661–691). Education Department, Government of Maharashtra. http://www.columbia.edu/itc/mealac/pritchett/00ambedkar/txt_ambedkar_waiting.html

Ásta. (2018). *Categories We Live By: The Construction of Sex, Gender, Race, and Other Social Categories*. Oxford University Press.

Baindur, M. (2015a). *Nature in Indian Philosophy and Cultural Traditions*. Sophia Studies in Cross-cultural Philosophy of Traditions and Cultures. Springer.

Baindur, M. (2015b). Nature, Body and Woman. An Indian Perspective on Value Dualisms. In *Science and Narratives of Nature* (pp. 33–55). Routledge.

Baindur, M. (2020). Philosophical Education in Traditional and Buddhist Schools of Thought in South Asia. In P. M. Sarangapani & R. Pappu (Eds.), *Handbook of Education Systems in South Asia, Global Education Systems*. Springer. https://doi.org/10.1007/978-981-13-3309-5_8-1

Baniwal, V., & Sharma, R. (2020). South Asian Education Thinkers. In P. M. Sarangapani & R. Pappu (Eds.), *Handbook of Education Systems in South Asia. Global Education Systems*. Springer. https://doi.org/10.1007/978-981-13-3309-5_78-1

Basu, A. (2005). A Century and a Half's Journey: Women's Education in India, 1850s to 2000. In B. Ray (Ed.), *Women of India: Colonial and Post-Colonial Period* (pp. 183–207). Project of History of Indian Science, Philosophy and Culture Centre for Studies in Civilizations.

Blackman, L. (2008). *The Body. The Key Concepts*. Berg.

Bowden, J. A., & Marton, F. (1998). *The University of Learning*. Psychology Press.

Brennen, A. (2002). Asian traditions of Knowledge: The Disputed Questions of Science, Nature and Ecology. *Studies in History and Philosophy of Biological and Biomedical Sciences, 33*, 567–581.

Cheema, Z. (2012). Picturing the Nation: The Visual Logic and Discontents of India's Nationalism. *Art History, 35*, 174–178. https://doi.org/10.1111/j.1467-8365.2011.00874.x

Colas, G. (2007). God's Body: Epistemic and Ritual Conceptions from Sanskrit Texts of Logic. *Paragrana, 16*(2), 53–63. https://doi.org/10.1524/para.2009.0004

Damasio, A. R. (1999). *The Feeling of What Happens: Body and Emotion in the Making of Consciousness*. Houghton Mifflin Harcourt.

Das, V. (2015). *Affliction. Health, Disease, Poverty*. Fordham University Press.

Deshpande, G. P. (Ed.). (2016). *Selected Writings of Jotirao Phule*. LeftWord Books.

Flood, G. (2006). *The Tantric Body. The Secret Tradition of Hindu Religion*. Taurus.

Griffiths, P. J. (1986). *On Being Mindless. Buddhist Meditation and the Mind-Body Problem*. Indological and Oriental Publishers.

Gupta, B. (2009). *Reason and Experience in Indian Philosophy*. Indian Council of Philosophical Research.

Guru, G. (2009). *Humiliation*. Oxford University Press.

Guru, G., & Sarukkai, S. (2012). *The Cracked Mirror. An Indian Debate on Experience and Theory*. Oxford University Press.

Guru, G., & Sarukkai, S. (2019). *Experience, Caste and the Everyday Social*. Oxford University Press.

Holdrege, B. A. (1998). Body Connections: Hindu Discourses of the Body and the Study of Religion. *International Journal of Hindu Studies, 2*(3), 341–386.

Kaikini, G. (2019). Gandhiji: Language and Education. In G. N. Devy & C. N. Ramachandran (Eds.), *Mahatma Gandhi in Kannada Literature. Shifting Perspectives* (pp. 327–337). Sapna Book House. Original in Kannada as Kaikini, G. (1970). Gandhiji: Bhashe Mattu Shikshana. In *Gandhi Tatwa Vishleshane*. Karnataka University (pp.1–28).

Kelly, G. J., & Licona, P. (2018). Epistemic Practices and Science Education. In M. R. Matthews (Ed.), *History, Philosophy and Science Teaching, Science: Philosophy, History and Education*. Springer. https://doi.org/10.1007/978-3-319-62616-1_5

Krishnamurti, J. (1974). *On Education*. Krishnamurti Foundation.

Krishnamurti, J. (1975). *Freedom from the Known*. Harper & Row.

Krishnamurti, J., & Bohm, D. (2014). *The Ending of Time. Where Philosophy and Physics Meet*. Krishnamurti Foundation.

Laine, J. (1998). Indian Philosophy of Mind. In *Routledge Encyclopaedia of Philosophy*. Routledge. https://doi.org/10.4324/9780415249126-F070-1

Larson, G., & Bhattacharya, R. S. (1987). *Samkhya. Encyclopaedia of Indian Philosophies. Vol IV*. Motilal Banarsidass Publishers.

Macaulay, T. B. (1835). *Minute upon Indian Education*. http://home.iitk.ac.in/~hcverma/Article/Macaulay-Minutes.pdf

Maldonado-Torres, N. (2011). Thinking Through the Decolonial Turn: Post-Continental Interventions in Theory, Philosophy, and Critique—An Introduction. *Transmodernity: Journal of Peripheral Cultural Production of the Luso-Hispanic World, 1*(2), 1–15.

McKinnon, L., & Bacon, L. (2015). The Move to Student-Centric Learning: Progress and Pitfalls. In *International Conference on e-Learning*. Academic Conferences International Limited.

Mehrotra, D. P. (2007). Origins of Alternative Education in India: A Continuing Journey. In S. Vittachi, N. Raghavan, & K. Raj (Eds.), *Alternative Schooling in India* (pp. 25–44). Sage.

Michaels, A., & Wulf, C. (Eds.). (2013). *Exploring the Senses. South Asian and European Perspectives on Emotions, Performativity and Rituals*. Routledge.

Nola, R. (2018). The Enlightenment: Truths Behind a Misleading Abstraction. In M. R. Matthews (Ed.), *History, Philosophy and Science Teaching*. Springer. https://doi.org/10.1007/978-3-319-62616-1_2

Pinderhughes, C. (2011). Toward a New Theory of Internal Colonialism. *Socialism and Democracy, 25*(1), 235–256. https://doi.org/10.1080/08854300.2011.559702

Prentiss, K. P. (1999). *The Embodiment of Bhakti*. Oxford University Press on Demand.

Ray, B. (Ed.) (2005). *Women of India: Colonial and Post-Colonial Periods*. Project of History of Indian Science, Philosophy and Culture Centre for Studies in Civilizations.

Ruitenberg, C. W. (2015). Toward a Curatorial Turn in Education. In T. Lewis & M. Laverty (Eds.), *Art's Teachings, Teaching's Art. Contemporary Philosophies and Theories in Education, 8*. Springer. https://doi.org/10.1007/978-94-017-7191-7_16

Sarukkai, S. (2018). Ekalavya and the Possibility of Learning. In S. C. Bhattacharya, V. Dalmiya, & G. Mukherji (Eds.), *Exploring Agency in the Mahabharat. Ethical and Political Dimensions of Dharma*. Routledge.

Sarukkai, S., & Akshara, K. V. (2020). *Indigenous Education Practices. An Introduction*. In P. M. Sarangapani & R. Pappu (Eds.), *Handbook of Education Systems in South Asia, Global Education Systems*. Springer. https://doi.org/10.1007/978-981-13-3309-5_1-1

Scarry, E. (1985). *The Body in Pain. The Making and Unmaking of the World*. Oxford University Press.

Stoljar, D. (2017). *Philosophical Progress. In Defence of a Reasonable Optimism*. Oxford University Press.

Synnott, A. (1993). *The Body Social. Symbolism, Self and Society*. Routledge.

Valeskar, P. (2012). Education for Liberation: Ambedkar's Thought and Dalit Women's Perspectives. *Contemporary Education Dialogue, 9*(2), 245–271. https://doi.org/10.1177/097318491200900206

Westley, H. (2008). *The Body as Medium and Metaphor*. Rodopi.

Zimmerman, F. (1987). *Jungle and the Aroma of Meats*. Motilal Banarsidass Publishers.

CPSIA information can be obtained
at www.ICGtesting.com
Printed in the USA
LVHW082027101222
734883LV00026B/122